Past Forward:
Articles from the
Journal of American History

Volume 1: From Colonial Foundations to the Civil War

Past Forward: Articles from the *Journal of American History*

Volume 1: From Colonial Foundations to the Civil War

EDITED BY JAMES SABATHNE AND JASON STACY

New York
OXFORD UNIVERSITY PRESS
in collaboration with *The Journal of American History*

Oxford University Press is a department of the University of Oxford. It furthers the University's objective of excellence in research, scholarship, and education by publishing worldwide.

Oxford New York
Auckland Cape Town Dar es Salaam Hong Kong Karachi
Kuala Lumpur Madrid Melbourne Mexico City Nairobi
New Delhi Shanghai Taipei Toronto

With offices in
Argentina Austria Brazil Chile Czech Republic France Greece
Guatemala Hungary Italy Japan Poland Portugal Singapore
South Korea Switzerland Thailand Turkey Ukraine Vietnam

For titles covered by Section 112 of the US Higher Education
Opportunity Act, please visit www.oup.com/us/he for the latest
information about pricing and alternate formats.

Published by Oxford University Press
198 Madison Avenue, New York, New York 10016
http://www.oup.com

Oxford is a registered trademark of Oxford University Press

Library of Congress Cataloging-in-Publication Data
Names: Sabathne, James, editor. | Stacy, Jason, 1970- editor.
Title: Past forward : articles from the Journal of American history / edited
   by James Sabathne and Jason Stacy.
Other titles: Journal of American history (Bloomington, Ind.)
Description: New York : Oxford University Press, 2017.
Identifiers: LCCN 2016017561 | ISBN 9780190299286 (v. 1) | ISBN 9780190299293 (v. 2)
Subjects: LCSH: United States--History.
Classification: LCC E173 .P275 2017 | DDC 973--dc23 LC record available at https://lccn.loc.
gov/2016017561

9 8 7 6 5 4 3 2 1

Printed in the United States of America
on acid-free paper

PAST FORWARD: ACKNOWLEDGMENTS

We appreciate the guidance from the good people at the Organization of American Historians, without whose help this project would not be possible. Ed Linenthal and Stephen Andrews provided important early encouragement, and Nancy Croker, throughout, proved to be an essential resource and advocate.

Many thanks to Brian Wheel, Brianna Provenzano, Tili Sokolov, Marissa Dadiw and the rest of the editorial staff at Oxford University Press for making such a beautiful book. Thanks also to Jeanine Alexander, Randall Briggs, Jeff Enright, Todd Hering, Stacey Jarvis, Rebecca Kelley, Stephen Klawiter, Betsy Newmark, Frank Shoemaker, and the 3 anonymous readers who reviewed the manuscript.

James Sabathne is glad for opportunity to publicly acknowledge those who guided and influenced him, especially his parents, Chris and Connie Sabathne, who offered boundless love and support and valuable life lessons from the outset. James also wishes to thank the community at the University of Cincinnati, especially Hope Earls, Roger and Judith Daniels, and Gene and Dottie Lewis, whose excellent companionship continue to feed his passion for scholarship and his belly. Likewise, James is thankful for his good friends Jason and Michelle Stacy, and his wife Tracy. Lastly, James thanks his many muses—those who inspired his ongoing search for interesting, meaningful, and thought-provoking history—the thousands of dynamic and engaging students in his classes at Jacobs, Auburn, and Hononegah high schools. Among these he found two very special favorites who taught him the most, Payton and Camden Sabathne.

Jason Stacy thanks his colleagues at Southern Illinois University Edwardsville for their support and good cheer and especially Michelle, Abigail and Margaret Stacy, whose love makes everything possible.

Most importantly, James and Jason wish to thank the authors who contributed their excellent historical scholarship to these volumes. We are excited to share their outstanding work with US history students.

CONTENTS

INTRODUCTION

✺

A Guide for Students on Active Reading and Reading Historically

In this introduction, we encourage you to think like a historian. The methods suggested here assume you are a student engaged in a formal study of US history, and likely at the college survey level. Successful history students read actively, engage in deep analytical thinking, and create memorable records of their thoughts for later reference. This introduction in particular, along with this book in general, will help you be a successful student of history.

ACTIVE READING

Reading academic history presents a complicated challenge. What is called simply "reading" actually includes interpretation, recognition of important parts, and remembering what you read for later reference. Due to the difficulty of combining reading, interpreting, thinking, and remembering, students often honestly report, "I read, but I don't remember what I have read." You can overcome this common experience by reading actively. Active reading allows you to complete a series of tasks that separate the processes of reading, interpreting, and remembering before recombining them in the form of notes. Active reading calls for concentrated reading of a short section of text, an interpretation of the short section, the translation of ideas into your own words, and, if you judge them important, a brief recording of those ideas. We favor active reading in the form of annotations on the pages of the text. Most students, given a bit of practice, find annotations written in the margins the fastest and most efficient form of active reading. Try these steps to help you annotate something you read:

1. Select a manageable section to read (usually a paragraph).
2. Focus on reading and interpreting that section quickly.
3. Decide whether any aspects of the section merit remembering. Usually paragraphs present an argument; what the author is trying to prove. The author's argument is most often what you will want to remember.
4. Convert what you want to remember into a brief version expressed in your own words.
5. Write your brief annotation in the margins (next to text source if possible).

Annotating in our recommended fashion suits the way most people read and learn. Rare individuals read and absorb a complicated and lengthy text in a single uninterrupted sitting. Most people, however, consume texts in a piecemeal fashion one section at a time. If you annotate, you can approach a long text one manageable part at a time and create an easily understood personal record in your own words. The process of translating the author's text into your own words will increase your ability to recall those ideas later. If you find yourself easily distracted, try the annotation methods above to help you later remember the challenging history you read. With a moment of focus, you can quickly interpret and record in the margins arguments and evidence of a single paragraph. Annotating will allow you to read in whatever time you have—ten minutes while riding a bus, fifteen minutes at your doctor's office, or twenty minutes while waiting in line at the department of motor vehicles. The annotations you create will be an easily accessible personal record of your reading. You will also find that your annotations are easier to study later and review quickly since the ideas in your annotations reflect your thinking and trigger your memory of a section.

We think there are many good reasons that you should look up unfamiliar vocabulary as a part of the process of interpreting the text and translating it into meaningful annotations. Using a dictionary will help you develop key skills related to interpreting and thinking. Your ability to understand and employ specific and nuanced vocabulary defines your capacity to think, learn, and express ideas. Difficult vocabulary you encounter often represents a particular expression of a concept. Historians use specific and nuanced words to express complicated ideas. Look up unfamiliar words to ensure you capture the author's meaning, to advance your ability to interpret sophisticated texts, and to aid your own thinking. Building your vocabulary in this way also heightens your ability to express complicated thoughts. If you do not have access to a dictionary, use context clues to make sense of unfamiliar words. Given widespread access to the Internet and dictionary applications, these times should be few and far between.

Although we recommend in-text annotations, some people prefer to record their notes in other locations. You might use sticky notes to record your annotations and stick them over the original paragraph, or record your notes on separate paper, or even make your notes digitally on a tablet or laptop. Whatever method you use to annotate a text, remember that the process of taking small sections and translating them into your own words aids both understanding and memory.

PAYING ATTENTION TO THE
PARAMETERS OF HISTORICAL ESSAYS

To practice good historical thinking, you should know the parameters of what you read. Here is a handy list of the common parameters of a piece of historical writing:

1. Author
2. Title

3. Topic and Subtopics (What)
4. Chronological Scope (When)
5. Geographic Setting (Where)

Although we recommend you note these five basic essay parameters, perhaps at the end of the essay itself, the annotations that you make while you read will often capture most of them. If it helps, apply a simple marking that calls your attention to the author and title. If the author includes the chronological scope in the title or subtitle (by including the dates "1840–1855," for example) connect the label "when" to the date range. Find room in the margins to write other essay parameters: "topic," "subtopics," "where," and, if the author did not provide the chronological scope as a part of the title, "when."

Historians often convey important information in the titles of their essays, which is one reason they are worth your attention. Sometimes they hint at their central argument in the beginning and sometimes they offer up the biggest topics. It is important to remember both the author and the title of an essay so that when you refer to an essay in a discussion, a dinner conversation, or in writing a response to an examination question, you can identify the author and title for your reader or listener.

Also remember that all writing by historians has a main topic, and often subtopics. The main topic is what you would describe as the single biggest unifying subject of the essay. If the author divides the essay into smaller component parts, note these as subtopics. A good place to organize your annotations of the main topic and subtopics of an essay is in the space at the beginning or the end of the essay itself.

Once you read and annotate an essay in this volume you will have noted its basic parameters (author, title, main topic and subtopics, when, and where), and the author's important ideas. These annotations can appear in the margins of the essay itself, though annotations of more general ideas and topics may be more usefully placed at the beginning or the end of the essay. No matter where you annotate, doing so will help you understand the essay and remember its important points and facts.

THINKING AS A BRIDGE FROM INTERPRETING TO REMEMBERING

We want you to think in a variety of ways to deepen your understanding of an author's ideas, hone critical historical thinking skills, and establish your thoughts in response to the essay. In the process, you will generate useful memories of what you read. Below are a few strategies to help you understand and remember a historical essay.

A great first step is to locate and label the author's thesis. Searching for, thinking about, committing to, and labeling an author's thesis requires you to process what the author wrote and understand the author's argument. Can you locate a statement, or statements, expressing the overriding argument of the author? Consider the entirety of the essay, and, if possible, locate the author's statement, or statements, that make up the thesis. When locating a potential thesis, consider carefully whether it suits the entirety of the essay. Most of the time, thesis statements encapsulate all of an author's arguments, so a thesis statement can be quite long, even multiple sentences or a whole paragraph.

Authors occasionally write historical essays in which they do not include a clearly stated thesis. You may find an essay with no stated thesis frustrating, and ought to consider raising that issue during a discussion of the piece, as well as noting the lack of a thesis in your annotations. Traditionally, authors state their thesis near the beginning of an essay. Some authors, however, structure their writing differently by elaborating on a number of introductory arguments (often summarizing what other historians have argued) before stating their thesis. Some historians only reveal the clear statement of their thesis in the very last pages or even sentences. If you locate a potential thesis near the end of an essay you might double check the beginning of the essay to see if you missed an earlier statement that amounts to the author's thesis. Sometimes a thesis can only be understood holistically, or after reading and understanding the entire essay. An essay whose thesis requires a holistic reading often contains certain themes that give some hint of the overall thesis. For example, if an author discusses women during the American Revolution, a holistic understanding of the entire essay may make the author's arguments about women during the American Revolution apparent.

Another strategy to help you understand and remember historical essays is to identifying the supporting arguments the author uses to support the thesis. Reread your annotations and mark each one that represents a major argument or idea. You can circle each annotation that interprets one of the author's main ideas, or place an asterisk next to them, or highlight them with a marker. Use whatever symbol works for you.

Once you have identified the author's thesis and supporting arguments, consider how an essay supports, refutes, changes, or adds to what you know about a topic and to your knowledge in general. Can you connect what you read to current events? Perhaps the essay shows stark differences from the course of current events. Another important way to think about the essay is to consider the ways in which the author's arguments and subjects connects to other history you read or know. Does this essay remind you of the work of any other historians? Or, does the content of the essay remind you of other historical events you studied in class? When you answer these questions, you will likely come up with examples since historical subjects connect both to events that came before and after. These connections allow you to engage in comparative thinking. What was similar about the events, both past and present? And what were significant differences between them? Another useful line of reasoning considers whether the current reading connects to your knowledge of other academic disciplines such as literature, philosophy, rhetoric, science, or art. Think about how the essay you read might influence your understanding of broad historical patterns. Did this essay show a continuation of the historical trends of prior eras? Did the essay bring to light some new developments and reveal important historical changes?

Historians also think historiographically. *Historiography* is the study of the study of history. When historians think historiographically, they read historical essays not only for content, but also for consideration of how other historians have used sources and the ways in which historical context shaped a particular historical analysis. Getting to know an author and their work will help you start to identify the ways in which history is a kind of discussion among historians. Academic history emerges from ongoing conversations and arguments of scholars. Historians build upon the research of their colleagues and give credit to the work of other historians in their essays and citations. Scholars researching the same topics arrive at varying conclusions, and sometimes note whose work they argue against in their writing. In making their arguments, using or supporting the work of earlier historians, and trying to disprove other researchers' ideas, scholars often refer to other authors. So, when you think historiographically, you will see that this book is a collection of discussions among historians with their own personalities and interests. Remembering which historians argued what about a particular topic will be your first step toward historiographical thinking.

Another aspect of historiographical thinking recognizes that the events and culture of a particular time and place exert an influence over a historian's work. You will notice in this book that there are short author biographies at the end of each essay. Many of the authors describe the ways in which historical events shaped their own historical writing. For example, one historian who lived during the Civil Rights Movement of the 1960s noted that this historical event shaped his interest in the Civil War and the emancipation of enslaved blacks in the South. In order to understand more fully a historical essay we advocate that you note the date of publication of any history you read. The questions historians ask and answer originate in their interests and concerns—as do the conclusions they reach.

Historiographical thinking also requires an analysis of the evidence a historian employs. For example, if a historian uses the *New York Times* to prove an argument about a coal strike in Pennsylvania, you might ask: why not use some newspapers from Pittsburgh as well? Why did this historian depend on sources from New York City? When you analyze a historian's sources, you will find ways in which the evidence employed offers insight about the history, the historian, and the nature of the field of history. Think about the numbers, variety, and types of sources the author used. Historians analyze sources and question, or assert, their sources' relative merits, and/or limitations, but in all cases, historians make choices when utilizing sources. These choices reflect a historian's sense of audience and purpose. Even the best sources speak to limited topics. Part of thinking historically involves analyzing and weighing the usefulness of a historian's chosen sources.

Lastly, we advocate that you engage in thinking related to evaluation and criticism. Judge the essay. What was successful about the essay? In what ways did the author fail? Did you like it, and why, or why not? Was it well written? Were the author's arguments sufficiently supported with historical evidence? Did the author express an analytical argument clearly? Did the author omit key information, or topics? If you were the historian . . . how would you have improved the essay?

In sum, by engaging in meaningful thinking and reflection you increase your creation of useful memories of history. Moreover, you practice analytical thinking, which will be useful in everything you do.

TECHNIQUES AIDING REMEMBERING

The easiest approach to increase your recall is to reread your annotations. You will find rereading annotations is much more efficient than rereading the original essay. Reread and study your annotations and you will increase your chances of remembering the basic essay parameters, thesis, topics and subtopics, and main ideas. Adding the products of your thoughts to your annotated essay increases the usefulness of studying the annotated essay. If margin space allows, add new features to your annotated essay, but if space is short, you can staple an extra page or pages to the essay. Consider including:

1. A list of the main ideas or a mini-outline, including the author's thesis and the most important supporting arguments.
2. A list of your ideas for discussion. This has the added advantage of recording not only the author's ideas, but also your personal analysis and thoughts about the essay.
3. A brief self-reflection at the end of your annotated essay. You reflection might be as short as a sentence or two in which you capture your impressions of the essay's ideas and arguments.
4. A single analytical, idea-focused paragraph. Integrate a brief treatment of the author's thesis and supporting arguments, with your thoughts and evaluations. Your paragraph should avoid retelling the content and instead focus on important arguments and ideas of the author, and your thoughts about those ideas. One paragraph is an appropriate length comprising a more likely "memorable" comprehensive piece of thinking about the essay. Students that distill the author's arguments as well as their thoughts and evaluations into one paragraph create a product of a size, length, and importance that is more "memorable."

Your annotated essays with accompanying reflective writing make great study tools for final exams or preparation for class discussions or debates. An annotated essay makes it easy to "refresh" your memory of something you read ten weeks ago, or even two years in the past. And, of course, these annotations will serve as the beginning of your own essays about the past. Once you have gathered an author's arguments, weighed the evidence, and reflected on the merits and the shortcomings of an essay, you have entered the historical dialogue. You are thinking like a historian!

CHAPTER ONE

✦◦

Slavery and Freedom: The American Paradox[1]

Edmund S. Morgan

American historians interested in tracing the rise of liberty, democracy, and the common man have been challenged in the past two decades by other historians, interested in tracing the history of oppression, exploitation, and racism. . . . We owe a debt of gratitude to those who have insisted that slavery was something more than an exception, that one-fifth of the American population at the time of the Revolution is too many people to be treated as an exception.[2]

We shall not have met the challenge simply by studying the history of that one-fifth. . . . Nor shall we have met the challenge if we merely execute the familiar maneuver of turning our old interpretations on their heads. The temptation is already apparent to argue that slavery and oppression were the dominant features of American history and that efforts to advance liberty and equality were the exception, indeed no more than a device to divert the masses while their chains were being fastened. To dismiss the rise of liberty and equality in American history as a mere sham is not only to ignore hard facts, it is also to evade the problem presented by those facts. The rise of liberty and equality in this country was accompanied by the rise of slavery. That two such contradictory developments were taking place simultaneously over a long period of our history, from the seventeenth century to the nineteenth, is the central paradox of American history.

The challenge, for a colonial historian at least, is to explain how a people could have developed the dedication to human liberty and dignity exhibited by the leaders of the American Revolution and at the same time have developed and maintained a system of labor that denied human liberty and dignity every hour of the day.

The paradox is evident at many levels if we care to see it. Think, for a moment, of the traditional American insistence on freedom of the seas. "Free ships make

[1]Interested students are encouraged to read this essay in the original form. Edmund S. Morgan, "Slavery and Freedom: The American Paradox," *Journal of American History* 59 (1) (June 1972), pp. 5–29.

[2]Particularly Staughton Lynd, *Class Conflict, Slavery, and the United States Constitution: Ten Essays* (Indianapolis, 1967).

free goods" was the cardinal doctrine of American foreign policy in the Revolutionary era. . . . At the time the colonists announced their claim to that station they had neither the arms nor the ships to make the claim good. They desperately needed the assistance of other countries, especially France, and their single most valuable product with which to purchase assistance was tobacco, produced mainly by slave labor. So largely did that crop figure in American foreign relations that one historian has referred to the activities of France in supporting the Americans as "King Tobacco Diplomacy," a reminder that the position of the United States in the world depended not only in 1776 but during the span of a long lifetime thereafter on slave labor.[3] To a very large degree it may be said that Americans bought their independence with slave labor.

The paradox is sharpened if we think of the state where most of the tobacco came from. Virginia at the time of the first United States census in 1790 had 40 percent of the slaves in the entire United States. And Virginia produced the most eloquent spokesmen for freedom and equality in the entire United States: George Washington, James Madison, and above all, Thomas Jefferson. They were all slaveholders and remained so throughout their lives. In recent years we have been shown in painful detail the contrast between Jefferson's pronouncements in favor of republican liberty and his complicity in denying the benefits of that liberty to blacks. . . .[4] What we need to explain is how such men could have arrived at beliefs and actions so full of contradiction.

Put the challenge another way: How did England, a country priding itself on the liberty of its citizens, produce colonies where most of the inhabitants enjoyed still greater liberty, greater opportunities, greater control over their own lives than most men in the mother country, while the remainder, one-fifth of the total, were deprived of virtually all liberty, all opportunities, all control over their own lives? We may admit that the Englishmen who colonized America and their revolutionary descendants were racists, that consciously or unconsciously they believed liberties and rights should be confined to persons of a light complexion. . . . [E]ven when we have probed the depths of racial prejudice, we will not have fully accounted for the paradox. . . .

Let us begin with Jefferson, this slaveholding spokesman of freedom. Could there have been anything in the kind of freedom he cherished that would have made him acquiesce, however reluctantly, in the slavery of so many Americans? The answer, I think, is yes. The freedom that Jefferson spoke for was not a gift to be conferred by governments, which he mistrusted at best. It was a freedom that sprang from the independence of the individual. The man who depended on another for his living could never be truly free. We may seek a clue to Jefferson's

---

[3]Curtis P. Nettels, *The Emergence of a National Economy 1775–1815* (New York, 1962), 19. See also Merrill Jensen, "The American Revolution and American Agriculture," *Agricultural History* 43 (Jan. 1969), 107–24.

[4]William Cohen, "Thomas Jefferson and the Problem of Slavery," *Journal of American History* 56 (Dec. 1969), 503–26; D. B. Davis, *Was Thomas Jefferson an Authentic Enemy of Slavery?* (Oxford, 1970); Winthrop D. Jordan, *White over Black: American Attitudes toward the Negro, 1550–1812* (Chapel Hill, NC, 1968), 429–81.

enigmatic posture toward slavery in his attitude toward those who enjoyed a seeming freedom without the independence needed to sustain it. For such persons Jefferson harbored a profound distrust, which found expression in two phobias that crop up from time to time in his writings.

The first was a passionate aversion to debt. Although the entire colonial economy of Virginia depended on the willingness of planters to go into debt and of British merchants to extend credit, although Jefferson himself was a debtor all his adult life—or perhaps because he was a debtor—he hated debt and hated anything that made him a debtor. He hated it because it limited his freedom of action. He could not, for example, have freed his slaves so long as he was in debt. Or so at least he told himself. But it was the impediment not simply to their freedom but to his own that bothered him. "I am miserable," he wrote, "till I shall owe not a shilling."[5]

Though Jefferson's concern with the perniciousness of debt was almost obsessive, it was nevertheless altogether in keeping with the ideas of republican liberty that he shared with his countrymen. The trouble with debt was that by undermining the independence of the debtor it threatened republican liberty. Whenever debt brought a man under another's power, he lost more than his own freedom of action. He also weakened the capacity of his country to survive as a republic. It was an axiom of current political thought that republican government required a body of free, independent, property-owning citizens.[6] A nation of men, each of whom owned enough property to support his family, could be a republic. It would follow that a nation of debtors, who had lost their property or mortgaged it to creditors, was ripe for tyranny. Jefferson accordingly favored every means of keeping men out of debt and keeping property widely distributed. He insisted on the abolition of primogeniture and entail; he declared that the earth belonged to the living and should not be kept from them by the debts or credits of the dead; he would have given fifty acres of land to every American who did not have it—all because he believed the citizens of a republic must be free from the control of other men and that they could be free only if they were economically free by virtue of owning land on which to support themselves.[7]

If Jefferson felt so passionately about the bondage of the debtor, it is not surprising that he should also have sensed a danger to the republic from another class of men who, like debtors, were nominally free but whose independence was illusory. Jefferson's second phobia was his distrust of the landless urban

---

[5]Julian P. Boyd, ed., *The Papers of Thomas Jefferson* (18 vols., Princeton, 1950–), X, 615. For other expressions of Thomas Jefferson's aversion to debt and distrust of credit, both private and public, see ibid., II, 275–76, VIII, 398–99, 632–33, IX, 217–18, 472–73, X, 304–05, XI, 472, 633, 636, 640, XII, 385–86.

[6]See Caroline Robbins, *The Eighteenth-Century Commonwealthman: Studies in the Transmission, Development, and Circumstance of English Liberal Thought from the Restoration of Charles II until the War with the Thirteen Colonies* (Cambridge, MA, 1959); J. G. A. Pocock, "Machiavelli, Harrington, and English Political Ideologies in the Eighteenth Century," *William and Mary Quarterly* 22 (Oct. 1965), 549–83.

[7]Boyd, ed., *Papers of Thomas Jefferson*, I, 344, 352, 362, 560, VIII, 681–82.

workman who labored in manufactures. In Jefferson's view, he was a free man in name only, Jefferson's hostility to artificers is well known and is generally attributed to his romantic preference for the rural life. But both his distrust for artificers and his idealization of small landholders as "the most precious part of a state" rested on his concern for individual independence as the basis of freedom. Farmers made the best citizens because they were "the most vigorous, the most independant, the most Virtuous. . . ." Artificers, on the other hand, were dependent on "the casualties and caprice of customers," If work was scarce, they had no land to fall back on for a living. In their dependence lay the danger. "Dependence," Jefferson argued, "begets subservience and venality, suffocates the germ of virtue, and prepares fit tools for the designs of ambition." Because artificers could lay claim to freedom without the independence to go with it, they were "the instruments by which the liberties of a country are generally overturned."[8]

In Jefferson's distrust of artificers we begin to get a glimpse of the limits— and limits not dictated by racism—that defined the republican vision of the eighteenth century. For Jefferson was by no means unique among republicans in his distrust of the landless laborer. Such a distrust was a necessary corollary of the widespread eighteenth-century insistence on the independent, property-holding individual as the only bulwark of liberty, an insistence originating in James Harrington's republican political philosophy and a guiding principle of American colonial politics, whether in the aristocratic South Carolina assembly or in the democratic New England town.[9] Americans both before and after 1776 learned their republican lessons from the seventeenth- and eighteenth-century British commonwealthmen; and the commonwealth men were uninhibited in their contempt for the masses who did not have the propertied independence required of proper republicans. . . .

That people in the lowest condition, the dregs of society, generally arrived at that position through their own vice and misconduct, whether in ancient Rome or modern Britain, was an unexamined article of faith among eighteenth-century republicans. And the vice that was thought to afflict the lower ranks most severely was idleness. The eighteenth-century's preferred cure for idleness lay in the religious and ethical doctrines which R. H. Tawney described as the New Medicine for Poverty, the doctrines in which Max Weber discerned the origins of the spirit of capitalism. But in every society a stubborn mass of men and women refused the medicine. For such persons the commonwealthmen did not hesitate to prescribe slavery. Thus Francis Hutcheson, who could argue eloquently against the enslavement of Africans, also argued that perpetual slavery should be "the

---

[8]Ibid., VIII, 426, 682; Thomas Jefferson, *Notes on the State of Virginia*, William Peden, ed. (Chapel Hill, NC, 1955), 165. Jefferson seems to have overlooked the dependence of Virginia's farmers on the casualties and caprice of the tobacco market.

[9]See Robbins, *The Eighteenth-Century Commonwealthmen*; Pocock, "Machiavelli, Harrington, and English Political Ideologies," 549–83; Michael Zuckerman, "The Social Context of Democracy in Massachusetts," *William and Mary Quarterly* 25 (Oct. 1968), 523–44; Robert M. Weir, "'The Harmony We Were Famous For': An Interpretation of Pre-Revolutionary South Carolina Politics," ibid. 26 (Oct. 1969), 473–501.

ordinary punishment of such idle vagrants as, after proper admonitions and tryals of temporary servitude, cannot be engaged to support themselves and their families by any useful labours."[10] James Burgh, whose *Political Disquisitions* earned the praises of many American revolutionists, proposed a set of press gangs "to seize all idle and disorderly persons, who have been three times complained of before a magistrate, and to set them to work during a certain time, for the benefit of great trading, or manufacturing companies, &C." . . .[11]

. . . [Jefferson] distrust[ed] . . . men who were free in name while their empty bellies made them thieves, threatening the property of honest men, or else made them slaves in fact to anyone who would feed them. Jefferson's own solution . . . was given in a famous letter to Madison, prompted by the spectacle Jefferson encountered in France in the 1780s, where a handful of noblemen had engrossed huge tracts of land on which to hunt game, while hordes of the poor went without work and without bread. Jefferson's proposal, characteristically phrased in terms of natural right, was for the poor to appropriate the uncultivated lands of the nobility. And he drew for the United States his usual lesson of the need to keep land widely distributed among the people. . . .[12]

The situation contemplated by Madison . . . was not irrelevant to those who were planning the future of the American republic. In a country where population grew by geometric progression, it was not too early to think about a time when there might be vast numbers of landless poor, when there might be those mobs in great cities that Jefferson feared as sores on the body politic. In the United States as Jefferson and Madison knew it, the urban labor force as yet posed no threat, because it was small; and the agricultural labor force was, for the most part, already enslaved. In Revolutionary America, among men who spent their lives working for other men rather than working for themselves, slaves probably constituted a majority.[13] In Virginia they constituted a large majority.[14] If Jefferson and Madison, not to mention Washington, were unhappy about that fact and yet did nothing to alter it, they may have been restrained, in part at least, by thoughts of the role that might be played in the United States by a large mass of free laborers.

---

[10]Francis Hutcheson, *A System of Moral Philosophy* (2 vols., London, 1755), II, 202; David B. Davis, *The Problem of Slavery in Western Culture* (Ithaca, NY, 1966), 374–78. I am indebted to David B. Davis for several valuable suggestions.

[11]James Burgh, *Political Disquisitions: Or, An ENQUIRY into public Errors, Defects, and Abuses* . . . (3 vols., London, 1774–1775), III, 220–21. See the proposal of Bishop George Berkeley that "sturdy beggars should . . . be seized and made slaves to the public for a certain term of years." Quoted in R. H. Tawney, *Religion and the Rise of Capitalism: A Historical Essay* (New York, 1926), 270.

[12]Boyd, ed., *Papers of Thomas Jefferson*, VIII, 681–83.

[13]Jackson Turner Main, *The Social Structure of Revolutionary America* (Princeton, 1965), 271.

[14]In 1755, Virginia had 43,329 white tithables and 60,078 black. Tithables included white men over sixteen years of age and black men and women over sixteen. In the census of 1790, Virginia had 292,717 slaves and 110,936 white males over sixteen, out of a total population of 747,680. Evarts B. Greene and Virginia D. Harrington, *American Population before the Federal Census of 1790* (New York, 1932), 150–55.

When Jefferson contemplated the abolition of slavery, he found it inconceivable that the freed slaves should be allowed to remain in the country.[15] In this attitude he was probably moved by his or his countrymen's racial prejudice. But he may also have had in mind the possibility that when slaves ceased to be slaves, they would become instead a half million idle poor, who would create the same problems for the United States that the idle poor of Europe did for their states. The slave, accustomed to compulsory labor, would not work to support himself when the compulsion was removed. This was a commonplace among Virginia planters before the creation of the republic and long after. "If you free the slaves," wrote Landon Carter, two days after the Declaration of Independence, "you must send them out of the country or they must steal for their support." . . .[16]

That fear, I believe, had a second point of origin in the experience of the American colonists, and especially of Virginians, during the preceding century and a half. If we turn now to the previous history of Virginia's labor force, we may find, I think, some further clues to the distrust of free labor among Revolutionary republicans and to the paradoxical rise of slavery and freedom together in colonial America.

The story properly begins in England with the burst of population growth there that sent the number of Englishmen from perhaps three million in 1500 to four-and-one-half million by 1650.[17] The increase did not occur in response to any corresponding growth in the capacity of the island's economy to support its people. And the result was precisely that misery which Madison pointed out to Jefferson as the consequence of "a high degree of populousness." Sixteenth-century England knew the same kind of unemployment and poverty that Jefferson witnessed in eighteenth-century France. . . . Alarming numbers of idle and hungry men drifted about the country looking for work or plunder. The government did what it could to make men of means hire them, but it also adopted increasingly severe measures against their wandering, their thieving, their roistering, and indeed their very existence. Whom the workhouses and prisons could not swallow the gallows would have to, or perhaps the army. When England had military expeditions to conduct abroad, every parish packed off its most unwanted inhabitants to the almost certain death that awaited them from the diseases of the camp.[18]

As the mass of idle rogues and beggars grew and increasingly threatened the peace of England, the efforts to cope with them increasingly threatened the liberties of Englishmen. Englishmen prided themselves on a "gentle government,"[19] a

---

[15]Jefferson, *Notes on the State of Virginia*, 138.

[16]Jack P. Greene, ed., *The Diary of Colonel Landon Carter of Sabine Hall, 1752–1778* (2 vols., Charlottesville, 1965), II, 1055.

[17]Joan Thrisk, ed., *The Agrarian History of England and Wales, Vol. IV: 1500–1640* (Cambridge, England, 1967), 531.

[18]See Edmund S. Morgan, "The Labor Problem at Jamestown, 1607–18," *American Historical Review* 76 (June 1971), 595–611, especially 600–606.

[19]This is Richard Hakluyt's phrase. See E. G. R. Taylor, ed., *The Original Writings & Correspondence of the Two Richard Hakluyts* (2 vols., London, 1935), I, 142.

government that had been releasing its subjects from old forms of bondage and endowing them with new liberties, making the "rights of Englishmen" a phrase to conjure with. But there was nothing gentle about the government's treatment of the poor; and as more Englishmen became poor, other Englishmen had less to be proud of. Thoughtful men could see an obvious solution: get the surplus Englishmen out of England. Send them to the New World, where there were limitless opportunities for work. There they would redeem themselves, enrich the mother country, and spread English liberty abroad.

The great publicist for this program was Richard Hakluyt. His *Principall Navigations, Voiages and Discoveries of the English nation*[20] was not merely the narrative of voyages by Englishmen around the globe, but a powerful suggestion that the world ought to be English or at least ought to be ruled by Englishmen. Hakluyt's was a dream of empire, but of benevolent empire, in which England would confer the blessings of her own free government on the less fortunate peoples of the world. It is doubtless true that Englishmen, along with other Europeans, were already imbued with prejudice against men of darker complexions than their own. And it is also true that the principal beneficiaries of Hakluyt's empire would be Englishmen. . . . Hakluyt's vision endured, of liberated natives and surplus Englishmen, courteously governed in English colonies around the world. Sir Walter Raleigh caught the vision. He dreamt of wresting the treasure of the Incas from the Spaniard by allying with the Indians of Guiana and sending Englishmen to live with them, lead them in rebellion against Spain, and govern them in the English manner.[21] Raleigh also dreamt of a similar colony in the country he named Virginia. Hakluyt helped him plan it. . . .[22]

Virginia from the beginning was conceived not only as a haven for England's suffering poor, but as a spearhead of English liberty in an oppressed world. That was the dream; but when it began to materialize at Roanoke Island in 1585, something went wrong. . . . When the English finally planted a permanent colony at Jamestown they came as conquerors, and their government was far from gentle. The Indians willing to endure it were too few in numbers and too broken in spirit to play a significant part in the settlement.

. . . Virginia offered a bleak alternative to the workhouse or the gallows for the first English poor who were transported there. During the first two decades of the colony's existence, most of the arriving immigrants found precious little English liberty in Virginia.[23] But by the 1630s the colony seemed to be working out, at least in part, as its first planners had hoped. Impoverished Englishmen

---

[20]Richard Hakluyt, *The Principall Navigations, Voiages and Discoveries of the English nation . . .* (London, 1589).

[21]Walter Raleigh, *The Discoverie of the large and bewtiful Empire of Guiana*, V. T. Harlow, ed. (London, 1928), 138–49; V. T. Harlow, ed., *Ralegh's Last Voyage: Being an account drawn out of contemporary letters and relations* (London, 1932), 44–45.

[22]Taylor, ed., *Original Writings & Correspondence*, II, 211–377, especially 318.

[23]Morgan, "The Labor Problem at Jamestown, 1607–18," pp. 595–611; Edmund S. Morgan, "The First American Boom: Virginia 1618 to 1630," *William and Mary Quarterly* 28 (April 1971), 169–98.

were arriving every year in large numbers, engaged to serve the existing planters for a term of years, with the prospect of setting up their own households a few years later. The settlers were spreading up Virginia's great rivers, carving out plantations, living comfortably from their cornfields and from the cattle they ranged in the forests, and at the same time earning perhaps ten or twelve pounds a year per man from the tobacco they planted. A representative legislative assembly secured the traditional liberties of Englishmen and enabled a larger proportion of the population to participate in their own government than had ever been the case in England. The colony even began to look a little like the cosmopolitan haven of liberty that Hakluyt had first envisaged. Men of all countries appeared there: French, Spanish, Dutch, Turkish, Portuguese, and African.[24] Virginia took them in and began to make Englishmen out of them.

It seems clear that most of the Africans, perhaps all of them, came as slaves, a status that had become obsolete in England, while it was becoming the expected condition of Africans outside Africa and of a good many inside.[25] It is equally clear that a substantial number of Virginia's Negroes were free or became free. And all of them, whether servant, slave, or free, enjoyed most of the same rights and duties as other Virginians. There is no evidence during the period before 1660 that they were subjected to a more severe discipline than other servants. They could sue and be sued in court. They did penance in the parish church for having illegitimate children. They earned money of their own, bought and sold and raised cattle of their own. Sometimes they bought their own freedom. In other cases, masters bequeathed them not only freedom but land, cattle, and houses.[26] Northampton, the only county for which full records exist, had at least ten free Negro households by 1668.[27]

---

[24]There are no reliable records of immigration, but the presence of persons of these nationalities is evident from county court records, where all but the Dutch are commonly identified by name, such as "James the Scotchman," or "Cursory the Turk." The Dutch seem to have anglicized their names at once and are difficult to identify except where the records disclose their naturalization. The two counties for which the most complete records survive for the 1640s and 1650s are Accomack-Northampton and Lower Norfolk. Microfilms are in the Virginia State Library, Richmond.

[25]Because the surviving records are so fragmentary, there has been a great deal of controversy about the status of the first Negroes in Virginia. What the records do make clear is that not all were slaves and that not all were free. See Jordan, *White over Black*, 71–82.

[26]For examples, see Northampton County Court Records, Deeds, Wills, etc., Book III, f. 83, Book V, ff. 38, 54, 60, 102, 117–19; York County Court Records, Deeds, Orders, Wills, etc., no. 1, ff. 232–34; Surry County Court Records, Deeds, Wills, etc., no. 1, f. 349; Henrico County Court Records, Deeds and Wills 1677–1692, f. 139.

[27]This fact has been arrived at by comparing the names of householders on the annual list of tithables with casual identifications of persons as Negroes in the court records. The names of householders so identified for 1668, the peak year during the period for which the lists survive (1662–1677) were: Bastian Cane, Bashaw Ferdinando, John Francisco, Susan Grace, William Harman, Philip Mongum, Francis Pane, Manuel Rodriggus, Thomas Rodriggus, and King Tony. The total number of households in the county in 1668 was 172; total number of tithables 435; total number of tithable free Negroes 17; total number of tithable unfree Negroes 42. Thus nearly 29 percent of tithable Negroes and probably of all Negroes were free; and about 13.5 percent of all tithables were Negroes.

As Negroes took their place in the community, they learned English ways, including even the truculence toward authority that has always been associated with the rights of Englishmen. Tony Longo, a free Negro of Northampton, when served a warrant to appear as a witness in court, responded with a scatological opinion of warrants, called the man who served it an idle rascal, and told him to go about his business. The man offered to go with him at any time before a justice of the peace so that his evidence could be recorded. He would go with him at night, tomorrow, the next day, next week, any time. But Longo was busy getting in his corn. He dismissed all pleas with a "Well, well, Ile goe when my Corne is in," and refused to receive the warrant.[28]

The judges understandably found this to be contempt of court; but it was the kind of contempt that free Englishmen often showed to authority, and it was combined with a devotion to work that English moralists were doing their best to inculcate more widely in England. As England had absorbed people of every nationality over the centuries and turned them into Englishmen, Virginia's Englishmen were absorbing their own share of foreigners, including Negroes, and seemed to be successfully moulding a New World community on the English model.

But a closer look will show that the situation was not quite so promising as at first it seems. It is well known that Virginia in its first fifteen or twenty years killed off most of the men who went there. It is less well known that it continued to do so. If my estimate of the volume of immigration is anywhere near correct, Virginia must have been a death trap for at least another fifteen years and probably for twenty or twenty-five. In 1625 the population stood at 1,300 or 1,400; in 1640 it was about 8,000.[29] In the fifteen years between those dates at least 15,000 persons must have come to the colony.[30] If so, 15,000 immigrants increased the

---

[28]Northampton Deeds, Wills, etc., Book V, 54–60 (Nov. 1, 1654).

[29]The figure for 1625 derives from the census for that year, which gives 1,210 persons, but probably missed about 10 percent of the population. Morgan, "The First American Boom," 170n–71n. The figure for 1640 is derived from legislation limiting tobacco production per person in 1639–1640. The legislation is summarized in a manuscript belonging to Jefferson, printed in William Waller Hening, *The Statutes at Large; Being a Collection of All the Laws of Virginia, from the first Session of the Legislature, in the Year 1619* (13 vols., New York, 1823), I, 224–25, 228. The full text is in "Acts of the General Assembly, Jan. 6, 1639–40," *William and Mary Quarterly* 4 (Jan. 1924), 17–35, and "Acts of the General Assembly, Jan. 6, 1639–40," ibid. (July 1924), 159–62. The assembly calculated that a levy of four pounds of tobacco per tithable would yield 18,584 pounds, implying 4,646 tithables (men over sixteen). It also calculated that a limitation of planting to 170 pounds per poll would yield 1,300,000, implying 7,647 polls. Evidently the latter figure is for the whole population, as is evident also from Hening, *Statutes*, I, 228.

[30]In the year 1635, the only year for which such records exist, 2,010 persons embarked for Virginia from London alone. See John Camden Hotten, ed., *The Original Lists of Persons of Quality . . .* (London, 1874), 35–145. For other years casual estimates survive. In February 1627/8 Francis West said that 1,000 had been "lately received." Colonial Office Group, Class 1, Piece 4, folio 109 (Public Record Office, London). Hereafter cited CO 1/4, f. 109. In February 1633/4 Governor John Harvey said that "this yeares newcomers" had arrived "this yeare." Yong to Sir Tobie Matthew, July 13, 1634, "Aspinwall Papers," *Massachusetts Historical Society Collections* 9 (1871), 110. In May 1635, Samuel Mathews said that 2,000 had arrived "this yeare." Mathews to ?, May 25, 1635, "The Mutiny in Virginia, 1635," *Virginia Magazine of History and Biography* I (April 1894), 417. And in March 1636, John West said that 1,606 persons had arrived "this yeare." West to Commissioners for Plantations, March 28, 1636, "Virginia in 1636," ibid. IX (July 1901), 37.

population by less than 7,000. There is no evidence of a large return migration. It seems probable that the death rate throughout this period was comparable only to that found in Europe during the peak years of a plague. Virginia, in other words, was absorbing England's surplus laborers mainly by killing them. The success of those who survived and rose from servant to planter must be attributed partly to the fact that so few did survive.

After 1640, when the diseases responsible for the high death rate began to decline and the population began a quick rise, it became increasingly difficult for an indigent immigrant to pull himself up in the world. The population probably passed 25,000 by 1662,[31] hardly what Madison would have called a high degree of populousness. Yet the rapid rise brought serious trouble for Virginia. It brought the engrossment of tidewater land in thousands and tens of thousands of acres by speculators, who recognized that the demand would rise.[32] It brought a huge expansion of tobacco production, which helped to depress the price of tobacco and the earnings of the men who planted it.[33] It brought efforts by planters to prolong the terms of servants, since they were now living longer and therefore had a longer expectancy of usefulness.[34]

It would, in fact, be difficult to assess all the consequences of the increased longevity; but for our purposes one development was crucial, and that was the appearance in Virginia of a growing number of freemen who had served their terms but who were now unable to afford land of their own except on the frontiers or in the interior. In years when tobacco prices were especially low or crops especially poor, men who had been just scraping by were obliged to go back to work for their larger neighbors simply in order to stay alive. By 1676 it was

---

[31]The official count of tithables for 1662 was 11,838. Clarendon Papers, 82 (Bodleian Library, Oxford). The ratio of tithables to total population by this time was probably about one to two. (In 1625 it was 1 to 1.5; in 1699 it was 1 to 2.7.) Since the official count was almost certainly below the actuality, a total population of roughly 25,000 seems probable. All population figures for seventeenth-century Virginia should be treated as rough estimates.

[32]Evidence of the engrossment of lands after 1660 will be found in CO 1/39, f. 196; CO 1/40, f. 23; CO 1/48, f. 48; CO 5/1309, numbers 5, 9, and 23; Sloane Papers, 1008, ff. 334–35 (British Museum, London). A recent count of headrights in patents issued for land in Virginia shows 82,000 headrights claimed in the years from 1635 to 1700. Of these nearly 47,000 or 57 percent (equivalent to 2,350,000 acres) were claimed in the twenty-five years after 1650. W. F. Craven, *White, Red, and Black: The Seventeenth-Century Virginian* (Charlottesville, 1971), 14–16.

[33]No continuous set of figures for Virginia's tobacco exports in the seventeenth century can now be obtained. The available figures for English imports of American tobacco (which was mostly Virginian) are in United States Bureau of the Census, *Historical Statistics of the United States, Colonial Times to 1957* (Washington, D.C., 1960), series Z 238–240, p. 766. They show for 1672 a total of 17,559,000 pounds. In 1631 the figure had been 272,300 pounds. Tobacco crops varied heavily from year to year. Prices are almost as difficult to obtain now as volume. Those for 1667–1675 are estimated from London prices current in Warren Billings, "Virginia's Deploured Condition, 1660–1676: The Coming of Bacon's Rebellion" (doctoral dissertation, Northern Illinois University, 1969), 155–59.

[34]See below.

estimated that one fourth of Virginia's freemen were without land of their own.[35] And in the same year Francis Moryson, a member of the governor's council, explained the term "freedmen" as used in Virginia to mean "persons without house and land," implying that this was now the normal condition of servants who had attained freedom.[36]

Some of them resigned themselves to working for wages; others preferred a meager living on dangerous frontier land or a hand-to-mouth existence, roaming from one county to another, renting a bit of land here, squatting on some there, dodging the tax collector, drinking, quarreling, stealing hogs, and enticing servants to run away with them.

The presence of this growing class of poverty-stricken Virginians was not a little frightening to the planters who had made it to the top or who had arrived in the colony already at the top, with ample supplies of servants and capital. They were caught in a dilemma. They wanted the immigrants who kept pouring in every year. Indeed they needed them and prized them the more as they lived longer. But as more and more turned free each year, Virginia seemed to have inherited the problem that she was helping England to solve. Virginia, complained Nicholas Spencer, secretary of the colony, was "a sinke to drayen England of her filth and scum."[37]

The men who worried the upper crust looked even more dangerous in Virginia than they had in England. They were, to begin with, young, because it was young persons that the planters wanted for work in the fields; and the young have always seemed impatient of control by their elders and superiors, if not downright rebellious. They were also predominantly single men. Because the planters did not think women, or at least English women, fit for work in the fields, men outnumbered women among immigrants by three or four to one throughout the century.[38] Consequently most of the freedmen had no wife or family to tame their wilder impulses and serve as hostages to the respectable world.

Finally, what made these wild young men particularly dangerous was that they were armed and had to be armed. Life in Virginia required guns. The plantations were exposed to attack from Indians by land and from privateers and petty-thieving pirates by sea.[39] Whenever England was at war with the French or

---

[35]Thomas Ludwell and Robert Smith to the king, June 18, 1676, vol. LXXVII, f. 128, Coventry Papers Longleat House, American Council of Learned Societies British Mss. project, reel 63 (Library of Congress).

[36]Ibid., 204–5.

[37]Nicholas Spencer to Lord Culpeper, Aug. 6, 1676, ibid., 170. See also CO 1/49, f. 107.

[38]The figures are derived from a sampling of the names of persons for whom headrights were claimed in land patents. Patent Books I–IX (Virginia State Library, Richmond). Wyndham B. Blanton found 17,350 women and 75,884 men in "a prolonged search of the patent books and other records of the times . . . ," a ratio of 1 woman to 4.4 men. Wyndham B. Blanton, "Epidemics, Real and Imaginary, and other Factors Influencing Seventeenth Century Virginia's Population," *Bulletin of the History of Medicine* 31 (Sept.–Oct. 1957), 462. See also Craven, *White, Red, and Black*, 26–27.

[39]Pirates were particularly troublesome in the 1680s and 1690s. See CO 1/48, f. 71; CO 1/51, f. 340; CO 1/52, f. 54; CO 1/55, if. 105–106; CO 1/57, f. 300; CO 5/1311, no. 10.

the Dutch, the settlers had to be ready to defend themselves. In 1667 the Dutch in a single raid captured twenty merchant ships in the James River, together with the English warship that was supposed to be defending them; and in 1673 they captured eleven more. On these occasions Governor William Berkeley gathered the planters in arms and at least prevented the enemy from making a landing. But while he stood off the Dutch he worried about the ragged crew at his back. Of the able-bodied men in the colony he estimated that "at least one third are Single freedmen (whose Labour will hardly maintaine them) or men much in debt, both which wee may reasonably expect upon any Small advantage the Enemy may gaine upon us, wold revolt to them in hopes of bettering their Condicion by Shareing the Plunder of the Country with them."[40]

Berkeley's fears were justified. Three years later, sparked not by a Dutch invasion but by an Indian attack, rebellion swept Virginia. It began almost as Berkeley had predicted, when a group of volunteer Indian fighters turned from a fruitless expedition against the Indians to attack their rulers. Bacon's Rebellion was the largest popular rising in the colonies before the American Revolution. Sooner or later nearly everyone in Virginia got in on it, but it began in the frontier counties of Henrico and New Kent, among men whom the governor and his friends consistently characterized as rabble.[41] As it spread eastward, it turned out that there were rabble everywhere, and Berkeley understandably raised his estimate of their numbers. "How miserable that man is," he exclaimed, "that Governes a People wher six parts of seaven at least are Poore Endebted Discontented and Armed."[42]

Virginia's poor had reason to be envious and angry against the men who owned the land and imported the servants and ran the government. But the rebellion produced no real program of reform, no ideology, not even any revolutionary slogans. It was a search for plunder, not for principles. And when the rebels had redistributed whatever wealth they could lay their hands on, the rebellion subsided almost as quickly as it had begun.

It had been a shattering experience, however, for Virginia's first families. They had seen each other fall in with the rebels in order to save their skins or their possessions or even to share in the plunder. When it was over, they eyed one another distrustfully, on the lookout for any new Bacons in their midst, who might be tempted to lead the still restive rabble on more plundering expeditions. When William Byrd and Laurence Smith proposed to solve the problems of defense against the Indians by establishing semi-independent buffer settlements on the upper reaches of the rivers, in each of which they would engage to keep fifty men in arms, the assembly at first reacted favorably. But it quickly occurred to the governor and council that this would in fact mean gathering a crowd of Virginia's wild bachelors and furnishing them with an abundant supply of arms and ammunition. Byrd had himself led such a crowd in at least one plundering foray during the rebellion. To put him or anyone else in charge of a large and

---

[40]CO 1/30, ft. 114–5.

[41]CO 1/37, ft. 35–40.

[42]Vol. LXXVII, 144–46, Coventry Papers.

permanent gang of armed men was to invite them to descend again on the people whom they were supposed to be protecting.[43]

The nervousness of those who had property worth plundering continued throughout the century, spurred in 1682 by the tobacco-cutting riots in which men roved about destroying crops in the fields, in the desperate hope of producing a shortage that would raise the price of the leaf.[44] And periodically in nearby Maryland and North Carolina, where the same conditions existed as in Virginia, there were tumults that threatened to spread to Virginia.[45]

As Virginia thus acquired a social problem analogous to England's own, the colony began to deal with it as England had done, by restricting the liberties of those who did not have the proper badge of freedom, namely the property that government was supposed to protect. One way was to extend the terms of service for servants entering the colony without indentures. Formerly they had served until twenty-one; now the age was advanced to twenty-four.[46] There had always been laws requiring them to serve extra time for running away; now the laws added corporal punishment and, in order to make habitual offenders more readily recognizable, specified that their hair be cropped.[47] New laws restricted the movement of servants on the highways and also increased the amount of extra time to be served for running away. In addition to serving two days for every day's absence, the captured runaway was now frequently required to compensate by labor for the loss to the crop that he had failed to tend and for the cost of his apprehension, including rewards paid for his capture.[48] A three week's holiday might result in a year's extra service.[49] If a servant struck his master, he was to serve another year. For killing a hog he had to serve the owner a year and the informer another year.[50] Since the owner of the hog, and the owner of the servant, and the informer were frequently the same man, and since a hog was worth at best less than one tenth the hire of a servant for a year, the law was very profitable to masters. One Lancaster master was awarded six years extra service from a servant who killed three of his hogs, worth about thirty shillings.[51]

The effect of these measures was to keep servants for as long as possible from gaining their freedom, especially the kind of servants who were most likely to cause trouble. At the same time the engrossment of land was driving many back to servitude after a brief taste of freedom. Freedmen who engaged to work for

---

[43]Hening, *Statutes*, II, 448–54; CO 1/42, f. 178; CO 1/43, f. 29; CO 1/44, f. 398; CO 1/47, if. 258–260, 267; CO 1/48, f. 46; LXXVIII, 378–81, 386–87, 398–99, Coventry Papers.

[44]CO 1/48 *passim*.

[45]CO 1/43, if. 359–365; CO 1/44, if. 10–62; CO 1/47, f. 261; CO 1/48, if. 87–96, 100–102, 185; CO 5/1305, no. 43; CO 5/1309, no. 74.

[46]Hening, *Statutes*, II, 113–14, 240.

[47]Ibid., II, 266, 278.

[48]Ibid., II, 116–17, 273–74, 277–78.

[49]For example, James Gray, absent twenty-two days, was required to serve fifteen months extra. Order Book 1666–1680, p. 163, Lancaster County Court Records.

[50]Hening, *Statutes*, II, 118.

[51]Order Book 1666–1680, p. 142, Lancaster County Court Records.

wages by so doing became servants again, subject to most of the same restrictions as other servants.

Nevertheless, in spite of all the legal and economic pressures to keep men in service, the ranks of the freedmen grew, and so did poverty and discontent. To prevent the wild bachelors from gaining an influence in the government, the assembly in 1670 limited voting to landholders and householders.[52] But to disfranchise the growing mass of single freemen was not to deprive them of the weapons they had wielded so effectively under Nathaniel Bacon. It is questionable how far Virginia could safely have continued along this course, meeting discontent with repression and manning her plantations with annual importations of servants who would later add to the unruly ranks of the free. To be sure, the men at the bottom might have had both land and liberty, as the settlers of some other colonies did, if Virginia's frontier had been safe from Indians, or if the men at the top had been willing to forego some of their profits and to give up some of the lands they had engrossed. . . .

There was another solution, which allowed Virginia's magnates to keep their lands, yet arrested the discontent and the repression of other Englishmen, a solution which strengthened the rights of Englishmen and nourished that attachment to liberty which came to fruition in the Revolutionary generation of Virginia statesmen. But the solution put an end to the process of turning Africans into Englishmen. The rights of Englishmen were preserved by destroying the rights of Africans.

I do not mean to argue that Virginians deliberately turned to African Negro slavery as a means of preserving and extending the rights of Englishmen. Winthrop Jordan has suggested that slavery came to Virginia as an unthinking decision.[53] We might go further and say that it came without a decision. It came automatically as Virginians bought the cheapest labor they could get. Once Virginia's heavy mortality ceased, an investment in slave labor was much more profitable than an investment in free labor; and the planters bought slaves as rapidly as traders made them available. In the last years of the seventeenth century they bought them in such numbers that slaves probably already constituted a majority or nearly a majority of the labor force by 1700.[54] The demand was so great that traders for a time found a better market in Virginia than in Jamaica or Barbados.[55] But the social benefits of an enslaved labor force, even if not consciously sought or recognized at the time by the men who bought the slaves, were larger than the economic benefits. The increase in the importation of slaves was matched by a decrease in the importation of indentured servants and consequently a

---

[52]Hening, *Statutes*, II, 280. It had been found, the preamble to the law said, that such persons "haveing little interest in the country doe oftner make tumults at the election to the disturbance of his majesties peace, then by their discretions in their votes provide for the conservasion thereof, by makeing choyce of persons fitly qualifyed for the discharge of soe greate a trust."

[53]Jordan, *White over Black*, 44–98.

[54]In 1700 they constituted half of the labor force (persons working for other men) in Surry County, the only county in which it is possible to ascertain the numbers. Robert Wheeler, "Social Transition in the Virginia Tidewater, 1650–1720: The Laboring Household as an Index," paper delivered at the Organization of American Historians' meeting, New Orleans, April 15, 1971. Surry County was on the south side of the James, one of the least wealthy regions of Virginia.

[55]See the letters of the Royal African Company to its ship captains, Oct. 23, 1701; Dec. 2, 1701; Dec. 7, 1704; Dec. 21, 1704; Jan. 25, 1704/5, T70 58 (Public Record Office, London).

decrease in the dangerous number of new freedmen who annually emerged seeking a place in society that they would be unable to achieve.[56]

If Africans had been unavailable, it would probably have proved impossible to devise a way to keep a continuing supply of English immigrants in their place. There was a limit beyond which the abridgment of English liberties would have resulted not merely in rebellion but in protests from England and in the cutting off of the supply of further servants. At the time of Bacon's Rebellion the English commission of investigation had shown more sympathy with the rebels than with the well-to-do planters who had engrossed Virginia's lands. To have attempted the enslavement of English-born laborers would have caused more disorder than it cured. But to keep as slaves black men who arrived in that condition was possible and apparently regarded as plain common sense.

The attitude of English officials was well expressed by the attorney who reviewed for the Privy Council the slave codes established in Barbados in 1679. He found the laws of Barbados to be well designed for the good of his majesty's subjects there, for, he said, "although Negros in that Island are punishable in a different and more severe manner than other Subjects are for Offences of the like nature; yet I humbly conceive that the Laws there concerning Negros are reasonable Laws, for by reason of their numbers they become dangerous, and being a brutish sort of People and reckoned as goods and chattels in that Island, it is of necessity or at least convenient to have Laws for the Government of them different from the Laws of England, to prevent the great mischief that otherwise may happen to the Planters and Inhabitants in that Island."[57] In Virginia too it seemed convenient and reasonable to have different laws for black and white. As the number of slaves increased, the assembly passed laws that carried forward with much greater severity the trend already under way in the colony's labor laws. But the new severity was reserved for people without white skin. The laws specifically exonerated the master who accidentally beat his slave to death, but they placed new limitations on his punishment of "Christian white servants."[58]

Virginians worried about the risk of having in their midst a body of men who had every reason to hate them.[59] The fear of a slave insurrection hung over them for nearly two centuries. But the danger from slaves actually proved to be less than that which the colony had faced from its restive and armed freedmen....

---

[56]Abbot Emerson Smith, *Colonists in Bondage: White Servitude and Convict Labor in America 1607–1776* (Chapel Hill, 1947), 335. See also Thomas J. Wertenbaker, *The Planters of Colonial Virginia* (Princeton, 1922), 130–31, 134–35; Craven, *White, Red, and Black*, 17.

[57]CO 1/45, f. 138.

[58]Hening, *Statutes*, II, 481–82, 492–93; III, 86–88, 102–3, 179–80, 333–35, 447–62.

[59]For example, see William Byrd II to the Earl of Egmont, July 12, 1736, in Elizabeth Donnan, ed., *Documents Illustrative of the History of the Slave Trade to America* (4 vols., Washington, 1930–1935), IV, 131–32. But compare Byrd's letter to Peter Beckford, Dec. 6, 1735, "Letters of the Byrd Family," *Virginia Magazine of History and Biography* 36 (April 1928), 121–23, in which he specifically denies any danger. The Virginia assembly at various times laid duties on the importation of slaves. See Donnan, ed., *Documents Illustrative of the History of the Slave Trade*, IV, 66–67, 86–88, 91–94, 102–17, 121–31, 132–42. The purpose of some of the acts was to discourage imports, but apparently the motive was to redress the colony's balance of trade after a period during which the planters had purchased far more than they could pay for. See also Wertenbaker, *The Planters of Colonial Virginia*, 129.

[S]laves were less troubled by the sexual imbalance that helped to make Virginia's free laborers so restless. In an enslaved labor force women could be required to make tobacco just as the men did; and they also made children, who in a few years would be an asset to their master. From the beginning, therefore, traders imported women in a much higher ratio to men than was the case among English servants,[60] and the level of discontent was correspondingly reduced. Virginians did not doubt that discontent would remain, but it could be repressed by methods that would not have been considered reasonable, convenient, or even safe, if applied to Englishmen. Slaves could be deprived of opportunities for association and rebellion. They could be kept unarmed and unorganized. They could be subjected to savage punishments by their owners without fear of legal reprisals. And since their color disclosed their probable status, the rest of society could keep close watch on them. It is scarcely surprising that no slave insurrection in American history approached Bacon's Rebellion in its extent or in its success.

Nor is it surprising that Virginia's freedmen never again posed a threat to society. Though in later years slavery was condemned because it was thought to compete with free labor, in the beginning it reduced by so much the number of freedmen who would otherwise have competed with each other. When the annual increment of freedmen fell off, the number that remained could more easily find an independent place in society, especially as the danger of Indian attack diminished and made settlement safer at the heads of the rivers or on the Carolina frontier. There might still remain a number of irredeemable, idle, and unruly freedmen, particularly among the convicts whom England exported to the colonies. But the numbers were small enough, so that they could be dealt with by the old expedient of drafting them for military expeditions.[61] The way was

---

[60]The Swiss traveler Francis Ludwig Michel noted in 1702 that "Both sexes are usually bought, which increase afterwards." William J. Hinke, trans. and ed., "Report of the Journey of Francis Louis Michel from Berne Switzerland to Virginia, October 2 (1), 1701–December 1, 1702: Part II," *Virginia Magazine of History and Biography* 24 (April 1916), 116. A sampling of the names identifiable by sex, for whom headrights were claimed in land patents in the 1680s and 1690s shows a much higher ratio of women to men among blacks than among whites. For example, in the years 1695–1699 (Patent Book 9) I count 818 white men and 276 white women, 376 black men and 220 black women (but compare Craven, *White, Red, and Black*, 99–100). In Northampton County in 1677, among seventy-five black tithables there were thirty-six men, thirty-eight women, and one person whose sex cannot be determined. In Surry County in 1703, among 211 black tithables there were 132 men, seventy-four women, and five persons whose sex cannot be determined. These are the only counties where the records yield such information. Northampton County Court Records, Order Book 10. 189–91; Surry County Court Records, Deeds, Wills, etc., No. 5 part 2, 287–90.

[61]Virginia disposed of so many this way in the campaign against Cartagena in 1741 that a few years later the colony was unable to scrape up any more for another expedition. Fairfax Harrison, "When the Convicts Came," *Virginia Magazine of History and Biography* 30 (July 1922), 250–60, especially 256–57; John W. Shy, "A New Look at Colonial Militia," *William and Mary Quarterly* 20 (April 1963), 175–85. In 1736, Virginia had shipped another batch of unwanted freedmen to Georgia because of a rumored attack by the Spanish. Byrd II to Lord Egmont, July 1736, "Letters of the Byrd Family," *Virginia Magazine of History and Biography* 36 (July 1928), 216–17. Observations by an English traveler who embarked on the same ship suggest that they did not go willingly: "our Lading consisted of all the Scum of Virginia, who had been recruited for the Service of Georgia, and who were ready at every Turn to mutiny, whilst they belch'd out the most shocking Oaths, wishing Destruction to the Vessel and every Thing in her." "Observations in Several Voyages and Travels in America in the Year 1736," *William and Mary Quarterly* 15 (April 1907), 224.

thus made easier for the remaining freedmen to acquire property, maybe acquire a slave or two of their own, and join with their superiors in the enjoyment of those English liberties that differentiated them from their black laborers.

A free society divided between large landholders and small was much less riven by antagonisms than one divided between landholders and landless, masterless men. With the freedman's expectations, sobriety, and status restored, he was no longer a man to be feared. That fact, together with the presence of a growing mass of alien slaves, tended to draw the white settlers closer together and to reduce the importance of the class difference between yeoman farmer and large plantation owner.[62]

The seventeenth century has sometimes been thought of as the day of the yeoman farmer in Virginia; but in many ways a stronger case can be made for the eighteenth century as the time when the yeoman farmer came into his own, because slavery relieved the small man of the pressures that had been reducing him to continued servitude. Such an interpretation conforms to the political development of the colony. During the seventeenth century the royally appointed governor's council, composed of the largest property-owners in the colony, had been the most powerful governing body. But as the tide of slavery rose between 1680 and 1720 Virginia moved toward a government in which the yeoman farmer had a larger share. In spite of the rise of Virginia's great families on the black tide, the power of the council declined; and the elective House of Burgesses became the dominant organ of government. Its members nurtured a closer relationship with their yeoman constituency than had earlier been the case.[63] And in its chambers Virginians developed the ideas they so fervently asserted in the Revolution: ideas about taxation, representation, and the rights of Englishmen, and ideas about the prerogatives and powers and sacred calling of the independent, property-holding yeoman farmer—commonwealth ideas.

In the eighteenth century, because they were no longer threatened by a dangerous free laboring class, Virginians could afford these ideas. . . . [A] century later, without benefit of rebellions, Virginians had learned republican lessons, had introduced schools and printing presses, and were as ready as New Englanders to recite the aphorisms of the commonwealthmen.

It was slavery, I suggest, more than any other single factor, that had made the difference, slavery that enabled Virginia to nourish representative government in a plantation society, slavery that transformed the Virginia of Governor Berkeley to the Virginia of Jefferson, slavery that made the Virginians dare to speak a political language that magnified the rights of freemen, and slavery, therefore, that brought Virginians into the same commonwealth political tradition with New Englanders. The very institution that was to divide North and South after the Revolution may have made possible their union in a republican government.

---

[62]Compare Lyon G. Tyler, "Virginians Voting in the Colonial Period," *William and Mary Quarterly* 6 (July 1897), 7–13.

[63]John C. Rainbolt, "The Alteration in the Relationship between Leadership and Constituents in Virginia, 1660 to 1720," *William and Mary Quarterly* 27 (July 1970), 411–34.

Thus began the American paradox of slavery and freedom, intertwined and interdependent, the rights of Englishmen supported on the wrongs of Africans. The American Revolution only made the contradictions more glaring, as the slaveholding colonists proclaimed to a candid world the rights not simply of Englishmen but of all men. To explain the origin of the contradictions, if the explanation I have suggested is valid, does not eliminate them or make them less ugly. But it may enable us to understand a little better the strength of the ties that bound freedom to slavery, even in so noble a mind as Jefferson's. And it may perhaps make us wonder about the ties that bind more devious tyrannies to our own freedoms and give us still today our own American paradox.

Edmund Morgan

Edmund Morgan (1916–2013) was born in Minneapolis, Minnesota, and studied at Harvard University under Perry Miller. His Ph.D. dissertation, "Religion and the Family in Seventeenth-Century New England," became his first book, *The Puritan Family* (1944). Morgan remained a student of colonial history throughout his career, publishing *Virginians at Home* (1952), *The Stamp Act Crisis: Prologue to Revolution* (1953), *The Puritan Dilemma: The Story of John Winthrop* (1958), among many others, including the seminal *American Slavery, American Freedom: The Ordeal of Colonial Virginia* (1975), which grew from the arguments in this essay. Morgan continued to publish into his eighties, including *Benjamin Franklin* (2002) and *American Heroes: Profiles of Men and Women Who Shaped Early America* (2009). Morgan won many prizes for his work, including the National Humanities Medal, a Pulitzer Prize, the Bancroft Prize, and the American Historical Association's Distinguished Scholar Award, among others. Morgan taught at the University of Chicago, Brown University, and Yale University and served as the president of the Organization of American Historians (1971–1972).[64]

QUESTIONS FOR CONSIDERATION

1. What, according to Morgan, is the "American paradox?"
2. In what way did the ideology of the "commonwealthmen," coupled with the institution of American slavery, help create this paradox for Americans in the eighteenth century?
3. Characterize the economic effects of population growth in England during the early seventeenth century. Compare the economic effects of population growth in early seventeenth century England to population growth in late seventeenth century Virginia. What were some similarities, and some important differences?
4. In what way was Bacon's Rebellion of 1676 a product of the success of Virginia colony? In what ways was the growth of the slave system after 1676 both socially and economically "automatic" according to Morgan?
5. How did the solidification of the slave system change the social context in which wealthy and poor whites interacted in the Virginia colony? Consult this statement by Morgan to help you construct your response:

> A free society divided between large landholders and small was much less riven by antagonisms than one divided between landholders and landless, masterless

---

[64]"Edmund Sears Morgan (1916–2013)," Jon Butler, *Perspectives on History*, December 2013, online at https://www.historians.org/publications-and-directories/perspectives-on-history/december-2013/in-memoriam-edmund-sears-morgan [accessed September 29, 2015].

men. With the freedman's expectations, sobriety, and status restored, he was no longer a man to be feared. That fact, together with the presence of a growing mass of alien slaves, tended to draw the white settlers closer together and to reduce the importance of the class difference between yeoman farmer and large plantation owner.

CHAPTER TWO

People of the Dawn, People of the Door: Indian Pirates and the Violent Theft of an Atlantic World[1]

Matthew R. Bahar

In the spring of 1759 a familiar supplicant stood before the legislature in Boston's State House. As royal governor of Massachusetts during the Seven Years' War (1756–1763), Thomas Pownall envisioned a lasting victory for his empire through the conquest of the Penobscot River valley in the colony's northeastern frontier, the very heart of the Wabanaki Indians' ancestral homeland. "For many Years a Den for Savages," he reminded his lawmakers, a "Rendevouz of the Eastern Indians when they come against our Frontiers," the region long loomed as a swarming nest of Indian outlaws. Circumstances there now necessitated the appropriation of assets for a strong garrison, Pownall argued, since "the Enimy have now no Outlet to ye sea but thro this River Penobscot; The Door being Shutt upon them in every other Part." Pownall's incessant agitation of the General Court (Massachusetts's legislature) to slam shut this final door eventually paid dividends. Bolstered by British military victories throughout this borderland in early 1759 and by the subsequent allotment of funds for the construction of Fort Pownall, the jubilant governor could finally declare in a victory speech that "this River was ye last & only door That the Enimy had left to ye Atlantic & I hope this is now fairly shutt upon them." Equally confident of the strategy's success, the legislature congratulated him for his defeat of the Indians now, they affirmed, "deprived of the only Opening they had left to the Atlantick." Pownall sought to infect his superiors at Whitehall with the same enthusiasm, boasting in a June letter of his triumphant closure of "the last & only Door which the Enimy had left to ye Atlantic."[2]

---

[1]Interested students are encouraged to read this essay in the original form. Matthew R. Bahar, "People of the Dawn, People of the Door: Indian Pirates and the Violent Theft of an Atlantic World," *Journal of American History* 101 (2) (Sept. 2014), 401–26.

[2]Speech of T. Pownall in the Council Chamber, June 1, 1759, in *Documentary History of the State of Maine, Containing the Baxter Manuscripts*, ed. James Phinney Baxter (24 vols., Portland, ME, 1908), XIII, 168–69. For Thomas Pownall's victory speech, see "Message from Thomas Pownall," Feb. 1, 1759, ibid., 149–50. Address of the Massachusetts General Court to Governor Thomas Pownall, June 12, 1759, Colonial Office Papers 5/889, f. 250 (British National Archives, Kew, England); Governor Pownall to Board of Trade, June 14, 1759, Colonial Office Papers 5/889, f. 236, ibid.

The curious anxieties voiced by Boston's political elite over the perilous consequences of Indian access to the ocean . . . point to a peculiar dimension of the
Wabanaki experience in the early modern world. The perseverance of this native
culture ashore, colonial leaders and Indians both came to understand, was predicated on its tenacity afloat. . . . For nearly two centuries, Wabanaki Indians
responded to the most threatening and most opportunistic effects of colonialism
by carefully orchestrating acts of maritime violence and theft. When their long-
standing conception of the ocean ran up against European—and later primarily
British—efforts to forcefully consolidate the Atlantic Ocean into a coherent and
far-flung imperial network, native marine-warriors shrewdly exploited colonial
and imperial conflicts to decimate European ships and sailors and reinforce
native command of the waves. Countless voices from all strata of imperial
society—from frantic colonial fishermen and settlers on up to nervous metropolitan officials—decried Indians' seemingly incessant devastation of the North
Atlantic fishery, their serial impressment of British seamen, their commandeer-
ing of British sailing vessels, and their destructive naval warfare. Native power
afloat thus wreaked havoc on Britain's ongoing struggle to integrate the Atlantic
into an extensive and seamless imperial economy.

Over the colonial period, Wabanaki came to appreciate Britain's maritime
presence. . . . Its sheer vulnerability . . . rendered it a valuable extractive economy
for native communities. This floating warehouse offered plundering Indian mariners convenient access to British sailing vessels, maritime labor, and material
goods, which were quickly incorporated into Wabanaki villages or pressed into
further service of native interests on their ocean. . . . Such opportunities allowed
Wabanaki to engineer a subsidiary maritime economy out of a larger Atlantic
commercial nexus.

. . . The native maritime vision—one in which the ocean and its variegated
opportunities functioned to serve Indian interests—frequently interrupted and
fiercely contested the vision of the newly arrived imperial neighbors. Pownall's
ambitious plan in 1759 . . . indicated the striking marine violence with which
Wabanaki pursued their vision. . . . [It] thus affords us both a glimpse into the
salty past of the People of the Dawn, a culture carefully cognizant of the potenti-
ality of their eastern horizons, and a more holistic understanding of the contestation, violence, and plurality shattering the Atlantic in a maelstrom of clashing
worlds and colliding ambitions.

The targets and timing of Wabanaki nautical assaults reveal a broad Atlantic
dimension to their blue-water campaign. After the initial phase of contact with
European explorers in the sixteenth and early seventeenth centuries, Indians
concentrated their attacks exclusively on the British maritime presence. This
strategy reflected native concerns with the steadily mounting pressures of British
colonization to their south, a threatening development that eclipsed in geographic
and demographic scale the French settlement of Wabanakia's northern fringes.
Indian communities further focused their seaborne violence by executing it only
during wider colonial conflicts. King Philip's War (1675–1678), King William's
War (1689–1697), Queen Anne's War (1702–1713), Governor Dummer's War

(1721–1726), King George's War (1739–1754), and the French and Indian War (1756–1763) all functioned as lucrative opportunities to both retaliate against New England's aggressive colonialism and plunder British vessels at sea. . . . [M]any of these clashes spanned the ocean and consequently linked Indian fortunes to European courts. In their adroit exploitation of empire, Wabanaki developed an efficient strategy to manage its most destabilizing effects.

Yet the same imperial competition that afforded Indians opportunities to augment their autonomy through violence also presented them with chances to secure it through diplomacy. When France's and Britain's Atlantic empires were not at war, Wabanaki communities played them off against each through carefully measured negotiations designed to strengthen native interests in a rapidly changing Northeast. Promises of wartime fidelity to the French officials in Acadia, for example, or gestures of goodwill and assurances of future neutrality to the British governor in Massachusetts aimed to elicit reciprocal obligations from both colonies. European authorities responded in kind, often guaranteeing high-quality and fairly priced trade goods, generous gifts, and the containment of colonial settlement. . . . Britain's persistent fear of upsetting this equilibrium—of fueling native suspicions about British designs and fostering already-warm Franco-Wabanaki relations—only encouraged the impunity with which Indian warriors raided and plundered British ships during wartime. For nearly a century Wabanaki endeavored to dictate the terms of engagement with colonial newcomers by shrewdly manipulating Europe's imperial politics. Their efforts often met with stunning success.[3]

The factors motivating Wabanaki maritime theft cannot be understood in isolation from these imperial dynamics. Material goods plundered during wartime offered Indian communities a degree of economic autonomy and cultural stability in the face of colonialism's constant pressures. By violently seizing European resources, Indians forged access to the ships, sailors, and cargo that granted authority on the waves, and thusly managed their need to negotiate for colonial goods with Acadians and New Englanders during peacetime. This effective scheme also served to bolster native diplomatic authority. Preying on the British Atlantic economy during wartime became a brutally convincing performance of Indians' indispensability as French allies and the risky consequences of discounting native power. The Wabanaki cultivation of an extractive economy in the soil of imperial conflict thus enabled them to undergird their strategic geopolitical position in the Northeast. A critical step in this process was recognizing the futility and folly of purging their world of European foreigners; at sea and on land, the

---

[3]On native diplomatic strategy, see Emerson W. Baker and John G. Reid, "Amerindian Power in the Early Modern Northeast: A Reappraisal," *William and Mary Quarterly* 61 (Jan. 2004), 77–106; Jenny Hale Pulsipher, "Gaining the Diplomatic Edge: Kinship, Trade, and Religion in Amerindian Alliances in Early North America," in *Empires and Indigenes: Intercultural Alliance, Imperial Expansion, and Warfare in the Early Modern World*, ed. Wayne E. Lee (New York, 2011), 18–47; and Christopher John Bilodeau, "The Economy of War: Violence, Religion, and the Wabanaki Indians in the Maine Borderlands" (Ph.D. diss., Cornell University, 2006).

presence of French and British colonizers had assumed a tremendous economic value and political import.

That the Atlantic world was a fundamentally European construction is accepted as an unchallenged tenet among the field's ardent supporters. Europe's monarchs, merchants, sailors, and cartographers, this established precept maintains, integrated the ocean's vast trade winds and currents into a seamless and coherent early modern superhighway connecting adjacent and disparate land-masses and, in the process, extended the breadth and wealth of Europe's empires.[4]

Atlantic historiography . . . overwhelmingly privileges the interests and aims of the European imperial project. . . . Conventional applications of this paradigm . . . has succeeded admirably in enriching our understanding of the Atlantic nexus in all its complexities, [but] it has also effectively read out people—indeed, entire societies—who possessed alternative visions of and ambitions for their own maritime worlds. From that development has surfaced a rational and organic Atlantic world of, by, and for the European empire and its subjects.[5]

Though this localized study of native seafaring theft serves to complicate these suppositions, it does not merely suggest that Indians are Atlantic too. It moves beyond recuperative history to contend that the Wabanaki maritime experience illuminates something larger and far more significant about the nature of the early modern Atlantic. . . . Wabanaki did not simply yield their vast watery frontier to strangers or allow it to impede their dynamic culture, any more than did their colonial counterparts. Indian naval warriors, mariners, and diplomats instead viewed it as a powerful catalyst for extending political and cultural autonomy and enriching their economic life. . . . When Indian efforts to define and defend the ocean's significance disrupted Britain's struggle to do the same, a profoundly contentious and brutally violent Atlantic space surfaced.

Beyond the methodological conundrums posed by current assumptions about the Atlantic world, scholarly ambivalence toward bridging Indian and Atlantic history is based largely in popular and academic conceptions of native culture. Put simply, we commonly envisage American Indians as a quintessen-tially terrestrial people. Contemporary political conversations involving Indian

---

[4]This idea is best articulated in David Armitage, "Three Concepts of Atlantic History," in *The British Atlantic World, 1500–1800*, ed. David Armitage and Michael J. Braddick (New York, 2002), 16; and Bernard Bailyn, *Atlantic History: Concept and Contours* (Cambridge, MA, 2005), 62–63. See also Bushnell, "Indigenous America and the Limits of the Atlantic World," 191.

[5]A survey of this trend in the canon of Atlantic history includes J. G. A. Pocock, *The Machiavellian Moment: Florentine Political Thought and the Atlantic Republican Tradition* (Princeton, 1975); Nicholas Canny and Anthony Pagden, eds., *Colonial Identity in the Atlantic World, 1500–1800* (Princeton, 1989); David Hancock, *Citizens of the World: London Merchants and the Integration of the British Atlantic Community, 1735–1785* (New York, 1995); Bernard Bailyn, "The Idea of Atlantic History," *Itinerario* 20 (March 1996), 19–44; Anthony Pagden, *Lords of All the World: Ideologies of Empire in Spain, Britain, and France, c. 1500–c. 1800* (New Haven, CT, 1998); Alison Games, *Migration and the Origins of the English Atlantic World* (Cambridge, MA, 2001); Jorge Cañizares-Esguerra, *Puritan Conquistadors: Iberianizing the Atlantic, 1550–1700* (Stanford, CA, 2006); and John H. Elliott, *Empires of the Atlantic World: Britain and Spain in America, 1492–1830* (New Haven, CT, 2007).

country nearly always accentuate land rights and the inextricability of sovereignty and territoriality. . . .

Fixations with the *terra firma* Indian also resound in Native American historiography. The most influential and enduring theoretical constructs preoccupying the field and orienting much of its scholarship over the last two decades sustain this familiar trope. Middle grounds, native grounds, divided grounds, crossroads, borderlands, and back countries . . . have also served to rivet the field's gaze on the continental interior and captivate its attention on adjoining processes. . . .[6]

Considering these prevailing perceptions inside and outside academia of native peoples, it is little wonder that . . . we are left with the assumption that Indians, as one Atlanticist has determined, simply "turned their back on the Atlantic" and gave "it no more than myopic glances." An image of Wabanaki pirates hijacking European sailing ships and plying the rough waters of the North Atlantic consequently risks consignment to a surreal realm of the fantastical; a picture of native marine-warriors at ship's helm successfully laying siege to colonial garrisons is naturally confined to the level of the absurd; and the notion of an Indian navy pressing British seamen into its ranks can be relegated to a world of the fanciful. Yet history is, indeed, often stranger than fiction.[7]

The colonial-era Wabanaki central to this study were a northeastern Algonquian culture comprising numerous hunter-gatherer peoples in the region of northern New England and the Canadian Maritimes. Their descendants today are referred to as the Eastern Abenaki, Penobscot, Maliseet-Passamaquoddy, and Mi'kmaq. In the early historic period, these people inhabited coastal and island settlements throughout the spring, summer, and fall and migrated to interior hunting camps for the winter. Prior to their sustained contact with European fishermen and adventurers in the sixteenth century, the Wabanaki and their ancestors long possessed a maritime-oriented culture expressed in their material life and spiritual beliefs. . . . Inland encampments relied marginally on anadromous marine life, including the alewife, shad, and Atlantic salmon, while coastal settlements journeyed to deeper waters on regular swordfish hunts and

---

[6]Prominent contributions to these paradigms include Richard White, *The Middle Ground: Indians, Empires, and Republics in the Great Lakes Region, 1650–1815* (New York, 1991); Richard White et al., "Forum: *The Middle Ground* Revisited," *William and Mary Quarterly* 63 (Jan. 2006), 9–80; James H. Merrell, *Into the American Woods: Negotiators on the Pennsylvania Frontier* (New York, 1999); Jane T. Merritt, *At the Crossroads: Indians and Empires on a Mid-Atlantic Frontier, 1700–1763* (Chapel Hill, NC, 2003); Kathleen DuVal, *The Native Ground: Indians and Colonists in the Heart of the Continent* (Philadelphia, 2006); Alan Taylor, *The Divided Ground: Indians, Settlers, and the Northern Borderland of the American Revolution* (New York, 2006); James F. Brooks, *Captives and Cousins: Slavery, Kinship, and Community in the Southwest Borderlands* (Chapel Hill, NC, 2002); Eric Hinderaker and Peter C. Mancall, *At the Edge of Empire: The Backcountry in British North America* (Baltimore, MD, 2003); Jeremy Adelman and Stephen Aron, "From Borderlands to Borders: Empires, Nation-States, and the Peoples in Between in North American History," *American Historical Review* 104 (June 1999), 814–41; and Jeremy Adelman and Stephen Aron, "Of Lively Exchanges and Larger Perspectives," ibid., 104 (Oct. 1999), 1235–39.

[7]Shammas, "Introduction," 10.

cod-fishing expeditions. Many communities sanctified the sea's centrality in their lives by constructing large marine mammal effigies. . . . [N]atives in this region commanded durable seafaring watercraft and possessed a refined nautical competency hundreds of years before their encounters with Europeans. . . . Wabanaki ancestors increasingly adapted to and utilized relatively new resources, including large sea mammals such as grey seals, harbor seals, porpoises, and even baleen whales. The ocean did not demarcate the edge of their cosmology: Its waters and coastal isles were a world in which to expand and inhabit, whose fecundity could be harnessed and cherished.[8]

Wabanaki oral tradition similarly reveals this long-standing maritime-centeredness. When dawn first broke on Wabanakia, Gluskap, the life-giving culture hero, emerged from the watery horizon in a tree-covered stone canoe. After coming ashore and instilling in the First People valuable life skills neces-sary to cultivate their world, Gluskap embarked on a series of aquatic adventures with various amiable and menacing characters at sea. As the sun set on his time with the People, the mythical hero departed with his stone canoe into the ocean's immense and boundless expanses, from whence it is believed he will one day return. Gluskap's landing thus bridged the cognitive chasm hitherto separating the mysterious unknown of this pelagic world from the Dawnland, the birthplace and home of its People. By imbuing the ocean with spiritual and material mean-ing, and by regarding its profoundly generative and life-giving power, the Wabanaki effectively imbricated their marine and terrestrial worlds in the very beginning. . . .[9]

This saltwater-saturated history shaped the context of possibilities within which Wabanaki comprehended early encounters with Europeans. During the sixteenth century, Indians gradually forged a valuable extractive economy by aggressively manipulating the presence of colonial newcomers in their waters. The fruits of this new economy could supplement native modes of mari-time production and consumption while enhancing Wabanaki seagoing

---

[8]Dean R. Snow, "The Ethnohistoric Baseline of the Eastern Abenaki," *Ethnohistory* 23 (Summer 1976), 291–305; Bruce J. Bourque, "Ethnicity on the Maritime Peninsula, 1600–1759," ibid., 36 (Summer 1989), 257–77; Bruce J. Bourque, *Twelve Thousand Years: American Indians in Maine* (Lincoln, NE, 2001), 105–9. On the maritime culture of the Wabanaki, see ibid., 37–101; Brian S. Robinson, "Early and Middle Archaic Period Occupation in the Gulf of Maine Region: Mortuary and Technological Patterning," in *Early Holocene Occupation in Northern New England*, ed. Brian S. Robinson, James B. Petersen, and Ann K. Robinson (Augusta, ME, 1992), 106–7; David Sanger, "Maritime Adaptations in the Gulf of Maine," *Archaeology of Eastern North America* 16 (Fall 1988), 81–99; Bruce J. Bourque, *Prehistory of the Central Maine Coast* (New York, 1992), 23; and Arthur E. Spiess and Robert A. Lewis, *The Turner Farm Fauna: 5000 Years of Hunting and Fishing in Penobscot Bay, Maine* (Augusta, ME, 2001), 134, 157–59.

[9]Charles G. Leland, *The Algonquin Legends of New England, or Myths and Folk Lore of the Micmac, Passamaquoddy, and Penobscot Tribes* (Boston, 1884), 28–33, 41–42, 130–31; Wilson D. Wallis and Ruth Sawtell Wallis, *The Micmac Indians of Eastern Canada* (Minneapolis, 1955), 482–83; Joseph Nicolar, *The Life and Traditions of the Red Man*, ed. Annette Kolodny (Durham, NC, 2007), 103–4, 116–20; Frank G. Speck, "Penobscot Transformer Tales," *International Journal of American Linguistics* 1 (Aug. 1918), 193; Pauleena MacDougall, *The Penobscot Dance of Resistance: Tradition in the History of a People* (Durham, NH, 2004), 35–38.

mobility. . . . [A] native community along coastal Acadia in 1583 carefully watched the approach of a French pinnace (a small ship used as a tender for larger ships) commanded by the trader and explorer Étienne Bellenger. The boat's emergence from the natives' maritime world, now frequently dotted by non-Wabanaki watercraft, figured as a potentially threatening, albeit valuable, opportunity to acquire material goods. Warriors attacked the boat, killed two Frenchmen, and decoyed the others before seizing and sailing away the vessel. This surprising dexterity at sea also shocked Bartholomew Gosnold's expedition to the southern Maine coast in 1602, when a crewman remarked how "sixe Indians, in a Baske-shallop with mast and saile . . . came boldly aboord us" with "an iron grapple" and demanded trade. Similarly astonished was Henry Hudson's crew as they rowed ashore near the mouth of the Penobscot River in 1609 to mend their sails and cut a new foremast. The adventurers turned and suddenly scoped "two French shallops full of the country people" sailing in swift pursuit. Though "they offered us no wrong, seeing we stood upon our guard," the natives exuded such authority by their command of the waves and of European nautical equipment, that the explorers felt impelled to quickly offer trade. . . .[10]

. . . By 1661 Father Biard . . . [m]arveling at the Indians' fluency with shallops . . . asserted that "they handle them as skillfully as our most courageous and active Sailors of France." Other Jesuits expressed similar awe at the Mi'kmaq's extraordinary command of the deep sea. "It is wonderful how these Savage mariners navigate so far in little shallops," they noted in 1659, "crossing vast seas without compass, and often without sight of the Sun, trusting to instinct for their guidance." Both native and newcomer had little doubt that Wabanaki possessed a considerable degree of authority over the processes and opportunities of their maritime world and could dictate the exchanges with its interlopers.[11]

During King Philip's War, Wabanaki began actively exploiting the seemingly interminable series of colonial conflicts that enveloped their homeland during the late seventeenth and eighteenth centuries. These wars afforded valuable opportunities for Indians eager to ramp up their predatory seaborne raids amid intensified British colonialism in northern New England. Marblehead fisherman Robert Roules suffered the consequences when Indians captured his rig "half laden with fish" in 1677. Several other New England mariners endured similar misfortunes

---

[10]D. B. Quinn, "The Voyage of Étienne Bellenger to the Maritimes in 1583: A New Document," *Canadian Historical Review* 43 (Dec. 1962), 332–33, 339–41; John Brereton, "Briefe and True Relation of the Discoverie of the North Part of Virginia, 1602," in *Early English and French Voyages: Chiefly from Hakluyt, 1534–1608*, ed. Henry S. Burrage (New York, 1967), 330; Henry Hudson, *The Third Voyage of Master Henry Hudson, Written by Henry Juet, of Lime-House*, in *Sailors Narratives of Voyages along the New England Coast, 1524–1624*, ed. George Parker Winship (Boston, 1905), 182.

[11]Father Pierre Biard to Father Christopher Baltazar, June 10, 1611, in *The Jesuit Relations and Allied Documents: Travels and Explorations of the Jesuit Missionaries in New France, 1610–1791*, ed. Reuben Gold Thwaites (73 vols., Cleveland, 1896–1901), I, 173; "Relation of What Occurred in the Mission of the Fathers of the Society of Jesus in the Country of New France, from the Summer of the Year 1661 to the Summer of the Year 1662," ibid., XLVII, 223; Father Hierosme Lallemant to Father Jacques Renault, Oct. 16, 1659, ibid., XLV, 65.

throughout that fishing season. By the end of King Philip's War, upward of twenty fishing ketches had been surprised and stolen. Wabanaki near Norridgewock in Maine employed an equally efficient fishing method when they stocked their community "full of codd fish out of 15 or 16 vessels they have taken" near the beginning of Governor Dummer's War in 1724. . . . Well into the eighteenth century, then, native warriors mined the British maritime presence as a convenient locus of wealth to enhance their long-standing cultivation of marine resources.[12]

Sailing craft plundered in this extractive economy could also be mobilized to strike back against the most disruptive pressures of British colonialism in the Dawnland. While Massachusetts reeled from the devastation of King Philip's War in southern New England, Indians in southern Maine marshaled a formidable navy and extended the conflagration to the sea in the fall of 1676. Mogg Heigon, a sagamore from the Saco River region, launched repeated naval offensives against British ships and settlements throughout the Gulf of Maine, blending retaliation for aggressive colonial encroachment on native hunting territories with a lucrative opportunity to confiscate British ships. "Captain Mog" split his force of one hundred warriors into two companies, sending one to attack Jewels Island in Casco Bay, while he proceeded with the other to the mouth of the Kennebec River where they attacked and seized a British fishing shallop. His crew then sailed to nearby Damaras Cove, "for they had intelegence of a catch and a sloop" anchored there. The Indians defeated the British crews, though they were only able to hijack the sloop. On October 12, a month after those initial victories, Mogg's quickly growing flotilla succeeded in laying siege to the British garrison at Black Point, the strongest fortification on the northeastern frontier. Later that day, in the campaign's culminating victory, the native forces commandeered a hefty thirty-ton ketch docked at Richmond's Island to load the supplies of a fleeing settler, Walter Gendal.[13]

Far from a haphazard ambush, the successful seizure of Gendal's large cargo ship required a considerable degree of forethought and coordination with the ocean's natural rhythms. Waiting until they observed "the Wind blowing in hard upon" the British so "they could not get out of the Harbour," the Indians commenced their attack by pouring heavy gunfire on the ship's crew. Meanwhile, another group of natives "manned out a Canoo with several Hands to cut their Cable" while others continued their bombardment of the vessel. The boat drifted ashore where waiting Indians boarded it and procured the surrender of the colonists.

---

[12]James Axtell, "The Vengeful Women of Marblehead: Robert Roules's Deposition of 1677," *William and Mary Quarterly* 31 (Oct. 1974), 650–52. "Statement of Robert Roules of Marblehead concerning the capture of fishing vessels at Cape Sable by the Indians," July 17, 1677, Massachusetts Archives Collection, 1629–1799, SC1-45X, vol. 69, f. 158 (Massachusetts State Archives, Boston). On fishing ketches stolen at the end of King Philip's War, see William Hubbard, *A Narrative of the Troubles with the Indians in New-England* (Boston, 1677), 236–37. Letter of Father Rallé, Aug. 23, 1724, in *Calendar of State Papers, Colonial Series, America and the West Indies, Vol. XXXIV: 1724–1725*, ed. Cecil Headlam (London, 1936), 429–32.

[13]"Francis Card's Declaration," Jan. 22, [1676], in *Documentary History of the State of Maine*, ed. Baxter, VI, 149; Horatio Hight, "Mogg Heigon—His Life, His Death, and Its Sequel," in *Collections of the Maine Historical Society*, 2nd ser. (10 vols., Portland, ME, 1894), V, 350–54; Horace P. Beck, *The American Indian as a Sea-Fighter in Colonial Times* (Mystic, 1959), 27–30.

Their latest prize was then quickly sailed up the coast. By enhancing their nautical acumen with prize vessels, Indians continued to elaborate on longstanding methods of mobility and warfare to combat dangerous new forces threatening their autonomy. Their mission succeeded in exploiting King Philip's War as a pretext to expel the colonial threat.[14]

Mogg was not above a bit of saber rattling to maximize the terror unleashed by his forces. Before releasing the British captive Francis Card from their ship, the Indian marines boasted that "they do in tend to take veseles and so to go to all the fishing ilandes and so to drive all the contre befor them." The impervious sagamore himself, Card related, "doth make his br[ag] and laf at the english and saith that he hath found the way to burn boston." Mogg's pyrotechnics never materialized; nor did he earnestly wish to follow through on such a proposition. Massachusetts had simply become too economically and politically important to Wabanaki interests. His threats did succeed in striking fear into the hearts and minds of colonial authorities and in opening the officials to negotiations. "I know not the cause of your so cruel Irruption upon our people," an alarmed Massachusetts government wrote, pleading with the commander to call off his warriors and indicating colonial officials' willingness to parley. Mogg's first order of business at these talks was ensuring the resumption of fair trade between the colony and Wabanaki communities in Maine. The tenacity of the sagamore's seafaring exploits demonstrated both the resiliency of Indian maritime power in Dawnland waters into the late seventeenth century and its capacity to garner diplomatic authority among colonial neighbors.[15]

When Captain Mogg's fleet harnessed an oceanic weather system to execute their attack at Richmond's Island, they utilized a skill that would serve native warriors well throughout each colonial and imperial conflict. Indians employed their intimate knowledge of the natural world, including a fluency with the region's rugged coastal geography, to augment an aggressive command of their maritime world and their plundering of European nautical technology. . . . During King William's War in 1688, Indian forces laid siege to two British sloops by positioning themselves at "a Turn of the Creek." Here they could "ly out of danger, so near 'em, as to throw Mud aboard with their Hands" while simultaneously making it "impossible for any of the Garrisons to afford 'em any relief." After making little headway in this posture, the Indians attempted a more creative approach. They constructed "a Great Fire Work, about Eighteen or Twenty Foot Square, and fill'd it up with Combustible matter, which they Fired" and carefully arranged "it in the way, for the Tide now to Floate it up, unto the Sloops." During Governor Dummer's War in July 1725, Captain Edward Winslow described how

---

[14]"Francis Card's Declaration," 149; Hight, "Mogg Heigon," 352–54; Hubbard, *Narrative of the Troubles with the Indians*, 46–7.

[15]"Francis Card's Declaration," 149, 150–51. Brackets in original. Massachusetts Archives Collection, SC1-45X, vol. 30, f. 225, Massachusetts Historical Society Photostats, Oct. 19, 1676 (Massachusetts Historical Society, Boston). Special thanks to the *Journal of American History*'s anonymous reader 5 for bringing this last source to my attention.

"two Shallops & a Scooner were . . . taken by a Scooner man'd with Indians" who immediately sailed them "in to the Harbour on the North Side of Monhegan [Island]" off the Maine coast, "which is the Place of their Rondezvouz." . . . The natural topography of Maine and Acadia's jagged shoreline provided countless rivers, bays, and coves ideal for staging assaults and secreting away even the most sizable of Wabanaki plunder.[16]

Sailing ships commandeered during wartime became so integrated into native society that their new owners were unwilling to relinquish them after a declaration of peace. As early as King Philip's War, British commissioners realized that regardless of the pressures they could exert on Wabanaki in treaty conferences, native delegates were far less yielding regarding watercraft acquired through right of conquest. . . . After hearing rumors of the arrival of Wabanaki delegates in Boston in 1725, the Marblehead fisherman Samuel Stacey informed the governor's office "That they have one of my Schooners in their Hands, which they took from me some Time ye Summer before last," indicating that Indians developed methods for the long-term preservation of their prizes.[17]

Nautical technology extracted from the British maritime presence was so critical to Wabanaki society that Indians took elaborate measures to preserve and conceal ships from their oftentimes befuddled enemies. After King Philip's War in 1677, Boston authorities organized a reconnaissance mission to coastal Maine, assuring one distraught fisherman there that they were "sensibly Affected with the Losse of your sonne, together with the takeing of your Ketch" by Indian mariners, and promising to determine "what they doe with your Vessells." Shortly after the outbreak of King William's War, a British officer stationed at Sagadehoc garrison near Casco Bay "went up the River from New Towne Garrison . . . to fetch Downe the Vessell ye Indians had taken and carry'd up the River," but he was repelled by a "parcell of Indians." . . . Col. Thomas Westbrook informed his supervisors in [1724] . . . that he "Diligently Searched after the Vessells belonging to this Province (that were taken by the Indians) but Could find none. . . ." Most of the ships lost forever to their British owners had been quickly ensconced among the maze of rivers, bays, and coves linking the inland forests to the ocean, a natural network with which Wabanaki were most fluent. These watercraft were simply too important to their captors' communities to be scuttled or abandoned.[18]

---

[16]Cotton Mather, *Decennium Luctuosum: An History of Remarkable Occurrences in the Long War, Which New-England hath had with the Indian Salvages, From the Year, 1688, to the Year, 1698* (Boston, 1699), 90, 94–5. On the 1725 episode, see statement of Capt. Edward Winslow, July 9, 1725, Massachusetts Archives Collection, SC1-45X, vol. 62, f. 421; *Boston Evening Post*, July 22, 1745, p. 2.

[17]"Letter A. Brockhollt & others to the Governor & Council," Aug. 18, 1677, in *Documentary History of the State of Maine*, ed. Baxter, VI, 191–92; Samuel Stacey to Dummer, Nov. 15, 1725, in *Letters of Colonel Thomas Westbrook and Others Relative to Indian Affairs in Maine, 1722–1726*, ed. William Blake Trask (Boston, 1901), 151.

[18]H. Burnett to a fisherman, Jan. 3, 1676, in *Documentary History of the State of Maine*, ed. Baxter, VI, 146–47; Elisha Andrewes to Your Honours, May 19, 1689, ibid., 480; John Minot to Dummer, July 16, 1724, in *Letters of Colonel Thomas Westbrook and Others Relative to Indian Affairs in Maine*, ed. Trask, 64; John Penhallow to Dummer, Aug. 16, 1724, in *Documentary History of the State of Maine*, ed. Baxter, X, 224; letter to Capt. Durrell, ibid., 214.

Aside from the ships and cargo so esteemed by native seamen, Indians also routinely pressed maritime labor from the floating warehouse to their east. Exercising physical domination over prisoners captured in battle and employing them in servile tasks were long central to the Wabanaki protocol of captive-taking, a custom extended to Atlantic waters with increasing frequency. Not long after the beginning of Governor Dummer's War in 1722, Governor Richard Philipps of Nova Scotia was already so distraught over the success of Indian press gangs that he issued a public proclamation denouncing their frequent harassment of the fishery with "the Assistance of the prisoners whom they take for Sailors" and promising swift justice for any French inhabitants who abetted the natives. The announcement did little good as three months later Phillips was still fuming when "Indians cruised upon the Fishing Ships with the Sloops and Prisoners they had first taken who they Compelled to serve as Mariners which Alarmed the Fishery at Canco."[19]

Yet other Indian warriors, perhaps those less nautically proficient, valued the highly technical sailing acumen of their British prisoners and exploited it effectively aboard their prize ships. During King Philip's War, for example, Captain Mogg's native crew pressed Thomas Cobbit and John Abbot into service aboard a small pinnace, "which the Indians made them to sayl for them." The following year, the fisherman Robert Roules described how his captors seized everyone on his ship and "commanded us to sail our vessel towards Penobscot" and later "compelled us to haile" an unsuspecting British ship on the horizon. By Governor Dummer's War, native warriors had developed a keen eye for experienced navigators. In one of the conflict's engagements, Indians surprised eight vessels anchored off the Fox Islands in Maine and took forty prisoners, "reserving the skippers and best sailors to navigate for them" before killing the rest. Anchored off the Nova Scotia coast in 1737, the sloop *Friends Adventure* was "Boarded in an hostile manner" by armed Indians who quickly overcame the slumbering crew. Well versed with the ship's rigging, the hijackers instantly "cutt away the fasts, hoisted sail" and forced its captain "to steer the Vessell about three Leagues" to a discreet cove where half the cargo was unloaded to awaiting Indians. After this stop, the mariners "brought the aforesaid Vesell to sail & forced him to steer her part of the way to a place called Cape Fendu," where they dispersed the remainder of the plunder to another native community.[20]

---

[19]Proclamation of Richard Philipps, July 15, 1722, Colonial Office Papers 5/752, f. 19(i); Abstract of a letter from Richard Philipps Gov. of Nova Scotia, Sept. 19, 1722, Frederick Lewis Gay transcripts, Nova Scotia Papers, vol. IV, f. 45 (Massachusetts Historical Society).

[20]For the "which the Indians made them" quotation, see William Hubbard, "A Narrative of the Troubles with the Indians in New-England, From Pascataqua to Pemmaquid," in *A Narrative of the Troubles with the Indians in New-England, from the first planting thereof in the year 1607, to this present year 1677. But chiefly of the late Troubles in the two last years, 1675, and 1676*, by William Hubbard (Boston, 1677), 57–58, 65. On Roules, see Axtell, "Vengeful Women of Marblehead," 650, 51. On Governor Dummer's War, see Samuel Penhallow, *The History of the Wars of New-England with the Eastern Indians* (Cincinnati, OH, 1859), 101. Deposition of Stephen Jones mariner Master of the Sloop Friends Adventure, June 18, 1737, Colonial Office Papers 217/31, ff. 126–28.

Ransoming hijacked ships for ready cash became a profitable option for Indian warriors by the early eighteenth century. The French fortress of Louisbourg on Ile-Royale (Cape Breton Island) emerged after 1713 as the principal entrepôt through which France provisioned its Wabanaki allies. Here Indians maximized the benefits of imperial alliance by cultivating a market for their stolen British ships. French officials at the precarious edge of empire had few qualms about participating in these transactions, routinely obliging native mariners demanding remuneration for their prizes. After stopping by their village to unload a rich cargo of powder, shot, and cannon from a "prize English ship" taken in November 1727, Indian sailors steered immediately for Louisbourg and hawked it for 3,500 livres. Gov. Joseph de Saint-Ovide paid two thousand livres of the ransom in cash, while the Indians "demanded the rest in goods." During King George's War in 1752, Indians near Port-Toulouse on Ile-Royale hijacked two British fishing schooners, dispensed with their crews ashore, and sold the vessels to the French for 5,200 livres. . . .[21]

The French colony's active role in this ransom economy was, of course, impelled by its imperial ambitions against Britain, the achievement of which increasingly depended on an ever-tenuous Wabanaki alliance. Colonial administrators acknowledged the indispensability of Indian warriors to the cause of empire as early as King William's War in the 1690s, the first conflict where Wabanaki and French forces coordinated their efforts against Britain. Jean Bochart de Champigny, intendant of New France during the war, jubilantly detailed for his superiors in France the devastation wrought by a native seaborne attack on New England ships and coastal forts. Other French colonial leaders echoed these sentiments in succeeding conflicts, and in peacetime they made clear their fear of perturbing Wabanaki communities in the slightest degree. . . .[22]

---

[21]On Louisbourg, see J. S. McLennan, *Louisbourg from Its Foundation to Its Fall, 1713–1758* (London, 1918); and Geoffrey Plank, *An Unsettled Conquest: The British Campaign against the Peoples of Acadia* (Philadelphia, 2001), 40–41, 62–65. "Monsieur de Saint-Ovide au Ministre concernant les Sauvages" (Mr. de Saint-Ovide to minister concerning the Indians), Nov. 20, 1727, Archives des colonies, series C11B, vol. 9, ff. 64–70v (National Archives of Canada, Ottawa). On King George's War, see "Monsieur Prévost au Ministre" (Mr. Prévost to minister), Sept. 10, 1752, Archives des colonies, series C11B, vol. 32, ff. 163–66.

[22]"Lettre de Monsieur de Champigny au Ministre, a Québec" (Letter of Mr. de Champigny minister, Quebec), Oct. 5, 1692, in *Collection de manuscrits contenant letters, mémoirs, et autres documents historiques relatives à la Nouvelle-France recueillis aux Archives de la Province de Québec ou copiés à l'étranger* (Manuscript collection containing letters, memoirs, and other historical documents relative to New France collected from archives of the province of Quebec or copies abroad) (4 vols., Quebec, 1883–1885), II, 89–90; "Mémoire concernant la distribution de présents aux sauvages" (Report concerning the distribution of presents to the Indians), 1717, Archives des colonies, series C11B, vol. 2, ff. 188–89. On warnings about the necessity of Indian alliances, see "Resumé des Lettres sur les Sauvages Abenaquis" (Summary of letters on the Wabanaki Indians), n.d., in *Collection de manuscrits contenant letters, mémoirs, et autres documents historiques relatives à la Nouvelle-France recueillis aux Archives de la Province de Québec ou copiés à l'étranger*, I, 468–69; Pulsipher, "Gaining the Diplomatic Edge," 19–47; and Kenneth M. Morrison, *The Embattled Northeast: The Elusive Ideal of Alliance in Abenaki-Euroamerican Relations* (Berkeley, CA, 1984).

Native seaborne offensives were neither chance encounters nor frivolous diversions from land-based warfare, but calculated and sustained operations with unambiguous objectives. Plundering material wealth, exacting retribution, and enhancing diplomatic authority among imperial rivals—indispensible strategies for managing colonialism by the late seventeenth century—could be achieved most effectively afloat. . . .

When Indians took the fight to the sea in each of the colonial wars, they continued to set their sights on the lucrative North Atlantic fishery, New England's commercial backbone and a vital component of Britain's Atlantic economy. The rich stores of cod and mackerel along Georges Bank and the Grand Banks attracted annual fishing expeditions from England starting in the early sixteenth century. Backed by London merchants, New England fishermen from coastal communities such as Marblehead and Gloucester staged a gradual takeover of the industry during the 1640s as England became embroiled in a decade of political turmoil unleashed by the Civil Wars (1642–1651). The economic effects of this transformation were quickly felt on both sides of the Atlantic. As early as 1641 Massachusetts governor John Winthrop reported an annual harvest of some 300,000 cod worth £6,750, while four years later the annual value of exported fish was pushing £10,000. . . . "The Chief Staple of this Country," as Massachusetts lieutenant governor William Stoughton referred to it in 1696, would continue to flourish over the next century. . . . By the end of the colonial period, fishing constituted the largest sector of New England's economy, with annual exports totaling over £160,000—roughly half of all exports by value. In Nova Scotia the percentage was far greater.[23]

But whatever affluence Britain enjoyed from this arm of its commercial network, the fishery was also the empire's Achilles' heel in Wabanaki waters. The concentration of European fishing fleets trolling the northeastern banks had long profited plundering Indian mariners, and throughout the colonial wars fishermen found their enterprise under sustained assault. These perennial attacks jeopardized the fishery's viability and contributed to its ongoing deterioration, setbacks that belied the industry's overall steady growth. Massachusetts fishermen in 1688, for example, chose to relinquish their employment entirely and plead with their government for compensation rather than risk their lives and equipment in the Wabanaki Atlantic. The Indian threat at sea forced these desperate men to stay "shut up in Garrison" throughout the season, "not permitted to go to Sea or to bring their Fish about to Boston, which Lyeth there upon Spoyle." Shortly after Queen Anne's War reached Wabanakia, a British

---

[23]"Address to the King," Sept. 24, 1696, in *Documentary History of the State of Maine*, ed. Baxter, V, 450; John J. McCusker and Russell R. Menard, *The Economy of British America, 1607–1789* (Chapel Hill, NC, 1985), 99–100, 108–15; Bernard Bailyn, *The New England Merchants in the Seventeenth Century* (Cambridge, MA, 1955), 76–82; Christine Leigh Heyrman, *Commerce and Culture: The Maritime Communities of Colonial Massachusetts, 1690–1750* (New York, 1984); Stephen Innes, *Creating the Commonwealth: The Economic Culture of Puritan New England* (New York, 1995), 298–300, esp. 298.

fishing community near the mouth of the St. John River quickly evacuated to a nearby island as "the Indians burnt all their Stages and Boats."[24]

Colonial leaders routinely amplified such warnings to their own superiors. With the outbreak of each war, governors, legislators, and military officials dreaded the thought of Wabanaki warriors closing in on the heart of their transatlantic economy. Edmund Andros's beleaguered government in Boston reminded Whitehall at the beginning of King William's War in 1689 that "our enemies are Eastern Indians" and "this country will be in danger of being overrun" if left unchecked. "Then farewell to the West Indian plantations, which cannot subsist without our provisions," Edward Randolph, a colonial administrator, argued to his superiors. . . . By Queen Anne's War, such terrors had not abated when Massachusetts governor Joseph Dudley petitioned his Assembly for "a good force of . . . Sloopes to attend the Coast Eastward to keep the Indians from the benefit of the sea." His supplications grew more frantic when later that year "about 200 Cape Sable Indians . . . came round the bay of Fundee and . . . debauched all the Eastern Coast from St. Croix to the Province of Main." After his diplomatic tour of Acadia in 1708, the Boston merchant Samuel Vetch likewise warned London of the miserable postwar state of New England's fishing economy. Thanks to Wabanaki seafaring assaults and the French support they often enjoyed, he alerted the Board of Trade that "their fishery is quite ruined." Although the British "had many hundreds of vessells, who formerly both catched and made their fish along this shore," they are currently "almost wholly debared this trade, to the unexpressible loss of New England in particular, and all the English Islands in generall, who used to be supplyed from thence with codd and mackrell, in great quantityes, and att low rates for the subsistance of themselves and slaves." Bidding adieu to the West Indies in an Indian sea of trouble was hardly the image metropolitan officials wished to see when envisioning their Atlantic empire.[25]

. . . People from all segments of colonial society—from fishermen and settlers to military officers and governors—supplemented their pleas with efforts to muster effective responses. During Queen Anne's War in August 1709, for example, Gloucester fishing captain Andrew Robbinson applied to the governor's office for a commission to arm his "good large Sloop" in a "warlike manner" to defend himself and his neighbors against the assaults of the "barbarous Salvages" off the

---

[24]"Petition of David Edwards," Oct. 22, 1688, in *Documentary History of the State of Maine*, ed. Baxter, VI, 442. For the "Indians burnt all" quotation, see *Boston News-Letter*, May 7, 1705, p. 2. John Wainwright to Dummer, July 13, 1724, in *Documentary History of the State of Maine*, ed. Baxter, X, 213.

[25]Copy of a letter from Boston, Oct. 24, 1689, in *Calendar of State Papers, Colonial Series, America and the West Indies*, vol. XIII: *1689–1692*, ed. J. W. Fortescue (London, 1901), 163–64. For the "good force" quotation, see "March 9, 1703 His Excellencys Speech to the Assembly," March 9, 1702, ibid., IX, 124–25. For the Cape Sable Indians quotation, see Col. Joseph Dudley to the Board, Sept. 15, 1703, ibid., 151–52. Letter from Capt. Samuel Vetch, July 27, 1708, in *Calendar of State Papers, Colonial Series, America and the West Indies*, vol. XXIV: *1708–1709*, ed. Cecil Headlam (London, 1922), 41–49.

coast of Cape Sables. The Indians, Robbinson complained, "frequently interrupt them in their Fishery, and commit outrages upon them." Emboldened by his robust new force, the fisherman was determined to "make Reprizal for the loss of his Vessell taken from him the year past, and to do other Spoiles upon the Enemy." . . .[26]

When the Wabanaki ramped up their plundering operations during Dummer's War in the mid-1720s, colonial officials struggled to match Indian naval prowess with an array of aggressive responses. Governor Phillips of Nova Scotia fitted out armed shiploads of volunteers in 1722 when "the Fishery became Impraticable from the Attacks and Barbarities the Indians made on all Vessels that were a Fishing," assaults that threatened the only commercial value the colonial outpost enjoyed. Massachusetts adopted an analogous approach when it encouraged the fisherman Samuel Hinckes and his band of volunteers to hunt and eradicate "indian pirets" in 1724. . . . Lt. Gov. William Dummer issued similar orders to an officer after receiving news "of severall Vessels man'd with Indians infesting the Eastern Coast to the great Disturbance & Loss of those concern'd in the Fishery."[27]

. . . British colonists could appropriate a proven rhetoric of piracy in their efforts to annihilate native maritime power. The trope of Wabanaki piracy surfaced during Dummer's War in the 1720s, conveniently coinciding with the "golden age" of piracy throughout the Atlantic in the wake of Queen Anne's War. This widespread eruption of seaborne theft and violence afforded imperial architects a timely discourse to discredit and criminalize the Wabanaki's now-formidable naval strength. Casting Indian maritime violence as the desperate and unprincipled acts of outlaws, as flagrantly "Illegall and Contrary to the Law of Nations," permitted colonial authorities to rationalize their losses to it without acknowledging native seafaring power as structured, systematic, and oftentimes impeding that of the colonists. A volunteer squadron was recruited . . . in July 1724 . . . not to engage a credible naval force but to go scouting "after indian pirets." . . . The rhetorical ploy of Indian piracy also of course implicitly acknowledged native warriors' destructive capacity in the British Empire's Atlantic economy.[28]

The Indian-as-pirate construct signified too the enduring dynamism and potency of native maritime authority and the increasing problem it posed to colonial authority in the Northeast. As late as October 1743, two decades after the decline of the golden age of piracy, Indian naval attacks near Nova Scotia so flourished that the colony's governor, Paul Mascarene, issued a public proclamation to British and French inhabitants who considered abetting them.

---

[26]The petition of Andrew Robbinson of Gloucester, Aug. 10, 1709, Massachusetts Archives Collection, SC1-45X, vol. 31, ff. 57–58.

[27]The humble petition of John Elliot of Topsham in the Country of Devon, July 22, 1722, Colonial Office Papers 5/752, f. 19; Samuel Hinckes to Dummer, Fort Mary, July 19, 1724, in *Documentary History of the State of Maine*, ed. Baxter, X, 212–13; "Letter to Capt. Durrell," n.d., ibid., 214.

[28]Marcus Rediker, *Villains of All Nations: Atlantic Pirates in the Golden Age* (Boston, 2004), 28, 35; Marcus Rediker, *Between the Devil and the Deep Blue Sea: Merchant Seamen, Pirates, and the Anglo-American Maritime World, 1700–1750* (New York, 1987), 254; "Letter from Samuel Hinckes," July 19, 1724, in *Letters of Colonel Thomas Westbrook and Others Relative to Indian Affairs in Maine*, ed. Trask, 63–64.

Furiously denouncing "the Indians in these their Piratical Villanys," particularly those "guilty of the like Piracys in time of serene Peace," Mascarene decreed that anyone who provided an outlet for goods "from the Indians so Piratically by them Robbed and taken" would risk prosecution for piracy. . . . Mascarene's carefully crafted language at once rendered Indian maritime power illicit and unlawful, while tacitly declaring its profound resilience and brutal effectiveness.[29]

Wabanaki understood their seaborne operations as characterized by continuity rather than as practices that suddenly transitioned to piracy in the 1720s. From the earliest period of European contact, they consistently organized their bluewater campaigns around the joint strategies of resistance and plundering to maintain and augment their established relationship to the Atlantic. Much of that approach may well have been prompted by a number of European pirates who frequented Dawnland waves. The legendary Dixey Bull, for example, "first pirate in New England waters," traveled from London to the Maine coast in 1631 and cultivated an extensive trading relationship with local Indians while simultaneously preying on colonial New England shipping. The crew of Dutchman Jurriaen Aernouts and Boston seamen John Rhoades similarly plied the Gulf of Maine and Acadian coastline in the 1670s, pillaging traders and attempting to conquer the sparsely colonized territory. In September 1723 the notorious Captain "Lowder the Pyrate" and his crew commandeered some twenty French vessels near Cape Breton along with several other British crafts, "particular[ly] a Scooner belonging to Boston." The enduring presence of such outlaws in Wabanakia introduced Indians to likeminded seafarers with similar ambitions, while revealing to them the sheer vulnerability—and richness—of the North Atlantic economy.[30]

Cultural maxims governing pirate life were also strikingly compatible with customary Algonquian attitudes regarding power, justice, economic subsistence, and the role of the individual in the community. Material collectivism, an aversion to personal acquisitiveness, authority through communal consensus, and retaliatory justice permeated the ethos of both Indian and pirate societies, uniting their values and interests for over a century in the Northeast. Regardless of colonial rhetoric, Wabanaki warriors did not newly resort to piracy after Queen Anne's War; they had always been "pirates" in their exploitation of the European maritime world and in their struggle to maintain their long-standing authority in the northwest Atlantic. What precisely constitutes piracy, of course, has always been predicated on the observer's economic and political perspective. In the face of increasing land dispossession, a deteriorating natural resource base, and ongoing attempts to sever their bonds with the ocean, native communities possessed entirely different notions of who the real pirates were.[31]

---

[29]Paul Mascarene's proclamation, Oct. 20, 1743, Colonial Office Papers 217/31, ff. 193–94.

[30]George Francis Dow and John Henry Edmonds, *The Pirates of the New England Coast, 1630–1730* (1923; New York, 1996), 20–53. On "Lowder the Pyrate," see *American Weekly Mercury*, Sept. 26, 1723, 2.

[31]Robert C. Ritchie, *Captain Kidd and the War against the Pirates* (Cambridge, MA, 1986), 123–25; Rediker, *Villains of All Nations*, 45, 62; Rediker, *Between the Devil and the Deep Blue Sea*, 263, 269, 279.

The rhetorical emergence of the "Indian pirate" during the golden age of piracy had repercussions far beyond what was said and written by colonial officials. When shored up with legal implications, as it was in a spectacle that shocked and infuriated the native Northeast in October 1726, the juridical rhetoric of Indian piracy served as another attempt to regulate and restructure the Wabanaki Atlantic in accordance with British modes of governance. In that month three Indian warriors stood trial before the viceadmiralty court in Boston, indicted for piracy. The accused were among a native force that nearly hijacked Captain Doty's vessel anchored off the Nova Scotia coast. After storming aboard and pressing the captain and crew into service, the Indians forced Doty to chase down another vessel on the horizon as they vowed "they would take her, and kill all the Hands on board and then give him his Vessel again." One of Doty's men who earlier escaped undetected to a small chamber below deck suddenly emerged with his guns blazing. Doty joined him as "three of the Indians jumped out of the Cabbin Window, they being then a Mile or two from the Shore, and the rest immediately submitted." Three Wabanaki prisoners were transported to Boston and ordered before the court of admiralty. At the conclusion of the trial, newspapers informed Bostoners that the pirates "were found Guilty" and "received [a] Sentence of Death." A few days later they were hanging from the public gallows.[32]

The reaction in Wabanaki communities was explosive. Rather than succeeding as a deterrent, the public trial and execution of Indian warriors orchestrated by an imperial judicial system in distant Boston escalated native fear of, and anger over, Britain's maritime colonialism. . . . [A] wave of retributive violence quickly swept through northeastern waters. Indians again targeted the fishery. Less than two months later, Governor Dummer received desperate news from the Annapolis Royal garrison of impending Wabanaki violence against "our Fisher Men in Revenge of ye Justice doen to ye French & Indian Pirates the last Fall." Those fears were further realized when "Indians of Cape Sables . . . committed divers barbarous acts of hostility upon an English vessel . . . and some other fishermen that were at anchor at Cape Sables." . . . The Boston piracy trial and its violent aftermath typified the ongoing contest to consolidate and define the contours of the Atlantic world, a struggle of incompatible and increasingly exclusive visions.[33]

In the wake of Dummer's War, the ambit of Wabanaki maritime violence shifted northeast. British military campaigns during the war devastated Indian villages in southern Maine, and many refugees fled northwest to join extended kin in French mission communities along the St. Lawrence River. Swelling colonial settlements along coastal Maine now displaced native summer encampments. These mutually reinforcing trends psychologically, economically, and

---

[32]*Boston News-Letter*, Sept. 8, 1726, p. 2; ibid., Oct. 6, 1726, p. 2.

[33]L. F. S. Upton, *Micmacs and Colonists: Indian-White Relations in the Maritimes, 1713–1867* (Vancouver, 1979), 44–45; letter from Lt. Gov. Dummer, May 23, 1727, in *Documentary History of the State of Maine*, ed. Baxter, X, 393–96, esp. 396; Gyles to Dummer, June 14, 1727, ibid., 403–5; Dummer to the Council of Trade and Plantations, Nov. 6, 1727, in *Calendar of State Papers, Colonial Series, America and the West Indies*, vol. XXXV: *1726–1727*, ed. Cecil Headlam (London, 1936), 391.

spatially distanced southern Wabanaki from the ocean to an unprecedented extent. Their seasonal migratory pattern linking the inland forests and the Atlantic—an annual cycle that defined Wabanaki life for generations—was increasingly interrupted by dammed rivers, sawmills, and commercial fishing stages. The sparse native population that remained in the southern borderlands experienced greater proximity to the locus of British power in New England, which, when coupled with limited access to the ocean, precluded the successful extension of warfare to the ocean.[34]

Geopolitical circumstances in northern Wabanakia were much different. The relatively weak position of the British in Nova Scotia and the presence of the French stronghold at Cape Breton created an environment where Mi'kmaq and other Wabanaki refugees from the southwest could sustain their seaborne violence. Their exploitation of the British maritime presence, increasingly executed during interludes of official imperial peace, signaled the abandonment of the former strategy that relied on the occasional outbreak of European imperial conflict. Instead, northeastern Wabanaki forged their own retributive and economic opportunities. Recognizing the native Atlantic's ongoing dissolution in Maine, Nova Scotia Indians desperately sought to circumvent that same fate. British fishermen remained the prime target. In 1737 Stephen Jones was plundered of goods worth fifteen hundred pounds when, one night, his "Sloop was Boarded in an hostile manner by six or seven Indians armed with Guns, Hatchets & Knives &c." When Jones offered resistance, one of his captors "presented a Pistoll to his Breast several times" and "threatn'd to knock his Brains out." Mr. Trefry, another ship master, endured a similar experience in 1742 when near Mines he encountered a number of "Indians who surprised his Sloop and Cut her Cables," most likely after noticing that he was sailing without anchors. Trefry was subsequently "very Ill used By the said Indians," who proceeded to confiscate the entire cargo.[35]

When another European conflict broke out in 1754 and spread throughout the Atlantic, northern Wabanaki again seized the exigencies of war in a final attempt to retain some semblance of their maritime world. An express sent to Boston authorities in 1758 notified them of a joint force of "St. Johns & Penobscot Indians who were to Rendevous at Mount Desart" in the mouth of the Penobscot River, where "they were to proceed in the two Sloops (which they had lately Taken)" to attack British garrisons in south central Maine. But by the war's conclusion in 1763, the opportunities linked to the Northeast's imperial equilibrium had disintegrated. The end of the French regime in the Northeast marked the closure of a milieu that had allowed for the survival of the Wabanaki's seafaring power.

---

[34]Bourque, *Twelve Thousand Years*, 194; David L. Ghere, "Diplomacy & War on the Maine Frontier, 1678–1759," in *Maine: The Pine Tree State from Prehistory to the Present*, ed. Richard W. Judd, Edwin A. Churchill, and Joel W. Eastman (Orono, ME, 1995), 133; David L. Ghere, "Myths and Methods in Abenaki Demography: Abenaki Population Recovery, 1725–1750," *Ethnohistory* 44 (Summer 1997), 529.

[35]At a council held by order of Lt. Gov. Lawrence Armstrong, June 10, 1737, Colonial Office Papers 217/31, ff. 117–18; Deposition of Stephen Jones, June 18, 1737, ibid., ff. 126–28; At a council held on April 9, 1742, Colonial Office Papers 217/39, no. 173(a).

Gone were the French markets for commandeered ships, sources of material aid, and military presence that checked British land encroachment in Acadia. And gone too was the system of playing imperial powers off each other mastered by Indian diplomats over the previous century.[36]

While the end of the imperial status quo eliminated the conditions nourishing native naval aggression, the task of severing Indians from the Atlantic demanded a more culturally destructive strategy. British efforts to dislodge the French from the Northeast during the Seven Years' War were executed in conjunction with renewed schemes to thwart Wabanaki access to the ocean. This long-standing policy had been most recently articulated in 1748 by Gov. William Shirley, who advocated unsuccessfully for a blockhouse along the mid-Maine coast as "a means of keeping them from the Sea Shore." But when his successor, Governor Pownall, triumphantly announced in 1759 the construction of Fort Pownall to finally slam shut "ye last & only door That the Enimy had left to ye Atlantic," he accomplished what his predecessors could not. The dynamic longevity of Wabanaki power in the Northeast, so damaging to British Atlantic designs, could not be uprooted by solely obliterating its communities or imperial allies. Required was a dismantling of their ancient relationship with the sea.[37]

The Wabanaki experience in the early modern world stands outside the narrative of many other native peoples who bid farewell to ancestral homelands and endured forced migrations across vast expanses of the American landscape. Theirs instead was one of removal onto land. The maritime traits that defined so much of their culture and gave meaning to the Dawnland for centuries dissolved in their coerced relocation from the waters of the East and subsequent terrestrial confinement. This transformation was completed by a fundamental deconstruction of their Atlantic vision until it was compatible with one very different. By 1763 Wabanaki were forced to reckon with a reality they struggled so long to prevent: the violent theft of a cherished world. Yet the outcome of this pelagic power struggle belies the stormy two centuries of theft, destruction, and chaos that buffeted Europe's Atlantic project and rendered its integration elusive. Indian campaigns of maritime violence left in their wake an utterly terrified and helpless corner of the colonial Northeast, so precarious that many Euro-Americans feared it was teetering on the precipice of destruction. We have long known that native people in early America shaped in profound ways nearly every military

---

[36]Pownall to Board of Trade, Sept. 12, 1758, Colonial Office Papers 5/889, ff. 179–80. On the Indians' playing-off system in North America, see, for example, Pulsipher, "Gaining the Diplomatic Edge"; Claudio Saunt, "'Our Indians': European Empires and the History of the Native American South," in *The Atlantic in Global History, 1500–2000*, ed. Jorge Cañizares-Esguerra and Erik R. Seeman (Upper Saddle River, NJ, 2006), 61–76; David J. Weber, *The Spanish Frontier in North America* (New Haven, CT, 1992); DuVal, *Native Ground*; Morrison, *Embattled Northeast*; Gilles Havard, *The Great Peace of Montreal of 1701: French-Native Diplomacy in the Seventeenth Century* (Montreal, 2001); and Daniel K. Richter, *The Ordeal of the Longhouse: The Peoples of the Iroquois League in the Era of European Colonization* (Chapel Hill, NC, 1992).

[37]"Governor Shirley's Speech, May 26, 1748," in *Documentary History of the State of Maine*, ed. Baxter, XI, 401–2. Speech of T. Pownall in the Council Chamber, June 1, 1759, ibid., XIII, 168.

conflict on North American soil and in many cases dictated the terms of engagement. Historians maintain too that Indians held the balance of power in the
northeastern borderlands well into the eighteenth century. But at sea their actions
were equally decisive. Wabanaki power afloat exposed an Atlantic world quite
striking to modern sensibilities, one very far from an organic, seamless, and
timeless entity facilitating the construction of European empires and their ascen-
dant global economies. To the region's native inhabitants and colonial newcomers, this extraordinarily generative and lucrative corner of the Atlantic was a
profoundly contested space, not only as two European empires frequently
declared it so in the war rooms of London and Versailles but also when Britain's
struggle to homogenize and incorporate its productive capacity collided with
Wabanaki attempts to protect and enhance their rich maritime heritage. The
rationalization of a British Atlantic world never progressed systematically, but
instead ran up against the hostility, disarray, and devastation unleashed by a
people equally resolute to define the ocean's significance.[38]

---

[38]On Indians' role in the balance of power in the northeastern borderlands, see Baker and Reid,
"Amerindian Power in the Early Modern Northeast," 77–106; Pulsipher, *Subjects unto the Same
King*; and Bilodeau, "Economy of War." On southeastern Indians, see Saunt, "Our Indians," 61–76;
and Patrick M. Malone, *The Skulking Way of War: Technology and Tactics among the New England
Indians* (Baltimore, MD, 1993). The historian Brian Connolly argues that conventional applications
of an Atlantic framework tend to naturalize modern-day global capitalism and its attendant social
relations in a coherent early modern Atlantic world. See Brian Connolly, "Intimate Atlantics:
Toward a Critical History of Transnational Early America," *Common-Place* 11 (2) (Jan. 2011), http://
common-place-archives.org/vol-11/no-02/connolly/.

Matthew R. Bahar

I am a historian of colonial America with an interest in the cross-cultural relations of American Indians and Euro-Americans. The role of violence in these exchanges serves as an important analytical framework in my research and writing. By exploring its uses, successes, and failures, violence can reveal for us the depths of human desire, fears and anxieties about others, and the formation and expression of identity. Much of what I enjoy about studying and teaching history is the opportunity to tell stories. My curiosity about the past grew out of the countless stories my grandparents shared with me about their lives. The world they recreated seemed so different from mine, but I later learned that a good historian must appreciate the utter strangeness of the past. History is fascinating because we need to exercise so much of our imagination to make sense of it; we need to empathize with people who sometimes held beliefs very different from our own; we need to look beyond our individual lived experiences of the world and make room for others. In my classroom and my writing, I am less interested in making the past speak directly to the present than I am in developing an appreciation for the complexity of the human experience. Students who come away from my classes should have much in common with those who study abroad in a cultural immersion program. I am a faculty member in the Department of History at Oberlin College.

QUESTIONS FOR CONSIDERATION

1. Describe the ways the Wabanaki people utilized British dependence on Atlantic trade to their advantage.
2. Characterize the Wabanaki relationship with the Atlantic Ocean, both economically and culturally, before European contact. How did this history before contact shape Wabanaki encounters with Europeans?
3. The Wabanaki and English were shaped by their encounter with each other. Describe the effect of this encounter on each.
4. Bahar describes New England's profit from fishing as the empire's "Achilles' heel." What evidence does he use to support this statement?
5. How did the British use the European "trope" of piracy to counter Wabanaki attacks? According to Bahar, why was the use of this trope particularly meaningful during the eighteenth century?
6. According to Bahar, what values did Wabanaki society share with European pirates? How might the Wabanaki reject this comparison?

7. Name two events that allowed the British to wrest control over the Atlantic seaboard from the Wabanaki.

8. According to Bahar, how does an understanding of Wabanaki "piracy" complicate and enhance our knowledge of the history of the North Atlantic during the seventeenth and eighteenth centuries?

CHAPTER THREE

From Captives to Slaves: Commodifying Indian Women in the Borderlands[1]

Juliana Barr

On July 21, 1774, fray Miguel Santa María y Silva, the leading Franciscan missionary stationed in the mission district of Los Adaes on the border between Texas and Louisiana, reported to the Spanish viceroy in Mexico City on his trip . . . as part of a delegation seeking renewed peace with powerful Wichita and Caddo nations. In 1769, in the aftermath of the Seven Years' War, Spain had officially established administrative control of the former French province of Louisiana, and the mission to reconfirm Wichita and Caddo alliances sought to represent the new unity of Spaniards and Frenchmen in Louisiana and Texas. . . . Rather than detail this first peace council sought by the Spanish government with leading Indian nations, the Franciscan spent page after page lamenting an "infamous traffic of the flesh" he had witnessed being carried on by Frenchmen living in and among Caddoan Indian villages. . . . To discredit Frenchmen, Santa María y Silva could have deplored the skyrocketing numbers of enslaved Africans and African Americans in Louisiana by the 1770s. Or, given the hostile relations between the Spanish government and many independent and powerful Indian nations in the lower Plains, the missionary could have bemoaned the fate of Spanish women and children from New Mexico who had been taken captive by Indians armed with guns obtained from French traders. Yet, strikingly, the traffic in humans on which Santa María y Silva chose to focus was one in Indian women and their children, captured by Indian warriors in the southern Plains and Texas and traded east as slaves to French buyers in Louisiana—women thus consigned to "perdition" by "such cruel captivity." . . .[2]

The scholarly focus on mediation and accommodation as women's characteristic activity in Indian-European relations often leads us to overlook the

---

[1] Interested students are encouraged to read this essay in the original form. Juliana Barr, "From Captives to Slaves: Commodifying Indian Women in the Borderlands," *Journal of American History* 92 (1) (June 2005), 19–46.

[2] Fray Miguel Santa María y Silva to Viceroy Antonio Bucareli y Ursúa, July 21, 1774, in *Athanase de Mézières and the Louisiana-Texas Frontier, 1768–1780*, trans. and ed. Herbert Eugene Bolton (2 vols., Cleveland, OH, 1914), II, 74–75.

importance of women in political economies of war and imperial rivalry.[3] Multiple coercive traffics in women became essential to European-Indian interaction long before Sacagawea fell into the hands of her captors. Recognition of the diversity of trafficking not only enriches our understanding of the gender dynamics of European-Indian diplomacy and conflict but also enables us to move beyond the homogeneous conception of slavery suggested by using only African American enslavement, specifically, racial chattel slavery (defined here as a form of property and system of compulsory labor entailing permanent and hereditary status) to explore bondage and unfreedom in America. . . .

The confluence of Spanish, French, and Indian peoples in the areas later known as Comanchería, Apachería, Spanish Texas, and French Louisiana makes them an ideal venue for exploring the forms that traffic in women might take and the kinds of currency that women might represent to Indian and European men who exchanged them. Distinct systems of captivity, bondage, and enslavement developed in a matrix of expanding Indian territories, French mercantilism, and Spanish defensive needs during the eighteenth century. At the end of the seventeenth century, steadily increasing numbers of Spaniards coming north from Mexico and Frenchmen coming south from Illinois and Canada began to invade the region and establish neighboring, competing provinces. At the same time, the territories of bands of Apaches and later Comanches and Wichitas were shifting to include increasingly large areas of present-day north and north-central Texas. As those groups converged in the eighteenth century, European and Indian men—as captors, brokers, and buyers—used captured and enslaved women to craft relationships of trade and reciprocity with one another. A key difference between such exchanges and those involving intermarriage was that the women whom men captured and enslaved were strangers or enemies to their kinship systems. When Indian bands brokered marital unions in the service of diplomacy, a woman's own family or band leaders usually negotiated on her behalf. . . . [E]nslaved Indian women in Texas and Louisiana remained outside the kin relations of the households that made them objects of exchange. . . .[4] Indians of another group suffer[ed] the loss of their women when their enemies sought to build trade ties with Europeans through captive women and children. If efforts to cement diplomatic and economic ties did not succeed—as often happened between Indians and Spaniards—military and state officials made punitive war, seeking out captives and hostages in retribution for failed negotiations. Thus hostility as much as accommodation was the context for the traffic in women. The political and commercial aspects of the exchanges also set them apart from most Indian practices of captivity and from European systems of enslavement: Indians did not take the women to

---

[3]Walter Johnson, "On Agency," *Journal of Social History* 37 (Fall 2003), 113–24. Brooks, *Captives and Cousins;* and Albert L. Hurtado, *Intimate Frontiers: Sex, Gender, and Culture in Old California* (Albuquerque, NM, 1999). Thomas P. Slaughter, *Exploring Lewis and Clark: Reflections on Men and Wilderness* (New York, 2003), 86–113. Donna Barbie, "Sacajawea: The Making of a Myth," in *Sifters: Native American Women's Lives*, ed. Theda Perdue (New York, 2001), 60–76.

[4]Gayle Rubin, "The Traffic in Women: Notes on the 'Political Economy' of Sex," in *Toward an Anthropology of Women*, ed. Rayna R. Reiter (New York, 1975), 174. Jane Fishburne Collier, *Marriage and Inequality in Classless Societies* (Stanford, 1988).

avenge or replace the dead, as they took most captives; nor did Europeans intend to use them as a servile labor force, as they used most slaves. Instead, the exchanges interwove the categories of captivity and slavery and thereby transformed Indian women into valuable commodities of cross-cultural war, diplomacy, and power.

Writing in 1774, Santa María y Silva demonstrated a certain disingenuousness in focusing only on Frenchmen, since Spaniards had been reducing select Indians from the region to bondage for much of the eighteenth century. But that misdirection highlights the way the trade in Indian women may explicate geopolitical relations among European and native powers in colonial America. In his attempts to accent Spanish-French differences, the Franciscan downplayed the contentious relations between Spaniards and neighboring Indians that had made the diplomatic mission to the Wichita and Caddo bands a necessity in the first place. In such a world, Indian women in the hands of enemy Indian men became key objects of captive raiding and hostage exchange as the women's Indian captors sought economic and diplomatic gain with both native and European allies. In the hands of Spanish and French buyers and enslavers, women faced fates from sexual servitude to consignment to labor camps to use as political capital in attempts to win or impose alliances or to signal the failure of those efforts. . . . I . . . explore the ways Spanish, French, and Indian men sought to forge or coerce bonds of obligation through a trade in female pawns. The diverse conditions to which such women were reduced reveal new ways of understanding bondage and unfreedom.

Our story begins with French-Indian captive trade across the Plains and along the Texas-Louisiana border. . . . Indian peoples took a few captives in warfare only for ritualized ceremonies of revenge or, less often, for adoption. Men rarely allowed themselves to be captured, preferring death on the battlefield; those captured most often were destined for torture, which furnished the opportunity for the honorable warrior's death denied them in battle (the honor acquired by enduring pain). In contrast, captors deemed women and children easier to incorporate into their communities. . . . Outside the realm of war, exchanges of women and children more often took a peaceful form, particularly in the service of diplomatic alliance. Intermarriage often united bands in political and economic relationships. . . . Children might also be exchanged . . . and adopted into their communities as signs of alliance and insurance of peace.[5]

[When] Henri de Tonti and several other Frenchmen arrived in Caddo lands in search of survivors of La Salle's expedition, Kadohadacho warriors tried to

---

[5]William C. Foster, ed., Johanna S. Warren, trans., *The La Salle Expedition to Texas: The Journal of Henri Joutel, 1684–1687* (Austin, TX, 1998), 227–29; Fray Francisco Casañas de Jesús María to the Viceroy of Mexico, Aug. 15, 1691, in "Descriptions of the Tejas or Asinai Indians, 1691–1722," trans. Mattie Austin Hatcher, *Southwestern Historical Quarterly* 30 (Jan. 1927), 217; Ralph A. Smith, trans. and ed., "Account of the Journey of Bénard de la Harpe: Discovery Made by Him of Several Nations Situated in the West," ibid. 62 (July 1958), 75–86; ibid. (Oct. 1958), 246–59; ibid. (Jan. 1959), 371–85; ibid. (April 1959), 525–41; David La Vere, *The Caddo Chiefdoms: Caddo Economics and Politics, 700–1835* (Lincoln, NE, 1998), 1–14, 33–35; Timothy K. Perttula, *"The Caddo Nation": Archaeological and Ethnohistoric Perspectives* (Austin, TX, 1992), 85, 217–20; Karl Schmitt and Iva Osanai Schmitt, *Wichita Kinship: Past and Present* (Norman, n.d.), 23; Gordon M. Sayre, *Les Sauvages Américains: Representations of Native Americans in French and English Colonial Literature* (Chapel Hill, NC, 1997), 14, 266.

persuade the Frenchmen to accompany them into war against Spaniards to the southwest of their lands. As enticement, the warriors promised the Frenchmen any money found, but "as for themselves," Tonti recorded, "they only wished to take the women and children as slaves." The Frenchmen declined, trying to make clear that the decision derived from a reluctance to take Christian captives, since the women and children targeted were in Spanish settlements. The Caddo men could not be blamed for presuming French interest in slaves, however, since the Frenchmen showed no reluctance to trade in enslaved or captive *Indians*. In fact, Tonti had brought with him two Kadohadacho women whom he had purchased from Arkansas Indians at his Illinois trading post on the Mississippi River. The Frenchman hoped that returning the women to their people would put him in the Caddos' good graces—and he was right; it did. It may also have helped establish an image of Frenchmen as purveyors of Indian slaves in the minds of Caddoan peoples.[6]

After the French province of Louisiana was established in 1699, French officials, following these earlier promising contacts, decided to orient their trade interests to the west and north. In 1706 the Spanish expedition leader Juan de Ulibarri reported to New Mexican officials that Wichitas in the southern Plains had begun to sell captive Apache women and children to the French. . . . Attempts to find routes to New Mexico put the French in contact with Indian bands whose reactions to the French newcomers further signaled their spreading reputation as slave raiders. In 1719, for instance, when the French trader Claude-Charles Dutisné first approached a northern Wichita village in the Plains, warriors twice raised a war club over his head as he struggled to convince them that he had not come to enslave them. A warning from neighboring Osages regarding French intentions, he soon learned, had preceded his arrival. . . .[7]

Frenchmen next attempted to open trade with Apaches, the very people who were losing relatives to French enslavement. In 1724 Étienne de Bourgmont sent a twenty-two-year-old woman and a teenage boy of sixteen whom he had purchased from Kansas Indians back to their village among Plains Apaches. Three months later, he traveled there and tried to build on this gesture in seeking trade relations with Apache leaders. Standing in the midst of trade goods he had carefully laid out for display—rifles, sabers, pickaxes, gunpowder, bullets, red cloth, blue cloth, mirrors, knives, shirts, scissors, combs, gunflints, vermilion, awls, needles, kettles, bells, beads, brass wire, and rings—Bourgmont both symbolically and rhetorically made the case that the Apaches would derive advantage from trade with Frenchmen. Apache leaders, though, saw quite a different gain to be had and quickly grabbed the

---

[6]Henri de Tonti, "Memoir Sent in 1693, on the Discovery of the Mississippi and the Neighboring Nations by M. D. La Salle, from the year 1678 to the Time of his Death, and by the Sieur de Tonty to the year 1691," in *The Journeys of Rene Robert Cavelier, Sieur de la Salle*, ed. Isaac Joslin Cox (2 vols., New York, 1973), I, 41–44, 46, esp. 42.

[7]Juan de Ulibarri, "The Diary of Juan de Ulibarri to El Cuartelejo, 1706," in *After Coronado: Spanish Exploration Northeast of New Mexico, 1696–1727*, trans. Alfred Barnaby Thomas (Norman, OK, 1935), 59–77; Charles Wilson Hackett, trans., *Pichardo's Treatise on the Limits of Louisiana and Texas* (4 vols., Austin, TX, 1931), II, 179–87; Mildred Mott Wedel, *The Wichita Indians, 1541–1750: Ethnohistorical Essays* (Lincoln, NE, 1988), 101; Kate L. Gregg, "The Missouri Reader: Explorers in the Valley, Part II," *Missouri Historical Review* 39 (July 1945), 511.

opportunity. "We will go to visit the French, and we will bring horses to trade with them," an Apache chief first informed Bourgmont. The next day, as negotiations continued, he neatly and publicly committed the French to supplying much more.... Standing before more than two hundred warriors and an equal number of women and children ... [at] the ceremonial meetings, the Apache leader announced: "You see here the Frenchman whom the Great Spirit has sent to our village to make peace with us.... Henceforth we shall be able to hunt in peace.... They will return to us our women and children whom they have taken from us and who are slaves in their country in exchange for horses that we will give them. The great French chief has promised this to us." But both men's machinations would be in vain.[8]

Despite Bourgmont's peaceful intentions and the Apache chief's persuasive rhetoric, French posts in western Louisiana had already become, and would remain throughout the eighteenth century, nuclei of a slave trade in Apache captives brought by Caddos, Wichitas, and later Comanches. Having identified the numerous and prosperous Caddoan peoples along the Red River as crucial targets for efforts to establish profitable trade alliances, Frenchmen had established a military post near a village of Natchitoches Indians in 1716, naming it Fort St. Jean Baptiste aux Natchitoches. They built a subsidiary trading post further upriver among Nasonis, another Caddo band, in 1719 (followed later by posts along the Red River at Rapides, Avoyelles, Ouachita, Opelousas, and Atakapas). A 1720 report of the French government addressing the commercial potential of the Natchitoches post and its hinterlands asserted that the most profitable trade with Indians there was in slaves, horses, deerskins, and bison hides.... Once Caddo, Wichita, and Comanche warriors had ascertained their own families' safety from French enslavement, they willingly obliged French desires by trading to them the enemy women and children they captured in war.[9]

---

[8]Étienne de Bourgmont identified the Indians as "Padoucas"—a French ethnonym that some scholars have asserted referred to Comanches. But Thomas W. Kavanagh and other Plains historians have convincingly argued that until 1750 it described Apaches. Frank Norall, trans., "Journal of the Voyage of Monsieur de Bourgmont, Knight of the Military Order of Saint Louis, Commandant of the Missouri River [which is] above That of the Arkansas, and of the Missouri [Country], to the Padoucas," in *Bourgmont, Explorer of the Missouri, 1698–1725*, by Frank Norall (Lincoln, NE, 1988), 125–61, esp. 152 and 154–55; Henri Folmer, "De Bourgmont's Expedition to the Padoucas in 1724, the First French Approach to Colorado," *Colorado Magazine* 14 (July 1937), 124–27; Henri Folmer, "Etienne Véniard de Bourgmont in the Missouri Country," *Missouri Historical Review* 36 (April 1942), 279–98; Thomas W. Kavanagh, *The Comanches: A History, 1706–1875* (Lincoln, NE, 1996), 65–66.

[9]Pierre François Xavier de Charlevoix, *History and General Description of New France*, trans. John Gilmary Shea (6 vols., New York, 1872), VI, 32–38; Daniel H. Usner Jr., *Indians, Settlers, and Slaves in a Frontier Exchange Economy: The Lower Mississippi Valley before 1783* (Chapel Hill, NC, 1992); archival material from Correspondence Générale, French Dominion, Mississippi Provincial Archives, vol. IX, 111, cited in Almon Wheeler Lauber, *Indian Slavery in Colonial Times within the Present Limits of the United States* (New York, 1913), 75; Sieur Jean-Baptiste Le Moyne de Bienville, "Memoir on Louisiana, the Indians and the Commerce that Can Be Carried on with Them," 1726, in *Mississippi Provincial Archives, French Dominion*, vol. III: 1704–1743, ed. Dunbar Rowland and A. G. Sanders (Jackson, MI, 1932), 532; Russell Magnaghi, "Changing Material Culture and the Hasinai of East Texas," *Southern Studies* 20 (Winter 1981); W. W. Newcomb and W. T. Field, "An Ethnohistoric Investigation of the Wichita Indians in the Southern Plains," in *Wichita Indian Archaeology and Ethnology: A Pilot Study*, ed. Robert E. Bell, Edward B. Jelks, and W. W. Newcomb (New York, 1974).

The Indian peoples with whom Frenchmen sought trade enjoyed powerful positions in the region, and almost all of them used the European presence to maintain and even strengthen those positions. Caddo, Wichita, and Comanche willingness to trade war captives to Frenchmen in exchange for European material goods indicates that the three groups—displaying a range of socioeconomic systems—did not secure captives with the intention of keeping them in their own communities for labor or other purposes. Caddoan peoples maintained three affiliated confederacies spread thickly over hundreds of square miles in present-day Louisiana, Texas, Arkansas, and Oklahoma. The multiple communities in those confederacies rested economically on steadily intensifying agricultural production and a far-reaching commercial exchange system, involving trade in hides, salt, turquoise, copper, marine shells, bows, and pottery with New Mexico, the Gulf Coast, and the Great Lakes.[10] By the end of the seventeenth century, Wichita-speaking peoples had moved into the lower southern Plains to establish fifteen to twenty consolidated, often palisaded, villages scattered across the northern regions of present-day Texas, most in fertile lands along rivers where they could successfully farm without jeopardizing their defensive capabilities. The trade connections Wichitas then developed over the first half of the eighteenth century with Frenchmen and Caddos to the east and newly allied Comanches to the west secured a steady supply of guns and horses as well as critical alliances needed to defend their populous and productive communities against Osage and Apache raids.[11] Like Wichitas, Comanches had moved onto the southern Plains by the early eighteenth century, operating as independent, bison-hunting groups loosely tied to one another in defensive and economic alliances.[12] By midcentury Comanche, Wichita, and Caddo bands had formed mutually beneficial trade relationships that brought European material goods, Plains hides, and Spanish horses together for exchange. All three also shared common enemies—multiple bands of Apaches living in mobile encampments across central Texas and western New Mexico—and all three took increasing numbers of Apache captives for trade in Louisiana.

The economic visions of Frenchmen in Louisiana dovetailed with those of native groups, as the French extended their involvement in the native trade networks that crisscrossed the southern Plains and lower Mississippi Valley. Though plantation agriculture increasingly garnered the attention of Frenchmen in

---

[10]La Vere, *Caddo Chiefdoms*; Perttula, "*Caddo Nation.*"

[11]W. W. Newcomb Jr., *The People Called Wichita* (Phoenix, AZ, 1976); Elizabeth A. H. John, "A Wichita Migration Tale," *American Indian Quarterly* 7 (Fall 1983), 57–63; Susan C. Vehik, "Wichita Culture History," *Plains Anthropologist* 37 (Nov. 1992), 311–32; F. Todd Smith, *The Wichita Indians: Traders of Texas and the Southern Plains, 1540–1845* (College Station, TX, 2000).

[12]Thomas W. Kavanagh, *Comanche Political History: An Ethnohistorical Perspective, 1706–1875* (Lincoln, NE, 1996); Morris Foster, *Being Comanche: A Social History of an American Indian Community* (Tucson, AZ, 1991); Gerald Betty, *Comanche Society: Before the Reservation* (College Station, TX, 2002); D. B. Shimkin, "Shoshone-Comanche Origins and Migrations," in *Proceedings of the Sixth Pacific Science Congress of the Pacific Science Association* (Berkeley, CA, 1940), 17–25.

south and central Louisiana, the Indian hide trade remained an important component of the province's economy to the end of the eighteenth century. Thus, a satellite system of trading posts gradually began to line the western and northern reaches of the French province with a mandate to establish and maintain the economic and diplomatic relations that underwrote that trade. The Frenchmen of the outlying posts did not have the numbers or force to subjugate Indians or dispossess them of their lands, nor did they wish to. Rather, they sought to establish profitable exchange, and as a result, they entered into egalitarian relations with dominant Caddo, Wichita, and, by extension, Comanche peoples. Frenchmen offered European trade goods that the Spaniards in Texas would not, thus stealing a march on their rivals to the west. French demographic and settlement patterns further contributed to their success as traders. In the Louisiana hinterlands, French social and familial intermixing with Indians was widespread, as the French built their trading and military posts in or near native villages and consequently joined with Indians not only for trade but also for subsistence, family building, and daily life. Community ties, in turn, brought Frenchmen into the heart of Indian political economies and offered foundations for long-lasting alliances.[13]

As such ties developed, bands of Caddos, Wichitas, and Comanches found female Indian captives to be as valuable as hides and horses in French markets in Natchitoches and other western Louisiana posts. In exchange, French trade offered native groups guns and ammunition essential not only for hunting but also for defense in the context of increasing competition and militarization among the region's native peoples. To its Indian participants, the developing slave trade represented two sides of native conventions of reciprocity.[14] Caddos, Comanches, and Wichitas obtained their trade goods from a range of sources:

[13]Usner, *Indians, Settlers, and Slaves in a Frontier Exchange Economy*, 116–22, 244–75; Joseph Zitomersky, "The Form and Function of French–Native American Relations in Early Eighteenth-Century French Colonial Louisiana," in *Proceedings of the Fifteenth Meeting of the French Colonial Historical Society, Martinique and Guadeloupe, May 1989*, ed. Patricia Galloway and Philip P. Boucher (New York, 1992). St. Jean Baptiste aux Natchitoches, c. 1722. In 1716 the French had established this military and trade post near a village of Natchitoches Indians. Through this post Indian slaves captured in Texas and the southern Plains entered western Louisiana. Map by J. F. Broutin. *Courtesy Northwestern State University of Louisiana, Watson Memorial Library, Cammie G. Henry Research Center.*

[14]Clarence H. Webb and Hiram F. Gregory, *The Caddo Indians of Louisiana* (1978; Baton Rouge, LA, 1986); Hiram Ford Gregory, "Eighteenth Century Caddoan Archaeology: A Study in Models and Interpretation" (PhD diss., Southern Methodist University, 1973); Dayna Bowker Lee, "Indian Slavery in Lower Louisiana during the Colonial Period, 1699–1803" (M.A. thesis, Northwestern State University of Louisiana, 1989). Patricia C. Albers, "Symbiosis, Merger, and War: Contrasting Forms of Intertribal Relationship among Historic Plains Indians," in *The Political Economy of North American Indians*, ed. John Moore (Lincoln, NE, 1993), 94–132; Marcel Mauss, *The Gift: The Form and Reason for Exchange in Archaic Societies*, trans. W. D. Halls (1924; New York, 1954); Marshall Sahlins, *Stone Age Economics* (Chicago, IL, 1972); and Claude Lévi-Strauss, *The Elementary Structures of Kinship*, trans. James Harle Bell and John Richard von Sturmer, ed. Rodney Needham (1949; Boston, 1969). La Vere, *Caddo Chiefdoms*; Daniel A. Hickerson, "Trade, Mediation, and Political Status in the Hasinai Confederacy," *Research in Economic Anthropology* 17 (1996), 149–68.

the hides from hunting, the horses from raids on Spanish settlements in Texas, and the captives from warfare with native enemies (primarily Apaches). One aspect of native conventions dictated that the three groups took captives only from those they designated enemies or "strangers" to systems of kinship and political alliance—thus they took captives only in the context of war. On the flip side, once captive women became desirable commodities in Louisiana, they also served as tools Comanche, Wichita, and Caddo men could use to build trade relations with Frenchmen. In the eighteenth century, therefore, the French markets gave new value to an old by-product of warfare.

The trade in women following their capture resulted in more than individual benefit or profit, however. Like diplomatic exchanges, the Indian slave trade brought together men of French and Indian nations in an exchange that served both utilitarian and prestige purposes. . . . Participation in exchanges made groups less likely to engage in confrontation and violence and brought them into metaphorical, if not real, relations of kinship. Caddo, Comanche, and Wichita men cast trade alliances in terms of fictive kinship categories of "brotherhood" and male sodalities. . . . The exchange process itself created relationships, binding men to each other in the act of giving and receiving. Practices of intermarriage, adoption, and symbolic kinship relations among different Indian peoples and among Europeans and Indians meant that "kinship" expanded to include relations beyond those of only familial (biological) descent. Economic ties could not be separated from political ones, and trading partners were also military and political allies. Quite simply, one did not fight with brothers, just as one did not trade with enemies. Conversely, the predominance of "Canneci" (Apache) women in the enslaved Indian population in Louisiana became so pronounced by midcentury that the governor of Louisiana, Louis Billouart de Kerlérec, identified it as the primary hindrance to any hope of adding Apache nations to the list of Louisiana's native trade allies. Since successful trade with some groups made trade with others impossible, the slave trade put its own limits on French commercial expansion. . . .[15]

On the other side of the Texas-Louisiana border, Indian enslavement exerted quite a different influence on the early invasion and settlement of the Spanish province of Texas. The advance of the Spanish frontier northward over the sixteenth and seventeenth centuries into the regions claimed as the provinces of Nueva Vizcaya, Coahuila, and Nuevo León (south of what became the province of Texas) had brought with it the spread of European diseases and the intrusion of slave-raiding expeditions seeking forced labor for Spanish mines and ranches—inexorable forces that preceded much of the colonization of those regions. Epidemics that began in the 1550s had, by the 1700s, scythed 90 percent of the

---

[15]Brooks, *Captives and Cousins*, 177–97; Louis Billouart de Kerlérec, "Projet de paix et d'alliance avec les Cannecis et les avantages qui en peuvent résulter, envoyé par Kerlérec, gouverneur de la province de la Louisianne, en 1753," in "Un Mémoire Politique du XVIII Siécle Relatif au Texas" (An eighteenth-century political memoir relating to Texas), by M. Le Baron Marc de Villiers du Terrage, *Journal de la Société des Américanistes de Paris* 3 (1906), 67–76.

native population of those northern regions of Mexico. Under law, moreover, the Crown might assign to Spaniards the labor and tribute of a specific Indian community in an arrangement termed an *encomienda*. Consequent Spanish demands for labor on farms and ranches and in mines brought their own brand of annihilation. By 1600 trafficking in enslaved Indians had become an established way of life in Nuevo León. Once the Spaniards there had killed off all the nearby Indian peoples by congregating them in crowded, unsanitary work camps where disease or overwork devastated their numbers, they extended the relentless reach of their slave raids ever northward. . . .[16]

Just as Indian groups had done when they encountered the early French traders on the Plains, Indians in Texas quickly learned what would be of value to the Spaniards whose expeditions had targeted the region even before permanent Spanish settlement was attempted in the 1690s. For some time rumors and evidence had been reaching them that the Europeans from Mexico and New Mexico were both buyers and actual enslavers of Indians. . . . [W]hen Spaniards first made contact with Caddo peoples along the Texas-Louisiana border in the 1690s, their reputation as slavers had apparently preceded them. . . .[17]

Others sought their own advantage in Spanish labor systems and thereby pulled native peoples from the southern Plains into an increasingly commercialized exchange system to the west in New Mexico. Many eastern Apache groups, who had been victims of Spanish slave raiding in New Mexico, began to bring their own captives to New Mexican markets. As early as the 1650s, the Franciscan missionary Alonso de Posada reported that in addition to hides and chamois skins, some Apaches now sought "to sell for horses some Indian men and women, girls and boys" taken from Wichita bands. . . .[18]

To the east, as Spaniards sought a toehold in Texas in the 1710s, they focused on building a cordon of mission-presidio complexes as bulwark to protect the silver mines of New Spain's northern provinces against French aggressors. Having failed to establish settlements among Caddos in the 1690s, Spaniards focused

---

[16]Peter Gerhard, *The North Frontier of New Spain* (Princeton, 1982), 328, 344–48; Daniel T. Reff, *Disease, Depopulation, and Cultural Change in Northwestern New Spain, 1518–1764* (Salt Lake City, UT, 1991); José Cuello, "The Persistence of Indian Slavery and Encomienda in the Northeast of Colonial Mexico, 1577–1723," *Journal of Social History* 21 (Summer 1988), 683–700; Susan M. Deeds, "Rural Work in Nueva Vizcaya: Forms of Labor Coercion on the Periphery," *Hispanic American Historical Review* 69 (Aug. 1989), 425–49; Peter Bakewell, *Silver Mining and Society in Colonial Mexico: Zacatecas, 1546–1700* (Cambridge, England, 1971); Vito Alessio Robles, *Coahuila y Texas en la época colonial* (Coahuila and Texas in the colonial period), (Mexico City, 1978); Silvio Zavala, *Los Esclavos Indios en Nueva España* (Indian Slaves in New Spain) (Mexico City, 1967), 179–349.

[17]Brooks, *Captives and Cousins*; L. R. Bailey, *The Indian Slave Trade in the Southwest* (Los Angeles, 1966); Nancy Parrott Hickerson, *The Jumanos: Hunters and Traders of the South Plains* (Austin, TX, 1994), 32–33, 48, 80, 103–4, 113–14; Fray Damián Mazanet to Don Carlos de Sigüenza, 1690, in *Spanish Exploration in the Southwest, 1542–1706*, ed. Herbert Eugene Bolton (New York, 1916), 282.

[18]Alfred Barnaby Thomas, trans., *Alonso de Posada Report, 1686: A Description of the Area of the Present Southern United States in the Late Seventeenth Century* (Pensacola, 1982), 36–37; Brooks, *Captives and Cousins*, 121–42.

instead on south-central Texas.... [T]he Spanish government faced serious problems attracting settlers, soldiers, and native converts to populate colonial centers so far north. The Spanish population of the Texas province at its height in 1790 was only 3,169. Spanish colonial development also remained rigidly hemmed in by far more populous and powerful Indian nations—both indigenous to the region (such as Caddos) and newly arrived (such as Lipan Apaches and later Comanches and Wichitas). Spaniards thus found that even in the limited areas claimed by Spanish settlement, their imperial policies regarding Indians involved, not imposing rule on others, but defending themselves against superior native rivals. The resulting weakness of New Spain's position in the region made it crucial for provincial authorities to secure peace and alliances with the independent and dominant native peoples that surrounded them.... Over the eighteenth century, then, Spaniards struggled to maintain their small foothold in the area against vying Apache, Caddo, Comanche, and Wichita powers.[19]

Of the four native powers, Lipan Apaches were the first to challenge the Spanish presence in Texas; as a result Spanish-Indian relations there took a different path than did the relations enjoyed by the French to the east, and the path led to a different form of bondage—one defined by punitive war.... Eastern Apaches living in what is now Texas had gained an early advantage among Indians there with horses acquired in the seventeenth century through trading and raiding in New Mexico. By the 1740s, "Lipan" had become the designation used by Spaniards to refer to the easternmost Plains Apache groups. Their economy centered on hunting and raiding for bison and horses, which did not allow permanent settlement, though they did practice semicultivation. Social units farmed and hunted in rancherías (a Spanish term for Indian encampments) that might cluster together for defense and ceremonial ritual. Usually numbering around four hundred people, such units aggregated ten to thirty extended families related by blood or marriage that periodically joined together for horse raids, bison hunts, and coordinated military action.... As horses rose in importance, so too did the raiding that maintained their herds and sustained their economy.[20]

Apache economies came under attack in the early eighteenth century, however, as Comanches and Wichitas migrated south to challenge Apache bands for the rich bison territories of northern and north-central Texas. Hostilities quickly

---

[19]Thomas R. Hester, "Texas and Northeastern Mexico: An Overview," in *Columbian Consequences, Vol. I: Archaeological and Historical Perspectives on the Spanish Borderlands West*, ed. David Hurst Thomas (Washington, D.C, 1989), 191–211; *The Indians of Southern Texas and Northeastern Mexico: Selected Writings of Thomas Nolan Campbell* (Austin, TX, 1988); Donald Chipman, *Spanish Texas, 1519–1821* (Austin, 1992), 182–83, 205–7, 249–50.

[20]Morris Edward Opler, "The Kinship Systems of the Southern Athabaskan-Speaking Tribes," *American Anthropologist* 38 (Oct. 1936), 620–33; Morris E. Opler, "Lipan Apache," in *Handbook of North American Indians*, ed. William C. Sturtevant, vol. XIII: *Plains*, ed. Raymond J. DeMallie (Washington, D.C., 2001), part 2, 941–52; Thomas F. Schilz, *Lipan Apaches in Texas* (El Paso, TX, 1987); Dolores A. Gunnerson, *The Jicarilla Apaches: A Study in Survival* (DeKalb, IL, 1974); Gary Clayton Anderson, *The Indian Southwest, 1580–1830: Ethnogenesis and Reinvention* (Norman, OK, 1999), 105–44; José Cortés, *Views from the Apache Frontier: Report on the Northern Provinces of New Spain*, ed. Elizabeth A. H. John, trans. John Wheat (Norman, 1989).

erupted that pitted Apaches against Comanches and Wichitas as well as Spaniards, ... gradually weaken[ing] Apaches' defenses, making them increasingly vulnerable to all three opponents. Apache women and children thus became the focus not only of raids by Comanche and Wichita warriors seeking captives for French markets in Louisiana but also of Spanish military campaigns seeking prisoners whom Spaniards could use to coerce or punish their Apache foes. Throughout the 1720s, 1730s, and 1740s, Lipan Apaches mounted raids on the horse herds of San Antonio de Béxar missions, civilian ranches, and presidio to sustain a supply of horses crucial to the mobility and defense of their family bands amid mounting conflicts. In turn, Spanish fear and frustration escalated when presidial forces proved unable to stop the warriors' attacks and led to desperate bids by Spaniards to stem the raids. Spanish officials, making war to achieve peace, ordered Apache women and children to be taken captive to force diplomacy, arguing that the best way to manipulate native groups was through their captive . . . kinswomen. . . .[21]

. . . Spaniards introduced captive-taking on a scale unimaginable to most Indian nations. To use captives for political coercion may have seemed a logical tactic to Spanish officials, who could refer to long traditions of prisoner and hostage exchange in European warfare. Yet, when Spanish forces attacked Apache rancherías, took captives, and then tried to force peace with the bands they had attacked, they sought to forge alliance through an act of hostility. Moreover, even by Spanish terms of hostage exchange, their captive policy was fundamentally unequal because it never represented an exchange of Indian women for Spanish women. Unlike the Comanche warriors in New Mexico who took Spanish women and children as well as horses as the booty of their raids, Apache men in Texas focused their raiding on horse herds.[22]

Not surprisingly, Spanish actions brought only more hostilities with Apaches. . . . As captivities lengthened from months into years, officials distributed the Apache women and children as "servants" among soldiers and civilians. . . . Spaniards, who had long found ways around the Crown's legal prohibitions against the enslavement of Indians, now rationalized their decision to keep such women and children in bondage by claiming the necessities of defense. By sleight of interpretation, they deemed the only *cautivos* in New Spain's northern provinces to be Spaniards captured by Indians—Apache women and children captured by Spanish forces were *prisioneros* (prisoners of war). . . .[23]

---

[21]William Edward Dunn, "Apache Relations in Texas, 1718–1750," *Quarterly of the Texas State Historical Association* 14 (Jan. 1911), 198–274.

[22]James William Brodman, *Ransoming Captives in Crusader Spain: The Order of Merced on the Christian-Islamic Frontier* (Philadelphia, 1986); Jarbel Rodriguez, "Financing a Captive's Ransom in Late Medieval Aragon," *Medieval Encounters: Jewish, Christian, and Muslim Culture in Confluence and Dialogue* 9 (April 2003), 164–81; Brooks, *Captives and Cousins*; Dunn, "Apache Relations in Texas"; Juliana Barr, "'Traces of Christians': A Spectrum of Indian Bondage in Spanish Texas," in *Indian Slavery in Colonial America*, ed. Alan Gallay (Lincoln, NE, forthcoming).

[23]Brooks, *Captives and Cousins*, 121–42; Gilberto M. Hinojosa and Anne A. Fox, "Indians and Their Culture in San Fernando de Béxar," in *Tejano Origins in Eighteenth-Century San Antonio*, ed. Gerald E. Poyo and Gilberto M. Hinojosa (Austin, TX, 1991), 109–10; Jesús F. de la Teja, *San Antonio de Béxar: A Community on New Spain's Northern Frontier* (Albuquerque, NM, 1995), 122–23.

The experiences of Apache family bands targeted by Spanish military policy are illustrated most poignantly by the story of one headed by the chief Cabellos Colorados. In 1737, accompanied by eight men and eight women, he approached San Antonio, seeking trade with Spanish residents there. The equal number of men and women in the party suggested their peaceful intent. Yet to find Apaches close to town just when Spanish forces were looking for someone to nab for past horse raids and Spanish officials were seeking to reestablish the effectiveness of their arms in the eyes of a desperate citizenry and doubting viceregal authorities was too providential an opportunity to pass up. When twenty-eight armed soldiers rode out, Cabellos Colorados and his men were clearly not expecting a fight and did not put up a defense; they were therefore quickly surrounded and captured. In further indication that Spaniards had no evidence to prove the group were raiders, they insisted on hearings to gather such evidence—something they had never felt necessary before.[24]

In June 1738 Prudencio de Orobio y Bazterra, the governor of Texas, thus proceeded to gather testimony on the "infidelity" of Apaches in violating a 1733 peace treaty that did not exist, and Cabellos Colorados and his people were the designated subjects of the frame-up. The "evidence" against them amounted to assertions based only on coincidence, rumor, and prejudice. First, Spaniards saw it as suspicious that, of the known Apache rancherías, that of Cabellos Colorados and his people was the closest to San Antonio. Second, soldiers testified that no "assaults" had taken place since their capture, so the raiders must be the ones in jail. Third, the presidial commander José de Urrutia identified Cabellos Colorados as a man of standing and reputation among Apaches—so much so that Urrutia claimed it was rumored that the leader had bragged to the *capitáne grande* of the Apache nation (a position that did not exist) that he would raid all the presidial horse herds of San Antonio, Coahuila, San Juan Bautista, and Sacramento (quite a task for one man), then slaughter all the inhabitants (a war tactic that did not exist among Apaches). Clearly, Cabellos Colorados was a powerful man whose downfall might powerfully enhance the reputation of the Spaniard who brought him down.[25]

In the meantime, Cabellos Colorados tried to negotiate with his captors, relying on female hostages as mediators by requesting that Spaniards allow one of the women to return to his ranchería to get horses with which to buy their freedom. Between the December capture and the June hearings, Apache women traveled back and forth between Apache and Spanish settlements, trying to exchange horses for the captives, but an attack on their ranchería by Caddos who killed twelve, captured two boys, and stole all their horses severely

---

[24]Don Prudencio de Orobio y Bazterra, Order for Investigation and Questionnaire, June 25, 1738, Proceedings concerning the Infidelity of the Apaches; Testimony of lieutenant Mateo Pérez, chief constable Vicente Alvarez Travieso, captain José de Urrutia, alférez Juan Galván, and corporal Juan Cortina, June 26–28, 1738, ibid.; Dunn, "Apache Relations in Texas," 244–45.

[25]Testimony of Mateo Perez, Vicente Alvarez Travieso, and José de Urrutia, *Proceedings concerning the Infidelity of the Apaches*; Dunn, "Apache Relations in Texas," 245–47.

limited their ability to produce enough horses to appease Spanish officials. Instead, the women brought bison meat for their captive kinsmen and bison hides as goodwill gifts for Spanish officials. In August an elderly man accompanied the women and brought news that, though they could not supply any horses, he had visited all the Apache bands and asked them to stop all raids, and he now offered this peace agreement to the officials in exchange for the captives. The governor refused. The elderly man then tried to exchange a horse and a mule for his elderly wife, who was among the captives. The governor refused again.[26]

No peace offering could offset the Spaniards' desire to punish someone for the deeds of Apache raiders who had made a mockery of their presidial forces in the preceding years. Ultimately, Orobio consigned Cabellos Colorados and his entire family to exile and enslavement. In his order of February 16, 1739, the governor refused to spare the women or even an infant girl, declaring that "the thirteen Indian men and women prisoners in the said presidio, [shall be taken] tied to each other, from jurisdiction to jurisdiction, to the prison of the capital in Mexico City, and that the two-year-old daughter of chief Cabellos Colorados, María Guadalupe, shall be treated in the same manner." The *collera* of Apache prisoners—seven men, six women, and one child—left on February 18 escorted by a mixed guard of soldiers and civilians. . . .[27]

Having proclaimed defensive needs as their *carte blanche* for wartime enslavements, militia groups made up of soldiers and civilians devastated Apache family bands, causing repeated loss of kinswomen and children, and nearly brought on their own destruction at the hands of infuriated Apache leaders and warriors until a peace treaty in 1749 ended hostilities for twenty years. During those twenty years, Apache leaders would strive without success to regain family members lost in the 1730s and 1740s. . . .[28]

. . . [I]n the late 1760s, . . . our two stories (and the two slave networks) come together. . . . For as long as French traders had been operating in the region, Spanish missionaries and military officials in Texas had been trying to effect alliances of their own in the hope of offsetting the influence of their French rivals. Throughout the first half of the century, however, such efforts had met with abject failure even as the Spaniards watched Indian-French ties steadily

[26]Statement of Don Prudencio de Orobio y Bazterra, Aug. 18, 1738, *Proceedings concerning the Infidelity of the Apaches*; Dunn, "Apache Relations in Texas," 245–46.

[27]Order of Governor Don Prudencio de Orobio y Bazterra, Feb. 16, 1739, *Proceedings concerning the Infidelity of the Apaches*; Benito de Fernández de Santa Ana to Viceroy Archbishop Juan Antonio de Vizarron, Nov. 24, 1739, in *Letters and Memorials of the Father Presidente Fray Benito de Fernández de Santa Ana*, ed. Leutenegger, 32.

[28]Dunn, "Apache Relations in Texas," 248–62; Elizabeth A. H. John, *Storms Brewed in Other Men's Worlds: The Confrontations of Indians, Spanish, and French in the Southwest, 1540–1795* (College Station, TX, 1975), 273–303, 336–405.

strengthen.[29] Reports filtered in from all across the Plains and New Mexico detailing how Frenchmen had expanded their native alliances and their slave trade.[30] Imperial Spanish officials feared that growing trade relations signaled military alliance and the potential for a united French-Indian attack on Spanish territories. Such laments remained focal points of Spanish rhetoric as they watched first Caddos, then Comanches and Wichitas, build economic ties to the French colony. The ever-increasing military power of Comanche and Wichita nations soon became far more daunting than that of the French, however. The armaments acquired through French trade had equipped Comanche and Wichita bands better for the raids that from the 1740s on plundered Spanish horse herds in civil and mission settlements in both Texas and New Mexico. By 1758 officials in Mexico City feared Comanche *invasion* of the Spanish provinces south of the Rio Grande.[31]

Yet without the finances to offer competitive trade of their own or the military power to stop French-Indian alliances by force, Spaniards in Texas found they could do little to offset French advantage. It was not until the 1760s that the cession of Louisiana from French to Spanish rule following the Seven Years' War opened up new possibilities for Spanish officials. Spanish law officially prohibited the enslavement and sale of Indians, and Alejandro O'Reilly, then serving as governor of Louisiana, extended that prohibition to the province with the formal assumption of Spanish power in 1769. Spanish officials saw an opportunity to cut off the trade that put guns into the hands of native groups deemed "hostile" to the Spanish government. . . . Spanish officials finally had the means to sever the commercial ties that had allied native bands in Texas and the southern Plains with Frenchmen. Thus in response to O'Reilly's edict, officials in Natchitoches forbade the trade in horses, mules, and slaves from those Indian nations, and

---

[29]Casañas de Jesús María to the Viceroy of Mexico, Aug. 15, 1691, in "Descriptions of the Tejas or Asinai Indians, 1691–1722," trans. Hatcher, 208; Juan Bautista Chapa, *Texas and Northeastern Mexico, 1630–1690*, ed. William C. Foster, trans. Ned F. Brierley (Austin, TX, 1997); Fray Francisco Hidalgo to the Viceroy, Nov. 4, 1716, in "Descriptions of the Tejas or Asinai Indians, 1691–1722," trans. Mattie Austin Hatcher, *Southwestern Historical Quarterly* 31 (July 1927), 60; Fray Isidro de Espinosa, "Ramón's Expedition: Espinosa's Diary of 1716," trans. Gabriel Tous, *Preliminary Studies of the Texas Catholic Historical Society* 1 (April 1930), 4–24; Don Domingo Ramón, "Captain Don Domingo Ramón's Diary of his Expedition into Texas in 1716," trans. Paul J. Foik, ibid., 2 (April 1933), 3–23; Fray Francisco Céliz, *Diary of the Alarcón Expedition into Texas, 1718–1719*, trans. Fritz Hoffmann (Los Angeles, 1935), 83.

[30]Don Antonio Valverde y Cosio, Governor of New Mexico, to Marquis de Valero, Nov. 3, 1719, in *Pichardo's Treatise on the Limits of Louisiana and Texas*, trans. Hackett, I, 193, 206; Testimonies of Luis Febre, Pedro Satren and Joseph Miguel Riballo before Governor Tomás Vélez Cachupín, April 13, 1749, and March 5, 1750, ibid., III, 299–320; testimony of Felipe de Sandoval, March 1, 1750, ibid., 320–24; Statement of Antonio Treviño to Governor Angel Martos y Navarrete, July 13, 1765, Béxar Archives.

[31]Pedro de Rivera, "Diary and Itinerary of What Was Seen and Examined During the General Inspection of Presidios in the Interior Provinces of New Spain," in *Imaginary Kingdom: Texas as Seen by the Rivera and Rubí Military Expeditions, 1727 and 1767*, ed. Jack Jackson (Austin, TX, 1995), 35; Marqués de Rubí, "Dictamen of April 10, 1768," trans. Ned. F. Brierley, ibid., 182–83; Paul D. Nathan, trans., Lesley Byrd Simpson, ed., *The San Sabá Papers: A Documentary Account of the Founding and Destruction of San Sabá Mission* (San Francisco, 1959), 71, 107–15, 136, 145.

they recalled from their subposts or homes among "hostile" Indians all licensed traders, hunters, and illicit "vagabonds"—many of whom the Natchitoches commander Athanase de Mézières described in 1770 as men "who pass their scandalous lives in public concubinage with the captive Indian women whom for this purpose they purchase among the heathen, loaning those of whom they tire to others of less power, that they may labor in their service, giving them no other wage than the promise of quieting their lascivious passion."[32]

Once at Natchitoches, the traders and hunters had to answer questions about their native trade relationships and to register their Indian slaves. In fear of losing their slaves, some Frenchmen sought to secure the women by whatever means possible. Though government officials recognized provisional ownership pending a royal decision on the status of enslaved Indians in the province, some men clearly chose not to let their fate rest on the vagaries of a royal decree. Many married their slaves or promised freedom if the women swore to remain with them as servants or consorts. Intimate relations thereby became a means of prolonging women's servitude. François Morvant, for instance, in 1770 declared his ownership of a twenty-five-year-old Apache woman named Marie Anne as well as their son, age twelve. Sometime thereafter, however, her status was transformed, as she was enumerated as Morvant's wife, "Ana Maria, of Apache nationality," in later Spanish censuses for the nearby settlement of Nacogdoches, Texas. Tellingly, though their relationship had existed for at least thirteen years, it was not until Morvant faced losing ownership of her that he married Marie Anne. By 1805 they had three more sons, a daughter, and one grandson living with them. Similarly, in 1774 Jacque Ridde freed an eighteen-year-old Apache girl, Angélique, whose ownership he claimed, but only after she pledged to remain in his service, and Pierre Raimond married Françoise, another Apache woman, following her manumission.[33]

Governing officials in Spain never ruled on the status of Indian slaves, and the extension of Spanish law into Louisiana freed no enslaved Indians except for a very few whose owners voluntarily manumitted them in the aftermath of O'Reilly's edict in 1769 or in 1787 when the ordinance was republished in response to a legal case involving runaway Indian slaves in St. Louis. The existence of a law tells us very little about whether the law was enforced or obeyed—and the reiteration of legal prohibitions suggests a lack of compliance. Between 1790 and 1794, a handful of slaves also sued successfully for manumission in Spanish courts on

---

[32]Alexandro O'Reilly, Proclamation, Dec. 7, 1769, in *Spain in the Mississippi Valley, 1765–1794*, ed. Lawrence Kinnaird (Washington, 1949), II, 126–27; Alejandro O'Reilly to Athanase de Mézières, Jan. 23, 1770, in *Athanase de Mézières and the Louisiana-Texas Frontier*, ed. and trans. Bolton, I, 135–36, 152; de Mézières to Governor of Louisiana Luis Unzaga y Amezaga, May 20, 1770, ibid., 166–68, esp. 166.

[33]On the actions of François Morvant, Jacque Ridde, and Pierre Raimond in 1770, see Lee, "Indian Slavery in Lower Louisiana during the Colonial Period," 83–85; and Mills, *Natchitoches, 1729–1803*, entries 1016, 1101, 1619, 1953, 2297, 2901. For the first and last appearances of the Morvant family in the town censuses, see Censuses of Nuestra Señora del Pilar de Nacogdoches for 1784 and 1805, Béxar Archives.

the grounds of Indian identity (their own or their mothers'), but all those cases were heard in New Orleans, and such legal opportunities did not exist for enslaved Indian women or their children in outpost settlements far from urban centers, such as Natchitoches. In the wake of the slave uprising in Saint Domingue in 1791, such opportunities quickly disappeared for all, as Spanish officials decided that any challenges to the slave system were dangerous. . . .[34]

In 1806 an Anglo-American report discussing the still-prevalent Apache women who had been "brought to Natchitoches, and sold amongst the French inhabitants, at forty or fifty dollars a head," concluded that the women had become "servants in good families, and taught spinning, sewing, &c. as well as managing household affairs, married natives of the country [Frenchmen and métis], and became respectable, well behaved women; and have now, grown up, decent families of children, have a language peculiar to themselves, and are understood by signs by all others."[35] Most enslaved women, however, appear in records only as the subjects of baptism at their French owners' behest or as mothers of natural children whose fathers usually, but not always, went unnamed in sacramental registers. Thus the lives of most enslaved Indian women rested on the whims of their owners, and a woman might find her world turned suddenly upside down if she were used to pay medical bills, exchanged for horses, seized for debt, or enumerated in a will.[36] The experiences of these women began in war, when they were torn from their communities by brutal force, and culminated in their sale into sexual and labor relations defined by coercion.

It was in response to such stories that fray Santa María y Silva had issued his denunciation of French traders after the Indian slave trade into Louisiana had become illicit in the 1770s. Yet, even Santa María y Silva, if pressed, would have

---

[34]Stephen Webre, "The Problem of Indian Slavery in Spanish Louisiana," *Louisiana History* 25 (Spring 1984), 117–35; Hans W. Baade, "The Law of Slavery in Spanish Louisiana, 1769–1803," in *Louisiana's Legal Heritage*, ed. Edward F. Haas (Pensacola, 1983), 43–86; Winston de Ville, ed., *Natchitoches Documents, 1732–1785: A Calendar of Civil Records from Fort St. Jean Baptiste in the French and Spanish Province of Louisiana* (Ville Platte, LA, 1994), 10, 17, 35.

[35]John Sibley, "Historical Sketches of the several Indian tribes in Louisiana, south of the Arkansas River, and between the Mississippi and River Grande," 1806, in *American State Papers*, vol. I (Washington, D.C., 1832), 721–31, esp. 723; Pueblo de Nuestra Señora del Pilar de Nacogdoches: List of Families in the Said Pueblo Taken by Captain and Commandant, Don José Joaquín Ugarte," Jan. 1, 1804, Béxar Archives; "Report of the Missions Occupied by the Priest of the College of Our Lady of Guadalupe de Zacatecas in Said Province [Texas], Their Progress to the End of 1804...," Dec. 31, 1804, ibid.; "Pueblo of Nuestra Señora del Pilar de Nacogdoches: Census of the families who live in the aforesaid pueblo, compiled by Commandant José Joaquín Ugarte," Jan. 1, 1805, ibid.; José María Guadiana, "Jurisdiction of the Pueblo de Nuestra Señora del Pilar de Nacogdoches: Houses located on the eastern side of the Sabinas River," Nov. 1805, ibid.; Sebastian Rodriguez, "Pueblo de Nuestra Señora de Pilar of Nacogdoches: Census of the families living in said town and its jurisdiction," Jan. 1, 1806, ibid.; "Report on the Barbarous Indians of the Province of Texas, Dec. 27, 1819," in "Texas in 1820," trans. Mattie Austin Hatcher, *Southwestern Historical Quarterly* 23 (July 1919), 47–53.

[36]A few men did register their paternity of children at baptism, see, for example, the children of Pierre Sebastian Prudhomme and Naillois, "an Indian woman," and Jean Baptiste Samuel and Jeanne, "a woman of the Canneci (Apache) nation," in Mills, *Natchitoches, 1729–1803*, entries 2245, 3444, 3049. For uses of women as objects of exchange, see Lee, "Indian Slavery in Lower Louisiana during the Colonial Period."

needed to acknowledge that as Spanish officials in Texas sought to stem the eastward flow of captive Indian women into Louisiana, they created in its stead a more deadly southward flow of hostages into Mexican prisons and labor camps.[37] Though French traders associated with the Natchitoches and Arkansas posts remained active covertly and British traders soon began pushing into the region, Comanche and Wichita economies were hindered. The need to diversify their trade contacts more and more turned Indian eyes to Spaniards in Texas. Though Comanches and Wichitas continued their raids on Spanish settlements in Texas to maintain their horse supply, the challenge of picking up the slack in arms and material goods formerly provided by Louisiana markets remained. To solve this problem, they found new ways to benefit from an exchange of women, selling war captives to Spaniards for horses and goods that Spanish officials preferred to term "ransom" and "redemption" payments. The new diplomatic traffic would put even more Apache women and children into Spanish bondage. Yet, it took years before economic exchange completely replaced battlefield violence among Spaniards, Wichitas, and Comanches.

During the transitional period of alternating war and diplomacy, Comanche and Wichita men at first took advantage of Spanish diplomatic needs to pursue personal rather than commercial ends. The tales of two Indian couples, one Wichita and one Comanche, illustrate the twists and turns that newly emerging captive exchanges might take in Spanish-Indian relations. Both stories unfolded over the spring and summer of 1772. That spring word reached a principal chief of a Taovaya (Wichita) band that his wife—who had been taken from him by Apache raiders—had been sold by her captors to a Spaniard in Coahuila. As the chief was soon to travel to San Antonio de Béxar as part of a diplomatic party sent to ratify the first treaty between Wichitas and the Spanish government, he recognized that Spanish officials' desperation for peace could be the means of saving his wife in circumstances where he himself could not. As soon as the chief reached San Antonio that summer, he explained his plight to the Spanish governor, Juan María de Ripperdá. "She is so much esteemed by him," Ripperdá reported to the viceroy, "that he assures me that she is the only one he has ever had, or wishes to have until he dies, and, as she leaves him two little orphans, he begs for her as zealously as he considers her delivery [return] difficult."[38]

The governor quickly grasped that the fate of the captive woman would determine the fate of the newly completed peace treaty and promised the Taovaya chief he would use the "strongest means" to secure her. If he failed to grant the chief's request for help, Ripperdá warned the viceroy, "all that we have attained and which is of so much importance, would be lost." Thus it was with exultation that Ripperdá wrote to the viceroy a month later, assuring his superior that, in answer to

---

[37]Moorhead, "Spanish Deportation of Hostile Apaches"; Christon I. Archer, "The Deportation of Barbarian Indians from the Internal Provinces of New Spain, 1789–1810," *Americas* 29 (Jan. 1973), 376–85.

[38]Barón de Ripperdá to Bucareli y Ursúa, July 5, 1772, in *Athanase de Mézières and the Louisiana-Texas Frontier*, trans. and ed. Bolton, I, 322.

his urgent requests, the governor of Coahuila had found and returned the chief's wife. Indeed, Ripperdá had orchestrated her delivery to his own home in San Antonio where she was to be turned over to her husband (surely to convince the Taovaya chief that it was the Texas official to whom he was beholden for his wife's return). Optimistically, the governor reiterated "that she may be the key that shall open the way to our treaties." In March 1773 Ripperdá finally concluded his private captive exchange, writing to the viceroy that the happy husband and a delegation of Taovayas were in Ripperdá's home and the Taovaya couple had been reunited.[39]

The governor might well choose to dwell on that auspicious moment, because his negotiation of a similar situation with Comanches had taken a far rockier, less promising path. In fact, Ripperdá very nearly bungled the whole thing. The second story began in February 1772 when a detachment from the Béxar presidio returned to the town of San Antonio with an unexpected prize—not Apache but Comanche captives—three women and one girl. Ripperdá already had three other Comanche women, captured months before, who had been held so long in one of the San Antonio missions that all three had been baptized and two married off to mission neophytes. Because of their baptisms, those three could not be returned to live among their people in what Spaniards considered apostasy, but the four new captives provided the governor an opening for diplomatic overtures to Comanche leaders. Since the Spanish government had recently completed new peace agreements with bands of Taovayas and Caddos, he hoped he might likewise attract (or coerce) Comanches to the negotiating table for the first time. Ripperdá therefore sent two of the women back to their village under military escort, carrying goodwill gifts to present to their chief, Evea, while he kept the other woman and little girl as hostages to draw the chief to San Antonio.[40]

A month later, Evea sent a response to San Antonio in the form of emissaries led by a woman carrying a cross and a white flag. The woman at the head of the party was one of the female captives freed by Ripperdá and was also the mother of the little girl still held hostage. Others in the party included the hostage girl's father, the husband of the other hostage woman held by the governor, and the brother of two of the three Comanche women held in the missions. The governor's gambit had not drawn out the chief, but he certainly had attracted a diverse group seeking to recover lost family members. Initially, meetings went well as the Comanche visitors reunited with Ripperdá's two hostages and exchanged diplomatic courtesies with the governor. As they departed, however, they sought retribution for their troubles by taking four hundred horses from the Béxar presidial herd. They also tried to liberate the three other Comanche women held in the mission, but Spanish soldiers thwarted that rescue operation. In despair at her

---

[39]Ripperdá to Bucareli y Ursúa, March 30, 1773, Béxar Archives; Ripperdá to Bucareli y Ursúa, July 5, Aug. 2, 1772, in *Athanase de Mézières and the Louisiana-Texas Frontier*, trans. and ed. Bolton, I, 322, 335; Ripperdá to governor of Louisiana Unzaga y Amezaga, Sept. 8, 1772, ibid., 348.

[40]Bucareli y Ursúa to Ripperdá, March 24 and April 28, 1772, Béxar Archives; Ripperdá to Unzaga y Amezaga, May 26, 1772, in *Athanase de Mézières and the Louisiana-Texas Frontier*, trans. and ed. Bolton, I, 273.

failed escape, one of the women from the mission tried to kill herself upon recapture by Spaniards. Unfortunately for the Comanche party, they too failed in their getaway. A group of Apache warriors attacked the party as it fled the region, killed seven men, captured half the horses and four of the women, and promptly turned them over to the Spaniards. Ripperdá, angered at what he labeled the Comanches' "treachery" for using women to feign peace, consigned all the women to different forms of bondage in Coahuila. The three missionized Comanche women were destined for Coahuila missions, accompanied by their neophyte husbands, while the others went to labor camps.[41]

Comanche leaders, however, did not give up, and in the summer of 1772, they traveled to San Antonio (this time in the company of Wichita allies) to retrieve the women now even farther from their reach in Coahuila. Chief Evea himself joined the conference. Following ceremonies reaffirming peace agreements with Wichita bands, Ripperdá attempted to shame the Comanche men by displaying the "false" white flag of truce carried earlier by the Comanche woman. Though he claimed to the viceroy to have sent the Comanches away empty-handed, the men he confronted—including the husband of one captive woman—ultimately had the advantage; the governor could not risk offending representatives of such a powerful Indian nation. Tellingly, in the same letter in which he bragged of cowing Evea with the false flag, Ripperdá reported that he had advised the governor of Coahuila to ensure that the Comanche woman was not baptized, so that she could be returned to her husband. Records fail to tell whether she was. If she was redeemed, it did not buy the Spaniards peace for long, since hostilities continued unchecked until 1785 when the two peoples signed their first peace treaty. The position of power enjoyed by Comanches and Wichitas stood in stark contrast to that of Apaches, as the Comanche and Wichita women who fell prey to Spanish bondage were few and Comanche and Wichita men more easily regained those who did.[42]

Spanish officials increasingly chose to negotiate truce and alliance with Comanche and Wichita warriors by ransoming from them any enemy captives they took in war. In the process, Spaniards also attained for themselves, by commercial rather than violent means, captive Indian women to use in diplomatic relations with the women's families and peoples. Most commonly, they purchased Apache captives from Comanche and Wichita men. Native captive raiding may have risen in response to Spanish attempts to broker deals with victims' family members. Fray Juan Domingo Arricivita asserted that while Apaches might take captives in war to sell to other nations, they equally took them "to exchange them for some of their relatives who have been made prisoners."[43] Spanish diplomatic traffic in women was not limited to transactions with

[41]Bucareli y Ursúa to Ripperdá, June 16, 1772, Béxar Archives; Ripperdá to Unzaga y Amezaga, May 26, 1772, in *Athanase de Mézières and the Louisiana-Texas Frontier*, trans. and ed. Bolton, I, 274.

[42]Ripperdá to Bucareli y Ursúa, July 5, 1772, in *Athanase de Mézières and the Louisiana-Texas Frontier*, trans. and ed. Bolton, I, 321–22.

[43]Fray Juan Domingo Arricivita, *Apostolic Chronicle of Juan Domingo Arricivita: The Franciscan Mission Frontier in the Eighteenth Century in Arizona, Texas, and the Californias*, trans. George P. Hammond and Agapito Rey (2 vols., Berkeley, CA, 1996), II, 25.

Comanches and Wichitas. For instance, when eighty Apache warriors led by seven chiefs captured a woman, one girl, and two boys in a revenge raid on a Tonkawa ranchería in 1779, Texas governor Domingo Cabello offered eight horses for the captives. He claimed to want the children because they "could become Christians by virtue of their youth," but his desire for the woman was purely political, since she could be restored to a Tonkawa band as "proof of friendship." Interestingly, the Apache men refused to give him any of the captives, not because eight horses was an unfair price, but because they saw little political gain to be had from the Spanish governor at that time. Further proof of the Apache men's careful assessment of where their interests lay came when chief El Joyoso chose instead to give one of the children, a ten-year-old Mayeye girl, to his "good friend Don Luis Menchaca," a Spanish merchant in San Antonio who had long traded with Apache peoples and shown them good faith (sometimes against the wishes of the provincial government). . . .[44]

Beyond telling of warfare and its spoils, the stories of enslaved Apache women and children document the ways European and Indian men used them as social and political capital in efforts to coerce and accommodate one another. Looking at how bands and empires or traders and diplomats transformed women into currency allows one to see multiple sources and forms of bondage: from pre-Columbian indigenous warfare that created captivity as an alternative to battlefield deaths, to captive raiding and commercial trade that created human commodities, to hostage taking and deportation that created prison labor. Pressed into service, women became objects for sex, familial reproduction, and reciprocal trade relations; gifts that made peaceful coexistence possible for their captors; or victims who paid the price for their captors' hostility. This diversity of slaveries unfolded from the confrontations and collusions of European and native political systems that structured economic behavior, battlefield enmity, and diplomatic maneuvering. Putting standardized categories of slavery and unfreedom to the test in complicated borderlands where two imperial powers sought to negotiate multiple configurations of Indian social and political organization shows how wanting those categories can be. Slavery in North America has been cast as a monolithic, chattel-oriented system of coerced labor, thus making it a distinctive and anomalous model when compared to forms of bondage instituted in other times and places. Meanwhile the forms of captivity and exchanges of women involved in European-Indian relations in the Americas have fallen into categories often perceived to be more benign. If bondage could prove such an infinitely variable institution in just one region of colonial North America, imagine what we may find as we piece together experiences across the entire continent. Explicating such diversity will bring American practices of slavery into better global perspective and more fruitful comparison with colonial geopolitics and cultural geographies around the world.

---

[44]Domingo Cabello to commandant general of the Interior Provinces, Teodoro de Croix, March 18, 1779, Béxar Archives; William W. Newcomb Jr. and Thomas N. Campbell, "Tonkawa," in *Handbook of North American Indians*, XIII, ed. DeMallie, part 2, 953–64.

Juliana Barr

I am an historian of American Indians and women, and my research focuses on using history, archaeology, and anthropology to study Indian-European relations in sixteenth-, seventeenth-, and eighteenth-century North America. I grew up in a home of educators; my mother is a high school mathematics teacher and my father is a university history professor. After graduating from the Plan II Honors Program at the University of Texas–Austin, I earned my Ph.D. in the first doctoral program in women's history established in the United States at the University of Wisconsin–Madison. I now teach at Duke University. My publications have at their heart the question of American Indian sovereignty and how European empires came to impinge on it (or not) over time. Scholars tend to associate issues of sovereignty only with the endpoint—nineteenth-century reservations—that transformed Indian lands into remnant outposts within the United States. Yet if we look at North America in 1800, three centuries after European colonization began, 75 percent of the continent remained under Indian rule as well as half of the so-called sovereign territory of the U.S. Thus the "colonial" period does not tell a story of inevitable European conquest; Indians continued to exert power within their own borders and over Europeans themselves long after 1492. This article comes partially from my book *Peace Came in the Form of a Woman: Indians and Spaniards in the Texas Borderlands*, which tells the story of what cross-cultural relations look like when Indians have the power to control them.

QUESTIONS FOR CONSIDERATION

1. Barr contends that the history of slavery in colonial North America has been limited in its scope. How does she propose to widen our understanding of North American slavery during the seventeenth and eighteenth centuries?
2. Characterize the ways in which Indians used captivity of other Native peoples before European contact in the Southwest.
3. How did the French use the institution of slavery in the Southwest? How did French slavery impact the institution of slavery for the Native people they encountered?
4. How did the Spanish use the institution of slavery in the Southwest? How did Spanish slavery impact the institution of slavery for the Native people they encountered?
5. In what ways did the cession of French Louisiana to Spain after 1763 reshape the status of some enslaved Native women, especially those owned by the French? In what ways did their status remain the same?
6. Characterize the ways in which the strengthened presence of the Spanish in the Southwest after 1763 shaped Apache, Comanche and Wichita relations with them?

7. According to Barr, "diversity of slaveries unfolded from the confrontations and collusions of European and native political systems that structured economic behavior, battlefield enmity, and diplomatic maneuvering." Choose one of these three (economic behavior, battlefield enmity, diplomatic maneuvering) and describe the way in which it shaped the enslavement of Indian women over the course of the seventeenth and eighteenth centuries.

CHAPTER FOUR

~◯

Suicide, Slavery, and Memory in North America[1]

Terri L. Snyder

Lots of slaves what was brung over from Africa could fly. There was a crowd of them working in the field. They don't like it here and they think they go back to Africa. One by one they fly up in the air and all fly off and gone back to Africa.

—Jack Tattnall, Georgia Writers' Project interview,
in Georgia Writers' Project, *Drums and Shadows:*
Survival Stories among the Georgia Coastal
Negroes (1940; Athens, GA, 1986), 108.

When ex-slaves were interviewed by the Federal Writers' Project in the 1930s, the subject of suicide rarely surfaced.[2] Exceptions to this silence about slave self-destruction came from the particular region of the Georgia and South Carolina Sea Islands where ex-slaves and their children related stories, similar to Jack Tattnall's, of Africans who literally had the power to take flight to escape enslavement. The flying African folktale probably has its historical roots in an 1803 collective suicide by newly imported slaves. A group of Igbo (variously, Ebo or Ibo) captives who had survived the middle passage were sold near Savannah, Georgia, and reloaded onto a small ship bound for St. Simon's Island. Off the coast of the island, the enslaved cargo, who had "suffered much by mismanagement," "rose" from their confinement in the small vessel, and revolted against the crew, forcing them into the water where they drowned. After the ship ran aground, the Igbos "took to the marsh" and

---

[1]Interested students are encouraged to read this essay in the original form. Terri L. Snyder, "Suicide, Slavery, and Memory in North America," *Journal of American History* 97 (1) (June 2010), 39–62.

[2]Interviews with African American informants in the 1930s were often rendered in "negro dialect," which, as Rhys Isaac has pointed out, used spelling conventions that were developed for minstrel shows. Following the example of Isaac and others, I have regularized spelling without changing the syntax or the idiom of the informants' interviews. Rhys Isaac, *Landon Carter's Uneasy Kingdom: Revolution and Rebellion on a Virginia Plantation* (New York, 2004), 193; and Timothy B. Powell, "Summoning the Ancestors: The Flying Africans' Story and Its Enduring Legacy," in *African American Life in the Georgia Lowcountry: The Atlantic World and the Gullah Geechee*, ed. Philip Morgan (Athens, GA, 2010), 259–62; Charles L. Perdue Jr., Thomas E. Barden, and Robert K. Phillips, *Weevils in the Wheat: Interviews with Virginia Ex-slaves* (Bloomington, 1976), 367–76.

71

drowned themselves—an act that most scholars have understood as a deliberate, collective suicide. The site of their fatal immersion was named Ebos Landing.[3]

The fate of those Igbo in 1803 gave rise to a distinctive regional folklore and a place name, but both individual and collective suicide were also part of the general history of North American slavery. From the start of the transatlantic slave trade, mariners, merchants, and masters exchanged reports of slave suicide along with their human traffic, and they noted alarmingly that captive Africans often responded to enslavement by destroying themselves. Some ship captains kept account of their cargo losses for investors and insurers; one study of surgeons' logs for the period 1792–1796 attributed 7.2 percent of deaths that occurred during capture, embarkation on the African coast, and along the middle passage to suicide. Particularly at loading points on the African coast and aboard ships during the middle passage, captive Africans' self-destruction was common enough to warrant the use of the earliest technologies for suicide prevention. Nets were strung on the decks of slave ships to forestall any captives who might leap to their deaths and the *speculum oris* was used to forcibly feed those who chose to starve themselves. While work by Michael Gomez and, more recently, Marcus Rediker and Eric Robert Taylor has underscored the frequency of suicide among captive Africans during the early stages of the transatlantic trade, little attention has been given to the meanings of self-destruction among newly imported slaves after disembarkation or among seasoned and former slaves born in colonial North America and, later, the United States. . . .[4]

---

[3]William Mein to Pierce Butler, May 24, 1803, folder 27, box 6, Series II: Plantation Management, Miscellaneous Correspondence 1802–1803, Butler Family Papers (Historical Society of Pennsylvania, Philadelphia). Michael A. Gomez, *Exchanging Our Country Marks: The Transformation of African Identities in the Colonial and Antebellum South* (Chapel Hill, NC, 1998), 117–18. Powell, "Summoning the Ancestors," 253–80; Timothy B. Powell, "Ebos Landing," June 15, 2004, *New Georgia Encyclopedia,* http://www.georgiaencyclopedia.org/nge/Article.jsp?id=h-2895&hl=y; and Malcolm Bell Jr., *Major Butler's Legacy: Five Generations of a Slaveholding Family* (Athens, GA, 1987), 131–32.

[4]Gomez, *Exchanging Our Country Marks,* 116–31. Marcus Rediker, *The Slave Ship: A Human History* (New York, 2007). Eric Robert Taylor, *If We Must Die: Shipboard Insurrections in the Era of the Atlantic Slave Trade* (Baton Rouge, LA, 2006). David Eltis, *The Rise of African Slavery in America* (Cambridge, England, 1999), 157n73. Richard H. Steckel and Richard A. Jensen, "New Evidence on the Causes of Slave and Crew Mortality in the Atlantic Slave Trade," *Journal of Economic History* 46 (March 1986), 58-62, Table 1, Table 3. William D. Pierson, "White Cannibals, Black Martyrs: Fear, Depression, and Religious Faith as Causes of Suicide among New Slaves," *Journal of Negro History* 62 (April 1977), 147–59. Stephanie E. Smallwood, *Saltwater Slavery: A Middle Passage from Africa to American Diaspora* (Cambridge, MA, 2007). John Thornton, "Cannibals, Witches, and Slave Traders in the Atlantic World," *William and Mary Quarterly* 60 (April 2003), 273–94. Alex Bontemps, *The Punished Self: Surviving Slavery in the Colonial South* (Ithaca, NY, 2001). Orlando Patterson, *Slavery and Social Death: A Comparative Study* (Cambridge, MA, 1982). Daniel E. Walker, "Suicidal Tendencies: African Transmigration in the History and Folklore of the Americas," *Griot* 18 (Spring 1999), 10–18. Vincent Brown, *The Reaper's Garden: Death and Power in the World of Atlantic Slavery* (Cambridge, MA, 2008). Terri L. Snyder, "What Historians Talk about When They Talk about Suicide: The View from Early Modern British North America," *History Compass* 5 (March 2007), 658–74. Donna Merwick, *Death of a Notary: Conquest and Change in Colonial New York* (Ithaca, NY, 1999). Howard I. Kushner, *Self-Destruction in the Promised Land: A Psychocultural Biology of American Suicide* (New Brunswick, 1989); Richard Bell, "The Double Guilt of Dueling: The Stain of Suicide in Antidueling Rhetoric in the Early Republic," *Journal of the Early Republic* 29 (Fall 2009), 383–410. Richard James Bell, "Do Not Despair: The Cultural Significance of Suicide in America, 1780–1840" (PhD diss., Harvard University, 2006).

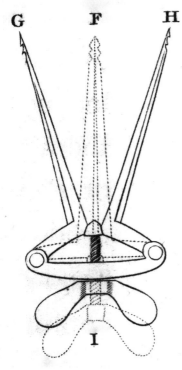

Figure 4.1

"The speculum oris was used in the forced feeding of suicidal enslaved people. According to a merchant who sold the instrument, "[S]laves were frequently so sulky, as to shut their mouths against all sustenance, and this with a determination to die; and it was necessary their mouths should be forced open to throw in nutriment, that they who had purchased them might incur no loss by their death." Thomas Clarkson, *The History of the Rise, Progress, and Accomplishment of the Abolition of the African Slave-Trade by the British Parliament* (London, 1808). Courtesy the Huntington Library, San Marino, California, Call no. 297390.

This article widens the traditional scope of evidence to consider slave self-destruction from multiple perspectives and chronological moments and more effectively places suicide within the long history of North American slavery. Slave suicide often has been rightly perceived as a form of defiance; indeed, Michael Gomez assesses suicide as "perhaps the ultimate form of resistance."[5] To contemplate the history of suicide within the context of North American slavery, however, I step outside of that resistance model and examine slave self-destruction through what I term slave suicide ecology: the emotional, psychological, and material conditions that fostered their acts of self-destruction. My consideration of ecology does not discount resistance as a precipitating factor in slave suicide, but it allows for a more nuanced exploration of slaves as individual subjects and encourages a more careful parsing of the role of power in acts of self-destruction. Certainly, kidnapping, forced migration, rape, brutality, starvation, natal alienation, and family separation gave enslaved men and women readily imaginable motives for suicidal responses to their captors and owners. But casting a wider ecology of slave suicide allows the inclusion of other, lesser known sources of power, including religious beliefs, gendered entitlements, family and household composition, physical pain, revolt, and imminent incarceration.

While slave suicide was a seemingly isolated choice driven by immediate, identifiable conditions, it nevertheless reverberated in significant local, regional, and national contexts and raised questions about a host of cultural and political issues: the nature of slave temperament, the legitimacy of the institution of slavery, and the extent of individual

---

[5]Gomez, *Exchanging Our Country Marks*, 120.

rights and liberties in the early republic and during the antebellum era. . . .[6] Those approaches uncover many of the social and political nuances of suicide in the United States, but they reveal little about the act of self-destruction and its various meanings within the context of slavery. Suicide by enslaved people might signal cultural continuity with ethnic African attitudes about choosing death rather than dishonor, or it might be seen as an entirely reasonable—if not outright revolutionary—response to enslavement. Suicide might have been a source of spiritual relief: a means for African-born individuals to transmigrate to Africa or a way for native-born Christians to reach heaven. Suicide might also be understood as an aggressive act toward others, as an expression of gendered entitlement, or as an escape from physical or emotional pain. Historically speaking, however, suicide was an act that held shades of discernable meaning and reflected the ecology of the enslaved self. Simultaneously, accounts of enslaved peoples' suicides carried a host of potent political and cultural meanings and came to symbolize, particularly for abolitionists, much of what was objectionable about the institution of slavery.

Beyond the immediate experience and perception of the act of self-destruction, ex-slave memories also reconfigured the intersections of slavery and suicide. Flying African folklore, in particular, illustrates how distinct cultural communities chronicled, compressed, and remembered the experience of self-destruction in slavery. Stories of flying Africans, like the types of African American folklore that were explored by Lawrence W. Levine and Sterling Stuckey, serve didactic purposes. Using Saidiya V. Hartman's argument that memory is not simply an inventory of what went before, but is, rather, a bridge from the past to the present that redresses the wrongs of history, the stories can also be seen as corrective measures.[7] In this sense, flying African folklore demonstrates the power of cultural memory to reshape past tragedies, transforming stories of suicide into stories of strength and propelling them into the future.

Taken together, the attitudes of onlookers to the slave trade, the viewpoints of enslaved people themselves, and the perspectives of ex-slaves can historicize our understanding of suicide within slavery and our paradigms for studying self-destruction in the American past. Moreover, the interplay among the perceptions, ecology, and memories of suicide within slavery can challenge us to rethink some of our assumptions about the peculiar institution and about the history of suicide in early North America.

---

[6]Kushner, *Self-Destruction in the Promised Land*; Bell, "Do Not Despair." David Andrew Silknat, "Suicide, Divorce, and Debt in Civil War–Era North Carolina" (Ph.D. diss., University of North Carolina, 2007). Roger Lane, *Roots of Violence in Black Philadelphia, 1860–1900* (Cambridge, MA, 1986), esp. 15. Roger Lane, *Violent Death in the City: Suicide, Accident, and Murder in Nineteenth-Century Philadelphia* (Cambridge, MA, 1979).

[7]Lawrence W. Levine, *Black Culture and Black Consciousness: Afro-American Folk Thought from Slavery to Freedom* (New York, 1977). Sterling Stuckey, *Slave Culture: Nationalist Theory and the Foundations of Black America* (New York, 1987). Saidiya V. Hartman, *Scenes of Subjection: Terror, Slavery, and Self-Making in Nineteenth-Century America* (New York, 1997), 73.

EVIDENCE

Heard about the Ibo's Landing? That's the place where they
bring the Ibos over in a slave ship and when they get here, they
ain't like it and so they all start singing and they march right
down in the river to march back to Africa, but they ain't able to
get there. They gets drown.

—Floyd White, Georgia Writers' Project interview,
in Georgia Writers' Project, *Drums and Shadows*, 185.

A comparison of the recollections of Jack Tattnall and Floyd White suggests that
evidence of slave suicide on plantations in early North America is impressionis-
tic and often competing. Over the course of slavery's long history in North
America, enslaved men and women, masters, legal authorities, and antislavery
activists held divergent interpretations of suicide by slaves—most often seen in
legal, political, and popular descriptions but also found in private papers and
plantation account books. A brief review of the evidence makes clear how incidents of slave suicide served different purposes and allows us to consider the
conclusions that might be drawn from those often contradictory and sometimes
ambiguous sources.

Legal sources, particularly legislative petitions, coroners' reports, and
breach-of-warranty lawsuits attest to the incidence of suicide by enslaved people
from the seventeenth century through the Civil War. At first glance, the sources
appear to report on slave suicide, but most of them also represent the actions of
slave owners (or potential owners) who were motivated to protect their financial
interests. . . . [P]etitions must be understood to convey only a fraction of the suicides that had occurred at the time. (See Table 4.1.) Similarly, coroners' reports
from county jurisdictions in North Carolina, South Carolina, and Virginia also
reflect the persistence of suicide by enslaved people in mainland North America
well beyond the colonial period.[8] (See Table 4.2.)

Breach-of-warranty legal cases provide yet another view of suicide in slavery from the mid-eighteenth century through the Emancipation Proclamation.
Early on, North American courts consistently recognized that slaves killed
themselves because of "cruel and improper treatment." Breach-of-warranty suits
attempted to affix responsibility for enslaved peoples' suicides on owners, overseers, or those who hired slaves and attempted to recover monetary damages. In
the 1741 case of *Viel v. Pery*, a plaintiff in Louisiana sought damages for the
death of Francois, an enslaved carpenter who cut his throat "in despair, whether
for ill-treatment or for other causes." Other ordinary southerners shared a similar perspective on slavery and suicide. In 1861 one young woman in New Orleans
saw an enslaved woman attempt to hang herself and concluded that the act was

---

[8]Inquest on Wilmouth, Dec. 3, 1858, C.R.054.928.1, Coroners' Inquests concerning Slave
Deaths, Iredell County Slave Records, 1823–1872 (North Carolina State Archives, Raleigh). Genovese, *Roll, Jordan, Roll*, 37–41. Peter Kolchin, *American Slavery, 1619–1877* (New York, 1993), 111–22.

Table 4.1   Suicide, Possible Suicide, and Slavery in Virginia, 1727–1776

SUICIDE AS A CAUSE OF DEATH	MEN	WOMEN	UNKNOWN	TOTAL
Certain	31	6	6	43
Possible	19	2	4	25
TOTALS	50	8	10	68

caused by the "ill-treatment of her devilish master." That some of the breach-of-warranty suits were litigated into the 1870s underscores the efforts of some masters and former masters to recoup their financial interests in deceased former bondpeople.[9]

Data from legal records must be treated with caution. Masters' claims that their slaves killed themselves and verdicts of suicide from coroners' inquests probably masked homicidal violence against slaves. Similarly, deaths that might be legally ruled as accidental may have been homicides or suicides. Some inquests were no doubt held at the request of masters who suspected foul play and wanted to sue for damages. The records also reflect the local tensions between slave owners and the juries who made final rulings (some not always in favor of masters, particularly after 1820 . . .). When the enslaved Rachel died of a blow to her head in 1834, for example, the jurors "rest[ed] their suspicion" on her owner Thomas Preay.[10]

In contrast, depictions of self-destruction by enslaved people in antislavery print culture served very different ends than the depictions in legal documents: those that appeared in print culture directly addressed the system of slavery and the experiences of enslaved persons. The published results of a 1791 British House

Table 4.2   Slave Suicide and Coroners' Inquests from Selected Southern Jurisdictions in the Colonial, Early Republic, and Antebellum Periods

	SUICIDE VERDICTS	
	SLAVES/TOTAL	PERCENTAGE OF INQUESTS ON SLAVES
North Carolina	10 / 45	22%
South Carolina	18 / 49	37%
Virginia	7 / 33	21%
TOTALS	35 / 127	28%

[9]Heloise H. Cruzat, trans. and ed., "Records of the Superior Council of Louisiana, XXXVII," *Louisiana Historical Quarterly* 11 (Jan. 1928), 141. *Ritchie v. Wilson*, 3 Mart. (N.S.), 585 (1825). Elliot Ashkenazi, ed., *The Civil War Diary of Clara Solomon: Growing Up in New Orleans, 1861–1862* (Baton Rouge, LA, 1995), 236. *Merrick v. Bradley*, 19 Md. 50 (1862); and *Ketchum v. Dew*, 7 Coldwell 237 (1870).

[10]Inquest on Rachel, Feb. 18, 1834, box 1, series L 20149, Coroners' Inquests, Fairfield County, South Carolina Court of General Sessions (South Carolina Department of Archives and History, Columbia). Genovese, *Roll, Jordan, Roll*, 37–41. Kolchin, *American Slavery*, 111–22.

of Commons investigation into the slave trade, for example, provided ample evidence that Africans responded to enslavement by destroying themselves. . . . Suicide ideation and specific accounts of self-destruction can be found in personal slave narratives as widely ranging as Olaudah Equiano's and Mattie J. Jackson's. Harriet Jacobs contemplated suicide, writing that slave self-destruction was a "frequent occurrence" in all slave states and relaying the story of one unnamed enslaved woman who, pursued by patrollers, "rushed to the river, jumped in, and ended her wrongs in death." Frederick Douglass cautioned slaves not to "abandon" themselves to suicide "as have many thousands of American slaves." The fugitive slave Charles Ball related the story of African-born Paul, who argued for the "propriety of destroying a life which was doomed to continual distress" and eventually hanged himself in the woods. Ball asserted that "self-destruction was much more frequent among the slaves in the cotton region than is generally supposed" and added that he did not "marvel that the slaves who are driven to the south often destroy themselves." His comments suggest that the social and cultural dislocations created by the transatlantic slave trade and the middle passage continued to shape the self-destructive impulses of slaves who were born in the United States and traded domestically. Still, even antislavery forces used the incidence of slave suicide for different purposes. Witnesses in the House of Commons investigation, for example, argued that slave suicide would diminish if the slave trade was ended and if the enslaved population was allowed to increase through reproduction rather than importation. They suggested that suicide among slaves would be lessened by stable family formation, a factor dependent on the reproductive labor of female slaves. However, as the testimonies of Jacobs, Ball, and Douglass make clear, such stability was illusive for slaves—two million of whom, according to Walter Johnson, were sold at interstate, local, and state-ordered sales from the end of the transatlantic trade through the Civil War.[11]

---

[11]Sheila Lambert, ed., *List of House of Commons Sessional Papers* (145 vols., Wilmington, DE, 1968–). Thomas Clarkson, *Abstract of the evidence delivered before a select committee of the House of Commons, in the years 1790 and 1791; on the part of the Petitioners for the Abolition of the Slave-Trade* (London, 1791). Olaudah Equiano, "Interesting Narrative of the Life of Olaudah Equiano, or Gustavas Vasa, the African," in *The Interesting Narrative and Other Writings,* ed. Vincent Caretta (New York, 2003), 48, 50, 56, 58–59. Mattie J. Jackson, "The Story of Mattie J. Jackson," in *Six Women's Slave Narratives,* ed. William L. Andrews (New York, 1988), 6. Olaudah Equiano's claim to have been born in Africa has been challenged most recently by Vincent Caretta; nonetheless, his suicide attempts are consistent with those considered by other slaves. See Vincent Caretta, *Equiano, the African: Biography of a Self-Made Man* (Athens, GA, 2005). Harriet Jacobs, *Incidents in the Life of a Slave Girl. Written by Herself.* (Boston, 1861), 61, 77–78, esp. 122. Letter from Frederick Douglass, Sept. 5, 1850, in *Frederick Douglass: Selected Speeches and Writings,* ed. Philip S. Foner and Yuvall Taylor (Chicago, 1999), 162. Charles Ball, *Slavery in the United States: A Narrative of the Life and Adventures of Charles Ball, a Black Man, Who Lived Forty Years in Maryland, South Carolina and Georgia, as a Slave Under Various Masters, and was One Year in the Navy with Commodore Barney, During the Late War* (New York, 1837), 329, 69, in *Documenting the American South: North American Slave Narratives,* http://docsouth.unc.edu/neh/ballslavery/menu.html. Walter Johnson, *Soul by Soul: Life inside the Antebellum Slave Market* (Cambridge, MA, 2001), 7.

THE PERCEPTION OF SLAVE SUICIDE

I have heard of them people. . . . My mother used to tell me about
them when we sat in this city market selling vegetables and fruit.
She say that there was a man and his wife and they got fooled
aboard a slave ship. First thing they know they was sold to a
planter on St. Helena. So one day when all the slaves was
together, this man and his wife say, "We going back home,
goodie bye, goodie bye," and just like a bird they flew out of sight.

—Carrie Hamilton, Georgia Writers' Project interview,
in Georgia Writers' Project, *Drums and Shadows*, 28.

During the early stages of North American colonization, European and Anglo-
American onlookers viewed suicide by captive Africans through an early modern
sensibility that emphasized hierarchies of domination and submission. Some empowered onlookers were simply perplexed by slave suicide, particularly suicides by
newly imported slaves. In 1698 the British politician Edward Littleton warned
planters that slaves hanged themselves and "no creature knows why," while the
Virginian William Mayo wrote matter-of-factly in 1731 that the "Negro Quaccoo
Hang'd himself the Women all in Health and all things goe on as well as can be
expected." Early newspapers were also at a loss to explain suicide by the enslaved.
A 1752 announcement in the *Virginia Gazette* noted that "a few days ago, a fine
negroe Man Slave, imported in one of the late Ships from Africa, belonging to a
Wheelwright, near this City, taking Notice of his Master's giving another Correc-
tion for a Misdemeanor, went to a Grindstone and making a Knife sharp cut his
own throat, and died on the Spot."[12] The language of the item seems to underscore
the deliberateness of the slave's self-destructive intentions: he watched, walked, and
sharpened his knife. While the story suggests that his suicide was a response to
witnessing a beating, its tone does not otherwise directly comment on his reasons
for so doing, suggesting that the *Gazette*'s readers required no further explanation.

Other observers of enslaved peoples' acts of self-destruction appealed to
essentialism. They explained suicide as a predilection of newly imported slaves of
a particular age or ethnicity rather than as a response to enslavement. Planters
were counseled to avoid purchasing older slaves who were "sullen and unteach-
able and frequently put an end to their own lives." As James Grainger's popular
poem *The Sugar Cane* (published in 1764 but reprinted in the United States as late
as the 1850s) expressed the matter:

But, planter, from what coast soe'er they sail,
Buy not the old: they ever sullen prove;

---

[12]Edward Littleton, *The groans of the plantations, or, A true account of their grievous and extreme sufferings by the heavy impositions upon sugar, and other hardships relating more particularly
to the island of Barbados* (London, 1698), 20. William Mayo to John Perratt, Aug. 27, 1731, no. mss2
M4547 a 1, Library and Manuscripts Collection (Virginia Historical Society, Richmond). *Virginia
Gazette*, July 10, 1752, p. 31; Rhys Isaac, "On Explanation, Text, and Terrifying Power in Ethno-
graphic History," *Yale Journal of Criticism: Interpretation in the Humanities* 6 (Fall 1993), 217–36.

With heart-felt anguish, they lament their home.
And oft by suicide their being end.[13]

Planters were also warned against obtaining captives from particular nations. *The Sugar Cane* counseled planters to "fly, with care, from the Moco nation," because "they themselves destroy" and to avoid "Coromontee" who "chuse death before dishonorable bonds." Merchants such as Henry Laurens of South Carolina wrote that Igbos were "quite out of repute from numbers in every Cargo . . . destroying themselves." Traders in the West Indies and planters in South Carolina avoided the Igbo precisely because they were reported to be suicidal. Even so, Virginians apparently were not dissuaded by such reports: between 1710 and 1760, 38 percent of all slaves imported to Virginia were Igbo.[14]

Aside from age and ethnicity, however, temperamental stubbornness was the characteristic most commonly ascribed to suicidal bondpeople, regardless of whether they were newly imported or native born. Self-destroying slaves were deemed to be willful, sullen, or simply insensible individuals who—through unconscious inability or conscious determination—railed against their station. The characteristic of stubbornness also linked self-destroying slaves to what early modern observers referred to as refuse slaves: seasoned yet undesirable slaves who were traded northward from ports in the Caribbean. By the early eighteenth century, slave dealers up and down the Atlantic seaboard had learned to avoid "refuse Negroes" because, as one merchant explained, they were "Hazardous. Criminalls or otherwise of Little Worth" and also "distempered or refractory."[15] Refuse slaves fit uneasily into early modern Anglo-American models of authority and were, therefore, easily cast aside. Their recalcitrance made them unfit for slavery, compromised the mastery of owners and overseers, and diminished the overall value of slaves as property. . . .

The connection between stubbornness and slavery was . . . reflected in the punishments that were meted out to self-destructive slaves, and slaves who took their own lives were used as visible deterrents for the rest of the community. In 1712, when the enslaved Roger hanged himself in the "old 40 foot Tobacco House," his overseer's response was swift and immediate: Roger's head was "cutt off and Stuck on a pole to be a terror to others." Through the Civil War era, the corpses of

---

[13]James Grainger, "A History of Sugar Cane, from a Poem called Sugar Cane," *Gentleman's Magazine* 24 (Oct. 1764), 487. James Grainger, *The Sugar Cane: A Poem in Four Books* (London, 1764), bk. 4, lines 66–71. John Gilmore, *The Poetics of Empire: A Study of James Grainger's* The Sugar Cane (London, 2000), 1–85. David Shields, *Oracles of Empire: Poetry, Politics, and Commerce in British America, 1690–1750* (Chicago, 1990), 72–78; *Debow's Review, Agricultural, Commercial, Industrial Progress and Resources* 9 (6) (1850), 668.

[14]Grainger, *Sugar Cane*, bk. 4, lines 81, 99. Donnan, ed., *Documents Illustrative of the History of the Slave Trade*, IV, 317. Gomez, *Exchanging Our Country Marks*, 114–15, 124. Sylvia Frey and Betty Wood, *Come Shouting to Zion: African American Protestantism in the American South and British Caribbean to 1830* (Chapel Hill, NC, 1998), 38. Philip D. Curtin, *The Atlantic Slave Trade: A Census* (Madison, WI, 1969), 188, 192.

[15]As quoted in Donald D. Wax, "Preferences for Slaves in Colonial America," *Journal of Negro History* 58 (Oct. 1973), 371–401, esp. 376. Lambert, *List of House of Commons Sessional Papers*, LXXXII, 196.

suicidal slaves were decapitated, dismembered, and displayed to punish the victim and to deter like-minded slaves. . . . Such practices attested to the community's need for a retributive justice that could only be obtained by punishing the body and the family of a self-destructive soul. . . . Historically, the act of desecrating or dismembering the corpses of rebellious or suicidal slaves serves as a reminder that the violence visited on the corpses of African Americans—typically equated with the lynchings of the postbellum years—has a history that stretches back to the earliest period of North American settlement. . . .[16]

While the association of suicide with stubbornness held fast throughout the era of North American slavery, perceptions of slave temperament did begin to change during the revolutionary period. The concept of refuse slaves shifted subtly, used more commonly for those slaves who were "sickly . . . by grief" or who had been "over crowded on board the ships." Particularly in the eighteenth-century Caribbean and in South America, slave self-destruction was increasingly viewed as a symptom of a pining rather than as a result of a stubborn temperament—a change that also reflects emerging views of suicide as consequence of mental disease, not a product of a willful temperament or diabolical inspiration. The tendency toward suicide by slaves was labeled "nostalgia" and had a distinct set of symptoms that still continued to encompass temperamental stubbornness. Slaves who manifested medical nostalgia killed themselves through outright refusals: they would not eat or move and by these actions they deliberately courted death.[17]

The evolving assessments of the temperament of enslaved people reflected eighteenth-century debates over both suicide and slavery. . . . Beginning in the last quarter of the eighteenth century, antislavery activists—including ex-slaves—used self-destruction to illustrate the wrongs of slavery, the denial of liberty, and the immorality of arbitrary power. Such themes—natural rights, the entitlements of the self, and the extent of individual liberty—were central to the cultural and political debates that mark the emergence of the modern era. On occasion, arguments about slavery and suicide literally invoked one another. When John Locke asserted that freedom from arbitrary power was a natural right, he used the example of a slave's choice to die to illustrate his point. Locke argued that whenever a slave found that the hardship of slavery outweighed the value of his life, "it is in his power, by resisting the will of his master, to draw on himself the death he desires."[18]

Sentimental depictions of enslaved peoples' suicides appeared in the print culture of the revolutionary and early republican eras. Even those who were convinced of slaves' innate stubbornness and were disdainful of abolitionism would have been

---

[16]Overseer's account, Selsdon Quarter, Dec. 6, 1712, Francis Porteus Corbin Papers (Rare Book, Manuscript, and Special Collections Library, Duke University, Durham, NC).

[17]Lambert, ed., *List of House of Commons Sessional Papers*, LXXXII, 24. Kushner, *Self-Destruction in the Promised Land*, 13–34. Watt, ed., *From Sin to Insanity*, 1–8. Mary C. Karasch, *Slave Life in Rio de Janeiro, 1808–1850* (Princeton, NJ, 1987), 318.

[18]S. E. Sprott, *The English Debate on Suicide: From Donne to Hume* (La Salle, 1961), 104. Peter Laslett, ed., *Two Treatises of Government*, by John Locke (1689; Cambridge, England, 1988), 284–85.

Figure 4.2

The cover of *The Dying Negro* illustrates the wrongs of slavery through images of the central figure's self-destruction and contextual representations of family separation, forced labor, and the overseer's whip. The turbulent skies and epigraph also reflect a challenge to traditional attitudes toward suicide. The slave offers his spirit to God and defiantly suggests that his voluntary death is unstained by sin: "To you this unpolluted blood I pour. To you that spirit which ye gave restore." The open heavens suggest that God is, at least, listening—and perhaps even yielding—to the slave's challenge. Thomas Day, "The Dying Negro, a Poem" (London, 1775). Courtesy the Huntington Library, San Marino, California. Call no. 315267.

hard put to ignore the different human temperament reflected in Thomas Day's wildly popular poem, *The Dying Negro*, which became an overnight sensation when it was first published in 1773. According to its epigraph, the poem, allegedly based on an actual event, was written by a slave in England who believed that he was free. He had been baptized and was about to marry his beloved, a white servant, when he was seized and readied for shipment back to the Americas. While awaiting transport on a ship in the Thames, he shot himself.[19] Both the news item of the actual event and Day's poem were widely reprinted in American newspapers, amplifying the contradictions of the chattel principle: Were enslaved individuals commodities or persons? The poem reflects the new assessments of slaves' emotional temperament that were emerging at the end of the eighteenth century, and it ultimately endows slaves with a sensibility that accentuates their humanity.

In popular print and in emerging abolitionist literature, the enslaved were increasingly depicted as prone to passionate apathy over disappointments in love, despair over family separation, and despondency stemming from physical and sexual brutality. Sensibility in slaves marked their humanity and explained their resort to suicide.... By attributing sentimental rather than stubborn emotional sensibilities to the enslaved, such representations of slave temperament attempted to measure the humanity of the enslaved and became persistent—if deeply flawed—images in abolitionist literature and legal forums. Of course, other onlookers denied slaves' emotional complexity or even the possibility of insanity based on the putative inferiority of their mental faculties.

It is also possible that these changing assessments of slave temperament affected the enslavers. As the eighteenth century gave way to the nineteenth,

---

[19] Day, *The Dying Negro*. Moira Ferguson, *Subject to Others: British Women Writers and Colonial Slavery, 1670–1834* (New York, 1992), 237–38.

Figure 4.3
The American Anti-Slavery Almanac for 1838 illustrated the suicide of the slave Paul, who, according to fellow slave Charles Ball, had "suffered so much in slavery that he chose to encounter the hardships and perils of a runaway. He exposed himself, in gloomy forests, to cold and starvation, and finally hung himself, that he might not again fall into the hands of his tormentor." *The American Anti-Slavery Almanac for 1836–1838*, (Boston, 1835). Courtesy The Huntington Library, San Marino, California. Call no. 218591.

masters became increasingly defensive about the suicides of their slaves; perhaps the mask of paternalism necessitated their denials of slave self-destruction. William Beverley, a member of one of Virginia's most powerful slave-owning families, testified in 1791 that "never one" report of slave suicide had ever reached him. That statement seems nearly inconceivable, however, from a well-born Virginian who was studying the law and whose family possessed approximately five hundred slaves. Writing later in the nineteenth century, Charles Ball is even more explicit on that point, asserting that "a certain degree of disgrace falls upon the master whose slave has committed suicide: the master is unwilling to let it be known, lest the deed should be attributed to his own cruelty."[20]

In the aftermath of the American Revolution, antislavery reformers and slaves challenged the centrality of stubbornness and, instead, used slave suicide to highlight the denial of personhood that was central to the institution of slavery. Doing so gave fresh meaning to Cato's choice, widely invoked in North American slave narratives, between liberty and death.[21] Antislavery print culture depicted suicidal slaves as closely linked to an emotional sensibility that was more often manifested in nostalgia and melancholy than in temperamental stubbornness. The image of slave suicide became a potent political shorthand for the wrongs of slavery. That slaves could all too often be driven to suicide was a reflection of their lack of liberty and their membership in humanity and, therefore, a key argument against the maintenance of the peculiar institution. . . .

---

[20]Bertram Wyatt-Brown, "The Mask of Obedience: Male Slave Psychology in the Old South," *American Historical Review* 93 (Dec. 1988), 1228–52. Testimony of William Beverley," in *List of House of Commons Sessional Papers*, ed. Lambert, LXXXII, 216. Ball, *Slavery in the United States*, 70.

[21]Jacobs, *Incidents in the Life of a Slave Girl*, 99; and Frederick Douglass, *Narrative of the Life of Frederick Douglass. Written By Himself* (Boston, 1845).

THE ECOLOGY OF SLAVE SUICIDE

My gran use to tell me about folks flying back to Africa. A man
and his wife was brung from Africa. When they find out they
was slaves and got treat so hard, they just fret and fret. One
day, they was standing with some other slaves and all of a
sudden they say, "We going back to Africa. So goodie bye,
goodie bye." Then they flied right out of sight.

—Mose Brown, Georgia Writers' Project interview,
in Georgia Writers' Project, *Drums and Shadows*, 18.

Despite the persistence and perceptions of enslaved peoples' acts of self-
destruction in early America, comprehending the subjectivities of those who responded to enslavement by destroying themselves remains difficult. Without
their own words to explain their actions, often we are left to look at the conditions surrounding their decisions—the emotional, psychological, and material
circumstances that fostered slaves' self-destruction. Using those exterior em-
bodiments—the ecology of slave suicide—to parse slave subjectivities is tricky,
but doing so will bring us closer to an understanding of the experience of self-
destruction within slavery.

Newly imported African slaves as well as native-born North American slaves
held a variety of attitudes toward suicide. Evidence suggests, as Michael Gomez
has demonstrated extensively, that some African groups held strong prohibitions
against suicide. Among the Igbo, participants in the 1803 group suicide, self-
destruction was a serious transgression. According to Gomez, however, the dislocations of the transatlantic slave trade eroded those traditional taboos. Other
African ethnic groups, including the Yoruba and the Ashanti, did not equate
suicide with jeopardizing one's soul, social standing, or family reputation.
Indeed, in some instances, suicide was deemed an honorable act, particularly if it
provided an escape from a dishonorable status such as that created by slavery.
Daniel E. Walker also argues that captive Africans who desired spiritual transmigration and a return to Africa took courses of action that they fully understood might lead to death. Walker considers the contempt for death as it was
manifested in the specific context of collective slave resistance and revolt. In that
sense, captives' behaviors can be seen as parallels to Huey P. Newton's definition
of revolutionary suicide: that it is better to fight the forces of oppression that lead
to despair rather than to endure them, even if the fight means risking death.[22]

Slaves might have understood that even death by suicide was preferable to
life under slavery because, however it was obtained, death brought the possibility
of transmigrating and returning home to Africa. They therefore prepared for
death in a ritualistic manner or with materials they believed would aid their journey. Ship captains and planters alike understood this motivation for suicide and

[22]Gomez, *Exchanging Our Country Marks*, 133–34. Walker, "Suicidal Tendencies," 13. Huey P.
Newton, *Revolutionary Suicide* (New York, 1973), 1–6.

dismembered the recovered corpses, telling slaves that desecration would prevent their return to Africa. There is no evidence that such a method of deterrence worked. Before killing themselves, for instance, newly imported slaves would put on or remove all of their clothes, place food and water nearby, or wrap chains around their waists; they believed that these actions and objects would sustain them through the transmigration, regardless of whether the act of self-destruction was individual or collective.

The idea of transmigration also often dictated the methods of suicide. Drowning was preferable because water was seen as the spiritual conduit back to Africa; hanging in the woods was also acceptable because it allowed for ritual preparation. . . . [M]ost slave narratives do not rebuke the act of committing suicide. Elizabeth Keckley matter-of-factly reports that her uncle hanged himself from the branch of a willow tree, and Frederick Douglass warned others away from the act, even as he acknowledged self-destruction as a reasonable response to slavery. . . .[23]

In many instances, the physical brutality and psychological horrors of slavery fostered self-destruction. The physician and author Jesse Torrey tells the story of one slave who was on the brink of being passed to a new master was asked by his current master to remove his shirt for one final beating; instead, he drowned himself in refusal. Torrey also gives several accounts of female slaves who leaped from windows, jumped into rivers, or cut their throats rather than face separation from their families. The subject of the 1825 lawsuit *Ritchie v. Wilson* was a female slave who drowned herself after "improper and cruel treatment," suggesting that she refused to tolerate further brutality. Similar themes surface in ex-slave narratives. . . . Ida Hutchinson Blackshear also recalled that one woman, a frequent runaway who vexed her would-be captors, "went to the slough and drowned herself" rather than let the patrollers "beat her and mark her up."[24]

Suicide often had a gendered calculus in North America. The denial of masculine prerogatives within marriage or sexual relations, for example, could lead some slaves to suicide. . . . The connections among slave suicide, masculinity, and honor can be seen at work in the 1851 case *Bunch v. Smith*. After Bob, his wife Binah, and their two children were sold as slaves, their new owner asked Bob whether he would like him as a master. Bob replied that the owner "would not suit." The master threatened to turn his dogs on Bob who responded that he "would run from no man." Bob then walked into the "negro house" and came

---

[23]Vincent Brown, "Spiritual Terror and Sacred Authority," 179–84. Frey and Wood, *Come Shouting to Zion*, 38–39. Smallwood, *Saltwater Slavery*, 186; Karasch, *Slave Life in Rio de Janeiro, 1808–1850*, 319. Elizabeth Keckley, *Behind the Scenes, or, Thirty Years a Slave and Four Years in the White House* (New York, 1868), 319; Foner and Taylor, *Frederick Douglass*, 162.

[24]Jesse Torrey, *A Portraiture of Domestic Slavery, in the United States, with Reflections on the Practicability of Restoring the Moral Rights of the Slave, without Impairing the Legal Privileges of the Possessor* (Philadelphia, 1817), 11, 41–45. *Ritchie v. Wilson*, 3 Mart. (N.S.), 585 (1825), p. 82, available at LexisNexis Legal Research. Perdue et al., *Weevils in the Wheat*, 34. Ida Blackshear Hutchinson interview by Samuel S. Taylor, May 11, 1938, transcript, p. 374, *Born in Slavery: Slave Narratives from the Federal Writers' Project, 1936–1938*, http://lcweb2.loc.gov/ammem/snhtml/snhome.html.

back out "with his throat cut." Gendered themes can also be found in the depictions of enslaved women in Jesse Torrey's portrait of slavery, particularly in the image of an enslaved mother, whom Robert H. Gudmestad refers to as "Anna," leaping from her window after being separated from her children. As Gudmestad has demonstrated, Anna's attempted suicide stirred a national debate over the morality of the domestic slave trade. A similar story is told by escaped slaves William and Ellen Craft: the house servant Antoinette avoided rape by breaking loose from her attacker and "pitch[ing] herself head foremost through the window" to her "bruised but unpolluted" death.[25]

Self-destruction was also part of a pattern of collective resistance by enslaved people. In Virginia, slaves attempted at least eleven collective revolts in the course of the eighteenth century, and suicide may have been a response to a failed insurrection. In 1736, an unnamed female slave broke into a storehouse, stole goods, wounded her master's son, burned a tobacco storehouse, murdered her children and other slaves, and drowned herself. In 1774, when her master was at church, a woman named Juda set fire to her house and her master's house, murdered her son, and deliberately "rushed into the dwelling house" to her certain death.[26] It is possible to read those slave actions as preludes to or instigators of collective revolt as much as it is possible to read them as purely individual acts of resistance. Many early slave suicides in the South were . . . a solitary act of self-directed violence performed in isolation. In contrast, the suicides of Juda and the unnamed female slave include elements that were common features of collective slave resistance: master-directed violence, arson, purloined goods. Moreover, the sequence of events surrounding those suicides begins with the seizure and destruction of material property; murder and self-murder are the final stages of the progression. . . .

Another aspect of self-destruction can be seen in the actions of enslaved men and women who killed themselves before the state or their masters had an opportunity to execute them. By 1754, the runaway slave Dick had lost both ears as punishment for repeated escapes. . . . [A]fter his final capture, according to

---

[25]Overseer's Account, Selsdon Quarter, Dec. 6, 1712, Corbin Papers. *Bunch v. Smith*, in *Judicial Cases concerning American Slavery and the Negro*, ed. Helen Tunnicliff Catterall (5 vols., Washington, D.C., 1926–1929), II, 425–26. Torrey, *Portraiture of Domestic Slavery*, 42–44. Robert H. Gudmestad, *A Troublesome Commerce: The Transformation of the Interstate Slave Trade* (Baton Rouge, LA, 2003), 35–61; Robert H. Gudmestad, "Slave Resistance, Coffles, and the Debates over Slavery in the Nation's Capital," in *The Chattel Principle: Internal Slave Trades in the Americas*, ed. Walter Johnson (New Haven, 2004), 72–90. William Craft, *Running a Thousand Miles for Freedom; or, the Escape of William and Ellen Craft from Slavery* (London, 1860), 21.

[26]Herbert Aptheker, *American Negro Slave Revolts* (New York, 1943), 209–43. James Sidbury, *Ploughshares into Swords: Race, Rebellion, and Identity in Gabriel's Virginia, 1730-1810* (Cambridge, England, 1997). Douglas Egerton, *Gabriel's Rebellion: The Virginia Slave Conspiracies of 1800 and 1802* (Chapel Hill, NC, 1993). Petition of William Cox, Suicide of Unnamed Slave Woman, in *Journals of the House of Burgesses of Virginia, 1727-1740*, ed. J. P. Kennedy and H. R. McIlwaine (Richmond, 1910), 254. Petition of George Mason, in *Journals of the House of Burgesses of Virginia, 1752-1758*, ed. J. P. Kennedy and H. R. McIlwaine (Richmond, VA, 1909), 259–60. Petition of Stephen Ham, Suicide of Juda, *Journals of the House of Burgesses of Virginia, 1773-1776*, ed. J. P. Kennedy and H. R. McIlwaine (Richmond, VA, 1905), 181–82.

the slave patroller who seized him, Dick "fell down in the Road, and either would not or could not go further." The patroller tied Dick to his horse's tail and dragged him to a nearby farm. On the way, Dick ingested a white substance and poisoned himself. If the patroller's claim is true, Dick's action suggests that he was prepared for the eventuality of death; the patroller remembered Dick "saying he was outlawed, and if he was carried to Prison he should certainly be hanged." In similar circumstances, other slaves also killed themselves before the state had an opportunity. In 1837, the *Rutherford (N.C.) Gazette* printed the story of Lucy, a runaway slave who hanged herself rather than face recapture. The newspaper commented on the "firmness" of her resolve, far beyond that "exhibited by any person," because the "place from which she suspended herself was not high enough to prevent her feet from touching the floor and it was only by drawing her legs up, and remaining in that position, that she succeeded in her determined purpose."[27] In 1860, the *Macon (Ga.) Daily Telegraph* reported that, while awaiting trial, the enslaved John "deliberately choked himself," in a manner similar to Lucy's.[28]

Perceptions of bondpeople who were moved to destroy themselves by virtue of age or ethnicity or out of mere stubbornness persisted throughout the antebellum period and competed with assessments that slave suicide resulted from the excessive cruelty of masters and the inhumanity of the institution of slavery itself. An examination of the ecology of enslave peoples' suicides, however, reveals the subjectivities that drove some of them to suicide and illuminates the intimate experiences of power that fostered self-destructive impulses. For some men and women, the path to choosing self-murder may have begun before embarkation in Africa; suicide was an integral part of their culture of colonization, an act fostered by the predictable brutality of enslavement, imminent punishment, household isolation, the stripping of gender entitlements, and physical pain. These circumstances continued to direct the self-destructive impulses of native-born slaves in the United States and shaped the memory of suicide through several postslavery generations.

THE MEMORY OF SLAVE SUICIDE

> My daddy use to tell me all the time about folks what could fly
> back to Africa. They could take wing and just fly off. . . . Lots of
> time he tell me another story about a slave ship 'bout to be
> caught by a revenue boat. The slave ship slip through back

---

[27]Petition of George Mason, in *Journals of the House of Burgesses of Virginia, 1752–1758*, ed. Kennedy and McIlwaine, 259–60. The patroller's account might be dismissed as false, but some evidence suggests the prevalence of poison among Igbo Africans in Virginia. See Douglas B. Chambers, *Murder at Montpelier: Igbo Africans in Virginia* (Jackson, MI, 2005), 67–71, 185–87; and Schwarz, *Twice Condemned*, 92–113. *Rutherford (NC) Gazette* cited in Theodore Weld, *Slavery and the Internal Slave Trade in the United States of North America* (London, 1841), 40.

[28]As quoted in Clarence L. Mohr, *On the Threshold of Freedom: Masters and Slaves in Civil War Georgia* (Athens, GA, 1986), 12–13.

river into creek. There was about fifty slaves on board. The
slave runners tie rocks 'round the slaves' necks and throw them
overboard to drown.

—Paul Singleton, Georgia Writers' Project interview,
in Georgia Writers' Project, *Drums and Shadows*, 17.

In coastal Georgia and South Carolina, ex-slave memories of the 1803 Igbo suicide are often—although not always—intertwined with versions of the flying African folktale and other memories of slavery, as the stories from Jack Tattnall,
Carrie Hamilton, Mose Brown, and Paul Singleton suggest. Historians, literary
scholars, and folklorists have noted the power of flying African folklore to transform an "experience of mass suicide into a tale of mythical transmigration." The
folklore redresses the dislocations caused by slavery, as captives literally rise
above their enslavement, transcending the natal alienation of the middle passage,
and returning to Africa. Because they serve as a form of reparation, the reliability
of the memories—and the flying African tales they contain—is less important
than their function as a bridge between the living and the dead. The folklore ultimately reflects one means of reshaping the memory of suicide in slavery.[29]

The ex-slaves interviewed by the Federal Writers' Project in the 1930s focus,
in part, on the dislocations that newly imported enslaved people faced and reflect
the ecology of their acts of self-destruction. Many ex-slaves recall flying Africans
as unseasoned slaves—such as Tony or the 1803 Igbo—who did not comprehend
the language, authority, or labor system of their captors. Mose Brown retold the
story of a man and his wife "brung from Africa"; Carrie Hamilton spoke about
another couple that was "fooled" onto a slave ship; and yet another ex-slave
recalled that the flying Africans were not "climatize[d]." According to the inter-
viewees, the flying Africans could not understand new world language or labor
systems. As one informant recalled, "they can't understand your talk and you
can't understand their talk" and "they did not know how to "work right." Informants' stories also focused on the shock of slavery's brutality: one noted that
"wild" Africans were chained in a house until they were "tame." . . .[30]

While we do not know the gender composition of the captive Igbo in 1803,
gender also figures importantly in ex-slave memories of flying Africans. In the ex-
slave telling, no single leader is remembered; instead, they refer to a couple, a man
and wife, and it is the ritual magic performed collectively—by men and women
together—that channels the power to escape enslavement and fly back to Africa. In
the version of the story remembered by Hamilton, the couple ("this man and his
wife"), together, decides "we going back home." In contrast, the Works Progress

[29]Walker, "Suicidal Tendencies," 15. Hartman, *Scenes of Subjection*, 73–78.

[30]Mose Brown, Georgia Writers' Project interview, in Georgia Writers' Project, *Drums and Shadows: Survival Stories among the Georgia Coastal Negroes* (Athens, GA, 1986), 18. Carrie Hamilton interview, ibid., 28–29; Prince Sneed interview, ibid., 79; Wallace Quarterman interview, ibid.,
150–51. Shad Hall, Georgia Writers' Project interview, ibid., 169. Jim Meyers, Georgia Writers'
Project interview, ibid., 191.

Administration interviewers' rendering of the flying Africans as well as folktales published in the 1940s are built on a more patriarchal model that focuses on one central male figure that empowers other enslaved men and women to fly. The Georgia Writers' Project interviewers, for example, describe the 1803 Igbo as a group of captives who were "led by their chief" as they deliberately walked into the water to their deaths. In one version of the flying African tale published in the 1940s, a woman "took her breast with her hand and threw it over her shoulder that the child might suck and be content" as she labored in the master's fields. Her child continues to nurse, even after taking flight, as do all of the children who "laughed and sucked as their mothers flew and were not afraid." Added to the sense of power that is conveyed by the ability to literally fly away from slavery is the power represented by African American women suckling over their shoulders—an image with deep and troublesome roots in the European imagination.[31] Taken together, these folkloric elements address the dislocations of slavery and reflect the ecology of suicide by enslaved people and imagine the restoration of family and community.

The memories of the ex-slaves interviewed in the 1930s revealed the complex intersections of folklore, slavery, and suicide. It is at just such a confluence, David Blight has noted, that historians may best be able to observe and explain the interplay between history and memory to "write the history of memory." The coastal ex-slaves interviewed during the 1930s compressed separate discursive events—the flying African tales, their personal and familial memories of slavery, and the 1803 Igbo collective suicide—in a way that was unique to the Georgia Sea Islands. . . . A further clue to this compression of memory can be found in the connection of the 1803 Igbo collective suicide, flying Africans, and a person called "Mr. Blue." The boat that carried the Igbo ran ashore on St. Simon's Island at a plantation owned by the Butler family. A Savannah written account of the event lists the surname Patterson for the captain of the ship and Roswell King (overseer of Butler Plantation) as the person who recovered the bodies of the drowned Igbo. None of those names appear in any of the ex-slave interviews; instead, Mr. Blue was the overseer mentioned by Walter Quarterman in connection with the flying Africans. "Well, at that time Mr. Blue he was the overseer and Mr. Blue put them in the field but he couldn't do nothing with them. They gabble, gabble, gabble, and nobody could understand them and they didn't know how to work right. Mr. Blue he go down one morning with a long whip for to whip them good." When the interviewers asked if Mr. Blue was a hard overseer, Quarterman replied that "he ain't hard, he just can't make them understand. They's foolish acting. He got to whip them, Mr. Blue. . . . He whip them good."[32]

---

[31]Hamilton interview, 29; B. A. Botkin, *A Treasure of Southern Folklore* (New York, 1949), 481–82. Jennifer L. Morgan, "'Some Could Suckle over Their Shoulder': Male Travelers, Female Bodies, and the Gendering of Racial Ideology, 1500–1700," *William and Mary Quarterly* 54 (Jan. 1997), 167–92.

[32]David W. Blight, "If You Don't Tell It Like It Is, It Can Never Be as It Ought to Be," in *Slavery and Public History: The Tough Stuff on American Memory*, ed. James Oliver Horton and Lois E. Horton (New York, 2006), 26. Paul Singleton, Georgia Writers' Project interview, 17. Quarterman interview, ibid., 150.

Alexander Blue was, in fact, the manager of the Butler estate from 1848 to 1859. Quarterman was born in 1844 and his recollection of Mr. Blue—more than a coincidence, surely—makes sense. As the last manager of the Butler plantation before the end of slavery, Blue's name would have been most prominent in the memories of ex-slaves who were interviewed in the 1930s, especially because he was the overseer—the immediate symbol of domination for most bondpeople.

The figure of Alexander Blue also exemplifies how ex-slaves may have connected stories of suicide with their own experiences of separation, interweaving their knowledge of flying Africans and the Igbo in transatlantic slave trade with their personal memory of domestic sale. That connection developed simultaneously with Blue's role in the sale of slaves for the Butler plantation. Living in Philadelphia and managing his Georgia estates in absentia, Pierce Butler was, by 1855, in serious financial trouble. Four years later, he sold 436 enslaved men and women (approximately half of the estate's holdings) in what became known as the largest slave sale in history. The Butler plantation bondpeople were separated, packed into railroad cars, and shipped to a racetrack outside of Savannah where they were sold over a period of four days. Some of the former Butler slaves still remained on St. Simon's Island in 1863, and they remembered the "great sale" as the "weeping time" and recalled, according to Col. Robert Gould Shaw, that a steady rain accompanied the sale of their "sons and daughters" and their "children and grandchildren."[33]

Alexander Blue likely oversaw the sorting of human property for the momentous sale on those rainy days. By attaching Blue's name to the flying African tale, the ex-slave Walter Quarterman forged a connection between himself, the captive Africans who arrived—and died—in 1803, and the Butler plantation slaves who were sold and dispersed in 1859. In that compression, water symbolically links memory and experience. The fatal immersion of the Igbo has its parallel in the rain that fell on the great sale, and water joins both the experience of the African-born Igbo and native-born, Christianized slaves' notions of the spiritual and redemptive qualities of baptism. Water creates a bridge between the Igbo, the flying Africans, and the ex-slaves in the 1930s; it also bridges suicide, sale, and the power to escape to home. In 1803, the Igbo chanted as they marched into the water—an element that is reconfigured in the flying African myth as a vocalization of the joy of return ("goodie bye, goodie bye"). . . . Such expression stands in stark contrast, however, to the sorrow of separation invoked by the idea of a "weeping time." If the flying African folklore provides a "reprieve from domination" for the Igbo as they fly back to Africa rather than drown, the reprieve is tempered by one ex-slave's recollections of Mr. Blue, whose figure loomed large over the dispersal of their families and communities in

---

[33]"American Civilization Illustrated: A Great Slave Sale," *New York Daily Tribune*, March 9, 1859, p. 5. Bell, *Major Butler's Legacy*, 319–40. For discussions of "the weeping time," see Russell Duncan, ed., *Blue-Eyed Child of Fortune: The Civil War Letters of Colonel Robert Gould Shaw* (Athens, GA, 1992), 344, 348; and J. C. Furnas, *Fanny Kemble: Leading Lady of the Nineteenth-Century Stage* (New York, 1982), 374.

Quarterman's own experience in slavery.[34] The great sale was not a suicide, of course, but the separation it engendered paralleled the permanence of a mythical return to Africa. Like many of those who were dispersed in the great sale, flying Africans were never seen again by those who watched and remembered their departure.

The flying African stories lie at the crossroads of memory and history. At that point, the tales are an attempt at some restoration of the losses from suicide and separation that were necessitated by the slave trade. The stories assert the power of culture to maintain community in the face of its forcible dislocation. Sullen stubbornness and sentimental despair—characteristically used to describe enslaved peoples' acts of suicide in the early modern and early Republican eras—have no role in the tales, although the ecology of slave suicide is present in the form of refusals, brutality, labor regimes, and separation. Flying African folklore allows for the possibility of escaping slavery through the supernatural power of refusal rather than through self-destructive violence. Like both the African- and North American–born slaves who contemplated or chose self-inflicted death, flying Africans also made a choice. Collective memory conferred upon them the power to fly—to escape slavery and to return home. Ex-slave memories and folklore perform the cultural work of remaking the history of the self, the family, and the community within slavery, ultimately transforming the crossroads of despair, suicide, and separation into an intersection of power, transcendence, and reunion.

---

[34]Hartman, *Scenes of Subjection*, 78.

Terri L. Snyder

I am an historian of colonial North America, with research and teaching interests in gender, slavery, the law in the early American South. My interest in these subjects of early American history sharpened when I attended a field school on historical archeology with James Deetz and deepened when I began studying with Linda K. Kerber at the University of Iowa, where I received my Ph.D. in American Studies. My first book, *Brabbling Women: Disorderly Speech and the Law in Early Virginia* focused on women before the bar; since its publication, I have continued to research and publish on women, race, and the courts in early eighteenth-century America. The research in this article can also be found in my book *The Power to Die: Slavery and Suicide in British North America*, which won the support of a National Endowment for the Humanities Faculty Award. I have spent most of my career in the Department of American Studies at California State University, Fullerton.

QUESTIONS FOR CONSIDERATION

1. According to Snyder, why have historians overlooked the phenomenon of suicide among enslaved peoples? How does she propose to broaden our understanding of this topic? What documents does she consult in her research?
2. During the eighteenth century, in what ways did Anglo-Americans understand suicide by enslaved people? How did this change in the nineteenth century?
3. Describe the "ecology" of suicide according to Snyder. How does the idea of an "ecology" help her present a complicated and multi-faceted understanding of suicide among enslaved people?
4. How did enslaved peoples remember suicide? What do these memories tell us about their perceptions of suicide? How were these perceptions different than the dominant white culture around them?
5. To what extent were the suicides Snyder describes a kind of resistance?

CHAPTER FIVE

The Transformation of
Urban Politics 1700–1765[1]

Gary B. Nash

That colonial politics were highly factional and unstable is a familiar theme in early American history. . . . An examination of . . . [two] cities which would become instrumental in the coming of the Revolution—Boston, and Philadelphia—yields compelling evidence that in the six decades before the Stamp Act crisis a "radical" mode of politics was evolving in the urban centers of colonial life.[2] This "transformation" involved activation of previously quiescent lower-class elements; the organization of political clubs, caucuses, and tickets; the employment of political literature and inflammatory rhetoric as never before; the involvement of the clergy and the churches in politics; and the organization of mobs and violence for political purposes. Although many of these innovations were managed by and for political elites and not intended to democratize colonial political life, the effect was to broaden the spectrum of, individuals actively involved in public affairs and to produce a political culture that was far from deferential, increasingly anti-authoritarian, occasionally violent, and often destructive of the very values which the political elite wished to preserve.

At election time in 1726, a prominent Quaker merchant in Philadelphia wrote an English friend that "we have our Mobs, Bonfires, Gunns, Huzzas . . . Itinerations and processions too-Trains made up (as 'tis said) not of the Wise, the Rich or the Learned, for the Gentleman while he was Governour took care to

---

[1]Interested students are encouraged to read the original. Gary B. Nash, "The Transformation of Urban Politics, 1700–1765," *Journal of American History* 60 (3) (Dec. 1973), 605–32.

[2]Eighteenth-century writers employed the term "radical" only infrequently; and when they did, they meant "root" or "basic." Thus Samuel Davies looked for an "outpouring of the Spirit" as the "grand, radical, all-comprehensive blessing" in 1757; and "Plain Dealer," writing from Philadelphia in 1764, asserted that the cause of Pennsylvania's troubles "is radical, interwoven in the Constitution, and so become of the very Nature of Proprietary Governments." See Alan Heimert, *Religion and the American Mind from the Great Awakening to the Revolution* (Cambridge, MA, 1966), 13; [Hugh Williamson], *Plain Dealer #2* (Philadelphia, 1764), 7. The term is used here to mean not only basic but also basic in its tendency to shift power downward in a society where politics had heretofore been corporate and elitist in nature.

discard all Such. . . ."[3] In this description Isaac Norris expressed his dismay that Governor William Keith, who no longer felt obliged to serve the interests of his employer, the widow of William Penn, had cultivated the support of a stratum of society that the "wise, Rich and Learned" believed had no place in the political process. Since 1723, in fact, Keith had been mobilizing support among lower-class workingmen in Philadelphia and newly arrived German and Scotch-Irish immigrants.

Elitist politicians and proprietary supporters complained bitterly of "Sir William's town Mob" and the governor's "sinister army," lamented that elections were "mobbish and carried by a levelling spirit," and charged that the "common People both in town & Country" were "blown up even to a degree of madness."[4] Of the 1726 elections Norris wrote that Keith had "perambulated" the city, "Popping into ye dramshops tiff & alehouses where he would find a great number of modern statesmen & some patriots settling affairs, cursing some, praising others, contriving laws & swearing they will have them enacted *cum multis aegis*." Worse still, Keith's electoral victory was celebrated by an exuberant procession, "mostly made of Rabble Butchers porters & Tagrags—thus triumphantly has he made his Gradations Downward from a Government to an Equal with Every plain Country Member." . . .[5]

This technique of mobilizing the politically inert became increasingly more important to eighteenth-century political life. For the Pennsylvania Quakers, who had overcome earlier disunity and formed a strong anti-proprietary party, the problem was how to maintain influence in a society where they were fast becoming a minority. For the proprietary party, the problem was how to develop popular sources of support in order to overcome Quaker domination of the assembly. Thus both factions, led by men of high position and reputation, nervously began to eye the Germans who were streaming into the colony after 1715. . . . That the Quakers continued to control the assembly throughout the half-century preceding the Revolution, despite their fading numerical importance, was attributable largely to their success in politicizing the Germans, who were more interested in farming than legislative assemblies but found themselves dragged into the thicket of politics.[6]

With even greater misgivings, the proprietary party courted the German community, which by the 1750s represented about 40 percent of the population

---

[3]Isaac Norris to Jonathan Scarth, Oct. 21, 1726, Letter Book, 1716–1730, Isaac Norris Papers (Historical Society of Pennsylvania, Philadelphia).

[4]Thomas Wendel, "The Keith-Lloyd Alliance: Factional and Coalition Politics in Colonial Pennsylvania," *Pennsylvania Magazine of History and Biography* 92 (July 1968), 298, 296n, 301.

[5]Norris to Scarth, Oct. 21, 1728, Letter Book, 1716–1730, Norris Papers.

[6]Arthur D. Graeff, *The Relations Between The Pennsylvania Germans and The British Authorities (1750–1776)* (Philadelphia, 1939); Dietmar Rothermund, *The Layman's Progress: Religious and Political Experience in Colonial Pennsylvania, 1740–1770* (Philadelphia, 1961); Glenn Weaver, "Benjamin Franklin-and the Pennsylvania Germans," *William and Mary Quarterly* 14 (Oct. 1957), 536–59; John J. Zimmerman, "Benjamin Franklin and the Quaker Party, 1755–1756," ibid., XVII (July 1960), 291–313.

in Pennsylvania. In private discourse and correspondence its leaders continued to regard the Germans as "an uncultivated Race" of uncouth peasants, incapable, as one put it, "of using their own Judgment in matters of Government. . . ."[7] But political requirements conquered social and ethnic reservations. . . . This drive for German support yielded only meager rewards in the political battles of the mid-1750s, but by 1764 the proprietary campaign was crowned with success. Benjamin Franklin and Joseph Galloway attributed their loss in the hotly contested election of that year to the "Dutch vote" which had swung against them.[8] Proprietary leaders would have preferred to exert political leverage from power bases where men were appointed out of regard for their background, accomplishments, and standing in the community—the council, city corporation, College of Philadelphia, hospital, and Library Company.[9] But gradually—and reluctantly— proprietary politicians learned to seek support from groups which they would have preferred to regard as inadmissible to political life. The problem of challenging the legislative strength of their opponents could not otherwise be solved.

Just as members of the proprietary party learned to overcome their scruples with regard to involving Germans in the political process, they learned to swallow reservations about soliciting the support of lower-class mechanics and laborers. Galloway, a Quaker party stalwart, took great delight in pointing out that the "Gentlemen of the best fortune" in the proprietary party, who in their public statements spoke for hierarchy and order in all affairs, "thought it not mean or dishonourable to enter the Houses of the Lowest Mechanics to solicit their Opposition" to the Militia Act of 1756.[10] By 1764 these artisans would become all-important in the attempts of the proprietary party to defeat their opponents. . . .

In Boston the process of activating the inactive proceeded along somewhat different lines but in the same direction. Unlike Philadelphia . . . Boston had a population that was ethnically homogeneous. Throughout the colonial period factional leaders appealed for the support of a mass of English voters only lightly sprinkled with Scotch and Irish. Boston was also different in that ever since an armed crowd had mysteriously gathered in April 1689 to command the streets of Boston and force Edmund Andros into exile, its citizens, at all levels of society, had been far less quiescent than their counterparts in other urban centers. This may be partially explained by the effect on the political life of the city which the town meeting fostered.[11] In Boston, as in no other city, open debate was heard and decisions were made by majority vote on many issues, ranging from passing a bylaw "to prevent playing football in the streets" to voting £10 to Susana Striker for a kidney

---

[7]Graeff, *Pennsylvania Germans*, 61–63.

[8]Labaree and others, eds., *Papers of Benjamin Franklin*, XI, 397; Weaver, "Franklin and the Pennsylvania Germans," 550.

[9]G. B. Warden, "The Proprietary Group in Pennsylvania, 1754–1764," *William and Mary Quarterly* 21 (July 1964), 367–89.

[10][Joseph Galloway], *A True and Impartial State of the Province of Pennsylvania: Containing an Exact Account of the Nature of Its Government, the Power of it Proprietaries, and Their Governors . . . also the Rights and Privileges of the Assembly and People . . .* (Philadelphia, 1759), 61.

[11]See G. B. Warden, *Boston, 1689–1776* (Boston, 1970), 28–33.

stone operation for her son, to taxing inhabitants for the erection of public buildings, poor relief, school teachers' salaries, and other expenses.[12] And whereas in . . . Philadelphia only a small number of municipal officers were elected, in Boston the voters installed not only selectmen, sheriffs, assessors, and constables, but surveyors of hemp, informers about deer, purchasers of grain, haywards, town criers, measurers of salt, scavengers, viewers of shingles, sheepreeves, hogreeves, sealers of leather, fenceviewers, firewards, cullers of stave hoops, auditors, and others.[13]

Thus in terms of a politically minded and active lower rank, Boston had already developed by the early eighteenth century what other urban centers haltingly and sporadically moved toward in the half century before 1765. . . . But if the clay with which leaders of political factions worked was of a somewhat different consistency in Boston, the problems of delving deeper in society to insure political victory was essentially the same. Thus the "soft money" faction led by Elisha Cooke, Oliver Noyes, Thomas Cushing, and William Clark "turned to the people as the only possible base of political strength in Boston and took it upon [themselves] to organize politics and elections in the town with unprecedented vigor and attention" in the 1720s.[14] In the following decade, when a series of economic issues in Boston came to a head, and in the 1740s, when the second currency crisis ripened, exceptional measures were again taken to call upon those not included in the ranks of respectability. "Interested Men," complained Peter Oliver in 1749, had "set the Canaille to insult" Thomas Hutchinson for his leadership of the conservative fiscal movement.[15] In this way political leaders recruited the support of lower-class artisans and mechanics whose bodies provided a new kind of political power, as demonstrated in three mob actions of the 1740s in Boston directed by men of stature in the community, and whose votes provided the margin of victory in the increasingly frequent contested elections. . . .[16]

Because all factions felt the necessity of broadening the political base, the dynamics of politics changed markedly. In a society in which the people at large acquiesced in the rule of the upper stratum, and in which social, economic, and

---

[12]William H. Whitmore and others, eds., *Reports of the Record Commissioners of Boston* (39 vols., Boston, 1880–1902), VIII, 12, 23, XII, *passim.*

[13]In Philadelphia the municipal corporation was self-perpetuating, but sheriffs, commissioners, assessors, and coroners were elected annually.

[14]Warden, *Boston*, 92.

[15]Douglas Adair and John A. Schutz, eds., *Peter Oliver's Origin & Progress of the American Rebellion: A Tory View* (San Marino, CA, 1961), 32.

[16]Eighteenth-century elections were by no means always contested. One measure of politicization is the frequency of contested elections. Defining a contested election as one in which the candidate was opposed and lost at least 25 percent of the vote, one can trace a rise in oppositional politics from the 1720s through the 1750s.

Boston Election Contests	
Decade	Number of Contested Seats
1720–1729	14/45 (31.1%)
1730–1739	23/48 (47.9%)
1740–1749	25/45 (55.6%)
1750–1759	24/40 (60.0%)

political leadership were regarded as indivisible, political decisions could be made quietly and privately. Elites would be held in check, of course, by periodic tests of confidence administered by the propertied part of the community. But when the upper layer of society split into competing factions, which were obliged to recruit the support of those previously inert or outside the political process, then politics became open, abusive in tone, and sometimes violent.

New techniques of political organization were required. Men began to form political "tickets," as happened in Pennsylvania as early as 1705, [and] in Boston at the end of the 1720s.... Leaders of the more conservative factions usually resisted this move in the direction of popular politics. Philadelphia conservatives James Logan and Norris, for example, decried the use of tickets that obliged the voter to "have eight men crammed down his throat at once."[17] The use of tickets was also accompanied by written balloting and the introduction of the caucus— closed at first—to nominate a slate of candidates. Thus Quaker leaders in the 1720s loudly declaimed Keith's "Electing-Club" in Philadelphia.[18] But within a few decades the anti-Quaker proprietary leaders would be complaining bitterly that the Quakers used their yearly meeting, which met during the week before assembly elections, as a political caucus—a practice condemned in 1755 as "the finest Scheme that could possibly be projected for conducting political Intrigues, under the Mask of Religion."[19] Yielding to the realities of political life, the proprietary leaders in 1756 adopted the tactics of their opponents and even outdid the Quaker party by calling for open rather than private caucuses. A notice in the *Pennsylvania Gazette* summoned the electorate to the Philadelphia Academy for an open-air, on-the-spot primary election. Ideological consistency was abandoned as Quaker party writers condemned the innovation in the next issue of the newspaper, only to be attacked by the aristocratic proprietary spokesman who defended the rights of the freeholders "to meet in a peaceable Manner to chuse their Representatives."[20] Seeing a chance for electoral success in the Quaker opposition to war appropriations, the proprietary leaders put scruples aside and resorted to tactics that heretofore had offended their sense of political propriety.

In Boston popular politics came under the control of perhaps the best organized caucus in the English colonial world. So far as the limited evidence indicates, the Boston caucus was organized about 1719 and functioned intermittently for about four decades before splitting into the North End Caucus and South End Caucus. The Boston caucus nominated candidates for the city's four seats in the General Court and proposed selectmen and other town officials at the annual elections. Operating in the taverns, it perfected a network of political influence

---

[17]Edward Armstrong, ed., *The Correspondence between William Penn and James Logan* (2 vols., Philadelphia, 1870–1872), II, 188, 336, 427.

[18]Norris to Joseph Pike, Oct. 28, 1728, Letter Book, 1716–1730, Norris Papers; *A Modest Apology for the Eight Members . . .* (Philadelphia, 1728).

[19][William Smith], *A Brief State*, 26; Peters to Thomas Penn, Aug. 25 and Nov. 17, 1742, Letter Book, 1737–1750, Richard Peters Papers (Historical Society of Pennsylvania, Philadelphia).

[20]*Pennsylvania Gazette*, Sept. 12, 19, 1756. See also William R. Steckel, "Pietist in Colonial Pennsylvania: Christopher Sauer, Printer, 1738–1758" (doctoral dissertation, Stanford University, 1949), 233–44.

through affiliations with the independent fire companies, the Merchants' Club, and other social organizations. . . .[21]

An even more significant element in transforming positions from a private to a public affair was the use of the press. Although the political press had been used extensively in seventeenth-century England, it was not widely employed in colonial politics until the 1720s. Before that an occasional pamphlet had directed the attention of the public to a controversial issue. But such early polemical efforts as Joseph Palmer, *The Present State of New England* (Boston, 1689), or Thomas Lloyd, *A Seasonable Advertisement to the Freemen of this Province* . . . (Philadelphia, 1689), were beamed at the General Court or the assembly, though their authors probably hoped also to cultivate the support of the populace at large. "Campaign literature"—direct appeals to the freemen at election time—was rare in Boston before 1710, [and] in Philadelphia before 1720. . . . But as issues became more heated and politicians discovered the need to reach a wider audience, the resort to the press became a fixed part of political culture. In Philadelphia, for example, where only five pieces of political literature had appeared in the first quarter of the century, the public was bombarded with forty-six pamphlets and broadsides between 1725 and 1728. Bostonians in 1721 and 1722 could spend their evenings in tavern discussions of any of the twenty-eight argumentative tracts on the currency crisis that appeared in those years. . . .

By the 1740s the printed word had become an indispensable part of campaigning. In every contested election pamphleteers industriously alerted the public to the awful consequences that would attend a victory by the other side. When the excise bill was under consideration in 1754, seventeen pamphlets appeared in the streets of Boston to rally public support against it. . . .[22] In Philadelphia the Paxton Massacre was argued pro-and-con in at least twenty-eight pamphlets, and in the election contest that followed in the fall of 1764 no less than forty-four pamphlets and broadsides were published, many with German editions.[23] A rise in polemical literature and election appeals is also evident in colonial newspapers which were increasing in number in the eighteenth century.[24]

---

[21]G. B. Warden, "The Caucus and Democracy in Colonial Boston," *New England Quarterly* 43 (March 1970), 19–33.

[22]Paul S. Boyer, "Borrowed Rhetoric: The Massachusetts Excise Controversy of 1754," *William and Mary Quarterly* 21 (July 1964), 328–51.

[23]Many, although by no means all, of the pamphlets are reprinted in John R. Dunbar, ed., *The Paxton Papers* (The Hague, 1957), or discussed in J. Philip Gleason, "A Scurrilous Colonial Election and Franklin's Reputation," *William and Mary Quarterly* 18 (Jan. 1961), 68–84.

[24]The sheer bulk of this literature grew rapidly in the second quarter of the century, though tapering off in Boston thereafter. Election day sermons are not included in the figures for Boston.

Decade	Boston	Philadelphia
1695–1704	6	2
1705–1714	12	2
1715–1724	40	2
1725–1734	28	43
1735–1744	37	15
1745–1754	38	15
1755–1764	26	109

This increase in the use of the press had important implications, not merely because of the quantity of political literature but also because the pamphlets and newspaper creeds were intended to make politics everyone's concern. The new political literature was distributed without reference to social standing or economic position and "accustomed people of all classes, but especially of the middling and lower estates, to the examination and discussion of controversial issues of all sorts."[25] Thus, those whom even the most conservative politicians would not have formally admitted to the political arena were drawn into it informally.

The anguished cries of politicians about the dangerous effects of this new polemical literature give a clue to the ambivalent feelings which the elite held in regard to the use of the press. An optimist like Franklin looked upon . . . pamphlets and newspaper fusillades as instruments "to prepare the Minds of the Publick,"[26] but most men assumed that man easily succumbed to his basest instincts and that the unthinking multitude, which included a vast majority of the population, was moved by passion rather than reason. . . .[27] And yet by the 1750s, and often before, even the most conservative leader could not resist the resort to the press, even though it might contradict his social philosophy. . . . In Philadelphia it was the proprietary party, espousing social conservatism and constantly warning about the anarchic and levelling designs of Quaker politicians, that raised the art of pamphleteering to new levels of sophistication in the 1750s. No one in Philadelphia could quite match the imperious William Smith for statements about the necessity of the ordered, deferential society; but no one did more to make the abusive pamphlet a part of the eighteenth-century political arsenal.[28]

Not only a quantitative leap in political literature but also an escalation of rhetoric made the use of the press a particularly important part of the new politics. As political literature became institutionalized, the quality of language and the modes of argumentation changed markedly. In the early eighteenth century pamphleteers exercised restraint, appealing to the public judgment and the "best interest of the country." Perhaps mindful of the revolutionary potential of the printed word, authors couched their arguments in legalistic terms. For example, in Boston, during the exchange of pamphlets on the currency crisis in 1714, hundreds of pages were offered to the public, but readers encountered nothing more virulent than charges that the opposition view was "strange and Unaccountable," "intolerable," "unreasonable and unjust," or that writers on the other side were guilty of "bold and wilful Misrepresentation." But by 1754 the anti-excise pamphleteers were raising images in the public mind of "Little pestilent Creature[s],"

---

[25]Carl Bridenbaugh, "The Press and the Book in Eighteenth-Century Philadelphia," *Pennsylvania Magazine of History and Biography* 65 (Jan. 1941), 5.

[26]Labaree and others, *The Papers of Benjamin Franklin*, VII, 374. Franklin came close to changing his mind concerning the beneficial effects of the political press when he became the target of a savage pamphlet offensive in 1764.

[27]For example, see *A View of the Calumnies Lately Spread in Some Scurrilous Prints against the Government of Pennsylvania* (Philadelphia, 1729).

[28]Writing to the proprietor in 1755, Smith confessed that "The Appeal to the public was against my Judgment." Paul A. W. Wallace, *Conrad Weiser, 1696–1760, Friend of Colonist and Mohawk* (Philadelphia, 1945), 115.

"dirty miscreants," and unspeakably horrible creatures ready to "cram [their] ... merciless and insatiable Maw[s] with our very Blood, and bones, and Vitals" while making sexual advances on wives and daughters.[29] In Philadelphia, Keith's political campaigns in the 1720s introduced a genre of literature that for the first time directly attacked men of wealth and learning. "According to my experience," wrote David Lloyd, "a mean Man, of small Interest, devoted to the faithful Discharge of his Trust and Duty to the Government, may do more good to the State than a Richer or more Learned Man, who by his ill Temper and aspiring Mind becomes an opposer of the Constitution by which he should act."[30] This was egalitarian rhetoric which inverted the social pyramid by rejecting the traditional notion that the maintenance of social order and political stability depended on vesting power in men of education and high status.

But this kind of language was a model of restraint compared to mid-century political vitriol. In newspapers and pamphlets, contending elites hurled insults at each other and charged their opponents, to cite one example from Philadelphia, with "Inveterate Calumny, foul-mouthed Aspersion, shameless Falsehood, and insatiate Malice. . . ."[31]

In effect, the conservatives' worst fears concerning the use of the press were being confirmed as the tactics of printed political discourse changed from attacking the legality or wisdom of the opposition's policies or pleading for the election of public-minded men to assailing the character and motives of those on the other side. The effect of the new political rhetoric was self-intensifying as each increase in the brutality of language brought an equivalent or greater response from the opposition. Gradually the public was taught to suspect not simply the wisdom or constitutional right of one side or the other, but the motives, morality, and even sanity of its leaders. The very high-placed individuals to whom the rank-and-file were supposed to defer were being exposed as the most corrupt and loathsome members of society.

In mob activity and threats of violence the radicalization of politics can be seen in its most dramatic though not its most significant form. It is well to make a distinction between spontaneous disorders expressive of deeply felt lower-class grievances and mob activity arranged and directed by political leaders to serve their own purposes. A connection existed between the two kinds of activity since political elites, witnessing random lower-class disorder, did not fail to note the effectiveness of collective force; and lower-class elements, encouraged or even rewarded by political leaders for participating in riotous activity, undoubtedly lost some of their awe and reverence for duly constituted authority, gaining a new sense of their own power.[32]

---

[29]Boyer, "Borrowed Rhetoric: The Massachusetts Excise Controversy of 1754," 341–44.

[30]*A Vindication of the Legislative Power* (Philadelphia, 1725).

[31]*Pennsylvania Journal*, April 22, 1756. The charges were made against Smith in return for "the Vomitings of this infamous Hireling" whose attacks on Franklin "betoken that Redundancy of Rancour, and Rottiness of Heart which render him the most despicable of his Species." Ibid.

[32]Pauline Maier, "Popular Uprisings and Civil Authority in Eighteenth-Century America," *William and Mary Quarterly* 27 (Jan. 1970), 3–35.

Mobs expressing class grievances were less common in the colonial cities than in rural areas, where land disputes and Indian policy were major sources of conflict throughout the eighteenth century.[33] The food rioting that was a persistent factor in the history of European cities of this period was almost unknown in Boston, . . . and Philadelphia.[34] Far more common was the sporadic violence directed at individuals identified with unpopular causes. Cotton Mather, who went unappreciated by a large part of Boston's population throughout his lifetime of religious and political eminence, had his house fire-bombed in 1721.[35] In 1749 Thomas Hutchinson, long identified with hard-money policies, watched ruefully as his house burned to the cheers of the mob while the fire company responded with a suspicious lack of speed.[36] James Logan and his wife spent a night under the bed when the mob bombarded their stately house with stones, convincing Logan that law and order in Philadelphia was as shattered as his window panes.[37] This kind of violence, along with unofficially sanctioned riots such as the annual Pope's Day battles between North End and South End in Boston, reflected the general abrasiveness of life in the eighteenth century and the frailty of law enforcement in the cities.[38]

Far more significant was violence inspired and controlled by the elite. This was often directed at imperial officers charged with carrying out unpopular trade or military policies. Thus Boston was more or less in the hands of the mob for three days in 1747, after the commander of the British fleet in the harbor ordered his press gang to make a nocturnal sweep through the streets. The mob, wrote Governor William Shirley, "was secretly Contenanc'd and encourag'd by some ill minded Inhabitants and Persons of Influence in the Town. . . ."[39] But mobs were also used in internal political struggles that did not involve imperial

---

[33]There are few parallels in the history of the colonial cities to the forays of the White Pine rebels in Massachusetts, the land rioters in New York and New Jersey in the 1740s, and the Paxton Boys in Pennsylvania. For accounts of these movements, see Joseph J. Malone, *Pine Trees and Politics: The Naval Stores and Forest Policy in Colonial New England, 1691–1775* (Plymouth, England, 1964); Irving Mark, *Agrarian Conflicts in Colonial New York, 1711–1775* (New York, 1940); Donald L. Kemmerer, *Path to Freedom: The Struggle for Self-Government in New Jersey, 1703–1776* (Princeton, NJ, 1940); Theodore Thayer, *Pennsylvania Politics and the Growth of Democracy, 1740–1776* (Philadelphia, 1953); and Brooke Hindle, "The March of the Paxton Boys," *William and Mary Quarterly* 3 (Oct. 1946), 461–86.

[34]Gordon S. Wood, "A Note on Mobs in the American Revolution," *William and Mary Quarterly* 23 (Oct. 1966), 635–42; and William A. Smith, "Anglo-American Society and the Mob, 1740–1775" (doctoral dissertation, Claremont Graduate School, 1965).

[35]*The Diary of Cotton Mather, 1709–1724*, Massachusetts Historical Society Collections (8 vols., Boston, 1900–1912), VIII, 657–58.

[36]Warden, *Boston*, 140.

[37]James Logan to James Alexander, Oct. 23, 1749, Letter Book, 1748–1750, James Logan Papers (Library Company of Philadelphia).

[38]R. S. Longley, "Mob Activities in Revolutionary Massachusetts," *New England Quarterly* 6 (March 1933), 102–3.

[39]Maier, "Popular Uprisings," 4–15; Charles H. Lincoln, ed., *The Correspondence of William Shirley: Governor of Massachusetts and Military Commander in America, 1731–1760* (2 vols., New York, 1912), I, 406.

policy. In Boston in the 1730s, when the issue of a public market dominated municipal politics, a band of night raiders sawed through the supports of the market houses in the North End and later demolished another building. When Governor Jonathan Belcher vowed to see justice done, letters circulated in the town claiming that five hundred men stood ready to oppose with force any attempt to intervene in the case.[40] In Philadelphia, Keith's "town mob," as his detractors called it, was sufficiently enlivened by their election victory in 1726 to burn the pillory and stocks—the symbols of authority and social control.[41] Two years later a dispute over a vacant assembly seat led to a campaign of intimidation and assault on Quaker members of the assembly by Keith's partisans. The Quakers complained that such "Indecensies [were] used towards the Members of Assembly attending the Service of the Country in *Philadelphia*, by rude and disorderly Persons," that it was unsafe to meet any longer in Philadelphia.[42] When the assembly met in the following spring, it faced an incipient insurrection. Keith's mob, according to James Logan, was to apply "first to the Assembly and then storm the Government," knocking heads, plundering estates, and putting houses to the torch, if necessary, to get what it wanted.[43] Only the hasty passage of an act authorizing the death penalty for riot and insurrection seems to have averted violence.

In 1742 Philadelphia was shaken by a bloody election day riot. It is a prime example of the elite's willingness to employ the mob.[44] Even before election day, rumors circulated that the Quaker party intended to maintain its majority in the assembly by steering unnaturalized Germans to the polls and that the proprietary party meant to thwart this attempt by engaging a pack of toughs. The rumors had substance. When the leaders of the two political factions could not agree on procedures for supervising the election, heated words and curses were exchanged; and seventy sailors wielding clubs and shouting "down with the plain Coats & broad Brims" waded into the Quaker crowd assembled before the courthouse.[45] When the Quaker leaders retreated inside, the sailors filled the air with a hailstorm of bricks. A counterattack was launched by Germans and younger Quakers, who momentarily forgot their pacifist principles. "Blood flew plentifully

[40]Warden, *Boston*, 121–24; Carl Bridenbaugh, *Cities in the Wilderness: The First Century of Urban Life in America, 1625–1742* (New York, 1938), 352.

[41]Patrick Gordon to John Penn, Oct. 17, 1726, Official Correspondence, 1, Penn Family Papers.

[42]Gertrude MacKinney, ed., *Votes and Proceedings of the House of Representatives of the Province of Pennsylvania, Pennsylvania Archives* (Eighth Series) (8 vols., Harrisburg, PA, 1931–1935), III, 1908. See also *The Proceedings of Some Members of Assembly, at Philadelphia, April 1728 Vindicated from the Unfair Reasoning and Unjust Insinuations of a Certain Remarker* (Philadelphia, 1728).

[43]Logan to John, Richard, and Thomas Penn, April 24, 1729, Official Correspondence, II, 55, Penn Family Papers.

[44]For two interpretations of the riot, see Norman S. Cohen, "The Philadelphia Election Riot of 1742," *Pennsylvania Magazine of History and Biography* 92 (July 1968), 306–19; and William T. Parsons, "The Bloody Election of 1742," *Pennsylvania History* 36 (July 1969), 290–306.

[45]Richard Hockley to Thomas Penn, Nov. 1, 1742, Official Correspondence, III, Penn Family Papers.

around," the proprietary secretary reported.[46] Conducting investigations later, the Quaker assembly concluded that the riot had been engineered by the leaders of the proprietary party. Though some historians have disputed this, two of the proprietor's chief officials in Pennsylvania privately admitted as much. . . .[47]

It would be a mistake to believe that political mobs were passive instruments manipulated by the elite. Though lower-class economic and social grievances only rarely achieved ideological expression in this period, the men who worked by night in Boston or Philadelphia surely gained a new sense of their own power. The urban artisan or laborer discovered that he was not only a useful but also often an essential part of politics. As early as 1729, James Logan sensed the implications of deploying "the multitudes." "Sir William Keith," he wrote, "was so mad, as well as wicked, most industriously to sett up the lowest part of the People; through a vain expectation that he should always be able to steer and influence them as his own Will. But he weakly forgot how soon the minds of such People are changed by any new Accident and how licentious force, when the Awe of Government . . . is thrown off, has been turned against those who first taught them to throw it off."[48]

Another important facet of the "new politics" of the pre-Revolutionary decades was the growing involvement of religious leaders in politics, something nearly all leaders deplored but nonetheless exploited. Of course religious leaders had never been isolated from political life in the early history of the colonies; but such efforts as they made to influence public affairs were usually conducted discreetly and privately. When clergymen published pamphlets on political subjects, they did so anonymously. The common assumption that it was inappropriate for clergymen to mix religion and politics was clearly articulated in 1722 when Cotton Mather and John Wise were exposed as two of the principal controversialists in the heated currency debate in Massachusetts. "Some of our Ecclesiasticks of late," wrote an anonymous pamphleteer, "have been guilty of too officious a meddling with State Affairs. To see a Clergy-man (Commedian-like) stand belabouring his Cushion and intermixing his Harrangue with THUNDERBOLTS, while entertaining his peaceable Congregation with things whereof he is . . . Ignorant . . . how ridiculous is the Sight and the Sound."[49] Such attacks on clerical involvement in politics would continue throughout the pre-Revolutionary period. But by mid-century church leaders were beginning to shed their anonymity and to defend their right to engage in "preaching politics," as Jonathan Mayhew put it in Boston in 1750.[50]

[46]Peters to the Proprietors, Nov. 17, 1742, Letter Book, 1737-1750, Peters Papers.

[47]Hockley to Thomas Penn, Nov. 1 and Nov. 18, 1742, Official Correspondence, III, 241-43, Penn Family Papers; Peters to Thomas Penn, Nov. 17, 1742, Letter Book, 1737-1750, Peters Papers.

[48]Logan to John, Richard, and Thomas Penn, April 24, 1729, Official Correspondence, II, 55, Penn Family Papers.

[49]Andrew McF. Davis, *Colonial Currency Reprints, 1682-1751* (4 vols., Boston, 1910-1911), II, 134.

[50]Quoted in Heimert, *Religion and the American Mind*, 15.

To some extent this politicization of the clergy can be attributed to the Great Awakening, for amidst the evangelical fervor of the early 1740s "religious controversies and political problems were blended in a unique pattern of interaction."[51] But perhaps more important was the fact that by the 1740s the fires of political contention were growing hotter, impelling factional leaders to enlist the services of religious leaders. In Philadelphia, the issue of war and defense appropriations in 1748, not the Great Awakening, brought the first full-scale exchange on a secular question between opposing denominational spokesman. In a dozen signed pamphlets Presbyterian and Quaker leaders such as Gilbert Tennent and Samuel Smith carried out a public dialogue on the necessity of military defense—a battle of words that thrust the clergy into the political arena.[52]

No more dramatic representation of a politicized clergy can be imagined than the jailing of the Anglican ecclesiastic William Smith by the Pennsylvania assembly in 1758. Writing anonymously, Smith had published two open-handed attacks on the Quaker party in 1755 and 1756 as part of the proprietary party's offensive against the Quaker-dominated assembly. He continued his assaults in 1757 and 1758 in the *American Magazine* and the *Pennsylvania Journal*. Determined to halt these attacks, the assembly charged Smith and one of his fellow writers with libel. During the course of a long trial and subsequent appeals to England, Smith carried out his duties and political ambitions from the Philadelphia jail.[53]

The clergy's increasing involvement in politics had a second dimension which was closely related to the Great Awakening. One of the side effects of the revivalist movement was an expansion of political consciousness within the lower reaches of society. The average city dweller developed a new feeling of autonomy and importance as he partook of mass revivals, assumed a new power in ecclesiastical affairs, and was encouraged repeatedly from the pulpit to adopt an attitude of skepticism toward dogma and authority. Doctrinal controversy and attacks on religious and secular leaders became ritualized and accepted in the 1740s.[54] It was precisely this that caused high-placed individuals to charge revivalists with preaching levelism and anarchy. "It is . . . an exceedingly difficult gloomy time with us . . .," wrote Charles Chauncey from Boston; "Such an enthu-

---

[51]Rothermund, *Layman's Progress*, 82.

[52]The debate can be followed in a series of pamphlets published in 1748. See, for example, William Currie, *A Treatise on the Lawfulness of Defensive War* (Philadelphia, 1748); Gilbert Tennent, *The Late Association for Defence, Encourag'd, or the Lawfulness of a Defensive War* (Philadelphia, 1748); and John Smith, *The Doctrine of Christianity, As Held by the People Called Quakers, Vindicated: In Answer to Gilbert Tennent's Sermon on the Lawfulness of War* (Philadelphia, 1748).

[53]William Renwick Riddell, "Libel on the Assembly: a Prerevolutionary Episode," *Pennsylvania Magazine of History and Biography* 52 (2, 3, 4) (1928), 176–92, 249–79, 342–60; William S. Hanna, Benjamin Franklin and Pennsylvania Politics (Stanford, CA, 1964), 134–37; Leonard W. Levy, *Freedom of Speech and Press in Early American History: Legacy of Suppression* (New York, 1963), 53–61.

[54]Rothermund, Layman's Progress, 55–60, 81–82; Heimert, *Religion and the American Mind*, 27–58, 239–93. The process was not confined to the cities. See Richard L. Bushman, *From Puritan to Yankee: Character and the Social Order in Connecticut, 1690–1765* (Cambridge, MA, 1967).

siastic, factious, censorious Spirit was never known here.... Every low-bred, illiterate Person can resolve Cases of Conscience and settle the most difficult Points of Divinity better than the most learned Divines."[55] Such charges were heard repeatedly during the Great Awakening, revealing the apprehension of those who trembled to see the "unthinking multitude" invested with a new dignity and importance. Nor could the passing of the Great Awakening reverse the tide, for this new sense of power did not atrophy with the decline of religious enthusiasm, but remained as a permanent part of the social outlook of the middle and lower strata of society.

The October 1764 elections in Philadelphia provide an opportunity to observe in microcosm all of the radicalizing tendencies of the previous three-quarters of a century. The city had already been badly shaken by the Paxton Boys, who descended on the capital to press demands for frontier defense and to take the lives of a group of Christian Indians, who were being sheltered by the government in barracks at Philadelphia. This exercise in vigilante government led to a Quaker-Presbyterian pamphlet war. Against this background the Quaker party decided to organize the October assembly elections around a campaign to replace proprietary with royal government.[56]

By the spring of 1764 the move to place Pennsylvania under royal government was underway, and political leaders in both camps were vying for popular support. Proprietary aristocrats, suppressing their contempt for the urban working class, made strenuous efforts to recruit artisan support and, for the first time, placed three ethnic candidates—two Germans and one Scotch-Irish—on their eight-man assembly slate. "The design," wrote a party organizer, "is by putting in two Germans to draw such a Party of them as will turn the scale in our Favor...."[57] The success of these efforts can be measured by the conversion to the proprietary cause of Carl Wrangel and Henry Muhlenberg, the Lutheran church leaders in Philadelphia, and Christopher Sauer, Jr., and Heinrich Miller, the German printers. By the end of the summer all of these men were writing or translating anti-Quaker pamphlets for distribution in the German community.[58]

The efforts of the proprietary party to search in the lower social strata for support drove Franklin and the assembly party to even greater lengths. In early April, Franklin called a mass meeting and sent messengers house-to-house to turn out the largest possible audience. The featured speaker was Galloway, who

[55]John C. Miller, "Religion, Finance and Democracy in Massachusetts," *New England Quarterly* 6 (1933), 52–53.

[56]Hindle, "The March of the Paxton Boys," 461–86; Hanna, *Benjamin Franklin and Pennsylvania Politics*, 154–68; James H. Hutson, "The Campaign to Make Pennsylvania a Royal Province, 1764–1770," *Pennsylvania Magazine of History and Biography* 94 (Oct. 1970), 427–63, 95 (Jan. 1971), 28–49.

[57]Samuel Purviance, Jr., to James Burd, Sept. 10, 1764, Vol. I, Shippen Family Papers (Historical Society of Pennsylvania, Philadelphia).

[58]Hutson, "Campaign to Make Pennsylvania a Royal Province," 452; Theodore Tappert and John W. Doberstein, trans. and eds., *The Journals of Henry Melchior Muhlenberg* (3 vols., Philadelphia, 1942–1945), II, 91, 99–102, 106–07, 123.

delivered an "inflammatory harangue" about the evils of proprietary government.[59] This was the opening shot in a campaign to gather signatures on a petition pleading for the institution of royal government. In the concerted drive to obtain signatures, according to one critic, "Taverns were engag'd, [and] many of the poorer and more dependent kind of labouring people in town were invited thither by night, the fear of being turn'd out of business and the eloquence of the punch bowl prevailed on many to sign"[60] The town was saturated with polemical literature, including three thousand copies of the assembly's biting message to the proprietor and their resolves for obtaining royal government. Franklin and Galloway published pamphlets designed to stir unrest with proprietary government, and Quakers, according to one observer, went door-to-door in pairs soliciting signatures for the royal government petition.[61] John Penn, the nephew of the proprietor, was shocked that Franklin's party went "into all the houses in Town without distinction," and "by the assistance of Punch and Beer" were able to procure the signatures of "some of the lowest sort of people" in the city.[62]

It was only a matter of time before the proprietary party, using fire to fight fire, circulated a counter-petition and far outstripped the efforts of Franklin and Galloway to involve the populace in politics. Everyone in Philadelphia, regardless of religion, class, or ideological predisposition, found himself being courted by the leaders of the two political factions.[63] Never in Pennsylvania's history had the few needed the many so much.

As the battle thickened, pamphleteers reached new pinnacles of abusiveness and scurrility. Franklin was reviled as an intellectual charlatan who begged and bought honorary degrees, a corrupt politician intimately acquainted "with every Zig Zag Machination," a grasping, conniving, egotistical climber, and a lecherous old man who promoted royal government only for the purpose of installing himself in the governor's chair.[64] His friends responded by labeling an opposition pamphleteer "a Reptile" who "like a Toad, by the pestilential Fumes of his virulent Slabber" attempted "to blast the fame of a PATRIOT" and describing William Smith, leader of the opposition, as a "consumate Sycophant," an "indefatigable" liar, and an impudent knave with a heart "bloated with *infernal Malice*" and a head full of "*flatulent Preachments.*"[65] As for the Presbyterians, they were redesignated "Piss-Brute-arians (a bigoted, cruel and revengeful sect)" by a Franklin

---

[59]John Penn to Thomas Penn, May 5, 1764, Official Correspondence, IX, 220, Penn Family Papers; John Dickinson, *A Reply to a Piece Called the Speech of Joseph Galloway, Esquire* (Philadelphia, 1764), 32–33.

[60]Dunbar, ed., Paxton Papers, 369; Hutson, "Campaign to Make Pennsylvania a Royal Province," 437–52.

[61]William Bingham to John Gibson, May 4, 1764, Shippen Papers.

[62]John Penn to Thomas Penn, May 5, 1764, Official Correspondence, IX. 220, Penn Family Papers.

[63]Autograph Petitions, 1681–1764, Penn Family Papers.

[64]Labaree and others, eds., *Papers of Benjamin Franklin*, XI, 380–84.

[65]Quoted in ibid., XI, 384; Gleason, "A Scurrilous Colonial Election and Franklin's Reputation," 82.

party pamphleteer who later reached the apogee of scatalogical polemics when he suggested that now was the time for Smith, president of the college and a director of the hospital, to consummate his alliance with the pamphleteer David Dove, who "will not only furnish you with that most agreeable of all Foods to your Taste, but after it has found a Passage through your Body . . . will greedily devour it, and, as soon as it is well digested, he will void it up for a Repast to the Proprietary Faction: they will as eagerly swallow it as the other had done before, and, when it has gone through their several Concoctions, they will discharge it in your Presence, that you may once more regale on it, thus refined."[66] One shocked outsider wrote to a friend in Philadelphia: "In the name of goodness stop your Pamphleteer's Mouths & shut up your presses. Such a torrent of low scurrility sure never came from any country as lately from Pennsylvan[i]a."[67]

Religious leaders were also drawn into the election campaign. A rural clergyman related that the proprietary leaders had convinced Presbyterian and Anglican ministers in Philadelphia to distribute petitions requesting the preservation of proprietary government. "The Presbyterian ministers, with some others," he lamented, held Synods about the election, turned their pulpits into Ecclesiastical drums for politics and told their people to vote according as they directed them at the peril of their damnation. . . ."[68] Church leaders such as Tennent, Francis Alison, and Muhlenberg wrote political pamphlets or sent circular letters on the election to every congregation in the province. St. Peters and Christ Church were the scene of pre-election rallies as denominational groups assumed an unprecedented role in politics.[69] A "Gentlemen from Transylvania" charged that Philadelphia's Anglican leaders had "prostituted their Temples . . . as an Amphitheatre for the Rabble to combat in. . . ."[70]

Inflammatory rhetoric, a large polemical literature, the participation of the churches in politics, mobilization of social layers previously unsolicited and unwelcome in political affairs, all combined to produce an election in which almost everybody's integrity was questioned, every public figure's use of power was attacked, and both sides paraded themselves as true representatives of "the people." The effects were dramatic: a record number of Philadelphians turned out for the election. The polls opened at 9 a.m. and remained open through the night as party workers on both sides shepherded in the voters, including the infirm and aged who were carried to the courthouse in litters and chairs.

---

[66][Isaac Hunt], *A Letter From a Gentleman in Transilvania To his Friend in America Giving Some Account of the Late Disturbances That Happen'd in that Government, with Some Remarks upon the Political Revolutions in the Magistracy, and the Debates That Happened about the Change* (Philadelphia, 1764); [Isaac Hunt], *A Humble Attempt at Scurrility* (Philadelphia, 1765), 36–37.

[67]Quoted in Gleason, "A Scurrilous Colonial Election and Franklin's Reputation," 82n.

[68]Quoted in Guy Soulliard Klett, *Presbyterians in Colonial Pennsylvania* (Philadelphia, 1937), 256.

[69]Thayer, *Pennsylvania Politics*, 97; Klett, *Presbyterians in Pennsylvania*, 256–57; Rothermund, *Layman's Progress*, 126–30; Thomas Stewardson, contributor, "Extracts from the Letter-Book of Benjamin Marshall 1763-1766," *Pennsylvania Magazine of History and Biography* 20 (2) (1896), 207–08.

[70][Hunt], *A Letter from a Gentleman in Transilvania*, 10.

By the next morning, party leaders were still seeking a few additional votes. Not until 3 p.m. on the second day were the polls closed.[71] When the returns were counted, both Franklin and Galloway had lost their seats to men on the proprietary ticket.[72] Franklin did not doubt that he had been defeated by defecting Germans and propertyless laborers "brought to swear themselves intituled to a Vote" by the proprietary leaders.[73] A bit of post-election doggerel caught the spirit of the contest: "A Pleasant sight tis to Behold/ The beggars hal'd from Hedges/ The Deaf, the Blind, the Young the Old:/ T' Secure their priveledges/ They're bundled up Steps, each sort Goes/ A Very Pretty Farce Sir:/ Some without Stockings, some no Shoes/ Nor Breeches to their A—e Sir."[74]

Although the election represents an extreme case and was affected by factors unique to the politics of proprietary Pennsylvania, it reflected a trend in the political life of other cities as well. Political innovations, involving a new set of organizational and propagandistic techniques, a vocabulary of vituperation, resort to violence, attacks on authority and social position, and the politicization of layers and groups in society that had earlier been beyond the political pale, had transformed the political culture of each of these cities in the half-century before 1765.

The extent of these changes can be measured, though imperfectly, by charting electoral participation.[75] In Boston, where the population remained nearly static at about 15,000 from 1735 to 1765, and the number of eligible voters declined markedly between 1735 and 1750 before beginning a slow upward climb, the number of voters participating in General Court elections showed a

---

[71]Tappert and Doberstein, eds., *Journals of Henry Melchoir Muhlenherg*, II, 122–23; William B. Reed, *Life and Correspondence of Joseph Reed* (2 vols., Philadelphia, 1847), I, 36–37; William Logan to John Smith, Oct. 4, 1764, John Smith Papers (Historical Society of Pennsylvania, Philadelphia); Labaree and others, eds., *Papers of Benjamin Franklin*, XI, 390–91. Benjamin H. Newcomb, "Effects of the Stamp Act on Colonial Pennsylvania Politics," *William and Mary Quarterly* 23 (April 1966), 257–72.

[72]Tappert and Doberstein, eds., *Journals of Henry Melchior Muhlenberg*, II, 123; Reed, ed., *Life and Correspondence of Joseph Reed*, I, 36–37. For the results of the city elections, see Isaac Norris, "Journal, 1764" (Rosenbach Foundation, Philadelphia).

[73]Labaree and others, eds., *Papers of Benjamin Franklin*, XI, 434.

[74]*The Election Medley* (Philadelphia, 1764).

[75]Robert E. Brown estimates that 56 percent of the adult males were eligible for the vote in Boston but later revises this upward to 75 percent or higher on the basis of literary evidence and inference. Robert E. Brown, *Middle-Class Democracy and the Revolution in Massachusetts, 1691–1780* (Ithaca, NY, 1955), 50, 58, 96. For Philadelphia the estimate is 75 percent. Chilton Williamson, *American Suffrage from Property to Democracy, 1760–1860* (Princeton, NJ, 1960), 33–34. The number of eligible voters in the cities probably never exceeded 75 percent of the taxables, and this percentage seems to have been declining in the eighteenth century as urban poverty and propertylessness increased. Williamson indicates that in Philadelphia in 1774 only 1,423 of 3,124 adult males (about 45 percent) were taxed for real or personal property. Williamson, *American Suffrage*, 33. Of course it is possible that many who were ineligible still voted, as was almost certainly the case in Philadelphia.

significant rise.[76] Although voter turnouts fluctuated widely from year to year, a series of peaks in 1732, 1748, 1757, 1760, and 1763 brought the number of voters from 650 in 1732 to 1,089 in 1763—a 66 percent increase during a period of population stagnation. It is also significant to note that from 1764 to 1775 the General Court elections in Boston never drew as many voters as in the years 1760 and 1763, or, for that matter, as in 1758.[77] These data throw doubt on traditional interpretations of the "democratization" of politics accompanying the movement, if we mean by that term the involvement of more people in the electoral process or the extension of the franchise. In the city and county of Philadelphia a similar rise in political participation can be traced. Four years in which knowledgeable observers remarked on vigorous campaigning and heavy voter turnouts were 1728, 1742, 1754, and 1764.[78] The table below indicates the uneven but generally upward drift of political participation as the eighteenth century progressed.

YEAR	TAXABLES	VOTERS	PERCENT OF TAXABLES VOTING
1728	2963	971	32.8
1742	5240	1793	34.2
1754	6908	2173	31.4
1764	8476	3874	45.7

Extant voting statistics for the city of Philadelphia, exclusive of the surrounding areas of Philadelphia County, are obtainable for only a few scattered years, but a comparison of 1751 and 1764, both years of extensive political activity, shows a rise in voting participation from 40.9 to 54.5 percent of the taxable inhabitants.[79] In 1765, when the proprietary and anti-proprietary parties waged another fierce struggle around the issues raised in the campaign of 1764, the percentage of taxable inhabitants voting in the county and city of Philadelphia increased to 51.2 and 65.1 percent. Never again in the pre-Revolutionary decade would involvement in the electoral process be so widespread, not even in the

---

[76]Warden, *Boston*, 127–29; Bridenbaugh, *Cities in the Wilderness*, 303n; Carl Bridenbaugh, *Cities in Revolt: Urban Life in America, 1743–1776* (New York, 1955), 5, 216; and *Boston Town Records*, XIV, 13, 100, 280.

[77]*Reports of the Record Commissioners of Boston*, VIII, XII, XVI, XVIII.

[78]Voters in Philadelphia participated in two assembly elections each October, one for the eight representatives for Philadelphia County and one for two "burgesses" from the city. Thus they were doubly represented in the assembly. These elections were usually held on successive days. Voting statistics are from newspapers, private correspondence, and Isaac Norris, "Journals." The number of taxables for the four years has been extrapolated from the known number of taxables for the years 1720, 1734, 1740, 1741, 1760, and 1767.

[79]Isaac Norris, "Journals, 1764." For another set of totals for Philadelphia County, which vary slightly, see Benjamin Franklin Papers, LXIX, 97 (American Philosophical Society, Philadelphia). The 1765 figures are from ibid., 98, and are reprinted in Labaree and others, eds., *Papers of Benjamin Franklin*, XII, 290–91n.

hotly contested special assembly elections for the city of Philadelphia in April 1776.[80] These figures suggest that the barometric pressure of political culture was on the rise during the half-century preceding the Stamp Act crisis and may, in fact, have reached its pinnacle, prior to the emergence of national political parties, in the early 1760s.

That an increasing percentage of qualified voters was participating in electoral politics not only by casting their votes but also by taking part in street demonstrations, rallies, and caucuses was emblematic of the changing political culture of the cities. Upper-class leaders, contending for political advantage, had mobilized the electorate and introduced new techniques and strategies for obtaining electoral majorities. Most of these leaders had little taste for the effects of this new kind of politics and perhaps none of them wished to bring political life to the kind of clamorous, unrestrained exercise in vitriol and slander that prevailed in Philadelphia in 1764 and 1765. But piecemeal they had contributed to a transformed political culture which by the 1760s they could only precariously control.

The transformation of politics was not restricted to the cities.[81] But it proceeded most rapidly in the urban centers of colonial life because it was in cities that men in power could influence large numbers of people; that printing presses were located and political literature was most widely distributed; that population density made possible the organization of clubs, mass meetings, and vociferous electioneering tactics; that numerous taverns provided natural nerve centers of feverish political activity; that disparities of wealth were growing most rapidly; and that new attitudes and behavioral patterns first found ideological expression. The countryside was far from immune to the new style of politics and a new political culture, but distances and population dispersion created organizational and communication problems which were far harder to solve than in urban places.

But change occurred everywhere, rendering an older mode of politics obsolete. Internal, local and intraclass as well as interclass struggles in colonial society had transfigured politics, creating almost by inadvertance a political culture which by 1765 already contained many of the changes in political style and behavior usually associated with the Revolutionary period.[82]

---

[80]See David Hawke, *In the Midst of a Revolution* (Philadelphia, 1961), 13–31.

[81]For example, see Kenneth A. Lockridge, *A New England Town, The First Hundred Years: Dedham, Massachusetts, 1636–1736* (New York, 1970), 93–164; and Edward M. Cook, Jr., "Social Behavior and Changing Values in Dedham, Massachusetts, 1700 to 1775," *William and Mary Quarterly* 27 (Oct. 1970), 546–80.

[82]For the view that the radicalization process should be associated with the post-1763 period, see Merrill Jensen, "The American People and the American Revolution," *Journal of American History* 57 (June 1970), 5–35.

Gary Nash

Growing up near Valley Forge, where Washington's Continental Army was encamped in the winter of 1777–78, I developed a virus I've never cured: to understand how ordinary people experienced and influenced the major events we encounter in our history books. I later encountered Margaret Mead's pronouncement that "Never doubt that a small group of thoughtful committed citizens can change the world. Indeed, it is the only thing that ever has." So I have been haunting archives near and far over the last half-century to restore to memory a great many ordinary individuals and social groups that have been disfavored by top-down narratives. My work began with studies of seventeenth-century Colonial America but has drifted into studies of revolutionary and post-revolutionary America, with a special emphasis on African Americans, Native Americans, and the laboring people of the seaboard cities. The governing idea here is not to eject our traditional heroes from the pantheon but to open up the pantheon so that there is room for a wide assortment of figures, powerful in their own ways, whose importance has been obscured. Apart from published scholarship, my work in recent years has turned toward public history. Especially rewarding have been opportunities to work with the National Park Service (NPS), which operates the world's largest outdoor classrooms in their hundreds of historical sites and parks. Having an opportunity to influence the messages told and the questions posed at the President's House and Liberty Bell exhibits at Independence National Historical Park in Philadelphia has been rewarding beyond expectation. Likewise, serving on the National Parks Second Century Commission, which published its report *Advancing the National Park Idea* in 2010, and coauthoring *Imperiled Promise: The State of History in the National Park Service* (2011) have been highlights of my latter years.

QUESTIONS FOR CONSIDERATION:

1. Traditionally, Pennsylvania was a proprietary colony under the control of the supporters of the proprietor, William Penn and his descendants. However, according to Nash the eighteenth century represented a period of political change in the colonial assembly. Characterize this changing political situation.

2. How did the factions of this changing political environment view recent German immigrants to Pennsylvania colony? And how did they view working-class artisans? In what ways did political necessity reshape politics in Pennsylvania?

3. How did the different political and ethnic context in Boston shape politics there differently? What were some similarities to politics in Philadelphia?

4. Describe some of the new techniques politicians in eighteenth century Boston and Philadelphia employed to gain, maintain, or extend political power.

5. Describe the ways in which the press was an essential part of these new techniques. How did the use of the press to gain, maintain, or extend political power shape politics in these colonies?

6. Give two examples of the "mob activity" Nash describes. To what extent were these activities a result of the new style of politics in the eighteenth century?

7. Nash also notes that religious leaders became increasingly involved in politics during this era. According to Nash, how did the Great Awakening create a context for greater religious political involvement?

8. To what extent did political partisanship and politicking contribute to the democratization of colonial politics in the generation before the American Revolution? Support your answer with evidence from Nash's article.

CHAPTER SIX

Popular Mobilization and Political Culture in Revolutionary Virginia: The Failure of the Minutemen and the Revolution from Below[1]

Michael A. McDonnell

In the fall of 1775, George Gilmer, friend and physician to Thomas Jefferson and himself a member of the gentry of Albemarle County, Virginia, wrote an address to his neighbors lamenting the lack of support for the new military establishment created that August by the colony's extralegal revolutionary government, the Third Virginia Convention. The problem, Gilmer believed, was the decline in popular enthusiasm for the cause manifested in the poor rate of enlistment for the new "minuteman" service: "I know not from what cause, but every denomination of the people seem backward; the Convention have altered the name Volunteers to that of Minute Men, and behold! what a wondrous effect it has had. Out of near three hundred Volunteers there are how many Minute Men? So few that I am afraid to name them." He noted the striking contrast between the ardor of a few months before and the present: "We were once all fire, now most of us are become inanimate and indifferent." . . .[2]

---

[1]Interested students are encouraged to read this essay in the original form. Michael A. McDonnell, "Popular Mobilization and Political Culture in Revolutionary Virginia: The Failure of the Minutemen and the Revolution from Below," *Journal of American History* 85 (3) (Dec. 1998), 946–81.

[2]George Gilmer, "Address of George Gilmer to the Inhabitants of Albemarle," [fall 1775], in "Papers, Military and Political, 1775–1778, of George Gilmer, M.D., of 'Pen Park,' Albemarle County, Virginia," ed. R. A. Brock, Virginia Historical Society, *Collections*, new series, 6 (1887), 122, 125. Gilmer was active in politics and served as a stand-in for Thomas Jefferson in the Virginia conventions of 1774–1775 while the latter served in the Continental Congress. We can safely date the address cited here as later than September 11, probably a few weeks later. On Gilmer's life, see Robert L. Scribner, ed., *Revolutionary Virginia: The Road to Independence, Vol. III: The Breaking Storm and the Third Convention* (Charlottesville, VA, 1977), 50.

Indeed, the minuteman service was designed to play a pivotal role in Virginia's defense amid escalating hostilities through the summer and fall of 1775. Established when popular enthusiasm for the war was high, it was supposed to be the truly revolutionary backbone of Virginians' defense of their liberties. Replacing the royally controlled militia as the ideological alternative to a standing army, the minute service was designed to ready eight thousand "citizen-soldiers" for service at short notice—men "in whose Hands the Sword may be safely trusted," as a creator of the service put it. Even the appellation "minuteman" was designed to evoke an image of the mass popular resistance to perceived British tyranny already immortalized in New England in the first skirmishes of the war—an image still strong in the pantheon of American historical myths.[3]

Virginia, too, was supposed to have its minuteman heroes. But the minute service in Virginia failed miserably and was quickly forgotten. Gilmer's complaints about poor recruiting for the minutemen in his county were paralleled throughout the colony, and the minute service never came close to attracting a full complement of men. Consequently, it entirely failed in providing for the colony's defense, pushing the gentry into relying wholeheartedly on the kind of paid, professional regular army vilified by revolutionary rhetoric. . . .[4]

[T]he reasons why the minuteman plan failed illustrate a more enduring conflict than the one against Britain: the one between the governors and the governed, between the gentry and the "lower" and "middling sorts." That conflict has been masked in its scale and detail by an elite bias in the available sources. Small farmers in Virginia in the eighteenth century left very few written records of their thoughts and experiences. Most Virginians, particularly non-gentry Virginians, lived in an oral-aural world—perhaps as many as 75 percent of adults in the colony could not even sign their names. . . .[5]

---

[3]George Mason to George Washington, Oct. 14, 1775, in *The Papers of George Mason, 1725–1792*, ed. Robert A. Rutland (3 vols., Chapel Hill, NC, 1970), I, 255–56. See Robert A. Gross, *The Minutemen and Their World* (New York, 1976), 59.

[4]George Gilmer to Thomas Jefferson, July 26 or 27, 1775, in *The Papers of Thomas Jefferson*, ed. Julian P. Boyd et al. (27 vols., Princeton, 1950–), I, 238.

[5]In defining groups in eastern Virginia, I have followed John Selby, who concluded that the "typical white Virginia male was a small farmer. . . . [who] had access to no more than a couple of hundred acres, at most a slave or two, and some cattle." Just under 50 percent of white males were small landowners, 10 to 20 percent tenants (concentrated in the Northern Neck), and 20 to 30 percent agricultural laborers or indentured servants. "Small farmers," or the "middling sort," were those in the first two groups; "poor whites," or the "lower sort," refers to the third group. The final 10 percent of white males were the gentry, who owned half the land in Virginia and almost half the personal property and occupied most important posts of leadership and authority at provincial and local levels. See Selby, *Revolution in Virginia*, 24. On the predominantly nonliterate world of Virginia, see Rhys Isaac, "Dramatizing the Ideology of Revolution: Popular Mobilization in Virginia, 1774 to 1776," *William and Mary Quarterly* 33 (July 1976), esp. 357–64. Emory G. Evans, "Trouble in the Backcountry: Disaffection in Southwest Virginia during the American Revolution," in *An Uncivil War: The Southern Backcountry during the American Revolution*, ed. Ronald Hoffman, Thad Tate, and Peter J. Albert (Charlottesville, VA, 1985), 180.

Yet the reasons for the failure of the minute service, particularly from the point of view of ordinary Virginians, though elusive, are not impossible to reconstruct. . . . By applying the methodology used by Rhys Isaac . . . we can find the alternative and often conflicting meanings of the Revolution for ordinary Virginians by placing their actions within the context of events. In this case, though it is difficult to reconstruct what ordinary Virginians thought about the war, we can determine when they did or did not fight. . . .[6]

Figure 6.1
The dress and accoutrements of this rifleman, probably from a backcountry or western Piedmont county, were typical of the volunteers who turned out in the independent companies. Courtesy Anne S.K. Brown Military Collection, Brown University Library.

Resistance to the minute service among the middling sort in Virginia . . . was not over whether or not to fight the British, but over how and on whose "terms" to do so. The conditions of service were often decisive in the choice of a farmer to fight or not. Throughout the Revolutionary War, small farmers in Virginia grounded their patriotism in the economic realities of small-scale farming (with few or no slaves and little other help). They desired a more egalitarian distribution of the burden of war, a more democratic and consensual military organization, and equality within the service. When policy makers did not take these considerations into account, ordinary Virginians refused to serve. They thereby demonstrated their commitment to an "alternative popular political culture," very similar to the one prevailing in the backcountry and very different from the expectations of the gentry.[7]

Contained within the small farmers' demands were the seeds of an ideal of political and social relations outside of military service very different from that held by the leading gentry. . . . Indeed, through their participation, or refusal to serve, in the military, ordinary Virginians . . . articulated alternative ideas about the political society in which they lived . . . , [and] exercised power to make those demands heard. Ultimately, small farmers' wartime resistance to unfavorable military policy . . . helped develop their ideas about the nature of political and social relations, demonstrated the limits of the authority of the gentry, and irrevocably changed postwar politics in the Old Dominion.

---

[6]My methodology has been influenced by Rhys Isaac, *The Transformation of Virginia, 1740-1790* (Chapel Hill, NC, 1982), esp. 323-59; Isaac, "Dramatizing the Ideology of Revolution," 357-64; and works of the new military historians, beginning with John Shy, *A People Numerous and Armed: Reflections on the Military Struggle for American Independence* (Ann Arbor, MI, 1990).

[7]Albert H. Tillson Jr., *Gentry and Common Folk: Political Culture on a Virginia Frontier, 1740-1789* (Lexington, KY, 1991); and Albert H. Tillson Jr., "The Militia and Popular Political Culture in the Upper Valley of Virginia, 1740-1775," *Virginia Magazine of History and Biography* 94 (July 1986), 285-306.

Figure 6.2
The Alternative of Williamsburg by Philip Dawe (1775) shows armed patriots forcing gentlemen-merchants to sign the commercial "Association" against imports. The "alternative" was to suffer the degradation of being tarred and feathered with materials hanging from the scaffold. Courtesy the Colonial Williamsburg Foundation. Museum Purchase.

Figure 6.3
George Washington in the Uniform of a British Colonial Colonel by Charles Wilson Peale (1772). Courtesy Washington-Custis-Lee Collection, Washington and Lee University, Lexington, VA.

... [T]he story of the failure of the minutemen challenges the traditional and enduring picture of an organically unified white Virginia society before and during the Revolution. . . .[8] [S]cholars have begun to question the homogeneity and harmony of prewar Virginia as they have looked at the diverse and diverging interests of growing groups of merchants, wheat growers, backcountry farmers, dissenting sectarians, laborers and the "lower sort," and even those who challenged that stability from within, enslaved Virginians. . . . [T]here are now clear indications that even among the white agricultural communities the "consensus" on which the gentry premised their authority to command was coming undone.[9]

For many of the ruling class, the Revolution may be seen as an attempt to reassert control, authority, and legitimacy. . . . [T]he gentry's approach to mobilizing for war shows a conservative and fearful group clinging to traditional notions of hierarchy, deference, and public virtue in an attempt to maintain an

---

[8]Herbert Sloan and Peter Onuf, "Politics, Culture, and the Revolution in Virginia: A Review of Recent Work," *Virginia Magazine of History and Biography* 91 (July 1983), 267. For the interpretation that created the image of a unified Virginia, see Charles Sydnor, *Gentlemen Freeholders: Political Practices in Washington's* Virginia (Chapel Hill, NC, 1952).

[9]Gordon S. Wood, "Rhetoric and Reality in the American Revolution," *William and Mary Quarterly* 23 (Jan. 1966), 28; Woody Holton, *Forced Founders: Indians, Debtors, Slaves, and the Making of the American Revolution in Virginia* (Williamsburg, Institute of Early American History and Culture, forthcoming).

increasingly challenged social and political culture. But the struggle with a politicized middling and lower class over mobilization during the Revolutionary War would further and finally erode that authority and demonstrate to the gentry the finality of their failure to govern by old standards and the pressing need to recast their leadership. The transition from a deferential to a more republican political culture was forged and fueled by conflict, not consensus.[10]

That transition—the conflict and its consequences in Virginia—brings into focus . . . all across the colonies and new states, popular upheaval and social protest before, during, and after the war was endemic and involved hundreds of thousands of ordinary people, male and female, black, white, and Native American. . . .[11] [T]he story of Virginia in the Revolution also helps show how internal conflict and social protest were crucial to that revolutionary settlement. . . . An examination of the minuteman establishment and the war in the Old Dominion in general will show that, as in the Philadelphia militia and elsewhere, the experiences and actions of ordinary people at war were as important as political and imperial issues in shaping the revolutionary transformations that took place.[12]

Both the origins of the minute service and the roots of its failure lay in the establishment that it was designed to replace, the "Independent Companies of Volunteers" that had begun forming between fall 1774 and summer 1775. This initial effort at organizing a military force was crucial in shaping subsequent military policy, for it set a precedent—frightening for the gentry, exemplary for small farmers. To understand the failure of the minute service, we need to understand why the independent companies were successful, what was really "altered," . . . between the "Volunteer" and minuteman companies, and why Virginia leaders sought to replace the volunteers with minutemen.

In the aftermath of the Boston Port Act, as relations began to worsen between the colonies and Britain during the summer and fall of 1774, Virginia's elite leadership confronted the problem of rallying popular support for . . . more disruptive resistance efforts. The last economic boycott, of 1768–1770, had ended ignominiously. . . . In summer 1774, there was every indication that stronger measures would be necessary, but the gentry could not take popular support for granted. In the dramatic days immediately following the news of the Boston Port Act, a report

---

[10]Jack P. Greene, *Imperatives, Behaviors, and Identities: Essays in Early American Cultural History* (Charlottesville, VA, 1992), 181–207.

[11]Carl Lotus Becker, *The History of Political Parties in the Province of New York, 1760–1776* (Madison, WI, 1909); Alfred F. Young, ed., *The American Revolution: An Exploration in the History of Radicalism* (DeKalb, IL, 1976); Alfred F. Young, ed., *Beyond the American Revolution* (De Kalb, IL, 1990); and the seminal work, Gary Nash, *The Urban Crucible: Social Change, Political Consciousness, and the Origins of the American Revolution* (Cambridge, MA, 1979).

[12]Steven Rosswurm, *Arms, Country, and Class: The Philadelphia Militia and the "Lower Sort" during the American Revolution* (New Brunswick, 1987). See also Gregory T. Knouff, "'An Arduous Service': The Pennsylvania Backcountry Soldiers' Revolution," *Pennsylvania History* 61 (Jan. 1994), 45–74.

was circulated in the Northern Neck that "The lower Class of People here are in a tumult on the account of Reports from Boston, many of them expect to be press'd & compell'd to go and fight the Britains!" Such reports must have worried the gentry, who could remember that the "lower Class of People" had singularly rejected their general calls to join the provincial army during the French and Indian War and had resisted efforts to conscript them to fight. . . . [I]n most places the militia, if functioning, had long since taken on a largely symbolic social role. . . . Consequently, drawing on lessons learned in the French and Indian War, the gentry moved cautiously and refused to call for mandatory service.[13]

Instead, they tried to mobilize popular *opinion* by beginning an informal movement, in September 1774, to form extralegal "Independent" or "Volunteer" companies of "Gentlemen." Rather than try to mobilize all men and risk upheaval, the gentry established military companies that were voluntary, exclusive, and amenable to their own sense of propriety. . . . [T]he volunteer companies were thus generally organized on very different terms than the colonial militia or previous volunteer or conscript armies. These companies were not designed for the "common" sort; they were established to "rouse the attention of the public," to "excite others by [their] Example," and to "infuse a martial spirit of emulation." These were preliminary preparations: one member of the gentry believed these companies to be useful, not because they would provide a first line of defense, but because they would "provide a fund of officers; that in case of absolute necessity, the people might be better enabled to act in defence of their invaded liberty." The gentry would thus ready themselves, train, and if war came, go forth among the people to assume leadership roles on the field of battle and in more traditional military organizations.[14]

Limited membership and the terms on which these companies came together reinforced the exclusivity of the independent companies. . . . In Dunmore County, which embodied one of the largest companies, only eighty-seven men enrolled out of an eligible fighting population of approximately eight hundred males. Similarly, the twenty-three men who enlisted in the company from Albemarle represented less than 1.8 percent of the county's 1,314 eligible males. The more material terms of enrollment seemed tailored to exclude less wealthy farmers and in effect played the role that property qualifications for office played in civil life: Among other accoutrements, each member of the unit had to provide his own uniform, in "Blue, turn'd up with Buff," complete with "Coat & Breeches & white Stockings," along with "a good Fire-lock and Bayonet" and six pounds of gunpowder, twenty pounds of lead, and fifty gun flints, "at the least." It was generally reported that

---

[13]McDonnell, "Politics of Mobilization in Revolutionary Virginia," chap. 1. *Virginia Gazette* (Rind), March 8, 1770, quoted in T. H. Breen, *Tobacco Culture: The Mentality of the Great Tidewater Planters on the Eve of Revolution* (New Brunswick, 1985); May 31, 1774, entry in *Journal and Letters of Philip Vickers Fithian, 1773–1774: A Plantation Tutor of the Old Dominion*, ed. Hunter Dickinson Farish (1943; Williamsburg, VA, 1957), 111. On the problems of raising men in the French and Indian War, see Titus, *Old Dominion at War*.

[14]Titus, *Old Dominion at War*, 144; George Mason, "Fairfax County Militia Association," Sept. 21, 1774, in *Papers of George Mason*, ed. Rutland, I, 210; George Mason, "Remarks on Annual Elections for the Fairfax Independent Company," [April 17–26, 1775], ibid., 229.

membership in the new independent companies was to be confined to "gentlemen of the first fortune and character." George Mason later boasted that his own company, from Fairfax County, when first formed "consisted entirely of Gentlemen."[15] Consequently, between September 1774 and April 1775, when actual fighting broke out, no more than a handful of volunteer companies were raised throughout Virginia.[16]

Because the new independent companies were established by the gentry, and for gentlemen alone, they were organized on a much more consensual and egalitarian basis than militia or regular army units. Service in an independent company was voluntary. . . . Unlike soldiers in the militia or other regular military units, the members of the company were not bound to serve by law but "by the sacred ties of virtue, Honor, and love to our Country," and "the words of Gentlemen." . . . Officers were to be "of their own Choice," selected "from among our Friends and acquaintaince, upon whose Justice, Humanity & Bravery we can relie." Moreover, members promised only to "obey the commands of the officers" that they themselves had "*elected* from the Inlisted Volunteers." Finally, some associators pledged to "adhere strictly" only "to such resolves which shall be *entered into by a Majority* of the Company."[17]

The radical nature of the independent companies . . . just prior to the outbreak of hostilities in Virginia, [when] George Mason wrote "Remarks on Annual Elections" of officers for his volunteer company, justifying the practice by appealing to broad principles of natural rights philosophy. Declaring that "All men are by nature born equally free and independent" and that all power was originally "lodged in, and consequently is derived from, the people," Mason argued that frequent appeals to the "body of the people" for their "approbation or dissent" were necessary to prevent the "abuse of authority, and the insolence of office." Moreover, yearly elections of officers would open "a door to the

---

[15]For the estimates of those eligible for military service in Dunmore and Albemarle counties, see the manuscript list published as "The Number of Men of Military Age in Virginia in 1776," *Virginia Magazine of History and Biography* 18 (Jan. 1910), 34–35. "Declaration of Subscribers to the First Independent Company of Dunmore County," [after Jan. 1775?], Dunmore County Committee of Safety Papers (Virginia Historical Society, Richmond); Mason, "Fairfax County Militia Association," 211; Mason to [Mr. Brent?], Oct. 2, 1778, in *Papers of George Mason*, ed. Rutland, I, 434. See also "Report of the Committee to inquire into the causes of the late disturbances. . . . June 1, 1775, "The Proceedings of the House of Burgesses of Virginia," in *Records of the States of the United States*, ed. William S. Jenkins (Washington, DC, 1949) (microfilm: Virginia, lb, reel 3, 1773–1781), I would like to thank Woody Holton for this reference.

[16]William C. White, "The Independent Companies of Virginia, 1774–1775," *Virginia Magazine of History and Biography* 86 (April 1978), 151; McDonnell, "Politics of Mobilization in Revolutionary Virginia," 35–36.

[17]White, "Independent Companies of Virginia," 152; "Terms of Inlisting," [April 1775], in "Papers, Military and Political, . . . of George Gilmer," ed. Brock, 82; Mason, "Remarks on Annual Elections for the Fairfax Independent Company," 229; George Mason, "Fairfax County Militia Plan 'For Embodying the People,'" [Feb. 6, 1775], in *Papers of George Mason*, ed. Rutland, I, 215–16; Mason, "Fairfax County Militia Association," 210–11; "Declaration of Subscribers to the First Independent Company of Dunmore County"; "The First Independent Company of Dunmore," *Virginia Magazine of History and Biography* 44 (April 1936), 102–4 (emphasis added).

return of officers of approved merit, and will always be a means of excluding unworthy men."[18]

Yet it was because the companies were generally small and composed of the "better sort" that the election of officers and a more consensual style of leadership were initially permitted. Mason implied that elections of officers would be acceptable only if a company was composed of gentlemen of equal merit: "In a company thus constituted, no young man will think himself degraded by doing duty in the ranks, which he may in his turn command, or has commanded." Among "equals," Mason could talk of popular elections; the company's exclusivity would allow a "safe" election as competition would be limited to equals of the "better sort," mirroring the safe, almost symbolic, political competitions at the polls in prerevolutionary Virginia. And if the companies consisted only of gentlemen, they could afford to leave regulations, rules, and even actions up to the decision of a majority, democratic vote. . . . While hostilities had yet to break out, the units resembled elite gentlemen's clubs, rather than formal military units.[19]

But the start of hostilities in April 1775 caught the gentry off balance, and a window of opportunity thus opened for small farmers. In Virginia British troops under the direction of the royal governor, John Murray, earl of Dunmore, executed a successful midnight raid on the Williamsburg public magazine, removing fifteen half barrels of stockpiled gunpowder only two days after Gen. Thomas Gage botched his similar foray into the Massachusetts countryside. . . . [N]ews of Dunmore's actions, quickly joined with reports of bloodshed from the north and, importantly, rumors that the governor had threatened to arm the slaves and use them against white Virginians, inflamed the colony and incited a new burst of enthusiastic militarism. . . . "Volunteers presented themselves from every direction," a soldier later recalled, and Gilmer wrote from Williamsburg that "Every rank and denomination of people [are] full of marshal notions."[20] The vehicles for those martial expressions were the democratically organized "Independent Companies of Volunteers," which now seemed to hold out a tantalizing and most immediate example of revolutionary ideology in practice.[21]

Those who now began to rally to arms, however, seemed to look and act different from the "gentlemen" who had previously predominated in the volunteer companies. In George Gilmer and Thomas Jefferson's Albemarle County, for example, membership in the volunteer company blossomed from the 23 who had originally signed on in April, to 74 . . . in June (and there was one report that nearly 300 volunteers eventually signed up). By June, however, only 12 of the original

[18]Mason, "Remarks on Annual Elections for the Fairfax Independent Company," 229–31.

[19]Ibid., 231–32.

[20]John Selby, *The Revolution in Virginia: 1775–1783*, (Williamsburg, VA, 1988), 1–6; Holton, *Forced Founders*; Peter Wood, "'Liberty Is Sweet': African-American Freedom Struggles in the Years before White Independence," in *Beyond the American Revolution*, ed. Young, 163–64; Gilmer to Jefferson, July 26–27, 1775, in Papers of Thomas Jefferson, ed. Boyd, I, 238.

[21]White, "Independent Companies of Virginia," 151; McDonnell, "Politics of Mobilization in Revolutionary Virginia," chap. 1.

company were present, and in the others' place stood an entirely different body of men. Property tax records from 1782 are available for 30 of the 62 new men, and land records for 21. Whereas on the average, each member of the earlier company owned almost 1,000 acres of land, the June soldiers owned only 322 acres each. The new men also owned an average of 5 slaves, 10 cattle, and 3 horses, compared with the 15 slaves, 27 cattle, and 8 horses owned by the average member of the earlier company. Moreover, whereas all the men from the earlier muster for whom tax records are available owned slaves, one-third of the new group owned none.[22]

Gone were the white-stockinged gentlemen volunteers. Some counties had lowered the "property" qualifications for joining the independent companies in anticipation of the outbreak of hostilities. . . . The stipulation that the recruits wear blue uniforms "turn'd up with Buff; with . . . Buff Waist Coat & Breeches, & white Stockings" was quietly dropped. In the growing crisis of April and May, most men seemed to ignore any such remaining regulations—if they were not voted out of existence by the swelling numbers of ordinary farmers who began to compose the independent companies. . . .[23]

In a more telling instance, the newly enlarged independent company of Albemarle . . . had been told by the local gentry-dominated county committee (one of the extralegal bodies created to correspond with other counties and colonies and to enforce the 1774 boycott) to disband and not to march out of the county. But the company, meeting after receiving these instructions, noted the members were still "at a loss what to do." The company therefore voted, and the majority were in favor of marching to Williamsburg, which they proceeded to do. . . . It was reported in June that . . . "the *Caroline* company refused to enlist, unless they were to be solely under the direction of officers of their own choosing." There is some evidence, too, suggesting that some companies elected officers on each occasion of marching, further exacerbating the problem of control.[24]

As imperial tensions mounted throughout June, volunteer companies marched to Williamsburg from nearby counties and set up camp on the edge of town. Their presence there, particularly their lack of discipline and of deference to civil authority, would force the gentry to reevaluate Virginia's military establishment. Arriving under the authority of their respective county committees or merely their elected commanding officers, the soldiers at Williamsburg quickly made a nuisance of themselves. Thomas Jefferson was told that the elected commanding officer of the volunteers, a Captain Scott, though his "goodness and merit is great, fear[s] to

---

[22]Gilmer, "Address of George Gilmer to the Inhabitants of Albemarle," 122; George Gilmer, "List of Volunteers Present at Muster, June 17, 1775," in "Papers, Political and Military, . . . of George Gilmer," ed. Brock, 85; "Terms of Inlisting," 82; Albemarle County Personal Property Tax Records, 1782; Albemarle County Land Tax Records, 1782.

[23]Mason, "Fairfax County Militia Plan 'For Embodying the People,'" 215–16; Isaac, "Dramatizing the Ideology of Revolution," 379–81.

[24]Scribner, ed., *Revolutionary Virginia*, III, 177. See also ibid., 71–72n. Proceedings of the Independent Company of Volunteers, [April 29, 1775], Diary and Memoranda of Gilmer; "Report of the Committee to inquire into the causes of the late disturbances."

offend, and by that many members are rather disorderly."[25] What the gentry feared was the lack of a clear chain of command with centralized control. If a commander could be replaced by the vote of his men and military actions decided by majority vote, there could be no discipline and no control over what these troops might do. . . .

In the eyes of the gentry, particularly the moderate Patriots, the independent actions of the volunteer companies threatened political and social stability because they were increasingly responsible for pushing Britain and Virginia further down the road to open conflict. Governor Dunmore had initially reacted to news of the marches of the independent companies by appealing for reinforcements from General Gage and Admiral Samuel Graves in Boston. He also made clearer and more public his threat to arm the slaves to spread "Devastation wherever I can reach," further inflaming Virginians, especially propertied moderate Virginians. Finally, after repeated incidents involving independent companies in Williamsburg, Dunmore fled from the town to an awaiting vessel, abandoning conciliatory efforts, he said, because his "house was kept in continual Alarm and threatened every Night with an Assault."[26] With Dunmore's flight, the possibility of reconciliation became even more remote.

But equally important, as the independent companies helped radicalize resistance . . . against Britain, they also began pushing for a stricter accounting of allegiances internally, polarizing the conflict within Virginia. Most often, they called for everyone to show patriotism by joining the independent companies and by ostracizing those who were slow in displaying their allegiance or approval. . . . [T]hose who were "backward" in their "Attendance" with the independent companies often compelled to do service with the threat of "Tar & Feathers" and other "popular Terrors" including "Scoff and Shame". . . . Many merchants around the colony who wished to remain neutral had apparently been "called upon" by volunteer companies "to enlist as Soldiers therein, under pain of incurring the Displeasure of the Said Company, and of being treated as Enemies to the Country." These were political acts. . . .[27] [T]o the gentry in Virginia, perhaps the most horrifying manifestation of the volunteer companies' newfound independence was the leveling entailed by increased attacks on neutral or unsympathetic individuals, particularly propertied ones. In such instances, volunteers recognized no socioeconomic barriers. . . .

The movement, in the eyes of the gentlemen, was becoming unwieldy, dangerous, and potentially subversive. The gentry felt that their control over the "ebullition of patriotism" . . . was slipping. Armed bands of men were taking the law into their own hands and radicalizing the resistance movement. . . . As early as the summer of

---

[25]Selby, *Revolution in Virginia*, 47–48; Scribner, ed., *Revolutionary Virginia*, III, 218–19; Gilmer to Jefferson, [July 26–27, 1775], in *Papers of Thomas Jefferson*, ed. Boyd, I, 237; "Meeting of Officers at Williamsburg," July 18, 1775, in *Papers, Political and Military, . . . of George Gilmer*, ed. Brock, 92–93.

[26]See Selby, *Revolution in Virginia*, 4–5, 42–43.

[27]June 8, 1775, entry in *Philip Vickers Fithian: Journal, 1775–1776*, ed. Albion and Dodson, (Princeton, NJ, 1934), 25, 34; petition of Charles Duncan, [Aug. 9, 1775], in *Revolutionary Virginia*, III, ed. Scribner, 410, 412; Rosswurm, *Arms, Country, and Class*, 54. See also Scribner, ed., *Revolutionary Virginia*, III, 490–91.

1774, one Virginian pointed out to the wealthy the danger of resistance: "even a slight commotion may expose part of your wealth to the ravages of the populace, or the plunder of a licentious army." . . . Similarly, in the aftermath of Patrick Henry's march on Williamsburg, James Madison explained that "The Gentlemen . . . whose property will be exposed in case of a civil war in this Colony were extremely alarmed." Even the House of Burgesses confessed the great "difficulty there is in restraining an incensed multitude."[28] The situation, of course, was exacerbated by the presence of slaves and indentured and convict servants, many of whom saw the coming "civil war" as an opportunity to gain their personal "independence. . . ."[29]

The answer to the problems inherent in the independent companies, the gentry believed, was the minutemen. Hoping to channel the manifest enthusiasm for the cause among the yeomanry, the gentry-dominated Third Virginia Convention called for eight thousand men (almost one-fifth of the colony's eligible fighting males) who would train for twenty days immediately and frequently thereafter. This force would be the backbone of the new military establishment, ready and trained to fight on short notice.[30] It was also believed that the ranks would be filled with those who had already shown a disposition to fight, particularly the common farmer, or the middling sort—men "in whose Hands the Sword may be safely trusted"—rather than the lower sort, those deemed economically expendable, who usually fought the wars of the eighteenth century. . . .[31]

But, because the gentry established the minute service in reaction to the disorder engendered by the independent companies, they imposed conditions that ignored the popular will and clashed with the more voluntaristic, egalitarian, and democratic principles that had underpinned the success of those companies. Thus, prescribed terms of service were introduced that compelled men to train and serve for longer periods of time than in the independent companies. New rules and regulations for the governance of forces in the field imposed strict discipline on the troops. Subordination would henceforth be enforced, and an

---

[28][Thomson Mason], "The British American, VII," *Virginia Gazette* (Rind), July 14, 1774, in *Revolutionary Virginia: The Road to Independence, Vol. I: Forming Thunderclouds and the First Convention, 1763–1774*, ed. Robert L. Scribner (Charlottesville, VA, 1973), 184. See also a revealing exchange of letters, first published in May and June 1775, ibid., III, 117, 180–82, 199–200. James Madison to Bradford, May 9, 1775, in James Madison, and William T. Hutchinson, ed,. *The Papers of James Madison.*(Chicago: University of Chicago Press, 1962), .I, 145, The House of Burgesses, "Report of the Committee to inquire into the causes of the late disturbances."

[29]Peter H. Wood, "'The Dream Deferred': Black Freedom Struggles on the Eve of White Independence," in *In Resistance: Studies in African, Caribbean, and Afro-American History*, ed. Gary Okihiro (Amherst, MA, 1986), 161–87; and Holton, *Forced Founders*, chap. 5.

[30]Selby, *Revolution in Virginia*, 51–52; William Waller Hening, ed., *The Statutes at Large: Being a Collection of all the Laws of Virginia, From the First Session of the Legislature, in the Year 1619* (1809–1823; 13 vols., Charlottesville, VA, 1969), IX, 9–48; Don Higginbotham, *The War of American Independence: Military Attitudes, Policies, and Practice, 1763–1789* (New York, 1971), 81–95.

[31]Mason to George Washington, Oct. 14, 1775, in *Papers of George Mason*, ed. Rutland, I, 255–56; Mason to Cockburn, Aug. 22, 1775, ibid., 251; Gilmer to Charles Carter, July 15, 1775, Diary and Memoranda of Gilmer; Reginald C. Stuart, *War and American Thought: From the Revolution to the Monroe Doctrine* (Kent, OH, 1982), xiii–xv; Shy, *People Numerous and Armed*, 277–80; and Robert Middlekauff, *The Glorious Cause: The American Revolution* (New York, 1982), 297–98.

elaborate hierarchy within the military was resurrected, all to come under the central direction of the Committee of Safety in Williamsburg. Most seriously, the new rules ended once and for all the popular election of officers of any rank.[32] The minute service was, in effect, a conservative reaction—perhaps a counter-revolution—to the disorder of the egalitarian and uncontrollable independent companies. . . .

Thus, while the gentry wished the ranks of the minute service to be filled with the same men who expressed enthusiasm for the cause through the independent companies, they changed the terms upon which those companies were founded. Although the gentry saw no contradiction in this new organization, the common farmer firmly and soundly rejected the new terms. By all accounts, the minute service failed miserably. . . . The Northampton County Committee of Safety complained of difficulties in completing the minute companies, "people in general being averse to the minute service." A contemporary from Fredericksburg noted on October 20, 1775, that "the Officers of The Minute men are much behind and by all accots will not be able to get the full compliment of men," adding that only "one district" out of fifteen was "compleated. . . ."[33]

The reasons for the failure of the minute service were many, but Gilmer aptly summed them up in the extraordinarily explicit speech he made in the fall of 1775 with which this essay began. In his address, Gilmer took note of all the complaints he had heard about the service among his neighbors and attempted to counter each in order to raise enthusiasm for the minute plan. In doing so, he allowed us a rare and revealing glimpse of the views of the normally "inarticulate" common farmer in Virginia, which, with the evidence of white Virginians' earlier enthusiasm for the independent companies and similar complaints later in the conflict, provides a clear portrait of small farmers' grievances and demands at the start of the war. What emerges quickly and clearly from Gilmer's speech is a picture of a Virginia deeply divided—between those dictating the terms upon which the colony would fight and those expected to bear the brunt of those terms.

In any voluntary call for manpower, inequality will prevail. Military service is a regressive form of taxation as everyone must make the same sacrifice, regardless of wealth. Though the minuteman plan called for "only" twenty days' initial training, small farmers generally found this difficult to manage. . . . They would train for a total of eighty days the first year and sixty days in later years. In return, the minutemen were to receive a modest pay, but only for the time they were out

---

[32]Hening, ed., *Statutes*, IX, 9–53.

[33]Northampton County Committee of Safety to the Continental Congress, Nov. 17, 1775, in "Virginia Legislative Papers," *Virginia Magazine of History and Biography* 14 (Jan. 1907), 253; Robert L. Scribner and Brent Tarter, eds., *Revolutionary Virginia: The Road to Independence, Vol. IV: The Committee of Safety and the Balance of Forces, 1775* (Charlottesville, VA, 1978), 246; Lewis to George Washington, Nov. 14, 1775, in *Pennsylvania Magazine of History and Biography* 53 (Jan. 1929), 93.

for training or in service. Most small farmers felt, in the words of Gilmer, that the service was "a heavy duty."[34]

Those were long periods to be away from farms. But the burden was far less for the policy-making wealthy planter with many slaves and overseers who could labor in his absence than it was for the small farmer. Despite popular images of Virginia as a "slave society," the bulk of the people were not generally slave owners, or owned one or two slaves at most. One recent study concludes that a "majority of the whites stood outside of the slave system at the time of the Revolution."[35] For many slave-holding planters, time away from the estate meant at worst lost profits; for small farmers with no help—whose "Corporeal Labours [were] necessary to sustain their families"—the basic subsistence of the family was at risk. . . . Petitioners from Chesterfield County in 1776 were explicit about who would be most hurt by military service: "the poorer sort who have not a slave to labour for them." Later in the war, one militia unit put the case succinctly: "We generally procure a sustenance for our Selves and families by the labour of our own hands and one days Labour is Necessary for the Next days support." . . .[36]

Yet it was less the military service that small farmers objected to than the attendant training. If enrolled in the minute service, farmers had to attend training or risk being fined. Most small farmers believed that such training was unnecessary and more than "a little burthensome," particularly once they had learned the "most essential parts" of soldiering. Gilmer believed that his neighbors thought that the "military anticks & ceremonies [were] altogether useless."[37] Small farmers wanted, in the words of northern Virginians protesting the new military establishment, to "go and Fight the Battle at once, and not be Shilly Shally, in this way, until all the Poor people are ruined." Indeed, small farmers were willing to fight, just as they had in the independent companies. Membership in a volunteer company called for little training or extra duty, at least none that was not voluntary. . . .[38]

---

[34]Hening, ed., *Statutes*, IX, 20–21; Gilmer, "Address of George Gilmer to the Inhabitants of Albemarle," 122–23, 125, 127.

[35]Richard S. Dunn, "Black Society in the Chesapeake, 1776–1810," in *Slavery and Freedom in the Age of the American Revolution*, ed. Ira Berlin and Ronald Hoffman (Charlottesville, VA, 1983), 67.

[36]For the statement about "Corporeal Labours," see James Innes to Jefferson, Feb. 21, 1781, in *Papers of Thomas Jefferson*, ed. Boyd, IV, 675; Petition from Chesterfield County, in Proceedings of the Fifth Virginia Convention, May 7, 1776, in *Revolutionary Virginia: The Road to Independence, Vol. VII: Independence and the Fifth Convention, 1776*, ed. Brent Tarter (Charlottesville, VA, 1983), 47.

[37]Petition from Chesterfield County, 47; George Gilmer, "Address to the Albemarle County Independent Company," April 18, 1775, in *Revolutionary Virginia*, III, ed. Scribner, 50–51.

[38]Lund Washington to George Washington, Feb. 29, 1776, in *Papers of George Washington*, ed. Abbot et al., III, 396. On the northern Virginians' protest, see Woody Holton and Michael McDonnell, "The Loudoun County Uprising and the Revolution in Virginia," typescript, 1997 (in Michael McDonnell's possession). William Henry to Theodorick Bland, June 17, 1779, Bland Family Papers (Virginia Historical Society). For a sample of the times when many small farmers turned out to fight, see McDonnell, "Politics of Mobilization in Revolutionary Virginia," chap. 7, esp. 246–49.

Small farmers particularly resented training that consisted of "learning" discipline, subordination, and "respect" for now-appointed officers. Moreover, they were being asked to do this and to pay the price of this unfair taxation even as gentlemen did not enlist and exemptions from service benefited the wealthy. . . . Those complaints . . . are key to understanding the mentality of the small farmer during the revolutionary crisis. Dissatisfaction with the conditions and terms of military service was and continued to be a paramount factor in limiting small farmers' desire and willingness to fight.

. . . Small farmers wanted the burden of service equally distributed through all ranks of society, with no exceptions. It was one thing to take time away to fight, but it was another to do so while wealthier neighbors stayed at home. . . . Surges of violent anti-Tory actions coincided with greater manpower demands, and they usually came from below.[39] Discontent with the minute service was capped by the perception that many of . . . the Patriot gentry were not serving. . . . Indeed, even by the end of 1776, it had become a commonplace "objection which many with us have of entering the service . . . that as the Danger of War approaches, men of Fortune refuse to afford that assistance, which is expected from them." Such a perception continued to plague the war effort and helped precipitate an incipient rebellion in the Northern Neck as aggrieved militia complained "that the Rich wanted the Poor to fight for them, to defend there property, whilst they refused to fight for themselves."[40]

Within the minute service, small farmers were equally irritated by the belief that when the gentry did take part in the new military service, it was invariably as appointed officers. Gilmer took note that many "declare the Gentlemen have more at stake and ought to fight to protect it, but that none enter the service but as officers," they being, it was said, "fond of officers' places." . . . Now that rules and regulations had been imposed and rigid discipline was expected, many of the gentry refused to "submit" to "standing in the ranks as common soldiers" as they had in the independent companies. The view of Francis Willis of Frederick County seems typical. In July 1775 he wrote to Robert Carter that he had "no objection to my Sons Henrys entring into the Service in the lowest as an Officer, from his own Behaviour then would depend his being advanced." However, he asserted, "I am absolutely in the strongest Terms against his enlisting as a common Soldier. . . ."[41]

---

[39] Scribner, ed., *Revolutionary Virginia*, III, 490–92, 497. On the timing of anti-Tory actions, see, for example, a petition from Caroline County, submitted during the militia call-outs to counter the 1781 British invasion, in *The Letters and Papers of Edmund Pendleton, 1734–1803*, ed. David John Mays (2 vols., Charlottesville, VA, 1967), I, 363–65.

[40] Gilmer, "Address of George Gilmer to the Inhabitants of Albemarle," 122–23; "Virginia Legislative Papers," *Virginia Magazine of History and Biography* 18 (Jan. 1910), 29–3 1; "Proceedings of a General Court Martial held in Leeds Town," June 18, 1781, Executive Papers (Virginia State Library).

[41] Gilmer, "Address of George Gilmer to the Inhabitants of Albemarle," 122, 124; Isaac, *Transformation of Virginia*, 105; Francis Willis to Robert Carter, July 19, 1775, Carter Family Papers (Virginia Historical Society).

[T]he fact that the gentry would serve only if they served as officers was particularly galling in light of the reintroduction of "distinctions" in the service by way of increased pay for officers. *Nobody* had been paid in the independent companies, but in the new military establishment, everyone was paid on a graded, hierarchical scale. In the minute service, for example, privates were to get a shilling and a quarter per day when in service, whereas their captains were to receive six shillings and their colonels fifteen shillings per day. Many complained of this difference. . . . When a full-scale riot broke out in February 1776, protesters in that county then argued that "the pay of officers and Soldiers should be the same, or what would be still better they should not be paid at all, there is no inducement for a poor Man to Fight, for he has nothing to defend." . . . Those complaints reflected a social vision that was far more egalitarian than the gentry's. . . .[42]

Gentlemen took a different view. They considered a wide pay disparity vital to the maintenance of hierarchy and thus of discipline. "Such as have been already in the service," Gilmer explained, "must know that without some distinction there can be no subordination." . . . Without it, no discipline can be observed; 'tis the life of an army." George Washington later argued that decent pay for officers was needed to preserve a distance between an officer and his men. If the officer was in no way distinguished, his men would "consider and treat him as an equal; and . . . regard him no more than a broomstick, being mixed together as one common herd; [thus] no order, nor no discipline can prevail." . . .[43]

The pay issue was clearly interwoven with the gentry's attempts to reassert control and authority over the revolutionary movement when they could no longer take that command for granted. Indeed, Gilmer and others' emphasis on the need for discipline, subordination, and hierarchy is yet another sign of the dual purpose of the minute service.[44] The gentry desired an army composed of men different from the members of the mercenary body that they opposed, yet a desire to maintain social order and a reliance on traditional means of fighting meant that discipline and distinctions in rank were absolutely vital to the war effort and ultimately, they felt, to the integrity of Virginia society. . . .

Though the gentry went into the conflict hoping that deference would secure their authority, they quickly turned to a greater reliance on law and coercion to maintain control. When the conflict began, the gentry fell back on a wish that deference would be sufficient to rouse popular enthusiasm and to keep it under control. Thus they had hoped in the independent companies to "infuse a martial spirit of emulation" and to "excite others by our Example," and in other military

---

[42]Hening, *Statutes*, IX, 9–10, 21–23; Leven Powell to Sally Powell, Dec. 5, 1775, photocopy (Virginia Historical Society). I would like to thank Woody Holton for this reference. Lund Washington to George Washington, Feb. 29, 1776, in *Papers of George Washington*, ed. Abbot et al., III, 395–96; Gilmer, "Address of George Gilmer to the Inhabitants of Albemarle," 126; Scribner and Tarter, eds., *Revolutionary Virginia*, IV, 142.

[43]Gilmer, "Address of George Gilmer to the Inhabitants of Albemarle," 126, 128; George Washington to the president of Congress, Sept. 24, 1776, in *Writings of George Washington*, ed. Fitzpatrick, VI, 108–9, 110.

[44]Greene, *Imperatives, Behaviors, and Identities*, 200–201.

matters, they hoped for ordinary Virginians' "implicit acquiescence and Concurrence," as Cumberland officials put it, in whatever was recommended. And, as Gilmer noted with regard to the minutemen, the gentry wanted and expected ordinary Virginians to "sacrifice their own ease and interests to their country's wellfare."[45] The gentry, however, wanted them to make sacrifices on imposed terms, especially after they saw the consequences of uncontrolled and unchecked militarism in the independent companies. When appeals to public virtue and deference failed to keep small farmers in check, the gentry tried to reimpose their authority through a traditional military establishment that reasserted the primacy of raw power. . . .

It was precisely the inequality, subordination, dependence, and involuntary service inherent in slavery that farmers were rallying against in the military. Small farmers refused to comply, refused to act deferentially, particularly when asked to make unequal sacrifices. They would serve, but not out of deference to what the gentry wanted, and only if they could do it on their own terms. George Washington himself perhaps best summed up the problems in the clash of cultures between the gentry and yeomanry. Remonstrating against the idea of raising "volunteers" in Virginia a little later in the war, Washington claimed that "Those who engage in Arms under that denomination . . . are uneasy, impatient of Command, ungovernable; and, claiming to themselves a sort of superior merit, generally assume, not only the Priviledge of thinking, but to do as they please." In their demands for no differences in pay, or no pay at all, the inhabitants of Albemarle, Loudoun, and other counties demanded just that. They demanded, not just the "Priviledge" but the right "of thinking" and, while making sacrifices, of doing "as they please."[46]

. . . Military preparations in 1775 and the subsequent history of wartime mobilization reveal a coherent pattern in small farmers' expectations and demands. They . . . wished for less hierarchy and subordination and more democratic, or at least consensual, modes of organization. Moreover, small farmers consistently demonstrated their commitment to "fare play," as one irate Piedmont carpenter-farmer later put it—not only equality within the service but also a fair distribution of the burden of service through all ranks of society. If these demands were not met, ordinary Virginians could simply refuse to serve, as they did in the minutemen, forcing the gentry to recognize that they could not take unquestioning and deferential popular support for granted.[47]

---

[45]Mason, "Fairfax County Militia Association," 210; Mason, "Remarks on Annual Elections for the Fairfax Independent Company," 229; "Proceedings of the Committees of Safety of Cumberland and Isle of Wight Counties," 16–17; Gilmer, "Address of George Gilmer to the Inhabitants of Albemarle," 122–23, 125, 127.

[46]George Washington to Patrick Henry, April 13, 1777, in *Writings of George Washington*, ed. Fitzpatrick, VII, 407–9.

[47]Tillson, "Militia and Popular Political Culture in the Upper Valley of Virginia," 306. See also Tillson, *Gentry and Common Folk*, chaps. 3–5. The comment about "fare play" was made in the heat of an incident over the apprehension of a deserter. "Information," Oct. 6, 1777, box 1, 1770s–, Suit Papers, Cumberland County Court Records (Virginia State Library).

The failure of the minutemen in Virginia had important consequences, both in the military short run and the political long run. Militarily, the refusal of small farmers to enter into the minute service in the expected numbers left the colony defenseless, threatened, and in the "greatest confusion" at the very moment when Governor Dunmore launched his counteroffensive . . . and officially proclaimed all slaves who would join with him against their masters free. In a panic, the gentry effectively scrapped the minuteman plan in the December 1775 convention and instead asked Congress to accept and pay for six more battalions of regular full-time troops. . . . [T]he gentry pleaded with Congress to authorize and to pay for more regular troops because the minutemen had failed to attract sufficient citizen-soldiers to defend the colony. The new professional troops raised were . . . stationed around the frontiers of Virginia, in a defensive posture with full-time pay. Thus they were literally to take the place of the minutemen but were paid by Congress and composed of the "lower sort" who would serve full time and for regular pay.[48]

The gentry thus abandoned the ideological ideal of the citizen-soldier and turned to a more traditional force of paid professional troops, and to a more traditional pool of people—the "poor, the unemployed, and the unlucky," the young, men "who could best be spared, and will be most serviceable," or, in the words of one of the gentry, "those Lazy fellows who lurk about and are pests to Society"— offering economic incentives in return for disciplined and obeisant service. . . . Thus small farmers' refusal to act as the gentry asked at a critical moment in the war shaped the contours of Virginia's military policy for the duration of the war.[49]

. . . Persistent and violent resistance to attempts to raise a full-time regular army also forced leaders to adopt destructive inflationary measures and seriously frustrated mobilization. Indeed, until the war moved south in 1780–1781, the gentry had to rely mainly on large bounties and material inducements to get men to serve in the army. Such policies contributed immeasurably to the horrendous inflation that plagued Virginia's wartime economy. . . .[50]

In the military crises of 1780 and 1781, when the Virginia Assembly was forced to implement a more universal draft policy that targeted the middling as well as the lower sort, resistance to military service—on the gentry's terms—once

---

[48]Lewis to George Washington, Nov. 14, 1775, *Pennsylvania Magazine of History and Biography* 53 (Jan. 1929), 93; Hening, ed., *Statutes*, IX, 86, 89,139; Scribner and Tarter, eds., *Revolutionary Virginia*, V, 190–91. On the struggle over the addition of Virginia's new troops to the Continental establishment, the situation in Virginia in fall 1775, and Dunmore's proclamation, see Selby, *Revolution in Virginia*, 58–79; and John Robert Sellers, "The Virginia Continental Line, 1775–1780" (Ph.D. diss., Tulane University, 1968), 54–63.

[49]Titus, *Old Dominion at War*, 45; Hening, *Statutes*, IX, 275–80; Edmund Pendleton to William Woodford, June 28, 1777, in *Letters and Papers of Edmund Pendleton*, ed. Mays, I, 215; John Chilton to his brother [Charles Chilton?], Aug. 11, 1777, in Keith Family of Woodburn, Fauquier County, Papers (Virginia Historical Society); Robert Honyman Diary, Jan. 2, 1776, microfilm f.l (Alderman Library),, Aug. 29, 1777, ff. 154–56.

[50]Pendleton to James Madison, Sept. 25, 1779, in *Letters and Papers of Edmund Pendleton*, ed. Mays, I, 308–9.

again became widespread. Pressure from below thoroughly disabled enforced mobilization in 1780 and 1781. Draft laws collapsed under the weight of "violent and riotous" behavior and the threat thereof, although ordinary Virginians again turned out as volunteers in more local skirmishes when necessary. Against mandatory laws Virginians reacted with evasive and resistance tactics. . . .

Problems over mobilization . . . also politicized small farmers. The farmers' frustration spilled over into other, more political realms. Called upon to make sacrifices for the Patriot cause, ordinary Virginians demanded a say in how that cause should be run. . . . Ordinary Virginians' politicization in the independent companies and the protest against the minutemen also help explain the popularity of Thomas Paine's *Common Sense*. . . . Events in Virginia in 1775 may have created fertile soil for a pamphlet that urged not just independence from Britain but also the creation of a new and far more democratic government. . . . The popular sovereignty and egalitarianism that small farmers in Virginia had called for in their military organization and in their protests over bearing the burden of the war were endorsed in Paine's *Common Sense*, which did more than any other document to equate independence and republicanism in the minds of the American people. . . .[51]

Such feelings found an outlet in April 1776, when an election was held for delegates to a new general convention. . . . Years later, Edmund Randolph recalled that the election of delegates for that convention, which ultimately decided on secession, "depended in very many, if not in a majority, of the counties upon the candidates pledging themselves . . . to sever . . . the colonies from Great Britain." Many incumbents who refused to endorse independence were turned out. . . . Altogether, forty-eight seats, or 38.1 percent of the convention, changed. . . . In a colony unused to contested elections and legislative turnover, particularly in the run-up to rebellion, these results were significant, and they caused anxiety amongst the gentry.[52]

Certainly, military issues were at the forefront of many of the contests. . . . Echoing the concerns of such members of the gentry as Gilmer and Washington over the "independence" of the volunteers, [Landon] Carter feared that the popular feeling was for an independence defined as "a form of Government, that by being independt of the rich men eve[r]y man would then be able to do as he pleasd"—an "independence," he confided in his diary, "in which no Gentleman should have the least share." . . . It was this convention that instructed Virginia's

[51]Jan. 22, 26, 1776, entries in *Journal of Nicholas Cresswell*, 136; March 12 and 28, 1776, entries in *Diary of Landon Carter*, ed. Greene, II, 999, 1006. On the impact of *Common Sense* in Virginia, see Holton and McDonnell, "Loudoun County Uprising."

[52]Edmund Randolph, *History of Virginia*, ed. Arthur H. Shaffer (Charlottesville, VA, 1970), 234; Josiah Parker to Landon Carter, April 14, 1776, Sabine Hall Papers; Robert Brent to R. H. Lee, April 28, 1776, in *Lee Family Papers*, ed. Paul P. Hoffman (microfilm, University of Virginia Library, Charlottesville, VA, 1966); Scribner, ed., *Revolutionary Virginia*, VI, 287–91. On the relatively quiet prerevolutionary elections, see John G. Kolp, "The Dynamics of Electoral Competition in Pre-Revolutionary Virginia," *William and Mary Quarterly* 49 (Oct. 1992), 652–74.

delegates in Congress to propose that the thirteen colonies declare independence and that began to frame a new, republican, government.[53]

Yet the politics of mobilization did not end with independence. Persistent and widespread resistance to gentry policy . . . prompted ordinary Virginians to take their grievances to the polls. During the war years a high rate of legislative turnover, most often coinciding with unpopular mobilization policies, especially draft laws, continued to mark Virginia politics, as "the people interest themselves in Elections at this time more than ever." By 1780, many gentry were complaining that the assembly was full of "men of mean abilities & no rank" or too many "ignorant or obscure". . . .[54] Such changes in the assembly may explain why new mobilization laws weighed heavily on the wealthy. . . .

. . . The prewar political consensus that had prevailed among elites vanished after the war. One recent study concludes that the "most striking thing about Virginia politics in the postwar period is that the harmony so characteristic of the prewar years is completely absent," a contrast made all the "more arresting" because of the continuity of membership.[55] Postwar Virginia was a changed place, and gentlemen as well as the lower and middling sorts thought differently about the political culture in which they lived, at the local, state, and national levels. . . . Postwar politics showed a move away from deferential politics and marked "the beginnings of sustained conflict between legislative factions over public policy, and of issue-oriented appeals to constituents."[56]

Small farmers left an indelible mark on the course and direction of the revolutionary movement. . . . In Virginia, both the middling and lower sorts used the war in different ways, at different times, in different places, to make their voices heard, to manipulate gentry attitudes and policies and to change the patterns of social interaction and political culture in the new state subtly but profoundly. . . .

Indeed, as historians have shown, all across the colonies and new states, internal conflict and social upheaval made resistance and rebellion a dual revolution, and never was this more apparent and dramatic than during the armed conflict itself. In all the colonies, the varied experiences of the middling and

---

[53]Landon Carter to George Washington, May 9, 1776, in *Papers of George Washington*, ed. Abbot et al., IV, 236–37, 240–41; May 1, 1776, entry in *Diary of Landon Carter*, ed. Greene, II, 1031; Holton, *Forced Founders*, esp. part III.

[54]Honyman Diary, April 15, July 4, 1780, ff. 395, 414; George Mason, "Remarks on the Proposed Bill for Regulating the Elections of the Members of the General Assembly," [June 1, 1780], in *Papers of George Mason*, ed. Rutland, II, 629–31, 631–32n; McDonnell, "Politics of Mobilization in Revolutionary Virginia," chap. 4.

[55]Sloan and Onuf, "Politics, Culture, and the Revolution in Virginia," 280.

[56]Ibid., 279. See also Norman K. Risjord, *Chesapeake Politics, 1781–1800* (New York, 1978); Norman K. Risjord, "How the 'Common Man' Voted in Jefferson's Virginia," in *America: The Middle Period; Essays in Honor of Bernard Mayo*, ed. John B. Boles (Charlottesville, VA, 1973), 36–64; and Jackson T. Main, "Sections and Politics in Virginia, 1781–1787," *William and Mary Quarterly* 12 (Jan. 1955), 96–112. See also Steven James Sarson, "Wealth, Poverty, and Labor in the Tobacco Plantation South: Prince George's County, Maryland, in the Early National Era" (Ph.D. diss., Johns Hopkins University, 1998).

lower sorts in the military and their varied outcomes—not always positive—brought revolutionary change. The Minutemen of Massachusetts went to war to retain their traditional way of life and ended up transformed by participation in the war. In Pennsylvania the most radical gains were made, as the lower sort in Philadelphia were mobilized and politicized and used their new bargaining power to affect politics and constitution making. Militia in backcountry Pennsylvania, however, used the Revolution to protect and expand their family farms and to intensify a racially motivated war with neighboring Native Americans. Throughout the colonies and new states, many poorer or younger whites and blacks joined local forces or the Continental Army in the hope of securing a steady income or a propertied stake in the new republic, while broadening their social and political horizons. . . .[57] Wherever the net has been cast so far, it is clear that while resistance and rebellion may have resulted in a war for independence, social conflict and internal upheaval made for a revolutionary war that profoundly changed American society.

---

[57]See Gross, *Minutemen and Their World*; Rosswurm, *Arms, Country, and Class*; Knouff, "Arduous Service"; and Edward C. Papenfuse and Gregory A. Stiverson, "General Smallwood's Recruits: The Peacetime Career of the Revolutionary War Private," *William and Mary Quarterly* 30 (Jan. 1973), 117–32.

Michael McDonnell

I was born in Wales and grew up in Canada, where I had some great history teachers at both high school and at the University of Ottawa (where I did my BA in history and philosophy). They were passionate about history and politics and cared deeply about their subjects. I then returned to Britain to do a DPhil at Balliol College, Oxford. While there, I learned a great deal about class and inequality and after a long research trip to Virginia, began to think very differently about race and class in the United States. I've always been interested in social history, but I think it is important to connect what's happening at the local level with larger political developments and ideas. Far too much of what we know about the past, and especially the eighteenth century, comes from elite sources. It is important to question these and try to write more balanced history that encompasses a range of perspectives and views, however difficult that might be at times. I have tried to do this in the book that followed this article, entitled *The Politics of War: Race, Class, and Conflict in Revolutionary Virginia* (2007), and another I've just finished called *Masters of Empire: Great Lakes Indians and the Making of America* (2015). I'm now happily ensconced at the University of Sydney, Australia, and have started another book looking at the Revolutionary War experiences of ordinary Americans. Research and writing American history from afar can be challenging at times, but I think it also gives me a different perspective on it. My students here also keep me on my toes by raising challenging questions—but that's what I love about history.

QUESTIONS FOR CONSIDERATION

1. According to McDonnell, how does resistance to minutemen duty by "lower" and "middling sorts" challenge "the traditional and enduring picture" of Revolution-era Americans?

2. How did the beginning of the Revolution change the social makeup of voluntary companies in Virginia? Describe how these changes transformed the power structure of these volunteer companies.

3. McDonnell calls the movement to create minutemen service "a conservative reaction." How did colonial elites initially conceive the minutemen service in Virginia as a form of social control?

4. What factors inclined small farmers to reject the new minutemen structure? What factors forced the gentry to request funding from Congress for a standing army? To what extent were these factors a result of social tensions within colonial Virginia itself?

5. Compare McDonnell's argument with Gary Nash's in "The Transformation of Urban Politics 1700–1765." What are some similarities in the tensions described in each article? What are some important differences? What do these similarities and differences tell us about the contexts in which the events described in each article take place?

CHAPTER SEVEN

◦◦

Aristocracy Assailed:
The Ideology of Backcountry
Anti-Federalism[1]

Saul Cornell

Historical accounts of the ratification of the federal Constitution have viewed Anti-Federalism through the eyes of the leading political figures who opposed adoption of the new frame of government. By focusing too narrowly on the delegates to the state ratifying conventions and leading Anti-Federalist politicians, studies of ratification have underestimated the depth of hostility to the new Constitution characteristic of grassroots Anti-Federalism. Discussions of Anti-Federalist political thought have also been obscured by the tendency to treat Anti-Federalism as a monolithic ideology.[2]

Since the Progressive Era, historians have vigorously debated who was more democratic: the Anti-Federalists or their Federalist opponents. Neo-progressive historians like Jackson Turner Main have cast the Anti-Federalists as the first genuine democratic populists and the Federalists as opponents of further democratization of American society. Against this view, consensus historians have generally followed the lead of Cecelia M. Kenyon who claimed that the Anti-Federalists

---

[1]Interested students are encouraged to read this essay in the original form. Saul Cornell, "Aristocracy Assailed: The Ideology of Backcountry Anti-Federalism," *Journal of American History* 76 (4) (March 1990), 1148–72.

[2]John P. Kaminski, "Antifederalism and the Perils of Homogenized History: A Review Essay," *Rhode Island History* 42 (Feb. 1983), 30–37. On the different connotations of the hyphenated and unhyphenated spellings (Antifederalist or anti-Federalist), see Forrest McDonald, "The Anti-Federalists, 1781–1789," *Wisconsin Magazine of History* 46 (Spring 1963), 206–14. The former usage implies substantial uniformity among opponents of the Constitution; the latter suggests little unity beyond a common antipathy to the Federalists' scheme of government. I have not followed McDonald's use of the lowercase a in "anti" because I believe that it has the effect of denying commonalities among opponents of the Constitution. In this article I have adopted the term Anti-Federalist as middle position between the two poles. When considering an abstract political theory derived from the opposition I have employed the term *Anti-Federalism*.

were "men of little faith" who distrusted the common people as much as their elected representatives.[3]

To understand the thinking of the opponents of the Constitution, especially their attitude toward democracy, we must abandon the idea that Anti-Federalists were united by a single, homogeneous political creed. Instead, we must identify the various subgroups within the Anti-Federalist ranks and explore the various ideologies that led individuals to oppose the Constitution. . . .

While east/west tensions accounted for much of the animosity felt by back-country folk toward the Constitution, it is also important to acknowledge the role of class antagonisms in shaping a distinctive populist variant of Anti-Federalist ideology. . . .

The leading Anti-Federalist representatives of the western interests, individuals like William Findley, were among the most democratic figures in Pennsylvania politics. Yet despite their democratic sympathies, men like Findley were members of a recognizable political elite, even if they were far closer to the social status of the people they represented than were members of the more established eastern political elites. The individuals who served in state government were members of a mediating class that stood well above the common folk. To uncover grassroots Anti-Federalist thinking it is essential to move beyond the lesser elite who dominated politics in the backcountry and to restore a voice to a segment of Anti-Federalism that has been rendered mute by the elitist bias of previous scholarship.[4]

The Carlisle Riot of 1788 affords a rich occasion for comparing the ideology of Anti-Federalists of the better and inferior sorts. Since violence in backcountry Pennsylvania attracted the attention of prominent Anti-Federalist politicians, the riot and its aftermath provide an unusual opportunity to contrast popular and elite attitudes among the opponents of the new Constitution. Furthermore, since events in Carlisle were often linked to Shays's Rebellion in the minds of contemporaries, rural unrest in backcountry Pennsylvania can also reveal the depth of concern over anarchy that united the Federalist and the Anti-Federalist political elites.

---

[3]Jackson Turner Main, *The Antifederalists: Critics of the Constitution, 1781–1788* (Chapel Hill, NC, 1961). Lee Benson, *Turner and Beard: American Historical Writing Reconsidered* (Glencoe, IL, 1960). Cecelia M. Kenyon, "Men of Little Faith: The Anti-Federalists on the Nature of Representative Government," *William and Mary Quarterly* 12 (Jan. 1955), 3–43; Martin Diamond, "Democracy and The Federalist: A Reconsideration of the Framers' Intent," *American Political Science Review* 53 (March 1959), 52–68; and James H. Hutson, "Country, Court, and Constitution: Antifederalism and the Historians," *William and Mary Quarterly* 38 (July 1981), 337–68. Herbert J. Storing, *What the Anti-Federalists Were For* (Chicago, 1981).

[4]On William Findley's political thought, see Gordon S. Wood, "Interests and Disinterestedness in the Making of the Constitution," *Beyond Confederation: Origins of the Constitution and American National Identity*, ed. Richard Beeman et al. (Chapel Hill, NC, 1987), 69–109.

THE CARLISLE RIOT

. . . Local politics in Carlisle were colored by the intensity of partisan conflict throughout Pennsylvania. The area west of the Susquehanna, including Carlisle, was a stronghold of the egalitarian political traditions associated with the state constitution of 1776. Much of the controversy in Pennsylvania politics during the decade after the Revolution revolved around proposals to revise the state constitution and replace its unicameral legislature with a bicameral system. At the root of this conflict was an argument about the role of representation in a republican government.[5] The debate turned on the question of how much democracy could be sustained in a republic before it would degenerate into mobocracy, tyranny, or aristocracy. Leading citizens in Carlisle, like many notable political figures throughout the United States who would support the Federalist cause, were concerned about the destabilizing impact of the more democratic aspects of revolutionary ideology on American society. Like their counterparts in other parts of the country, nationalists in Carlisle sought to counter the forces of democratization by championing the idea of ordered liberty, a deferential conception of politics, and the ideal of disinterested republican virtue. These positions set them against the popular traditions of egalitarianism that had played a crucial role in the revolutionary struggle against Britain and that typified grassroots Anti-Federalism. . . .[6]

At about five o'clock in the evening on December 26, 1787, a group of Federalists gathered in Carlisle's center for a celebration marking Pennsylvania's ratification of the new federal Constitution. The mood was festive: drums beat and bells rang as Federalists awaited the cannon salute that would honor the new Constitution. The celebratory mood shifted, however, when an angry crowd of Anti-Federalists came on the scene and ordered the Federalists to disband. Confident in the superiority of their cause and undaunted by their opponents, the Federalists resolutely stood their ground. . . .[7]

Although the Federalists had won a resounding victory in the state ratifying convention, the area west of the Susquehanna was an acknowledged Anti-Federalist stronghold. Carlisle itself was divided; the town's elite was strongly Federalist while popular sympathies lay largely with the Anti-Federalists. As one observer noted, "in Cumberland county all are against it, except a small group in Carlisle."[8]

---

[5]On Pennsylvania politics, see Robert L. Brunhouse, *The Counter-Revolution in Pennsylvania, 1776–1790* (Harrisburg, PA, 1942); Douglas M. Arnold, "Political Ideology and the Internal Revolution in Pennsylvania: 1776–1790" (Ph.D. diss., Princeton University, 1976); and Richard A. Ryerson, "Republican Theory and Partisan Reality in Revolutionary Pennsylvania: Toward a New View of the Constitutionalist Party," in *Sovereign States in an Age of Uncertainty*, ed. Ronald Hoffman and Peter J. Albert (Charlottesville, VA, 1981), 95–133.

[6]Merrill Jensen, John P. Kaminski, Gaspare J. Saladino, *The Documentary History of the Ratification of the Constitution*, (Madison: Wisconsin Historical Society Press, 1976).

[7]Jensen et al., eds., *Documentary History of the Ratification*, II, 671, 675.

[8]*Pennsylvania Gazette*, March 26, 1788.

When the two groups met in the streets of Carlisle, tensions were already high. The Anti-Federalists were angry and easily provoked; they were still smarting from their recent defeat in the state convention. Federalist arrogance exacerbated matters. When confronted by local Anti-Federalist opposition, Federalists insisted that "they would fire the cannon in spite of any who would oppose them; and if they would not clear the way, they would blow them up." The Anti-Federalists responded by pelting Federalists with pieces of wood and the confrontation escalated into a full-scale riot. Armed with staves and bludgeons, the Anti-Federalists easily routed the Federalists and drove them from the scene.

At noon the next day, the Federalists gathered once more to celebrate; this time the heavily armed group succeeded in hailing the new government with a volley of musket fire and an artillery salute. Afterwards, the Federalists retired to a tavern where they toasted leading Federalists, the new frame of government, and the future prosperity of the United States. Carlisle Federalists raised their glasses to demonstrate their respect for order and their deference to their leaders, men like George Washington and James Wilson. They praised the prospects of greatness awaiting a powerful federal union, when "the flag of the United States" would "fly triumphant in all the ports of the world. . . ."[9]

In response to the Federalist demonstration, the Anti-Federalists mounted a counterdemonstration. Led by a local militia captain, the opponents of the Constitution staged a procession complete with effigies of James Wilson and of Pennsylvania's chief justice, Thomas McKean, men who had helped secure ratification in Pennsylvania. The Federalist leaders were treated as the leaders of a conspiracy to foist an aristocratic government on the people. Such treachery demanded severe punishment, and the Anti-Federalist crowd overlooked no detail in preparing the figures for public judgment. The two effigies were dressed in garb appropriate to their high stations. A local Federalist reported that "the Effigie of the Chief Justics was pretty well Dressed a good Coat but not black a pretty good hat & wig & Rufld Shirt." The crowd jeered as the figures of the two Federalists were paraded through town in a cart and repeatedly lashed. After being humiliated before the assembled crowd, the two effigies were hanged and then delivered to a funeral pyre while "the dead bell tolled until they were totally consumed to ashes. . . ."[10]

Anti-Federalists in Carlisle showed little interest in the vision of national greatness that inspired many Federalists. Rather than accept the Federalist ideal of a large republican empire administered by a small elite, Anti-Federalists defended the ideal of a confederation of small republics in which republican liberty and popular participation were the defining characteristics of political life. The nature of the Anti-Federalists' political protest provides one measure of the ideological distance separating them from Federalists. Not content to defer to their social betters, local Anti-Federalists drew upon popular traditions of "rough music" to express their resentment against the elitism of their opponents. An essential feature of the plebeian cultural traditions of the Anglo-American world,

---

[9]Jensen et al., eds., *Documentary History of the Ratification*, II, 672–73, 681.

[10]Ibid., 675, 678; see also microform supplement, doc. nos. 271, 409.

the rituals of rough music, such as tarring and feathering, were usually administered to individuals who had violated commonly accepted community values.[11]

The ritual use of effigies by the rioters was designed to affirm the values of
community, equality, and democracy. The public humiliation of the figures of
Wilson and McKean provided a focus for popular animosity and allowed the protesters in Carlisle to identify two individuals who, they believed, were leaders in
the Federalists' attempt to foist an aristocratic government on the people. The two
Federalist leaders were subjected to a symbolic trial and executed for conspiring to
undermine the liberty of the people. Like legal punishment, the ritual was designed
to reaffirm the values of the community and to provide a warning. In the minds of
the protesters, the battle to defeat the Constitution was not yet over. . . .

The colorful plebeian rituals of status reversal enacted by Anti-Federalists
also served to undercut the deferential political message implicit in Federalist
ideology. Anti-Federalists reacted angrily to the aristocratic leanings of their
opponents and took every opportunity to berate Federalists for their "proud and
Lordly" ideas. Many Anti-Federalists resented the attempt by the Federalists to
use the prestige of great men to gain support for the Constitution. . . .[12]

The actions of the rioters were an explicit rejection of Federalist pleas for deference. The men who took to the streets in Carlisle accepted the warning of the
influential Anti-Federalist author "Centinel," who noted that "the wealthy and
ambitious . . . in every community think they have a right to lord it over their
fellow creatures." Indeed, they followed his advice quite literally and refused "to
yield an implicit assent to the opinions of those characters. . . ." The rioters proudly
asserted that they "would pay no respect to their rank, nor make any allowance for
their delicate constitutions," adding that "it was laughable to see Lawyers, Doc-
tors, Colonels, Captains & c. & c. leave the scene of their rejoicing in such haste."[13]

With the community bitterly divided by the riot, local authorities faced a
difficult problem: Should the instigators of the riot, the Anti-Federalists, be

---

[11]E. P. Thompson, "The Moral Economy of the English Crowd in the Eighteenth Century,"
Past & Present, 50 (Feb. 1971), 76–136; E. P. Thompson, "Patrician Society, Plebeian Culture," *Jour-
nal of Social History* 7 (Summer 1974), 382–405; and Alfred E. Young, "English Plebeian Culture and
Eighteenth-Century American Radicalism," in *The Origins of Anglo-American Radicalism*, ed.
Margaret Jacob and James Jacob (London, 1984), 185–212. Pauline Maier, *From Resistance to Revo-
lution: Colonial Radicals and the Development of American Opposition to Britain, 1756–1776*
(New York, 1972); Edward Countryman, "The Problem of the Early American Crowd," *Journal of
American Studies* 7 (April 1973), 77–90; and Paul Gilje, *The Road to Mobocracy: Popular Disorder in
New York City, 1763–1834* (Chapel Hill, NC, 1987).

[12]Aristocrotis [William Petrikin], *The Government of Nature Delineated; or, An Exact Picture of
the New Federal Constitution* (1788), in *The Complete Anti-Federalist*, ed. Herbert J. Storing (6 vols.,
Chicago, 1981), III, 196–213. Storing failed to identify the author as William Petrikin. For evidence
supporting the attribution, see Jensen et al., eds., *Documentary History of the Ratification*, II, 674.

[13][Samuel Bryan], "Centinel," in *Complete Anti-Federalist*, ed. Storing, II, 137. The "Centinel"
was among the most widely distributed Anti-Federalist works and was especially popular among
Carlisle Anti-Federalists. William Petrikin, a leader of the riot, wrote to a prominent Pennsylvania
Anti-Federalist to request "a few of the Centinals" since "they are much admired here." William
Petrikin to John Nicholson, Feb. 24, 1788, in *Documentary History of the Ratification*, ed. Jensen et
al., II, 695; ibid., microform supplement, doc. no. 409.

prosecuted to the full extent of the law or should the incident be forgotten in the hope of restoring harmony to the community? The prospect of a divisive trial did not appeal to a number of leading Federalists. . . . Nonetheless, depositions were taken, and on January 23, 1788, a warrant for the arrest of the leaders of the Anti-Federalist mob was issued.[14]

The twenty-one men named in the writ were rounded up for prosecution and charged with assembling "in a riotous, routous, and unlawful manner" and fomenting "great terror and disturbance on the inhabitants of the said borough of Carlisle." The presiding judge in the case offered the defendants the opportunity to leave jail on bail. Seven prisoners refused the offer, proclaiming that since "they were prosecuted to gratify party spite, they were determined not to enter bail on the occasion."[15]

Local Anti-Federalists turned to the community for support. Organizing themselves through the militia, the Anti-Federalists elected representatives to meet with local Federalist leaders and negotiate the release of the jailed Anti-Federalists. A number of respectable persons on both sides of the question, fearful of further violence, signed a petition to release the prisoners. After the agreement was formally ratified, a contingent of militia numbering between two hundred and fifty and fifteen hundred men marched to the jail to secure the release of the prisoners, singing a song composed by the rioters that mocked the Federalists' aristocratic bearing. . . . Anti-Federalists rejoiced at their symbolic victory. The huge crowd that marched on the jail to secure the release of prisoners was a visible affirmation of the strength of the Anti-Federalist cause. The parade provided another occasion to humiliate their opponents and thereby to demonstrate popular hostility toward the Federalist vision of order and deference.[16]

Political rituals provide one set of clues that help reveal the underlying political dynamic at work in Carlisle. While Federalists engaged in rituals of deference, the Anti-Federalists employed rituals of status reversal. Contemporary observers on both sides of the ratification debate were struck by the clear class divisions that separated Federalists from Anti-Federalists in the Pennsylvania backcountry. The hostility to the new Constitution was most acute among men of the "lower and middling sort." One hostile observer noted that rioters were small property holders who "have but few lots. . . ."[17]

Evidence obtained from the 1787 tax lists for Carlisle provides an unusual opportunity to assess the social origins of Anti-Federalism in one backcountry

---

[14]Walter Stewart to William Irvine, Jan. 30, 1788, in *Documentary History of the Ratification*, ed. Jensen et al., II, microform supplement, doc. no. 380.

[15]Pennsylvania Supreme Court to Sheriff Charles Leeper, Jan. 23, 1788, in *Documentary History of the Ratification*, ed. Jensen et al., II, 685. The prisoners' statement is reprinted, ibid., 700.

[16]Ibid., 708. Ibid., 699. John Montgomery to James Wilson, March 2, 1788, ibid., 701–6; John Shippen to Joseph Shippen, March 3, 1788, ibid., 706–7; and ibid., microform supplement, doc. nos. 491, 544, 554, 556, 629, 652.

[17]"John Penn's Journal of a Visit to Reading, Harrisburg, Carlisle, and Lancaster in 1788," *Pennsylvania Magazine of History and Biography* 3 (1879), 284–95, esp. 292. Montgomery to Benjamin Rush, June 12, 1787, in *Documentary History of the Ratification*, ed. Jensen et al., II, microform supplement, doc. no. 691.

Table 7.1   Median Level of Assessed Tax for Selected Taxpayers in Carlisle, 1787

GROUP	MEDIAN TAX (£)	INTERQUARTILE RANGE (£)	N
All taxpayers (includes freemen and householders)	68.6	19.7–176.2	281
Householders	100.0	50.0–229.35	226
Federalist petitioners	749.1	322.8–802.69	9
Anti-Federalist petitioners	187.0	93.6–245.6	8
Anti-Federalist rioters	103.8	27.5–125.3	14

Source: Cumberland County Tax Lists 1787, microfilm copy (Historical Society of Pennsylvania, Philadelphia).
Note: The assessment was made in pounds; I have converted shillings to a decimal figure in pounds. The interquartile range represents the range over which the central 50 percent of the data is spread.

locality. (See Table 7.1.) The Carlisle rioters represented a cross section of the population that ranged from freemen to moderately prosperous yeomen. Anti-Federalists who signed petitions to gain the release of the rioters tended to be somewhat better-off and were concentrated within the ranks of the middling and the prosperous yeomanry. Anti-Federalism in Carlisle, however, drew its most vocal support from the lower and middling inhabitants of the town. By contrast, Federalists who signed the same petition were largely drawn from the wealthiest stratum of Carlisle society. The median assessed tax for those Federalists was roughly four times as much as that of Anti-Federalist petitioners and roughly seven times that of the jailed rioters. Both the striking class-conscious rhetoric of the rioters and the tax lists suggest that there was an important class dimension to the struggle between Federalists and Anti-Federalists in Carlisle.[18]

Table 7.2   Frequency of Selected Accusations in Anti-Federalist Rhetoric[a]

CATEGORY	%
Aristocracy	49
Well born	35
Great names	23

Source: These figures are based upon content analysis of 80 Anti-Federalist attacks on the Consitution or its supporters published in the Pennsylvania press between September 26 and December 26, 1787, appearing in Merrill Jensen et al., *The Documentary History of the Ratification of the Constitution* (16 vols., Madison, 1976–), and its microform supplement.
[a]Since each article usually contained more than one epithet, the percentages listed above add up to more than 100%.

---

[18]Cumberland County Tax Lists 1781, microfilm copy (Historical Society of Pennsylvania, Philadelphia). Only fourteen of twenty-one rioters were found on the Carlisle tax lists. The seven missing individuals may have been either too poor to make it onto the evaluations or nonresidents. The names of Federalist and Anti-Federalist petitioners were obtained from a petition signed by respectable persons associated with each side, and the names of the rioters were obtained from the arrest warrant, see notes 13 and 12 above. Figures for householders were obtained by excluding from the tax lists the figures for freemen (that is, nonhouseholders).

ANTI-FEDERALISM AND PLEBEIAN POPULISM

... The difference between attacks on aristocracy and those on natural aristocracy illustrates an aspect of the ratification debate that has often been confused in recent scholarly discussions. One could attack the new Constitution for concentrating too much power in the hands of government and thus establishing an aristocracy of governmental officials, or one could attack the Constitution for favoring the interests of a specific social class, loosely defined as the natural aristocracy. The difference between the two critiques is crucial to understanding Anti-Federalism as a heterogeneous ideology. Concern about the dangers of aristocracy was a republican commonplace and was closely tied to the fear of corruption that was central to republican discourse. Virtually all Americans accepted the legitimacy of that concern even if they disagreed about how to guard against such danger. The problem of natural aristocracy was far more complicated and politically divisive.[19]

The most systematic discussion of the interrelated concepts of aristocracy and natural aristocracy by any Anti-Federalist can be found in the writings of the "Federal Farmer," who observed that:

> There are three kinds of aristocracy spoken of in this country—the first is a constitutional one, which does not exist in the United States. . . . the second is an aristocratic faction; a junto of unprincipled men, often distinguished for their wealth and abilities, who combine together and make their object their private interests and aggrandizement.[20]

The third category in the "Federal Farmer's" scheme, natural aristocracy, was far more difficult to define. The "Federal Farmer" acknowledged that the exact composition of this class "is in some degree arbitrary; we may place men on one side of this line, which others may place on the other." The "Federal Farmer" estimated that the class numbered about "four or five thousand men," including high-ranking politicians like state governors; the most important officers of Congress; state senators; the officers of the army and militia; superior judges; and the most eminent professional men, wealthy merchants, and large property holders. In large measure this class was defined against the middling sort, which included the yeomanry, subordinate officers of the military and militia, mechanics, and many of the traders and merchants. The bottom category in the Anti-Federalist's scheme was the inferior sort, which included the dependent poor and unskilled laborers. Although few Anti-Federalists were as systematic in their thinking as the "Federal Farmer," many shared his belief that natural aristocracy was best understood as a distinctive, if ill-defined, social class, which the Constitution clearly favored.

The concept of natural aristocracy also figured prominently in Federalist thinking. The most detailed analysis occurred in John Adams's *Defence of the*

---

[19]E. P. Thompson, "Eighteenth-Century English Society: Class Struggle without Class," *Social History* 3 (May 1978), 133–66. Craig Calhoun, *The Question of Class Struggle: Social Foundations of Popular Radicalism during the Industrial Revolution* (Chicago, 1982). Gary J. Schmitt and Robert H. Webking, "Revolutionaries, Antifederalists, and Federalists: Comments on Gordon Wood's Understanding of the American Founding," *Political Science Reviewer* 9 (Fall 1979), 195–229, esp. 216–18.

[20]"Federal Farmer," in *Complete Anti-Federalist*, ed. Storing, II, 267.

Constitutions of Government of the United States of America. Adams identified a class of natural aristocrats whose wealth, education, reputation, and talents set them apart from the common people. Adams defended the salutary effects that this class would have on government if its members were sequestered in an upper house of the legislature and allowed to play their natural role as a check on a popularly elected lower house.

When Adams and other Federalists discussed natural aristocracy they often blurred two distinct interpretations of who ought to be included as its members: society's social and political elite or men of wisdom, talent, and virtue. His use of the term included both an aristocracy of privilege and an aristocracy of merit. . . . Federalists exploited the ambiguous meaning of the term by arguing that republicanism required a government composed of a natural aristocracy of virtuous leaders. When pressed in public debate, most Federalists followed the example of James Wilson who argued that a government ruled by a natural aristocracy was "nothing more or less than a government of the best men in the community . . . most noted for wisdom and virtue."[21]

A reliance on the so-called natural aristocracy was compatible with the Federalist belief that the new Constitution's system of representation should effectively filter out men with parochial views and elevate men of refined views who would best discern the common good. To promote the election of "men of intelligence and up-rightness," Federalists followed Wilson's recommendation that "experience demonstrates that the larger the district of election, the better the representation. It is only in remote corners of a government, that little demagogues arise. Nothing but real weight of character can give a man real influence over a large district." Wilson's views were shared by James Madison (writing as "Publius") who counseled the necessity of enlarging the "public views, by passing them through the medium of a chosen body of citizens, whose wisdom may best discern the true interest of their country." In practice, Madison's "chosen body of citizens," the men who possessed "the weight of character" discussed by Wilson, were more likely to be found among the educated, affluent, and leisured elite.[22]

---

[21]John Adams, *A Defence of the Constitutions of Government of the United States of America* (2 vols., London, 1787–1788). The first volume appeared shortly before the Constitutional Convention. See John R. Howe, Jr., *The Changing Political Thought of John Adams* (Princeton, NJ, 1966); Gordon S. Wood, *The Creation of the American Republic, 1776–1787* (Chapel Hill, NC, 1969), 567–92; Joyce Appleby, "The New Republican Synthesis and the Changing Political Ideas of John Adams," *American Quarterly* 25 (Dec. 1973), 578–95; and Peter Shaw, *The Character of John Adams* (Chapel Hill, NC, 1976). James Wilson, speech in the Pennsylvania State Convention, in *Documentary History of the Ratification*, ed. Jensen et al., II, 488–89.

[22]Jensen et al., eds., *Documentary History of the Ratification*, II, 488–89. For similar statement by Wilson, see Adrienne Koch, ed., *Notes of the Debates in the Federal Convention of 1787 Reported by James Madison* (Athens, OH, 1966), 74, 85. For Madison's comment, see James Madison, Alexander Hamilton, and John Jay, *The Federalist*, ed. Jacob Cooke (Middletown, OH, 1961), 62. Lance Banning, "The Hamiltonian Madison: A Reconsideration," *Virginia Magazine of History and Biography* 92 (Jan. 1984), 3–28. See also Robert J. Morgan, "Madison's Theory of Representation in the Tenth *Federalist*," *Journal of Politics* 36 (Nov. 1974), 852–85; Jean Yarbrough, "Representation and Republicanism: Two Views," *Publius* 9 (Spring 1979), 77–98; and Gordon S. Wood, "Democracy and the Constitution," in *How Democratic Is the Constitution?* ed. Robert A. Goldwin and William A. Schambra (Washington, D.C., 1980), 1–17.

At the root of the Anti-Federalist critique of that elite, and of the ideology of natural aristocracy, lay a distinctive vernacular sociology. Anti-Federalist radicals, such as the Carlisle rioters, sought to ensure that representatives would do more than serve as spokesmen for the interests of individual localities. The radicals argued that true representation required that legislators actually resemble their constituents. When populists suggested that the legislature ought to be an exact mirror of society, they were speaking in a literal, not a figurative, sense. Since no one class possessed an exclusive monopoly on virtue, they reasoned, representative bodies ought to include a wide range of individuals from different social classes.

... While Anti-Federalists thundered against natural aristocracy, Federalists countered with the claim that they were proponents of an aristocracy of merit, what we would now call meritocracy. Federalists argued that the Anti-Federalist alternative to an aristocracy of merit, the idea of the legislature as an exact mirror of society's diverse interests and classes was incompatible with the republican ideal of virtue. Implicitly this debate turned on whether the necessary qualities of virtue, talent, and wisdom were evenly distributed throughout the various classes in society. Federalists believed that these qualities were disproportionately found in the upper stratum of society, while the populists among the Anti-Federalists maintained that there were enough virtuous men within the different classes to warrant broader representation. ...

The vernacular sociology of Anti-Federalists presented an inverted mirror image of the Enlightenment political sociology of Federalists like Madison and Wilson. Anti-Federalist populists and Federalists were in essential agreement about the impact of the Constitution's new scheme of representation: it would, both sides believed, enhance the prospects for electing members of the society's natural aristocracy and diminish the power of local politicians.[23]

... Carlisle Anti-Federalists did not have to look very far to find ardent supporters of [the Federalists'] ... theory of natural aristocracy. Charles Nisbet, president of nearby Dickinson College, took every opportunity to remind local inhabitants of the necessity of an educated governing elite drawn from the ranks of society's natural aristocracy.

A recent immigrant from Scotland and a staunch Presbyterian, Nisbet saw the world quite differently than did the Carlisle rioters. While they fulminated at lawyers, clergymen, and university men, Nisbet extolled the virtues of governance by a leisured and learned elite. Where the rioters saw an overbearing elite in control of political life, Nisbet saw a society that veered dangerously close to a Hobbesian state of nature. In Nisbet's view, "This new world ... is unfortunately composed, like that of epicurus, of discordant atoms, jumbled together by chance and tossed by inconstancy in an immense vacuum, it greatly

---

[23]Jack Rakove, "The Structure of Politics at the Accession of George Washington," in *Beyond Confederation*, ed. Beeman et al., 261–94.

wants a principle of attraction and cohesion."[24] According to Nisbet's view, the New World threatened to level all distinctions and thus plunge society into anarchy.

To offset the leveling tendency of the frontier, Nisbet regularly intoned the sober principles of traditional republicanism to his students at Dickinson College. While the Constitutional Convention met, Nisbet reminded students in his class on public law that "it is certain that men of learning, leisure and easy circumstances . . . if they are endued with wisdom, virtue & humanity, are much fitter for every part of the business of government, than the ordinary class of people." It is hardly surprising that Anti-Federalists felt that "Dickinson Coledge will be a Choice nursery for Federal officers and rulers." The commencement services held at the college during the spring of 1788 confirmed their suspicions. As one Anti-Federalist observed, "the great Drift of all their discourses was to prove the mass of the people to be void of every liberal Sentiment" and "destitute of understanding and integrity."[25] The concept of natural aristocracy articulated by Federalists was embedded within an ideology that posited a strong link between education, knowledge, and republican virtue. In addition to the martial and yeoman ideals of the citizen, republicanism also accorded a special role to the "republican man of letters" whose extensive reading habits conferred on him a cosmopolitan sensibility.[26] In his role as the president of Dickinson College, Charles Nisbet became the leading spokesman for the concept of natural aristocracy within Carlisle and served as a model of the "republican man of letters." Nisbet was not the only Federalist who espoused that ideal. One of its most ardent exponents was Federalist Benjamin Rush, a leading supporter of the Constitution in Pennsylvania and a trustee of Dickinson College. Rush hoped to use education and the popular press to mold the character of citizens and believed that it was "possible to convert men into republican machines" so that they might "perform their parts properly in the great machine of government."[27] The choice of a

---

[24]James Smylie, "Charles Nisbet: Second Thoughts on a Revolutionary Generation," *Pennsylvania Magazine of History and Biography* 98 (April 1974), 189–205, esp. 193. See also "Charles Nisbet to the Students after Vacation," in *Documentary History of the Ratification*, ed. Jensen et al., II, microform supplement, doc. no. 182; Charles Nisbet to Alexander Addison, Dec. 7, 1787, ibid., 259; Nisbet to the Earl of Buchan, Dec. 25, 1787, ibid., XV, 87–90.

[25]Smylie, "Charles Nisbet," 193; Petrikin to Nicholson, May 8, 1788, in *Documentary History of the Ratification*, ed. Jensen et al., II, microform supplement, doc. no. 675.

[26]Edmund S. Morgan, *Inventing the People: The Rise of Popular Sovereignty in England and America* (New York, 1988), 153–208. Richard D. Brown, "From Cohesion to Competition," in *Printing and Society in Early America*, ed. William Joyce et al. (Worcester, 1983), 300–309, esp. 304; and David Paul Nord, "A Republican Literature: Magazine Reading and Readers in Late-Eighteenth-Century New York," in *Reading in America: Literature and Social History*, ed. Cathy N. Davidson (Baltimore, MD, 1989), 114–39.

[27]Benjamin Rush, "Thoughts upon the Mode of Education Proper in a Republic," in *Essays on Education in the Early Republic*, ed. Frederick Rudolph (Cambridge, MA, 1968), 9–23, esp. 17. In addition to Rush, several other prominent Federalists served as trustees of Dickinson College during this period, including John Dickinson and James Wilson, and among local Federalists, John Armstrong and John Montgomery. Charles C. Sellers, *Dickinson College: A History* (Middletown, OH, 1973), 481–84.

mechanical metaphor was especially appropriate since it captured the essentially hierarchical nature of the Federalist vision of politics.

The most outspoken critic of the concept of natural aristocracy in Carlisle was William Petrikin, a leader of the Anti-Federalist election riot. Petrikin was the embodiment of a different, radical egalitarian, version of the "republic of letters." Unlike Nisbet, Petrikin was schooled in the popular press and proudly proclaimed that he was a "mechanic . . . who never spent an hour in coledge."[28] He eagerly consumed the popular political literature of his day. The popular press did not, however, convert Petrikin into a "republican machine." The egalitarian vision of the "republic of letters" that Anti-Federalists like Petrikin rallied around encouraged an active role for common folk who would exercise their own capacity for civic virtue by reading popular political literature, writing for the popular press, and even seeking public office. In fact, Petrikin was sufficiently inspired by what he read to take up his own pen to denounce the proponents of natural aristocracy in Carlisle. . . .[29]

. . . In one of the first pieces [Petrikin] . . . published after the riot, he adopted the name the "Scourge," defended the actions of the "friends of liberty," and attacked the Federalists for "having the learned professions on their side." He charged that Federalists in Carlisle had the support of "all the attorneys then in town and all the auxiliaries they could procure" and compared their ideas to those of a "Solon, a Lycurgus . . . or an Adams."[30]

Since formal education was clearly a prerogative associated with wealth and social standing, the "Scourge" saw the invocation of venerable republican figures such as Solon and Lycurgus as yet another attempt by the affluent to equate formal education with virtue. Unlike his Federalist opponents, Petrikin felt that politics required no recourse to classical allusion. Like the other participants in

---

[28]Jensen et al., eds., *Documentary History of the Ratification*, II, microform supplement, doc. no. 675. Little is known about Petrikin's early life; see the biographical sketch in John Blair Linn, *History of Centre and Clinton Counties, Pennsylvania* (Philadelphia, 1883), 219. Lucy Simler, "Tenancy in Colonial Pennsylvania: The Case of Chester County," *William and Mary Quarterly* 43 (Oct. 1986), 542–69. R. Eugene Harper, "The Class Structure of Western Pennsylvania in the Late Eighteenth Century, 1783–1796" (Ph.D. diss., University of Pittsburgh, 1969). Thomas L. Purvis, "Patterns of Ethnic Settlement in Late-Eighteenth-Century Pennsylvania," *Western Pennsylvania Historical Magazine* 70 (April 1987), 107–22; and Bernard Bailyn, *Voyagers to the West: A Passage in the Peopling of America on the Eve of the Revolution* (New York, 1986), 25–27, 176–85, 204–38. Owen Ireland, "The Crux of Politics: Religion and Party in Pennsylvania, 1778–1789," *William and Mary Quarterly* 42 (Oct. 1985), 453–75. Robert Kelley, *The Cultural Pattern in American Politics: The First Century* (New York, 1979); and Forrest McDonald, *Novus Ordo Seclorum: The Intellectual Origins of the Constitution* (Lawrence, KS, 1985), 157.

[29]Stanley Fish, *Is There a Text in This Class? The Authority of Interpretive Communities* (Cambridge, MA, 1980); Roger Chartier, "Intellectual History or Sociocultural History? The French Trajectories," in *Modern European Intellectual History: Reappraisals and New Perspectives*, ed. Dominick La Capra and Steven L. Kaplan (Ithaca, NY, 1982), 13–46; and Janice Radway, "American Studies, Reader Theory, and the Literary Text: From the Study of Material Objects to the Study of Social Processes" in *American Studies in Transition*, ed. David E. Nye and Christen Kold Thomsen (Odense, Denmark, 1985), 29–51.

[30]Jensen et al., eds., *Documentary History of the Ratification*, II, 685–92.

the Carlisle riot, he proudly asserted that virtue and knowledge were not the sole possessions of a small elite class of natural aristocrats. Anti-Federalists did not believe that figures from the republican past monopolized political wisdom any more than they believed that education or wealth signaled greater wisdom in their own society. When Anti-Federalists did invoke classical republican figures, they favored the defenders of the late Roman republic, such as Brutus, men who symbolized the battle against tyranny. In marked contrast, Federalists favored figures such as Publius, the great founders and lawgivers of republican antiquity.[31]

Although Anti-Federalists admired Brutus, the historical figure depicted in Plutarch's Lives mattered less to Anti-Federalist populists than the spirit of "Brutus" dwelling in all stalwart republicans.[32] When Carlisle Anti-Federalists praised the dissenting members of the state ratifying convention who voted against adoption of the Constitution, they took great pride in noting that "scholastic learning and erudition" were set against the "simple reason" of "a very few country farmers and mechanics." . . . Any citizen concerned about the state of the republic could author a piece, assume the pen name "Brutus," and alert his fellow citizens that the republic or liberty was jeopardized. The tradition of pseudonymous writing closed the distance between readers and authors, allowing any concerned citizen to step forward and enter an ongoing debate as an equal participant. Thus one can readily understand Anti-Federalists' outrage when a number of Federalist printers sought to abandon the convention of printing anonymous or pseudonymous pieces. "Philadelphiensis" thought that the Federalist effort to abolish the use of pseudonyms embodied "the genius and spirit of our new government" and that it would please the "well born." In opposition, he championed the belief that "it is of no importance whether or not a writer gives his name; it is with the illustrations and arguments he affords us, and not with his name, that "we have any concern." Requiring authors to sign their names would discourage "men of ability, of a modest, timid, or diffident cast of mind . . . from publishing their sentiments. . . ."[33]

Although several modern commentators have acknowledged that the opponents of the Constitution were wedded to an intensely localistic ideology, most scholars have mistakenly viewed Anti-Federalist localism as the polar opposite of Federalist cosmopolitanism.[34] Anti-Federalist localism was not an expression of a narrow parochial and insular world view. Localist ideology owed much to Whig oppositional thought, especially the rhetoric of country ideology. The pervasive fears of centralized authority, standing armies, and excessive taxation were only

---

[31]McDonald, *Novas Ordo Seclorum*, 67–70.

[32]McDonald, *Novas Ordo Seclorum*, 67–70. Writing as "Aristocrotis," Storing, ed., *Complete Anti-Federalist*, III, 198. Donald S. Lutz, "The Relative Influence of European Writers on Late Eighteenth-Century American Political Thought," *American Political Science Review* 78 (March 1984), 189–97.

[33]Robert Gross, "The Authority of the Word: Print and Social Change in America, 1607–1880," 1984, (in Saul Cornell's possession), 125–35; and "Philadelphiensis," *Complete Anti-Federalist*, ed. Storing, III, 103–4.

[34]Jackson Turner Main, *Political Parties before the Constitution* (Chapel Hill, NC, 1973), 32.

the most obvious instances of Anti-Federalism's debt to this older Whig tradition. It would, however, be a mistake to view Anti-Federalist ideology as a mere echo of an older English struggle between "court and country." . . .[35] The essence of Anti-Federalist localist ideology was captured by the ardent states' rights advocate Luther Martin, who argued that the American people were accustomed to "have their seats of government near them, to which they might have access, without much inconvenience." Martin's vision of localism was congruent with that of Massachusetts Anti-Federalist James Winthrop, who saw localism as the natural consequence of the diversity of American society. It is hard to maintain that Anti-Federalist localists were narrow-minded provincial politicians while recognizing Winthrop, the librarian of Harvard College, and Martin, a respected figure in the Maryland legal community, as leading theorists of Anti-Federalist localism.[36] Both men illustrate the existence of an important strain of cosmopolitan localism among the Anti-Federalist elite.

A simple localist/cosmopolitan dichotomy not only fails to capture the complexity of many leading Anti-Federalists, but it also obscures the nature of the popular Anti-Federalist ideology espoused by such individuals as William Petrikin and the Carlisle rioters. The localism of the Carlisle rioters was closely tied to their egalitarian populist ideas. Although distinctly localistic in outlook, Anti-Federalists were not provincial in their cultural views; they did not envision localities as isolated and insular communities. Their localism stressed the importance of face-to-face relationships and the values of neighborliness even as they defended the necessity of expanding communication between individual communities. In this way, local autonomy could be maintained without fostering provincialism. Even the localism of the most populist-minded Anti-Federalists was closely tied to their own egalitarian defense of the "republic of letters." . . .

Anti-Federalist populist localism was based on a "mandate" or "actual" theory of representation. According to it, representatives were to act as agents of their constituents. In the view of most Anti-Federalists, members of the legislature had to be sufficiently steeped in the values of the locality, immersed in its economic and social life, to serve as true spokesmen for community interests.

---

[35]Bernard Bailyn, *The Ideological Origins of the American Revolution* (Cambridge, MA, 1967); J. G. A. Pocock, *The Machiavellian Moment: Florentine Political Thought and the Atlantic Republican Tradition* (Princeton, NJ, 1975); J. G. A. Pocock, ed., *Three British Revolutions: 1641, 1688, 1776* (Princeton, NJ, 1980); J. G. A. Pocock, *Virtue, Commerce, and History* (Cambridge, England, 1985); and Wood, *Creation of the American Republic*. Robert Shalhope, "Toward a Republican Synthesis: The Emergence of an Understanding of Republicanism in American Historiography," *William and Mary Quarterly* 29 (Jan. 1972), 49–80; Robert Shalhope, "Republicanism and Early American Historiography," ibid., 39 (April 1982), 334–56; and the special issue "Republicanism in the History and Historiography of the United States," ed. Joyce Appleby, *American Quarterly* 37 (Fall 1985), 461–598. Hutson, "Country, Court, and Constitution," and Richard Beeman "Introduction," in *Beyond Confederation*, ed. Beeman et al., 3–19, esp. 16.

[36]Jack P. Greene, *Peripheries and Centers: Constitutional Development in the Extended Politics of the British Empire and the United States, 1607–1788* (Athens, GA, 1986); [Luther Martin], "The Genuine Information," *Complete Anti-Federalist*, ed. Storing, II, 48; James Winthrop], "Agrippa," ibid., IV, 76–77, 93.

To achieve that goal, populists argued, representatives had to resemble those they represented. The ideology of localism rejected the republican ideal of disinterestedness. Only by guarding the many diverse local interests in society, Anti-Federalists believed, could Americans maintain liberty.[37]

Challenges to the claim that disinterested gentlemen of refined views were more capable of representing the people than were the people themselves resonated in the minds of backcountry folk. Such ideas were not unique to the backcountry of Pennsylvania. Indeed, similar ideas could be found throughout the backcountry from Maine to Georgia. Amos Singletary, an Anti-Federalist from Sutton, Massachusetts, in the heart of Shaysite Worcester County, warned that "these lawyers, and men of learning, and moneyed men, that talk so finely, and gloss over matters so smoothly," would "get into Congress themselves" and would become "the managers of this Constitution, and get all the power and all the money into their own hands, and then they will swallow up all us little folks."[38]

The rhetoric of populists in Carlisle was tinged with similar inchoate class consciousness. At the root of their crudely formulated class critique was the claim that an identifiable class of natural aristocrats that included lawyers, men of learning and monied men were engaged in a systematic plot to increase their own power and dilute the influence of the people in government. . . .[39]

The plebeian populism that motivated so much of the popular opposition to the Constitution created an important division within the ranks of the Anti-Federalists. It divided those (such as Petrikin) hostile to the concept of natural aristocracy from those whose fear that the Constitution promoted aristocracy did not lead them to challenge the ideal of natural aristocracy.

Anti-Federalists like Virginia's George Mason feared that the government created by the Constitution would "commence in a moderate Aristocracy" and would probably degenerate into an "oppressive Aristocracy." Mason is quite properly thought of as a "man of little faith." He did not, however, fear natural aristocracy. A wealthy cosmopolitan planter like Mason expected society's leaders to be drawn from the gentlemanly elite. What worried Mason was the traditional republican fear of corruption. In his mind, any group of men who were given too much power would seek aggrandizement and elevate their own interests above those of society. The solution to Mason's objections was a more effective system of checks on government and a written bill of rights to protect individual liberty. Hardly a populist democrat, Mason was a critic of the democratic excess that characterized American politics during the Confederation period. At the Constitutional Convention, Mason acknowledged "that we had been too democratic," but he also cautioned against moving too far "into the

---

[37]See Hanna F. Pitkin, *The Concept of Representation* (Berkeley, CA, 1967), 60–61, 146–47.

[38]Jonathan Elliot, ed., *The Debates in the Several State Conventions* . . . (5 vols., Philadelphia, 1836–1845), II, 102.

[39]Montgomery to Wilson, March 2, 1788, in *Documentary History of Ratification*, ed. Jensen et al., II, 705.

opposite extreme."[40] Mason's elitist republicanism stood in stark contrast to the populist sentiments of the Carlisle rioters. The debate over natural aristocracy was only one instance of a basic rift separating elite Anti-Federalists from grass-roots Anti-Federalists.

LIBERTY VERSUS ORDER: RESPONSES TO BACKCOUNTRY VIOLENCE

If the issue of natural aristocracy divided Anti-Federalists, the plebeian traditions of protest enacted by the Carlisle rioters were even more divisive. Events like the Carlisle riot touched a sensitive nerve in leading figures on both sides of the ratification struggle. It is hardly surprising that Federalists viewed such events as signs of the need for a stronger union. What is surprising is the reaction of leading Anti-Federalists to those events. Anti-Federalist reactions were often indistinguishable from those of Federalists. The fear of aristocracy and concern for liberty that inspired elite opposition to the Constitution paled when the Anti-Federalists were presented with the specter of anarchy. For Anti-Federalists of the better sort, the actions of the rioters were a sobering reminder of the necessity and difficulty of balancing liberty and order.[41]

Shays's Rebellion left a profound imprint on the minds of many Americans, and the fear of anarchy and disorder created by the western Massachusetts insurgents influenced members of political elites on both sides of the ratification struggle. The climate of fear created by Shays's Rebellion accounts for the coverage of the Carlisle riot in the press as far south as Georgia and as far north as Maine. Many Federalists viewed the rioters as "mobites" and "levellers."[42]

The horror of Federalists was more than matched by the reactions of leading Anti-Federalists, especially in Massachusetts, where Shays's Rebellion had left an especially deep impression. To an experienced politician like Elbridge Gerry, a man of the "better sort," the Carlisle riot was a bitter reminder of the leveling tendencies among the populace. Although an outspoken opponent of the Constitution, Gerry shared the Federalist belief that the nation's political problems stemmed from an "excess of democracy." His commitment to republican ideas stopped well short of the democratic leanings of the Carlisle rioters. . . . When he learned that the "people threatend the Justice in Carlisle to pull down his House, & the houses of the federalists," Gerry expressed grave concern that "we shall be in a civil War," but he hoped that God would "avert the evil." Rather than

---

[40]"George Mason's Objections to the Constitution of Government Formed by the Convention, 1787," in *Complete Anti-Federalist*, ed. Storing, II, 13; Koch, ed., *Notes of the Debates in the Federal Convention of 1787 Reported by James Madison*, 39.

[41]Wood, *Creation of the American Republic*, 471–518. Robert A. Feer, "Shays's Rebellion and the Constitution: A Study in Causation," *New England Quarterly* 42 (Sept. 1969), 388–410. Thomas P. Slaughter, *The Whiskey Rebellion: Frontier Epilogue to the American Revolution* (New York, 1986).

[42]The Federalist description of the riot by an "Old Man" was reprinted thirty-seven times by March 10, 1788, in papers from Georgia to Maine. On the distribution of the piece, see Jensen et al., eds., *Documentary History of the Ratification*, XV, 225; ibid., microform supplement, doc. nos. 392, 334.

solidifying opposition to the Constitution, the Carlisle riot drove a wedge between the majority of backcountry Anti-Federalists and the most respected Anti-Federalist leaders.[43]

Despite the fears of prominent Anti-Federalists, popular support for the rioters was strong in the Pennsylvania backcountry. William Petrikin observed that in the aftermath of the riot "almost every day . . . some new society . . . [is] being formed" to oppose "this detastable Fedrall conspiracy." Anti-Federalist Richard Baird noted that "on the West side of the Susquehanna in this state there is at least nine out of every ten that would at the risk of their lives & property" oppose the new Constitution.[44]

In the wake of the peaceful resolution of events in Carlisle, backcountry Anti-Federalists mounted a petition campaign to void the actions of the state ratifying convention. In the short space of twelve days, Anti-Federalists gathered more than six thousand signatures to petitions in six counties. Leading Federalists in Huntingdon County sought to frustrate the campaign by destroying Anti-Federalist petitions. The actions of the "federal junto" aroused the indignation of local inhabitants who turned to the traditions of rough music to vent their anger. "A number of people . . . collected, and conducted upon the backs of old scabby ponies the EFFIGIES of the principals of the junto." When this procession passed the local court-house, officers of the court apprehended the "effigy-men." The response of the local community was decisive. "Immediately the county took the alarm, assembled, and liberated the sons of liberty, so unjustly confined." The release of the prisoners was greeted with "loud huzzas and repeated acclaimations of joy from a large concourse of people." These self-styled sons of liberty reenacted the same traditions of direct community action that inspired Anti-Federalists in Carlisle. Once again Anti-Federalists took to the streets, marched to the jail, and forced the release of their fellow citizens who had been unjustly imprisoned by an "aristocratic junto."[45]

Backcountry Anti-Federalists did not limit their actions to petition campaigns and street demonstrations. Events like the Carlisle and Huntingdon riots gave additional impetus to the move to call a second convention to revise the federal Constitution. Encouraged by the plans for a convention in Harrisburg, Carlisle Anti-Federalists offered up the following toast in celebration: "may such amendments be speedily framed . . . as may render the proposed Constitution of the United States truly democratical."[46] Leading Anti-Federalists from throughout Pennsylvania and several newcomers to Pennsylvania politics did convene in

---

[43]Koch, ed., *Notes of the Debates in the Federal Convention*, 39. Elbridge Gerry to S. R. Gerry, Jan. 28, 1788, Samuel R. Gerry Papers (Massachusetts Historical Society, Boston, MA).

[44]Petrikin to Nicholson, Feb. 24, 1788, in *Documentary History of the Ratification*, ed. Jensen et al., II, 695–96; Richard Baird to Nicholson, Feb. 1, 1788, ibid., 712.

[45]Ibid., 709–25.

[46]Merrill Jensen and Robert A. Becker, eds., *The Documentary History of the First Federal Elections, 1788–1790* (3 vols., Madison, 1976–), I, 242.

Harrisburg to discuss the future of their opposition to the new Constitution. One of the newcomers was a feisty representative from Carlisle, William Petrikin.[47]

Petrikin wanted the convention to adopt a radical program to unite Anti-Federalists throughout the country and to call a new convention to amend the Constitution. Petrikin's more radical position was defeated by the moderate forces led by a Philadelphia merchant, Charles Pettit. Like most other Anti-Federalist leaders, Pettit sought to distance himself from events such as the Carlisle riot. Men like Pettit were alarmed by the depth of hostility in the backcountry and feared the prospects of anarchy. Pettit felt that to "reject the New Plan and attempt again to resort to the old would . . . throw us into a State of Nature, filled with internal Discord." Pettit captured the view of many leading Anti-Federalists when he later confided to George Washington that "even after the vote of adoption by the State Convention, a large proportion of the people, especially in the western counties, shewed a disposition to resist the operation of it, in a manner which I thought indicated danger to the peace of the State."[48]

Ironically, the very success of the Carlisle rioters ultimately proved their own undoing. The fear of anarchy aided the moderates at Harrisburg and effectively ensured the demise of the second convention movement. Rather than encourage extralegal action on the part of backcountry populists, leading Anti-Federalists opted to compromise and take up their role as a "loyal opposition party."[49]

Elbridge Gerry, George Mason, and Charles Pettit were representative of Anti-Federalists of the "better sort." They interpreted events like the Carlisle riot as a reminder of the precarious balance between liberty and order. The Anti-Federalism of these men had little to do with any populist notions of democracy. Such "men of little faith" sought to steer a political course between unfettered democracy and tyranny. The fear of popular anarchy was as intense among the Anti-Federalist political elite as among the Federalist leadership. . . .[50]

THE LEGACY OF PLEBEIAN POPULISM

If we are to understand why popular antagonism to the Constitution spilled into the streets we must attempt to see the struggle through the eyes of the men who risked their lives to oppose a form of government that, they thought, veered toward a new aristocratic order.

---

[47]Ibid., I, 257–81. Paul Leicester Ford, *The Origin, Purpose, and Result of the Harrisburg Convention of 1788: A Study in Popular Government* (Brooklyn, 1890); Linda Grant DePauw, "The Anticlimax of Antifederalism: The Abortive Second Convention Movement, 1788–89," *Prologue* 2 (Fall 1970), 98–114; and Steven R. Boyd, *The Politics of Opposition: Antifederalists and the Acceptance of the Constitution* (Millwood, 1979), 142–44.

[48]Charles Pettit to Robert Whitehill, June 5, 1788, Robert Whitehill Papers (Hamilton Library, Cumberland County Historical Society). See also Pettit to George Washington, March 19, 1791, in *Documentary History of the Ratification*, ed. Jensen et al., II, microform supplement, doc. no. 706.

[49]Lance Banning, "Republican Ideology and the Triumph of the Constitution, 1789 to 1793," *William and Mary Quarterly* 31 (April 1974), 167–88.

[50]Kenyon, "Men of Little Faith."

The rioters in Carlisle, like the supporters of Shays and many Anti-Federalists throughout the backcountry, were extremely hostile toward the federal Constitution. Although the eruption of violence in Carlisle grew out of local circumstances and events, the ideology that inspired this violent outburst and the rhetoric evoked to articulate local grievances were hardly unique to Carlisle. The rhetoric and symbols of protest appropriated by the rioters filled the popular press. Similar indictments of the new Constitution could be found in every major Anti-Federalist newspaper. Backcountry Anti-Federalists of the "lower and middling sort" articulated a vision of populist democracy that was decidedly egalitarian and localistic. They challenged the idea that wealth, education, or prestige were appropriate measures of civic virtue and resisted the attempt by Federalists to frame a political system that shifted political power away from local communities. This position set backcountry opponents of the Constitution against Federalists who championed a vision of representative government that sought to encourage deference for men of "refined views" who would transcend local interests.

The ideological divide separating Federalists from Anti-Federalists cannot, however, be understood solely in terms of a battle between populist democrats and supporters of deference and order. Not everyone within the Anti-Federalist ranks championed populist democratic sentiments. Many leading Anti-Federalists were as concerned about the dangers of democratic excess as were leading Federalists. Many Anti-Federalists of the better sort were "men of little faith," who saw the federal Constitution as a threat to individual liberty and a dangerous departure from traditional Whig opposition to powerful centralized governments. Anti-Federalists of the better sort, like the young John Quincy Adams, took great pains to make clear that their "strong *antifederalist*" sentiments were based upon "very different principles than those of your Worcester insurgents [Shaysites]." Indeed, it was precisely because of the popularity of Anti-Federalist sympathy among former Shaysites, that men like John Quincy Adams felt that continuing opposition to the Constitution "would be productive of much greater evils," no matter how "dangerous the tendency" of the new frame of government.[51]

As for Anti-Federalist populists, although they did not succeed in their efforts to block ratification, their political vision should not be ignored. The populist sentiments that inspired backcountry Anti-Federalists would continue to be a potent force in American political culture. A scant few years would pass before the anger and frustrations of common folk would again lead men into the streets to vent their hostility against the new federal government. The reverberations of Anti-Federalism can clearly be heard in the Whiskey Rebellion. In fact, the Anti-Federalist challenge to the Constitution, like the Whiskey Rebellion, was only the first of many populist challenges that shaped the course of American politics.

---

[51]John Quincy Adams to Oliver Fiske, Feb. 17, 1788, Adams folder, Miscellaneous Manuscripts (American Antiquarian Society, Worcester, MA).

Localism and egalitarianism, the cornerstones of Anti-Federalist populism, provided inspiration for a distinctly American style of radical politics, one fashioned around the idea of participatory democracy and equality. Similar ideas would echo in the rhetoric of Jacksonian democracy and the Populist movement of the late nineteenth century.[52]

---

[52]Slaughter, *Whiskey Rebellion*, 205–11. Dorothy Fennell, "Herman Husband's Antifederalism and the Rebellion in Western Pennsylvania," paper presented at the annual meeting of the Organization of American Historians, Philadelphia, April 1987 (in Cornell's possession). Jennifer Nedelsky, "Confining Democratic Politics: Anti-Federalists, Federalists, and the Constitution," *Harvard Law Review* 96 (Dec. 1982), 340–60. Richard Ellis, "The Persistence of Antifederalism after 1789," in *Beyond Confederation*, ed. Beeman et al., 295–314. John Ashworth, *Agrarians' & Aristocrats' Party Political Ideology in the United States, 1837–1846* (Cambridge, England, 1983). Lawrence Goodwyn, *The Populist Moment: A Short History of the Agrarian Revolt in America* (New York, 1978). Saul Cornell, "The Changing Historical Fortunes of the Anti-Federalists," *Northwestern University Law Review* (forthcoming).

Saul Cornell

Saul Cornell is the Paul and Diane Guenther Chair in American History at Fordham University. He has taught at the College of William and Mary, Ohio State University, Leiden University in the Netherlands as a Fulbright Scholar, and has been a Senior Visiting Research Scholar at Yale Law School and the University of Connecticut Law School. Professor Cornell is the author of two prize-winning books in early American constitutional history, *The Other Founders: Anti-Federalism and the Dissenting Tradition in America, 1788–1828,* (1999) and *A Well Regulated Militia: The Founding Fathers and the Origins of Gun Control in America* (2006). He has also published *Whose Right to Bear Arms Did the Second Amendment Protect?* (2000) and has coedited a collection of essays on the Supreme Court's landmark Heller decision, *The Second Amendment Goes to Court: Critical Essays on District of Columbia v. Heller* (2013). His scholarly articles have appeared in *The Journal of American History, The William and Mary Quarterly, The Law and History Review, The Northwestern University Law Review, The UCLA Law Review, The Fordham Law Review, The Yale Journal of Law and the Humanities,* and *Constitutional Commentary.* Professor Cornell is also the coauthor of popular college level American history textbook, *Visions of America.*

QUESTIONS FOR CONSIDERATION

1. According to Cornell, what have historians primarily debated regarding the ratification of the Constitution? What are some of the limitations of this debate? What new focus does Cornell recommend to overcome these limitations?

2. What anxieties were Federalists reacting to when they supported the new Constitution? What anxieties did the new Constitution raise among those collectively known as Anti-Federalists?

3. How did Anti-Federalist protesters in Carlisle manifest their anger at local Federalists? What purpose did "rough music" serve, according to Cornell, for these protesters?

4. While both Federalists and Anti-Federalists rejected the idea of an aristocracy, how did the idea of a "natural aristocracy" prove a point of conflict between the two? In what way did the two sides differ on the concept of representation and who would serve as representatives in the new government?

5. In what ways did Anti-Federalists expect "localism" to protect the rights proclaimed by the Declaration of Independence? How did the new Constitution threaten this localism in the eyes of these Anti-Federalists?

6. Compare the Carlisle riot to other protests described in this book. Specifically consider articles by Gary Nash and Terry Bouton. What continuities and changes over time do you see when comparing these protests?

CHAPTER EIGHT

A Road Closed: Rural Insurgency in Post-Independence Pennsylvania[1]

Terry Bouton

Something remarkable happened in the Pennsylvania countryside in the years following the federal Constitutional Convention of 1787: Large numbers of farmers closed the main roads that led into and out of their communities. During an eight-year period, fall 1787 through fall 1795, rural Pennsylvanians obstructed roads at least sixty-two times.[2] The road closings were not confined to any particular county or region: Farmers blocked highways in new backcountry settlements and in the established communities surrounding Philadelphia. And while road closings were more frequent in the central and frontier parts of the state, barriers appeared in roadways only twenty-five miles beyond the Quaker city. (See map.)

The obstructions were usually formidable, often making roads impassable for many months at a time. Throughout Pennsylvania, farmers constructed six-foot-high fences that stretched fifty feet across the highway. Some farmers felled trees across roads or hauled timber into log piles that sometimes measured thirty feet wide and forty feet long. Others blocked roads with heavy stones, brush, and decaying logs. Still others scarred roadways with eight-foot-wide, five-foot-deep ditches large enough to halt any wagon or coach. One group in the southeastern county of Chester shoveled enough dirt out of the main highway to Philadelphia that they created an impassable crater measuring fifty feet in circumference and seven feet deep. Farmers in two other eastern counties flooded roads by carving out canals to nearby waterways. On the western frontier, people dug into a hillside, causing an avalanche at a narrow passage. And on a highway in the central county of Cumberland, farmers dumped fifteen wagonloads of manure, creating a four-foot-high wall of stink.[3]

---

[1]Interested students are encouraged to read this essay in the original form. Terry Bouton, "A Road Closed: The Rural Insurgency in Post-Independence Pennsylvania," *Journal of American History* 87 (3) (Dec. 2000), 855–87.

[2]This figure was derived from dockets and papers from the county quarter sessions courts for thirteen of the twenty counties beyond Philadelphia: Bedford, Bucks, Berks, Chester, Cumberland, Dauphin, Huntingdon, Lancaster, Mifflin, Northampton, Northumberland, Washington, and York. It does not include the seven counties beyond Philadelphia for which relevant court papers have not survived or are extremely fragmentary: Allegheny, Delaware, Fayette, Franklin, Montgomery, Luzerne, and Westmoreland.

[3][Please see Pennsylvania county court records from 1787 to 1795 as documented in the original.]

Map 8.1

Road Closings in Pennsylvania by County November 1787 to November 1795. Source: County quarter sessions court records, 1787–1795, for the thirteen counties whose records are complete for those years.

In the late eighteenth century, when roads were lifelines for rural communities, closing any of the few highways that ran through the countryside was a serious matter. Roads brought wagons bearing spices, sugar, salt, kettles, axes, and plows to places where such necessities were not produced. They kept rural neighborhoods tied to the larger world by bringing news of grain prices, national politics, and wars in Europe, along with letters from distant relatives. They allowed farmers to take their wheat flour, corn whiskey, and livestock to market. In this way, roads brought the money that farmers needed to repay their mortgages and that artisans needed to purchase the tools of their trades. By themselves, the many petitions for new highways that Pennsylvanians drafted during the 1790s—even as they closed roads across the state—stand as a testament to how important highways were to rural people.

Given the significance of roadways in late-eighteenth-century America, why did farmers throughout Pennsylvania expend so much energy in obstructing highways and keeping them closed for long periods of time? Why would rural people sever lines of communication and willfully jeopardize their ability to supply their communities and get goods to market? In short, why did people so dependent upon the world outside their local neighborhoods take such extreme measures to isolate themselves?

These mysterious road closings, it turns out, are part of a much larger pattern of rural protest by Pennsylvania farmers who saw the developments of the later 1780s and 1790s as a betrayal of the American Revolution. . . . I argue that rural insurgency in Pennsylvania grew out of an economic crisis, the severity of which historians have greatly underestimated. Scholars have . . . overlook[ed] nearly two decades of sustained protest by farmers across the state aimed at halting that crisis. Inevitably, missing such critical pieces of the historical canvas has skewed the interpretive portrait of farm protest, most notably the "Whiskey Rebellion" of

1794 and "Fries's Rebellion" of 1799. The omissions have made rural insurgency seem shallow: spontaneous isolated outbursts that quickly subsided. Insurgent farmers appear . . . as "Whiskey Rebels," an image that implicitly . . . trivializes their protest. I argue that, ultimately, this . . . distorts our understanding of the Revolution by misrepresenting rural discontent with the Revolution's outcome and concealing its full dimensions.[4]

This essay . . . demonstrate[es] how government policies helped to induce mass property foreclosure throughout the state, undermining both the perception and the reality of rural independence. In response to this crisis, farmers across Pennsylvania developed multi-tiered networks to shield their property and their vision of the Revolution. Facing stiff opposition from many local, state, and national elites, insurgent farmers resorted to increasingly desperate strategies— such as blocking roads. In the end, however, they found that their organizing efforts could not match those of the revolutionary elite, who drafted new laws and constitutions in ways that outlawed the most effective forms of agrarian resistance. In 1794 and again in 1799, rural Pennsylvanians made their final stands in what historians have misleadingly called the Whiskey and Fries "rebellions." In the minds of many farmers, the defeat of those insurgencies, each by a federal army, closed a road toward a more just and democratic future.

In postwar Pennsylvania, the dominant fact of life everywhere in the state was a profound scarcity of money and credit. . . . "The situation of this Country at present is very alarming for the want of Money," explained a frontier merchant in Pittsburgh in 1787. "Very few in this Town can procure Money to go to market. And as to pay . . . a Debt it is out of the question." Two hundred miles to the east in the town of Carlisle, things were little better. Here, one observer declared that money was "almost invisible." . . . The scarcity even struck the burgeoning metropolis of Philadelphia. . . . In December 1782, the merchant Stephen Collins observed that the "scarcity of money is now the cry & rings through the city almost as much as the bells do in the case of fire." . . . Three years later in September 1787, sitting in an office only a few blocks from where delegates were completing their draft of a new federal constitution, Collins wrote that "times have grown so bad, money so scarce [that] amazing quantities of real estate of every kind [are] selling at both public and private sale."[5]

---

[4]Thomas P. Slaughter, *The Whiskey Rebellion: Frontier Epilogue to the American Revolution* (New York, 1986), 4–5, 28–60; Stanley Elkins and Eric McKitrick, *The Age of Federalism* (New York, 1993), 451–88, 695–700; Paul Douglas Newman, "Fries's Rebellion and American Political Culture, 1798–1800," *Pennsylvania Magazine of History and Biography* 119 (Jan./April 1995), 37; Dorothy Fennell, "From Rebelliousness to Insurrection: A Social History of the Whiskey Rebellion, 1765–1802" (Ph.D. diss., University of Pittsburgh, 1981).

[5]Robert Galbraith, Pittsburgh, to George Woods, Dec. 4, 1787, in *The Documentary History of the Ratification of the Constitution, vol. II: Ratification of the Constitution by the States, Pennsylvania*, ed. Merrill Jensen et al. (18 vols., Madison, 1976–), II (microfiche supplement, document 253, frame 1167); John Armstrong, Carlisle, to William Irvine, Aug. 16, 1787, vol. IX, Irvine Family Papers (Historical Society of Pennsylvania, Philadelphia, PA); Stephen Collins, Philadelphia, to Jinks & Forrester, Dec. 11, 1782, vol. LX, Letter Books, Stephen Collins & Sons Papers (Manuscript Division, Library of Congress, Washington, D.C.); Collins to Charles Wright, Sept. 7, 1787, LXII, ibid.

Forced property sales were not limited to Philadelphia: the scarcity of money had unleashed a statewide epidemic of foreclosures. . . . If debtors proved unable to acquire the funds to pay judgments against them, county sheriffs were called in to foreclose possessions or land. . . . In the eastern county of Berks, a decade of debt litigation from 1782 to 1792 produced 3,400 writs of foreclosure for a taxable population that averaged about 5,000 families—or enough to foreclose 68 percent of the taxable population. . . . In Northumberland County on the northern frontier, from 1785 to 1790, the sheriff delivered more writs of foreclosure (2,180) than there were taxpayers (2,140).[6]

Things were even worse in the frontier counties west of the Appalachian Mountains. In Westmoreland County, over the decade spanning 1782 to 1792, judges issued a remarkable 6,100 separate orders to foreclose goods and lands for a population of about 2,800 taxpayers. Tracing those writs to individual households, it becomes apparent that the county sheriff foreclosed at least 1,200 different families—or 43 percent of Westmoreland's taxable population.[7] (See graph.)

Westmoreland court records also reveal the tales of misery behind these numbers. In a frontier county, where people typically possessed little of value, the things that the sheriff piled into his wagon often represented all that people owned: chairs and tables, bed frames and feather mattresses, mugs, plates, and spoons. Much of what the sheriff confiscated represented items needed to make a living: horses and wagons, weaving looms and carpentry tools, distillery equipment and grindstones for mills. When the sheriff auctioned goods, the small number of bidders with ready cash meant that sales routinely brought only one-half to one-tenth of the item's traditional value, if property sold at all. As a result, 92 percent of the time that goods were sold at auction, the selling price failed to cover the debt. The same was true for the one-in-ten Westmoreland citizens whose land was auctioned: 67 percent of land sales did not earn enough to repay the debt. As this process repeated, the sheriff frequently found himself in the homes of farmers who owned nothing worthy of drawing a bid, as happened more than 1,200 times during this decade. With no means of covering their unpaid debts and taxes, many farmers found themselves in jail. In Westmoreland County, from 1782 to 1792, the sheriff imprisoned at least 270 debtors on 360 different occasions. . . .[8]

While this litany of hardship angered many farmers, rural discontent was deepened by the popular belief that the waves of foreclosure had been generated by deliberate government efforts to reduce the supply of money and credit. . . . [S]ince 1723, when the colony's first public loan office was created, "money" had generally meant paper currency issued by the colonial government, while "credit" included the long-term low-interest loans farmers could obtain from the colony by using their land as collateral. In an economy facing a perpetual shortage of

---

[6]Berks County Execution Dockets (Berks County Government Services Building, Reading, PA); County Execution Dockets (Northumberland County Courthouse). These figures represent orders processed, not the actual number of people foreclosed . . .; each case typically generated multiple foreclosure orders.

[7]Westmoreland County Execution Dockets, 1782–1792 (Westmoreland County Courthouse, Greensburg, PA).

[8]Figures compiled from Westmoreland County Execution Dockets.

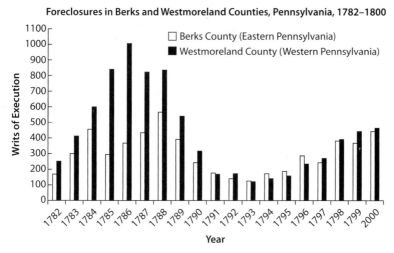

Figure 8.1
Foreclosures in Berks and Westmoreland Counties, Pennsylvania, 1782–1800.
Source: County execution dockets, 1782–1800, for Berks and Westmoreland counties.

gold and silver, Pennsylvania's "land bank" and the paper currency it lent had proven critical to the financial well-being of farmers throughout the colony. . . .[9]

Despite the centrality of paper money and public credit to the health of the economy, state leaders (representing Pennsylvania's two main political factions) persistently reduced the supply of both during the postwar decades. Although the leaders of the warring Republican and Constitutionalist factions advocated competing economic programs, those men—bankers, merchants, lawyers, landlords, and prominent commercial farmers—shared a commitment to protecting their common interests as creditors. They united to protect themselves as moneylenders by reducing the supply of paper currency in order to limit inflation and by narrowing the scope of the state loan office, their primary competition in the credit market. Leaders of the two factions also worked toward advancing their interests as public creditors (those who held the certificates representing the Revolutionary War debt) in ways that exacerbated the monetary scarcity.

The controversy about the war debt surrounded the millions of dollars in promissory notes that a near-bankrupt Continental Congress had issued to soldiers, farmers, and merchants to finance the war for independence. Because of Congress's severe financial problems, all war debt certificates instantly fell in worth, some to as low as one-thirtieth of their face value. During and after the war, cash-strapped farmers and artisans sold their certificates at those low going rates, causing the paper to concentrate in the hands of wealthy Americans who possessed the resources to engage in such risky and potentially lucrative speculation

---

[9]E. James Ferguson, *Power of the Purse: A History of American Public Finance, 1776–1790* (Chapel Hill, NC, 1961), 3–24; Leslie Van Horne Brock, *The Currency of the American Colonies, 1700–1764* (New York, 1975); Mary M. Schweitzer, *Custom and Contract: Household, Government, and the Economy in Colonial Pennsylvania* (New York, 1987), 115–67; and John J. McCusker and Russell R. Menard, *The Economy of British America, 1607–1789* (Chapel Hill, NC, 1985), 338–39.

as purchasing the certificates. In Pennsylvania, as elsewhere, the degree of consolidation was astounding. By 1790, over 96 percent of Pennsylvania's $4.8 million in war debt certificates was held by just 434 people. The top twenty-eight investors (nearly all of whom were Philadelphia merchants, lawyers, and brokers) owned over 40 percent of the entire Pennsylvania war debt. Foremost among them were politicians: the Republicans Morris, George Clymer, Thomas FitzSimons, and William Bingham and Constitutionalists such as Charles Pettit and Blair McClennachan. Despite purchasing certificates at pennies on the dollar, those men lobbied for a yearly interest payment of 6 percent and the eventual redemption of the slips of paper at their full face value. Such provisions, if implemented, would have meant that a speculator who had purchased a $100 face-value certificate probably for between $10 and $17 (and perhaps for as little as $4) would receive a yearly interest payment of $6 and, in time, the entire $100 principal.[10]

. . . Amassing the funds to redeem the war debt meant the swift collection of back taxes . . . and the enactment of new taxes to pay the interest and principal—all of which removed more hard money and currency from the economy. The demands of public creditors to be paid in gold and silver or, if necessary, paper money that was as valuable as possible led state leaders to avoid printing new currency. And when the state did print new money, it was designed primarily for bondholders, not the average farmer. . . .

The sum effect of these policies was a dramatic reduction in the amount of money in circulation, particularly the paper currency that was so central to the health of the rural economy. To put the paper money cuts in perspective, on the eve of the Revolutionary War, at a time when Pennsylvanians complained of a "scarcity" of money, there had been approximately $5.33 in government currency in circulation per person. By comparison, in 1786 there was only about $1.88 worth of paper money for every man, woman, and child. By 1790, currency reductions and a rapidly growing population had dropped the circulation of government money to a mere $0.31 per person. The limited supply of currency and public credit kept interest rates during the first decade after the war at shocking levels: from 5 to 12 percent *per month*, rather than the usual 6 percent *per year*. Needless to say, while those rates were detrimental to most debtor farmers, they benefited many large-scale creditors, especially the political leaders associated with Philadelphia's Bank of North America: the merchants Morris, FitzSimons, and Clymer and the lawyer James Wilson—men who in 1787 served as Pennsylvania's delegates to the federal Constitutional Convention.[11]

---

[10]The best analysis of certificate holding patterns is Ferguson, *Power of the Purse*, 35–40, 53–55, 59–69, 251–86. For the market value of securities in Pennsylvania, see *Independent Gazetteer*, Feb. 15, 1783, Feb. 12, 1784, Jan. 8, 1785; *Carlisle Gazette*, Feb. 22, 1786; Pennsylvania General Assembly, *Minutes of the General Assembly*, Dec. 4, 1784, March 16, 1785 (Philadelphia, 1785). For individual certificate holdings of the war debt in Pennsylvania, see Certificate Exchange Proposals, 1789–1793, Records of the Comptroller General.

[11]McCusker and Menard, *Economy of British America*, 338–39; Pennsylvania Comptroller General, *A View of the Debts and Expenses of the Commonwealth of Pennsylvania, and the Funds and Revenues of the Same, December 1786* (Philadelphia, 1786).

The men who drafted those policies firmly believed that they were acting in the best interests of the state and the nation. According to such men as Robert Morris, the most powerful political figure in Pennsylvania, any policy that benefited the economic interests of the elite was good for the nation, even if it produced widespread hardship for ordinary citizens. Articulating what was conventional wisdom among many of his colleagues, Morris asserted that America would become a great nation only when government "distributed" wealth into the hands of affluent men who knew how to make the "most productive" use of money. . . . Specifically, Morris believed that the affluent would follow "the strong Principle of Self Love and the immediate Sense of private Interest" and use government to wrest from ordinary citizens the funds they needed to build a great nation. As Morris liked to say, the formula for national greatness was simple: "The Possession of Money will acquire Influence. Influence will lead to Authority, and authority will open the Purses of the People."[12]

Herein lies the last factor driving agrarian protest: many Pennsylvanians considered Morris's vision of government and the crisis it produced to be a direct violation of the principles they assumed had been guiding the Revolution. York County farmers declared that the "Independence" they had sacrificed their "blood and treasure to secure" was being lost as their property was sold to pay the "grievous and insupportable load of taxes" that provided a financial windfall to war debt speculators. Farmers in Cumberland County condemned state officials for the "almost total annihilation of private credit, the pressure of taxes, and the extreme scarcity of circulating specie." They asserted that these policies undermined liberty by allowing a "merciless, rapacious creditor . . . to sacrifice the property of his debtor, by a public sale" and, thereby, reducing "Great numbers of . . . good people . . . from a state of competency to beggary." Likewise, thousands of Pennsylvania farmers signed petitions asserting that the state's attempt to replace the traditional system of paper money and public credit with Robert Morris's Bank of North America was "incompatible with the nature of our government" because it worked to "destroy" economic "equality" and, by doing so, allowed "a few private citizens to acquire an influence in . . . the government subversive of the dearest rights of the people." In a similar way, many farmers saw their political liberties threatened by the state's "unjust and improper" policy of "selling Back Lands in great quantities to companies"—a practice they saw as "destructive of an essential principle in every republican government: the equal division of landed property." In short, farmers across Pennsylvania believed that government was undermining their political liberty by using its powers to concentrate wealth in a few hands, rather than ensuring that ordinary citizens obtained the economic independence that gave freedom its meaning.[13]

---

[12]Robert Morris to Thomas Jefferson, June 11, 1781, in *Papers of Robert Morris*, ed. Ferguson et al., I, 143; Morris to John Jay, July 13, 1781, ibid., I, 287; Morris to the President of Congress, July 29, 1782, ibid., VI, 63; Robert Morris, "Observations on the Present State of Affairs," Jan. 13, 1783, ibid., VI, 306.

[13]York County Petition, 1784 (microfilm, reel 3), Records of the General Assembly (Pennsylvania Historical and Museum Commission); *Carlisle Gazette*, April 2, 1788. For text of petitions against the Bank of North America, see *Pennsylvania Evening Herald*, Feb. 23, 1785, Feb. 10, 1786; *Carlisle Gazette*, Aug. 20, 1794; Terry Bouton, "Tying Up the Revolution: Money, Power, and the Regulation in Pennsylvania, 1765–1800" (Ph.D. diss., Duke University, 1996), 12–48, 172–265, 402–40.

Of course, this was not an all-inclusive ideal: Pennsylvania farmers were concerned only about preserving political liberty and economic equality for white men. . . . When it came to defending this vision, farmers across Pennsylvania turned to an idea of citizen rights that was also far more expansive than many elite Americans would allow. Behind rural protest was a belief that the Revolution (and the Pennsylvania Constitution of 1776 in particular) gave ordinary people extensive rights to resist policies that threatened economic equality and political liberty. The 1776 state charter stated that "the people" had the "sole, exclusive, and inherent right of governing and regulating" state policy. It specified that government policies must work for the "common benefit" of the "community" and "not for the particular emolument or advantage of any . . . set of men who are only part of that community." And if government violated those provisions, the 1776 constitution proclaimed that "the people" had the right to "take such measures as to them may appear necessary to promote their safety and happiness." As will become apparent, many farmers took all this literally, believing that the state constitution sanctioned a wide range of resistance, from civil disobedience to road closings to taking up arms.[14]

This conception of democracy produced agrarian protest that unfolded in two distinct phases. The first phase covered the period from the end of the war to Pennsylvania's ratification of the federal Constitution in the fall of 1787. The second phase, which included the road closings, ran from the fall of 1787 to the uprisings of 1794 and 1799.

During the first phase, from 1783 to the fall of 1787, rural protest generally took the form of complex defensive networks that shielded the property of farm communities. While in part these networks sought to stop property confiscation for private debts, farmers focused most of their attention on limiting foreclosures resulting from state and federal tax policies. Most farmers undoubtedly considered mass private debt foreclosure to be objectionable. But they seemed even more offended by the prospect of public officials foreclosing families to provide a windfall for speculators in the war debt—especially men who had purchased certificates from farmers at pennies on the dollar. Consequently, farmers in locales throughout Pennsylvania organized themselves to save their horses, blacksmith hammers, and land. In the process, many tried to reaffirm the idea that only widespread economic independence would preserve their political liberty. . . .

Evidence . . . reveals a common structure to the defensive networks that farmers created. In the immediate postwar years, farmers constructed what can be thought of as concentric rings of protection around their communities. Each individual ring corresponded to a different stage in a foreclosure process that began with tax collection and ended with sheriffs' auctions. Starting from the outer ring and working inward to the last barrier shielding property, the first ring was created by county revenue officials who refused to collect taxes or to disclose to the state the names of those who could not pay. If their efforts failed, locally

---

[14]Council of Censors, *The Constitutions of 1776 and 1790* (Harrisburg, PA, 1825).

elected county justices often formed a second ring by rejecting requests to prosecute delinquent taxpayers and tax collectors. If justices did not include themselves in the network, witnesses and juries occasionally used their power over the legal process to create a third ring. If juries did not act, sheriffs and constables sometimes constituted a fourth. Finally, if all those rings failed, farmers constructed a fifth and final ring of defense . . . violent resistance. . . . [T]he rings of protection—a clear example of popular democracy in action—formed a sturdy barrier that lasted from 1783 through the fall of 1787 and defended both property and rural notions of a just society. . . .

[T]he rings of protection that farmers built between 1783 and 1787 were impressive. This was true even of the outermost ring constructed by county revenue officials, people whose financial well-being depended upon successful tax collection. Although it meant losing income from commissions, local revenue officers in nearly every county tried to protect their constituents by refusing to collect taxes, submit their ledgers for inspection, or prosecute delinquent taxpayers. In Bucks County, just twenty miles outside Philadelphia, the commissioners of taxes declared in 1783 that the "absolute scarcity of Money" made it "hard and impolitic to execute Rigours of the Law upon the Collectors." . . . Across the Susquehanna River in Cumberland County, officers reported that "money is so scarce" that taxes could not be collected "without Indictments," a prospect those officers found "very disagreeable."[15]

Revenue officers in the westernmost counties issued the strongest statements against state tax policies and neglected their official duties with the most enthusiasm. One official in Huntingdon County was so distressed by inflicting "great cruelties" on his neighbors that he resigned his post, asserting that he was "an unfit person for such business" as bringing "ruin on poor families." . . . In Washington County in 1785, when the state attorney general commanded tax officials to surrender their ledgers, they rebuffed the order and instead accepted fines for delinquency. Two years later, those men continued their resistance, promising to protect "a poor distressed people That is Willing To Do Everything in Their power" to pay their taxes, but who could not acquire the necessary funds.[16]

In most cases, however, resistance by county revenue officials proved temporary. Revenue laws made it relatively easy for state leaders to sue county tax officers for neglecting their duties. Furthermore, when county revenue officials took office, state law required that they sign hefty bonds that mortgaged their own property against the faithful performance of their duties. Consequently, when

---

[15]Commissioners of Bucks County to John Dickinson, July 31, 1783, in *Pennsylvania Archives: First Series*, ed. Samuel Hazard (12 vols., Harrisburg, PA, 1852–1856), X, 75; John Agnew, Cumberland Co., to Nicholson, Oct. 2, 1786, file 5, box 4, General Correspondence, Records of the Comptroller General.

[16]John Cadwallader, Huntingdon Co., to John Nicholson, May 22, 1788, file 13, box 9, General Correspondence, Records of the Comptroller General; Sept. 1785, Washington County Quarter Sessions Papers; Andrew Swearingen, Washington Co., to Nicholson, Feb. 4, 1787, file 12, box 4, General Correspondence, Records of the Comptroller General.

ordered by the state to do their jobs, county officers typically relented and initiated lawsuits against local tax collectors to avoid being sued themselves.[17]

... [C]ounty justices of the peace sometimes assumed responsibility for protecting their communities. . . . [18] In the foothills of the Appalachians in Bedford County, no amount of prodding could make Justice James Martin retreat from his idea of how a democracy should function. Throughout 1785 and 1786, Martin refused to take action against any delinquent collector or taxpayer in his jurisdiction. To defend his neighbors, Martin was even willing to make himself appear as a country bumpkin: He told revenue officials he did not understand the tax laws; he missed court appearances; and he claimed to have mislaid tax rolls. In the summer of 1787, however, an informal street-corner meeting between the justice and worried citizens exposed Martin's deception. At this meeting (overheard by a county revenue officer), Martin tried to reassure neighbors who were afraid that he would foreclose them for unpaid taxes. As the eavesdropper reported, Martin

> wondered what sort of Assembly we had got that made such Laws. . . . Lord have mercy on us (says he wringing his hands) the country will be ruined. I do not know what to do. The collectors all make returns of the Delinquents & I don't know what to do. I have put one Township off with telling them I did not understand the Law, but I'll tell you what (says he) I will not sue one of you until I am sued.

Martin did better than this. By stalling the legal process, he gave several hopelessly delinquent taxpayers and collectors time to sell their property and flee the county. In these multiple ways, Justice Martin became a man Bedford citizens could trust to uphold rural notions of the Revolution by repelling laws that foreclosed the county.[19]

When justices of the peace chose to enforce tax laws, as most inevitably did, the defensive networks usually held together, sometimes because court witnesses and juries stepped forward to form their own ring of protection. For example, one Northampton County tax official reported in February 1786 that it was extremely difficult to get witnesses to testify against neighbors on matters involving unpaid taxes. . . .[20]

In the event that trial juries voted to convict taxpayers or collectors, the defense network sometimes remained intact through the action (or rather

---

[17]For examples of the reluctance of county officers to put the law into force, see Commissioners of Bucks County to John Dickinson, July 31, 1783, in Samuel Hazard, *Pennsylvania Archives: First Series : Selected and Arranged from Original Documents in the Office of the Secretary of the Commonwealth, Conformably to Acts of the General Assembly, February 15, 1851, and March 1, 1852,* (Philadelphia: Printed by J. Severns, 1852), X, 75; [and other examples as cited in the original essay].

[18]"Agreeable to the request of the Honorable the Committee on Ways and Means," Dec. 1786, file 8, box 4, General Correspondence, Records of the Comptroller General. See also Brown, *Redeeming the Republic,* 64–65. [And letters to John Nicholson as cited in the original essay.]

[19]Bedford County commissioner to the Pennsylvania Comptroller General: Thomas Crossan to Nicholson, Aug. 22, 1787, file 6, box 5, ibid.; Crossan to Nicholson, Sept. 15, 1787, file 10, box 5, ibid.

[20]Robert Levers, Northampton Co., to Nicholson, Feb. 15, 1786, file 6, box 3, ibid.

inaction) of county law enforcement. For their part, county sheriffs, who were among the wealthiest officers in county government, joined the protective effort infrequently. . . . By contrast, constables, typically the poorest officers in county government, were far more likely to refuse to deliver warrants or arrest taxpayers. Ironically, it was precisely their relative poverty that made constables such an effective part of the defensive network. The treasurer of Bedford County explained in April 1787 that "Constables are generally chosen out of the Lowest Class of people" and, therefore, they generally did not own property that could be confiscated by a lawsuit when they failed to perform their jobs. "What law can compel the poorest man that has nothing to pay?" asked this officer, experienced with the fact that his threats to sue propertyless constables carried little weight. In Northampton County, constables used the power of their poverty to "Indulge their neighbors" by refusing to foreclose them for unpaid taxes. In Washington County, the entire corps of constables exercised similar indulgence by boycotting court during the entire January 1786 session.[21]

If constables did their jobs, farmers often took it upon themselves to construct a last ring of protection. Tax officials from Cumberland County explained one strategy: "should their neighbors' property be exposed to sale," rural people turned out in great numbers and crowded the premises, but they would "not offer to purchase." Instead, farmers would "combine together and not give a single bid." Between 1783 and 1787, the officers of at least eight different counties . . . all reported that farmers would not bid on property foreclosed for taxes. Moreover, since county officers could not arrest people for failing to bid at an auction, they found it nearly impossible to stop the practice. . . .[22]

If these efforts failed, some farmers resorted to physical resistance. Most of the cases involved individual men and women trying to protect their property by hurling rocks, wielding sticks, or throwing punches at the county officials who attempted to uphold the law.[23] During 1786 and 1787, farmers also turned to traditional eighteenth-century forms of crowd action. In early 1786, the Pennsylvania comptroller general John Nicholson threatened to sue county tax officials unless they collected "every shilling" their counties owed within the year, triggering a surge of lawsuits against taxpayers and collectors. In response, farmers occasionally responded with "rough music." For example, in April 1786, farmers in Washington County accosted one tax collector, mutilating his hat and then

---

[21]Thomas Crossan and David Stewart, Bedford Co., to Nicholson, April 24, 1787, file 17, box 4, ibid.; Jacob Arndt Jr., Northampton Co., to Nicholson, Aug. 25, 1786, file 16, box 3, ibid.; Arndt to Nicholson, April 21, 1787, file 17, box 4, ibid.; Jan. 1786, Washington County Quarter Sessions Dockets and Papers. Tax rolls in western Pennsylvania confirm that sheriffs were among the wealthiest officers of county government and constables among the poorest: R. Eugene Harper, *The Transformation of Western Pennsylvania, 1770–1800* (Pittsburgh, PA, 1992), 168.

[22]Richard Parker, Cumberland Co., to John Nicholson, May 13, 1788, file 16, box 6, General Correspondence, Records of the Comptroller General; Alexander McKeehen and George Logue, Cumberland Co., to Nicholson, March 21, 1789, file 13, box 6, ibid.; Commissioners of Bucks County to John Dickinson, July 31, 1783, in *Pennsylvania Archives: First Series*, ed. Hazard, X, 75.

[23]For the incidents of assaults on county officials, see Jan. 1783, April 1785, Bedford County Quarter Sessions Dockets and Papers; [And other examples as cited in the original article].

cutting off the hair on one side of his head. The crowd then paraded the man through the county wearing his mangled hat, passing him from township to township, and compelling him to drink at every tavern the procession crossed. When the thoroughly intoxicated collector and the ever-growing crowd reached the border to neighboring Westmoreland County, the farmers set the tax collector free with "Threats of utter Desolution should he dare to return to our County." . . .[24]

In York County, conflict between farmers and revenue officers nearly exploded into civil war. In December 1786, York tax officials tried to thwart bidderless auctions by moving sheriffs' sales from the homes of foreclosed farmers to the county courthouse. In response, approximately two hundred farmers from the surrounding townships marched into the town of York to enforce their protective network. This group, which included a number of men of "good moral Carrectors, and of considerable Proppery," paraded through town armed with guns and clubs, before breaking up the auction of some cattle and returning home. When county officials tried to move another auction in January 1787, farmers once again descended on the town and freed foreclosed livestock. "This disorder," concluded one York officer, "I am nearly warranted to say is become epidemic. . . ."[25]

Under such circumstances, what could the state do? Preventing this wide array of community resistance was not a simple matter. State leaders had little faith that they could call on county militias to enforce their laws. In 1784 and 1785, when they had ordered militia units from Bucks and Northampton counties to enforce another unpopular policy . . ., the militias had refused to march. In petitions, Bucks County militiamen had declared that they were "Sensibly touched with abhorrence of the Idea of Staining their hands with the blood of their Countrymen & fellow Subjects" to settle "the quarrel of a set of landjobbers," noting that the orders to march "arose from a dispute about private property" and were antithetical to the "Very Spirit of our Laws & [state] Constitution." In 1786, state leaders undoubtedly reasoned that farmers . . . were unlikely to march against their fellow Pennsylvanians. Moreover, state leaders understood that, in most places, they could not call out the militia to ensure the success of a sheriff's auction or compel tax collection precisely because, as in York County, it

---

[24]Circular, March 30, 1786, Letter Book, Records of the Comptroller General; Dorsey Penticost, Washington Co., to Council, April 16, 1786, in *Pennsylvania Archives: First Series*, ed. Hazard, X, 757. For eighteenth-century forms of "charivari" or "rough music," see E. P. Thompson, "Patrician Society, Plebian Culture," *Journal of Social History* 7 (Summer 1974), 382–405; and E. P. Thompson, "Rough Music Reconsidered," *Folklore* 103 (1) (1992), 3–26. For examinations of "rough music" in eighteenth-century America, see Alfred F. Young, "English Plebian Culture and Eighteenth-Century Radicalism," in *The Origins of Anglo-American Radicalism*, ed. Margaret Jacob and James Jacob (London, 1984), 185–212; and Fennell, "From Rebelliousness to Insurrection," 4–43, 98–122.

[25]Michael Hahn, York Co., to John Nicholson, Dec. 15, 1786, in *Pennsylvania Archives: First Series*, ed. Hazard, XI, 98; *Pennsylvania Mercury*, June 8, 1787.

was the militia units themselves that stopped auctions and blocked tax collection in the first place.[26]

The state treasurer explained in 1784 that all the defensive efforts had combined to produce "almost a total stop in the Collecting of Taxes."[27] Reluctant revenue officials, lenient judges, defendant-friendly juries, disobedient law officers, bidderless auctions, community censure, and self-directed militia units all effectively immobilized the revenue system.... For... the merchant, banker, bondholder, and politician Thomas FitzSimons..., statewide taxpayer resistance was a cause of alarm to... men like himself, who counted on the tax returns to fund their yearly interest payment on the war debt certificates they held.[28]

Such "alarm" prompted many Pennsylvania creditors, whether they identified themselves politically as Republicans or Constitutionalists, to push for revisions to the Articles of Confederation and the Pennsylvania Constitution of 1776. Many large-scale public and private creditors believed that those documents left government too weak to collect taxes or private debts. Men like FitzSimons saw their ambitions frustrated by a decentralized revenue system where power was entrusted to local officials, a civil police force composed of relatively autonomous constables and militia units, and a legal infrastructure that could not easily break the rings of community protection. Such factors help explain why many state leaders joined the movement for a new federal Constitution and why Pennsylvania's delegation to the Constitutional Convention in Philadelphia included the state's largest private and public creditors. Indeed, five of the eight delegates from Pennsylvania were men with close ties to the Bank of North America in Philadelphia: Thomas FitzSimons, Robert Morris, Gouverneur Morris, George Clymer, and James Wilson. The Constitution that those men helped to draft prohibited states from printing paper money and paved the way for making the war debt a federal responsibility.... [T]he federal Constitution broke through the rings that Pennsylvania farmers had constructed to defend their property from foreclosure. Federally appointed revenue agents, prosecutors, and judges (responsive to the national leaders who appointed them) oversaw the collection of new federal taxes. If rural communities opposed the new tax measures, the Constitution allowed the president to command militia units from any state to put down resistance in another. In sum, the federal Constitution provided what

---

[26]For the refusals of Northampton and Bucks County militiamen to march in 1784, see Honorable John Boyd and Lt. Col. John Armstrong to President Dickinson, Aug. 7, 1784 (frame 409, reel 21), Records of Pennsylvania's Revolutionary Government. For petitions of Bucks County militiamen, see "Petition of Sundry Inhabitants of the Township of Lower Milford in the County of Bucks to President of the Supreme Executive Council," April 15, 1785 (frame 39, reel 22), ibid.; and "Richmond Township, Bucks County," 1785 (frame 496, reel 22), ibid.

[27]David Rittenhouse, state treasurer, to President Dickinson, April 27, 1784, quoted in Brown, *Redeeming the Republic*, 63.

[28]"State of the Accounts of the Treasury... from 1782... to 1785," in *Pennsylvania Archives: Third Series*, ed. Egle, V, 368–73; "Account of Taxes Paid by the Several Counties, from Jan. 1, 1787 to Sept. 6, inclusive," Sept. 20, 1787, in Pennsylvania General Assembly, *Minutes of the General Assembly* (Philadelphia, 1787); "County Tax Accounts, Balances, Effective Supplies Taxes, 1785–1789," County Tax Accounts, Records of the Comptroller General.

men such as Robert Morris had long desired: money, power, and the authority needed to "open the Purses of the People."[29]

Not content with the provisions of the federal Constitution, political leaders in Pennsylvania enacted their own state measures to complete the destruction of the protective rings. While Pennsylvanians were debating ratification of the federal Constitution in late 1787, the state comptroller general John Nicholson began a new campaign to use "every effort to enforce the speedy collection" of all outstanding taxes. He initiated special procedures to "destroy or prevent" local resistance, such as moving property auctions away from sympathetic rural neighborhoods to commercial centers where willing bidders lived.[30] Over the next several years, state leaders further dismantled rural defenses by passing a series of laws that established stiff penalties for revenue officers, judges, constables, and sheriffs who refused to perform their duties.[31] Finally, the new Pennsylvania Constitution of 1790 negated the power of locally elected justices of the peace by transferring much of their authority to new state-appointed judges. In these sundry ways, state leaders hoped to displace the broad notions of citizenship specified in the 1776 state constitution with a much narrower set of democratic rights.

The new political environment that emerged in the fall of 1787 brought popular protest in Pennsylvania to an important turning point, signaling the start of a new and more desperate phase of rural insurgency. With state and national leaders working to destroy rural defenses, farmers were forced to develop increasingly ambitious, creative, and confrontational strategies to defend their communities. Ultimately, by the mid-1790s, many Pennsylvania farmers concluded that the only way to defend their liberties was armed resistance against the policies of state and national leaders.

The first efforts to protect rural communities during this new phase, however, provided no hint of the drama to come. Farmers simply tried to rejuvenate the traditional rings of protection. . . . The transformation of agrarian protest occurred when state leaders rewrote laws to outlaw such official resistance, compelling rural Pennsylvanians to develop more creative strategies. It was at this moment that farmers across the state began blocking roads with fences, ditches, and log piles. Farmers hoped that road closings would give them a new way to

---

[29]Morris, "Observations on the Present State of Affairs," Jan. 13, 1783.

[30]John Nicholson to Thomas Mifflin, Sept. 17, 1788, Letter Book, Records of the Comptroller General; Nicholson to Richard Parker, Cumberland Co., June 19, 1788, ibid.; Nicholson to Commissioners of Cumberland County, March 31, 1789, ibid.; Nicholson to Christopher Devring, Northumberland Co., May 16, 1789, ibid.

[31]"A Supplement to the Act Entitled 'An Act to Enforce the Due Collection and Payment of Taxes Within this Commonwealth,'" Oct. 4, 1788, in *Statutes At Large of Pennsylvania*, ed. Mitchell and Flanders, XIII, 145–49; "A Supplement to the Act Entitled 'A Supplement to the Act Entitled "An Act to Enforce the Due Collection and Payment of Taxes Within this Commonwealth,"'" March 28, 1789, ibid, XIII, 292–94; "An Act Relating to the Securities to be Given by Sheriffs and Coroners," March 5, 1790, ibid., XIII, 455–57; "An Act to Provide a More Effectual Method of Settling the Public Accounts of the Commissioners and Treasurers of the Respective Counties," March 30, 1791, ibid., XIV, 41–46.

stop sheriffs' auctions. Consequently, in most counties, farmers created barriers between their neighborhoods and the commercial centers where bidders were likely to reside. Many farmers tried to quarantine the towns that contained the county courthouses where John Nicholson had ordered property auctions to be moved. Accordingly, from 1788 to 1794, obstructions appeared in the roads leading to and from courthouses. . . . [F]armers blocked roads leading from ferry stations or felled trees across the main routes connecting one county to another. In eastern counties, inhabitants tended to obstruct the main highways that led to and from Philadelphia. With roads blocked, it made little difference that bidders acquired furniture, grain, or livestock at low prices; barricaded roads meant that buyers would be unable to get their bargains home.

Other road closers had an even more ambitious goal: disrupting the court system altogether. In several counties, obstructions in the road prevented court attendance or provided a convenient excuse for jury members and constables who failed to show for required courthouse appearances. For example, in Northumberland County in the spring and summer of 1792, inhabitants dug ditches and erected fences on at least five of the main roads that led to the courthouse at Sunbury. Subsequently, at the April court session, twenty-three of thirty-five jurors failed to appear. At the next court session, held in August, the empty seats in the jury box were now mirrored by eleven vacant spaces on the benches where township constables were supposed to sit.[32]

Achieving such results required considerable organization. It was not enough to assemble large groups of farmers to spend days cutting down trees or digging deep ditches in well-packed highways; keeping roads blocked for long periods of time meant that this resistance had to be a communitywide affair. . . . In eastern Chester County, when one man was arrested for digging a crater in the road measuring fifty feet in circumference and seven feet deep, forty-two men signed a petition calling for his release. In 1793 in the central county of Huntingdon, citizens in one township assembled in a unique way to ensure that their blocked highways remained obstructed: at the annual election for the township's "road supervisor" (the county official responsible for clearing the highways of debris), the entire electorate refused to cast a single vote, leaving the office vacant and the roads closed. . . .[33]

In those ways, road closings became for many rural people a way of constructing an additional ring for a defensive network that was rapidly being torn apart. In places where new laws, procedures, judges, and tax collectors had dismantled every other ring of protection, obstructed roads became the last barrier shielding property that was scheduled for the auction block. The remarkable effort demonstrated by rural citizens in shutting highways and the great inconveniences they endured by isolating themselves demonstrate just how desperate many farmers had become. . . .

---

[32]April, Aug. 1792, Northumberland County Quarter Sessions Dockets and Papers.

[33]1789, Chester County Quarter Sessions Papers; Nov. 1793, Huntingdon County Quarter Sessions Dockets and Papers.

... [An] extralegal court actually went into operation in early 1794 in several counties west of the Appalachians. The first of these courts was probably the Mingo Creek Society, formed in February 1794 by citizens in Washington County who were "harassed with suits from justices and courts, and wished a less expensive tribunal." This new court was not created for the purpose of allowing debtors to shirk their responsibilities and defraud their creditors. Instead it represented a serious effort to find a just and democratic solution for all parties. The society's constitution established that the officers who administered debt mediation were to be elected by the public at large. These new "judges" would oversee a jurisdiction corresponding to the district for regular elections and militia service. And, as the society's constitution proclaimed, citizens were supposed to turn to this informal court before they took matters to the regular legal system. "No district citizen," the constitution read, was to "sue, or cause to be sued before a single justice of the peace, or any court of justice, a citizen of the district, before applying to the society for redress."[34]

It appears that the court functioned as intended. The docket books for the official Washington County court reveal that numerous creditors dropped debt suits (and paid stiff penalties for doing so) to comply with the new society. . . . Moreover, shortly after this court opened in 1794, a similar extralegal court also appeared in neighboring Allegheny County. The report from a "meeting of the society from the four counties" (Allegheny, Washington, Fayette, and Westmoreland) announced that plans for similar courts were in the works. . . . Thus, by the opening months of 1794, it appeared that many people in western Pennsylvania were developing new organizations dedicated to promoting widespread economic independence. Those new institutions were not the product of a lawless rabble. Rather, they were an attempt by ordinary people to construct the kind of society where difficult problems were solved peacefully and democratically.[35]

While the destruction of the protective rings led to new attempts for peaceful solutions, it also produced many episodes of violence against public officials. Before 1787, violence against constables, sheriffs, tax collectors, and judges had formed only a small part of defensive efforts. Indeed, from 1781 through 1787, there were only twenty-three cases of violence against officials in surviving court records from thirteen counties. By comparison, in the seven years after Pennsylvania ratified the federal Constitution, the number of attacks on public officials in those counties nearly tripled, reaching sixty-three separate incidents of violence. Nearly half of the cases involved individuals or groups of people trying to "rescue" incarcerated debtors or foreclosed property. Desperate to protect their

---

[34]"Constitution of the Mingo Creek Society," Feb. 28, 1794, in Hugh Henry Brackenridge, *Incidents of the Insurrection in the Western Parts of Pennsylvania in the Year 1794* (3 vols. bound in one, Philadelphia, 1795), III, 25, and appendix, 148–49.

[35]Washington County Execution Dockets, 1791–1794 (Washington County Courthouse, Washington, PA); Brackenridge, *Incidents of the Insurrection*, III, 25.

idea of the Revolution, those people openly challenged a legal system that they saw as an undemocratic tool for exploiting debtors.[36]

Ultimately, the new government's efficiency in wresting property from rural Pennsylvanians brought desperate people to armed resistance, first in 1794 in the "Whiskey Rebellion" and again in 1799 in "Fries's Rebellion." Both insurgencies have long been misunderstood because historians have failed to appreciate the scope of the economic distress experienced by rural Pennsylvanians and the previous efforts of farmers to foster economic equality. On the surface, the protests seem to have been directed at a specific set of laws: in the case of the "Whiskey Rebellion," the 1791 excise tax on distilled spirits; and in "Fries's Rebellion," a revenue law that taxed people based on the number of windows in their houses. Understood within a broader context, however, the insurgencies emerge as the last rings of protection for defending property and a popular agrarian vision of the American Revolution.

In western Pennsylvania, many farmers saw the excise tax and the entirety of Alexander Hamilton's program to fund the war debt as an extension of policies they had opposed during the previous decade. Accordingly, when delegates from the counties of Washington, Westmoreland, Fayette, and Allegheny met in 1791 and 1792, they crafted a petition that specified the continuity of their grievances. The petitioners assailed the privately run Bank of the United States as an "evil" institution for monopolizing credit in the "hands of a few persons" who used their power to unduly "influence" the political process. They saw the provisions for paying off war debt certificates at full face value as an "insulting" and transparent attempt by a few wealthy and powerful men to "gratify" themselves with "ambitious and interested measures." Petitioners observed that Hamilton's funding program did little more than "make fortunes" for bond speculators while saddling the general public . . . with more taxes to pay the "unreasonable interest of the public debt." To petitioners, the new excise tax on distilled spirits (one of the sources by which this interest would be paid) was, thus, the "base off-spring of the funding system" to reward bond speculators at the public's expense. They declared that this tax, along with all the other measures, would exacerbate the already acute "scarcity of a circulating medium" and "bring immediate distress and ruin on the Western Country."[37]

Just as the primary arguments used by western Pennsylvanians remained consistent throughout the 1780s and 1790s, so too did their tactics for shielding property during the "excise protest." The farmers—many of them old enough to recall colonial resistance to the Stamp Act in 1765—urged those appointed to the position of excise collector to refuse the office. They drafted notices

---

[36]I compiled these figures from quarter sessions dockets and papers for the following counties: Bedford, Berks, Bucks, Chester, Cumberland, Dauphin, Huntingdon, Lancaster, Mifflin, Northampton, Northumberland, Washington, and York.

[37]"Minutes of the Meeting [of western counties delegates] at Pittsburgh, Sept. 7, 1791," in *Pennsylvania Archives: Second Series*, ed. John B. Linn and William Henry Egle (19 vols., Harrisburg, PA, 1874–1893), IV, 20–2 1; "Minutes of the Meeting at Pittsburgh, 21, 22 Aug. 1792," ibid., 30–31.

proclaiming that anyone attempting to collect the tax would be treated "with the contempt they deserve" by having their businesses boycotted. When a few federal officers disregarded this warning, some people resorted to physical measures to compel adherence to the protective network. The most violent of those episodes included ritualized attacks by groups of people who, like revolutionary patriots, blackened their faces and dressed as Indians or clad themselves in women's clothing. Many collectors avoided punishment by resigning their commissions. Those who did not often found themselves relieved of the money they had collected and the ledgers containing the names of delinquent distillers. If excise men adamantly refused to provide money or ledgers, the disguised crowds usually exacted some form of retribution. Some collectors were beaten, others tarred and feathered; one man was stripped naked and tied to a tree; another had his hair cut off; and still another was publicly branded with a hot fireplace poker.[38]

Within limits, western Pennsylvanians also continued to obstruct the legal system to stop enforcement of the excise law. When prosecutors brought charges against people accused of attacking excise collectors (in state, not federal, courts), they often could not get convictions. Grand juries routinely refused to indict those accused of the attacks. Witnesses failed to testify. When state and federal officials subsequently ordered state judges to press for conviction, some judges took no action, declaring "it was not our duty to hunt after prosecutions." Citing widespread opposition from all quarters, one state judge complained that he could not obtain "clear evidence" to convict anyone in his jurisdiction of crimes committed against federal collectors. . . .[39]

Seen in this context, the resistance against the excise appears as but part of this much larger pattern of rural insurgency in Pennsylvania. In August 1794, when [David] Bradford, his road-closing colleagues, and an army estimated at seven thousand farmers marched through the town of Pittsburgh, they were culminating more than a decade of protests against the revolutionary settlement of the postwar years.

Less than five years later, in early 1799, long-standing protests in the eastern counties of Berks, Bucks, Northampton, and Montgomery reached a similar moment of crisis. As in the 1794 protest in the western counties, the immediate issue was new taxes. And like the western insurgency, the eastern protest was filled with references to past transgressions by the state and federal government. Protesters declared that new tax policies were continuing a pattern of "Congress and the government" making "laws to rob the people" and leaving them "as bad

[38]See editorial note in Linn and Egle, eds., *Pennsylvania Archives: Second Series*, IV, 1–10. See also Slaughter, *Whiskey Rebellion*, 109–15; Fennell, "From Rebelliousness to Insurrection," 4–43, 98–122.

[39]Judge Alexander Addison to Gov. Thomas Mifflin, Nov. 4, 1792, in *Pennsylvania Archives: Second Series*, ed. Linn and Egle, IV, 36–39. See also James Brison to Miffin, Nov. 9, 1792, ibid., 44–45; David Redick to Alexander Dallas, Nov. 14, 1792, ibid., 46–47; and Judge Thomas Smith to Mifflin, Dec. 10, 1792, ibid., 54–57.

off as they were in Europe."[40] Many newspaper editorials compared the new taxes to the previous ones that had made fortunes for speculators in the Revolutionary War debt. Some writers flatly asserted that it was wrong for Congress to offer five million dollars in new war bonds that paid a steep annual interest of 8 percent. They declared that the government had no business providing a yearly "tribute to the amount of 100,000 dollars" in interest payments to *usurious nabobs* who hoped to increase their wealth through "the House and Land Tax" on ordinary citizens. The "gentry ought to be ashamed," concluded one writer who saw these laws as self-interested attempts to saddle the public with new taxes for personal gain. . . . Whatever the specific formulation, many easterners were angered that, with each new tax law, it seemed that the "Speculator goes free and the industrious farmer is become the object of taxation." Little was new in any of this analysis. These were precisely the arguments that farmers throughout Pennsylvania had been making since the end of the Revolutionary War.[41]

Finally, like the insurgents in western Pennsylvania, many farmers in the east drew the conclusion that defending the legacy of the Revolution required them to confront state and national leaders. John Fries, the purported leader of the movement, declared that the new federal tax signaled the moment to make a stand against the men who controlled Congress. "If we let them go on," he stated, "things would be as in France" where the people were "as poor as snakes." Many of Fries's neighbors in Northampton County shared this belief, pledging that they would "rather die than submit" to the new taxes, noting that "they had fought against such laws" in the Revolution and that, if necessary, they would fight again.[42]

Most rural protesters in both the east and the west probably never thought that there would actually be any fighting. Many western farmers did not think their government would send troops against its own citizens. Others in 1794 believed that, once the army arrived, the ordinary soldiers who filled its ranks would join the protest.[43] Similar beliefs emerged in the east in 1799: many insurgents thought that, if federal troops came, an army of farmers from beyond the Appalachians would rush to assist their agrarian brothers.[44]

---

[40]Testimony of Jacob Eyerly in *The Two Trials of John Fries on an Indictment for Treason*, ed. Thomas Carpenter (Philadelphia, 1800), 222; Deposition of Jacob Snyder, Oct. 7, 1799, Insurrection in Western Pennsylvania, Rawle Family Papers (Historical Society of Pennsylvania).

[41]*Aurora*, Jan. 12, Feb. 4, Feb. 21, Feb. 27, 1799. Emphasis in original.

[42]Deposition of Israel Robert, n.d., Insurrection in Western Pennsylvania, Rawle Papers; Fries quoted by Testimony of James Williamson in *Two Trials of John Fries*, ed. Carpenter, 187. Due to blurred print in the original document, it was unclear whether the word in the Fries quote was "snakes" or "shakers."

[43]Brackenridge, *Incidents of the Insurrection*, appendix VIII, 138, 139; Deposition of Isaac Meason, frame 346, reel 1, M–986, Criminal Case Files of the U.S. Circuit Court for the Eastern District of Pennsylvania, 1791– 1840 (National Archives, College Park, MD); William Bradford to Secretary of State, Sept. 5, 1794, Pennsylvania Whiskey Rebellion Collection (Manuscripts Division, Library of Congress).

[44]Deposition of Adam Hetzel, April 11, 1799, Insurrection in Western Pennsylvania, Rawle Papers; Testimony of Cephas Childs in *Two Trials of John Fries*, ed. Carpenter, 74; Testimony of Israel Roberts, ibid., 114.

In all these perceptions—about their government, the soldiers in the army, and the potential of mutual support among farmers—rural Pennsylvanians were badly mistaken.

When federal troops came, as they did during both the "rebellions," Pennsylvania farmers discovered that they could construct no ring of defense powerful or subtle enough to stop a large federal army. . . . Many farmers, both east and west, assumed that ordinary folk across the state wanted a government that promoted widespread economic equality. And, as the evidence presented here reveals, in many ways that assumption was not wrong. But in the new political environment created by the federal Constitution, common beliefs required organization to be effective. Because farmers in the east and west never found a way to link their efforts, the rings of protection they formed around themselves remained too weak to withstand the new government and its pro-creditor legal system. After the armies left their neighborhoods, many rural Pennsylvanians undoubtedly tried to keep their ideas about economic morality and political liberty alive. But they did so in a society now securely governed by a very different set of rules from the kind of economic democracy they had envisioned.[45]

Understanding Pennsylvania's rural insurgency in this way has the potential to transform how we think about the revolutionary settlement of the 1780s and 1790s. Much of the current scholarship on the American Revolution frames its conclusion as an unambiguous victory for ordinary Americans and their desires for a government that left them free to pursue their own economic self-interest.[46] Most rural Pennsylvanians of the revolutionary generation thought otherwise. Compared to the vision of 1776, as limited as it was, the revolutionary settlement of the 1780s and 1790s seemed to them a hollow and incomplete victory at best. During those years, many farmers saw their faith in economic equality challenged by political leaders who placed the interests of large-scale creditors ahead of the rural majority. They saw their economic independence eroded by mass property foreclosure. They saw their beliefs about political liberty undermined by government policies that concentrated wealth and political power at the top of society. And when they tried to shield their property and

---

[45]Farmers would challenge the political and economic dominance of a moneyed elite during the Jacksonian period and again during the Populist movement in the century's dosing decades, both times falling short of their objectives. For relevant studies, see, for example, Naomi Lamoreaux, *Insider Lending: Banks, Personal Connections, and Economic Development in Industrial New England* (New York, 1994); John Mack Faragher, *Sugar Creek: Life on the Illinois Prairie* (New Haven, CT, 1986); Charles C. Bolton, *Poor Whites of the Antebellum South: Tenants and Laborers in Central North Carolina and Northeast Mississippi* (Durham, NC, 1994); and Lawrence Goodwyn, *Democratic Promise: The Populist Moment in America* (New York, 1976).

[46]The assumption that ordinary Americans were advocates of economic liberalism underlies much recent scholarship on the Revolution and its aftermath. For relevant examples, see Joyce Appleby, *Inheriting the Revolution: The First Generation of Americans* (Cambridge, MA, 2000); Gordon S. Wood, *Radicalism of the American Revolution* (New York, 1991); and Elkins and McKitrick, *Age of Federalism*.

their ideals, farmers saw their notions of democratic citizenship, as expressed through their protective networks, dismantled by new constitutions and new laws. In short, rural Pennsylvanians witnessed the creation of a new government that systematically undermined the democratic society that they were trying to create.

The ultimate defeat of their vision for the Revolution, however, came not in the statehouse or on the battlefield, but in the history books. For two hundred years, historians have marginalized rural people, diminished their ideas, and discounted their protests. Pennsylvania's mass insurgencies have done little to change the central interpretations of the American Revolution because historians have tended to treat them as aberrations: spontaneous isolated outbursts—short hiccups of dissatisfaction that ended as quickly as they began. . . . As a result, when writing about the Revolution in Pennsylvania, historians have generally excluded from the story line the attempts of rural citizens—probably the majority of the state—to enact their own idea of a good society.

This agrarian vision (both its possibilities and its limitations) and the way it was contained by the creation of a new government deserve a central place in our understanding of the revolutionary settlement, precisely because the story in Pennsylvania was not an aberration. Farmers across the nation expressed dissatisfaction with the Revolution's final chapters; similar movements pushing for an alternative kind of democratic society developed, to one extent or another, in every state during the postwar decades. Many of those insurgencies are well known, such as the Massachusetts Regulation (long minimized as "Shays's Rebellion").[47] Others, like the road closings and rings of protection in Pennsylvania, have only recently been unearthed. No doubt similar efforts remain undiscovered in neglected county court records and unpublished government documents. Recovering the full scope of those various movements will permit us, perhaps for the first time, to understand the supposedly unrelated outbursts as part of a larger process. Only then will we begin to comprehend what farmers wanted from the Revolution and why so many rural people felt betrayed, rather than liberated, by the Revolution's outcome.[48]

---

[47]For the way the naming of popular insurgency during the American Revolution has obscured its content and meaning, see Ronald P. Formisano, "Teaching Shays/The Regulation," *Uncommon Sense* 106 (Winter 1998), 24–35. For elite attempts to tame the memory of the Revolution, see Alfred F. Young, *The Shoemaker and the Tea Party: Memory and the American Revolution* (Boston, 1999).

[48]This essay joins a growing body of scholarship seeking to understand how ordinary farmers interpreted the economic provisions of the revolutionary settlement: see, for example, Szatmary, *Shays' Rebellion*; Alan Taylor, *Liberty Men and Great Proprietors: The Revolutionary Settlement on the Maine Frontier, 1760–1820* (Chapel Hill, NC, 1990); Bellesiles, *Revolutionary Outlaws*; and Robert A. Gross, ed., *In Debt to Shays: The Bicentennial of an Agrarian Rebellion* (Charlottesville, VA, 1993).

Terry Bouton

My essay in this volume was inspired by petitions sent to the new national government in 1791 and 1792 from upset farmers, who, several years later, would rise in an armed protest that Treasury Secretary Alexander Hamilton lampooned as the "Whiskey Insurrection." In those petitions, farmers had raised an array of grievances against Hamilton's economic policies. Their main point was that new government was perpetuating widespread distress and concentrating wealth and power to such a frightening extent that democracy itself was at risk. For two hundred years, historians have rejected those charges as provincial paranoia and dismissed the farmers as "Whiskey Rebels." None of these scholars, however, had ever investigated the merits of the farmers' claims of mass property foreclosure and economic hardship. Instead, they had simply assumed that the Rebels were wrong and Hamilton was right. That's where I came in. Rather than dismissing the claims, I did what I was taught good historians were supposed to do: question assumptions, investigate, and search for actual evidence. And so, rather than take Hamilton's word for it, I set off across Pennsylvania to scour county court houses to see if things were as bad as the farmers claimed. What I found in musty old dockets led me to launch other investigations that ended up overturning much of what I had been taught about the nation's founding. You can read the full story of what I discovered in my book, *Taming Democracy: "The People," the Founders, and the Troubled Ending of the American Revolution* (Oxford, 2007).

QUESTIONS FOR CONSIDERATION

1. According to Bouton, what larger context shaped the road closings in post-independence Pennsylvania?
2. Characterize the economic changes in the years after the Revolution. What caused these changes? And what was their effect?
3. Who did rural Pennsylvania farmers blame for their woes? In what ways did they frame their protest in the language of the recent Revolution? Who did they exclude from this language?
4. Characterize the first phase of agrarian protest according to Bouton. How did authorities respond to these protests?
5. Bouton claims that "[t]he new political environment that emerged in the fall of 1787 brought popular protest in Pennsylvania to an important turning point." What events precipitated this turning point? And how did protests and reaction to them change after this turning point?
6. According to Bouton, how have historians furthered the ultimate defeat of eighteenth century rural protests in Pennsylvania?

CHAPTER NINE

"The Common Rights of Mankind": Subsistence, Shad, and Commerce in the Early Republican South[1]

Harry L. Watson

In the summer of 1787, while delegates to the federal convention in Philadelphia struggled in the arena of high politics to balance conflicting demands for public liberty and the common good, the free inhabitants of Orangeburg District, South Carolina, were angry about a more local version of that perennial problem. "No individual has a Right to Arrogate or Assume to himself an exclusive & partial Right," they fumed, "whereby he may deprive the People in its vicinage of those just Rights & Privileges which as Citizens of a free & independent State they are entitled to." The specific problem was a dam, which stretched across the Edisto River and created a fall of water to power Ferguson's Mills, incidentally blocking the movement of rafts and fish on the river. As a result of this dam, petitioners from the upstream neighborhoods bitterly protested, "they are totally cut off from availing themselves of the common Rights of Mankind."[2]

By some lights, the dam for Ferguson's Mills was essential to the rural economy, as much a part of the pastoral landscape as cornfields or framed houses. Its water-powered saws cut logs into lumber for sale to local customers, to downstream owners of Sea Island plantations, and perhaps to more distant consumers. In addition, mills such as Ferguson's often supplied local families with cornmeal for their daily bread, and they also ground wheat flour, an article that southern farmers were more likely to export than to eat themselves.

Many of Ferguson's neighbors saw the matter differently. Most obviously, the dam prevented other sawmill operators, located upstream, from floating their products to market. Petitioners complained to the legislature that the Edisto dam deprived them of something even more important, "the Benefits and

---

[1] Interested students are encouraged to read this essay in the original form. Harry L. Watson, "'The Common Rights of Mankind': Subsistence, Shad, and Commerce in the Early Republic South," *Journal of American History* 83 (1) (June 1996), 13–43.

[2] Petition from the Orangeburg District, on the Edisto River, General Assembly Petition 1787-08-01 (South Carolina Department of Archives and History, Columbia).

Emoluments arising from a Fishery." Expanding on this theme, residents a few years later declared that the offending dam even deprived them "of *a necessary of Life*, which their fellow citizens living upon other water courses 200 miles above the said Mills enjoy in the Greatest plenty."[3]

The "necessary of Life" that the Orangeburg petitioners demanded was the American shad, *Alosa sapidissima*, a species of Atlantic Ocean fish that ascends rivers every spring, from Florida to Canada. . . . [S]had were extremely abundant before the nineteenth century and fed Indians, pioneers, and slaves alike. Together with their cousins the alewives and the blueback herring, shad penetrated eastern rivers in massive spawning runs and were freely available to anyone who could operate a fish trap, cast a hook and line, or wield a hand-held dip net. The itinerant artist David Hunter Strother captured the likeness of one such happy fisherman in his illustrated account of a trip to North Carolina published in 1857. (See Figure 9.1.) Salted shad and herring were regarded as cheap food for the laboring poor as late as the mid-nineteenth century, when a leading commercial fisherman of North Carolina declared them "cheaper than bacon." Judging from the controversy they generated in early republican state legislatures, shad and herring played a[n] . . . important role.[4]

Complaints against the Edisto Sawmills were not isolated incidents, but manifestations of a widespread regional controversy over milldams and fishing rights that produced hundreds of angry petitions to legislatures in the South Atlantic area between 1750 and 1850. Some aspects of the dispute surfaced in almost every southeastern state at almost every legislative session in this period, leading each state to erect complex thickets of special legislative acts to regulate the competing claims of fishermen and millers.[5] The issue demonstrated the

---

[3]Ibid.; "The humble Petition of the Inhabitants of Orangeburgh District living above the Edisto Saw Mills," General Assembly Petition 1792-87-01, Ibid. Emphasis added.

[4]Porte Crayon [David Hunter Strother], "North Carolina Illustrated. I—The Fisheries," *Harper's New Monthly Magazine* 14 (March 1857), 438–47; Edward Wood, *To the President of the State Agricultural Society of North Carolina* (Edenton, 1871) (broadside, North Carolina Collection, Wilson Library, University of North Carolina, Chapel Hill). On fish in the southern food supply, see Sam Bowers Hilliard, *Hog Meat and Hoecake: Food Supply in the Old South, 1840–1860* (Carbondale, IL, 1972), 85–87; Charles H. Stevenson, "Fisheries in the Ante-Bellum South," in *The South in the Building of the Nation, Vol. V: Southern Economic History, 1607– 1865*, ed. James C. Ballagh (Richmond, VA, 1909), 267–71; and Joyce E. Chaplin, *An Anxious Pursuit: Agricultural Innovation and Modernity in the Lower South, 1730–1815* (Chapel Hill, NC, 1993), 351–53.

[5]William Waller M. Hening, comp., *The Statutes at Large; Being a Collection of All the Laws in Virginia, from the first Session of the Legislature in the Year 1619* (13 vols., Richmond, VA, 1820–1823); William L. Saunders and Walter Clark, comps., *The Colonial and State Records of North Carolina* (30 vols., Raleigh, NC, 1886–1914); Thomas Cooper and David J. McCord, comps., *The Statutes at Large of South Carolina* (10 vols., Columbia, SC, 1836–1841); Augustin Smith Clayton, comp., *A Compilation of the Laws of Georgia, Passed by the Legislature Since the Political Year 1800, to the Year 1810, Inclusive* (Augusta, GA, 1813); Oliver H. Prince, comp., *A Digest of the Laws of the State of Georgia* (Milledgeville, GA, 1822); Henry Potter, J. L. Taylor, and Bartlet Yancey, comps., *Laws of the State of North Carolina* (2 vols., Raleigh, NC, 1821); Samuel Shepherd, comp., *The Statutes at Large of Virginia from October Session 1792 to December Session 1806, Inclusive* (3 vols., Richmond, VA, 1835–1836); and Lucius Q. C. Lamar, comp., *A Compilation of the Laws of the State of Georgia. . . .* (Augusta, GA, 1821).

Figure 9.1
North Carolina yeoman carrying shad.
Courtesy Rare Book Collection, Wilson Library,
University of North Carolina Library at Chapel Hill.

place of fish in southern diets, but the controversy also had a deeper meaning. The damming of southeastern creeks and rivers and the campaign to keep them open reflected a major transition in social and economic history, as the backcountry South shifted from an economy based on pioneer subsistence to one based on slavery and the market. Voluminous petition campaigns reveal that this transition was heavily contested by southern yeomen who feared and resented the threat mills posed to their independence and livelihoods. They fought back with some success, using petitions and the languages of republican virtue and liberal rights bequeathed them by the American Revolution. But their petitions of protest had diminishing effects, as the power and ideology of the "market revolution" undermined their appeals and the full ecological dimensions of the shad problem escaped them. In other words, petitions against enterprises such as the Edisto Sawmills represented more than the pique of frustrated sportsmen; they were eloquent testimony to the interaction of nature, politics, and market forces in the transformation of early republican society. . . .

Edisto fishermen and of other up-country shad lovers['] . . . complaints were directly tied to the advancing market because the mills they protested made flour and lumber for export and ground meal to feed large forces of slaves. The petitions and political rhetoric that upland southerners used to defend their communal access to fish, moreover, were direct legacies of the American Revolution, and the relative success or failure of these methods gives us an unusual measure of the significance of democratic politics in the lives of ordinary people of the early republic. Finally, since long-standing traditions of riparian law put the disposition of streams and fishing grounds squarely within the legislature's purview, the fishery disputes had a public, political dimension (and a paper trail in the public archives) that some market-related changes did not have.

The conflict between millers and fishermen forced southern lawmakers to locate "the common Rights of Mankind." Did "rights" belong to property holders as individuals, protecting them in the unrestricted use of their privately owned lands and machinery? Or were there "common Rights," the collective property of a community, that gave inhabitants a collective claim on flowing streams and protected their access to traditional forms of subsistence? English law had placed strict limits on private rights over flowing water, but how far would these restrictions apply in a growing American economy? Unlike the judges of this era, who aggressively supported the cause of increased economic development, elected politicians were reluctant to impose tidy solutions to difficult questions; they preferred to find a middle ground that offered something valuable to all the voters involved.[6] In the ensuing compromises, the only clear losers (besides the shad) were the farmer-fishermen, who were frustrated by an ineffective legal and political struggle for their "rights," outmaneuvered by commercial predation on the fish, and overwhelmed by an ecological crisis to which they themselves had unwittingly contributed.

In its widest context, the quarrel over mills and shad in the early republican South is more than a simple fish story. The persistence, ingenuity, and initial success of yeoman petitioners in protecting their access to migratory fish are significant testimonials to the limited power of market-based society and to the contested character of its rise. The ultimate failure of the fishermen to protect the fish, however, is an equally powerful clue to the weaknesses that beset their communities, and to the sources of the slave owners' strength. . . . [T]he millers and slaveholders who led the attack on traditional southern fishing practices pursued their interests vigorously and showed no complaisant paternalism to those who stood in their way. Nor were the protesting fishermen crippled by deference, but defended themselves with vigor and some success. . . . Plantation slavery was a key feature of the commercialized agriculture that threatened the yeomen's pursuit of subsistence, and slavery had a powerful impact on the choices they faced in the changing economy. . . . [E]xpanding plantations offered little in the way of employment or market outlets for displaced yeomen. . . . As historians have long noted, articulate protests against the plantation system and the institution of slavery that sustained it were nearly impossible in the antebellum backcountry. The system of racial privilege and cultural hegemony that stifled objections to the peculiar institution kept yeomen's complaints against the loss of their fishing rights limited to narrowly focused petitions that never fully confronted the roots of their problems.

In the late-eighteenth- and early-nineteenth-century South, disputes over dams and fish typically erupted in yeoman communities above the fall line, where local producers faced a transition from semisubsistence to market-oriented agriculture. Since the beginnings of European settlement in the mid-eighteenth century, families in those communities had grown food crops for their own consumption, and many of them had eschewed the purchase of slaves. Most shipped no more than a small surplus to seaboard markets. Residing in tight-knit, often densely interrelated communities and relying on what Steven Hahn called "habits of mutuality" for common survival, white yeoman families of the upper South's backcountry tended to work, vote, pray, marry, and fight together as late as the mid-nineteenth century. Their way of life encouraged intense clan loyalties and strong community attachments. For the first several generations of settlement, lifestyles in these frontier regions reminded sophisticated visitors such as William Byrd and Charles Woodmason of the customs of "savage" Native Americans. In

---

[6]Morton Horwitz, *The Transformation of American Law, 1780–1860* (Cambridge, MA, 1977), 34–53; Gordon Wood, *The Radicalism of the American Revolution* (New York, 1992), 188–89, 324–25.

fact, these backcountry settlers did adopt important elements of the Indians' economy, including the use of slash-and-burn techniques for the culture of maize, the regular hunting of wild game, and the annual harvest of migratory fish. . . .[7]

Like maize, shad and herring were also part of the Indian legacy to European settlers, and they inspired the conflict between fishing rights and dams. Both species are *anadromous*, that is, the adults spend most of their lives in remote parts of the ocean but swim up freshwater streams in spring to lay their eggs and fertilize them. Shad are larger than herring; modern specimens range between three and four pounds, but early accounts reported individuals as heavy as fourteen pounds. . . . [E]ighteenth- and nineteenth-century observers reported shad runs as far inland as Wilkesboro, North Carolina, 451 miles up the Great Pee Dee and Yadkin rivers from the Atlantic Ocean. . . .[8]

Native Americans were the first to harvest the annual bounty of these migrating fish, and they transmitted their skills to the English colonists who displaced them. In 1585, the English artist John White depicted Algonquian Indians of the Albemarle Sound region using traps and spears to capture a canoeful of shad and preserving their catch by "brovvyllinge" it on a wooden frame. Over a century later, the explorer John Lawson reported the purchase of two dozen "ready barbaku'd" shad from a passing Indian and foretold the development of a large herring fishery in the waters of North Carolina. "The Herrings in *March* and *April* run a great way up the Rivers and fresh Streams to spawn," he explained, "where the Savages make great Wares, with Hedges that hinder their passage only in the middle, where an artificial Pound is made to take them in; so that they cannot return." After another generation of settlement, Brickell reported that "the civilized *Indians*" were teaching their skills to English colonists, "making Weares to catch Fish . . . for a small consideration . . . , after a method peculiar to the Indians only."[9]

By the middle of the eighteenth century, migratory fish were recognized as an important source of food for white families who had established themselves in the upper country of Virginia and the Carolinas. Still relying heavily on what they could gather directly from the forests and streams, these families sought government protection for their access to the annual migrations. Other

---

[7]Robert C. Kenzer, *Kinship and Neighborhood in a Southern Community: Orange County, North Carolina, 1849–1881* (Knoxville, TN, 1987). William Byrd, "History of the Dividing Line," in *The Prose Works of William Byrd of Westover: Narratives of a Colonial Virginian*, ed. Louis B. Wright (Cambridge, MA, 1966), 184; Charles Woodmason, *The Carolina Backcountry on the Eve of the Revolution*, ed. Richard J. Hooker (Chapel Hill, NC, 1953), 15; Timothy Silver, *A New Face on the Countryside: Indians, Colonists, and Slaves in South Atlantic Forests, 1500–1800* (Cambridge, England, 1990), 96–97, 104–7, 135.

[8]*North Carolina Geological and Economic Survey, 1891–1925*, vol. II: Hugh M. Smith, *The Fishes of North Carolina* (Raleigh, NC, 1907), 122–29; Charles H. Stevenson, "The Restricted Inland Range of Shad due to Artificial Obstructions and Its Effects on Natural Reproduction," *Bulletin of the United States Fish Commission*, 17 (1897), 265–71.

[9]Paul Hulton, *America, 1585: The Complete Drawings of John White* (Chapel Hill, 1984), 73, 75, 181; John Lawson, *A New Voyage to Carolina*, ed. Hugh Talmage Lefler (Chapel Hill, 1967), 66, 93, 160, 163, 218; Brickell, *Natural History of North Carolina*, 42.

households fought these efforts and embraced the superior efficiency of water-powered machinery. Eliminating the onerous chore of hand grinding corn, grist-mills offered a convenience to those who owned pack animals for the journey to and from the mill and whose crops were large enough to spare the miller's toll. Mills could also grind wheat into flour or, as in the case of Ferguson's Mills, saw logs into lumber. Water-ground cornmeal was normally eaten locally, but wheat flour was an export product that gained popularity in the late eighteenth century as planters grew disenchanted with tobacco.[10] Milldams were therefore more than simple elements of the pastoral landscape; they were crucial advance engines of the market economy. . . .

An important trend in southern state government had a major bearing on the battle over dams and fish. The American Revolution had seen a significant shift of political power in the South, downward in the social structure and west-ward into the region's isolated backcountry. In North Carolina, constitution writ-ers moderated the landholding requirement for suffrage while legislators created seventeen new counties between 1775 and 1790, lifting western representation in the legislature closer to parity with that of the more conservative eastern section. In South Carolina, gentry leaders extended the right to vote to all white men. . . . In Georgia, leaders revised the state constitution repeatedly to accommodate the expansion of white population into each successive area acquired from the Indi-ans. . . . These changes were all consistent with a larger movement toward more democratized politics for white men throughout the United States.[11]

As egalitarian political culture took shape, white yeomen used their enhanced political standing to pursue personal and public goals. Petitions demanding special action by a state legislature were a favorite tactic. In requests supported by one to several hundred signatures, citizens asked lawmakers to pass private bills to authorize payment for wartime damages, or to emancipate favored slaves, or to legitimize out-of-wedlock children, or to pardon popular felons, or to grant divorces. Beyond these personal objectives, yeoman communities also used petitions to demand protection for their collective autonomy and material secu-rity. Backwoods communities petitioned for strengthened fence laws, for exam-ple, or measures against hog thieves. . . .[12]

---

[10]Harry Roy Merrens, *Colonial North Carolina in the Eighteenth Century: A Study in Historical Geography* (Chapel Hill, NC, 1964), 111–19.

[11]Fletcher M. Green, *Constitutional Development in the South Atlantic States, 1776–1860* (Chapel Hill, NC, 1930); Jackson Turner Main, "Government by the People: The American Revolu-tion and the Democratization of the Legislatures," *William and Mary Quarterly* 23 (July 1966), 391–407.

[12]Ruth Bogin, "Petitioning and the New Moral Economy of Post-Revolutionary America," *Wil-liam and Mary Quarterly* 45 (July 1988), 391–425; "The Petition of Sundry Inhabitants of the County of New Hanover," H. Dec. 13, 1791, box 3, Petitions (Miscellaneous), session of Dec. 1791–Jan. 1792, General Assembly Session Records (State Archives, North Carolina Division of Archives and His-tory, Raleigh; the H. preceding a date indicates that a petition was originally introduced in the North Carolina House of Commons); "The petition of the Subscribers. . . .," Sept. 1792, H. Nov. 24, 1792, box 4, Petitions, session of Nov. 1792–Jan. 1793, Ibid.; and "To the Honourable the Genll. Assembly of the State of No. Carolina now Siting," H. Nov. 27, 1792, ibid.

The petition campaign for southern shad, which began in the mid-eighteenth century, was a central part of this larger political effort. A Virginia statute of 1752 complained that "the upper part of the rivers Appomattox and Pamunkey are become useless to the inhabitants of this colony, by means of mill-dams, fish hedges, and other obstructions" and appointed a clutch of Randolphs, Nelsons, Wormeleys, and related gentlemen as trustees responsible for clearing the rivers and opening passages in the dams. Similar statutes of 1759, 1761, 1769, and 1772 addressed the same problem on the Rapidan, Meherrin, Nottoway, Rivanna, and Hedgman rivers.[13]

As settlement extended southward, comparable legislation appeared on the statute books of the Carolinas and Georgia, often becoming law about a generation after the beginnings of permanent white settlement in an area. A 1782 statute in North Carolina, entitled "An Act to amend the several Acts passed within this State, to prevent the stoppage of the passage of Fish up the Several Rivers therein mentioned," stiffened the penalties for blocking streams to correct for the effects of revolutionary inflation. A South Carolina law of 1796 responded to petitions from . . . [four] counties and imposed a penalty of eight pounds per day on anyone blocking Big Lynches Creek "by fish dams, mill dams, hedges, and other obstructions" between February 15 and April 1 of every year. Similar legislation in 1796 and 1800 mentioned further petitions from [four] . . . districts . . . and [six] rivers. In Georgia, a typical provision from 1802 . . . declared that "the keeping open the River Savannah, is of the greatest importance to the citizens of the back country, as well in consequence of navigation, as the advantages resulting to the citizens generally, by having an annual supply of fish therefrom," and imposed fines and jail terms on those who might block the river. . . .[14]

The language of fish petitions makes clear that the signers regarded themselves as poor people who intended to eat their fish, not to sell them. An appeal from Lunenburg and Mecklenburg counties in Virginia described "the great benefit and advantage" of fish to everyone along the banks of the Meherrin River, "but more Especially, the poorer Sort, whose families were chiefly supported thereby."[15] . . .

By contrast, the defenders of milldams identified themselves as large planters and other participants in marketplace prosperity who needed the assistance of mill machinery far more than they hungered for a mess of fish. . . . North Carolina petitions from the year 1810 allow us to measure the relative economic standing of fish supporters and mill supporters. One set pertained to a sizable

---

[13]Hening, *Statutes at Large*, VI, 291–93, VII, 321–22, 409–10, VIII, 581–83.

[14]Saunders and Clark, *Colonial and State Records of North Carolina*, XXIV, 460; Cooper and McCord, comps., *Statutes at Large of South Carolina*, V, 217–18, 278–79, 383, 508–9, 647–48, 700–701; Clayton, *Compilation of the Laws of Georgia*, 80–81.

[15]"The Petition of the freeholders and inhabitants of the Counties of Lunenburg and Mecklenburg," Oct. 31, 1776, Lunenburg County Legislative Petitions, 1776–1806 (Library of Virginia); "To his Excellency Josiah Martin. . . ." [1771], in Colonial and State Records of North Carolina, comp. Saunders and Clark, IX, 87–88; "The Petition of the Inhabitants of Moore and Other Counties. . . .," Petitions, session of Nov. 1792–Jan. 1793, General Assembly Session Records.

dam at the Great Falls of the Tar River . . . [on] the western edge of North Carolina's coastal plain . . . where the introduction of large-scale cotton production by
slave labor was beginning to put pressure on an earlier economy based on family
farming. The documents are unusual because texts and numerous signatures
survive from participants on both sides of the controversy, while an indication of
the signers' wealth is readily available in the manuscript returns of the United
States Census. . . .

In 1807, . . . investors built a sizable dam at the falls, which replaced an earlier
structure and provided energy to a pair of gristmills, one on each side of the river.
The dam was equipped with a "slope," a wide, ramplike chute or spillway that fish
could use to cross dams with safety. In 1810, however, a massive petition from 405
inhabitants of upstream Nash County complained that the new slope was ineffective and demanded that the General Assembly require that the dam be opened
entirely every spring, "that fish may have a free pasage up and down the said
River dureing the Run of fish in said River, which your petitioners Humble Con-
ceve would Tend to the Conveance of Your petitioners to Receve apart of the
fish." An identically worded petition from Franklin County, still farther
upstream, added 135 names to the list of aggrieved citizens.[16]

A counterpetition from Nash and Edgecombe counties rejected the arguments of the foregoing protests. The 459 signers declared that authorized commissioners had duly approved the slope's design when the dam was rebuilt in
1807. "For General usefulness," they claimed, the mills at the Great Falls of the
Tar were "excelled by few if any in the State," and they applied an elementary
form of cost-benefit analysis to judge the relative merits of mills and fish. "Were
the whole dam removed," they reasoned, "the numbers of fish that would pass up,
would not . . . be Sufficient to remunerate the persons who should attempt to take
them—Whereas by any regulation . . . having a tendency to injure the aforesaid
Mills, hundreds of people would be either intirely deprived or put to Considerable difficulty in Getting their Corn or wheat Ground." . . .[17]

Edgecombe and Nash counties contained nearly identical proportions of
slaves in 1810—41.1 and 39.8 percent, respectively—and slaveholders and nonslaveholders could be found on both sides of the dispute. Milldam supporters,
however, were far more likely to own human property than were their opponents.
Of the 225 signers of the petition in favor of the mill (from Edgecombe and Nash
counties) who could be located in the 1810 census, 62.7 percent were slaveholders.
But of the 247 signers of the petition against the mill (from Nash county only)
who could be located in that census, only 35.7 percent were slaveholders. The two
groups likewise differed in the mean number of slaves held: mill supporters

---

[16]Kemp Plumer Battle, "A History of the Rocky Mount Mills," in Herbert Bemerton Battle, *The
Battle Book: A Genealogy of the Battle Family in America* (Montgomery, 1930), 177–82; "The Petition
of Sundry the Inhabetants of Nash County," Dec. 4, 1810, General Assembly Session Records; "The
petition of Sundry Inhebitents of Franklin County," Dec. 4, 1810, ibid.

[17]"To the Honorable the Genel Assembly of the State of North Carolina" [1810], box 3, session
of Nov.–Dec. 1810, General Assembly Session Records; "We the inhabitants of the Counties of Nash
& Edgecombe," ibid.

owned an average of 5.9 slaves each, while fish supporters (including the signers from Franklin County) owned an average of 2.9. Evidently, wealthy farmers saw the advantages of good gristmills far more clearly than their poorer neighbors. Legislators were likewise more sympathetic to millers than to fishermen; they rejected all three petitions on technicalities, a solution that left the existing dam and slope in place.[18]

The language used by petitioners to defend their access to the shad runs stressed that the community's rights to its food supply were superior to the private property rights of mill owners. Many petitions declared that fish were a gift from God or "Nature" to humanity in general. In 1776, 236 petitioners from Sussex County, Virginia, described the shad runs as "this great blessing & advantage which kind providence intended bountifully to bestow on all such as should live on or near the [Nottoway] river." The North Carolina petitioners from Nash and Franklin counties likewise referred to "the fish that the allmity intended for all man kind." . . .

Petitioners likewise demanded protection in the name of republican equality. "We are rougued out of a part of our rights," cried residents of North Carolina's Yadkin and Pee Dee river valley in 1830, as they demanded an amended fish law "Such as will give Every free person equal Justice." Remonstrating against the operator of a seine, or massive commercial fishing net, who cut off their customary access to shad, Edgecombe County fishermen "deem[ed] it unjust that they should be denied this great blessing and their neighbor be permitted in violation of the spirit of the Constitution to enjoy a monopoly." An 1825 protest against a milldam in Surry County, North Carolina, likewise demanded that the legislature "consider the many in prefferance of one Individual."[19]

South Carolina grievants were even more adamant in their claims of republican equality. In 1792, the inhabitants along Big Lynches Creek called themselves "Justly Entitled to an Equal Distribution of Justice with Other Men" and insisted "on the goodness & wisdom of the Legislature to Devise some method of Redress which shall be Permanent & lasting." . . .[20] No matter how much state legislators may have sympathized with the interests of commercial

---

[18]All identified signers of these petitions were white men. The 1810 manuscript census returns listed by name only heads of households, but many signers may have lived in the households of others. This would account for the relatively low number of identifiable signers. The value of *t* for these two groups was 4.1, indicating a significant difference of means at the .0001 level. Manuscript Population Schedules, Edgecombe County, North Carolina, Third Census of the United States, 1810 (microfilm: reel 40, M 252), Records of the Bureau of the Census, RG 29 (National Archives, Washington, D.C.); Manuscript Population Schedules, Nash County, North Carolina, Third Census of the United States (reel 41, M 252), ibid.

[19]"To the Honorable the General Assembly of North Carolina," Nov. 1830, Petitions (Miscellaneous), box 6, session of Dec. 1830–Jan. 1831, General Assembly Session Records; "Your memorialists citizens of the county of Edgecombe. . . . ," ibid.; "The Remonstrance and petition of Sundry of the Inhabitants of Surry County," House Committee Reports (Propositions and Grievances—Miscellaneous), box 4, session of Nov. 1825–Jan. 1826, ibid.

[20]"The Petition of the Inhabitants of Big Lynches Creek," Dec. 4, 1792, General Assembly Petition 1792- 215-01 (South Carolina Department of Archives and History).

mill operators, they were normally reluctant to offend such large numbers of complaining constituents. Their preferred solution was to require the installation of slopes, thus preserving the interests of millers and fishermen alike. Alternatively, millers could agree to open sluices or gates in their dams to allow the passage of boats and fish in season. . . . In 1787 North Carolina enacted a general statute that authorized counties to appoint commissioners to inspect streams and to keep the deepest quarter of all major riverbeds open for the passage of fish during a specified season in the spring. South Carolina passed a similar law in 1827. In addition, all the southeastern states continued to pass local and private laws to regulate fishing and milling on particular rivers and streams, with Georgia relying exclusively on such measures.[21]

The only problem with these political compromises was that they did not work. Stubbornly, the fish proved much less responsive to petitions than were the legislators. As population rose in the South Atlantic states and a rising level of commercial activity increased pressure on the region's river systems, petitioners on both sides of the issue agreed that the number of shad was steadily declining, regardless of the slopes and sluices in the existing milldams.[22] . . . "Of late years," agreed petitioners from Little River in Fairfield district in 1811, "It has become a rare thing for a Shad to be caught in that river except within a few miles of its mouth." Instead of blaming milldams, however, they pointed to the practice of felling timber into streams and the excessive use of fish traps where the Little River joined the Broad.[23]

Mill owners seized upon uncertainty over the cause of dwindling shoals to argue that dams were not to blame for the problem and that mills were more important to the region than the few fish that might still penetrate the backcountry. . . . By 1828, supporters of a mill at Grendol Shoals on the Pacolet River near Spartanburg, South Carolina, assured themselves that other downstream dams had ended the local shad fishery long ago. "I do not consider the passage of fish of any importance since the erection of the 'Columbia Dam,'" wrote one. "It is very seldom we hear of a Shad being caught."[24]

---

[21]Saunders and Clark, *Colonial and State Records of North Carolina*, XXIV, 902–3; Cooper and McCord, *Statutes at Large of South Carolina*, VI, 340–41; Lamar, *Compilation of the Laws of the State of Georgia*, 487–90.

[22]The design of fishways for shad was difficult. In 1897, Charles H. Stevenson of the United States Fish Commission reported that numerous expensive devices to help shad over major dams were ineffective. Stevenson, "Restricted Inland Range of Shad," 268.

[23]"The petition of the inhabitants of Sussex County," Oct. 31, 1776, Sussex County Legislative Petitions 1776; "Petition of Sundry Inhabitants of Winton county," General Assembly Petition 1794-157-01 (South Carolina Department of Archives and History); Petition of the Inhabitants of Abbeville and Laurens districts n.d., General Assembly Petition 1800-137, ibid.; Petition of the Inhabitants of Fairfield district, Nov. 10, 1811 General Assembly Petition 1811-116, ibid.

[24]Petition from Union, Newberry, and Laurens districts, Nov. 20, 1808, General Assembly Petition 1808-30 (South Carolina Department of Archives and History); Petition of Robert Ellison and others of Darlington County, General Assembly Petition 1797-13, ibid.; Samuel M. Gowdey to John H. Farnandis, Jan. 16, 1828 attached to General Assembly Petition ND-1030, ibid.

Balancing the profits from mills against the presumed lack of profits from fish, mill supporters applied a balance-sheet logic that ignored the use value of shad to impoverished local fishermen, as well as the intangible rewards they derived from the camaraderie of the fishing experience. In 1783, led by Richard Bennehan, founder of one of North Carolina's most opulent mercantile and planter dynasties, mill supporters from the upper Neuse River valley defended their proposal for a new mill on the site of "Daniels fish camp" by remarking that the "mill will be much more profit then the fish that come up said river." More than four decades later, defenders of the mill at Grendol Shoals averred that "the few fish that would pass that high . . . would not pay for in twenty years the value of the loss that would be sustained by the country adjacent in one year on account of the destruction of the mills."[25]

. . . [Mill supporters] associated fishing with the survival among poor men of a collective culture in which the gathering of free food from the rivers doubtless mixed with generous indulgence in liquor, boasting, and horseplay, possibly followed by outbursts of fighting and other violations of public order. State protection of the shad runs, . . . [mill supporters] claimed, "affords an inducement to idleness, by tempting the attendance of numbers, at the fisheries, for days together, whose attention at that season is greatly needed in their farms, and who are, perhaps, not rewarded with a half a dozen of fish." Clearly indicating their moral disapproval, these signers believed that public policy should discourage behavior they regarded as lazy and irresponsible and prompt a more enterprising spirit of industry and individualism among the poor. The artist David Hunter Strother strongly reinforced this view of fishing with his depiction of shad fishing in late antebellum North Carolina, which contrasted the somnolence of the individual fisherman with the industrial efficiency of the commercial operation based on slave labor. (See Figure 9.2.)[26]

These arguments touched the heart of the quarrel over mills and fish, for a deep clash of values lay beneath the surface dispute between rival claimants for the benefits of public policy. The emergent culture of the marketplace stood on one side, celebrating hard work and personal advancement. The culture of an older subsistence community, long disparaged as "Lubberland" by elite observers, took the other side, depending on natural abundance, the rhythms of nature, and the consumption needs of its members to regulate its work life.[27]

---

[25]"Petition from Wake County and adjoining parts of Orange & Granville," box 1, Miscellaneous Petitions, session of April–May 1783, General Assembly Session Records. For Richard Bennehan, see Jean Anderson, *Piedmont Plantation: The Bennehan-Cameron Family and Lands in North Carolina* (Durham, NC, 1985), 1–14. Petition of the Union district, General Assembly Petition ND-1030-27 (South Carolina Department of Archives and History).

[26]*Laws Made and Passed by the General Assembly of the State of Maryland . . . 1825* (Annapolis, 1826), 83; Petition of the Union, Newberry, and Laurens districts, Nov. 20, 1808, General Assembly Petition 1808-30 (South Carolina Department of Archives and History). Emphasis added. Strother, "North Carolina Illustrated," 435, 437.

[27]Byrd, "History of the Dividing Line," 204–5.

Figure 9.2
Reinforcing the image of traditional, individual fishermen as
lazy and inefficient, David Hunter Strother depicted a bald
eagle robbing the fish trap of this sleeping Tarheel in 1857.
Courtesy Rare Book Collection, Wilson Library, University of North
Carolina Library at Chapel Hill.

In the decades between the American Revolution and the age of Jackson, the culture of subsistence clearly persisted in the southern backcountry, but the culture of the marketplace just as clearly grew stronger. The trend appeared earliest in Virginia, where late-eighteenth-century demands for open rivers began to treat the needs of fishermen as secondary to the draft requirements of boat traffic. By the 1790s, petitions from Southside counties drained by tributaries of the James and the Roanoke commonly asked for roads, ferries, town charters, and inspection stations for tobacco and flour, rather than protection for migrating shad. By 1796, tobacco plantations were expanding in the upper Roanoke Valley, and most petitioners ignored the fishing issue as they begged the assembly "to lessen if possible the expense & difficulty of transporting the produce of their lands to market." Similar requests appeared in neighboring capitals. . . .

Intensified agriculture in the backcountry also had an unintended effect on stream ecology that few petitioners remarked on, though it undoubtedly affected the behavior of the shad. Edward Wood, an experienced commercial fisherman on Albemarle Sound, reported in 1871 that "the fish . . . always avoid . . . muddy water." According to Wood, "the freshets of the Roanoke river frequently prove disastrous to the success of the fishermen, pouring large quantities of muddy water into the Sound, which color the water for forty miles below its mouth."[28]

Floods and sandbars resulted from the stripping of forest cover in the southern watersheds, which led to increased storm runoff, soil erosion, and torrents of muddy water. By the early nineteenth century, the extensive clearing of southern forests by farmers searching for "new ground" to replace "old fields" had led to complaints of timber shortage. . . . According to later investigations,

---

[28]Wood, *To the President of the State Agricultural Society of North Carolina*, n.p.; Petition from the residents of Little River in Fairfield District, General Assembly Petition 1811-116 (South Carolina Department of Archives and History). See also petition from the Orangeburg District, on the Edisto River, General Assembly Petition 1787-08-01, ibid.

nothing could be worse for the shad. "During heavy rains the plowed soil upon the hillsides is easily washed into gullies," one early fish scientist observed, "filling them beyond their capacity and bringing into them masses of earth and other debris, thus covering the spawning-grounds. The freshets are soon over, and the flow of water in the streams becomes so small that shad are not induced to proceed so far up as formerly."[29] Obviously, the yeoman farmers of the backcountry shared responsibility for the destruction of the southern forest with their more commercially minded neighbors, unwittingly contributing to the ecological crisis they so earnestly deplored. It is possible, indeed, that farmers who lost access to shad responded by clearing more land and cultivating more crops to make up the difference—either to exchange for the salted, or "pickled," products of commercial fishermen or to feed to hogs in final preparation for slaughter. In doing so, they would have made the problems of erosion and runoff even worse.[30]

The commercialization of fishing itself, however, was the most glaring and probably the most important factor in the decline of the shad population. Though most yeoman fishermen intended to eat their catches at home, some ambitious settlers had quickly realized that the annual shoals of shad could become the basis for a thriving business in pickled fish. . . . The construction of elaborate and expensive stone fish traps in South Carolina rivers likewise reflected the efforts of some inland entrepreneurs to develop a profitable fishing industry.[31]

The most extensive shad fisheries did not develop on inland rivers, however, but in the protected coastal sounds and estuaries that the shad and herring entered to begin their lengthy journey to the branch heads. Chesapeake Bay and the large rivers, such as the Potomac, that emptied into it as well as Albemarle and Pamlico sounds in North Carolina were ideal spots for commercial shad and herring fisheries, for wide expanses of relatively shallow water made it easy to manipulate large seines there, and broad sandy beaches offered suitable locations for landing and cleaning the catch. As early as 1807, Albemarle Sound became the center of a major business. By 1840, the United States census reported the production of 73,350 barrels of pickled fish in North Carolina, chiefly in the counties on the sounds. Virginians added 30,315 more barrels, while South Carolina and Georgia reported no more than 425 and 14 barrels, respectively. Wholesale distributors in Baltimore and the ports of Virginia marketed the salted catch

---

[29]Silver, *New Face on the Countryside*, 114–15; Petition from Lunenburg County, Dec. 14, 1811, in Lunenburg County Legislative Petitions, 1807–1821 (Library of Virginia); Clayton, comp., *Compilation of the Laws of Georgia*, 521; Stevenson, "Restricted Inland Range of Shad," 268.

[30]I am indebted to David Weiman for this observation.

[31]"The Petition of Sundray Inhabetents Freholders in the County of Pittsylvany," Oct. 21, 1791, Pittsylvania County Legislative Petitions, 1776–1793. See also "The petition of the inhabitants of Sussex County," Oct. 31, 1776, Sussex County Legislative Petitions, 1776; and "The petition of the Inhabitants of the County Halifax," Oct. 10, 1791, Halifax County Legislative Petitions, 1776–1791. Lamar, comp., *Compilation of the Laws of the State of Georgia*, 487. In an 1839 case commissioners of fish sluices were successfully sued for trespass, for their unlawful destruction of commercial fish traps in the Congaree River. See *Boatwight v. Boohman*, 24 S.C.L. (Rice) 447–48 (1839).

to customers throughout the upper South, many of them planters seeking inexpensive rations for their slaves.[32]

The methods used by commercial fishermen to collect such vast stocks of fish differed considerably from the hand-held "dip nets" of subsistence fishermen in the interior. Early producers set "wares, dams, or stoppages" across stream channels to trap entire shoals of fish. Later operators preferred to "shoot" a massive seine across the main channel of a given stream or estuary, thereby capturing virtually everything that swam in it. In the practice known as "double seining," workers used windlasses to haul in one net while others shot out a second net, thereby preventing the passage of more fish while the first seine was unloaded. Working around the clock in the shoaling season, big operators at favored landing sites near the mouths of rivers could thus monopolize the bounty of the waters. (See Figure 9.3.) A large force of male and female slaves to set and haul the nets and clean, salt, and pack the catch for sale was an essential part of such large-scale operations. (See Figure 9.4.)[33]

Commercial fishing had a dramatic impact on the sound region and the lower reaches of the rivers that fed the sounds. In contrast to the picture of idle yeomen frolicking on inland riverbanks, waiting days for a half a dozen shad, the scene at major fisheries was intense and overpowering. As early as 1807, the youthful James Cathcart Johnston, . . . wrote his cousin James Iredell Jr. about the latter's anticipated return from college. "You will see Roanoke in all its glory—cover'd with Seines—its bank strewed with fish carts—fish & fish guts—more fragrant than the roses & lilies with which poets & romance writers have decorated their streams & rivulets." The offal that Johnston joked about, however, would soon be highly prized by Albemarle planters, who purchased it to restore the fertility of their depleted fields.[34]

Generally speaking, North Carolina legislators recognized the injustice of monopolistic fishing practices and sought to limit them when prodded by petitions. As early as 1764, the colonial assembly banned the use of double seines in fishing season by "avaricious persons" in the waters of the Meherrin, Pee Dee,

---

[32]U.S. Department of State, *Compendium of the Enumeration of the Inhabitants and Statistics of the United States, as Obtained at the Department of State, From the Returns of the Sixth Census* (Washington, D.C., 1841), 158, 170, 182, 194, 206. On commercial shad and herring fisheries in the nineteenth century, see Mark T. Taylor, "Seiners and Tongers: North Carolina Fisheries in the Old and New South," *North Carolina Historical Review* 69 (Jan. 1992), 1–36.

[33]For the techniques of small fishermen, see "The Petition of Thomas Mercer & Others of the County of Camden," Petitions, box 3, session of Nov. 1810–Jan. 1811, General Assembly Session Records. For commercial fishing practices, see the acts that sought to regulate them. *Laws of North Carolina*, 1764, ch. XIII; ibid., 1766, ch. XXI; ibid., 1770, ch. XXI. For examples in the early republican period, see ibid., 1819, ch. XCVIII, ch. XCIV, ch. CIII; ibid., 1820, ch. LIII, ch. CV, ch. CXXII; ibid., 1821, ch. LVIII, IXIII. For the late antebellum period, seeJos. B. Skinner, *Letter on the Subject of the Albemarle Fisheries* (n.p., 1846); North Carolina General Assembly, "Report of the Select Committee on Fisheries," Senate Document no. 22 (Raleigh, NC, 1852); and Strother, "North Carolina Illustrated," 438–47.

[34]James Cathcart Johnston to James Iredell Jr., April 12, 1807, Charles E. Johnston Collection, Private Collections (State Archives, North Carolina Division of Archives and History); *Read v. Granbermy*, 30 N.C. (8 Ired.) 109 (1847); Capeheart v. Jones' Executor, ibid., 383.

Figure 9.3
Commercial fisheries in North Carolina operated all night in shoaling season, using large gangs of slaves, most of them male, to haul the seines. Courtesy Rare Book Collection, Wilson Library, University of North Carolina Library at Chapel Hill.

and Catawba rivers. William, Tryon, the same royal governor who crushed the North Carolina Regulators, shared the commercial values of leading coastal fishermen. He thus vetoed a bill to restrict the operation of seines, "esteeming it prejudicial to the general interest of the country and destructive of that spirit of industry and commerce so much wanted to be encouraged in this colony."[35]

Figure 9.4
Large numbers of female slaves cleaned and salted the catch from commercial shad and herring fisheries. Courtesy Rare Book Collection, Wilson Library, University of North Carolina Library at Chapel Hill.

---

[35]Laws of North Carolina, 1764, ch. XIII; William Tryon to Lord Hillsborough, Nov. 30, 1769, in *Colonial and State Records*, comp. Saunders and Clark, VIII, 153–54.

Following independence, and well into the nineteenth century, the North Carolina General Assembly sought to balance the needs of commerce and subsistence by protecting customary practices that allowed all watermen an equal chance at catching fish, while it condemned the greed that inspired persistent efforts to obtain a monopoly. An 1820 preamble thus denounced "many evil-minded persons [who] ... increase their own profits and injure others" and firmly forbade certain methods of placing nets that petitioners had denounced as unfair. A crazy quilt of private acts proliferated to regulate fishing on each major river, generally restricting the use of double seines and seines that extended more than three-quarters of the way across a main channel ... from late February to mid-May. Legislation also commonly banned the operation of seines on Sunday during the same period, not only to honor the sabbath but also to allow some shoals to escape upstream for other fishermen. Like their counterparts in other states, North Carolina legislators were normally willing to require mill owners either to open sluices in their milldams during the spring fishing season or to furnish the dams with slopes to accommodate the upstream migrations.[36]

Despite the legislature's efforts to ensure a fair distribution of the catch, sound fishermen were increasingly successful in monopolizing the annual run of shad and herring. An 1840 report to the legislature claimed that the seventeen fisheries of Albemarle Sound had employed 765 hands to pack 25,500 barrels of fish in the previous season.... Six years later, more than 1,000 slaves were employed, while the number of seines in Albemarle Sound reached seventy by 1852. Choice fishing sites traded hands for steep prices.... The industry had become concentrated in the hands of the largest planters of the shoreline.... In the face of such competition, upstream yeomen stood little chance.[37]

The results of this business were quickly apparent. The Select Committee on Fisheries reported in 1852 that the rivers that had once overflowed with shad, rockfish, and herring were now virtually empty.... Even so, the size of the catch had radically declined, and the price of salted fish had doubled from an unstated level "but a few years ago." Though commercial fishermen maintained that fish still constituted "a necessary article of food ... [for] the most indigent of our citizens," the power to obtain these fish directly from streams had disappeared.[38] For all practical purposes, shad were now available solely through the market economy....

The committee charged with devising a solution ..., applying the logic of Victorian laissez-faire, they concluded that the best way to ensure an equal share of fish for everyone was to suspend *all* regulation of the fishing industry, except

---

[36]There were petitions or private acts respecting fish, seines, and milldams at virtually every session of the North Carolina General Assembly. For details, see *Laws of North Carolina*, 1764–1860, and General Assembly Session Records, *passim*.

[37]"To the Honbl the General Assembly of the State of North Carolina," Nov. 17, 1840, Petitions, box 5, session of Nov. 1840–Jan. 1841, General Assembly Session Records; Skinner, "Letter on the Subject of the Albemarle Fisheries," 7; North Carolina General Assembly, "Report of the Select Committee on Fisheries," 182.

[38]North Carolina General Assembly, "Report of the Select Committee on Fisheries," 182.

for a ban on the use of nets and seines between sundown on Saturday and midnight on Sunday. This reform would protect the sabbath and make the catch as large as possible, giving all inhabitants of the state an equal chance to buy whatever fish they could afford. Needless to say, this recommendation closely followed the suggestions of the fishing industry's own lobbyists.[39]

. . . So far as state policy on fishing was concerned, this report marked an end to the independence and empowerment that had once been established by republican government and the subsistence economy. Well into Reconstruction, state lawmakers indulged popular hopes by adopting more measures to promote the passage of fish up inland rivers, but laws alone could not restore what earlier generations had called "the common Rights of mankind."[40] As the legislators acknowledged, poor North Carolinians who bought fish instead of catching them were themselves hooked on the need for a cash income and the "hard earnings" that market dependency entailed. Despite a long history of protest, the evolution of commercial fishing had left them no choice, and those who looked cheerful were undoubtedly making the best of a painful situation. What the American Revolution had granted, the market revolution was taking away.

The transformation of Tarheel fishing found its echo in other patterns of state life. As petitions for pardons, divorces, and the erection of fish ladders declined, the number of requests for turnpike roads and bank charters went up. Yeomen occasionally protested when such "privileged monopolies" trod excessively on popular liberties, and resentment of their inroads stimulated the growth of Andrew Jackson's Democratic party. For the most part, however, North Carolina yeomen found that relations with their more privileged neighbors were increasingly mediated through the institutions of the market. Their republican traditions had ill prepared them for the shift, and they had no ready means of answering when legislators applied the rhetoric of equality to guarantee the monopolies of planter-fishermen and other representatives of commercial privilege. . . .

The success of inland shad fishermen in protecting "the common Rights of mankind" should not be underestimated, however. From the middle of the eighteenth century to the middle of the nineteenth, southern colonial assemblies and legislatures had met the demand for protection of their rivers with a welter of local legislation requiring fish slopes, fish sluices, fishing seasons, fish commissioners, limits on seining, and seemingly endless similar measures. The campaign at the Edisto Sawmills was among these victories; South Carolina legislators insisted that a channel around the offending dam be available for both boats and fish, specified its hours of operation, and appointed commissioners to enforce the

---

[39]Ibid., 183–84.

[40]See, for example, "An Act to Remove Obstructions in the Pedee, Yadkin, and Wharie Rivers for the Purpose of Allowing Shad and Other Fish Free Passage Up the Same," *Public Laws of the State of North Carolina . . . , 1870–71* (Raleigh, NC, 1871), ch. 262, 418–20. The act required open passages of gradually diminishing widths in the channels of specific rivers extending from the South Carolina line to the town of Wilkesboro at the foot of the Blue Ridge.

regulation.[41] But such victories held little meaning in the long run. Eventually, the shad stopped coming despite the sluices, and upstream fishermen found no means to coax them back.

The yeomanry's emphasis on "common rights" to take fish that were assumed to come in unlimited numbers "from God" had been a creative and successful appropriation of republican political principles. Though rewarded with political success, this strategy could not address the fundamentally biological issues of fish reproduction and stream health that would ultimately control the presence of fish in southern rivers. The fish, after all, did not come directly "from God." They came instead from fish eggs, which had to be deposited and fertilized in appropriate spawning beds and had to be allowed to mature for a return trip to the sea before any new generation of shad could be brought to southern rivers. Milldam petitions were normally silent on the subject of fish reproduction, and neither yeomen nor commercial fishermen showed more than a foggy awareness of the biological reasons for the shad migrations. Consequently, neither group was intellectually or culturally prepared to devise solutions that would take into account the shad's needs along with their own. . . .[42]

More immediately, the yeomanry's emphasis on common rights proved vulnerable to economic reasoning that glorified markets as the most appropriate means for distributing the resources of nature. If the "public" should be the ultimate beneficiary of the fish, it was easy to argue that the marketplace served a much wider public than the inhabitants of any particular stream bank; the market should therefore have privileged access to the fish that God had sent to men in general. . . .

The fishermen's ultimate inability to fend off the milldams that interfered with their catches likewise reflected their difficulty in opposing the system of agriculture of which milldams were part. Machine-ground corn and "merchant's mills" for grinding wheat were aspects of an expanding and more commercialized farming complex that yeomen did not fully resist. The new system had its undeniable advantages. Women who were spared the backbreaking labor of grinding corn by hand must have been especially grateful for the relief afforded by a water-powered mill. Many successful male farmers, who began to patronize the new mills and substituted pork or store-bought fish for the shad that used to appear in the river, undoubtedly shared similar views. For poor men, however, the end of the shad runs brought a corresponding loss of personal dignity and independence. "The poorest Planter has as much Right to the delicaccies of this Country, as the richest," John Brickell had boasted in 1737, "nay the very Labourer is intituled to the Same Privilege."[43] With the shad gone, the ability of antebellum poor whites to make the same claim was diminished, though not destroyed.

---

[41]General Assembly Report 1792–3 (South Carolina Department of Archives and History).

[42]Stevenson, "Restricted Inland Range of Shad," 270; Charles Epes, "Officials Begin Restocking Shad," *Richmond Times-Dispatch*, July 21, 1992; Louis D. Rubin Jr., "On Catching Shad Fever at Fishing Creek," *Southern Living* 13 (March 1978), 52–56.

[43]Brickell, *Natural History of North Carolina*, 46.

Human bondage stood at the center of the agricultural system that displaced the shad. As analysis of the Tar River . . . petitioners of 1810 demonstrates, slave-holders were far more likely to favor milldams than nonslaveholders. When the shad stopped coming inland to feed the white poor, moreover, they were caught at the coast by slaves to feed more slaves throughout the region. Yet slavery was scarcely mentioned in the petition wars over fish and milldams. In facing threats to their customary chance to fish for subsistence, as in so many other aspects of antebellum life, yeomen protested the impact of slavery on their lives, but only in muted terms.

. . . Aside from marginal opportunities as overseers and day laborers, the expanding plantation offered few [job opportunities] to the yeoman families in its path. In the South, the frustrated yeoman could make the transition from fish and hand-ground cornmeal to cotton and wheat flour, or he could make his retreat to the beckoning West, hoping to recreate in Trans-Appalachia the world of independence that had eluded him near the seaboard. If he chose to remain, the purchase of slaves and increasing sensitivity to the power of the marketplace would be indispensable to his success. Alternately, he might remain as a yeoman inside an expanding plantation belt, struggling to maintain his sense of white male equality while acknowledging the actual superiority of others, in a complex set of rituals and relationships we are only beginning to understand.[44]

. . . The term ["market revolution"] will obscure more than it explains, how-ever, if we forget that the kinds of markets and the things being marketed varied significantly from section to section, and even from neighborhood to neighbor-hood. So far as the shad were concerned, a dam was a dam, whether North or South, and the effect on reproduction and migration patterns was the same. For the fishermen who sought the shad, however, the purposes of the dam and the social and economic system it represented could make a profound difference. In the North, the closing of a stream might be balanced against the opening of job opportunities. In the South, a similar dam might open the way for domestic con-veniences, marketing advances, and a network of paternal dependency upon the miller (and the slaveholder who stood behind him) that could not easily be calculated. . . .

Slavery, then, left its irresistible imprint on southern fishing. Like the mills themselves and their convenient products, slaves were an alluring menace to the yeoman way of life. They might undermine a traditional economy, but they offered obvious advantages to any free person who successfully exploited them. It would not be fair or accurate to say that yeoman fishermen ultimately chose slavery over shad, for the choice was never that simple. The petition campaigns demonstrate that the expansion of slave-based commercial agricul-ture was strongly contested in its day. But when the biological obstacles to the fishes' reproduction combined with the attractiveness of slave-based "prog-ress," disappearance of the shad, and so much else, was the unavoidable consequence.

---

[44]McCurry, *Masters of Small Worlds.*

To put it another way, the early republican period saw a critical moment of negotiation between the South's slaveholders and nonslaveholders. In the decades that immediately followed the American Revolution, the implied promises of republicanism clashed sharply with received traditions of deference and emerging patterns of commercial enterprise. In the ensuing confusion, petitioning became a favored political instrument for plain folk seeking to protect their independence from wealthier challengers. The outcome of these decades of negotiation saw the yeomanry's political equality increasingly secure, while their economic independence remained a hostage to the vagaries of the market. Implied support for slavery was an integral part of this development. The modest evidence of dams and fish testifies to the fragility of such an outcome, but the plain folk could obtain little better in the remaining years before secession.

Harry L. Watson

I am an historian of the early American republic, especially the antebellum South. Much of my work has centered around politics and government because I've come to believe that the quest for power has deep implications for almost everything else in a professed democracy. I'm probably best known for *Liberty and Power: The Politics of Jacksonian America*, a story about pivotal events in a formative period that tried to combine traditional narrative with newly-formed insights about social and economic development. Mrs. Lois Puryear taught me very well at my Greensboro, North Carolina high school, but John L. Thomas and William C. McLaughlin, both outstanding undergraduate teachers at Brown University, first inspired me to dream about the history profession. My doctoral adviser, Robert Wiebe of Northwestern University, fanned that passion even more. I have been exceedingly fortunate to spend my career at the University of North Carolina at Chapel Hill, where I am now Atlanta Alumni Distinguished Professor of Southern Culture. This article literally started as a fishing expedition. Looking for traces of the Old South's common whites, I stumbled across a trove of fishing petitions which I tried to understand through social, economic, and political history. Now I am completing the first half of an AP and college-level textbook of U.S. history, which I began long ago in a vain attempt to learn "everything" about my field. Now I know that's impossible, but the effort has been fun.

QUESTIONS FOR CONSIDERATION

1. Characterize why the inhabitants of Orangeburg District, South Carolina, considered a dam across the Edisto River to have "totally cut [them] off from availing themselves of the common Rights of Mankind?" What political and economic circumstances led to their claim?
2. Describe the origins of shad fishing in the colonial South.
3. How did the American Revolution shape the political status of rural Southerners? How did this changing status shape the debate over shad fishing versus mill owners during the late eighteenth century?
4. Characterize the effects of both the new market economy and the slave economy shad fishing.
5. Mill owners and shad fisherman portrayed each other in negative terms. Characterize each according to the other. In what ways were these negative depictions a product of their context?
6. How did the legislature try to balance the interests of the following: subsistence shad fisherman, mill owners, and those who fished commercially? How successful were these attempts?

7. Watson claims, "Human bondage stood at the center of the agricultural system that displaced the shad." How does he support this claim? Why didn't white subsistence fisherman make a similar claim?

8. Compare the protests on the part of subsistence shad fisherman in this article to the protests in the articles by Nash, McDonnell, and Bouton. What similarities and differences can you find between them? What accounts for the similarities and differences?

•⌒

CHAPTER TEN

The Evangelical Movement and Political Culture in the North During the Second Party System[1]

Daniel Walker Howe

The prominence of evangelical Christian piety is one of the major continuities in American life from colonial to national times. Indeed, for all the attention that has been devoted to the so-called Great Awakening and its effects, it seems likely that its nineteenth-century counterparts were even "greater" in their impact on American culture and politics. John M. Murrin once remarked that the Great Awakening and its legacy probably had even more to do with the Civil War than with the Revolution, and it is a perceptive comment.[2] The later evangelicals became more self-conscious shapers of society and opinion than their eighteenth-century predecessors, for they increasingly strove to subject social institutions and standards to divine judgment and to "reform"—that is, reshape—them accordingly. The purpose of this essay is to comprehend the impact of the evangelical movement on American political culture during the period of the second party system, from approximately 1830 to approximately 1860.

I will argue that in the northern United States during that era, evangelical religion interacted with economic development to polarize the population, creating the basis for two broad alliances. The members of the two alliances differed not only on questions of religion and religiously inspired reform efforts but also on questions of politics. Their disagreements shaped American society throughout the nineteenth century and beyond because the alliances offered divergent visions of how individuals and society should respond to modernization. The evangelicals were in many ways the champions of modernization, that is, of changes in the structure of society and individual personality that emphasized discipline and channeled energies by the deliberate choice of goals and the rational selection of

---

[1] Interested students are encouraged to read this essay in the original form. Daniel Walker Howe, "The Evangelical Movement and Political Culture in the North During the Second Party System," *Journal of American History* 77 (4) (March 1991), 1216–39.

[2] John M. Murrin, "No Awakening, No Revolution? More Counterfactual Speculations," *Reviews in American History* 11 (June 1983), 161–71.

means. Their opponents were more skeptical about such transformations and the accompanying economic inequality and regimentation of human life. . . .[3]

This essay addresses the oft-expressed current desire for fresh syntheses in American history. It draws upon existing knowledge instead of presenting new information, but my goal is to reconceptualize our knowledge, rather than simply to summarize or survey it, in a way that will help focus future inquiries. In developing my synthesis, I have been led to adopt a very broad definition of political culture. . . .

DEMOCRACY, DISCIPLINE, AND EVANGELICAL REFORM

In both the eighteenth and the nineteenth centuries, revivalism and democracy were interrelated phenomena. Each asserted popular claims against those of the elite, pluralism against orthodoxy, charisma against rationalism, competitiveness against authority, an innovative Americanism against European tradition. Such is the thrust of a vast body of distinguished scholarship by authors from William Warren Sweet to Perry Miller, from Richard Bushman to Patricia Bonomi and Nathan O. Hatch.[4] Indeed, the more active popular participation in American political life became, the more important moral and religious issues came to be in politics. It was no accident that religion became a more potent political force in the era of the second party system than it had been at the time of the adoption of the Constitution. It was a natural consequence of the increasingly democratic nature of American politics.[5]

Yet, the popular quality of the evangelical movement was only one side of it. Revivals did not spring forth from the populace spontaneously; they were "worked up." Revivals took place not simply because there was a receptive audience but also because evangelists promoted them. These evangelists had on their agenda a reformation of life and habits, both individual and communal. They continued the historic concern for church discipline characteristic of the early Protestant Reformers. Voluntary discipline represented Protestantism's alternative to the

---

[3]Eric Foner, "The Causes of the Civil War: Recent Interpretations and New Directions," in *Beyond the Civil War Synthesis: Political Essays on the Civil War Era*, ed. Robert P. Swierenga (Westport, CT, 1975), 15–32; James M. McPherson, *Ordeal by Fire: Civil War and Reconstruction* (New York, 1982), 5–22; Daniel Walker Howe, ed., *Victorian America* (Philadelphia, 1976); and Richard D. Brown, *Modernization: The Transformation of American Life, 1600–1865* (New York, 1976).

[4]William Warren Sweet, *Religion in the Development of American Culture, 1765–1840* (New York, 1952); Perry Miller, *The Life of the Mind in America: From the Revolution to the Civil War* (New York, 1965); Richard Bushman, *From Puritan to Yankee: Character and the Social Order in Connecticut, 1690–1765* (Cambridge, MA, 1967); Patricia Bonomi, *Under the Cope of Heaven: Religion, Society, and Politics in Colonial America* (New York, 1986); Nathan O. Hatch, *The Democratization of American Christianity* (New Haven, CT, 1989). Alan Heimert, *Religion and the American Mind. From the Great Awakening to the Revolution* (Cambridge, MA, 1966).

[5]See Stephen Botein, "Religious Dimensions of the Early American State," in *Beyond Confederation: Origins of the Constitution and American National Identity*, ed. Richard R. Beeman, Stephen Botein, and Edward C. Carter II (Chapel Hill, NC, 1987), 315–30.

authoritarianism of traditional society. If popular enthusiasm was the "soft side" of the great evangelical movement, the new discipline was its "hard side."[6]

The new discipline of the evangelical movement had far-reaching consequences. It reshaped the cultural system of the Victorian middle class in Britain and America, and it also influenced the working class in important ways. The reforms it inspired profoundly affected society and politics in both countries. We remember its morality as strict, and indeed it was—most notably in the novel restraints it imposed on the expression or even mention of sexuality and the use of alcohol. But even its most punitive severity was redemptive in purpose, as the words *reformatory* and *penitentiary* suggested. The obverse of Victorian discipline was the proper development of the human faculties. Education, self-improvement, even liberation, went along with discipline. Imposing discipline on a drunken husband could be liberating for his battered wife; the husband was liberated too, since as a sober man he could regain the use of his moral faculties. The evangelical reformers characteristically opposed physical violence, campaigning against corporal punishment of children, wives, sailors, and prisoners. They preferred such mental coercion as solitary confinement to flogging and hanging. Didactic would-be civilizers, they embodied their values in such institutional monuments as schools, universities, missions, hospitals, and insane asylums. Most consistent of all the Victorian reformers were the abolitionists and the feminists. They applied the principles of human self-development, the fulfillment of noble potential and the repression of base passions, to various races and both genders.[7]

The usefulness of evangelical moral reform to the new industrial capitalism of the nineteenth century has not escaped notice, and a vast historical literature analyzes it in terms of bourgeois "social control." Prosouthern and anti-evangelical historians have used that analysis to discredit abolitionists and other reformers for a long time. But the interpretation has taken on new vigor during the past generation with the reception of neo-Marxism and the social thought of Michel Foucault in the American academy. Its recent advocates have included Michael Katz, David J. Rothman, Anthony F. C. Wallace, Paul Johnson, and—of its most sophisticated and broadly ranging form—David Brion Davis. Davis's monumental volumes on slavery and antislavery in the modern world accord full respect to the moral integrity of the abolitionists and the justice of their cause. But they also portray the abolitionists as inadvertently promoting the hegemony of bourgeois capitalism. Through natural human limitations coupled with a measure of self-deception, the reformers were

---

[6]Terry Bilhartz, *Urban Religion and the Second Great Awakening* (Rutherford, NJ, 1986); and Richard Carwardine, "The Second Great Awakening in the Urban Centers," *Journal of American History* 52 (Sept. 1972), 327–40. Bruce Steiner, "The New Divinity's Impact upon the Laity: Lay Resistance and Resulting Change," paper delivered at the annual meeting of the Organization of American Historians, Cincinnati, April 1983 (in Bruce Steiner's possession).

[7]Ian Bradley, *The Call to Seriousness: The Evangelical Impact on the Victorians* (London, 1976). Myra Glenn, *Campaigns against Corporal Punishment: Prisoners, Sailors, Women, and Children in Antebellum America* (Albany, NY, 1984); Louis P. Masur, "The Revision of the Criminal Law in Post-Revolutionary America," *Criminal Justice History* 8 (1987), 21–36; David Brion Davis, *From Homicide to Slavery: Studies in American Culture* (New York, 1986), 17–40.

blind to the full implications of what they were doing. Without their being aware of it, the antislavery crusaders provided a moral sanction for new capitalist methods of exploitation. Their critique of chattel slavery indirectly legitimated wage slavery. In this interpretation, social control, if no longer a conscious motive, is no less a consequence of the reformers' actions and helps explain their success.[8]

The interpretation of antebellum reform as social control, in both its non-Marxian and neo-Marxian forms, has provoked an enormous critical reaction. Typically, this criticism has argued that the reformers were motivated by moral principle, rather than ambition for worldly power. Many critics of the social control thesis have sought to explain the evangelicals' behavior in psychological, frequently psychoanalytic, categories. In this view, the goal of evangelical commitment was a new personal identity, rather than class interest.[9]

The present state of historiography leaves unresolved two different perceptions of evangelical Christianity. The scholarship on the eighteenth century treats evangelical Christianity as a democratic and liberating force, whereas much of the literature on the evangelical movement of the nineteenth century emphasizes its implications for social control. Did some dramatic transformation of the revival impulse come about at the turn of the century? I would argue not; historians have concentrated on the "soft" and "hard" sides of evangelicalism in the eighteenth and nineteenth centuries, respectively, but both were consistently present. Evangelical Protestantism did not mysteriously mutate from a democratic and liberating impulse into an elitist and repressive one when it moved from the eighteenth to the nineteenth century. Austerity and self-discipline were present even in eighteenth-century evangelicalism; individual autonomy was asserted even in nineteenth-century evangelicalism. The problem is that our idea of social control, implying *one* person or group imposing constraints on *another*, is appropriate for some aspects of the reform impulse, such as the treatment of the insane, but not all. It does not take account of the embrace of *self*-discipline, so typical of evangelicals.

---

[8] Avery Craven, *The Coming of the Civil War* (New York, 1942); Charles C. Cole, *The Social Ideas of the Northern Evangelists* (New York, 1954); and Clifford Griffin, "Religious Benevolence as Social Control," *Mississippi Valley Historical Review* 44 (Dec. 1957), 423–44. Michael Katz, *The Irony of Early School Reform* (Cambridge, MA, 1968); David J. Rothman, *The Discovery of the Asylum* (Boston, 1971); Anthony F C. Wallace, *Rockdale* (New York, 1978); Paul Johnson, *A Shopkeeper's Millennium* (New York, 1978); David Brion Davis, The Problem of Slavery in the Age of Revolution (Ithaca, NY, 1975), esp. 251–54, 346–57. See also David Brion Davis, *Slavery and Human Progress* (New York, 1984), 109. E. P. Thompson, *The Making of the English Working Class* (London, 1980).

[9] Martin J. Wiener, ed., "Humanitarianism or Control? A Symposium on Aspects of Nineteenth-Century Social Reform in Britain and America," *Rice University Studies* 67 (Winter 1981), 1–84. See also Lois Banner, "Religious Benevolence as Social Control: A Critique of an Interpretation," *Journal of American History* 60 (June 1973), 34–41; James B. Stewart, *Holy Warriors: The Abolitionists and American Slavery* (New York, 1976); and Lawrence Frederick Kohl, "The Concept of Social Control and the History of Jacksonian America," *Journal of the Early Republic* 5 (Spring 1985), 21–34. On the quest for identity among reformers, evangelical and nonevangelical, see Waldo E. Martin, Jr., *The Mind of Frederick Douglass* (Chapel Hill, NC, 1984); Robert Abzug, *Passionate Liberator: Theodore Dwight Weld and the Dilemma of Reform* (New York, 1980); Lewis Perry, *Radical Abolitionism: Anarchy and the Government of God in Antislavery Thought* (Ithaca, NY, 1973); and Martin Duberman, ed., *The Antislavery Vanguard* (Princeton, NJ, 1965).

The essence of evangelical commitment to Christ is that it is undertaken voluntarily, consciously, and responsibly, by the individual for himself or herself. (That, after all, is why evangelicals, in any century, are not content to let a person's Christianity rest on baptism in infancy.) If we can substitute the more comprehensive category *discipline for social control*, we will be in a better position to understand the evangelical movement and the continuities between its colonial and antebellum phases. We will also be able to deal with the important psychological issues of personal identity that have been raised by the critics of the social control interpretation. Evangelical Christians were and are people who have consciously decided to take charge of their own lives and identities. The Christian discipline they embrace is both liberating and restrictive. Insofar as the discipline is self-imposed, it expresses the popular will; insofar as it is imposed on others, it is social control. The reforms undertaken by nineteenth-century evangelicals were typically concerned to redeem people who were not functioning as free moral agents: slaves, criminals, the insane, alcoholics, children, even—in the case of the most logically rigorous of reformers, the feminists—women. The goal of the reformers was to substitute for external constraint the inner discipline of responsible morality. Liberation and control were thus two sides of the same redemptive process. . . .[10]

ECUMENICISM VERSUS CONFESSIONALISM

The evangelical movement in the antebellum United States was in many respects the functional equivalent of an established church. Although voluntary rather than compulsory in its basis, the evangelical movement shared with the traditional religious establishments of European countries the goal of a Christian society. Nineteenth-century evangelicals defined that goal as something to be achieved, rather than something to be maintained. To meet the goal entailed a gigantic effort of organization. The revival established what contemporaries called "a benevolent empire" an interlocking network of voluntary associations, large and small, local, national, and international—to implement its varied purposes. The objectives of these voluntary societies ranged from antislavery to temperance, from opposing dueling to opposing Sunday mails, from the defense of the family to the overthrow of the Papacy, from women's self-help support groups to the American Sunday School Union, from the American Bible Society to the National Truss Society for the Relief of the Ruptured Poor.[11]

---

[10]The tiny bands of supporters of free love and anarchy carried this logic to drastic extremes, rejecting the institutions of marriage and government as coercing behavior that should come from inner discipline.

[11]On the organizing effort, see Donald C. Mathews, "The Second Great Awakening as an Organizing Process," *American Quarterly* 21 (Spring 1969), 23–44; and Robert Wiebe, *The Opening of American Society: From the Adoption of the Constitution to the Eve of Disunion* (New York, 1984), 229–32. Charles I. Foster, *An Errand of Mercy: The Evangelical United Front, 1790–1837* (Chapel Hill, NC, 1960); Richard L. Power, "A Crusade to Extend Yankee Culture," *New England Quarterly* 13 (Dec. 1940), 638–53; Ronald G. Walters, *American Reformers, 1815–1860* (New York, 1978). On the transatlantic dimension, see Frank Thistlethwaite, *The Anglo-American Connection in the Early Nineteenth Century* (Philadelphia, 1959).

The organization of Christian evangelism involved a whole new soteriology, that is, a new theory of the operation of divine grace. Earlier evangelists, even the great Jonathan Edwards, had waited upon the fluctuating action of the Spirit to create a revival. Nineteenth-century evangelists, typified by Charles G. Finney, institutionalized their revivals with an eye to making them permanent, efficient, and continuous. . . .[12] At a time when little else in American society was organized, when there were no nationwide business corporations except the national bank and no nationwide government bureaucracy except the post office, the evangelical movement was organized, vocal, and nationwide.

The evangelical organizing process was the religious precursor and counterpart of the so-called American System, the political program of Henry Clay and the Whig party. Both represented an imposition of system and direction on a formless society. Addressing religious and moral issues on the one hand, and banking, the tariff, internal improvements, and land sales on the other, the evangelical movement and the American System stood for conscious planning and collective purpose, rather than laissez-faire. What is more, both put their trust in the same leadership class of prosperous mercantile laity.[13] The Whigs may have been slower than the Democrats to accept the legitimacy of political parties partly because the Protestant benevolent societies provided Whigs with an alternative mode of organizing in pursuit of their social objectives. Certainly the Whigs were no less modern than the Democrats in their outlook, no less issue-oriented, and no less willing to make use of the new media of communication.[14] But the rise of political parties could only undercut the influence of voluntary associations, each focused on a single cause. The distrust of party organization that some historians have observed among Whigs was commonest among the evangelicals.[15]

One feature of the evangelical movement suggestive of an established church was its Protestant ecumenicism.[16] Led by laymen and, in a remarkable number of cases, laywomen, the evangelical movement was largely emancipated from control by the denominationally organized clergy. The laity were disposed toward

---

[12]James H. Moorhead, "Social Reform and the Divided Conscience of Antebellum Protestantism," *Church History* 48 (Dec. 1979), 416–30. Max Weber, *Economy and Society*, trans. Ephraim Fischoff (3 vols., Berkeley, CA, 1978), III, 1121–39.

[13]See Bertram Wyatt-Brown, *Lewis Tappan and the Evangelical War against Slavery* (Cleveland, OH, 1969); Peter Dobkin Hall, *The Organization of American Culture: Private Institutions, Elites, and the Origins of American Nationality* (New York, 1982); and Robert F. Dalzell, Jr., *Enterprising Elite: The Boston Associates and the World They Made* (Cambridge, MA, 1987).

[14]See, for example, David Paul Nord, "Evangelical Origins of Mass Media in America, 1815–1835," *Journalism Monographs* 85 (May 1984), 1–30; and more generally, R. Laurence Moore, "Religion, Secularization, and the Shaping of the Culture Industry in Antebellum America," *American Quarterly* 41 (June 1989), 216–42.

[15]For a different perspective on Whigs' antiparty sentiments, see Lynn Marshall, "The Strange Stillbirth of the Whig Party," *American Historical Review* 72 (Oct. 1967), 269–87. The antiparty attitudes of the Whigs are sometimes exaggerated and wrongly attributed to antimodern attitudes.

[16]A possible British counterpart were the ecumenical and evangelical Anglican reformers described in Richard Brent, *Liberal Anglican Politics: Whiggery, Religion, and Reform, 1830–1841* (Oxford, England, 1987).

interdenominational cooperation by considerations both practical and principled. In practical terms, ecumenicism made for efficiencies of scale. In ideological terms, it reflected a decline of interest in the theological distinctions that had often formed the basis for denominational differentiation accompanied by a rising sense of American nationality and national moral responsibility. For the American evangelical movement, the nation had taken on the character of a Christian community, within which members shared moral responsibility and a legitimate concern with mutual discipline.

Evangelical ecumenicism and the discipline that went with it were controversial. The Great Awakening had split Americans into New Lights and Old, and the Second Great Awakening was every bit as divisive. Just as some people objected to the imposition of political control by the Whig American System, some objected to the imposition of the religious and moral discipline of the evangelical movement. If the evangelical movement was the American religious "establishment," its opponents were the American "dissenters." . . .

Many political issues of the second party system involved judgments of moral value. Among the moral issues that shaped the second party system as it emerged in the 1820s were anti-Masonry, sabbatarianism, antislavery, and the white opposition to Indian removal (an opposition led by Presbyterian missionaries). Different ethnic or religious communities judged such issues differently. According to what has become known as the ethnoreligious interpretation of antebellum politics, those communities became the building blocks of party. Mutual antagonisms among the communities led them to regard each other as "negative reference groups." Voters lined up with the party opposing the party of their principal negative reference group. Thus Irish Catholic immigrants voted Democratic while their despised competitors, the free blacks, voted Whig— prompting many Scots-Irish Presbyterian immigrants to vote Whig in reaction against the Irish Catholic Democrats.[17]

In real life, of course, ethnoreligious hostilities did not exist in a vacuum; they were affected by the changing economic climate of the times. In the minds of contemporaries, moral issues and economic issues were not entirely separate categories. Given the connection between evangelical moral discipline and the complex processes we have been calling modernization, it is logical that

---

[17]Kathleen S. Kutolowski, "Antimasonry Re-Examined: The Social Bases of the Grass-Roots Party," *Journal of American History* 71 (Sept. 1984), 269–93; Bertram Wyatt-Brown, "Prelude to Abolitionism: Sabbatarian Politics and the Rise of the Second Party System," ibid., 58 (Sept. 1971), 316–41; Richard R. John, "Taking Sabbatarianism Seriously: The Postal System, the Sabbath, and the Transformation of American Political Culture," *Journal of the Early Republic* 10 (Winter 1990), 517–67; David J. Russo, "Major Political Issues of the Jacksonian Period and the Development of Party Loyalty in Congress," *Transactions of the American Philosophical Society* 62 (May 1972), 3–51. Lee Benson, *The Concept of Jacksonian Democracy: New York as a Test Case* (Princeton, NJ, 1961). Ronald P. Formisano, "Toward a Reorientation of Jacksonian Politics: A Review of the Literature:" *Journal of American History* 63 (June 1976), 42–65; and Robert P. Swierenga, "Ethnocultural Political Analysis," *Journal of American Studies* 5 (April 1971), 59–79. The broadest application of the ethnocultural interpretation is Robert Kelley, *The Cultural Pattern in American Politics: The First Century* (New York, 1979).

economic policies were judged by religious criteria. Even issues we think of as economic, such as bank notes, bankruptcies, and acts legitimating preemption of public lands, had their moral dimensions in antebellum America. Even movements we think of as ethnoreligious, such as nativism, had their economic dimension: Irish immigrants were not only Catholics but also low-wage laborers; in both guises they seemed threatening to native Protestant workingmen. . . .

The supporters and opponents of the evangelical revival constituted the two largest of all the mutually hostile moral communities or reference groups identified by the ethnoreligious interpretation. The multiplicity of religious bodies sorted themselves out into two camps, prorevival and antirevival, that then meshed with the two-party political system. By the time of the classic Whig-Democratic confrontation in 1840, the evangelicals were openly and actively enlisted in the Whig campaign, their opponents arrayed on the Democratic side. . . .[18]

The opponents of the revival may be characterized as confessionalists, people who attached primary importance to bearing witness to the truth as they saw it. Their interest in theological distinctions had not declined, and they were unwilling to subsume their differences under the ecumenical banner of the revival. Often their religious loyalties were underscored by ethnic identifications. Among the confessionalists were Roman Catholics, Old School Presbyterians, Missouri Synod Lutherans, Dutch True Calvinists, Antimission Baptists, Latter-day Saints, and Orthodox Jews.[19]

It is not possible to define the opponents of the revival entirely in denominational terms, since its support was not defined in denominational terms either. In New England, where the establishment of religion was a literal, not a metaphorical, political issue until 1833, Methodists and Baptists were dissenters and Democrats. Elsewhere the pattern of local negative reference groups was different. In the Old Northwest, southern settlers who arrived after 1830, regardless of denominational affiliation, generally resisted both the evangelical movement and the Whig party. For our purposes, the handful of avowed freethinkers in the United States count as confessionalists, since they too were critics of the revival. In the same camp were those of the unchurched whose only interest in religion was to resist intolerance and meddlesome moralism. What all these disparate groups—traditionalists, southerners, anti-clericals, and "nothingarians" had in common was a determination to preserve their independence in defiance of the evangelical juggernaut. To them evangelical ecumenicism looked like religious imperialism. As the Jeffersonian Republicans had rallied deists and sectarians in opposition to the Anglican and Congregational establishments of the late

[18]See Richard Carwardine, "Evangelicals, Whigs, and the Election of William Henry Harrison," *Journal of American Studies* 17 (April 1983), 47–53; and Ronald P. Formisano, *The Birth of Mass Political Parties: Michigan, 1827–1861* (Princeton, NJ, 1971), 102–36.

[19]Walter Conser, *Church and Confession: Conservative Theologians in Germany, England, and America, 1815–1866* (Macon, GA, 1984). Benton Johnson, "Ascetic Protestantism and Political Preference," *Public Opinion Quarterly* 26 (Spring 1962), 3 5–46; Paul Kleppner, *The Cross of Culture: A Social Analysis of Midwestern Politics* (New York, 1970); and Richard Jensen, "Religious and Occupational Roots of Party Identification," *Civil War History* 16 (Dec. 1970), 325–43.

eighteenth century, the Jacksonian Democrats became the party of those opposed to the ecumenical evangelical "establishment" of the antebellum era.[20]

The very theology of the evangelical movement had important political implications. Evangelicals often embraced postmillennialism, which teaches that the Second Coming of Christ will occur at the end of the thousand years of peace foretold in Scripture. The implication is that human efforts on behalf of social justice form part of the divine plan to bring about the day of the Lord. Premillennialism, the more traditional doctrine, teaches that the Second Coming will occur before the thousand years of peace and is necessary to usher it in, implying a less optimistic view of human progress. Postmillennialism became a prominent feature of main-stream evangelicalism in the United States and Britain during the nineteenth century and brought a new sense of religious urgency to social reform. . . . With traditions of paternalism weak . . . in the United States, Americans depended . . . more on post-millennial moralism to motivate reform.[21]

. . . Evangelicalism and its attendant impulse toward discipline and reform flourished most among Christian bodies that defined themselves as voluntary, lay-controlled societies of committed believers; confessionalism was associated with a view of the church as a universal institution, bearing witness to objective truths, whose clergy dispense grace through sacraments. This distinction was classically formulated by Ernst Troeltsch, who called the former bodies "sects" and the latter "churches." There is reason to believe that the sects have historically done more to encourage their members to politically active citizenship.[22]

The cultural approach to politics would lead us to view party affiliation as a function of membership in a community sharing common values. Careful local studies indicate that such membership was often determined by a combination of mutually reinforcing moral and economic motives. Within a cultural interpretation, how much importance to attach to formal religious beliefs and traditions must vary with circumstances.[23]

One thing is certain: The cultural interpretation has not revitalized the consensus approach to American history; on the contrary, it has vindicated the perception of the Progressive historians that American history has been characterized

---

[20]Donald J. Ratcliffe, "Politics in Jacksonian Ohio: Reflections on the Ethnocultural Interpretation," *Ohio History* 88 (Winter 1979), 5–36, esp. 17. William G. McLoughlin, *New England Dissent, 1630–1833: The Baptists and the Separation of Church and State* (2 vols., Cambridge, MA, 1970).

[21]Ernest L. Tuveson, *Millennium and Utopia* (Berkeley, CA, 1949); James Moorhead, *American Apocalypse: Yankee Protestants and the Civil War* (New Haven, CT, 1978); Boyd Hilton, *The Age of Atonement: The Influence of Evangelicalism on Social and Economic Thought, 1795–1865* (Oxford, England, 1988).

[22]Louis P. Masur, *Rites of Execution: Capital Punishment and the Transformation of American Culture, 1776–1865* (New York, 1989), 141–59; Ernst Troeltsch, *The Social Teaching of the Christian Churches*, trans. Olive Wyon (New York, 1960); the book was first published in German in 1911.

[23]Robert Doherty, "Social Bases for the Presbyterian Schism of 1837–38: The Philadelphia Case," *Journal of Social History* 2 (Fall 1968), 69–79; David Montgomery, "The Shuttle and the Cross: Weavers and Artisans in the Kensington Riots of 1844," ibid., 5 (Summer 1972), 411–46; and data on Rochester in Johnson, *Shopkeeper's Millennium*, 3–14, 89–94, 136–41. Michael Holt, *Forging a Majority: The Formation of the Republican Party in Pittsburgh* (New Haven, CT, 1969).

by profound conflict. If the simple liberal versus conservative dichotomy of early Progressive historians is no longer satisfactory, if both Whigs and Democrats are now seen to have some "liberal" and some "conservative" aspects, it does not follow that the two parties were altogether nonideological, still less that both were namby-pamby "moderates" with similar programs. The antebellum parties disagreed sharply over a wide range of issues, and their partisans hated each other cordially. The cultural interpretation has, however, placed our understanding of Whig/Democratic conflicts on a basis of world view broadly conceived rather than economic interest narrowly defined. It is as if the axis defining their polar opposition had rotated to a new position in our minds.[24]

Dedicated as they were to particularism and diversity, the confessional Democrats found doctrines of little government congenial. The natural rights philosophy of the Jacksonians asserted the individual's claims to be protected against interference from officious ecumenical reformers. An emphasis on the separation of church and state was the logical complement of this philosophy, for it removed everything having to do with religion from the potential interference of government. Thus, in place of the Puritan and evangelical religious tradition that the Whigs drew upon, the Democrats invoked the political ideas of the Enlightenment.

On the whole, historians of the Democratic party have found less reason to discuss religion than historians of the Whig party. The political strategy of the Democrats—indeed their very *raison d'être*—dictated a political secularism. Thus, for example, Jean H. Baker's study of the political culture of the antebellum northern Democrats scarcely mentions religion. Had she looked into the question, Baker would probably have been led to a view enunciated by Sean Wilentz. Stressing the diversity of religious opinion in the New York City Working Men's party, Wilentz concludes that "the artisans' disparate religious views provided a rough analogue to their democratic politics, opposed to all men of 'insolent morality' who would ratify their presumed social superiority with the Word of God."[25] When the Working Men's party did not succeed as a separate organization, it merged into the Democratic party. The freedom such people prized was "freedom from"; the goal of the Whigs was "freedom to."

In the great competition between ecumenicists and confessionalists, the initiative lay with the evangelicals. One difference between that America and our

---

[24]See Joel H. Silbey, *The Partisan Imperative: The Dynamics of American Politics before the Civil War* (New York, 1985). The classic Progressive interpretation of the second party system is Arthur Schlesinger, Jr., *The Age of Jackson* (Boston, 1945). For recognition of the political dimension of the evangelical movement, see his chapter "The Whig Counterreformation," ibid., 267–82. The many studies confirming partisan division include Joel H. Silbey, *The Shrine of Party: Congressional Voting Behavior, 1841–1852* (Pittsburgh, PA, 1967); Herbert Ershkowitz and William G. Shade, "Consensus or Conflict? Political Behavior in the State Legislatures during the Jacksonian Era," *Journal of American History* 58 (Dec. 1971), 591–621; and Donald J. Ratcliffe, "The Role of Voters and Issues in Party Formation: Ohio, 1824," ibid., 59 (March 1973), 847–70.

[25]Jean H. Baker, *Affairs of Party: The Political Culture of the Northern Democrats in the Mid-Nineteenth Century* (Ithaca, NY, 1983); Sean Wilentz, *Chants Democratic: New York City and the Rise of the American Working Class* (New York, 1984), 86.

own was the dominant culture-shaping power of antebellum evangelical Christianity. The ecumenical evangelicals then formed what Ronald P. Formisano has termed the "core" of the national culture; the confessionalists occupied the "periphery." The analogy already suggested with the Whig economic program (the American System) continues helpful: Arthur M. Schlesinger, Jr., interpreted the politics of the Jacksonian age as a conflict pitting the powerful "business community" against all the other interest groups in society, who were forced to make common cause to protect themselves. In the cultural interpretation, the evangelicals become the counterparts of Schlesinger's business community, and the confessionalists, the alliance of out-groups. This analogy should not compel us to regard the confessionalists as the heroes of the story. But it should remind us not to focus exclusively on the evangelical core, that the religions of the periphery have a fascinating cultural history (or rather, histories) of their own.[26]

The core/periphery metaphor has been applied to many other countries as well and lends itself to comparative study. For example, Robert Kelley has shown how the British Liberals, the Canadian Liberals, and the American Democrats were all parties of the ethnocultural periphery and therefore defenders of pluralism. An analogy between the American Whigs and the British and Canadian Tory parties can also be drawn, since they all endorsed national homogeneity and government intervention in the economy, but religion complicates the analogy. The established Church of England, overwhelmingly Tory in politics, had an evangelical wing, but many English evangelicals were religious Dissenters, part of the cultural periphery and aligned with the Liberal party. Throughout the English-speaking world, issues of religious establishment, whether formal or (as in most of the United States) informal, conditioned the political impact of the evangelical movement and the reaction against it. In the United States the cultural core was occupied by evangelical sectarian bodies that had usually been on the periphery in Europe, while churchly confessional religions like Lutheranism and Roman Catholicism, which had defined the core in their homelands, found themselves on the periphery here.[27]

Any major party in a two-party political system is bound to be a diverse coalition. The American Whig party included many voters who were not directly involved in the evangelical united front. Some of these Whigs, for example, Unitarians and Quakers, shared the perfectionist aspirations of the evangelicals but not their creed. These heterodox groups had derived from their evangelical past

---

[26]Ronald P. Formisano, *The Transformation of Political Culture: Massachusetts Parties, 1790s–1840s* (New York, 1983). How several out-groups have reinforced their identities by using mainstream American society as a negative reference group is the theme of a model study that avoids idealizing either side: R. Laurence Moore, *Religious Outsiders and the Making of Americans* (New York, 1986).

[27]Robert Kelley, *The Transatlantic Persuasion: The Liberal-Democratic Mind in the Age of Gladstone* (New York, 1969). Other important comparative works include Seymour M. Lipset and Stein Rokkan, eds., *Party Systems and Voter Alignments: Cross-National Perspectives* (New York, 1967); and Michael Hechter, *Internal Colonialism: The Celtic Fringe in British National Development, 1536–1966* (Berkeley, CA, 1975).

both individual and social perfectionist aspirations, which they had then magnified and radicalized. Sometimes excluded from evangelical organizations, these groups were particularly prominent in the more radical associations of the benevolent empire, addressing women's rights and antislavery. That such people became Whigs (and later, Republicans) confirms that it was the evangelicals' quest for discipline and perfection, rather than their theological orthodoxy, that had political implications. Significantly, however, the heterodox perfectionists did not display as high a level of Whig party loyalty as the evangelicals, and they were often drawn into minor reform parties.

The Whig party also included some people who were not evangelical even in a generalized sense. Contemporaries were aware of this and took account of it; it became the basis for the important distinction they drew between "Conscience" Whigs and "Cotton" Whigs in the North. Cotton Whigs included groups that identified with the cultural core of bourgeois British-American Protestantism but remained critical of evangelical didacticism, especially the crusade against slavery. Episcopalians and Princeton Old School Presbyterians provide examples of this cultural conservatism. In general, such groups were not so strongly Whig as the evangelicals were; many Episcopalians and Old School Presbyterians, for example, were Democrats. Some of them switched from Democratic to Whig or Republican affiliation only after large-scale Irish Catholic immigration had produced an important negative reference group for them.[28]

Historically derived from the Anglican/Episcopal church and like it manifesting an ambiguous relationship to the second party system was the Methodist Episcopal church. The ambiguous political consequences of Methodism were related to ambiguities in the religion itself. Though evangelical in faith, the Methodists, like the Episcopalians, were more churchly than sectarian in Troeltsch's ecclesiological classification. In England, the Methodist leadership long remained Tory; though religious Nonconformists, Methodists seldom joined political forces with the other English Dissenting sects. Methodism offered dignity and plenteous grace to ordinary people (thereby alarming some of the more authoritarian Anglicans), but it did not mobilize them politically. The Methodist separation from the established Church of England occurred slowly and reluctantly; neither there nor in the United States did Methodism identify clearly with either the core or the periphery. In antebellum America, party politics tended to be the last resort of evangelical reformers. Northern Methodists remained content longer with evangelical voluntarism and were slower than many other evangelicals to embrace political partisanship. Eventually, however, northern Methodists began to behave politically like other evangelicals. The Methodist clergy seem to have moved into the Whig party more readily than their laity. After the emergence of the third party system, the Republicans succeeded in rallying northern Methodists more effectively than the Whigs had ever done. Postbellum Methodists, like other

---

[28]Kelley, *Cultural Pattern in American Politics*, 170–74; and Paul Kleppner, *The Third Electoral System, 1853–1892: Politics, Voters, and Political Cultures* (Chapel Hill, NC, 1979), 164, 174, 177, 186. Formisano, *Birth of Mass Political Parties*, 314–16, citing unpublished work by Alexandra McCoy.

American reformers, turned even more than their predecessors toward political action and the state as an agency of discipline.[29]

With the understanding we have gained of the evangelical movement and its diverse opponents, we are now better able to appreciate the connection between style and substance in antebellum political culture. The hullabaloo of political campaigns in the second party era—the torchlight parades, the tents pitched outside town, the urgent calls for a commitment—was borrowed by political campaigners from the revival preachers. Far from being irrelevant distractions or mere recreation, the evangelical techniques of mass persuasion that we associate with the campaigns of 1840 and after provide a clue to the moral meaning of antebellum politics. . . .

From this perspective, we can see that issues of moral value did not arise in American politics only with the decade of the 1850s, though they took on a more momentous urgency than ever then. It was not the emergence of moral issues as such that wrecked the second party system, but the emergence of two particular issues, nativism and the choice between restriction and expansion of slavery, that the leadership of the existing parties felt it necessary to avoid. These were not exclusively or narrowly moral issues—they combined self-interest and ideology, secular and religious motives in the mutually reinforcing way that appealed so powerfully to the Americans of the day. They rose to salience during an era of prosperity (1844–1857) when the economic aspects of the old party debate seemed less urgent. Meanwhile the temperance movement too was becoming increasingly politicized, through the demand for prohibition by states on the model of the Maine Law. The temperance issue could readily have been accommodated within the existing Whig and Democratic party structure. But that structure provided no framework to debate either the effects of immigration or the extension of slavery. The public, having become accustomed to expressing moral convictions (positive and negative) in political terms, asserted its independence of the second party system. The evangelical movement, and the values and feelings it aroused, proved stronger and more durable than the Whig party that had been associated with it for a generation. When the leaders of the Whig party proved insufficiently responsive to the demands of their constituents, voters deserted the Whigs (and in some cases the Democrats) for the American and Republican parties.[30] The fact that the American party drew so much more support from Prot-

---

[29]Formisano, *Birth of Mass Political Parties*, 153–55. On the political conservatism of English Methodism, see Thompson, *Making of the English Working Class*, 385–440. Donald G. Mathews, *Slavery and Methodism: A Chapter in American Morality* (Princeton, NJ, 1965). Richard Carwardine, "Methodist Ministers and the Second Party System," in *Rethinking Methodist History*, ed. Russell E. Richey and Kenneth E. Rowe (Nashville, TN, 1985), 134–47. On Methodists as Republicans, see Kleppner, *Third Electoral System*, 73, 74, 148, 177; and Ralph Morrow, *Northern Methodism and Reconstruction* (East Lansing, MI, 1956). G. I. T. Machin, *Politics and the Churches in Great Britain, 1832–1868* (Oxford, England, 1977), esp. 195–96.

[30]William E. Gienapp, *The Origins of the Republican Party* (New York, 1986). See also Paul Goodman, "Moral Purpose and Republican Politics in Antebellum America, 1830–1860," *Maryland Historian* 20 (Fall/Winter 1989), 5–39.

estant working-class voters than the earlier workingmen's parties had done suggests that a political mobilization was more effective when it combined its economic appeal with an ethnoreligious one.

TOWARD A BROADER CONCEPTION
OF POLITICAL CULTURE

. . . The cultural interpretation has enriched our understanding of antebellum politics in several ways. First, it underscores the practical effects of ideas and moral values, making American political history seem more ideological than it was once the fashion to admit. Second, it demonstrates more clearly than ever the continuities between the second and third party systems, including those between Whigs and Republicans. This awareness strengthens the third contribution of recent scholarship, which is the new interest taken in the Whig party. No longer are the Whigs seen simply as the conservative opponents of Jacksonian progress. As Louise Stevenson puts it:

> Whiggery stood for the triumph of the cosmopolitan and national over the provincial and local, of rational order over irrational spontaneity, of school-based learning over traditional folkways and customs, and of self-control over self-expression. Whigs believed that every person had the potential to become moral or good if family, school, and community nurtured the seed of goodness in his moral nature.[31]

Such a description encompasses more than views on public policy; it depicts a value system with private as well as public aspects. The values that the evangelical Whig tradition sought to implement in the antebellum North derived from a conjunction of ancient Christianity with the cognitive expansion and disciplinary needs of the modern market society. Over its long history going back to the European Reformation, the Puritan/evangelical tradition did not simply adapt to, or borrow from, modernity and democracy; it actively helped form them.[32] Individualism, voluntarism, and contractualism were features of the Reformed religious tradition in early modern Europe before they were taken over by the secular political philosophers of possessive individualism. In antebellum America, that tradition continued to contribute to shaping the culture of the modern world.

---

[31]Louise Stevenson, *Scholarly Means to Evangelical Ends: The New Haven Scholars and the Transformation of Higher Learning in America, 1830–1890* (Baltimore, MD, 1986), 5–6. Major L. Wilson, *Space, Time, and Freedom: The Quest for Nationality and the Irrepressible Conflict* (Westport, CT, 1974); Michael F. Holt, *The Political Crisis of the 1850s* (New York, 1978); and Samuel P. Huntington, "Paradigms of American Politics," *Political Science Quarterly* 89 (March 1974), 1–26. Eric Foner, *Free Soil, Free Labor, Free Men: The Ideology of the Republican Party before the Civil War* (New York, 1970); and Gienapp, *Origins of the Republican Party.*

[32]There is no clear-cut date in American history for switching terminology from "Puritan" to "evangelical." I use both terms here because of the time span to which I refer.

The nineteenth-century evangelical movement represents the modernizing phase in the history of Christianity. In the antebellum North, the modernization of religion was a precursor of, a facilitator of, and a model for the modernization of politics, economics, and the media of communication. Richard L. McCormick, in his impressive survey of what he calls "the party period" of American political history, comments that the driving force in nineteenth-century political life was a "new vision" of an activist government advocated by Whigs and Republicans. That new vision of government had been pioneered, I would add, by a new vision of a moral society advocated by Christian evangelists invoking historic Protestant doctrines of individual rebirth and community discipline.[33]

The evangelical movement of the early nineteenth century reflected a momentous change in the relation of Troeltsch's sects to the rest of society. In Europe, the sects had been peripheral to society, had struggled for independence from the state, and had frequently disavowed state power. In the United States, the sects were in a position to shape the culture for their society as a whole and embraced the opportunity. They enlarged their conception of discipline to include the legal coercion of nonmembers. In colonial and early national times, some of them enjoyed certain privileges of religious establishment; during the era of the second party system, they pursued something resembling a functional establishment of religion.

Recently we have learned to attribute the public spirit of antebellum and colonial America to the classical republican tradition. That secular tradition was complemented in important ways by the Puritan/evangelical religious tradition, which often coexisted with it in the English-speaking world. Both traditions valued public virtue, private discipline, balanced government, and widespread participation. Much of the political debate of this era, partisan and sectional alike, was cast in the terms of classical republicanism. But it is not clear that the classical republican tradition supplied motivation for political participation, so much as a rationale for it.[34] Republicanism was a paradigm for understanding political life and a vocabulary for explaining it. Northerners and southerners, Whigs and Democrats, labor and capital, modernizers and antimodernizers, evangelicals and confessionalists spoke the language of republicanism. Every group interpreted it in a distinctive way and claimed to be its rightful heir. Republicanism, invoking the body of classical knowledge common to all

---

[33]See Gregory Singleton, "Protestant Voluntary Organizations and the Shaping of Victorian America," in *Victorian America*, ed. Howe, 47–58. Richard L. McCormick, *The Party Period and Public Policy* (New York, 1986), 89–140, esp. 132.

[34]Compare McCormick, *Party Period and Public Policy*, 112. On republicanism the seminal work is J. G. A. Pocock, *The Machiavellian Moment: Florentine Political Thought and the Atlantic Republican Tradition* (Princeton, NJ, 1975). Republicanism and its relationship to liberalism have been more thoroughly explored for the period before 1815 than after, but see Holt, *Political Crisis of the 1850s*; Howe, *Political Culture of the American Whigs*; Wilentz, *Chants Democratic*; Steven Watts, *The Republic Reborn: War and the Making of Liberal America, 1790–1820* (Baltimore, MD, 1987); and Dorothy Ross, "Liberalism," in the *Encyclopedia of American Political History*, ed. Jack P. Greene (3 vols., New York, 1984), I, 750–63.

educated people in the nineteenth century, was readily synthesized with both the natural rights philosophy of the Enlightenment and the Protestant tradition of discipline.[35] Since all sides in all debates made use of the classical republican vocabulary, it is difficult to see how classical republicanism could have helped people choose sides—though it clearly helped them argue their cases once they had chosen.

The evangelical movement and the resistance to it can help us understand the conflicting motivations that led people to choose the sides they did and hold onto them with tenacity. The political culture formed by the clash between the evangelical movement and its adversaries was one that generated a high level of excitement and participation.... [H]istorians have looked back with nostalgia to a political system that involved the public so much more effectively than our own. Of course voters might have innumerable reasons for wanting an active (or inactive) government besides the implementation (or frustration) of the evangelical agenda. But at a minimum, the evangelical agenda, media, and institutions provided models showing how to influence people, how to involve them, and how to get things done.[36]

McCormick has called for more investigation into "the organizations to which nineteenth-century Americans turned for expression of their ideological goals." Such organizations were by no means all political parties. As Alexis de Tocqueville observed, a host of issue-oriented voluntary associations connected individuals with public participation in antebellum America. The evangelical benevolent empire was by far the largest network of these. It fostered a sense of active purpose among groups who had never before experienced it, notably women and free blacks. Whatever its implications for social control, evangelicalism also contributed to social empowerment, and the latter has been less thoroughly studied. Too often historians have taken it for granted that the Democratic party was the only agency for broadening popular participation in antebellum public life. An innovative essay by Carroll Smith-Rosenberg, "The Cross and the Pedestal," is an example of how historians are breaking free from this limitation. She uses anthropological theory to describe the ways in which the great revival provided religious forms for female self-assertion in early capitalist America.[37]

---

[35]See James T. Kloppenberg, "The Virtues of Liberalism: Christianity, Republicanism, and Ethics in Early American Political Discourse," *Journal of American History* 74 (June 1987), 9–33; Daniel W. Howe, "Classical Education and Political Culture in Nineteenth-Century America," *Intellectual History Newsletter* 5 (Spring 1983), 9–14.

[36]William E. Gienapp, "Politics Seems to Enter into Everything: Political Culture in the North, 1840–1860," in *Essays on American Antebellum Politics*, ed. Stephen Maizlish and John Kushma (Arlington, VA, 1982), 14–69. Michael F. Holt, "The Election of 1840, Voter Mobilization, and the Emergence of the Second American Party System," in *A Master's Due: Essays in Honor of David Herbert Donald*, ed. William J. Cooper et al. (Baton Rouge, LA, 1985), 16–58. For a wonderful evocation of nineteenth-century participatory politics, see Michael E. McGerr, *The Decline of Popular Politics: The American North, 1865–1928* (New York, 1986), 3–41.

[37]McCormick, *Party Period and Public Policy*, 136; Alexis de Tocqueville, *Democracy in America*, trans. Henry Reeve, ed. Phillips Bradley (2 vols, New York, 1945), I, 198–205 and passim. See Carroll Smith-Rosenberg, *Disorderly Conduct: Visions of Gender in Victorian America* (New York, 1985), 129–64.

The next step in the evolution of antebellum political history should be to define political culture to include all struggles over power, not just those decided by elections. The women's movement, the struggles for racial justice and the rights of labor, conflicts for control of churches and voluntary organizations, even power struggles among members of the family—all these and more were relevant to the modernization of American life in this period. That the authority of government in the antebellum United States was so remarkably weak and decentralized is all the more reason to take account of other arenas in which power was contested. As Harry Watson has observed in studying the South, antebellum "state authority was mediated through so many local agencies of control that its influence appeared as a smooth extension of the other patterns that held every other aspect of neighborhood life in its place." Traditional political history, the history of government power, will be illuminated, not obscured, by being set in such a context. . . . Indeed, in the antebellum United States, electoral politics was often only the last resort . . . of movements that had failed to accomplish their objectives in other ways. And the broader the context in which political culture is studied, the more it will be found that religion was an important determinant of purposes and behavior. . . .[38]

The cultural and moral tradition of Reformed religion was carried on by the reformers in the antebellum Whig party. In that tradition, public policies were frequently concerned not only with society and politics but also with personality and personal discipline. Antebellum debates over public policy often addressed what had originally been private concerns. Political agitation for legal prohibition of alcohol, for example, was an outgrowth of an evangelical disciplinary impulse that was originally voluntary and individual. In an earlier work, I tried to show how the private struggles of prominent Whigs to shape their own personalities mirrored the public conflicts of their time and the resolutions the Whig party offered for them. . . .[39]

A broader conception of political culture can help illuminate not only partisan and sectarian conflicts but also sectional tensions. Some abolitionists rejected party politics and refused even to vote. But surely we would want to define their crusade in some broad sense as political; it was certainly perceived as such by the South. Besides slavery, another source of the cultural contrasts between the North and South lay in their different receptivity to changing gender relationships. The Whig and Republican modernizing culture placed a higher value on female self-expression than did the Democratic traditional one. Modernization of gender roles, bringing increasing autonomy to women, occurred faster in the North. Women were more active as leaders in the northern evangelical movement than in the southern resistance to it. (Conversely, the southern cult of honor—among both the gentry and the common folk—placed more emphasis on

---

[38]Watson, *Jacksonian Politics*, 9. Daniel Scott Smith shows the decline in nineteenth-century United States fertility occurred first in ethnoreligious groups that also supported economic and political modernization. See Daniel Scott Smith, "Cultural Bases of 19th Century U.S. Fertility Decline," 1988 (in Daniel Walker Howe's possession).

[39]Howe, *Political Culture of the American Whigs*.

the expression of physical "manliness" than northern culture did.) Northern Whig women like Harriet Beecher Stowe and Sarah Josepha Hale made popular literature an instrument of evangelical didacticism, in their own expression, a "moral influence." In fact, the relationship between the evangelical movement and the empowerment of women has been one of the most rewarding areas of historical research during the past generation.[40]

The middle period of American history was a time of dramatic innovation—economic, moral, and institutional, as well as political. The innovations were especially obvious in the North, and the evangelical movement provided the motivation and the model for many of them. Far from being reactionary, as has sometimes been thought, the religion of the great revival was an engine driving rational change, a force for modernization. The conflicts—public and private, communal and individual—that this force unleashed were central to the political culture of the era.[41]

---

[40]Jane Tompkins, *Sensational Designs: The Cultural Work of American Fiction* (New York, 1985); and, William R. Taylor, *Cavalier and Yankee: The Old South and American National Character* (Garden City, NJ, 1961). Watson, *Liberty and Power*, 178, 182, 221–22. Cott, *Bonds of Womanhood*; Ryan, *Cradle of the Middle Class*; Carroll Smith-Rosenberg, *Religion and the Rise of the City* (Ithaca, NY, 1971), 97–124; Ross Paulson, *Women's Suffrage and Prohibition* (Glenview, IL, 1973); Ellen DuBois, *Feminism and Suffrage: The Emergence of an Independent Women's Movement in America* (Ithaca, NY, 1978); and Blanche Hersh, *The Slavery of Sex: Feminist Abolitionists in Nineteenth Century America* (Urbana, IL1978).

[41]Daniel Walker Howe, "Religion and Politics in the Antebellum North," in *Religion and American Politics: From the Colonial Period to the 1980s*, ed. Mark Noll (New York, 1990), 121–45.

Daniel Walker Howe

I'm a historian of the United States, specializing in the "Middle Period" between 1763 and 1876, that is from the causes of the Revolution to Reconstruction after the Civil War. My father was a newspaperman who loved history. I remember him sitting me on his lap and telling me about Hannibal crossing the Alps with elephants to fight the Romans. My father died when I was only eight, but he had already put me on track to study history. I went to East Denver High School; we didn't have any AP courses then. I won a scholarship to Harvard. My widowed mother didn't earn much money as a secretary, so the scholarship made a huge difference. After college, I served in the Army (luckily, we weren't fighting any wars just then), got a master's degree at Oxford and then went to the University of California at Berkeley for my Ph.D. Professor Henry May supervised my doctoral dissertation. He taught intellectual and religious history; that's the kind of historian I've mostly remained. I write about religion as a force in history, not to win converts to a particular denomination. My first job was at Yale, the second at the University of California, Los Angeles, and for my third job I returned to Oxford. I've taught American religious history and have published other articles and books on that subject. My biggest book, called *What Hath God Wrought*, includes religion along with other kinds of history: social, political, diplomatic, and military.

QUESTIONS FOR CONSIDERATION

1. Howe claims that his article will be a "synthesis." What will he synthesize and for what reason?
2. According to Howe, the evangelical movement of the early nineteenth century had a "hard" and a "soft" side. Characterize each. How did each shape society during the early nineteenth century?
3. Soteriology posits a theory of the operation of divine grace and salvation. Ecumenism is an ideology accepting many Christian sects. In what ways did a new soteriology, revivalism, and ecumenism assist evangelicals in their pursuit of broad social reform?
4. What groups formed an "antirevival" or "confessionalist" faction in reaction to evangelical social reform? What interests shaped this faction?
5. How did the theological differences between evangelical and confessionalist factions manifest themselves politically? Economically? Which, according to Howe, inhabited the "core" of national culture and who inhabited the "periphery?" What contextual factors accounted for these positions?

6. According to Howe, how does an understanding of antebellum culture help us understand antebellum politics? Characterize the relationship between the two.

7. Name two examples that Howe provides to illustrate his contention that "the history of parties and governments will be illuminated by the recognition that electoral politics is only one possible form of struggle for power over others or autonomy for self."

CHAPTER ELEVEN

✦◠

Limits of Political Engagement in Antebellum America: A New Look at the Golden Age of Participatory Democracy[1]

Glenn C. Altschuler and Stuart M. Blumin

The expansion of democracy during the decades preceding the Civil War has long been a central theme of American historical literature, and in recent years political historians have vastly increased our knowledge of emerging demo-cratic institutions and processes by examining the partisan battles of that era. Virtually all historians agree that political engagement, which went well beyond voting, was both widespread and deeply felt within the electorate. Jean H. Baker observes "that nineteenth-century Americans gave closer attention to politics than is the case today, thereby guaranteeing a broader, deeper under-standing of issues. . . . party rallies were better attended than Sunday services or even meetings of itinerant preachers," and elections "became secular holy days." Politics and, especially, partisan commitment colored many other as-pects of American life. "More than in any subsequent era," writes William E. Gienapp, "political life formed the very essence of the pre–Civil War genera-tion's experience." . . .[2]

As described by historians, antebellum institutions and practices largely fulfilled the democratic promise of the many new state constitutions that had extended the suffrage to nearly all white men. Virtually everywhere in the United States, regularly convened political party caucuses and nominating conventions, supervisory central committees, party newspapers, and campaign techniques

---

[1]Interested students are encouraged to read this essay in the original form. Glenn C. Altschuler and Stuart M. Blumin, "Limits of Political Engagement in Antebellum America: A New Look at the Golden Age of Participatory Democracy," *Journal of American History*, 84 (3) (Dec. 1997), 855–85.

[2]Jean H. Baker, *Affairs of Party: The Political Culture of Northern Democrats in the Mid-Nine-teenth Century* (Ithaca, NY, 1983), 23, 269, 271; William E. Gienapp, "'Politics Seem to Enter into Everything': Political Culture in the North, 1840–1860," in *Essays on American Antebellum Politics, 1840–1860*, ed. Stephen E. Maizlish and John J. Kushma (College Station, TX, 1982), 66; Michael E. McGerr, *The Decline of Popular Politics: The American North, 1865–1928* (New York, 1986), 13.

seemed to assure that elected officials would serve, as Andrew Jackson said, as "delegates fresh from the people," ever mindful that they must respond to popular will. To assure this, the pyramidal structure of the candidate nomination process rested upon the broadest possible base. At the grass roots, Robert H. Wiebe argues, American parties functioned as a "lodge democracy," in which "leaders were made and unmade by their brothers, and all parties in the process assumed an underlying equality." A congressional candidate, for example, was ordinarily nominated by a congressional district convention made up of delegates from each of the district's counties. In most states, each of those delegates had in turn been selected at a county convention made up of delegates from each of the county's townships. In presidential elections, the pyramid of delegations could reach four levels. But if the pyramid was sometimes tall, its base was invariably broad, for the most local convention or caucus—the one that set all the others in motion—was open to all members of the party. Local editors urged all to attend and were delighted to be able to report a courthouse or a district school packed with enthusiastic citizens. "All one needed to get into politics," Wiebe insists, "was to get into it."[3]

The ensuing election campaign, moreover, was carefully designed to involve the people. Although important elements of "class theater" reflective of older, deferential relations may have remained visible within the campaign spectacle, McGerr argues, the campaign also "underscored the power of the North's workers and farmers," who came not only for the entertainment but also for "the intellectual stimulation of an open air, hour-long oration on the tariff" and the opportunity to have elites acknowledge their freedom and power. The partisan press was another popular element, not only because of its significance during campaigns, but also because as public educator, it discussed political issues and provided summaries or transcripts of legislative proceedings and presidential and gubernatorial messages even during periods of political quiescence. "The pages of the press," McGerr concludes, "made partisanship seem essential to men's identity." Finally, the frequency of elections assured that political quiescence would not last long. The election cycle varied from place to place, but everywhere in the United States there were annual local elections, usually in the late winter or spring, and everywhere there was some state, congressional, or presidential election each year in the late summer or fall. Frequent elections meant that Americans were "perpetually acting" in a ritual of democratic reaffirmation. The political calendar, concludes Joel Silbey, "ensured that Americans were caught up in semipermanent and unstinting partisan warfare somewhere throughout the year every year."[4]

---

[3]Joel H. Silbey, *The Partisan Imperative: The Dynamics of Amenican Politics before the Civil War* (New York, 1985), 13. Robert H. Wiebe, *Self-Rule: A Cultural History of American Democracy* (Chicago, 1995), 74, 81.

[4]McGerr, *Decline of Popular Politics*, 30–33, 17; Wiebe, *Self-Rule*, 74; Joel H. Silbey, *The American Political Nation, 1838–1893* (Stanford, CT, 1991), 48.

The claim that antebellum politics approximated the ideal of participatory democracy is now nearly a paradigm in American political history.[5] To be sure, many political historians recognize departures from the democratic ideal. Some acknowledge that party elites directed and occasionally manipulated political events, but they see in the relation between leaders and followers a democratic equilibrium. Others incline to accept Ronald P. Formisano's characterization of persisting deference and of a more oligarchic balance of forces. There is an ongoing and increasingly rich debate over the nature of political power in this era that has the potential to threaten the democratic paradigm.[6]

What is largely missing from the debate, however, and from the historical literature generally, is any sustained analysis of the nature and depth of popular political engagement, and of the possibility—even during this period of high voter turnout, spectacular campaigns, frequent elections, and a pervasive political press—that some American voters were disengaged from political affairs. We contend that the political engagement of antebellum Americans varied significantly, and that the recognition of this variation leads to fundamental questions about Americans and their politics, questions that we here begin to explore. How did Americans engage with politics? What were the mechanisms of, and the popular responses to, partisan mobilization and the fit between political culture and culture in general? Can we identify Americans who were politically disengaged, and can we take stock of the sources of their disengagement? Were there differing types of political activism among those who took citizenship seriously, and should this typology include a subcommunity of "politicians"? Did party activists themselves, in their very efforts to secure partisan identity and mobilize voters, recognize the existence of apathy and skepticism among the electorate? Was partisan loyalty, for some, an easy alternative to a thoughtful and time-consuming engagement in public affairs, rather than a vehicle for commitment? In sum: How can we understand the "space" that politics occupied in American society and culture during this "golden age" of participatory democracy?[7]

---

[5]Phillip Shaw Paludan, "A People's Contest": The Union and Civil War, 1861–1865 (New York, 1988), 10. Similarly, William G. Shade asserts with no documentation that "over one-third of the white adult males took part in party organizations as members of county committees." William G. Shade, Democratizing the Old Dominion: Virginia and the Second Party System, 1824–1861 (Charlottesville, VA, 1996), 83. Gienapp, "'Politics Seem to Enter into Everything,'" 43–44. Michael F. Holt, The Political Crisis of the 1850s (New York, 1978), 6, 36.

[6]See, for example, Richard P. McCormick, The Second American Party System: Party Formation in the Jacksonian Era (Chapel Hill, NC, 1966); Silbey, American Political Nation; William E. Gienapp, The Origins of the Republican Party, 1852–1856 (New York, 1987); Ronald P. Formisano, The Transformation of Political Culture: Massachusetts Parties, 1790s–1840s (New York, 1983); Edward Pessen, Jacksonian America: Society, Personality, and Politics (Homewood, IL, 1969); Paul Bourke and Donald DeBats, Washington County: Politics and Community in Antebellum America (Baltimore, MD, 1995); Kenneth J. Winkle, The Politics of Community: Migration and Politics in Antebellum Ohio (New York, 1988); Thomas E. Jeffrey, State Parties and National Politics: North Carolina, 1815–1861 (Athens, GA, 1989); and Harry L. Watson, Liberty and Power: The Politics of Jacksonian America (New York, 1990).

[7]The best analysis, in our view, is Formisano's discussion of geopolitical cores and peripheries in The Transformation of Political Culture. Lester W. Milbrath, Political Participation: How and Why Do People Get Involved in Politics? (Chicago, 1965). Gienapp, "Politics Seem to Enter into Everything," 65.

Because the engaged and enthusiastic citizen, but not his or her more passive, skeptical, or even hostile neighbor, has been so well served in the historical literature, in the present essay we will focus on the *limits* of popular political participation and interest. We will examine the organization of political affairs in three communities of the North, South, and West (Greenfield, Massachusetts; Augusta, Georgia; and Marietta, Ohio) during the three-year election cycle beginning with the first fully organized, mass-appeal presidential campaign (1840–1842); in six communities (adding Kingston, New York; Clarksville, Tennessee; and Dubuque, Iowa; and substituting Marion, Ohio, for Marietta) during 1850–1852; and in seven communities (adding Opelousas, Louisiana) during 1858–1860. These communities range from small cities that functioned in the 1840s and 1850s as regional or subregional entrepôts to the smallest county seats capable of sustaining two party newspapers. In number, geographic spread, and difference from one another, they provide much of the range of political experience near the base of the pyramid of partisan organization in the late antebellum United States. This is not to say that they are representative of the nation as a whole. The very fact that they were newspaper publication centers and county seats differentiates them from the still smaller towns and hamlets, and the scattered family farmsteads that lay beyond them within their own counties. These small and medium-sized political centers participated disproportionately in the political life of their counties, and their newspapers, each intended to be the party's voice to an entire county, focused disproportionately on, and circulated disproportionately within, the towns in which they were published. The towns studied here are a biased sample, therefore, in which political engagement was *greater* than in the nation as a whole.[8]

What was the extent and nature of political engagement in these not-quite-representative American towns? Central to our customary understanding of the "party in the electorate" is the assumption that it was in essence a popular institution, expressive of a broadly participatory political culture.[9] Certainly, the grass-roots caucuses, campaign clubs, mass rallies, and other democratic elements of the partisan system seem tailored to, and perhaps even by, an engaged electorate. Yet our inquiry into the ways in which party institutions actually functioned reveals limits to popular activity and interest, visible even amid heated election campaigns but particularly evident in the delegate and candidate nomination process. The partisan press, often despite itself, reveals the failure of political parties in all sections of the country to organize fully at the grass roots, to attract many voters to or widespread interest in local nominating caucuses and conventions, or even to assure that the elected delegates participated in conventions closer to the apex of the party pyramid. These difficulties are evident in both the earlier and later years of party development.

---

[8] Glenn C. Altschuler and Stuart M. Blumin, "'Where Is the Real America?': Politics and Popular Consciousness in the Antebellum Era," *American Quarterly* 49 (June 1997), 225–67.

[9] J. Sorauf, "Political Parties and Political Analysis," in *The American Party Systems: Stages of Political Development*, ed. William Nisbet Chambers and Walter Dean Burnham (New York, 1967), 37–38.

In our two northeastern communities, the small Connecticut River town of Greenfield, Massachusetts, and the larger Hudson River town of Kingston, New York, both major parties were organized at the town level, and both routinely called their adherents into caucus several times a year to choose delegates who would nominate candidates for a variety of offices. Only rarely, though, did a partisan editor report a "spirited" or "well attended" town caucus. Party editors would have been glad to boast of large and enthusiastic caucuses. But when they addressed the subject, it was almost always to exhort and complain, as did the Greenfield Whig editor in 1841 who urged attendance upon those who claim "it is not my business. . . . Whose business is it if it is not yours?" This was a common exhortation throughout the period. The Kingston Republican editor pleaded in 1852: "We hardly have the face to ask it. Give us a few hours. Go to your caucus meetings and come together one evening." . . . Absence from town caucuses was not an exclusively Whig-Republican problem. The Greenfield Democratic editor told us more than he intended when he claimed that an 1851 Democratic town caucus was "more fully attended than usual."[10]

The problem was even worse than poor attendance, for outside the county seat it was by no means certain that a town caucus would be held. Greenfield was one of twenty-six towns in Franklin County, but only once during the nine years we examined did either party convene more than nineteen town caucuses, and the number fell as low as thirteen. In June 1860 the *Franklin Democrat* described "the largest and most enthusiastic" Democratic congressional nominating convention "which has been held in this District for many years" before reporting that it consisted of delegates from seventeen of the sixty-eight towns in the district.[11] As many as sixteen caucuses were held during these years among the eighteen towns of Kingston's Ulster County, but thirteen was a more typical number. Greenfield and Kingston invariably held their caucuses, and so too did the nearby towns of Deerfield, Massachusetts, and Saugerties, New York, and a few other reliable (and generally larger than average) towns in each county. But in some of the smaller and more remote towns, caucuses were not to be relied upon, and in a few they were rare.

Not only did town caucuses fail to meet, but in many instances delegates chosen by caucuses failed to attend the conventions to which they had been sent. Convention reports usually do not permit a precise calculation of delegate attendance, but it is clear from reported delegate and convention vote totals that many delegates stayed home. Towns ordinarily selected three or more delegates to county and district conventions in Massachusetts and New York (Greenfield usually selected seven or eight), but the average number of attending delegates was frequently less than three per represented town. Only twenty-one votes were

---

[10]*Greenfield Gazette & Mercury,* Oct. 19, 1841; *Kingston Democratic Journal,* May 5, 1852, Aug. 10, 1859; *Franklin Democrat,* Aug. 4, 1851. For a description of a "spirited" caucus, see ibid., Sept. 22, 1851.

[11]The exception was the Whig county convention of October 1840, when 23 towns were represented. However, the total vote at this convention was 47, which suggests that all or some towns were underrepresented. See *Greenfield Gazette & Mercury,* Oct. 13, 1840. Franklin Democrat, June 1, 8, 1860.

cast at a Whig county convention in Greenfield in 1841, and Franklin County's Democratic congressional convention of 1850 attracted only sixty-seven delegates from the forty-three towns that had caucused to send delegates. At an 1858 Franklin County Republican state senatorial convention to which twenty-three towns sent delegates, the total number of votes cast was thirty-two, little more than one per town. . . .[12] Editors of party newspapers recognized this problem, and they often urged town caucuses to select delegates "who will be sure to attend the conventions."[13]

Farther west and in the South, the problem was even more acute. In Marietta, Ohio, the Whig county convention of 1841 selected every Washington County voter as a delegate to the legislative district convention before resolving that "the elderly men, in particular, are earnestly solicited to attend." A decade later the Marion Whig editor could still call for a more thorough organization in response to the lamentable "disposition on the part of the Whigs to stay at home."[14] Meanwhile, the Democrats in Marion moved from a primary to a caucus and convention system because Democratic voters failed to turn out for primaries. How effective the move was in overcoming apathy is suggested by the county convention's decision, recalling that of the Washington County Whigs a decade earlier, to appoint every Democrat in Marion County as a delegate to the congressional district nominating convention in 1852. At their 1859 county convention, the Democrats allowed "any Democratic voter" to cast the vote of his township if that township was "not represented by delegates." For its part, the younger Republican party managed to achieve (or to claim to have achieved) full or nearly full township representation at its county conventions, but it experienced difficulties higher up the pyramid. In March of 1860 the Republicans selected 14 delegates and 14 alternates to their congressional district convention, yet the convention report lists only one Marion County delegate, who appears to have cast all of Marion's 14 votes.[15] As the population of the frontier town of Dubuque grew from three to thirteen thousand during the 1850s, both major parties had difficulty in developing a full apparatus. After an election loss by a candidate who had not been nominated by a convention, editor A. P. Wood chided Dubuque County Whigs for their lack of organization: "[F]rom this time out, so long as we have anything to do with politics, we are against every and all

---

[12]*Greenfield Gazette & Mercury*, May 4, 1841; *Franklin Democrat*, Oct. 14, 1850; *Greenfield Gazette & Courier*, Oct. 12, 1858; *Kingston Democratic Journal*, Sept. 7, 1859. At the Democratic county convention of 1850, the towns of Kingston and Saugerties had their three delegates. But each town had selected 33. *Ulster Republican*, Sept. 11, 1850.

[13]*Franklin Democrat*, Aug. 10, 1860; *Greenfield Gazette & Mercury*, Oct. 19, 1841; *Greenfield Gazette & Courier*, Oct. 25, 1842; *Franklin Democrat*, Oct. 25, 1842, Aug. 9, 1858.

[14]*Marietta Intelligencer*, May 27, 1841; *Marion Buckeye Eagle*, Aug. 2, 1850. The *Marion Democratic Mirror* reported only eight of fifteen townships represented at a Whig county convention in 1852 and only eight delegates at a similar convention in 1850. *Marion Democratic Mirror*, Sept. 17, 1852, Sept. 20, 1850. The Eagle reported ten townships represented at the 1852 convention and remained silent about the 1850 convention. *Marion Buckeye Eagle*, Sept. 16, 1852, Sept. 20, 1850.

[15]*Marion Democratic Mirror*, July 2, Aug. 9, 1850, Sept. 19, 1851, Sept. 3, 1852; ibid., Aug. 16, 1860. *Marion Republican*, March 1, 1860, Sept. 30, 1858, Sept. 29, 1859, Sept. 13, 1860.

half-way proceedings. Sink or swim, live or die, we shall go in for regular Whig nominations, and a prompt and energetic support of them when made. . . ."[16]

Dubuque Whigs apparently became better organized, but the Republicans who succeeded them later in the decade experienced the same difficulties. Only four of seventeen townships were represented at a Republican county convention in 1858, and fully twenty-seven of the thirty-two delegates were from Dubuque (an only slightly exaggerated pattern of overrepresentation from the county's political center). Two years later, according to the local Democratic paper, the same convention attracted delegates from only three towns. There were few Democratic embarrassments of a similar magnitude, but the Democratic editor did admit that "apathy has gone so far as to leave whole precincts unrepresented in many of the [Democratic] county and district conventions." . . . Perhaps these westerners, newcomers and older settlers alike, imported from eastern states both the partisan system and its defects.

The difficulties experienced by southern parties reflected the pressures of the sectional crisis, but they also seem to reflect institutional realities separable from events. In the aftermath of the Compromise of 1850, Whigs, especially, found themselves casting about for new bases of party organization even where, as in Augusta, they outpolled the Democrats. But the Democrats of the southern towns examined here were, if anything, even more tentative in their organization than the Whigs. In Augusta in late 1850 and 1851, Whigs (or Constitutional Unionists), but not Democrats, organized for a special congressional election, sent local delegates to a state representative nominating convention, and held caucuses to elect delegates to the Richmond County convention. Similarly, in Clarksville, Tennessee, the Democratic editor complained in 1851 that "our party is without any efficient organization" and observed after the fall election that the Democratic county central committee "was so silent during the late canvas that we had forgotten that it was in existence. . . ."[17]

In Clarksville as late as the 1850s, conventions were called by unnamed party leaders, after "conferring with many persons," rather than by a regularly consti-tuted central committee. The Tennesseans' convention system differed from that of our other localities in another interesting way. Delegations selected to attend higher conventions were invariably huge. A county convention in 1859 of the Opposition (a successor to the Whigs), for example, sent ninety-two men to a state convention and then invited "all other gentlemen . . . who may be able to attend" to act as delegates. In 1860 the Constitutional Union county convention named seventy-nine delegates to a congressional district convention, while local Democrats selected sixty and seventy-two named delegates, plus every other Democrat in the county, for state conventions during these two years. This shotgun strategy may have been the only means of securing an acceptable delega-tion. Of all those Democrats, named and unnamed, empowered to represent

<hr/>

[16]*Weekly Dubuque Tribune*, April 30, 1851, May 8, 1850.

[17]*Augusta Daily Chronicle and Sentinel*, March 5, 1850, July 23, Aug. 20, 1851; *Clarksville Jef-fersonian*, June 11, July 16, Nov. 5, 1851, June 23, May 12, 1852.

Montgomery County, Tennessee, at the state convention in 1860 only nine actually attended. . . .[18]

The last of the seven towns, Opelousas, Louisiana, being both southern and western (and small, with an 1860 town population of fewer than eight hundred), was politically the least organized. If there is little information in local newspapers about attendance at caucuses and conventions, it is in part because there were not many such meetings to report on either side. The Opposition was distinctly less active than the Democrats here, but even Democrats had difficulty mobilizing voters in the nomination system. Apparently dormant throughout 1858, in 1859 the Democrats of St. Landry Parish, which included Opelousas, selected delegates to a judicial district convention to be held in Baton Rouge and met occasionally thereafter. But the most striking evidence of political organization found in the local press refers, not to the political parties, but to the eight nonpartisan parish vigilance committees (constituted to fight crime and track down runaway slaves), said to number some five hundred of St. Landry's citizens. "Opelousas was thronged by representatives" of the vigilance movement in May 1860, wrote the *Opelousas Courier* in language never used to describe a Democratic party meeting.[19] As it did on a variety of American frontiers, the vigilance movement may have provided St. Landry with an alternative form of government and an alternative politics as well. We should not be surprised to find the more customary institutions of politics relatively lethargic in such a setting.

Why were the "working days of the party" of so little interest to so many citizens in all seven towns? The absence of competition—electoral domination of a town or county by a single party or the certainty of a party's nomination of a particular candidate—no doubt contributed at times to the lethargy of ordinary citizens and perhaps even of some party activists. But thin attendance at local caucuses and delegates' failure to attend conventions were general patterns, and in the selected towns they were as evident in close contests as in dull ones with predictable outcomes. They continued, too, despite much editorial pleading—to local party voters that the upcoming election was going to be close, and to delegates that their presence was necessary to provide the psychological advantage of a well-attended convention. A rather different explanation appears with surprising clarity in the partisan press itself. Most direct was the *Dubuque Daily Times*, which wrote in 1859 that "the better portion" of the electorate "retire in disgust from the heat and turmoil of political strife. They leave primary meetings, and County, District and State Conventions to political gamblers and party hacks. . . ." Whether describing their own party or the opposition, local editors drew upon a broad understanding of politicians' control of seemingly open meetings, and they frequently related this understanding to the tendency of many citizens simply to avoid what a Clarksville editor (referring to the other party) named "party despotism under a show of popular consultation." Why would Kingston's

---

[18] *Clarksville Jeffersonian*, Jan. 12, 1859; *Clarksville Chronicle*, March 11, Feb. 11, 1859; *Clarksville Jeffersonian*, June 8, 1859, Jan. 11, 25, July 18, 1860.

[19] *Opelousas Courier*, May 19, 1860.

Democratic voters wish to attend congressional conventions once they had read in their party's paper that the geographic distribution of congressional nominations for the next ten years had been set? Augusta readers well understood the *Constitutionalist*'s advice not to attend Opposition meetings: "Such of them as may visit them, will only be spectators."[20]

The newspapers provide another perspective on this phenomenon in the formal reports submitted to them by party conventions. Although historians have characterized these meetings as typically open to genuine debate and contention, the conventions in our towns adhered fairly closely to a standard form that reveals, in some ways unintentionally, their close management. Each meeting began with one of the assembled being called to the chair, and with another being made secretary. Then, if the meeting had to select delegates, a motion would be made and invariably carried to empower the chair to select a delegate committee. The chair immediately appointed such a committee, which would retire, often "for a few moments," before returning to propose a list of delegates. In the dozens of conventions whose reports we have read, this list was approved in every instance without discussion or dissent. If the meeting were to pass upon party resolutions, the chair would appoint another committee, which would in many instances almost immediately offer a list of resolutions long enough to occupy a column or so of newspaper space. There might be discussion of the resolutions and some proposed additions or changes, but most often they were accepted without alteration or dissent. Too many delegates to such meetings, commented the Augusta Whig editor in 1840, "content themselves with approving the object and acquiescing in the result."[21]

Candidates for elected office, too, were often nominated with the same smooth harmony, and the nominee was sometimes "loudly called for" and fully prepared to give a speech. To be sure, candidacy nominations were often contested, and they sometimes provided an occasion for genuine dissent, but contestants for nomination almost always played the game according to the rule that called for timely withdrawal of losers and approval of the winner by acclamation. Often the maneuvering went on before the convention, and the latter's role was merely to ratify what had already been done. An "exception to prove the rule" may be the nomination of Greenfield's S. O. Lamb by a poorly attended Democratic state senatorial convention in 1858. Lamb won eighteen of the twenty-two votes before being declared the unanimous choice of the convention. His nomination, claimed the *Franklin Democrat*, "was entirely spontaneous, resulting from

---

[20]*Dubuque Daily Times*, Aug. 25, 1859; *Franklin Democrat*, July 18, 1859; *Clarksville Chronicle*, Oct. 1, 1858. Despotism is the central simile in this analysis of local caucuses by the New Orleans Picayune, reprinted in the *Opelousas Courier*, Oct. 2, 1858: "Primary assemblies are a mere blind for the eyes of the masses. They seem to rule, but like the Roman Senate in the time of the first Caesars, only record the edicts of masters. . . . he who dreams the people had anything to do with the result, labors under a pleasant but irrational hallucination." *Ulster Republican*, Dec. 31, 1851; *Augusta Daily Constitutionalist*, March 1, 1860.

[21]Silbey, *American Political Nation*, 60, 121, 221; and Silbey, *Partisan Imperative*, 65. *Augusta Daily Chronicle & Sentinel*, April 23, 1840.

no previous consultation so far as we could ascertain, and we have good reasons for believing was entirely unexpected by him."[22] Even if this dubious claim is to be believed (Lamb was the publisher of the *Democrat* and one of Greenfield's most powerful politicians), it is obvious that "previous consultation," not spontaneity, was the norm in Connecticut Valley political conventions.

The charge that the caucus and convention system was really "party despotism under a show of popular consultation" compels us to look more closely at the delegates, officers, speakers, and members of committees at political meetings. Were such activities performed frequently by a few men, or occasionally by many? How representative of the broader population, in social and economic terms, were the men who did these things? To pursue these questions we will examine the political participants in two of the communities we studied, Augusta and Marion, during the three-year election cycle preceding the Civil War. We recorded their names and activities from local newspapers, and we traced them to the manuscript schedules of the 1860 federal census. . . .

In Augusta's Richmond County, 110 men, some 3 percent of the population of white, voting-age males in the county, conducted the affairs of party meetings at the local level or were appointed as delegates to conventions higher in the political pyramid. About a fourth of them (twenty-seven), forming less than 1 percent of the electorate, participated in three or more conventions and accounted for half of all the positions held by Richmond County men in delegations, conventions, and committees. Tracing these men to the census, moreover, yields a collective profile suggestive of an elite political inner circle: of the twenty-three we located, eleven were lawyers, two were the publishers of the two party newspapers, one was the local postmaster, one was the mayor of Augusta, and eight were merchants and planters in the highest quintile (four were in the highest decile) of reported total wealth. . . .[23] It is difficult to define the boundaries of such a group, but one could draw them still more tightly to include an especially active group of only seven men, consisting of five of the lawyers, one of the publishers, and the mayor. We . . . point to a narrowly based system with an extraordinary concentration of lawyers, partisan publishers, officeholders, and rich men at its activist core.

In social characteristics, those who participated in only one or two political meetings were not very different from those who participated in three or more. In the larger group of 110, more than half (sixty-one) played some role in only one meeting, which suggests a degree of diffusion of activity within the very small minority of Richmond County's voters who were delegates, officers, or committee members. We believe that this diffusion resulted from pressure not so much

---

[22]*Franklin Democrat*, Oct. 18, 1858.

[23]Manuscript Population Schedules, Richmond County, Georgia, Eighth Census of the United States, 1860 (microfilm: reel 135, M 653), Records of the Bureau of the Census, RG 29 (National Archives, Washington, D.C.); U.S. Department of Interior, Census Office, *Population of the United States in 1860* (Washington, 1864), 60–61. Paul Bourke and Donald DeBats observe a political elite in Washington County, Oregon, where the party organizers, delegates, and nominees "accounted for much of the wealth, professional skill, and experience to which the county could lay claim." Bourke and DeBats, *Washington County*, 149. See also Winkle, *Politics of Community*.

from below as from above, that is, from attempts by party leaders to cast about for potential party workers. Whether recruited or self-selected, though, they were hardly a representative lot. We succeeded in tracing 88 of the 110 participants to the 1860 census. Of these, one-third were professionals (twenty-five lawyers and four physicians); five-eighths were merchants, planters, manufacturers, and other businessmen; and one-twentieth were clerical workers. Not one was a skilled or unskilled worker or even an independent hand-working artisan, although more than 42 percent of the adult white male work force in Richmond County was made up of such workers and artisans.[24] (Lawyers constituted 28 percent of the group and 2 percent of the general work force.) More than half reported property that placed them within the highest wealth decile in the county, and more than three-fourths placed within the highest quintile. Most of the few men who reported little or no property were young businessmen and professionals, including several young lawyers still living in the homes of their wealthy (and politically active) fathers.

Marion's nomination system was only slightly less concentrated than Augusta's, even though it added another (township) level of organization. A little under 6 percent of the local electorate, forty-two men, served as officers, committeemen, or delegates in and from the Ohio town during these years. As in Augusta, more than half (twenty-two) participated in only one meeting, while the eight men who played a role in more than two caucuses or conventions (again, about 1 percent of the electorate) accounted for nearly half of the positions. Of them, four were lawyers, one was a political editor, one was a doctor, and two were farmers in the highest decile of reported wealth. The larger group of forty-two was also similar to the Augusta group in its relative wealth (a little less concentrated at the top of a significantly less unequal society) and nearly identical to it in its occupational profile. The only significant difference in the latter was the appearance among the Marion delegates, officers, and committeemen of one nearly unpropertied artisan, Philip Dombaugh, a twenty-nine-year-old printer. Dombaugh, who attended one Democratic convention, almost certainly worked in the pressroom of the *Marion Mirror*.[25]

In Marion no less than in Augusta, the nomination process was carried out by a very small group of men drawn from the upper reaches of local society, and in particular disproportion from those lawyers whose offices clustered around

[24]Manuscript Population Schedules, Richmond County, Georgia, Eighth Census of the United States, 1860. Of the 110 participants, three men were listed in the census with artisanal occupational titles, but their reported wealth strongly suggests that these men were in reality manufacturers, retailers, or nonmanual businessmen of some sort. The men were a "carriage maker" whose property placed him in the top 5 percent in the distribution of wealth among adult white males; a "butcher" who placed in the top 10 percent; and a "gunsmith" in the top 20 percent. For a discussion of manufacturing or retailing "artisans" and the sometimes misleading nature of artisanal labels in historical sources, see Stuart M. Blumin, *The Emergence of the Middle Class: Social Experience in the American City, 1760–1900* (New York, 1989), 68–73.

[25]Manuscript Population Schedules, Marion County, Ohio, Eighth Census of the United States, 1860 (microfilm: reel 1006, M 653), Records of the Bureau of the Census.

the courthouse that was the site of most political meetings. Other men attended these meetings, to be sure, and in some instances local editors may have truthfully claimed a "large and enthusiastic" gathering of party faithful who were not named in caucus and convention reports. Editors, though, as frequently complained of thinly attended meetings and provided suggestive evidence in convention reports and delegate lists of a nomination system that did not attract many ordinary citizens. . . . [I]n this important phase of the antebellum political process, democracy was apparently somewhat muffled in the presence of an oligarchic system that most voters came to regard as someone else's business.[26]

Political mobilization had a phase that followed the nomination process—the campaign and the election—when larger numbers of citizens read newspapers that intensified political debate and exhorted the faithful to devote their minds and energies to the coming crisis. . . . The campaigns and elections we have observed through the party papers confirm the prevailing notion of an energetic spectacle, a phenomenon particularly evident during the presidential campaigns of 1840 and 1860. Let us look for a moment at the 1860 campaign. In all our towns it began early, in the spring, with Republican rallies held to celebrate the nomination of Abraham Lincoln. In Marion an already organized Young Men's Republican Club marched with beating drums to the courthouse, where they and other Republicans listened to speeches, passed a resolution to ratify the nomination, and finished the evening with a bonfire in the public square. This was typical, as were subsequent events. Within a week the *Marion Republican* was calling for organization of a local contingent of the Republican marching club, the Wide-Awakes, and before the end of June the paper reported a regular schedule of Thursday evening torchlight marches by the Marion Wide-Awakes. These recurring events were supplemented by occasional grand rallies that drew thousands from all over the county. The pace was maintained until the very end. "ONE FIRE MORE!" urged the *Marion Mirror* in announcing a procession of Invincibles, the Democratic counterpart of the Wide-Awakes, on the evening before the election.[27]

It is difficult for the historian to avoid being impressed by such a campaign spectacle. But a closer look at the whole range of elections in the era suggests qualifications about the depth and extensiveness of popular engagement in campaign rituals. One is that presidential campaigns varied in their fervor and length, the much-analyzed 1840 and 1860 elections being especially long and intense. Unlike either, the 1852 contest between Franklin Pierce and Winfield Scott was a relatively mild affair. In Greenfield, for example, a Scott and Graham Club was founded in late June, but it appears to have been dormant until early August, and the Whig paper was still calling in early September for a meeting to organize the campaign. The Democrats did not answer with a Granite Club until

---

[26]Silbey, *Partisan Imperative*, 65–66; and Silbey, *American Political Nation*, 46–71, 115–24
[27]*Marion Republican*, May 24, 31, June 30, 1860; *Marion Mirror*, Nov. 1, 1860.

mid-October.[28] In Greenfield and in all the other towns we examined, there were fewer campaign events than in 1840 or 1860, and far fewer evidences of popular enthusiasm. . . .

With rare exceptions campaign clubs appeared only in presidential elections, and torchlight parades and mass rallies were smaller and much less frequent in the off years. In many nonpresidential campaigns there were no torchlight parades at all. Off-year campaigns also began later. Whig nominating conventions in 1851 for governor and other state offices were held in mid-September in Massachusetts, and Franklin County towns got around to their state legislative nominations still later, in the case of Deerfield, only days before the November election. . . .[29]

Further qualifications emerge from examining the spectacle. One is the high degree of management in political campaigns. Editors repeatedly stressed the importance of organization, but they also tried to portray campaign events as spontaneous displays of popular enthusiasm. This description in the *Mirror* of a pole raising by Marion Democrats is no more overheated than most:

> Very little effort was put forth to attract hither a crowd beyond the bare announcement that there would be a pole raising and that the Hon. H. B. Payne would be present and address the Democracy that day; and yet . . . before 10 o'clock in the morning delegations from the country began to pour in by thousands. . . . The Republicans stood back in perfect amazement . . ., for never was there such an uprising, such a spontaneous outburst of the popular will.[30]

This was an unusual campaign rally if so large a crowd was produced with "very little effort" by party organizers. Nearly always, crowds at major campaign events were swollen by the carefully arranged importation of party workers from nearby towns and counties, who were visible alongside those who showed up on their own initiative, enhancing the appearance of massive and spontaneous popular support for the party's candidate. Support may have been genuine, but it was seldom entirely spontaneous. Editors, indeed, sometimes boasted of prearrangements. On the eve of a campaign visit by Stephen Douglas himself, the *Dubuque Herald* based its prediction of a massive turnout on some surprisingly precise information: "We understand that 200 are coming from Lansing, 700 from Independence, 600 from Bellevue, 1,000 from Maquoketa, . . . 500 from Galena & so on."[31] These numbers were probably exaggerated, but the *Herald* reveals here something important about the way campaign events worked. Local party leaders loaned their activists to the leaders of other towns to help swell their rallies, expecting payment in kind when they planned their own affairs. The visual impact of the resulting crowd could be impressive in a small town, and the crowd

---

[28]*Greenfield Gazette & Courier*, June 28, Aug. 2, Sept. 6, 1852; *Franklin Democrat*, Oct. 18, 1852.

[29]*Greenfield Gazette & Courier*, Sept. 15, 22, Oct. 13, 27, Nov. 3, 1851. McGerr, *Decline of Popular Politics*, 22–99.

[30]*Marion Mirror*, Aug. 16, 1860.

[31]*Dubuque Herald*, Oct. 9, 1860.

Figure 11.1
In August, 1860, during the presidential campaign, both
Douglas Invincibles and Lincoln Wide-Awakes marched in a
nonpartisan military parade. *Frank Leslie's Illustrated Newspaper*,
Sept. 1, 1860, p. 249. Courtesy Cornell University Libraries.

provided local editors with evidence of jammed streets and public squares. What
was left unsaid was that many of the same people were being counted repeatedly
in one town after another.

The elements of party rallies were also significant. It has often been observed
that campaign events were designed to be entertaining, but it is perhaps insufficiently stressed that many elements of the political rally had nothing to do with
public issues or specific candidacies, and some of the more attractive lacked
political symbolism. . . . Balloon ascensions, the central attractions of some of the
largest rallies, were devoid of political connotation; indeed, they were as likely to
be seen at county fairs as at political rallies. But they drew the people, as did brass
bands, barbecues, and even the simple prospect of a routine-interrupting big
crowd in town. Party leaders well understood that speeches or even specifically
political icons would not attract the masses in sufficient numbers, and they readily resorted to whatever would do so. . . .

Like political rallies, political campaign clubs were made attractive in apolitical ways. The young men and boys who joined the Wide-Awakes, Invincibles,
and other marching clubs were sold inexpensive uniforms and taught impressive
march maneuvers. In Marion the Wide-Awake uniform consisted of an oilcloth
cape and cap and a red sash, which along with a lamp or torch cost $1.33. Their
"worm fence march" can be imagined, as can a nice connection to Lincoln as
rail-splitter—a connection that does remind us of the log cabin and hard cider
symbolism of earlier days. The more important connection, however, is to the
"militia fever" of the 1850s. Many Americans, North and South, delighted in
military uniforms and titles, musters and parades, and the formal balls militia
companies sponsored during the winter social season. Their younger brothers no
doubt delighted in aping the militia members, so far as $1.33 would allow, while
their parents rejoiced to see youthful rowdyism channeled into a military form of
discipline. The regular campaign clubs, meanwhile, offered a different

Figure 11.2
Lincoln Wide-Awake clubs in Hartford, Connecticut, march in
military formation, July 1860. *Frank Leslie's Illustrated Newspaper,*
August 11, 1860, p. 246. Courtesy Cornell University Libraries.

attraction. One of the first items of business, once the club was organized, was to invite "the ladies" to meetings. Many members were single young men, and the campaign occurred during a relatively slow social season following the picnics, steamboat excursions, and other outings of summer, and preceding the balls sponsored by militia companies, fire companies, and fraternal lodges in winter. Campaign clubs helped to extend and connect the social seasons for single young men and women, and they gave both an occasion for high-spirited travel. . . .[32]

The reports of massive turnouts for political events were often exaggerated. Partisan editors regularly claimed great success for their own rallies while describing their opponents' efforts as a "fizzle," and on occasion two very different crowd estimates can be obtained for the same event. The major Democratic mass rally in Marion in 1860 was set at 8,000 by the Democratic editor. When the *Marion Republican* claimed the same number for the "Glorious Republican Rally" a month later, it insisted that the Democratic rally had been only half as large. It is impossible to say how accurate these estimates were, but it can be noted that there were as many claims of meetings in half-filled rooms and of parades through nearly deserted streets as there were boasts of courthouses and streets bursting with enthusiastic partisans. . . .[33]

If larger numbers of citizens participated in campaigns than in caucuses and nominating conventions, still larger numbers showed up on election day to vote. Clearly, this was an age of unusually high voter turnout, and this fact more than

---

[32]*Marion Republican*, Aug. 23, June 30, 1860; *Dubuque Herald*, Sept. 15, 1860.
[33]*Marion Mirror*, Aug. 16, 1860; *Marion Republican*, Sept. 20, 1860.

any other has undergirded the proposition that antebellum Americans were widely and deeply engaged in political affairs. Again, though, we can qualify this connection by taking a closer look at what happened in communities on election day. Most obviously, voters came to the polls and voted. But if many did so on their own initiative, the political parties behaved as though the electorate would not appear to vote, let alone participate in other political activities, in the absence of their own strenuous exertions. Throughout the period editors implored voters to go to the polls. Their appeals implied that politics would command the attention of some voters only on election day. "Who," asked Greenfield's Whig editor in 1841, "cannot give one day in three hundred and sixty-five to his Country? He, who thinks his business prevents him, 'saves at the spigot but lets out at the bung hole.'" "Let no business, no engagement, no pleasure, prevent you from exercising your right as a free citizen," urged the *Augusta Daily Chronicle & Sentinel* a week before the 1860 election. . . .[34] [O]rganization was the overriding theme of election day exhortations, and the specific modes of organizing to maximize the party's vote were of greater significance than anything that appeared in the paper.

Local political parties attempted to maximize their turnout by systematic assignments of responsibility for specific lists of voters. Poll lists were drawn up, according to school districts or other geographic subdivisions of the town or county, and each list was given to district vigilance committees or other groups of activists. These men were responsible for distributing tickets, tallying votes, challenging possible illegal voters brought in by the opposing party, and above all for making sure their own party's voters got to the polling place. A small-town and rural environment made this system work well across much of the United States, especially where the roads were good and the population not too dispersed. . . . Consider Greenfield, a township of some eight hundred voters. If each party's list ran to four hundred of these voters, then twenty election-day workers could be made responsible for only twenty voters apiece. If only half of those voters came to vote on their own initiative, the remainder could easily be called upon, exhorted, and driven to the polls.[35] Under these conditions, and considering also the visibility of each man's actions in such a community, it may well have been more bothersome not to vote than to vote. . . .

As in the campaign, organizers provided election day attractions quite different from the mere exercise of civic or partisan duty. Partisan editors never admitted that their own parties practiced election day "treating," but they invariably accused their opponents of attracting voters with free food and drink, especially the latter. "Whiskey was as free as water" for illegal Irish voters during the 1859 election, complained the *Marion Republican*, "and, brutally drunk, they were led

---

[34]*Greenfield Gazette & Mercury*, Nov. 2, 1841; *Augusta Daily Chronicle & Sentinel*, Oct. 30, Nov. 4, 1860; *Clarksville Chronicle*, Nov. 2, 1860; *Kingston Democratic Journal*, Oct. 27, 1858.

[35]We have been unable to determine how many people in the towns we selected worked at the polls on election day. The above example makes it clear, however, that only a small number, fewer than any local party's activist core, was required to contact and transport all reluctant voters. Workers, including teenage boys, were sometimes hired to perform these tasks.

Figure 11.3
"The Election—At the polls." *Harper's Weekly* 1 (45)
(November 7, 1857). Courtesy Cornell University Libraries.

up to the polls like so many CATTLE, a . . . ticket put into their hands, and they COMPELLED to vote it." Democrats were more notorious for treating, but it was practiced by both sides "The one that gin the last treat, old hoss, is the fellow I go's in for," responded one Dubuque citizen to the *Times* editor's question. Elections also attracted those who wished to gamble on the outcome, a practice the party papers encouraged when they printed betting offers as paid advertisements. Betting was widespread, and it may have contributed to turnout, for as the *Boston Herald* pointed out in a piece reprinted in the *Franklin Democrat*, "a man may buy his own vote, and his own influence—much more actively exercised than it would be for the money of another—for the side which will win his stakes, without regard to what he considers to be right."[36] Finally, and apart from all the party efforts to get voters to the polls, men went to talk, to conduct some business or another, or simply to take a break, knowing that others would be doing so as well.

And yet the parties worried a great deal about the turnout of their own voters—about being outhustled and outmaneuvered by the other side—in ways that suggest little faith in the self-directed participation of knowledgeable and interested voters. In an age when ballots were printed by party newspapers and distributed by party workers, opportunities existed for deceptions in the titling of ballots and the listing of candidates. In Marietta in 1840 the Whig editor warned his party's voters against "split tickets" that placed William Whittlesey, the Democratic candidate for state representative, among the names of Whigs running for other offices. "No Whig will vote for Mr. Whittlesey *if he knows it.*" Similarly, the Greenfield Republican editor reminded voters in 1858 that in the previous year's election the Democrats had printed ballots that imitated the type font of the Republican ballot but substituted some Democratic for Republican candidates. This, it appears, was a common practice based on the assumption by parties that there were sufficient numbers of

---

[36]*Marion Republican*, Oct. 13, 1859; *Dubuque Daily Times*, Aug. 19, 1859; *Franklin Democrat*, Nov. 23, 1860. See also Gienapp, "Politics Seem to Enter into Everything," 32.

Figure 11.4
"The Election—Naturalization office, day before election."
Harper's Weekly 1:45 (November 7, 1857). Courtesy Cornell
University Libraries.

inattentive or ill-informed voters on the other side to allow one or two of their own candidates to sneak into office in this way. . . . Editors who advised their party's voters to compare the ballots they were handed to the one printed in the newspaper clearly believed that some voters did not know who the candidates were. . . .[37]

High voter turnout, then, did not necessarily indicate a widespread and deep engagement in politics on the part of the American people. What it may more powerfully indicate, indeed, is the extraordinary achievement of American political parties in mobilizing voters, some of whom were uninterested in, skeptical about, or even averse to political affairs. Here we concur with many political historians who have emphasized the significance of party development in the antebellum era and underscore the importance of understanding how the political parties functioned as institutions. Where our interpretation differs from most is on the relationship between parties and the American electorate. The parties, we would argue, developed their elaborate structures and techniques for nominating candidates, devising platforms, conducting campaigns, and maximizing election-day turnout in response to the challenge of an electorate that could be skeptical or indifferent. Parties appeared and developed, not from the passionate politics of a uniformly engaged citizenry, but from variations of engagement; that is, from the efforts of those who were deeply committed to political affairs to reach and influence those who were not.[38]

The recognition of variations in, and limits to, political engagement should stimulate historians to explore anew the relations between the institutions of

---

[37]*Marietta Intelligencer*, Oct. 8, 1840; *Greenfield Gazette & Courier*, Nov. 1, 1858; *Augusta Daily Constitutionalist*, Nov. 6, 1852.

[38]Joel Silbey comes closest to this recognition in asserting that "party leaders worked assiduously to stimulate and reinforce what might otherwise have remained inert." Silbey, *American Political Nation*, 170. Unlike Silbey, however, we place the emphasis in the phrase "partisan imperative" on the second word rather than the first, and we believe that political historians need to recognize more fully the potential and actual resistance to organizing efforts by political parties.

politics and the people that participated in political affairs. . . . The institutionalization of the nation's politics may well have acted . . . on the relation between many Americans and public affairs. In an important sense, Americans "purchased" their political decisions from political parties, whose leaders and other activists offered an array of candidates, programs, and images—to say nothing of entertainments and whiskey—in return for their votes. . . . Americans could leave the work to the "professionals" and go about their other business. Parties, therefore, were instruments for Americans who wished to perform, but not become absorbed in, their duties as citizens. The irony is profound—political parties succeeded as engines of popular mobilization by demanding less of those it called to the electoral crusade.[39]

This instrumental view of political parties is crucial to understanding their role in American life, but it needs qualification in at least two ways. First, parties were not so fully developed, or so successful in organizing the nation's political life, or so exclusively devoted to organizational imperatives, that they preempted older modes of authority or newer elite and popular pressures to address public issues. Even in larger communities, public leadership had long been highly personal, and the institutionalization of political leadership in the party era did not entirely efface older, deferential relations between elites and ordinary citizens. . . . It is clear, in these early decades of party development, that some partisan leaders were not, or were not in every sense, political professionals, and that local political activism did not necessarily sharpen the popular perception of a political system run by wire-pullers and hacks. The highly visible presence of a courthouse gang of lawyers and editors—their offices clustered around the physical epicenter of the entire county's political life—no doubt reinforced the perception of political professionalism, but this same visibility may also have reinforced the prominence of lawyers and other activists as community leaders, along with old communal habits of deference to such men.[40]

Nor were party institutions impervious to democratic pressures. The governments of the antebellum era—and in particular the national government—were small, and their operations and effects relatively removed from the daily lives of most citizens. Richard L. McCormick accurately characterizes government's role in this age as "that of promoting development by distributing resources and privileges to individuals and groups." The granting of public lands, franchises, and special privileges and immunities, the raising or lowering of specific tariffs, and the appointment and removal of public officials—these were the day-to-day business of antebellum government, and they constituted a system that touched lightly and usually indirectly upon the vast majority of Americans who had few claims to make to their legislators or other public officials. The small size and remoteness of government was surely a source of political disengagement and of the willing and effortless "purchase" by many citizens of a

---

[39]Judith N. Shklar, *American Citizenship: The Quest for Inclusion* (Cambridge, MA, 1991), 3.

[40]Ronald P. Formisano, "Deferential-Participant Politics: The Early Republic's Political Culture, 1789–1840," *American Political Science Review* 68 (June 1974), 473–87.

party's political "package." But public issues, and even popular movements, did arise in this era and did impose themselves on a political system that both resisted and facilitated their expression. . . .[41] Several of the great movements of the era, and in particular the deepening conflict over human slavery, asserted themselves upon and sometimes through political parties. However institutionalized they may have become, the parties could not invariably resist being reshaped, and even remade, by popular feeling.

A second qualification of the instrumental relation between parties and ordinary citizens is different. Americans could expect more from their parties than the mere packaging of candidates, platforms, and images, but they could also expect less. The voters' relationship to party was frequently complicated by a well-understood "grammar" of corruption that derived from the comic carica-tures of wily, self-seeking politicians sketched by Seba Smith, through his fic-tional mouthpiece, Jack Downing, and other political humorists in the earliest days of mass political mobilization.[42] However effectively local leaders may have preserved the respect of their less powerful neighbors, they did so in the face of this ascending image of the selfishly corrupt politician, an image that was gener-alized to political institutions and was visible during and even after the seasons of political strife. Historians who have focused on the passions of the American political campaign, for whom the election is both climax and denouement in the electoral drama, have tended to overlook an important aspect of the election *aftermath*, namely, the rapidity and seeming determination with which Ameri-cans turned away from politics once the votes had been counted and the results announced. . . . [E]ditors stressed that in the popular disengagement from politics at the close of the campaign lay the strength of American political institutions and values. Americans, after all, knew that the temporary melodrama of politics was less important than the continuing narrative of their day-to-day lives (the metaphor favored by editors was the froth of the campaign temporarily disturb-ing the surface of a great quiet sea of private life). They knew also that the politi-cians from whom they "purchased" candidates, images, and party platforms many times offered shoddy goods. It is striking how frequently the partisan press itself invoked the image of the corrupt politician who deepened the gulf of mis-understanding and distrust between political leaders and ordinary people. . . .[43]

---

[41]Richard L. McCormick, *The Party Period and Public Policy. American Politics from the Age of Jackson to the Progressive Era* (New York, 1986), 204; Formisano, *Transformation of Political Culture*, 22.

[42]Seba Smith's highly influential Jack Downing "letters" appeared first in his newspaper, the Portland Courier, before being collected as *The Select Letters of Major Jack Downing, of the Down-ingville Militia, Away Down East, in the State of Maine. Written by Himself* (Philadelphia, 1834). Smith's satiric sketches of political venality, and those of countless imitators, appeared throughout the antebellum era in party newspapers all over America.

[43]See, for example, *Gleason's Pictorial Drawing-Room Companion*, Oct. 23, Dec. 4, 1852, Dec. 3, 1853; *Frank Leslie's Illustrated Newspaper*, July 12, 1856, Nov. 13, 1858; *Clarksville Chronicle*, Aug. 12, 1859; *Rondout Courier*, Nov. 8, 1850; and *Greenfield Gazette & Mercury*, Nov. 10, 1840. See also Altschuler and Blumin, "'Where Is the Real America?'" James Vernon, *Politics and the People: A Study in English Political Culture, c. 1815–1867* (New York, 1993). *Clarksville Jeffersonian*, Nov. 11, 1860.

... [T]he simultaneous ascendancy of the political spectacle and the grammar of corruption in the America of Jack Downing gave rise to another relation to politics, best captured, we believe, by Joshua Gamson's discussion of "engaged disbelief" as a mode of popular participation in celebrity culture. Gamson distinguishes among believers who uncritically accept the messages in texts about famous persons they do not personally know, believers who accept a "discernible authenticity" in the face of perceived distortions and manipulations, and skeptics who retain enough interest in the techniques of artifice to participate in a highly qualified, ironic fashion, maintaining a core of disbelief that permits apparent acquiescence—hence, "engaged disbelief." The relevance of Gamson's distinctions to antebellum political culture is suggested by the role of "humbug" in nineteenth-century America. Self-interested deception had no doubt increased in this age of easily counterfeited bank notes, confidence rackets in cities and on steamboats, mesmerism, phrenology, and national advertising for cure-all patent medicines appearing in newspapers alongside editorial claims of massive turnouts for party rallies. Much of this was vicious and exploitative, but as Neil Harris observes, the era's greatest artist of humbug, P. T. Barnum, understood "that American audiences did not mind the cries of trickery; in fact, they delighted in debate. Amusement and deceit could coexist; people would come to see something they suspected might be an exaggeration or even a masquerade." Not only gullibility but also skepticism—not only belief but also disbelief—such were the foundations of Barnum's astonishing career. That some Americans approached politics in much the same way—rising to its deceptions as they might not have to sober exposition and debate—is suggested by the many references to humbug, and to Barnum himself, in antebellum political discourse. "There is a man in Pennsylvania who was nominated for governor eight months ago, and hasn't been lied about yet!" complained Kingston's *Ulster Republican*. "Where's Barnum?"[44]

This political attitude is different from the enthusiastic commitment to party that suffused the period according to most political history. Americans who were attuned and attracted to humbug purchased tickets to the political circus, but they did not allow themselves to be gulled, even while they enjoyed the show. This metaphor of circus and of tickets purchased is also appropriate to the meaning of party membership. Although political parties were similar to many other institutions that proliferated in the antebellum United States, they were also different. Ordinary partisans were not organizational members in the usual sense. They did not pay dues, attend weekly or monthly meetings, or assume obligations for carrying out the organization's purpose, and there were no criteria for or even a process of admission. For ordinary Democrats, Whigs, or Republicans, the party did not even exist as an accessible institution except during the political season.[45] On some partisans outside the activist core, the party nonetheless

---

[44]Joshua Gamson, *Claims to Fame: Celebrity in Contemporary America* (Berkeley, CA, 1994). T. J. Jackson Lears, *Fables of Abundance: A Cultural History of Advertising in America* (New York, 1994). Neil Harris, *Humbug: The Art of P. T. Barnum* (Boston, 1973), 61–62; *Ulster Republican*, Dec. 4, 1850.

[45]Maurice Duverger, *Political Parties: Their Organization and Activity in the Modern State*, trans. Barbara North and Richard North (New York, 1954). Philip J. Ethington, *The Public City: The Political Construction of Urban Life in San Francisco, 1850–1900* (New York, 1994), 70–71.

made claims of membership—motivating them to attend local caucuses and rallies and to vote the party ticket, perhaps even with a serious sense of doing the people's business. To others, the party was an emporium of showy goods, some overpriced and falsely advertised—or a Barnum circus to go to when it happened to be in town. That they bought some of those goods and went to the political circus suggests neither high purpose nor gullibility. We must recognize among some Americans a more detached involvement and a more ironic appreciation of the Barnums of politics.

Barnum's own relationship to politics was that of the detached, disbelieving participant. A fairly frequent officeholder (he served in the Connecticut legislature and as mayor of Bridgeport, and he was nominated for Congress), he remained skeptical of politicians. Speaking at the reopening of the American Museum in the midst of the 1860 presidential campaign, Barnum observed:

> Four years ago I furnished a title for the "woolly horse candidate," and now the opposite parties are charged with having drawn on the museum for their "what is it" electoral ticket. After the election is over, I may possibly make reprisals by securing several of the defeated candidates and exhibiting them as about the smallest specimens of the dwarf genus ever seen since my little friend Tom Thumb made his debut in this establishment. If, like Madame Tussaud of London, I had a separate apartment called "the chamber of horrors," I might perhaps engage certain greedy and corrupt office-holders and swindling lobby members, who swallow whole blocks of houses in a single gulp; but as I make it a point to reject unpleasant monstrosities, I can give them no place in the museum.[46]

Barnum's interweaving of parties and politicians with the famous curiosities of his museum expresses the popular association of politics and humbug and underscores our argument that the connections between the campaign spectacle and voting in the antebellum era—and, more generally, the behavioral and cultural patterns of political engagement—were manifold, complex, and sometimes ironic. Parties at once energized and replaced political participation; electoral campaigns stimulated both enthusiasm and skepticism, sometimes in the same minds; American democracy found its greatest validation in the peaceful and apolitical aftermath of the strident political campaign.

Perhaps these complications tended toward resolution later in the nineteenth century and in the early twentieth, when campaigns no longer maintained the pretense of a spontaneous local spectacle, and citizens turned out to vote in decreasing numbers. Such an interpretation would at first glance seem to preserve current notions of a democratic "golden age" followed by "the decline of popular politics." But a different argument is also possible. Bernard Bailyn has pointed out that American political culture manifested Whig opposition theories episodically, in disputes with colonial governors during the first half of the eighteenth century, before expressing those theories more consistently and forcefully in the 1760s and 1770s when altered circumstances in the imperial

---

[46]*Franklin Democrat*, Sept. 21, 1860.

relationship gave them a new salience and legitimacy. Similarly, antebellum Americans manifested some forms of political disengagement—neglect of party conventions, for example, but not reduced voter turnout—while later generations responded to altered circumstances that legitimized a more general withdrawal. The political parties had become more fully professionalized, and many local activists of the sort who had used the party to exercise a traditional communal leadership had redirected their energies to their "own" legal and medical professional associations.[47] An alienating grammar of corruption was sustained and enhanced not only by notable scandals but also structurally by post–Civil War pensions and other innovations that gave the central government a more significant and more visible fiscal presence, and by the removal of the issue of slavery, with its peculiar power to energize and provide a moral imperative to politics. These and other institutional developments of the late nineteenth century perhaps helped resolve the ironies of a somewhat fragile antebellum political culture and pattern of behavior by lending greater force to the underlying political skepticism and hostility.[48] We would emphasize the presence of that skepticism and hostility in the antebellum era and their significance to the trajectory of popular politics in American history. They suggest not a simple rise and decline but a complex intersection of forces in all generations, and the need for a political history that recognizes the particular way in which Americans of each era engaged with and disengaged from political affairs.

---

[47]Bernard Bailyn, *The Origins of American Politics* (New York, 1968), esp. 124–61; Robert Wiebe, *The Search for Order, 1877–1920* (New York, 1967). See also Burton J. Bledstein, *The Culture of Professionalism: The Middle Class and the Development of Higher Education in America* (New York, 1976).

[48]Theda Skocpol, *Protecting Soldiers and Mothers: The Political Origins of Social Policy in the United States* (Cambridge, MA, 1992). Holt, *Political Crisis of the 1850s.*

Glenn C. Altschuler

Glenn Altschuler received his Ph.D. in American history from Cornell in 1976 and has been an administrator and teacher at the university since 1981. While Dean of the School of Continuing Education and Summer Sessions he has continued to research, write, and teach. In 1998, he became the Thomas and Dorothy Litwin Professor of American Studies. In 2006, he was named a Stephen H. Weiss Presidential Fellow, Cornell's most prestigious award for undergraduate teaching. He is the author or coauthor of ten books and more than eight hundred essays and reviews notably including: *Cornell: A History, 1940–2015* (coauthored with Isaac Kramnick, Cornell University Press, 2014); *The GI Bill: A New Deal for Veterans* (coauthored with Stuart M. Blumin, Oxford University Press 2009); *All Shook Up: How Rock 'n' Roll Changed America* (Oxford University Press, 2003); *Rude Republic: Americans and Their Politics in the Nineteenth Century* (coauthored with Stuart M. Blumin, Princeton University Press, 2000); and, *Changing Channels: America in TV Guide* (coauthored with David I. Grossvogel, University of Illinois Press, 1992).

Stuart M. Blumin

The 1960s was an exciting time to enter the history profession, and as a young man I participated eagerly in several of the "new social history" movements that were then emerging; perhaps most of all, in attempts to gain new understandings of the role of cities in nineteenth-century America, and of the day-to-day experiences of Americans who lived in cities and towns of various sizes and types. However, after writing several books in this vein, I became increasingly dissatisfied with the continuing separation between this kind of history and the more traditional narrative of America's political development. In collaboration with my friend and Cornell University colleague, Glenn Altschuler, I set out to examine patterns of American political life from the social historian's point of view. The result was the essay included in this volume, and a book entitled *Rude Republic: Americans and Their Politics in the Nineteenth Century*. Glenn and I also collaborated in writing a book about the GI Bill, but by then I was also turning back to my earlier interest in cities, this time from the perspective of art history, and of the broader sweep of European and American history. The result thus far has been a book entitled *The Encompassing City: Streetscapes in Early Modern Art and Culture*, and an exhibition, at Cornell's Herbert S. Johnson Museum of Art, entitled *Mirror of the City: The Printed View in Italy and Beyond, 1450–1940*. Though I am retired from Cornell, I continue to work on this fascinating subject.

QUESTIONS FOR CONSIDERATION

1. What do Altschuler and Blumin claim is missing from the histories of political democracy during the first half of the nineteenth century? What argument do they make in terms of the "political engagement" of antebellum Americans?
2. What problems did politicians and political parties face when trying to drum up interest among voters? How did they seek to overcome these problems?
3. According to Altschuler and Blumin, how did regional differences between the North, South and West shape political participation? Who tended to be most politically active in these regions? What accounts for their engagement?
4. If, as Altschuler and Blumin argue, voter enthusiasm was not as pronounced as other historians have claimed, what might account for this misconception?
5. How did P. T. Barnum exemplify the complexity of democratic politics during the first half of the nineteenth century?
6. By the middle of the nineteenth century, white males universally enjoyed suffrage in the United States. In what ways had political culture and democratic politics changed from the late eighteenth and early nineteenth centuries, and in what ways had politics remained the same?

CHAPTER TWELVE

National Identity on a Shifting Border: Texas and New Mexico in the Age of Transition, 1821–1848[1]

Andrés Reséndez

INTRODUCTION

Traditionally, we have told the story of how nations emerged as a triumphant tale of domination exerted by a determined center over reluctant peripheries and by persuasive officials over skeptical masses. The literature depicts state formation and nation building as originating from the core outward and from top to bottom. Sitting at the apex of all political and social organizations, the state has been granted the leading role. After all, it was the state that built the infrastructure linking the center to all corners of the nation, increasing the network of communications within a territory and thus helping integrate a national market. Under the auspices of the state, a nationalist ideology was fashioned and disseminated to all prospective citizens. And it was the state bureaucracy, employing novel means of communication such as mass education, that perpetuated the nation unto subsequent generations. Whether accounts spotlight institutions or identities, the underlying theme is centralization: The national state wins out over lesser political organizations and potential challengers, and the people divest themselves of previous ethnic or local loyalties as the nation becomes their overriding identity.[2]

This core-periphery, top-down model has recently come under criticism. In particular, E. J. Hobsbawm has made a crucial methodological point: Although nations tend to be promoted from above, they nevertheless have to be analyzed and understood from below, "in terms of the assumptions, hopes, needs,

---

[1]Interested students are encouraged to read this essay in the original form. Andrés Reséndez, "National Identity on a Shifting Border: Texas and New Mexico in the Age of Transition, 1821–1848," *Journal of American History* 86 (2), Rethinking History and the Nation-State: Mexico and the United States as a Case Study: A Special Issue (Sept. 1999), 668–88.

[2]For the most forceful formulation of this view, see John Breuilly, *Nationalism and the State* (Chicago, 1982), 1–2. See also Anthony D. Smith, *National Identity* (Reno, 1991), 59–61

longings and interests of ordinary people, which are not necessarily national and still less nationalist." People's perceptions (and not nationalist propaganda) constitute the most critical yardstick against which we can measure the success of attempts at national construction. . . .[3]

An approach that pays attention to both state designs and responses from local communities is badly needed to rethink the story of how Mexico's Far North became the American Southwest. This episode has long been explained through a sweeping narrative, that of American expansionism. Undoubtedly, expansionism was a powerful "mood" that prevailed in the United States throughout the first half of the nineteenth century. But expansionism has been used in the historiography as a catchall, explain-all concept to describe the social psychology of early Americans, to elucidate the relations between American settlers and Native Americans, and to provide a rationale for the policy pursued by the United States toward the Spanish/Mexican possessions.[4] The dramatic territorial exchanges of this era have been presented almost as logical outcomes of that irresistible ideology; they thus require no further explanation. Worse still, by emphasizing how Anglo-Americans expanded their domain, we have left unexamined how other peoples reacted to this offensive, often confining non-Anglo-Americans to the role of passive victims as they watched their homelands being taken away.[5]

Yet when we look closely at this process, we obtain a starkly different image. Expansionism, at least on Mexico's northern frontier, meant first and foremost economic penetration that afforded local Hispanic and Native American elites the opportunity to profit. This circumstance led those local elites consciously to shift their allegiances to accommodate their interests, even in the face of opposition from other members of their own ethnic groups. Economic expansion provided the medium in which cross-cultural alliances were forged along Mexico's northern frontier. Rather than idle players, local elites were active agents who made choices of far-reaching consequences.

---

[3]E. J. Hobsbawm, *Nations and Nationalism since 1780: Programme, Myth, Reality* (Cambridge, England, 1990), 10. See Peter Sahlins, *Boundaries: The Making of France and Spain in the Pyrenees* (Berkeley, CA, 1989), 8–9. On Mexico, see David A. Brading, *The Origins of Mexican Nationalism* (Cambridge, England, 1985); Peter F. Guardino, *Peasants, Politics, and the Formation of Mexicos National State: Guerrero, 1800–1857* (Stanford, CA, 1996); Florencia E. Mallon, *Peasant and Nation: The Making of Postcolonial Mexico and Peru* (Berkeley, CA,1995); Florencia E. Mallon, "Peasants and State Formation in Nineteenth-Century Mexico: Morelos, 1848–1858," *Political Power and Social Theory* 7 (1988), 1–54; Alan Knight, "Peasants into Patriots: Thoughts on the Making of the Mexican Nation," *Mexican Studies/Estudios Mexicanos* 10 (Winter 1994), 135–6 1; and Guy Thomson, "Bulwarks of Patriotic Liberalism: The National Guard, Philharmonic Corps, and Patriotic Juntas in Mexico, 1847–88," *Journal of Latin American Studies* 22 (Feb. 1990), 31–68.

[4]Albert K. Weinberg, *Manifest Destiny: A Study of Nationalist Expansionism in American History* (Baltimore, MD, 1935); Frederick Merk, *Manifest Destiny and Mission in American History: A Reinterpretation* (New York, 1963); and David M. Pletcher, *The Diplomacy of Annexation: Texas, Oregon, and the Mexican War* (Columbia, MO, 1973). Pletcher's book constitutes the most authoritative recent study of the war. Gastón Garcia Cantú, *Las invasiones norteamericanas en México* ["The American Invasions of Mexico"] (Mexico City, 1971). Andreas V. Reichstein, *Rise of the Lone Star: The Making of Texas* (College Station, TX, 1989), 197–202.

[5]David J. Weber, *Myth and the History of the Hispanic Southwest* (Albuquerque, NM, 1987), 94–95.

Just as we have tended to oversimplify the United States' drive for Mexico's territory, we have assumed that the northern frontier provinces were unproblematically a part of Mexico, as if national identity had emerged full-blown right after Mexico gained independence from Spain in 1821. Recent investigations have started to shed light on conflicts between the provinces and the national government or, more precisely, between local and national elites. Municipal and state authorities resisted the intervention of the national government on several fronts, from elections of local officials to the regulation of economy or the organization of the military.[6] In its most basic form, this tension between local and national elites acquired a clear nationalist dimension. In the fractious political environment of early-nineteenth-century Mexico, national leaders began to equate local and regional autonomy with territorial disintegration of the country and, accordingly, started to brand some power brokers in the Far North as separatists.

We need to recast the story of Mexico's northern frontier, paying attention to how the Mexican and the American national projects collided there and how conflicts played out at the local level. Did different provinces experience the change of sovereignty in the same manner? Did different social groups among Hispanics understand their loyalties and national attachments in the same way? Did Native Americans play the same role in California, New Mexico, and Texas as these provinces were being incorporated into the United States? Instead of a simple tale of domination in which a handful of resourceful Anglo-Americans managed to conquer an enormous territory, we have to unearth a far richer story of cross-cultural and cross-class alliances and counteralliances, each side struggling to define and shape whatever nation was emerging in its locality. In the following pages I attempt to trace some of the struggles over the nation, focusing on the cases of Texas and New Mexico. My contention is that communities in these two provinces were caught between two opposing forces. On the one hand, a web of local and regional economic interests increasingly tied Texas and New Mexico to the economy of the United States, thus affecting the livelihood and ultimately the loyalty of key social groups within the Hispanic, Anglo-American, and Native American communities. On the other hand, the Mexican government responded to this challenge by fashioning a defensive, antiforeign, patriotic rhetoric and by fostering rituals aimed at creating a sense of nationhood.[7]

---

[6]Horst Pietschmann, "Protoliberalismo, reformas borbónicas y revolución: La Nueva España en el **útltimo** tercio del siglo XVIII" ["Protoliberalism, Bourbon Reforms, and Revolution: New Spain in the Last Third of the Eighteenth Century"], in *Interpretaciones del siglo XVIII mexicano: El impacto de las reformas borbónicas* ["Interpretations of the Mexican Eighteenth Century: The Impact of the Bourbon Reforms"], ed. Josefina Zoraida Vazquez (Mexico City, 1991), 27–66; and Brian R. Hamnett, "Factores regionales en la desintegración del régimen colonial en la Nueva España: El federalismo de 1823–24" ["Regional Factors in the Disintegration of the Colonial Regime in New Spain: The Federalism of 1823–24"], in *Problemas de la formación del estado y de la nación en Hispanoamérica [Problems in the Formation of State and Nation in Hispanic America]*, ed. Inge Buisson et al. (Bonn, Germany, 1984), 305–17. Josefina Zoraida Vázquez, "Iglesia, ejército y centralismo" ["Church, Army, and Centralism"), *Historia Mexicana* 39 (July–Sept. 1989), 205–34.

[7]Andrés Reséndez, "Caught between Profits and Rituals: National Contestation in Texas and New Mexico, 1821–1848" (PhD diss., University of Chicago, 1997).

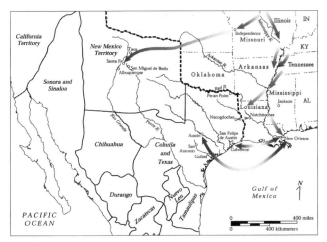

Map 12.1
Mexico in the 1820s. In 1824, the old provinces of Coahuila and
Texas were united as the enormous state of Coahuila and Texas,
which enjoyed considerable autonomy. In contrast, New Mexico
was considered a territory under the tutelage of national
authorities. The lifting of trade barriers in the early republican
period greatly expanded commerce between those Mexican
political units and the United States.

STRUGGLING FOR THE HEARTS AND MINDS

In the aftermath of independence, Mexico's political leadership, a clique of independence heroes and ardent nationalists, became fully aware of the difficulties of
bringing the northern frontier into the national fold. They did not delude themselves about the fact that the enormous arc of provinces from Texas to Alta California was exposed to the designs of other nations and most alarmingly to those
of the United States. They also knew that the northern frontier society was committed to deeply entrenched regional attachments, *las patrias chicas*. The people
of the frontier gave primacy to their cherished identities as *tejanos*, *nuevomexicanos*,
or *californios*, and understandably viewed with a certain skepticism newer and
more abstract appellations such as *mexicano/a*.[8] And finally, the heterogeneity of
frontier society made the task of forging the nation there quite daunting. In
Texas, for instance, the part of the population that was called "Mexican" was a
tiny minority, amounting to some two thousand inhabitants mostly concentrated

---

[8]By *tejanos*, *nuevomexicanos*, and *californios*, I refer to the Spanish-speaking populations of Texas,
New Mexico, and California respectively. These terms will not be italicized hereafter. Gerald E. Poyo and
Gilberto M. Hinojosa, eds., *Tejano Origins in Eighteenth-Century San Antonio* (Austin, TX, 1991); Jesu's
F. de la Teja, *San Antonio de Bixar: A Community on New Spains Northern Frontier* (Albuquerque, NM,
1995), esp. chap. 7; Jesus F. de la Teja and John Wheat, "Bexar: Profile of a Tejano Community, 1820–1832,"
Southwestern Historical Quarterly 89 (July 1985), 7–34; and Timothy M. Matovina, *Tejano Religion and
Ethnicity: San Antonio, 1821–1860* (Austin, TX, 1995). Gilbert R. Cruz, *Let There Be Towns: Spanish
Municipal Origins in the American Southwest, 1610–1810* (College Station, TX, 1988), esp. 127–70.

in the San Antonio–Goliad region. In comparison, the Texas Indian population was larger, far more diverse, and dominant in a greater geographic area. Similarly, the Anglo-American immigrants who came to Texas in waves during the 1820s and early 1830s ended up outnumbering Mexican Texans ten to one on the eve of the Texas Revolution of 1835–1836. New Mexico's demography was more favorable to the construction of the Mexican nation, but there was considerable heterogeneity. The Hispanic population amounted to close to 30,000 inhabitants. Yet Hispanics coexisted with the 10,000 Pueblo Indians living in twenty settlements who maintained significant autonomy. Moreover, Hispanics and Pueblo Indians were surrounded by nomadic groups that were generically called *barbarous, gentile*, or *errant* nations, including the powerful Comanche confederation, the Navajo, and the Apache. Although nomadic Indians were not generally considered Mexican citizens, they nevertheless, as contemporaries put it, formed part of "the extended Mexican family" whose members could one day become citizens if they were to abandon their wandering ways, pledge allegiance to the Mexican government, and convert to Catholicism.[9]

Thus many of Mexico's early leaders at the national, provincial, and local levels attempted to impose uniformity and nationalist devotion along the northern frontier. One vehicle to create national awareness was the printed word. Newspapers, journals, gazettes, and random manifestos proliferated throughout the northern frontier during the first half of the nineteenth century. . . . [R]egardless of their political orientation, editors and writers always cloaked themselves in the nationalist mantle. . . . Although the printed word undoubtedly helped foster a sense of nationhood in Texas and New Mexico, it is hard to contend that such publications played a decisive role, for very few people knew how to read and write. Even if we assume that the contents of the publications were spread by word of mouth beyond the actual readers, the number was nonetheless rather small. Geographic dispersion and cultural disparities added insurmountable barriers. Pueblo and nomadic Indians, for instance, simply could not participate in this virtual community of readers and writers, while Anglo-American colonists in Texas and New Mexico had their own publications where the symbology of the Mexican nation was greatly diluted, if it appeared at all, or where a different and incompatible national project was promoted.[10]

---

[9]Juan Nepomuceno Almonte, *Informe secreto sobre la presente situación de Texas* [*Secret Report on the Present Conditions of Texas*] [1834], ed. Celia Gutierrez Ibarra (Mexico City, 1987), 20, 26, 31; and David J. Weber, *The Mexican Frontier, 1821–1846: The American Southwest under Mexico* (Albuquerque, NM, 1982), 159–62, 166–67. Lansig Bloom, "New Mexico under Mexican Administration, 1821–1846," *Old Santa Fe* 1 (July 1913), 27–30. Juan Nepomuceno Almonte to Manuel Armijo, Nov. 12, 1839, *Mexican Archives of New Mexico* (microfilm, 43 reels, State of New Mexico Records Center, 1970), reel 26, p. 135.

[10]Since 1835 New Mexicans had had newspapers such as *El Crepúsculo de la Libertad* (Santa Fe) and *La Verdad* (Santa Fe). In Texas no Spanish-language newspapers were printed under Mexican rule, but Texans received publications from Coahuila, Tamaulipas, and New Orleans, where O. de A. Santangelo, an Italian expatriate and supporter of Mexican federalism, published *Correo Atlántico*. Benedict Anderson, *Imagined Communities: Refections on the Origin and Spread of Nationalism* (London, 1983), 61–65.

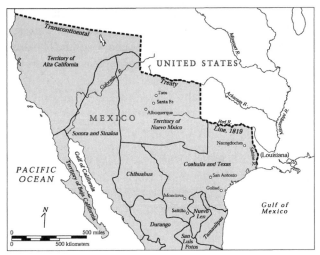

Map 12.2
Mexico's northern frontier in the 1820s was a complicated ethnic tapestry. Hispanic communities such as Santa Fe, Albuquerque, and San Antonio and Anglo-American communities such as San Felipe de Austin lived alongside nomadic, or seminomadic indigenous peoples such as the Navajo, Comanche, and Cherokee.

Primary education became a more deliberate vehicle to bolster national loyalties. In Texas and New Mexico an educational crusade flourished between 1827 and 1834. Public schools "of first letters" opened their gates in San Antonio, Goliad, and Nacogdoches in the late 1820s. In New Mexico, public schools were established in Santa Fe, Albuquerque, and Santa Cruz de la Cañada as well as in the pueblos of Zía, Jémez, and Zuñi. Once inside the classroom, there was no ambiguity about the school's twofold purpose, stated in articles 6 and 7 of the statutes issued by New Mexico's territorial assembly: "to observe the Christian doctrine within school, to teach the principal mysteries of our holy Catholic faith, devotion and respect toward the sacred images of Christ and his holy Mother . . . and to instill in pupils the love that they must profess toward the fatherland, giving them ample illustration of our federal system and the liberality of our government so they will grow up to become valuable citizens." However, the educational crusade was short-lived. By 1834 most public schools in Texas and New Mexico operated very precariously or had closed down. Scarce funds were frequently diverted toward more immediate concerns such as fighting Indians or paying the troops their back wages.[11]

For the vast majority of the frontier inhabitants, neither the print media nor the schools went very far in promoting a sense of nationhood. For them, the

---

[11]The legislative body in New Mexico changed names: *diputación provincial*, 1822–1824; *diputación territorial*, 1824–1837; *junta départamental*, 1837–1843; *asamblea departamental* 1843–1846. School statutes, Santa Fe, Nov. 4, 1827, *Mexican Archives of New Mexico*, reel 7, frames 3–5. See Josefina Zoraida Vázquez, *Nacionalismo y educación en México* [*Nationalism and Education in Mexico*] (Mexico City, 1975).

most pervasive and perhaps the only indications of the existence of the Mexican nation were rituals and symbols. Officials in Texas and New Mexico introduced an endless succession of reminders of the nation: flags, coins, elections, commemorations of the birthdays and deaths of independence heroes. The crowns that had hitherto embellished public buildings and carriages during colonial times were mercilessly erased, and the word "imperial" was systematically replaced by "national." Emblems planned to the last detail and always boasting the eagle standing on a prickly pear devouring a serpent—symbolizing the foundation of the Aztec empire—sprung up even in the smallest and most remote villages.[12]

Nationalizing rituals were first deployed in the nation's capital and quickly became an important weapon in the hands of skillful politicians such as Agustin de Iturbide, Antonio López de Santa Anna, and Maximilian of Habsburg—to name just the three most notorious—who showed a knack for ritualism and excruciating ceremony and pomp. From Mexico City the ritualistic onslaught was projected across the entire national domain. Even before the end of Spanish domination in 1821, the Mexican provisional governing junta was prompt to announce that the insurgent army would enter the capital in a triumphal parade to be celebrated on September 27 and exhorted all towns and villages that had not already sworn independence to do so on that day. The junta provided meticulous instructions to state and local authorities as to how the ceremonies should be conducted. . . .[13]

It is exceedingly difficult to ascertain how people felt about these ceremonies. [New Mexican] Governor Agustín Melgares somewhat sardonically remarked that it was his hope that those "exteriorities" revealed genuine support for "our holy cause." Indeed, it is likely that such newfound patriotism was at least partly a fabrication of zealous local and state officials desirous of showing their constituencies in a good light to their superiors. But regardless of private feelings, Independence Day celebrations in Texas and New Mexico quickly became elaborate and ritualized affairs organized by patriotic committees that labored for months every year to reach all segments of society. All of this required substantial outlays of money by leading citizens, who were thus able to show how solvent and patriotic they were. Repetition and anticipation became powerful conduits. From the enthusiasm displayed in San Antonio for the festivities of September 16, 1835, one would not have suspected that Texas was in the throes of a major rebellion. In addition to the usual tolling bells, pyrotechnic fires, and cannon shots, a mass with *Te Deum*, and the party and dance *de rigueur*, a gas-filled globe was released from the main plaza to commemorate Mexico's deliverance from Spain. Even more enthusiastic was the Independence

---

[12]Decree on militias, Aug. 3, 1823, *Mexican Archives of New Mexico*, reel 2, frame 78.

[13]Provisional Governing Junta to Governor of New Mexico, Oct. 6, 1821, ibid., reel 1, frames 171–74; *Gaceta Imperial de México* (Mexico City), March 23, 1822. This document has been translated and annotated: David J. Weber, "An Unforgettable Day: Facundo Melgares on Independence," *New Mexico Historical Review* 48 (Jan. 1973), 27–44.

Day celebration of 1844 in Santa Fe, which lasted six entire days, including three days of bullfights.[14]

Like the Independence Day celebrations, other civic ceremonies functioned as important means to instill patriotic sentiments in the checkered frontier population. One by-product of the political instability that engulfed Mexico during its first decades as an independent nation was the large number of political ceremonies and commemorations mandated throughout the national domain. A partial list would include Iturbide's coronation as emperor in 1822, the allegiance ceremony to the 1824 constitution, the celebration of the defeat of the Spanish reconquest attempt of 1829, the allegiance ceremony to the 1835 constitution, the interment of Iturbide's ashes in Mexico City's cathedral in 1838, and the allegiance ceremony to the 1844 constitution. Moreover, local and state officials improvised ceremonies whenever they saw the need. For instance, Col. José de las Piedras, military commander of the heavily Anglo-American district of Nacogdoches in Texas, decided to make local residents swear allegiance to the state constitution and to reacquaint them with the national constitution of 1824. One morning in 1827, under the threat of expulsion from the state if they failed to show up, Colonel Piedras gathered all settlers of Ayish Bayou, Sabinas, and Tajaná. Since the overwhelming majority could not speak Spanish and hence would not be able to utter the customary oath, Colonel Piedras had each settler sign a leaf of paper that contained an assertory oath in English. In his report Colonel Piedras noted that the public spirit did not seem entirely appropriate, "their coolness and apathy indicates to me that this act was not to their liking."[15]

Staged civic celebrations were bolstered by everyday ceremonies meant to heighten people's national loyalties. These included simple rituals such as that for taking legal possession of land, in which grantees were required to shout, "Long live the president and the Mexican nation" before they could become legitimate owners. Common religious events were ideal for this purpose. Priests expounded on the nation in daily sermons and at marriages, baptisms, and other ceremonies. Indeed, Catholicism and Mexicanness became tightly intertwined. Religion was an expedient way to distinguish between Mexicans and, say, Indians (that is, "pagans") or Protestant Anglo-Americans, and the terms *cristiano* and *mexicano*

---

[14]William H. Beezley, Cheryl English Martin, and William E. French, eds., *Rituals of Rule, Rituals of Resistance: Public Celebrations and Popular Culture in Mexico* (Wilmington, DE, 1994), xiii–xxii. For the American case, see David Waldstreicher, *In the Midst of Perpetual Fetes: The Making of American Nationalism, 1776–1820* (Chapel Hill, NC, 1997); and Len Travers, *Celebrating the Fourth: Independence Day and the Rites of Nationalism in the Early Republic* (Amherst, MA, 1997). On patriotic rituals in Mexico City, see Michael Costeloe, "The Junta Patriótica and the Celebration of Independence in Mexico City, 1825–1855," *Mexican Studies/Estudios Mexicanos* 13 (Winter 1997), 21–53. Minutes of the patriotic committee for the celebration of Independence Day, San Antonio, Aug. 16–22, 1835, Béxar Archives (microfilm, 172 reels, University of Texas Archives Microfilm Publication, 1967–1971), reel 166, frames 363–65; Minutes of the patriotic committee for the celebration of Independence Day, Santa Fe, July–Sept., 1844, *Mexican Archives of New Mexico*, reel 37, frames 564–649. On the political uses of the bullfight in Spain, see Adrian Shubert, *At Five in the Afternoon: A Social History of Spanish Bullfighting, 1700–1900* (New York, forthcoming), 274–325.

[15]Col. Jose de las Piedras to Gen. Anastasio Bustamante, Dec. 10, 1827, item 2, folder 673, box 40, Herbert E. Bolton Papers (Bancroft Library, University of California, Berkeley).

were frequently used interchangeably. In concrete policy terms this meant that all Native or Anglo-Americans wishing to become Mexican citizens had to convert to Catholicism. Religious and patriotic symbols were frequently juxtaposed. For example, in his Independence Day sermon of 1832, Father Antonio José Martínez of Taos compared Miguel Hidalgo, the hero of independence, to no less a figure than Jesus Christ. According to the priest, both figures preached their doctrines to the people courageously and both died at the hands of their enemies: "behold here the mysterious resemblance which gives reason enough evidence to compare Hidalgo to Jesus: the former saved the human race, the latter saved the American people, the continent of Anáhuac." . . . But in the Far North, Catholicism remained the very gateway to citizenship throughout the Mexican period.[16]

Notwithstanding these attempts at national construction, sweeping economic changes tended to foil such efforts, imposing capricious cross-national alliances and intranational cleavages and in general making the logic of the market—free trade, free movement of peoples, unencumbered exploitation of natural resources—prevail over the designs of nationalist officials. Mexico's national leaders generally supported the pursuit of capitalist development in the northern frontier, but toward the 1830s, as they became more wary of real or imagined secessionist tendencies in the North, they attempted to regulate the region's integration with the economy of the United States and put obstacles in the way of increasing Anglo-American immigration. However, in so doing national officials met with decided resistance from local and regional Hispanic and Indian elites as well as Anglo-American newcomers who had interests revolving around commerce and land and depended on laissez-faire policies for their well-being.

Initially, commerce provided the impetus for change. The Spanish colonies in America were long barred from trading with the United States and European countries other than Spain, and although the Bourbon monarchs did away with some trade regulations in the 1760s and 1770s, freedom of commerce outside the empire came only after independence from Spain. Trade liberalization had a particularly strong impact on Mexico's northern provinces as they were tantalizingly close to the United States, which was rapidly becoming one of the most dynamic trading areas in the world. In New Mexico the beginning of a new commercial era can be dated with precision. The people of Santa Fe were still digesting the news of separation from Spain in mid-November 1821 when word spread of an approaching caravan of Missouri merchants. This time New Mexico's governor allowed the Anglo merchants to trade with the locals unmolested. It was the beginning of the Santa Fe Trail, which within a few years became the most important trading route between the United States and northern Mexico. The caravans from Missouri kept coming every year and turned into sizable capital ventures moved by hundreds of wagons and protected by military escorts. In 1822 the value of the

---

[16]Malcolm Ebright, "New Mexican Land Grants: The Legal Background," in *Land, Water, and Culture: New Perspectives on Hispanic Land Grants*, ed. Charles L. Briggs and John R. Van Ness (Albuquerque, NM, 1987), 54; for the sermon by Martinez, see Santiago Valdez, *Biografía del Reverendo Padre Antonio José Martínez* [*Biography of Reverend Father Antonio Jose Martinez*] (Taos, NM, 1877), 54–56.

merchandise imported into New Mexico was estimated at fifteen thousand dollars, two years later that figure had doubled, and by 1826 it had doubled again. The merchandise brought to Santa Fe in 1843 was worth close to half a million dollars, a thirtyfold increase since independence.[17] Texas replicated what had happened in New Mexico as it fell into the commercial orbit of New Orleans. In 1822 Father Refugio de la Garza, the first representative of Texas to the Constituent Congress in Mexico City, was instructed to secure for his province freedom of commerce with the United States. Within a year the skillful priest had prodded an oblivious congress into exempting Texans from paying any import duties for a period of seven years, thus creating a trading rush of far-reaching consequences.[18]

Commerce brought a new set of social relations and interests to these provinces. In New Mexico the Santa Fe Trail was at first monopolized by an exclusive group of Anglo-American traffickers and a few Frenchmen who had preceded them. They controlled the bulk of the profits and wielded commensurate political influence. But New Mexico's traditional Hispanic elite soon made the transition from land-based and sheep-raising enterprises to commercial ventures. Manuel Armijo, three times governor of New Mexico, was the most striking example. He rapidly found a way to profit from the Santa Fe Trail, as the crafty governor began to sell foreign goods to other parts of northern Mexico where he had previously sold only sheep.[19] He was hardly alone. Such families as the Chávez, Ortiz, Otero, and Perea became successful international merchants in their own right. By 1843, nuevomexicano merchants accounted for a full 45 percent of New Mexico's total exports and 22 percent of all shipments of foreign goods going into Mexico's interior.[20]

Texas went through a similar transition. By 1826 Anglo-Americans dominated the trading business in San Antonio and Goliad, introducing merchandise at various times of the year. But as in New Mexico, it did not take long before

[17]Max L. Moorhead, *New Mexico's Royal Road* (Norman, OK, 1958), 55–151. Lansig Bloom, "New Mexico under Mexican Administration," *Old Santa Fe* 2 (Oct. 1914), 121.

[18]Instructions to Deputy Refugio de la Garza, Jan. 30, 1822, pp. 8–17, file 190, box 2q297, Nacogdoches Archives Transcripts (Barker Texas History Center, University of Texas, Austin); and Refugio de la Garza to *ayuntamiento* of San Antonio, April 30, Aug. 8, 1822, *Béxar Archives*, reel 71, frames 494–96, reel 72, frames 455–57. Jose Antonio Saucedo to Juan Martin de Veramendi, April 13, 1825, ibid., roll 80, frames 548–49.

[19]Manuel Alvarez to Secretary of State, July 1, 1843, Despatches from United States Consuls in Santa Fe, 1830–1846 (microfilm: roll M 199), Records of the Department of State, RG 59 (National Archives, Washington, D.C.).

[20]The data on nuevomexicano merchants' trade is derived from statistical analysis of customs receipts, or *guías*, for 1843, the most complete yearly set available. Data and analysis in computer-readable form are available from the author on request. In the 1840s Anglo-American merchants often complained that the trade was falling into the hands of Mexicans. See Mark L. Gardner, ed., *Brothers on the Santa Fe and Chihuahua Trails: Edward James Glasgow and William Henry Glasgow, 1846–1848* (Niwot, CO, 1993), 200n12. Marc Simmons, *The Little Lion of the Southwest: A Life of Manuel Antonio Chaves* (Chicago, 1973), 64–67. Daniel Tyler, "Anglo-American Penetration of the Southwest: The View from New Mexico," *Southwestern Historical Quarterly* 75 (Jan. 1972), 325–38. Notes to the San Antonio census, San Antonio, July 31, 1826, pp. 41–43, file 197A, box 2q298, Nacogdoches Archives Transcripts; and José María **Sánchez**, *Viaje a Texas en 1828–1829* [*A Journey to Texas in 1828–1829*] (Mexico City, 1939), 29.

entrepreneurial native sons staged a return to the commercial arena. Indeed by the early 1830s Anglo-American merchants squarely competed against a powerful tejano clique. These men had developed extensive trading networks comparable to those of their Anglo counterparts, webs stretching from New Orleans suppliers to Texas customs officers and store owners. This tejano group became a formidable power to reckon with.[21]

Although relations between Anglo and Hispanic merchants in both Texas and New Mexico were sometimes contentious, the two groups generally got along well and often forged profitable and long-lasting partnerships. In many respects the two groups of merchants were complementary. While Anglo-Americans could make introductions and pave the way for their Hispanic counterparts with suppliers in Missouri and Louisiana, Hispanic traders could reciprocate, helping their Anglo-American colleagues deal with Mexican customs officers and other authorities. The two groups were forced to travel together and to extend credit to one another. Many Anglo-American merchants married into nuevomexicano and tejano families.[22] Above all, the merchants, regardless of ethnicity, were keenly opposed to outside meddling that threatened to interrupt the flow of profits coming from the north.

The emergence of a trading economy in Texas and New Mexico stimulated land deals, which provided yet another network of common interests. In Coahuila and Texas, state officials contracted with private developers or *empresarios* whose task was to settle at least one hundred families and to establish self-sustaining colonies in exchange for land. The majority of both *empresarios* and colonists turned out to be Anglo-American. The *empresario* system completely changed the face of Texas. In the 1810s Texas had been an undeveloped province with enormous *baldíos* (vacant lands) visited only by occasional Indian groups, hunters, and adventurous Texans. Within a few years, most of the land was parceled out among numerous settlers who showed claims under the authority of overlapping *empresario* contracts and other land development schemes. State officials in Coahuila and Texas created a powerful patronage system on the basis of land distribution.[23] In secretive deliberations, state legislators and the gover-

---

[21]Philip Dimitt Collection (Barker Texas History Center).

[22]Jane Dysart, "Mexican Women in San Antonio, 1830–1860: The Assimilation Process," *Western Historical Quarterly* 7 (Oct. 1976), 365–75; Janet Lecompte, "The Independent Women of Hispanic New Mexico, 1821–1846," ibid., 12 (Jan. 1981), 20–37; Rebecca McDowell Craver, *The Impact of Intimacy: Mexican-Anglo Intermarriage in New Mexico, 1821–1846* (El Paso, 1982); and Ramón Gutiérrez, *When Jesus Came, the Corn Mothers Went Away: Marriage, Sexuality, and Power in New Mexico, 1500–1846* (Stanford, CA, 1991), 271–97. Sandra Jaramillo, "Bound by Family," unpublished paper, 1994 (in Andrés Reséndez's possession).

[23]Mary Virginia Henderson, "Minor Empresario Contracts for the Colonization of Texas, 1825–1834," *Southwestern Historical Quarterly* 31 (April 1928), 295–324; Reichstein, *Rise of the Lone Star*; Malcolm D. McLean, *Papers Concerning Robertson's Colony in Texas* (16 vols., Fort Worth and Arlington, 1974–1990); Vito Alessio Robles, *Coahuila y Texas desde la consumación de la independencia hasta el tratado de paz de Guadalupe Hidalgo* [*Coahuila and Texas from Independence to the Treaty of Guadalupe Hidalgo*] (2 vols., Mexico City, 1945). Ricki S. Janicek, "The Development of Early Mexican Land Policy: Coahuila and Texas, 1810–1825" (PhD diss., Tulane University, 1985); and Ricki S. Janicek, "The Politics of Land: Mexico and Texas, 1823–1836," paper presented at the meeting of the Texas State Historical Association, Austin, Feb. 1996 (in Reséndez's possession).

nor conferred princely land grants, approved colonization enterprises, granted exclusive rights to navigate Texas rivers, and made profitable appointments for customs and land officials. From these transactions emerged a web of economic as well as political alliances that ran from state officials to *empresarios*, land commissioners, and colonists themselves, including widely diverse groups from tejano landowners to Anglo-American developers and speculators to Indian allies such as the Cherokees, who also secured a grant.

New Mexico went through a similar, if less studied, land drive. Prosperous merchants, both nuevomexicano and Anglo-American, sought to invest some of their profits in New Mexico's traditional economic activity, sheep raising, which in turn fueled demand for land. On the one hand, this pressure led to an increasing encroachment on communal lands that had been granted to Pueblo Indians by the Spanish Crown. Since the 1820s, choice Pueblo lands had become contested by non-Indians, a trend that was felt with greatest force toward the end of the Mexican period.[24] On the other hand, New Mexico's authorities began to grant enormous tracts of land to Anglo-American developers alone or in partnership with nuevomexicanos. . . .[25] Indeed, most of the Anglo-American and nuevomexicano land grantees, as well as some disgruntled Pueblo Indian leaders, played key roles in the dramatic sovereignty struggles of New Mexico in 1846–1848.

Commercial and land transactions hindered the consolidation of the Mexican nation in Texas and New Mexico. This occurred not so much because there were cozy partnerships between local authorities and foreign businessmen as because the prosperity of those provinces hinged on the continuation and accretion of economic ties with the United States. Prominent tejanos and nuevomexicanos, with their Anglo-American partners, staked their future on the development of those provinces along federalist lines, which meant unrestricted trade with the United States, increasing immigration of Anglo-Americans, and flexible land policies that insured property rights for foreigners and recent arrivals. Given the demographic and economic imbalance between Hispanics and Anglos, this policy would eventually result in an overwhelming preponderance of Anglo-Americans along the frontier. On the eve of the Texas Revolution, northeastern Texas was largely inhabited by Anglo colonists who had prospered in a thriving cotton and cattle economy. In the years immediately before the Mexican-American War, northern New Mexico was falling inexorably into the hands of wealthy Anglo-American merchants and some of their nuevomexicano partners.

---

[24]G. Emlen Hall and David J. Weber, "Mexican Liberals and the Pueblo Indians, 1821–1829," *New Mexico Historical Review* 59 (Jan. 1984), 5–32; G. Emlen Hall, "The Pueblo Grant Labyrinth," in *Land, Water, and Culture*, ed. Briggs and Van Ness, 67–138. G. Emlen Hall, *Four Leagues of Pecos* (Albuquerque, NM, 1984); and Myra Ellen Jenkins, "Taos Pueblo and Its Neighbors, 1540–1847," *New Mexico Historical Review* 41 (April 1966), 85–114.

[25]Harold H. Dunham, "New Mexican Land Grants with Special Reference to the Title Papers of the Maxwell Grant," *New Mexico Historical Review* 30 (Jan. 1955), 1–22. Malcolm Ebright, *Land Grants and Lawsuits in Northern New Mexico* (Albuquerque, NM, 1994), 27.

These developments did not go unnoticed in centralist circles, and they eventually elicited a strong nationalist reaction. Lucas Alamnan, the minister of the interior, was the most adamant and influential voice of this political backlash. In 1830 he observed that

> instead of sending conquering armies, [North Americans] have recourse to other means . . . they begin by introducing themselves in a territory that they desire and establish colonies and trading routes. . . .

Such nationalist rhetoric was quickly appropriated in Texas and New Mexico and injected into local disputes. Citizens who felt displaced by outsiders repeatedly resorted to patriotic rhetoric to strengthen their claims. For instance, many tejanos of Goliad became very receptive to centralist harangues that emphasized patriotism because the community had a long-standing land dispute with the foreign-born *empresario* Green DeWitt. In fact, Carlos de la Garza, a Goliad resident, became the most conspicuous centralist tejano leader during the entire Texas Revolution. Likewise the Mexican military in San Antonio was able to raise two companies of "volunteers for the Nation" who remained loyal to the centralist government. Nationalist rhetoric was similarly appropriated and deployed in New Mexico to settle local and regional political scores, often masking pecuniary disputes, but also for ideological reasons. . . . [P]atriotic rhetoric became a potent cement binding local, regional, and national political groups who often pursued different immediate objectives but were all united under the same banner: to preserve the territorial integrity of Mexico.[26]

REBELLION, WAR, AND NATIONAL IDENTITY

The Texas Revolution would set the terms of the national identity struggles in Mexico's Far North in the decades to follow. Most traditional histories either trace the revolt of 1835–1836 to cultural or ethnic incompatibility between Mexicans and Americans or adopt a sweeping Manifest Destiny explanation, casting the revolution as merely a step in the westward drive of Anglo-Americans into Spanish America.[27] Yet a growing interest in Mexican Texans has shown that the revolution was not carried out exclusively by dissatisfied Anglo colonists but that tejanos as well were actively involved. Indeed, the initial momentum to organize state militias and resist the central government's authority, even if that entailed

---

[26]Lucas Alamán to Gen. Manuel Mier y Terán, Feb. 13, 1830, p. 4, folder 673, box 40, Bolton Papers. Ana Caroline Castillo Crimm, "Finding Their Ways," in *Tejano Journey, 1770–1860*, ed. Gerald E. Poyo (Austin, 1996), 119–20; Andrés Tijerina, "Under the Mexican Flag," ibid., 44–46; Andrés Tijerina, *Tejanos and Texas under the Mexican Flag, 1821–1836* (College Station, TX, 1994), 123–24; and Paul D. Lack, *The Texas Revolutionary Experience: A Political and Social History, 1835–1836* (College Station, TX, 1992), 163. On the San Antonio volunteers, see ibid., 165–66. Antonio José Martínez to José Antonio Laureano de Zubiría, Sept. 2, 1845, in Valdez, *Biografía del Reverendo Padre Antonio José Martínez*, 42.

[27]Eugene C. Barker, *Mexico and Texas, 1821–1835* (New York, 1965); Samuel H. Lowrie, *Culture Conflict in Texas, 1821–1836* (New York, 1932); and William C. Binkley, *The Texas Revolution* (Baton Rouge, LA, 1952).

using force, originated in Coahuila and the San Antonio-Goliad region, not in the Anglo colonies. Indians also played a crucial part in this story. Historians have begun to elucidate the tangle of alliances and counteralliances between Indians and revolutionists. Inevitably, with the addition of new protagonists, the story has lost some of its past simplicity. As David Weber has pointed out, the Texas Revolution was not a clear-cut ethnic or racial rebellion "pitting *all* Anglos against *all* Mexicans, *all* white against *all* non-white"; it was an unwieldy coalition of Anglo-American colonists, tejanos, and Indian tribes fighting against the national government and its local and regional allies.[28]

The origins of the Texas Revolution have to be traced back to the clash between regional and national elites in Mexico, especially as their struggle affected the network of interests that had flourished in Texas in the 1820s.Those who advocated autonomy for the states and defended local interests against national encroachment—a heterogeneous group that came to be known as "radical liberals" or "federalists"—began to chafe after the offensive launched by their "centralist" opponents in the early 1830s.[29] The short-lived administration of Anastasio Bustamante in 1830–1832 moved precisely in that centralizing direction. He established a ring of military garrisons in Texas, opened customs houses to regulate and tax commerce with the United States, and sought to reduce the preponderance of Anglo-Americans in Texas by promoting Mexican and European colonization and forbidding any further immigration from the United States. . . . [I]n 1834–1836 . . . [t]he national government instituted reforms that threatened to alter the fundamental economic and political relations prevalent in Coahuila and Texas . . . until Texas seceded from Mexico.[30]

Having said this, however, we should avoid another form of historical reductionism—following contemporary rhetoric—that described the Texas Revolution as a quest for freedom against military despotism from Mexico's heartland. First,

---

[28]Lack, *Texas Revolutionary Experience*, 156–207; Jesus F. de la Teja, ed., *A Revolution Remembered: The Memoirs and Selected Correspondence of Juan N. Seguín* (Austin, TX, 1991); and Tijerina, *Tejanos and Texas under the Mexican Flag*, 137–44. Dianna Everett, *The Texas Cherokees: A People between Two Fires, 1819–1840* (Norman, OK, 1990); and Mary Whatley Clarke, *Chief Bowles and the Texas Cherokees* (Norman, OK, 1971). Weber, *Myth and the History of the Hispanic Southwest*, 144. James E. Crisp, "Anglo-Texan Attitudes toward the Mexican, 1821–1845" (PhD diss., Yale University, 1976); and Arnoldo De Leon, *They Called Them Greasers: Anglo Attitudes toward Mexicans in Texas, 1821–1900* (Austin, TX, 1983).

[29]As a political system, "centralism" was not instituted until 1835, but the label had been in use since the late 1820s. Reynaldo Sordo, *El congreso en la primera república centralista [Congress during the First Centralist Republic]* (Mexico City, 1993). Michael P Costeloe, *The Central Republic in Mexico, 1835–1846: Hombres de Bien in the Age of Santa Anna* (Cambridge, England, 1993). Nettie Lee Benson, "Texas As Viewed from Mexico, 1820–1834," *Southwestern Historical Quarterly* 90 (Jan. 1987), 219–91.

[30]See Law of April 6, 1830, translated in McLean, Papers Concerning Robertson's Colony in Texas, III, 494–99. See also "Representación dirijida por el ilustre Ayuntamiento de la ciudad de Béxar al honorable Congreso del Estado" [*Representation Sent by the Illustrious Municipality of the City of Béxar (San Antonio) to the Honorable State Congress*], edited and translated, in *Troubles in Texas, 1832: A Tejano Viewpoint from San Antonio*, ed. David J. Weber and Conchita Hassell Winn (Austin, TX, 1983), 58. On the federalists' policies toward Coahuila and Texas, see Robles, *Coahuila y Texas*, I, 483–97.

the nationalist rhetoric employed by centralists commanded enormous popular support, especially given the truly scandalous speculation and the rapid Americanization of Texas. Even within Coahuila and Texas a vocal antifederalist faction responded enthusiastically to the patriotic harangues to regain Texas for Mexico. Second, federalists and revolutionists in Texas—whether Anglo, tejano, or Indian—may all have been fighting under the collective banner of "freedom," but "freedom" was often linked to self-interest. . . . [E]vidence of the importance of pecuniary interests is widespread and impressive. . . . [M]uch of the discontent leading up to the revolution revolved around tariff collection. Both Anglo-American and tejano merchants objected to the establishment of customs houses, and both remained generally supportive of the revolution even as secession from Mexico became permanent. Undoubtedly, in the course of the fighting, ethnic and racial tensions surfaced, but initially Texans made a revolution to protect their freedoms, their beliefs, and their interests; in the process they took the momentous decision to create a new nation.[31]

Ten years after the Texas Revolution, in the summer of 1846, Col. Stephen W. Kearny found himself marching along the Santa Fe Trail, commanding a small army, with instructions from the United States government to take possession of New Mexico. War had begun between Mexico and the United States. On August 18, about two thousand weary and dusty American soldiers marched unopposed into Santa Fe. Their commander formally took possession of the territory of New Mexico. The Army of the West had conquered New Mexico "without the firing of a shot or the shedding of a single drop of blood," according to a contemporary description that historians have repeated ever since. Yet five months later, an anti-American rebellion broke out in the northern and western districts of New Mexico. The uprising eventually claimed the lives of the recently appointed American governor of New Mexico, several other Anglo-American residents, and at least two nuevomexicano "collaborationists." The two episodes, the unopposed march of American troops into Santa Fe and the Taos rebellion, marked the two ends of the pendulum swing in the sovereignty struggles unfolding in New Mexico.[32] The war created an environment in which local political grievances, economic interests, and evolving identities played themselves out throughout Mexico's Far North against the backdrop of an impending invasion and possible annexation to the United States. It is tempting to interpret the war

[31]Reichstein, *Rise of the Lone Star*, 181–202; McLean, *Papers Concerning Robertson's Colony in Texas*, esp. XIII, 71–124. David Montejano, *Anglos and Mexicans in the Making of Texas, 1836–1986* (Austin, TX, 1987), 15. Weber, *Mexican Frontier*, 338n34; and Barker, *Mexico and Texas*, 107–8. Andrés Reséndez, "Traitor Merchants? Tejano Merchants in the Texas Revolution," paper presented at the meeting of the Texas State Historical Association, Austin, Feb. 1996 (in Reséndez's possession).

[32]Report of Stephen W. Kearny quoted in E. Bennett Burton, "The Taos Rebellion," *Old Santa Fe* 1 (Oct. 1913), 176. For narratives, see Howard R. Lamar, *The Far Southwest, 1846–1912: A Territorial History* (New Haven, CT, 1966); and three classics: Ralph Emerson Twitchell, *The Military Occupation of New Mexico, 1846–1851* (Denver, CO, 1909); Ralph Emerson Twitchell, *The Leading Facts of New Mexican History* (2 vols., Cedar Rapids, IA, 1911–1912); and Hubert H. Bancroft, *History of Arizona and New Mexico, 1530–1888* (San Francisco, CA, 1889). Michael McNierney, ed., *Taos 1847: The Revolt in Contemporary Accounts* (Boulder, CO, 1980).

squarely as a conflict between two clearly defined nations, and it is easy to understand the ensuing territorial exchange as solely a military outcome. And yet, from the perspective of the border society—rather than that of Mexico City or Washington, D.C.—what we find is an army of invasion negotiating with local and regional actors whose loyalties did not always conform to simple national lines.

Much in the attitudes of leading nuevomexicanos toward Kearny's Army of the West in the summer of 1846 has to be traced back to a network of interests that had developed among key nuevomexicano officials and Anglo-American merchants and residents during the 1840s. Some days before the arrival of the Army of the West, Manuel Alvarez, the Spanish-born consul of the United States in Santa Fe, tried to persuade Governor Armijo not to resist. Alvarez found Armijo "vacillating to the last" and utterly undecided. Although the consul admitted that he could not persuade the governor to turn over the Department of New Mexico to the Americans, he asserted that he had had more success with "other officers" and Armijo's "confidential advisers." Santiago (James W) Magoffin, a seasoned merchant of the Santa Fe Trail who had been commissioned by President James K. Polk to use his connections to win the northern provinces over to the American side, reported that prior to Kearny's arrival he had met many of the "rich" and the militia officers of New Mexico and, with only one exception, had found that they would be perfectly satisfied if the area became a territory of the United States. Magoffin told nuevomexicano officers that they would be happy under the star-spangled banner because their property would be respected, their houses would rise in value, and the political system would change for the better. Robert B. McAfee, another merchant, sarcastically summed up this phenomenon for President Polk: "Touch their money and you reach their hearts. Make it their interest to have peace and we will soon have it."[33]

The events that followed are not entirely clear. The governor began preparations to face the American army of occupation at a formidable pass called el Cañón, fifteen miles east of Santa Fe. Yet two days before the showdown would have occurred, Governor Armijo took the momentous decision to disband the volunteers he had summoned. With seventy soldiers the governor retreated to Chihuahua, thus clearing the path of the invading army.[34]

---

[33]Alvarez to James Buchanan, Sept. 4, 1846 (roll M 199), Despatches from United States Consuls in Santa Fe. On the Spanish-born consul, see Thomas E. Chávez, *Manuel Alvarez, 1794–1856: A Southwestern Biography* (Niwot, CO, 1990). J. W. Magoffin to W. L. Marcy, Aug. 26, 1846, Magoffin Papers, Twitchell Collection (New Mexico State Records Center and Archives); Testimony of Lt. Manuel García de Lara, Proceedings against Armijo, Mexico City, March 1847 (microfilm: file 2588, roll 11) Archivo Histórico de la Defensa Nacional (Bancroft Library). A fuller collection of the original documents is in the Archivo Histórico de la Defensa Nacional, Secretaría de la Defensa Nacional, Mexico City. Robert B. McAfee to James K. Polk, June 22, 1847, Magoffin Papers.

[34]Many nuevomexicanos spoke about outright treason and claimed that Armijo had sold the department for 25,000 pesos. See Proceedings against Armijo (file 2588, roll 11), Archivo Histórico de la Defensa Nacional, Bancroft Library. On Armijo's options and constraints at that juncture, see Daniel Tyler, "Governor Armijo's Moment of Truth," *Journal of the West* 11 (April 1972), 307–16.

McAfee may have been accurate in describing the outlook of the privileged few whose interests depended on the Santa Fe Trail, but displaced elites and commoners thought otherwise. In the aftermath of the American takeover, significant discontent surfaced throughout New Mexico. The Pueblo Indians of Taos, for instance, resented the encroachment of Anglo-American and Mexican merchants on their land. . . .

New Mexico's Catholic establishment also fiercely opposed annexation to the United States. Even before the military occupation of New Mexico, Father Martínez had been the most outspoken critic of Armijo's administration for "caving in" to the Americans and had delivered a series of sermons "arousing the people to a determined resistance." He warned his congregation of impending disasters and told them of his nightmares about the national government disposing of New Mexico. As the embattled priest interpreted New Mexico's situation with some hyperbole, a mob of "heretics were ready on its confines to overrun this unfortunate land." Father Martínez's patriotic rhetoric drew on a wellspring of religious symbology and Pueblo Indian mythology.[35]

The most telling example of this merger of patriotism, religion, and ancient mythology is found in a mysterious document that appeared in Jémez, San Juan, and probably other pueblos as well. The document was dated May 25, 1846, barely ten days after the United States declared war on Mexico. It was the story of Montezuma "to be told to the Pueblos of the great province of New Mexico, so that they understand that they are and shall be recognized as part of Montezuma's nation to whom they are to render full obedience." . . . [E]ven a cursory examination provides insights into how myths were used to create identity. . . .[36]

As to the exact role that the Montezuma legend played in the Pueblos' participation in the 1847 revolt, we know very little. Unfortunately, once the rebellion was put down, the Pueblo leaders were summarily tried, declared guilty of treason to the United States, and hanged without anyone recording their depositions. And yet the participation of Pueblo Indians in the Taos rebellion shows how Native Americans became key players in the struggles over national identity in the Southwest. It underscores the wellspring of myths and symbols brought forth by the contacts between various groups in this area, and it shows how these myths and symbols were merged and combined with one another, creating new and unexpected national meaning.

[35]Alvarez to Buchanan, Feb. 9, 1846 (roll M 199), Despatches from United States Consuls in Santa Fe, 1830–1846. For a warning against interpreting Martínez as simply a staunch Mexican nationalist, see Angélico Chávez, *But Time and Chance: The Story of Padre Martínez of Taos* (Santa Fe, CA, 1981), 81–87. Charles Bent to Alvarez, Feb. 26, 1846, file 74, Read Collection (New Mexico State Records Center and Archives).

[36]"Historia de Montezuma," May 25, 1846, folder 788, box 2q240, Bandelier Transcripts (Barker Texas History Center). On the sources, see Charles H. Lange, Carroll L. Riley, and Elizabeth M. Lange, *The Southwestern Journals of Adolph F Bandelier* (4 vols., Albuquerque, NM, 1984), IV, 513–17. See also Twitchell, *Leading Facts of New Mexican History*, I, 401–3.

CONCLUSION

The conflicts that rocked Mexico's northern frontier in the first half of the nineteenth century, including the Texas Revolution and the Taos rebellion, were ultimately struggles over sovereignty and identity. These events cannot be reduced to ethnic conflicts between Hispanics, Native Americans, and Anglo-Americans. The surprising decision of tejano merchants to support the Anglo-American drive to secede from Mexico in 1835–1836 or the Pueblo Indians' intention to restore Mexico's sovereignty over New Mexico in 1847 seem to defy common sense because their loyalties did not conform to previous ethnic solidarities. For this reason those events well illustrate how much national identity depended on economic arrangements as well as an imagery able to speak to the needs and longings of diverse peoples.

The Mexican government, having inherited the Spanish imperial bureaucracy and its political-religious mental world, attempted to forge a Mexican identity in the northern frontier by developing patronage lines leading from the center to the remote provinces by using the overlapping administrative structures of church, military, and civil government; by promoting civic and religious rituals derived chiefly from the independence struggle; and by fashioning—often unwittingly—a defensive, antiforeign, nationalist rhetoric that was appropriated by border communities and political groups to advance their own interests and agendas. Yet, this nationalist project went against the grain of a network of economic, social, and political cross-cultural alliances brought about by the prodigious economic development of the frontier region and its growing integration into the economy of the United States.

Adopting the perspective of the people living in these border provinces, we can recast the sovereignty struggles as a vast project to organize society. The decision to become Mexican or American or Texan was not only a question of placing or imagining oneself within one collectivity; most critically, it involved choices about the organization of the economy, the contours of the political system, and religious and moral values. And in making all of those critical choices, different social groups, classes, and ethnicities that coexisted in Mexico's Far North had different and often conflicting ideas. Tejanos, federalists, indigenous communities, nuevomexicanos, centralists, merchants, *empresarios*, Anglo-Americans, and common people attempted to shape the nation to their own wishes and their best interests. In this frontier world where interests, political ideology, and national allegiances were inextricably intertwined, the deployment of Mexicanist rhetoric—or its absence—became another weapon in their everyday life struggles. The nation did not emerge full-blown right after emancipation from Spain in 1821, nor was it purposefully constructed according to blueprint laid out by the "Mexican founding fathers," it was simply a by-product of complicated alliances and counteralliances contingent on a set of local arrangements in constant flux.

Andrés Reséndez

I grew up in Mexico City where I studied a BA in international relations and briefly went into politics and served as a consultant for historical soap operas. I got my Ph.D. in history at the University of Chicago and have taught at Yale, the University of Helsinki, and at the University of California–Davis where I am currently a professor in the Department of History. My first book, *Changing National Identities at the Frontier* (Cambridge University Press, 2005), explores how Spanish-speakers, Native Americans, and Anglo-American settlers living in Texas and New Mexico came to think of themselves as members of one national community or another in the years leading up to the United States–Mexico War. My most recent book, *A Land So Strange* (Basic Books, 2007), looks at North America at the dawn of European colonization and through the eyes of the last four survivors of a disastrous expedition to Florida in the 1520s. I am currently finishing a book manuscript, *The Other Slavery* (Houghton Mifflin Harcourt, forthcoming 2016), about the enslavement of hundreds of thousands of Indians in the Caribbean, Mexico, and the US Southwest between the sixteenth and nineteenth centuries.

QUESTIONS FOR CONSIDERATIONS

1. Characterize the traditional "story of how nations emerge" as described by Reséndez. What alternative "story," according to Reséndez, has arisen recently? What compromise between these two does he propose? And whose history does he propose to tell regarding the Mexican borderlands in particular?

2. After Mexican independence in 1821, how did the Mexican government seek to instill in the people of the Mexican borderlands a sense of common identity? To what extent were these attempts successful?

3. What economic factors ultimately divided the people of the Mexican borderlands between those who supported independence from Mexico and those who supported Mexican nationalism? Name one factor that divided the people of the Mexican borderlands in the 1840s between those who supported annexation by the United States and those supported union with Mexico.

4. Compare the economic interests of elites in the Mexican borderlands to those of the Spanish and French of the seventeenth and eighteenth century in Barr's article "From Captives to Slaves: Commodifying Indian Women in the Borderlands." How did these interests shape the Mexican borderlands of both in ways both similar and different?

CHAPTER THIRTEEN

✦◯

Young American Males and Filibustering in the Age of Manifest Destiny: The United States Army as a Cultural Mirror[1]

Robert E. May

Asked the meaning of the term *filibuster* modern Americans are likely to conjure up images of politicians rendering long-winded speeches to delay the passage of legislation. Prior to 1900, however, *filibuster* was most frequently applied to American adventurers who raised or participated in private military forces that either invaded or planned to invade foreign countries with which the United States was formally at peace. . . .

Filibustering reached its apex before the Civil War, when thousands of Americans risked their lives in expeditions. The most notorious filibuster was William Walker. Walker invaded Mexican Lower California and Sonora in 1853–1854, cast his lot in a Nicaraguan civil war in the spring of 1855, emerged commander-in-chief of the army in a coalition government that October, and had himself inaugurated as president of Nicaragua the following July. However, Walker represented a generation of filibusters. Filibuster activity touched . . . Mexico . . ., Nicaragua, . . . Cuba, Ecuador, Canada, Honduras, and Hawaii. "The fever of Fillibusterism is on our country. Her pulse beats like a hammer at the wrist, and there's a very high color on her face," noted the *New-York Daily Times* in an editorial that could have been dated any time between the Mexican War and Civil War.[2]

Filibustering defied international law, United States statutes, and presidential proclamations. Though only Walker's Nicaragua expedition achieved even short-term success, and although many of the expeditions met bloody ends, filibustering disrupted United States relations with England, Spain, France, and

---

[1] Interested students are encouraged to read this essay in the original form. Robert E. May, "Young American Males and Filibustering in the Age of Manifest Destiny: The United States Army as a Cultural Mirror," *Journal of American History* 78 (3) (Dec. 1991), 857–886.

[2] *New-York Daily Times*, March 4, 1854, p. 4.

many of the countries of middle and South America . . ., provoked outbreaks of anti-Americanism in Central America, and had a host of domestic ramifications. Filibustering sparked heated debate in Congress, state legislatures, and southern commercial conventions . . ., helped make and unmake presidents and contributed significantly to the breakdown of sectional relations, which eventuated in the American Civil War.[3]

. . . [Filibustering represents] a mid-nineteenth-century United States cultural phenomenon. . . . [H]istorians tend to judge filibustering by the number of adventurers who actually arrived in foreign domains, without taking into account their support networks or the persons who joined filibuster units that disbanded prematurely. . . . What has been obscured is filibustering's place in American social history, both North and South.[4]

Rather than restrict filibustering to the sideshows of America's pre–Civil War drama, historians need to respect its salience and probe its meaning. Filibustering contributed to the rhythm of antebellum life. Newspapers and periodicals published countless news items and editorials about filibuster plots, battles, and trials. Filibuster rallies, recruiting and bond drives, serenades, lectures, parades, and stage plays touched communities throughout much of the country. Filibustering provided the nation with heroes, martyrs, and villains. . . . A United States naval officer reflected, "I have forgiven the crime & delusion of the invaders for the immeasurable courage & uncomplaining spirit in which they all to a man met their deaths." . . . Intellectuals also found that filibustering commanded their attention. Washington Irving concluded that the filibusters signaled a "spirit of mischief" at loose in the country. . . . In the late antebellum period, filibustering helped define what it meant to be an American. As a cynic

---

[3]Ray Emerson Curtis, "The Law of Hostile Military Expeditions As Applied in the United States," *American Journal of International Law* 8 (Jan. 1914), 1–2, 8; Paul Neff Garber, *The Gadsden Treaty* (Philadelphia, 1923), 97–98; Kenneth Bourne, *Britain and the Balance of Power in North America, 1815–1908* (Berkeley, CA, 1967), 187–94; Richard W. Van Alstyne, "American Filibustering and the British Navy: A Caribbean Analogue of Mediterranean Piracy," *American Journal of International Law* 32 (Jan. 1938), 138–42; Dexter Perkins, *The Monroe Doctrine, 1826–1867* (1933; reprint, Gloucester, MA, 1965), 244–46, 324–31; James W. Cortada, *Two Nations over Time: Spain and the United States, 1776–1977* (Westport, CT, 1978), 66–68, 72–74.

[4]John Hope Franklin, *The Militant South, 1800–1861* (Cambridge, MA, 1956), 96–128; Robert E. May, *The Southern Dream of a Caribbean Empire, 1854–1861* (Baton Rouge, 1973); Rollin G. Osterweis, *Romanticism and Nationalism in the Old South* (Baton Rouge, LA, 1949), 172–85; Joe A. Stout, *The Liberators: Filibustering Expeditions into Mexico, 1848–1862, and the Last Thrust of Manifest Destiny* (Los Angeles, 1973). Works emphasizing filibustering's relationship to national culture include Charles H. Brown, *Agents of Manifest Destiny: The Lives and Times of the Filibusters* (Chapel Hill, NC, 1980); William H. Goetzmann, *When the Eagle Screamed: The Romantic Horizon in American Diplomacy, 1800–1860* (New York, 1966), 74–88; and Richard Slotkin, *The Fatal Environment: The Myth of the Frontier in the Age of Industrialization* (New York, 1985), 242–61. Many other books and articles treat antebellum filibustering. Of especial importance are William O. Scroggs, *Filibusters and Financiers: The Story of William Walker and His Associates* (New York, 1960); and Basil Rauch, *American Interest in Cuba, 1848–1855* (New York, 1948).

put it in *Harper's Weekly,* "The insatiable spirit of filibusterism . . . forms one of the most amiable virtues of our beloved fellow-countrymen."[5]

Above all, historians need to study filibustering's appeal and meaning to America's young males. . . . [T]he great number of. . . [filibustering soldiers], as might be expected in highly dangerous, physically demanding, and illegal ventures, were young. . . . The average age of the eighty-four filibusters taken prisoner in Narciso López's 1851 expedition to Cuba was 25.9 years. As would happen later in the Civil War, adolescents who had no business soldiering signed up for expeditions. "At the age of fifteen I ran away . . . to join an aggregation of young gentlemen but little older than myself, who enlisted under the banner of General Walker," one of them later recalled, noting that his group was "caught . . . like a bunch of truant kids" while passing down the Mississippi River. . . .[6]

Perhaps the most telling indication of filibustering's broad appeal to the nation's young males is its impact on the officers and enlisted men of the United States Army. At first glance, the army would seem a most unlikely institution to foster filibustering. The service had a history of anti-filibustering responsibilities that dated back to the Washington administration, and the prevention of filibusters emerged as one of the army's most important peacetime missions by the late 1830s. One might well expect the nation's officers and enlisted men to despise their filibuster antagonists. Yet sympathy for filibustering infiltrated army ranks. Some soldiers even resigned commissions and deserted ranks to join filibuster expeditions. While it would be misleading to brush the whole army with the stain of filibustering because of the derelictions and sentiments of a portion of its personnel, it would also be wrong to exempt United States soldiers from filibustering's spell. The army held up a cultural mirror to its nation. To understand the army's place in the story of filibustering is to render more comprehensible the meaning of filibustering to America's civilians.[7]

To antebellum white males coming of age, filibustering seemed less bizarre than it does to the modern mind. For one thing, longstanding American traditions of geographical and social mobility, heightened by the transportation revolution of the early nineteenth century, facilitated filibustering. Accustomed to

---

[5]Samuel Francis Du Pont to Charles Henry Davis, Sept. 10, 1851, Samuel Francis Du Pont Papers (Hagley Museum and Library, Wilmington, DE); Washington Irving to Charles A. Davy, Sept. 12, 1851, Washington Irving Papers (Alderman Library, University of Virginia, Charlottesville); Samuel Longfellow, ed., *Life of Henry Wadsworth Longfellow, with Extracts from His Journals and Correspondence* (2 vols., Boston, 1886), II, 231; *Harper's Weekly,* Jan. 10, 1857. For one striking example of how the media popularized and the public lionized the filibusters, see "A Visit to General Walker and Suite," *Frank Leslie's Illustrated Newspaper,* June 27, 1857, pp. 56, 55.

[6]William Walker, *The War in Nicaragua* (1860; reprint, Tucson, AZ, 1985), 23; Enclosure in Foxhall A. Parker to William A. Graham, Sept. 25, 1851, Letters Received, Squadron Letters, Records of the Secretary of the Navy, RG 45, microfilm 89, reel 92 (National Archives); Asbury Harpending, *The Great Diamond Hoax and Other Stirring Incidents in the Life of Asbury Harpending,* ed. James H. Wilkins (1915; reprint, Norman, OK, 1958), 5.

[7]Robert W. Coakley, *The Role of Federal Military Forces in Domestic Disorders, 1789–1878* (Washington, D.C., 1988), 25–28, 77–83, 110–19.

changing home and occupation, young American males found it easy to regard filibustering as just another move. The violent traditions and martial spirit of the United States fostered filibustering. . . . [Y]oung Americans could not help but absorb the lessons of their country's history of subjugating and exploiting darker-skinned peoples in the name of progress. Many Americans simply assumed that the superiority of their race and governmental institutions gave them the moral right to filibuster abroad. As one newspaper put it in a lengthy elegy to a young man who died filibustering in Central America:

> Just South of Texas is a Land,
> We call it Nicaragua, and
> Men live there who but little know
> How they should rule. Hence, to o'erthrow
> The tyrant Dolt, brave Walker's cause
> Did win Columbia's warm applause.[8]

. . . But more than history and tradition nudged young American men into filibuster expeditions. The pre–Civil War period brought rapid modernization, immigration, urbanization, and social disorder to the country—an ideal milieu for filibustering. Just as some youths sought identity in a fluid social environment by joining volunteer militia and fire companies or by frequenting taverns or illegal boxing matches, others cast their fate with filibuster companies. Certainly most immigrants-turned-filibusters seem to have regarded their units as a haven from the nativism and job discrimination that pervaded antebellum American municipal life. Filibuster recruiters promised wages, rations, and, sometimes, land, mines, and other riches to gullible enlistees. . . . German, Hungarian, and Irish immigrants played a visible role in filibuster expeditions departing such mid-Atlantic ports as New York City, Philadelphia, and Baltimore.[9]

The appeal of filibustering crossed class lines. Sons of planters, merchants, and prominent politicians joined clerks, apprentices, and immigrants in filibuster invasions. Some college students dropped out of their institutions to participate. A "young man . . . of the senior class left here quite abruptly a week ago and it is supposed that he put out for Cuba," a Princeton student noted at the time of López's last expedition to the island. Filibustering appealed to youthful idealism. A University of Mississippi student contacted the leader of a

---

[8]George W. Pierson, "Mobility," in *The Comparative Approach to American History*, ed. C. Vann Woodward (New York, 1968), 106–20; George R. Taylor, *The Transportation Revolution, 1815–1860* (New York, 1951); Richard Maxwell Brown, *Strain of Violence: Historical Studies of American Violence and Vigilantism* (New York, 1975); W. Eugene Hollon, *Frontier Violence: Another Look* (New York, 1974); Reginald Horsman, *Race and Manifest Destiny: The Origins of Racial Anglo-Saxonism* (Cambridge, MA, 1981), 158–248; Bruce Collins, *White Society in the Antebellum South* (London, 1985), 78–81; *Columbus* [Miss.] *Democrat*, June 6, 1857.

[9]Rowland Berthoff, *An Unsettled People: Social Order and Disorder in American History* (New York, 1971), 177–232; Michael Feldberg, *The Turbulent Era: Riot and Disorder in Jacksonian America* (New York, 1980); Joseph F. Kett, *Rites of Passage: Adolescence in America, 1790 to the Present* (New York, 1977), 39, 87–94; Elliott J. Gorn, *The Manly Art: Bare-Knuckle Fighting in America* (Ithaca, NY, 1986), 129–47.

Cuban filibustering expedition, John A. Quitman, arguing that "a people struggling beneath repression should not only receive the sympathies, but the strong arm of assistance of the republican institutions" of the United States. . . . Though engaged in illegal activity, the filibusters sometimes inspired public adulation, which only fed the illusory fires of chivalry. At times, crowds of well-wishers lined the docks to cheer filibusters off. . . . "We have got almost there and are going filibustering now sure," one filibuster penciled home from a Nicaragua-bound steamer, exultant that his party had managed to evade the authorities in California.[10]

Filibustering, in short, involved a cross section of young American males. Texans and Californians, to be sure, dominated forays into Mexico. Several expeditions designed to protect or expand slavery attracted a high percentage of southerners. John Quitman's planned attack on Cuba was both a response to rumors that Spanish officials might emancipate the island's slaves and an effort to add a new slave state or two to the Union. Walker's cause became a southern crusade after he reestablished slavery in Nicaragua. But to define filibustering as an episode in American regionalism is to obscure the almost infinite variety of reasons that led young men to join expeditions. Unhappy family lives, broken romances, debts, and troubles with the law were as likely to make a filibuster as was proslavery fanaticism. The potential spoils of war attracted filibusters just as they have enticed countless soldiers and sailors through the ages. . . .

Officers and enlisted men in the United States Army, although they often felt the pressures that made filibusters of young American men, were obliged to foil filibustering expeditions. The pre–Civil War army's anti-filibustering mission derived primarily from the Neutrality Act of 1818 and specific instructions from the War Department. Section 8 of the 1818 legislation declared it "lawful for the President of the United States, or such other person as he shall have empowered for that purpose, to employ . . . part of the land or naval forces of the United States . . . for the purpose of preventing the carrying on of any such expedition or enterprise from the territories or jurisdiction of the United States against the territories or dominions of any foreign prince or state, or of any colony, district, or people, with whom the United States are at peace." War Department orders, generally issued in response to reports reaching Washington of pending

---

[10]John T. McMurran, Jr., to Lemuel P. Conner, Sept. 10, 1851, Lemuel Conner Papers (Hill Memorial Library, Louisiana State University, Baton Rouge); A. J. McNeil to Quitman, June 10, 1854, John Quitman Papers (Mississippi Department of Archives and History, Jackson); [M. C. Taylor, ed.], "Col. M. C. Taylor's Diary in Lopez Cardenas Expedition, 1850," *Register of the Kentucky State Historical Society* 19 (Sept. 1921), 79, 80; Marcellus French, "Expedition of the Alamo Rangers," ed. Franklin a Gray Bartlett, *Overland Monthly* 21 (May 1893), 517–23; W. H. Burt to James Wilson, Jr., Oct. 16, 1855, James Wilson, Jr., Papers (New Hampshire Historical Society, Concord).

filibusters or filibusters in progress, regularly reminded high-ranking officers of their anti-filibustering responsibilities.[11]

Accustomed to obeying orders, army officers generally complied with specific anti-filibustering instructions. . . . While some officers genuinely sympathized with the natives of countries attacked by filibusters or worried that filibustering would impair American foreign trade or ignite a war for which the nation was unprepared, more were troubled by convictions that private military expeditions tarnished the honor of the nation that they had dedicated their careers to defend. . . . Ethan Allen Hitchcock, commander of the army's Pacific Division in the early 1850s, brought an especially intense ideological commitment to his anti-filibustering responsibilities. He perceived that illegal expeditions damaged American foreign relations and worried that the expeditions would endanger the Republic by raising anew sectional friction over slavery expansion. . . .[12] Gen. Persifor F. Smith, commanding the department of Texas in November 1855, informed Washington that stationing troops on the border to intercept unlawful expeditions collided with his responsibility to protect interior farmers from Indian attack.[13]

The Crabb expedition to Mexico proved particularly vexatious to the army. In March 1857, former California state senator Henry A. Crabb invaded Sonora with some ninety followers. Although Crabb soon surrendered to Mexican authorities, and although Crabb and his force (other than a sixteen-year-old boy) were then executed, the expedition complicated affairs for United States troops. In August 1857 soldiers from Fort Buchanan, New Mexico Territory, had to be dispatched to investigate the murder of four Americans staying at Sonoita (just

[11]"An Act in Addition to the 'Act for the Punishment of Certain Crimes against the United States,' and to Repeal the Acts Therein Mentioned," *Annals of Congress*, 15 cong., 1 sess., II, April 20, 1818, pp. 2567–70; W. W. Bliss to William Freret and John Walker, May 8, 1851, Letters Sent, Records of the Office of the Secretary of War, RG 107 (National Archives); Charles M. Conrad to David E. Twiggs, April 15, 1852, ibid.; Graham to Twiggs, Aug. 11, 1852, ibid.; U.S. Congress, House, *Correspondence between the Late Secretary of War and General Wool*, House Executive Document 88, Serial Set 956, 35 cong., 1 sess., 1858, p. 6.

[12]Ambrose P. Hill to Thomas Hill, Feb. 4, 1852, Ambrose P. Hill Papers (Virginia Historical Society, Richmond); Francis T. Bryan to William S. Bryan, May 12, 1854, William S. Bryan Papers (Southern Historical Collection, University of North Carolina, Chapel Hill); John R. Hagner to Peter V. Hagner, Aug. 20, 1855, Peter V. Hagner Papers, ibid.; Peter V. Hagner to Aleck Hagner, Jan. 24, 1854, ibid.; Joseph H. La Motte to Ellen La Motte, Dec. 22, 1851, La Motte-Coppinger Papers (Missouri Historical Society, St. Louis); Malcolm Edwards, ed., *The California Diary of General F. D. Townsend* (Los Angeles, 1970), 95; Edward L. Hartz to Samuel Hartz, May 2, 1859 [1860], Edward L. Hartz Papers (Manuscript Division, Library of Congress); John C. Pemberton to Israel Pemberton, June 1, 1850, Pemberton Family Papers (Historical Society of Pennsylvania, Philadelphia); Ethan Allen Hitchcock to Bladen Dulany, Sept. 30, 1853, Letters Received, Squadron Letters, Records of the Secretary of the Navy, microfilm 89, reel 36; W. A. Croffut, ed., *Fifty Years in Camp and Field: Diary of Major-General Ethan Allen Hitchcock, U.S.A.* (New York, 1909), 389–90, 410–11; "The Memoirs of Brigadier-General William Montgomery Gardner," typescript (United States Military Academy Library, West Point, NY).

[13]Persifor R Smith to Lorenzo Thomas, Oct. 17, 1855, enclosed with Jefferson Davis to William L. Marcy, Nov. 9, 1855, Miscellaneous Letters, Records of the Department of State, RG 59, microfilm 179, reel 148 (National Archives).

on the American side of the border of Sonora and what is today Arizona) by Mexican soldiers in revenge for the Crabb affair. Subsequent Mexican reprisals against United States citizens, fueled by rumors that Americans were planning new filibusters into Sonora, caused Secretary of War John B. Floyd to send Capt. Richard S. Ewell, commanding at Fort Buchanan, to call on Sonoran governor Ignacio Pesqueira and lodge a protest. Mexican officials at Hermosillo arrested and imprisoned Ewell. It took the threat of a naval broadside on Guaymas to spring Ewell after four days in custody.[14]

Once it became evident that a filibuster expedition had commenced, [many] army commanders took corrective action. In late May 1855, for instance, upon learning about the imminent departure from New York City of the Henry L. Kinney expedition to Nicaragua, Winfield Scott, commanding general of the army, requested permission from the War Department and President Franklin Pierce to deploy troops from Fort Hamilton on Long Island in New York harbor to interdict Kinney. Later that year the department of Texas issued orders that Captain [Sidney] Burbank deploy forces to prevent [James] Callahan's invasion of Mexico and cut off reinforcements to Callahan from the American side of the Rio Grande.... As Walker's force fled toward the United States—Mexican border near San Diego in the spring of 1854 following the collapse of the filibuster's invasion of Sonora, Gen. John E. Wool dispatched Capt. Justus McKinstry to the boundary to take Walker into federal custody.[15] ...

Since many of the expeditions left United States territory by sea, army officers frequently collaborated with their naval counterparts. Thus in 1851 army and navy officers exchanged information about Jose Maria Jesus Carvajal, who led a mixed force of Mexican and American revolutionaries across the Rio Grande to capture Camargo and attack Matamoros, as part of his project to fashion a Republic of the Sierra Madre. Army officers similarly coordinated efforts with customs officials.... In September 1853, when the United States collector at San Francisco lacked a revenue cutter in port to stop Walker's expedition to Mexico, he turned to General Hitchcock for assistance. Hitchcock seized the *Arrow*, a brig that Walker had chartered for the enterprise, and had it anchored away from the shore in the harbor under the command of Lieutenant George P. Andrews....[16]

---

[14]Edward E. Dunbar to Charles B. Smith, Aug. 27, 1857, U.S. Congress, House, *Execution of Colonel Crabb and Associates*, House Executive Document 64, Serial Set 955, 35 cong., 1 sess., 1858, pp. 58–61; E. D. Townsend to J. V. D. Reeve, Oct. 10, 1859, filed May 12, 1860, Miscellaneous Letters, Records of the Department of State; Farrelly Alden to Lewis Cass, Nov. 26, 1859, Despatches from United States Consuls in Guaymas, Records of the Department of State, microfilm 284, reel 1.

[15]Crist, ed., *Papers of Jefferson Davis*, V, 435; Winfield Scott to Charles Boarman, May 31, 1855, Charles Boarman Letter books (Manuscript Division, Library of Congress); Alfred Gibbs to Burbank, Oct. 7, 1855, enclosed with Jefferson Davis to Marcy, Nov. 9, 1855, Miscellaneous Letters, Records of the Department of State, microfilm 179, reel 148; Buell to Burbank, Oct. 8, 1855, ibid.

[16]K. Jack Bauer, ed., *The New American State Papers: Naval Affairs* (10 vols., Wilmington, 1981), II, 147–48; Charles Platt to Parker, May 29, 1851, Letters Received, Squadron Letters, Records of the Secretary of the Navy, microfilm 89, reel 92; William Smith to Parker, Nov. 18, 1851, ibid.; Dulany to J. C. Dobbin, Oct. 22, 1853, ibid., reel 36; Bliss to Freret and John Walker, May 8, 1851, Letters Sent, Records of the Office of the Secretary of War.

Yet, given the frequency of filibustering expeditions, it would be misleading to argue that the army successfully enforced the Neutrality Act. Part of the difficulty related to the magnitude of the filibustering challenge. If the ports on the Atlantic, Gulf, and Pacific coasts, as well as the Canadian and Mexican boundaries, are conceptualized as the filibuster frontier, it becomes apparent that the army lacked the resources to cope effectually with filibustering. Personnel cuts after the Mexican War left the army with fewer than ten thousand men, hardly the manpower necessary to police all potential filibuster departure points. Congress, in 1855, increased the army's size to 17,867 officers and men—a still inadequate figure. It was especially difficult . . . to seal the Mexican border. Teresa Griffin Viele, married to a first lieutenant stationed at Ringgold Barracks in Texas in 1851–1852, recalled:

> Our government ordered that officers should be stationed with a certain number of men and pieces of artillery all along the river to prevent American citizens from crossing to the Mexican side. . . . This however was . . . almost an impracticable thing on so extensive a line; the most they could achieve was to prevent large armed bodies from crossing. Smaller parties could not be stopped, and it was very easy for these to rendezvous and organize on the other side.

General David E. Twiggs, commanding the department of Texas in July 1858, informed the War Department that his troops would never be able to prevent filibusters from crossing the Rio Grande since virtually every mile of the "stream" was then fordable. Besides the army had other responsibilities to divert it from anti-filibustering efforts. In Texas, most garrisons were customarily stationed in the state's interior, rather than on the Mexican border, as a hedge against Comanche raids on settlements. With some justice, Secretary of State Daniel Webster urged the Mexican government to consider "the vast extent of the frontier" before condemning American authorities for failing to detect filibusters before they crossed the border.[17]

Pro-filibuster public opinion further interfered with army actions against filibustering. When some of López's followers were stranded in Key West following their invasion of Cuba, the local population provided food, shelter, and money for passenger fares to the mainland, even though the filibusters, according to one of López's men, "were expecting daily United States troops to arrive and make them prisoners." Consistent acquittals of filibusters by juries negated several army efforts to repress filibustering. . . .[18]

---

[17]Russell F. Weigley, *History of the United States Army* (New York, 1967), 189–90; Walter Millis, *Arms and Men: A Study of American Military History* (New York, 1956), 109–10; Clarence C. Clendenen, *Blood on the Border: The United States Army and the Mexican Irregulars* (London, 1969), 7, 9, 11; [Teresa Griffin Viele], *"Following the Drum": A Glimpse of Frontier Life* (New York, 1858), 208–9; King to Withers, July 28, 1858, Letters Received, Records of the Adjutant General's Office, microfilm 567, reel 582; Robert E. Lee to Annie Lee, Feb. 22, 1860, Lee Family Papers (Virginia Historical Society); Manning, ed., *Diplomatic Correspondence*, IX, 100, 175.

[18][F. C. M. Boggess], *A Veteran of Four Wars: The Autobiography of F. C. M. Boggess* (Arcadia, 1900), 25–26; Shearer, "Carvajal Disturbances," 227, 229; Edward S. Wallace, *Destiny and Glory* (New York, 1957), 162.

Wavering by authorities in Washington, particularly during the Pierce administration, also impeded effective enforcement of the Neutrality Act. Secretary of War Jefferson Davis helped thwart filibustering to Cuba and approved steps taken by General Smith and Captain Burbank against the Callahan expedition to Mexico. Nevertheless, Davis held latent pro-filibuster sentiments, ultimately exposed in public addresses endorsing William Walker. In April 1854 Davis lashed out at General Wool for being overzealous about stopping filibusters from California to Mexico. . . . The Pierce administration similarly hampered General Scott's efforts against the Kinney expedition. . . .[19]

No army commander encountered more problems with hostile public opinion, uncooperative civil officials, and unclear signals from Washington than did General Hitchcock during his stint in California. After Hitchcock seized Walker's ship at San Francisco, he was advised by the collector of the port and the United States district attorney that the filibusters and their supporters intended to retake the *Arrow* by force and that it would be best to return the vessel if so challenged. Convinced that both officials had become filibuster sympathizers, Hitchcock refused concessions. Tempers flared. Hitchcock noted:

> He [the collector] intimated that he had protected me from the effects of public opinion for having seized the vessel, whereupon I struck my fist down, saying "Damn public opinion!" adding that I would under no circumstances surrender the vessel, and that if any body of men undertook to get possession of her it would be at their peril.

Hitchcock alerted Lieutenant Andrews to expect an attack on the *Arrow*, urging him to hold the *Arrow* if it could be accomplished "without useless bloodshed." Hitchcock's reward for detaining the vessel four days until the district attorney reluctantly agreed to institute legal proceedings was a torrent of abuse by the local newspapers, a local judge, and the United States senator from California, John B. Weller. Hitchcock found himself facing a contempt proceeding in California's superior court and a trespass suit brought against him by Walker for thirty thousand dollars in damages. Furthermore, the district attorney delayed inspecting the *Arrow's* cargo long enough for Walker to transfer his arms to the schooner *Caroline* on which the filibuster departed for Lower California on October 16, 1853. Compounding Hitchcock's filibuster headaches, Weller's fellow senator from California, William Gwin, had the audacity to request that the general provide a "safe conduct" to Henry Crabb (then a California state legislator)

---

[19]Clement Eaton, *Jefferson Davis* (New York, 1977), 99–107; Jefferson Davis endorsement, Nov. 3, 1855, Letters Received, Records of the Adjutant General's Office, microfilm 567, reel 529; Crist, ed., *Papers of Jefferson Davis*, V, 63–64, 88, 291–92; Lynda Lasswell Crist and Mary Seaton Dix, eds., The Papers of Jefferson Davis, vol. VI (Baton Rouge, LA, 1989), 119, 140, 146, 165–66, 166–67n; Dunbar Rowland, ed., *Jefferson Davis, Constitutionalist: His Letters, Papers, and Speeches* (10 vols., Jackson, 1923), II, 374; Hinton, "Military Career of John Ellis Wool," 265–75; Marcus Cunliffe, *Soldiers & Civilians: The Martial Spirit in America, 1775–1865* (New York, 1973), 31–56, 101–11; Cooper to Scott, May 30, June 1, 185 5, Letters Received, Records of the Office of Secretary of War, microfilm 221, reel 175; Scott to Cooper, May 31, 1855, ibid.; James T. Wall, *Manifest Destiny Denied: America's First Intervention in Nicaragua* (Washington, D.C., 1981), 54–57.

so that Crabb could attempt "an independent move on Sonora." Hitchcock again held his ground but began to despair that the burden of preventing filibusters lay on his shoulder alone.

> A pretty thing indeed, that I should be dragooned into giving such a protection to a leading man of a hostile force against Sonora!—and at the solicitation of a senator of the United States! But they have not succeeded. As the matter now stands I am almost alone in this community in opposing the expedition.

Hitchcock hoped that at least Washington approved his position, but he was insecure about the reaction of an administration of announced expansionist proclivities. Hitchcock wrote General Scott that he had given "mortal offence" to all the leading politicians in California and was quite ready to be relieved.[20]

Given this record of the army's sustained efforts to repress filibustering in the face of resistance by the public and inadequate help from federal civil officials, it is tempting to exempt the army from America's filibustering sin. Yet even the army reflected America's filibustering culture. A surprising amount of pro-filibuster sentiment infiltrated the officer corps and enlisted ranks in the pre–Civil War period.

Before the Civil War, army service and filibustering represented competing career options. That young men chose one over the other often had more to do with circumstance than with preference. When Robert Farquharson contacted Quitman in February 1855, he asked if Quitman would let him join his Cuba filibuster force or if Quitman would pull strings to get him a lieutenant colonelcy in one of the army's new regiments. Either alternative would have sufficed. Obviously the army played second fiddle in the case of a new officer posted to Fort Leavenworth in 1858: "Mr. [Secretary of War John B.] Floyd has appointed in our regiment a gentleman from Richmond whose connection with Quitman . . . was well known; in fact the gentleman went to Greytown [Nicaragua] last May but was too late Walker having surrendered." . . .[21]

During the pre–Civil War era, it was by no means clear to young American males aspiring to be soldiers that they would better serve their country or their own interests by joining the army rather than a filibuster cohort. Commissions and promotions were hard to come by in a shrinking army, and peace with foreign nations limited the battlefield experience they might gain to skirmishes

---

[20]Croffut, ed., *Fifty Years in Camp and Field*, 400–403; "Memoirs of Brigadier-General William Montgomery Gardner," 56; Edwards, ed., *California Dairy of General E. D. Townsend*, 91–94; Brown, *Agents of Manifest Destiny*, 192–93. Secretary of War Jefferson Davis endorsed Gen. Ethan Allen Hitchcock's handling of the *Arrow* matter and dispatched Gen. John E. Wool to relieve Hitchcock. Croffut, ed., *Fifty Years in Camp and Field*, 405; Crist, ed., *Papers of Jefferson Davis*, V, 274. The contempt complaint against Hitchcock was dropped on November 8. Brown, *Agents of Manifest Destiny*, 193.

[21]Robert Farquharson to Quitman, Feb. 7, 1855, John Quitman Papers (Houghton Library, Harvard University); George Washington Hazzard to J. D. Howland, Jan. 25, 1858, George Washington Hazzard Papers (United States Military Academy Library); Crist, ed., *Papers of Jefferson Davis*, V, 402.

against native Americans on the Plains. Small-scale engagements in isolated western regions held little promise for fame or glory. But filibuster commanders such as Walker and Quitman presented themselves as professional soldiers and urged that their ventures be considered as alternatives to army service, while filibuster exploits attracted front-page headlines. Filibuster leaders and recruiters emphasized the possibilities for advancement awaiting filibuster personnel, sometimes pegging pay and rations precisely to army scales. "How would you like to go to Cuba?" one discharged American officer who had fought in Mexico wrote another about a year after hostilities terminated. "There is an expedition on foot and if you will go—just say the word. The inducements are, aside from the glory—two grades higher than you go out; I am authorized to offer you a first Lieutenantcy with two grades higher in the Army of the new Republic—Pay & emoluments same as the Army of the United States." Many men responded instinctively to such incentives. New Yorker Elijah D. Taft, for instance, solicited an officer's slot with Walker, explaining, "I have been fifteen years in commission in the Militia of this State . . . and as I have made that arm of the service my constant study for some years I should like to put in practice in Nicaragua the benefit of these years of study." Filibustering had a similar appeal to graduates of private military academies. Pre–Civil War males who joined the army rather than filibuster expeditions, therefore, may well have previously given filibustering serious consideration. . . .[22]

America's soldiers shared civilian ideologies of Anglo-American racial superiority and Manifest Destiny. Capt. Joseph H. La Motte reported from Ringgold Barracks that much was being said around the post about "the indomitable energy & perseverance of the Saxon race." Lieutenant Theodore Talbot announced, "Our 'Manifest destiny' bids fair for fulfillment." Cognizant of the army's conquests in the recent Mexican War, many officers anticipated additional territorial quests ahead. Even before the war ended, Gen. William Jenkins Worth earned press notice for wanting the annexation of Cuba and Central America. . . . William Tecumseh Sherman must have been sensitive to filibustering's immorality since he wrote that he favored the acquisition of Cuba by "fair means." Yet, he also confessed revealingly that the island promised such benefit to his country that he sometimes found himself hoping that the filibusters would succeed in conquering the Spanish colony.[23]

---

[22]Quitman to Alexander K. McClung, Feb. 4, 185 5, John Quitman Papers (Houghton Library); Isaac H. Trahue to Quitman, July 1, 1854, ibid.; Slotkin, *Fatal Environment*, 256; Brown, *Agents of Manifest Destiny*, 49; Earl W. Fornell, "Texans and Filibusters in the 1850's," *Southwestern Historical Quarterly* 59 (April 1956), 418; John S. Slocum to Albert Tracy, June 27, 1849, Albert Tracy Papers (Manuscript Section, New York Public Library, New York, NY); Elijah D. Taft to George B. Hall, Feb. 12, 1856, Appleton Oaksmith Papers (Perkins Library); *Columbus* [Miss.] *Democrat*, June 6, 1857.

[23]Joseph H. La Motte to Ellen La Motte, Dec. 22, 1851, La Motte-Coppingen Papers; Robert V. Hine and Savoie Lottinville, eds., *Soldier in the West: Letters of Theodore Talbot during his Service in California, Mexico, and Oregon, 1848–53* (Norman, 1972), 161; *New Orleans Daily Picayune*, Jan. 27, 1848; Reginald C. Stuart, *United States Expansionism and British North America, 1775–1871* (Chapel Hill, NC, 1988), 234; William Tecumseh Sherman to his brother, May 6, 1851, Oct. 22, 1852, William T. Sherman Papers (Ohio Historical Society, Columbus).

Nowhere in the army establishment was there more satisfaction about the Mexican War than at the United States Military Academy at West Point. Before the conflict with Mexico, the institution had been subjected to severe civilian criticism. Antagonists contended that the academy engendered aristocracy, that free education at the public's expense was unconstitutional, and that the education was wasted because so many graduates left the military for more remunerative employment in the private sector. Several state legislatures passed resolutions calling for the institution's abolition. However, West Pointers came into their own in the Mexican War, achieving so much recognition that their fame all but eliminated the movement to terminate the academy.[24]

Mexican War legend helped mold West Point into a breeding ground for Manifest Destiny apostles. While some cadets and officers at the Point found talk of further expansion repulsive, many coveted more territory for their country. If it took war to effect such growth, so much the better because war would provide opportunities for promotion and fame. . . . On July 4, 1855, Cadet Guilford D. Bailey of New York made territorial expansion the focus of his Independence Day oration. Fellow cadet James H. Wilson noted in disgust, "Mr Cadet Bailey delivered the oration it was nothing but a piece of bombast . . . he is in favor of taking Cuba by force."[25]

From Manifest Destiny West Pointers had to make only a short ideological jump to filibuster destiny. In his July 4, 1859, oration, first classman William W. McCreery expressed his hope that the United States take Cuba by a "fair fight" rather than by filibuster. But he was also quick to reject assertions that "the American filibuster" was a "ruthless pirate" and to explain that most filibusters were simply hotheaded romantics of "generous" intent. . . . And, once graduated, West Pointers found little cause to put filibuster emotions behind them. "[James E.] Slaughter is here, the 2 Lieutenant of the Company," Ambrose Hill reported home from the Texas frontier in 1852. "He is . . . a terrible Filibuster." Teresa Viele recalled that many of the officers stationed with her husband at Ringgold Barracks felt a conflict between pro-filibuster private feelings and their army obligations. When she once alerted some filibusters as to the whereabouts of an army patrol on their track, the officers merely "winked" at her behavior.[26]

For southerners in the army, a sectionalist imperative reinforced filibuster inclinations. While some southern army officers shed their sectional mentality

[24]Stephen E. Ambrose, *Duty, Honor, Country: A History of West Point* (Baltimore, 1966), 106–46; Cunliffe, *Soldiers & Civilians*, 172–75; Ambrose P. Hill to Thomas and Fannie Hill, March 16, 1847, Hill Papers.

[25]James Harrison Wilson Diary, July 4, 1855 (Historical Society of Delaware, Wilmington); Cyrus B. Comstock Diary, June 6, 1854, Elizabeth Comstock Papers (State Historical Society of Wisconsin, Area Research Center, Lacrosse). An extract from a typed copy of the diary was provided me by Professor William Skelton, University of Wisconsin, Stevens Point.

[26]"An Address Delivered by Cadet W. W. McCreery of the First Class, to the Corps of Cadets of the U.S. Military Academy, West Point, N.Y., on 4th July, 1859" (United States Military Academy Library); Ambrose P. Hill to Thomas Hill, Feb. 4, 1852, Hill Papers; [Viele], *"Following the Drum,"* 208, 211.

through the process of serving their nation, others clung tightly to their regional affiliation. Army captain Thomas Claiborne told fellow Tennessean John Overton that he hoped that "our people" would "go to work & help Bill Walker" and advised Overton to "help the good cause" while mentioning his own regret at not being in a position to do something tangible for Walker himself. Should Walker maintain his position in Nicaragua, Claiborne asserted, it would "ensure the integrity of the whole South." Similarly, South Carolina native James Longstreet thought filibustering might help Chihuahua secede from Mexico so that it might become a slave state. . . .[27]

Given the empathy for filibustering within the army, it is not surprising that some army officers ignored the spirit of their orders and provided filibusters with aid and comfort. When a group of destitute, returning Cuba filibusters arrived at Charlotte Harbor on Florida's west coast in 1850, they were pleasantly surprised by the hospitality provided by an army captain, who landed there with a group of soldiers shortly afterwards. The officer drank with them, sympathized with their cause, informed them that he expected orders for their arrest, and intimated that they should depart so that he would not have to commit such a "repugnant" act. The filibusters took this advice and traveled to Tampa, where they encountered another congenial officer, General Twiggs, then at Fort Brooke. "I called this morning to see Gen. Twig, and found him very talkative," one of the filibusters noted in his diary. Twiggs told the filibusters that their decision to flee Cuba was premature, provided them with three days' rations, and advised them to leave town before he would be forced to arrest them. A year later, Twiggs's lethargic response to the planned departure of López's ship, the *Pampero*, from New Orleans helped enable López to launch his final, and fatal, Cuban expedition.[28]

At times, army officers and enlisted men acted out their expansionist fantasies by joining expeditions. The process began in the waning days of the Mexican War, as thousands of young volunteers were mustered out of the service while their officers pondered restricted promotion opportunities for the indefinite future. The thoughts of some soldiers turned to the Mexican state of Yucatán (which had seceded from Mexico in 1846 and been neutral during the Mexican War) and Cuba. In Yucatán, warfare had broken out between the white governing class and native Mayan Indians. Yucatán whites established contact with American military personnel in Mexico. Meanwhile the Havana Club, a Cuban organization dedicated to replacing Spanish rule with incorporation into the United States, sent an agent to Mexico to contact Gen. William J. Worth. Meeting with Worth in Jalapa, the Cuban

[27]K. Jack Bauer, *Zachary Taylor: Soldier, Planter, Statesman of the Old Southwest* (Baton Rouge, 1985), 289–90; Thomas Claiborne to John Overton, n.d., enclosed with Annie Claiborne to her sister, Feb. 5, 1857, Thomas Claiborne Papers (Southern Historical Collection); James Longstreet to William Porcher Miles, Feb. 27, 1860, William Porcher Miles Papers, ibid. John Overton took Thomas Claiborne's advice to heart and threw a dinner for Walker in 1858 following the filibuster's return from his second Nicaraguan expedition. John Berrien Lindsley Diary, Feb. 11, 1858, Lindsley Family Papers (Tennessee State Library and Archives, Nashville, TN).

[28][Boggess], *Veteran of Four Wars*, 26–27; [Taylor], ed., "Col. M. C. Taylor's Diary," 87; Rauch, *American Interest in Cuba*, 160.

agent offered $3 million in return for Worth's recruiting a filibuster army of five thousand troops to invade the island and crush its Spanish garrison....[29]

By late May 1848, American army circles in Mexico City were buzzing with filibuster rumors. "There are officers in the city of Mexico trying to raise companies to go to Yucatán," noted one American soldier in his journal. The *Daily American Star*, the American organ in Mexico City, reported that some American soldiers had already enrolled in the Yucatán filibuster force and that the filibusters were hoping to recruit a party of four to five hundred men. Soldiers who wanted to "spend the summer in a delightful country, rather than return to their homes in the dull season" were advised to drop by the Star office for enlistment information. Filibuster plots persisted into early June, though there seems to have been confusion over whether the destination would be Yucatán or Cuba....[30]

In the war's aftermath, however, officers and enlisted men continued to demonstrate interest in Cuba filibusters. Lieutenant William L. Crittenden resigned his commission in March 1849, served briefly in the New Orleans customhouse, and then met his death as a battalion commander during López's final expedition to Cuba in August 1851.... Meanwhile, American soldiers did filibuster in Yucatán. Two lieutenants in the army's Thirteenth Infantry Regiment, Joseph A. White and David G. Wilds, accepted commissions in the Yucatán service. They recruited over five hundred discharged soldiers at $8 per month plus a 320-acre land bonus. The volunteers sailed from New Orleans in December 1848, spent a couple of months in inconclusive counter-guerrilla warfare against the Mayas, suffered casualties, and never received the expected remuneration. Most of the survivors returned to the Crescent City in March 1849.[31]

When John Quitman succeeded López as commander of the Cuba filibusters, the connection between the army and filibustering became even more pronounced. One of the nation's most successful generals in the Mexican War, Quitman had earned a reservoir of respect from the army's regular officer corps, even though he served as a volunteer for most of the war and was mustered out of the service at the end of the conflict. Filibusters anticipated that once Quitman joined their ranks, the cream of the United States Army would flock to his standard. Quitman accepted a commission from the Cuban Junta, an organization of Cuban exiles, in August 1853. Subsequently, some of Quitman's favorite wartime comrades, including officers still in the regular army, flocked to the filibuster standard.

[29]Brown, *Agents of Manifest Destiny*, 33–34; Rauch, *American Interest in Cuba*, 75–76; Mary W. Williams, "Secessionist Diplomacy of Yucatán," *Hispanic American Historical Review* 9 (May 1929), 133–43. Basil Rauch speculates that the Cubans selected William Jenkins Worth because he had recently quarreled with his superior—Gen. Winfield Scott. Worth had even been temporarily under military arrest. Rauch, *American Interest in Cuba*, 75.

[30]Manning, ed., *Diplomatic Correspondence*, XI, 439–40, 53, 59; Philip S. Foner, *A History of Cuba and Its Relations with the United States* (2 vols., New York, 1962–1963), II, 42–43; Lewis Pinckney Jones, "Carolinians and Cubans: The Elliotts and Gonzales, Their Work and Their Writings" (PhD diss., University of North Carolina, 1952), Part I, 32–33, 81–83.

[31]Foner, *History of Cuba*, II, 58; George Washington Cullum, *Biographical Register of the Officers and Graduates of the US. Military Academy from 1802 to 1867* (2 vols., New York, 1868), II, 139; Brown, *Agents of Manifest Destiny*, 33–38. *Washington Daily National Intelligencer*, March 24, 1849, p. 3.

Cadmus M. Wilcox, assistant instructor of military tactics at West Point, who had fought with Quitman at Chapultepec, requested seventy days' leave to reconnoiter Cuba on Quitman's behalf and gave serious thought to resigning his commission and becoming a filibuster. "I look on Cuba as our future field of glory & usefulness & am almost disposed to wait no longer but to turn Phillibuster at once" he wrote to Quitman in May 1854. "I would like to hear from you on Cuba matters . . . I really think that we ought not to buy it. The sooner we take it the better." Wilcox retained his commission, but others proved bolder. Lt. Gustavus Woodson Smith, a West Point graduate who had been brevetted a captain for his Mexican War accomplishments, was an assistant professor of engineering at the military academy. Upset over poor promotion prospects, Smith also found teaching excruciatingly boring and frustrating: "Nothing of consequence doing here. Quiet, dull, & stupid. Cadets ignorant, & ill natured—resenting, as an affront not to be submitted to, any attempt to teach them. Ain't they going to graduate in 6 weeks." On December 18, 1854, Smith resigned his commission to join Quitman's staff. That very day, Captain Mansfield Lovell, a classmate of Smith's at West Point who had been Quitman's aide-de-camp for part of the war, took the same step.[32]

Only two months separated the cancellation of Quitman's Cuba project in March 1855 and the launching of William Walker's Nicaragua enterprise. For some restless souls in the army, the temptation of an apparently successful filibuster expedition proved irresistible. Nicaragua enticed adventure-craving cadets at the military academy like George D. Bayard. In April 1856, two months prior to his scheduled graduation, Bayard alerted his mother that he might not give active service much of a chance before turning filibuster. His letter beautifully expresses the filibuster impulse within army circles.

> Several of us talk of going to Nicaragua. If I am not pleased with my Corps I think I will probably resign & go there. I could easily obtain a Captains commission & there is a good opening. Walker is greatly in want of scientific men & then he will want especially in organizing his ordnance and artillery. With that commission one or two campaigns there would be more pleasant than Indian fighting in New Mexico & the probabilities are that some thing would "turn up" there & in our Army there is no hope of anything of that kind. Even should I not be pleased with the life there I could resign & return benefited at least by military experience which would come in play in the event of a war, in the mean time devoting my attention to Law. This however is the worst side of the picture for I think in Nicaragua to a young man of energy & talent, "there is no such word as *fail*." Besides the opportunity of distinguishing myself there would be fine opportunities for making a fortune. It is a fine country & wealthy Gold mines have already been discovered. What do you say to Nicaragua?

[32]Robert E. May, *John A. Quitman: Old South Crusader* (Baton Rouge, LA, 1985), 181–82; John Henderson to John A. Quitman, July 2, 1850, Quitman Papers (Mississippi Archives); Cadmus M. Wilcox to John A. Quitman, May 8, 1854, ibid.; G. W. Smith to C. A. L. Lamar, Feb. 21, 1855, ibid.; J. W. McDonald to G. W. Smith, March 13, 1855, ibid.; Harry Maury to G. W. Smith, March 23, 1855, ibid.; J. E. H. Claiborne, *Life and Correspondence of John A. Quitman* (2 vols., New York, 1860), II, 389–90; John A. Quitman to F. Henry Quitman, Feb. 19, 1855, John Quitman Papers (Historical Society of Pennsylvania); Cullum, *Biographical Register*, II, 45, 46.

Bayard graduated and stuck things out in the service. But other soldiers took the step that Bayard had only contemplated. When naval commodore Hiram Paulding evacuated destitute filibusters from Central America in 1857 after the collapse of Walker's regime, he noted that a filibuster colonel was "late an officer in the U.S. Army." Half a year later, when Paulding forced Walker's surrender at Punta Arenas following the filibuster's reinvasion of Nicaragua, he took into custody the Mexican War hero Thomas Henry, who had served in the regular army until October 1855, as well as other former United States army soldiers. In lodging a complaint with President James Buchanan about Paulding's interference, Walker noted that some of the men apprehended had at one time "led your soldiers across the continent. . . ."[33]

. . . [Once] Walker arrive[d] on American soil in . . . [1857] he started to organize men and materiel for a return to Nicaragua. That summer and fall, four former Mexican War officers and future Civil War generals—Johnson Kelly Duncan . . ., George B. McClellan (who had resigned his lieutenancy in January 1857 and become chief engineer of the Illinois Central Railroad), Gustavus Smith, and Lovell—corresponded about joining Walker and rescuing the tropics from the "mongrel occupants" who stood in the way of the area's regeneration. "The fact is Mac," Duncan urged McClellan, "if we don't embrace some chance like this, our day and generation will pass amidst the quiets of peace, . . . our lives will be devoted to the accumulation of dollars and cents." Duncan suggested that McClellan might become Walker's highest-ranking subordinate and that the army group might even take control of the movement if Walker faltered. It is difficult to determine how many other army officers were making plans to accompany Walker's next filibuster. One of Walker's principal organizers reported, "We shall have a much better class of men in the next expedition already we have one major, four captains, and eight Lieutenants all in good standing now in the United States army who hold themselves ready to resign and march when the order is given to move." The Duncan-McClellan-Smith-Lovell coterie dropped out of the scheme prior to Walker's departure in November, to the relief of another future Civil War notable, Lieutenant Colonel Joseph Johnston. Johnston had been kept posted on his compeers' preliminary planning but had concluded that Walker was no better than a "robber."[34]

---

[33]George D. Bayard to Jane Dashiell Bayard, April 20, 1856, Bayard Papers; Hiram Paulding to Isaac Toucey, June 28, 1857, Letters Received, Squadron Letters, Records of the Secretary of the Navy, microfilm 89, reel 97; New York Times, Jan. 7, 1858, p. 2; K. Jack Bauer, The Mexican War: 1846–1848 (New York, 1974), 267; Heitman, Historical Register and Dictionary of the United States Army, I, 524; Brown, Agents of Manifest Destiny, 415; Don Russell, ed., Five Years a Dragoon ('49 to '54) And Other Adventures on the Great Plains by Percival G. Lowe (Norman, OK, 1965), 117, 118.

[34]Stephen W. Sears, George B. McClellan: The Young Napoleon (New York, 1988), 49–50, 52–53; C. J. Macdonald to Amy Morris Bradley, July 8, 1857, Amy Morris Bradley Papers (Perkins Library); Heitman, Historical Register and Dictionary of the United States Army, I, 388; William Walker to Johnson Kelly Duncan, Feb. 1, 1858, William Walker Miscellaneous Manuscripts (Historical Society of Pennsylvania).

No sooner had the Duncan group turned away from Walker than it trained its sights on Mexico. In early 1858, Lovell and Johnston negotiated with Mexican Liberals about inserting four thousand American filibusters into the Mexican civil war on the Liberals' side. McClellan, promised a leading role in the force, became excited about the prospects of military service "in a righteous cause & with fair prospect of distinction." The project fell through that February due to Mexican suspicions of the plotters' intent. . . .[35]

Without the interruption of the Civil War, army involvement in filibuster machinations would most likely have persisted indefinitely. Perhaps it would have escalated. Even after the conflict, officers and enlisted men continued to make an occasional contribution to filibustering, either through involvement in expeditions or through lax enforcement of legislation. The difference was that the age of Manifest Destiny had dissolved into new forms of expansion, and filibustering itself had a greatly reduced hold on the American scene.[36]

---

[35]John S. Thrasher to Quitman, Feb. 19, 1858, Quitman Papers (Mississippi Department of Archives and History); Sears, *George B. McClellan*, 55–57; Gilbert E. Govan and James W. Livingood, *A Different Valor. The Story of General Joseph E. Johnston, C.S.A.* (Indianapolis, 1956), 23–26.

[36]Stuart, *United States Expansionism*, 248; Richard H. Bradford, *The Virginius Affair* (Boulder, 1980), 11; Andrew F. Rolle, "Futile Filibustering to Baja California, 1888–1890," *Pacific Historical Review* 20 (May 1951), 163; Peter Gerhard, "The Socialist Invasion of Baja California, 1911," ibid., 15 (Sept. 1946), 297, 304; Robert Wooster, "The Army and the Politics of Expansion: Texas and the Southwestern Borderlands, 1870–1886," *Southwestern Historical Quarterly* 93 (Oct. 1989), 151–67.

Robert May

I am a historian of the nineteenth-century United States, with a particular interest in the nation's territorial expansion. I've spent my entire career at Purdue University, where I've been especially active in departmental, college, and university honors programs. Although I can't pinpoint what first interested me in history, from the time I was a boy I liked reading biographies and visiting historic sites (like the Thomas Paine house in my hometown of New Rochelle, New York). What I never would have dreamed, as a boy, was that one day I would be teaching college courses in Southern history and American military history. No one in my immediate family had a military background, and I spent my entire childhood and college years in the urban North. Maybe I was attracted to Southern and military history because they seemed so exotic to me. The subject of one of my books, John A. Quitman, not only owned plantations and slaves, but also went off to fight in the Texas Revolution without telling his wife and organized a private military (or "filibustering") invasion of a foreign country. I can't imagine doing such things. Understanding the unfamiliar is what most fascinates me about history. In recent years, I have become absorbed with filibustering, the subject of this article, and how such illegal invasions affected US politics, foreign relations, culture, and the Civil War. After writing this article for the *Journal of American History*, I wrote a book about filibustering titled *Manifest Destiny's Underworld*.

QUESTIONS FOR CONSIDERATION

1. According to May, why should historians consider filibustering more than one of the "sideshows of America's pre–Civil War drama"?
2. What social factors stimulated filibustering in the first half of the nineteenth century. Describe at least three.
3. The US military had a conflicted relationship with filibustering; some supported filibustering, some were adamantly against it. Characterize both sides of the argument.
4. May claims that filibustering attracted both civilians and soldiers for reasons tied to social context. Describe at least three contextual factors that made filibustering attractive to civilians in the mid-1850s. To what extent were these factors the same for members of the military?

CHAPTER FOURTEEN

✌

The Two Faces of Republicanism: Gender and Proslavery Politics in Antebellum South Carolina[1]

Stephanie McCurry

The history of republican political ideology and culture in the antebellum South may seem a long way from the concerns of contemporary theorists, but it is not so far, perhaps, as it appears at first glance. After all, theories of government and citizenship, in modern republics as in ancient ones, have been grounded in assumptions about the relation of public and private spheres, or civic sphere and household. In Aristotle's Politics, for example, according to Jurgen Habermas, "Status in the *polis* was . . . based upon status as the unlimited master of an *oikos*. Moveable wealth and control over labor power were no substitute for being the master of a household and of a family."[2]

In the antebellum South, where the defense of domestic institutions and relations were matters of the utmost political significance, one finds even more compelling reason to eschew conventional historiographical boundaries, and particularly those that separate the public from the private sphere and the history of women and gender relations from that of "high" politics. In the Old South, "high" politics was the politics of the household, and all relations of power in

---

[1]Interested students are encouraged to read this essay in the original form. Stephanie McCurry, "The Two Faces of Republicanism: Gender and Proslavery Politics in Antebellum South Carolina," *Journal of American History* 78 (4) (March 1992), 1245–64.

[2]Jurgen Habermas, *The Structural Transformation of the Public Sphere: An Inquiry into a Category of Bourgeois Society*, trans. Thomas Burger and Frederick Lawrence (Cambridge, MA, 1989), 3. J. G. A. Pocock makes the same point in *The Machiavellian Moment: Florentine Political Thought and the Atlantic Republican Tradition* (Princeton, 1975), 68. Some of these themes have been pursued by Hannah Pitkin, *Fortune is a Woman: Gender and Politics in the Thought of Niccolò Machiavelli* (Berkeley, 1984); and Carol Pateman, *The Sexual Contract* (Stanford, 1988), esp. x. The debate over the republican or liberal character of nineteenth-century American political ideology rages on; for the briefest introduction, see Drew McCoy, *The Elusive Republic: Political Economy in Jeffersonian Virginia* (Chapel Hill, 1980); Joyce Appleby, *Capitalism and a New Social Order: The Republican Vision of the 1790s* (New York, 1984); and Lance Banning, "Jeffersonian Ideology Revisited: Liberal and Classical Ideas in the New American Republic," *William and Mary Quarterly* 43 (Jan. 1986), 3–19.

what we would call the "private sphere," including those of men and women, were inevitably politicized. Indeed, the gender and class relations contained in southern households were the distinctive social conditions to which proslavery politicians pointed as permitting the South, and the South alone, to retain the proper political arrangements of republican government.

The slave South was commonly represented as the last republic loyal to the principle of government by an exclusive citizen body of independent and equal men. However inadvertently, that portrait revealed the two faces of republicanism in the antebellum South. The first gazed outward on the public sphere and countenanced a purportedly egalitarian community of enfranchised men. This is the familiar face of slavery republicanism privileged by antebellum politicians and, for the most part, by historians. But to view the political edifice solely from that perspective is to remain captive to the designs of its proslavery architects. For southern men, like other republicans, established their independence and status as citizens in the public sphere through the command of dependents in their households. The modern slave republic was defined above all else, as its defenders never tired of saying, by the boundary that separated the independent and enfranchised minority from the majority of dependent and excluded others. Republicanism had another, more conservative face that gazed inward on the private sphere and countenanced inequality and relations of power between masters and their dependents: slaves, women, and children.

Any assessment of antebellum southern political culture, and especially of the yeoman-planter relations on which it hinged, must confront the republican edifice whole. This broader perspective is most pressing with respect to the politics of the yeoman majority. As independent proprietors, yeoman farmers were (and knew themselves to be) empowered by the exclusionary boundaries of the public sphere. Their republicanism, no less than that of the planters, was centrally configured around the politics of the household and around the public meaning of domestic dependencies.[3]

The South Carolina low country, from which much of the material in this essay is drawn, provides a dramatic case in point. Nowhere did proslavery republicanism find more momentous expression; and nowhere was its social basis more starkly displayed in ways that confound a conventional focus on the public sphere in the interpretation of the yeomanry's politics. In that coastal region of vast rice and cotton plantations, where in 1860 more than seven of every ten people were black and enslaved, social and political inequality reached staggering proportions. Not only was the great majority of the population—slaves and

---

[3]On the household as the constituent unit of antebellum southern society and the locus of gender relations, see Elizabeth Fox-Genovese, "Antebellum Southern Households: A New Perspective on a Familiar Question," *Review* 7 (Fall 1983), 215–53; Elizabeth Fox-Genovese, *Within the Plantation Household: Black and White Women of the Old South* (Chapel Hill, 1988), esp. 37–99; Steven Hahn, *The Roots of Southern Populism: Yeoman Farmers and the Transformation of the Georgia Upcountry, 1850–1890* (New York, 1983); and Stephanie McCurry, "The Politics of Yeoman Households in Antebellum South Carolina," in *Divided House: Gender and the Civil War*, ed. Catherine Clinton and Nina Silber (New York, forthcoming).

women—propertyless and disfranchised, and the political culture thereby defined primarily in terms of whom it excluded; but the concentration of wealth in land and slaves was so advanced (the top 10 percent of property holders owned more than 70 percent of the real wealth in one mainland parish) that it gave decisive shape to relations between yeomen and planters as well as between masters and slaves. Even in the aristocratic low country, yeoman farmers constituted the majority of the white population, and their relations with planters formed a crucial dimension of political life.[4]

Social inequality was not comfortably confined to black and white and limited to the private sphere, as those who define slave society primarily in terms of race would argue. White society in the slave South was not a "herrenvolk" or racial "democracy," to use George Fredrickson's much-adopted term, that bound white, mostly propertied men in relations of rough equality.[5] Rather inequality and relations of power took many forms in the South Carolina low country and indeed all over the black belt South where similar social patterns prevailed.[6] They not only gave definitive shape to the public sphere but permeated its boundaries and infused its culture. To confront that pervasive inequality is to raise searching

---

[4]For the statistics on race, see *Eighth Census of the United States, 1860* (Washington, 1864), 1, 452; on wealth, see Federal Manuscript Census, South Carolina, Beaufort District, [St. Peter's Parish], Schedule of Population, 1860, Records of the Bureau of the Census, RG 29 (National Archives); and on the yeomanry as the white majority, see Federal Manuscript Census, South Carolina, Beaufort District, [St. Peter's Parish], Schedules of Population, Agriculture, and Slaves, 1860, Records of the Bureau of the Census, RG 29 (National Archives). These statistics are discussed at greater length in Stephanie McCurry, "Defense of Their World: Gender, Class, and the Yeomanry of the South Carolina Low Country, 1820–1860" (PhD diss., State University of New York at Binghamton, 1988), esp. 46, 58, 54.

[5]George Fredrickson, *The Black Image in the White Mind: The Debate on Afro-American Character and Destiny, 1817–1914* (New York, 1971), esp. 61. Frederickson introduced this term to southern history, where it quickly gained currency. Its adherents, from the liberal and republican camps, are united by a shared assumption that slavery is a system of racial, as opposed to class, relations and that race marks the primary social division of the Old South. In addition to Frederickson, the liberalism school includes James Oakes, *The Ruling Race. A History of American Slaveholders* (New York, 1982); the "republicanism" school includes J. Mills Thornton III, *Politics and Power in a Slave Society: Alabama, 1800–1860* (Baton Rouge, 1978); J. William Harris, *Plain Folk and Gentry in a Slave Society: White Liberty and Black Slavery in Augusta's Hinterlands* (Middletown, 1985); and Lacy K. Ford, Jr., *Origins of Southern Radicalism: The South Carolina Upcountry, 1800–1860* (New York, 1988). Class analyses include Eugene D. Genovese, *The Political Economy of Slavery: Studies in the Economy and Society of the Slave South* (New York, 1965); Eugene D. Genovese, *Roll, Jordan, Roll: The World the Slaves Made* (New York, 1974); Eugene D. Genovese, "Yeoman Farmers in a Slaveholders Democracy," *Agricultural History*, 49 (April 1975), 331–42; and Steven Hahn, *The Roots of Southern Populism*.

[6]In the Alabama black belt, for example, the top tenth of household heads owned more than 60 percent of the wealth in 1860, and in the South Carolina up-country (the heart of the cotton South), it reached 55 percent by 1850 and increased markedly by 1860. William L. Barney, "Toward the Civil War: The Dynamics of Change in a Black Belt County," in *Class, Conflict, and Consensus: Antebellum Southern Community Studies*, ed. Orville Vernon Burton and Robert C. McMath, Jr. (Westport, 1982), 147–51; Ford, *Origins of Southern Radicalism*, 50, 262; Gavin Wright, *Political Economy of the Cotton South: Households, Markets, and Wealth in the Nineteenth Century* (New York, 1978), 29–36; and Randolph F. Campbell, *A Southern Community in Crisis: Harrison County, Texas, 1850–1880* (Austin, 1983), 15–73.

questions about such interpretations as those of Fredrickson and others that locate the yeomanry's politics and commitment to the slave regime in the purportedly egalitarian public sphere of the slave republic and the "democratic" culture and ideology it engendered. To confront the relations of power in yeoman households, including gender relations, and the political privileges to which they entitled male household heads is to reveal a yeoman republicanism rather more complicated and rather less distinctly egalitarian and "democratic." And it is to offer an interpretation that comports more with the manifest social and political inequality of the black belt South. Yeomen in the low country knew, better than their up-country peers, that the slave republic was defined by its exclusionary boundaries. But the patterns revealed in the low country speak nonetheless to a characteristic of republican political culture all over the South. . . .

Republican and proslavery politics already had a long and intimate relationship in South Carolina by the beginning of the antebellum period. Indeed, the vision of the slave republic around which sectional consciousness cohered in the early 1830s had been taking shape in political struggle within the state at least since the constitutional reforms of 1808, and, more alarmingly and visibly, in congressional debate over slavery in the Missouri controversy.[7] But the crucial moment was the nullification crisis; then, in the midst of the state's greatest religious revival, South Carolina's antebellum political culture and ideology was forged.

As fire-eater politicians (not a few of whom were, like Robert Barnwell Rhett, newly born again) met the challenge of an unprecedented political mobilization, they embraced the language of evangelicalism, and with it the faith of its primarily yeoman congregants.[8] Evangelicalism and popular politics were thereafter indissociable in South Carolina. As the ideological work of slavery took on new urgency in those years, so proslavery arguments, infused with evangelical references, acquired the discursive shape that they would maintain until the Civil War. While fire-eaters and moderates would continue to contest the particular political uses of proslavery ideology right down to the successful secession

---

[7]Mark D. Kaplanoff, "Charles Pinckney and the American Republican Tradition," in *Intellectual Life in Ante- bellum Charleston,* ed. Michael O'Brien and David Moltke-Hansen (Knoxville, 1986), 85–122; Rachel N. Klein, *Unification of a Slave State: The Rise of the Planter Class in the South Carolina Backcountry, 1760–1808* (Chapel Hill, 1990), esp. 238–68; and Mark D. Kaplanoff, "Making the South Solid: Politics and the Structure of Society in South Carolina, 1790–1815" (PhD diss., Cambridge University, 1979), esp. 265.

[8]James Petigru Carson, ed., *Life, Letters, and Speeches of James Louis Petigru, the Union Man of South Carolina* (Washington, 1920), 85–86, 103–4, 128–29; William Mumford Baker, *The Life and Labours of the Reverend Daniel Baker . . . Prepared by his Son* (1858; reprint, Louisville, 1961), 133, 155–57, 160–66, 180; William John Grayson, "The Autobiography of William John Grayson," ed. Samuel Gaillard Stoney, *South Carolina Historical and Genealogical Magazine* 49 (Jan. 1948), 33–40. Robert Barnwell Rhett's conversion is noted in Baker, Life of Baker, 188–89. Beech Branch Baptist Church, Beaufort District, Church Book, Sept. 2, 1833, in Baptist Church, Hampton County, Beech Branch, Records, 1814–1918 (South Caroliniana Library, Columbia, SC); William W. Freehling, *Prelude to Civil War. The Nullification Controversy in South Carolina, 1816–1836* (New York, 1965), 73–74.

campaign of 1860, the representation of the Christian slave republic, forged in the fires of nullification, was beyond contestation. Proslavery republicanism had become the state religion. In 1852, in the tense aftermath of the first secession crisis, James Henley Thornwell, minister of the First Presbyterian Church of Columbia and the state's leading Presbyterian spokesman, looked back with satisfaction on the state's struggle for a self-conscious and self-confident sectional identity. The world's condemnation of slavery, he recalled, had forced southerners into a consideration of "the nature and organization of society" and "the origin and extent of the rights of man." But they had emerged from that philosophical essay, Thornwell concluded, "feeling justified in our own consciences" and confident "that we have been eminently conservative in our influence upon the spirit of the age."[9] Proslavery ideology and republican politics were inextricably intertwined in antebellum South Carolina.

Evangelical ministers did the main work of the proslavery argument, contributing more than half of the tracts ever written on the subject in the United States and leaving their imprint clearly on the more secular remainder. Indeed, the Biblical defense of slavery was the centerpiece of an organic or familial ideology that encompassed far more than the relation of master and slave.[10] Thornwell, among others, insisted that the central tenet of that conservative social theory, that "the relation of master and slave stands on the same foot with the other relations of life," was grounded in scriptural proof. "We find masters exhorted in the same connection with husbands, parents, magistrates," and "slaves exhorted in the same connection with wives, children and subjects."[11] Such stitching together of all social relations into the seamless fabric of southern

---

[9]James Henley Thornwell, "Slavery and the Religious Instruction of the Coloured Population," *Southern Presbyterian Review* 4 (July 1850), 110–11.

[10]Larry E. Tise, *Proslavery: A History of the Defense of Slavery in America, 1701–1840* (Athens, GA, 1987), esp. xvii. For a good introduction to the literature on the biblical defense of slavery, see, William S. Jenkins, *Pro-Slavery Thought in the Old South* (1935; reprint, Gloucester, 1960); Eugene D. Genovese, *The World the Slaveholders Made* (New York, 1969); Eugene D. Genovese, *'Slavery Ordained of God': The Southern Slaveholders' View of Biblical History and Modern Politics* (Gettysburg, 1985); Drew G. Faust, "Evangelicalism and the Meaning of the Proslavery Argument: The Reverend Thornton Stringfellow of Virginia," *Virginia Magazine of History and Biography*, 85 (Jan. 1977), 3–17; Drew Gilpin Faust, ed., *The Ideology of Slavery: Proslavery Thought in the Antebellum South, 1830–1860* (Baton Rouge, 1982); and Jack P. Maddex, "'The Southern Apostasy' Revisited: The Significance of Proslavery Christianity," *Marxist Perspectives* 2 (Fall 1979), 132–41.

[11]James Henley Thornwell, "Report on Slavery," *Southern Presbyterian Review* 5 (Jan. 1852), 383–84; Iveson L. Brookes, *A Defence of the South Against the Reproaches and Encroachments of the North* (Hamburg, SC, 1850), esp. 28; see also Iveson L. Brookes, *A Defence of Southern Slavery: Against the Attacks of Henry Clay and Alexander Campbell . . .* (Hamburg, SC, 1851), 19–20; Thomas Smyth, *The Sin and the Curse: or, The Union, The True Source of Disunion, and Our Duty in the Present Crisis* (Nov. 1860), reprinted in *Complete Works of Rev. Thomas Smyth, D.D.*, ed. J. William Flinn (10 vols., Columbia, SC, 1908–1912), VII, 544. Similar arguments were used by politicians: see William Harper, "Memoir on Slavery," *Southern Literary Journal* 3 (Jan. 1838), 65–75, esp. 68–69; ibid. (Feb. 1838), 81–97, esp. 89–90; ibid. (March 1838), 161–75; ibid. (April 1838), 241–51; ibid. (May 1838), 321–28; James Henry Hammond, "Hammond's Letters on Slavery," in *The Proslavery Argument as Maintained by the Most Distinguished Writers of the Southern States* (Philadelphia, 1853), 125–26, 154–5 5, 161–63.

society became the mainstay of the proslavery argument, and it drew proslavery advocates inexorably into a struggle with abolitionists in which the stakes were no less than the nature of society and the republic itself. Thornwell characteristically minced no words: "The parties in this conflict are not merely abolitionists and slaveholders," he railed from the heated perspective of the 1850s. "They are atheists, socialists, communists, red republicans, Jacobins on the one side, and the friends of order and regulated freedom on the other." His view of the conflict was widely shared by ministers of every denomination and politicians of both radical and moderate stripe.[12]

Throughout the antebellum period in South Carolina, ministers and politicians scored the philosophy of natural rights and universal equality as "well-sounding but unmeaning verbiage." "Is it not palpably nearer the truth to say that no man was ever born free and that no two men were ever born equal?" low-country politician William Harper asked in what became a famous contribution to proslavery literature.[13]

Instead of natural rights and universal equality, Harper, Thornwell, and others offered an elaborate theory of providential relations and particularistic rights. As Charleston minister John B. Adger explained, all human beings did not have the same rights, but only the specific ones that attached to their role. In the Christian republic, wives did not have the rights of husbands, or slaves the rights of masters: a husband had "the rights of a husband . . . a father the rights of a father; and a slave, only the rights of a slave." Slavery thus occupied no anomalous category in low-country social thought, and its defense became inseparable from that of Christian and conservative social order."[14]

The real measure of the effectiveness of proslavery arguments, as politicians were acutely aware, was their social breadth. . . . In reaching beyond masters and slaves to all relations of southern households, proslavery ideologues bid for the loyalties of all white male adults. They repeatedly reminded white southerners of all classes that slavery could not be disentangled from other relations of power

---

[12]Thornwell, "Report on Slavery," 391. For radical politicians' views, see Hammond, "Hammond's Letters on Slavery," esp. 174; Robert Barnwell Rhett, "Address to the People of Beaufort and Colleton Districts Upon the Subject of Abolition," Jan. 15, 1838, Robert Barnwell Rhett Papers (South Caroliniana Library), esp. 6–7. For moderates' views, see Robert Nicholas Olsberg, "A Government of Class and Race: William Henry Trescot and the South Carolina Chivalry, 1860–1865" (PhD diss., University of South Carolina, 1972), 100–104, 115, 122–23; John Townsend, The South Alone Should Govern the South (Charleston, 1860), 9–10.

[13]Harper, "Memoir on Slavery," esp. 71, 68; see also Whitemarsh B. Seabrook, An Essay on the Management of Slaves and Especially on Their Religious Instruction (Charleston, 1834), 6; John B. Adger, "The Christian Doctrine of Human Rights and Slavery," Southern Presbyterian Review 11 (March 1849), esp. 570–71; Whitefoord Smith, National Sins: A Call to Repentance . . . (Charleston, 1849), 18; Thornwell, "Slavery and Religious Instruction," 108–9, 130, 133–36, 140–41; Thornwell, "Report on Slavery," 387–88, 390–91; Brooks, Defence of the South, 8, 19–22, 30, 34; Hammond, "Hammond's Letters on Slavery," 109–10; and James Henry Hammond, Are Working Men Slaves? The Question Discussed by Senators Hammond, Broderick and Wilson (n.p., 1858), 3.

[14]Adger, "Christian Doctrine," esp. 573; see also Benjamin Morgan Palmer, "Thanksgiving Sermon" (1860), quoted in Thomas Cary Johnson, The Life and Letters of Benjamin Morgan Palmer (Richmond, Va., 1906), 212–13.

and privilege and that it represented simply the most extreme and absolute form of the legal and customary dependencies that characterized the Old South—and their own households.

The conjoining of all domestic relations of domination and subordination enabled proslavery spokesmen to tap beliefs about the legitimacy of inequality. . . . In the dual task of painting both the abolitionist image of social disorder and their own benevolent and peaceful social order, proslavery spokesmen returned repeatedly to gender relations, exploiting assumptions about the "natural" relations of men and women. On the common ground of gender they sought to ensure that every white man recognized his own investment in the struggle over slavery.

William Harper demonstrated the power of that approach, playing the trump card of gender inequality to give conclusive lie to the philosophy of the Declaration of Independence. "What is the foundation of the bold dogma so confidently announced?" he asked. "Females are human and rational beings. They may be found . . . better qualified to exercise political privileges and to attain the distinctions of society than many men; yet who complains of the order of society by which they are excluded from them?"[15] The transhistorical subordination of women was presented as incontestable proof that social and political inequality were natural.

In the lexicon of metaphors for slavery, marriage took pride of place, a discursive construction historians have rarely recognized.[16] No other relation was more universally embraced as both natural and divine, and none so readily evoked the stake of enfranchised white men, yeomen and planters alike, in the defense of slave society. By equating the subordination of women and that of slaves, proslavery ideologues and politicians attempted to endow slavery with the legitimacy of the family and especially marriage and, not incidentally, to invest the defense of slavery with the survival of customary gender relations.[17] In this sense, the subordination of women bore a great deal of the ideological weight of

---

[15]Harper, "Memoir on Slavery," 68–69.

[16]Harper, "Memoir on Slavery," 68–69, 89–90, 165; L. S. M. (Louisa Susannah McCord], "Enfranchisement of Woman" (1852), reprinted in *All Clever Men Who Make Their Way: Critical Discourse in the Old South*, ed. Michael O'Brien (Fayetteville, 1982), 337–56; Richard Fuller, quoted in J. H. Cuthbert, *Life of Richard Fuller, D.D.* (New York, 1879), 194–96; Hammond, "Hammond's Letters on Slavery," 125–26, 154–55; Thornwell, "Report on Slavery," 383–85; William M. Wightman, *Life of William Capers, D.D.* (Nashville, 1859), 296. Thornton Stringfellow, "A Brief Examination of Scripture Testimony on the Institution of Slavery," in *Ideology of Slavery*, ed. Faust, 156–57, 144–45; Henry Hughes, "Treatise on Sociology," in ibid., 262–63; George Fitzhugh, "Southern Thought," in ibid., 291–95; and George Fitzhugh, *Cannibals All!: Or, Slaves Without Masters* (1857; reprint, Cambridge, MA, 1960), 95–97.

[17]I mean the analogy of women and slaves to be understood specifically as an ideological construction. I do not mean to suggest that free women's legal or social position was analogous to that of slaves. Different interpretations have been offered by Anne Firor Scott, *The Southern Lady: From Pedestal to Politics, 1830–1930* (Chicago, 1970), esp. 45–79; and Catherine Clinton, *The Plantation Mistress: Women's World in the Old South* (New York, 1982), esp. 16–35.

slavery, providing the most concrete example of how public and private distinctions were confounded in political discourse and culture.

Women's nature and appropriate social role became . . . a matter of political concern all over the country in the antebellum period. But they assumed added political significance in the South where their fate was shackled to that of slavery. While southern republican discourse, like its northern variants, had long depended on gendered language and images, the specific analogy of slaves with women, masters with husbands, and slavery with marriage appears, in the late 1830s, to have replaced an older emphasis on the family in general and fathers and children in particular.[18] Perhaps the shift marked the need to put a more modern and benevolent face on familial authority. . . . But there can be no doubt that it reflected as well the need to put proslavery on the broadest possible social basis and the utility of the metaphor of marriage in that unceasing effort.

Although ministers continued to use the familial metaphor generally defined . . ., they increasingly focused specifically on the relation of husbands and wives. For in the family, that "model state," Benjamin Morgan Palmer explained, "subjection to law" originated with the authority of man "as the head of the woman." . . .[19]

The metaphor of marriage had much to recommend it to southern ideologues. But it was not without its problems, as they admitted; the most obvious was that the submission of wives was voluntary while that of slaves was not. Nevertheless, the problem of the analogy of husband and wife was more easily negotiated than that of parent and child. After all, male children grew up to lay claim in adulthood to the prerogatives of husbands, fathers, and masters. Female children, on the other hand, became wives; they remained, like slaves, as perpetual children, at least in relation to masters. . . . Females thus provided the only constant point of reference for naturalizing subordination.[20]

At another level, though, one cannot help but speculate that ideologues found a great deal more psychological satisfaction in likening slaves to women than to children. For the rebelliousness of women, like that of slaves, was a specter only summoned to be banished. By insisting that women *chose* to submit (a suspect formulation when one considers the options), men were, in effect, denying the personal power they knew women to have over them, however

[18]See the familial metaphors in Richard Furman, *Exposition of the Views of the Baptists Relative to the coloured Population of the United States* (Charleston, 1833), 10; Kerber, *Women of the Republic*; Ruth H. Bloch, "The Gendered Meanings of Virtue in Revolutionary America," *Signs*, 13 (Autumn 1987), 3 7–58; Jean Gunderson, "Independence, Citizenship, and the American Revolution," 59–77; Stansell, *City of Women*, 20–30.

[19]Wightman, *Life of Capers*, 296; Benjamin Morgan Palmer, *The Family in its Civil and Churchly Aspects* (Richmond, 1876), 15, 10–11. Although published after the war, Palmer's book was based on sermons delivered in the antebellum period and contains such chapters as "Authority of Masters" and "The Subjection of Slaves." The relevant secondary literature on paternalism is extensive, but see especially Genovese, *Roll, Jordan, Roll*.

[20]On the education of planter sons for masterhood, see Steven Stowe, *Intimacy and Power in the Old South: Ritual in the Lives of the Planters* (Baltimore, 1987).

temporarily, in romantic and sexual love. Dependence on women was unmanly; manhood orbited around the display of independence. Hence, arguments about female submission not only naturalized slavery; they confirmed masculinity.[21] Little wonder that proslavery ideologues went to such lengths to prove that women's subordination was grounded in nature and sanctioned by God. Their heart was surely in the job. . . .

Marriage did lend itself nicely to comparison with slavery, or rather the proslavery view of marriage did, and ideologues were quick to exploit it. God had ordained a position for slaves in the inevitable hierarchy of society, they argued, with particular rights and duties attached to it. Slaves, like women, were fitted by nature to conform comfortably to their place, and slavery, like marriage, was a relationship of "reciprocal interest" which ensured that a "due subordination is preserved between the classes which would otherwise be thrown into sharp antagonism." From their perspective, though not, perhaps, from that of white southern women, marriage was a benign metaphor for slavery. For while the metaphor enshrined male dominance and female subordination, it attempted to cast both in a benevolent light.[22]

Yet the likeness of women and slaves, despite ideological claims, did not ultimately reside in the subjects' natural fitness for subordination, but rather in the masters' power to command it. "Is it not natural that a man should be attached to that which is his own?" William Harper queried, wresting benevolence from the self-interest that allegedly secured for women and slaves protection from their masters' brutality. "Do not men everywhere contract kind feelings to their dependents?" If women found this an imperfect protection, as Harper inadvertently admitted, slaves found it worse than none at all. But the striking feature of the analogy was their common status as "his," as "dependents" who lacked, as Harper said repeatedly, self-ownership. A "freeman" was one who was "master of his own time and action. . . . To submit to a blow would be degrading to a freeman," he wrote, "because he is the protector of himself." But it was "not degrading to a slave—neither is it . . . to a woman."[23] Thus in proslavery discourse the metaphor of marriage worked in complex ways. It did not, in the last analysis, constrain the masters' boundless power; rather it confirmed that power by locating the only restraint on the exercise of it exclusively in the hands of masters themselves. The metaphor's multivalence, and particularly its manipulation of benevolence and power, explains its political efficacy.

In their efforts to impress on ordinary southerners the seamlessness of the social fabric, proslavery ideologues were afforded assistance from the most

---

[21]For an interesting discussion of the psychological dimensions of manhood and independence in republican discourse, see Elizabeth Colwill, "Transforming Women's Empire: Representations of Women in French Political Culture, 1770–1807" (Ph.D. diss., State University of New York at Binghamton, 1990).

[22]Palmer, *The Family*, 35–37, 45, 125, 147–68. For one yeoman woman's heroic struggle for a submissiveness supposedly instinctual, see Mary Davis Brown Diary, Mary Davis Brown Papers (South Caroliniana Library).

[23]Harper, "Memoir on Slavery," 94, 89–90, 163–68.

unlikely of quarters. In the 1830s, a handful of Garrisonian abolitionists also came to the conviction that the fate of dependents, slavery, and the subordination of women were inseparable, and that conventional gender relations were at stake in the national struggle over slavery. . . . Abby Kelley, a committed Garrisonian and a leading figure in the antebellum women's rights movement, articulated the radical meaning most concretely in acknowledging a debt of gratitude to slaves: "In striving to strike his irons off, we found most surely that we were manacled ourselves." Garrisonians' yoking of the subordination of women and slaves and their public commitment to a dual emancipation proved a perfect foil for proslavery politicians.[24]

If all men should have "equal rights," more than one South Carolinian worried, "then why not women?" That some northern women abolitionists, and some male ones too, asked the same question lent credibility to proslavery threats.[25] The Garrisonians' radical actions in the late 1830s and 1840s lent new fervor and detail to standard comparisons of the natural, divine, and benevolent social order of the slave South and the chaos of the revolutionary North, now embodied in the dual specter of abolitionism and feminism. No more dramatic illustration of the political significance of domestic, and especially gender, relations could have been imagined. South Carolinian politicians exploited it for all it was worth.

It was not difficult for ministers and politicians to convince low-country yeomen, among others, that abolitionists really threatened a violent end to Christian society as they knew it. . . . [T]he outraged and fearful response to Garrisonian feminism was not confined to South Carolina, nor even below the Mason-Dixon line; it was mirrored north of slavery, providing compelling evidence of how deeply gender undergirded conceptions of social and political order. . . . Resistance to Garrisonians was by no means limited to the ranks of conservative clergymen, though; in the early 1840s, conflict over the issue of women's rights provoked a split within the ranks of the broader antislavery

---

[24]Abby Kelley quoted in Blanche Glassman Hersh, *The Slavery of Sex: Feminist-Abolitionists in America* (Urbana, 1978), 20–21. Use of the analogy by first-generation women's rights activists is exemplified in the writings of Sarah Grimké and Angelina Grimké. See Elizabeth Ann Bartlett, ed., *Sarah Grimké: Letters on the Equality of the Sexes and Other Essays* (New Haven, 1988); and Angelina Grimké, *Letters to Catherine Beecher*, reprinted in *The Feminist Papers: From Adams to de Beauvoir*, ed. Alice S. Rossi (New York, 1973), 319–22. The literature on abolitionism and women's rights is now vast, but see Gerda Lerner, *The Grimké Sisters from South Carolina* (New York, 1967); Ellen C. DuBois, *Feminism and Suffrage: The Emergence of an Independent Women's Movement in America* (Ithaca, 1978); Nancy Hewitt, *Women's Activism and Social Change: Rochester, New York, 1822–1872* (Ithaca, 1984); Jean Fagan Yellin, *Women and Sisters: The Antislavery Feminists in American Culture* (New Haven, 1989); Lori D. Ginzberg, *Women and the Work of Benevolence* (New Haven, 1990).

[25]29 Quotation from Gay, "Tangled Skein," 131; Dew, "On the Characteristic Differences between the Sexes." The best evidence is the commonplace yoking of abolitionism and feminism, often through ridicule and humor. See *Orangeburg Southron*, June 11, 1856, Feb. 13, 1860; *Beaufort Enterprise*, Oct. 10, 1860; John L. Manning to his wife, May 29, 1860, Box V, Folder 172, Williams-Chesnut-Manning Families Papers (South Caroliniana Library).

movement as well.[26] . . . Garrisonian abolitionists and women's rights advocates nonetheless issued ringing challenges, as their proslavery adversaries charged, to traditional authority and privilege—to chattel property, the church, and most threatening of all, it would seem, to male supremacy.[27]

. . . [O]ne of the most powerful and coherent proslavery tracts to come out of South Carolina, a virtual model of conservative reasoning, was written to meet the challenge of the woman suffrage movement. Louisa Susannah Cheves McCord argued in her 1852 article that "The Enfranchisement of Women" was "but a piece with negro emancipation." . . . [T]he evidence she adduced was an amalgam of by then classic proslavery positions. She began with the usual mocking references to natural rights: "Mounted on Cuffee's shoulders, in rides the Lady. The genius of communism bows them both in, mouthing over Mr. Jefferson's free and equal sentence"; and moved to the inevitable contrast of northern and southern society. Whereas southerners were "conservatives" who had accepted God-given "distinctions of sex and race" and sought reform by working with "Nature's Laws," northerners, she explained, held unnatural principles that inevitably produced unnatural spectacles. Here McCord took an old genre to new depths, calling suffragists those "petticoated despisers of their sex . . . would-be men . . . moral monsters . . . things which nature disclaims." Women on top, the world indeed turned upside down, McCord conjured up the most fundamental image of social disorder to demonstrate that reform threatened nothing less than revolution and to remind southerners that where all relations of power were connected, the assault on privilege would not stop short of anarchy or the threshold of their own households.[28]

In the most literal sense, the subordination of women was at issue in the struggle over slavery; in another sense, however, the larger question was the social and political status of dependents, men and women alike, and thus the proper parameters of the republican polity. Although the debate was a national one, the conservative South clearly had more to gain than the North from the politicization of gender relations in the antebellum period.

---

[26]See Ronald G. Walters, *The Antislavery Appeal: American Abolitionism after 1830* (New York, 1978), 3–18; Tise, *Proslavery*, esp. 261–85. To compare northern and southern indictments, see Howe, Endowments of Women, esp. 11; "From a Pastoral Letter, 'The General Association of Massachusetts (Orthodox) to the Churches Under Their Care'" (1837), reprinted in *Feminist Papers*, ed. Rossi, 305–6; and Leonard Richards, *Gentlemen of Property and Standing: Anti-Abolitionist Mobs in the North* (New York, 1970), 56–61.

[27]Jonathan A. Glickstein, "'Poverty is not Slavery': American Abolitionists and the Competitive Labor Market," in *Antislavery Reconsidered. New Perspectives on the Abolitionists*, ed. Lewis Perry and Michael Fellman (Baton Rouge, 1979); David Brion Davis, *The Problem of Slavery in the Age of Revolution, 1770–1823* (Ithaca, 1975), esp. 435–68.

[28][McCord], "Enfranchisement of Woman," 344, 347, 342; Howe, *Endowments of Women*, 10–12. Scholarly treatments of McCord include Fox-Genovese, *Within the Plantation Household*, 242–89; and Richard Lounsberry, "Ludibria Rerum Mortalium: Charlestonian Intellectuals and Their Classics," in *Intellectual Life in Antebellum Charleston*, ed. O'Brien and Moltke-Hansen, 325–69. On gender reversal as the classic representation of the world turned upside down, see Natalie Zemon Davis, *Society and Culture in Early Modern France* (Stanford, 1965), 124–51.

Nationally the debate over women's emancipation strengthened conserva-tive resolve on a whole range of social and political issues, the most important of which was slavery. In the North, however, it caused division within antislavery ranks, marking for the majority the limits of democratic republican commitment to the rights of man. But in the South, in the absence of any women's movement, ideas about the natural subordination of women contributed . . . to the ideological and political cohesion of the proslavery cause.

No social relation has ever had such difficulty shedding its apparently "natu-ral" character as that between man and woman. Then as now, unexamined assumptions about natural gender differences and conventions were invoked through language to naturalize other social relations—class and race, for example—organizing difference hierarchically and lending it the cast of immu-tability and inevitability.[29] That was precisely what proslavery ideologues attempted to do in their association of women and slaves. The philosophy of natural rights foundered everywhere in the western world in the Age of Revolu-tion on the shoals of women's right to the status of individual and citizen.[30] By engaging their adversaries at that point, proslavery politicians put their claims about natural inequality . . . on ground few wanted to see move. Their success, however, ultimately depended on the social breadth and depth of the commit-ment to the ideas and conventions they invoked. Here lies the real contribution of a gender analysis of the proslavery argument. For the recognition that the social relations of the private sphere profoundly shaped political ideas and actions in the public sphere has important and largely unexamined implications for the political ideology and culture of the South Carolina low country and, especially, for the position of the yeoman majority within it.

Low-country yeoman farmers may never have read a sermon by Thornwell or a tract by Harper, but they almost certainly heard a sermon at their local Baptist church by the likes of Reverend Iveson Brookes or a speech at a July Fourth bar-becue by a prominent politician such as Robert Barnwell Rhett. The gulf between high and low culture was just not that great; evangelical values played a central role in both. . . . [I]n evangelical churches, whose extant records give us a rare glimpse of their communities, male yeomen demonstrated an unequivocal com-mitment to hierarchical social order and to conservative Christian republican-ism. Unlike intellectuals and planter politicians, these low-country farmers articulated their world view piecemeal, in framing covenants to govern admis-sion, fellowship, and representation and in the dispensation of gospel discipline. And they did so in the colloquial language of familialism. They represented Christian society most commonly as an extended family replete with paternal

---

[29]Scott, *Gender and the Politics of History*, esp. 53–68, and the series of articles in n. 2 above.

[30]Landes, *Women and the Public Sphere*; Pateman, Sexual Contract; Colwill, "Transforming Women's Empire"; Kerber, *Women of the Republic*; Linda Kerber, "'History Can Do It No Justice': Women and the Reinterpretation of the American Revolution," in *Women in the Age of the American Revolution*, ed. Ronald Hoffman and Peter J. Albert (Charlottesville, 1989), 3–42.

head and fixed ranks of dependents, a formulation that bore striking resemblance to the organic ideology of published proslavery ministers and politicians. In their Baptist, Methodist, and, less often, Presbyterian congregations, the yeoman majority, or rather its enfranchised male members, eschewed any attempt to interpret equality in social terms. Instead they assigned privileges and duties and meted out discipline according to secular rank, station, and status.[31]

This should come as no surprise, despite historians' usual insistence on the egalitarian impulses of southern yeomen. In their churches as in their households, marketplaces, and electoral districts, black belt yeomen moved as independent and enfranchised men amid a sea of dependent and disenfranchised people. Whether slaveholders or not, yeoman household heads were, as they proudly claimed, masters themselves. Politicians acknowledged and confirmed this identity in representing the defense of slavery as the defense of all kinds of power and privilege, domestic and public. Masterhood is thereby revealed as a complex identity, literally engendered in all those independent "freeman" by virtue of personal domination over dependents in their own households. It was moreover ritually confirmed in the exercise of the political rights to which masterhood entitled them. Out of that same social matrix, located resolutely in the household and the private sphere, the yeomanry's commitment to slavery was similarly engendered. For the hidden assumptions and values that underlay their political choices were forged in the relations that engaged them most directly—with the few slaves they may have owned, but just as important, with the women they presumed it their natural right to rule. In the struggle over slavery, yeoman farmers understandably saw the struggle to perpetuate their privilege both at home and at the ballot box.

Viewed within a holistic social context rather than exclusively in relation to planters, yeoman farmers come into focus as part of a small minority in plantation districts privileged by the qualifications of republican citizenship.[32] Little wonder that they exhibited a profound commitment to natural hierarchy and inequality even as they cherished equal rights as independent men. The political ideology of yeomen in plantation areas was thus a contradictory one. . . . Yeomen did indeed press overweening planters for a greater share of power and resources, and they pressed them for recognition of their rights as masters. But they also found common cause with planters in maintaining and policing the class, gender, and racial boundaries of citizenship in the slave republic. Their commitment to the slave regime owed as much to its legitimation of dependence and inequality in the private sphere as to the much-lauded vitality of male independence and

---

[31]This discussion is based on a quantitative analysis of the social composition of membership of 60 low-country and middle district churches and on textual analysis of church constitutions and dispensation of gospel discipline. See, for example, Beech Branch Baptist Church Book, esp. Nov. 11, 1809, Beech Branch Baptist Church Records; McCurry, "Defense of Their World," 172–334, esp. 237.

[32]Lacy K. Ford, Jr., "Republics and Democracy: The Parameters of Political Citizenship in Antebellum South Carolina," in *The Meaning of South Carolina History: Essays in Honor of George C. Rogers, Jr,* ed. David R. Chesnutt and Clyde N. Wilson (Columbia, SC, 1991), 121–45.

formal "democracy" in the public sphere. As good republicans, yeomen appreciated both of Columbia's faces.

It was a common trope of political tracts that the only true republic was a slave republic, for only a slave republic maintained the public sphere as a realm of perfect equality. But invariably in republican discourse, independence betrayed its intimacy with dependence, and equality with inequality. "No social state without slavery as its basis," Baptist minister Iveson Brookes offered, as if to make the point, "can permanently maintain a republican form of government."[33] Yeoman farmers, like most enfranchised southerners, were aware of what republican independence entailed.

Many historians, however, see only the public face of slavery republicanism, perhaps because they employ such a narrow definition of "the political," one more theirs than antebellum southerners'. As a result, they mistake ideology for description of social and political reality; the common interpretation of the South as a herrenvolk or white man's democracy bears an unsettling resemblance to the portrait proslavery politicians themselves drew.[34] But the slave republic was emphatically not a democracy, racial or otherwise, as its defenders readily acknowledged in boasting of the restriction of political rights to a privileged few as its distinctive and superior characteristic.

From the earliest skirmishes of the nullification crisis, antitariff South Carolinians such as the editorialist "Leonidas" laid claim to a distinctive republicanism. In the North, Leonidas observed in 1828, "liberty is a principle." In the slave South, where free men possessed of "habits of command" had developed a "privileged superiority," liberty is "a privilege, a passion, and a principle." South Carolina's freemen would never consent to be made "the dastard-trampled slaves of wool-weavers and spindle-twirlers." Constituted as "freemen" by slavery, they would show themselves, Leonidas predicted, to be the natural guardians of the republic against the corruption of the state and its dominant interests. . . .[35]

During the struggle over the abolitionists' congressional petition campaign of 1838, Robert Barnwell Rhett introduced what became an enduring focus on social relations and particularly the distinction between the antagonistic and antirepublican social relations of the free labor North and the harmonious and republican ones of the slave labor South.[36] It was an argument to which proslavery politicians increasingly turned as the sectional struggle deepened and, not incidentally, as the problem of enfranchised dependents fueled restrictionist

---

[33]Brookes, *A Defence of the South*, esp. 45–46; Speech of Gen. Robert Y. Hayne, *Charleston Mercury*, Feb. 3, 1830; W. C. Dana, *A Sermon Delivered in the Central Presbyterian Church, Charleston, S.C., Nov. 21st, 1860* . . . (Charleston, 1860).

[34]Michael Wayne recently challenged the dominant interpretation of herrenvolkism but did not take issue with the explanatory value of herrenvolkism itself or with exclusively racial interpretations of proslavery ideology. See Michael Wayne, "An Old South Morality Play: Reconsidering the Social Underpinnings of Proslavery Ideology," *Journal of American History* 77 (Dec. 1990), 838–63.

[35]Leonidas, *Charleston Mercury*, July 14, 1828.

[36]Rhett, "Address to the People of Beaufort," 7–9. Harper adopted a strikingly similar position in "Memoir on Slavery."

impulses in northern politics in the 1840s and 1850s. James Henry Hammond, planter, congressman, governor, senator, ideologue, gave it perhaps its most vivid formulation in his writings and speeches from the mid-1840s to the late 1850s.

Slavery everywhere exists in fact if not in name, Hammond reminded his fellow United States senators in an 1858 debate: "Your whole class of manual laborers and 'operatives' as you call them, are essentially slaves." To enfranchise slaves, as the free labor states were compelled to do, threatened a "fearful crisis in republican institutions" and invited revolution at the ballot box. Hammond sketched frightful portraits of the festering and explosive class politics of industrial England's cities, whose fate awaited, if it had not already visited, Boston, Philadelphia, and New York. The republic could not long survive such developments without the restraining conservative influence of the South. The genius of the southern system, Hammond insisted, was to have recognized the necessity of enslaving the poor and to have found a race of people "adapted to that purpose." Race was not, in his analysis, an essential but only a fortuitous characteristic of the slave labor system. It ensured that the South's dependent classes were confined within households under the governance of a master, where they could be deprived, as were women everywhere, of political rights. "Our slaves do not vote," Hammond pointed out. "In the slaveholding states . . . nearly one half of the whole population, and those the poorest and most ignorant, have no political influence whatever, because they are slaves." The half of the population who did vote were, as a result, if not rich, nonetheless part of a privileged class of independent men, "elevated far above the mass." Such men could be trusted, as they must be in a republic, to "preserve a stable and well-ordered government."[37]

Slavery was above all else, in Hammond's account, a system of class and labor relations that had become, to the inestimable benefit of the South, a system of race relations as well. It was that convergence that made the South an exemplary republic, one committed to universal manhood suffrage yet able to restrict it to independent men—a herrenvolk democracy, if you will. "History presents no such combination for republican liberty," Rhett boasted, "than that which exists at the South. The African for the laborer—the Anglo-Saxon for the master and ruler." Slavery was the "cornerstone of the republican edifice." As Hammond, Thornwell, and numerous other South Carolina politicians and ministers agreed, the "primitive and patriarchal" social relations of the South prevented the republic from going down the French road of corruption (to use Thornwell's memorable phrase) from a "representative to a democratic government. . . ."[38]

---

[37]Hammond, *Are Working Men Slaves?*, 3–4; Hammond, "Hammond's Letters on Slavery," esp. 110–11.

[38]Rhett, "Address to the People of Beaufort," 13; Hammond, "Hammond's Letters on Slavery," 110–11, 162–63; Thornwell, quoted in Palmer, ed., *Life and Letters of Thornwell*, 310–11. Barbara Fields has argued that slavery must be recognized as a system of class relations, despite the obfuscations of racial ideology; see Barbara J. Fields, "Ideology and Race in American History," in *Region, Race, and Reconstruction: Essays in Honor of C. Vann Woodward*, ed. J. Morgan Kousser and James M. McPherson (New York, 1982), 143–78; and Barbara J. Fields, "Slavery, Race, and Ideology in the United States of America," *New Left Review* 181 (May/June 1990), 95–118.

The principle of exclusion was articulated, significantly, in the gendered language of republican discourse. Such terms as "manly independence" and "womanly weakness" served in political tracts and speeches to construct, legitimize, and patrol the boundaries of the republican community, excluding not just women but all those who bore the stigma of dependence. Robert Barnwell Rhett was a master of the genre and demonstrated his skill in regular calls to arms. In an early antitariff speech he wove gender, class, and politics into a republican tapestry in which unmanly men, guilty of "abject submission" to northern "tyranny," were not just rendered effeminate but "crushed and trampled slaves." Those, however, who left "despair . . . to the weak," those who "as freemen" would never consent to "lay the bones of a slave beside those of a free ancestry," only those were true republican men. Dependencies were deliberately conflated by the gendered language of republicanism; independence, by contrast, remained brilliantly distinct. As Rhett had put it in a speech the previous June to his constituents at Walterborough Court House, the seat of Colleton District, the tariff must be resisted as "an infringement on our privileges as men." "Impotent resistance" or "submissive patience" was a fit response only of women or slaves. It was in no small measure in defense of that conception of republicanism that southern citizens rallied in the name of republican manhood.[39]

When a politician took the platform at a meeting, muster, or Fourth of July barbecue and claimed to speak "as a freeman," the salutation was not simply an invitation to his largely yeoman audiences to regard him as one among equals. It was that, but it was also an evocation of shared privilege, an invitation to see themselves as part of the elite: as freemen in a society in which the majority were not free.[40] It was, moreover, a constant reminder of their stake in social hierarchy, political exclusivity, and slavery. "Slavery is with us a powerful element of conservatism," William Henry Trescot, a low-country planter and historian, wrote, because "the citizen with us belongs . . . to a privileged class."[41] This was an argument with great appeal to yeomen.

The banner of "free men" was an emblem of the conservatism of "American republicanism," waved to distinguish it from "French democracy," or mobocracy, as so many low-country planters referred to the bastardized politics of the North. Thus the "MEN of the South," yeomen and planters, were challenged repeatedly to "set aside womanly fears of disunion" in favor of "manly and resolute action,"

---

[39]Extracts of speech of Robert Barnwell Smith [R. B. Rhett], *Charleston Mercury*, Aug. 6, 1829, and Robert Barnwell Smith [R. B. Rhett], "An Address of Sundry Citizens of Colleton District to the People of South Carolina," *Charleston Mercury*, June 18, 1828; see also Leonidas, *Charleston Mercury*, July 17, 1828; Townsend, *The South Alone Should Govern the South*, esp. 6, 9, 17–18, 30–35, 40. For a pioneering treatment of manhood and honor, see Bertram Wyatt-Brown, *Southern Honor: Ethics and Behavior in the Old South* (New York, 1982).

[40]Extracts of speech of Robert Barnwell Smith, *Charleston Mercury*, Aug. 6, 1829. The quotation beneath the banner headline of the Williamsburg Kingstree Star read "Let Every Freeman Speak." For examples from the nullification crisis, see the addresses and speeches reprinted in the *Charleston Mercury*, June 18, 1828, July 17, 1828, Aug. 4, 1828, Feb. 17, 1830.

[41]William H. Trescot quoted in Olsberg, "Government of Class and Race," 78; see also Hammond, "Hammond's Letters on Slavery," 104–5.

not, as many historians have argued, of an egalitarian and democratic regime, but of a hierarchical and republican one. Their loyalties were secured to a regime in which the rights of citizens were awarded only to those few who were fully masters of themselves and their dependents.[42]

Yeoman farmers were committed to the defense of social hierarchy and political privilege, including slavery, in large measure because of the relations of personal domination on which their own independence rested. But the prerogatives of power around which the public sphere was constructed could not be denied within. Thus the very values in which yeomen and planters found agreement also drew yeomen into a political culture and ideology in which planter prerogatives were difficult to resist. They were left, as a result, with few resources to represent effectively their specific interests as small farmers in a region of great planters, and they were over-matched in every aspect of South Carolina politics.[43] Empowered by a system that rewarded privilege, yeoman farmers found themselves overpowered by vastly more privileged planters.

A gendered approach to political history draws our attention to what we acknowledge in our own political system but usually deny in historical analysis. It is that values expressed in the public sphere reflect complex and deep-seated beliefs about a whole range of relationships and issues, many of which are considered private: marriage, sexuality, parental authority, motherhood, manhood, and the very concept of privacy. . . . The holistic approach that a gendered analysis compels is particularly pertinent to the interpretation of republicanism.

The meaning of republicanism was contested repeatedly over time and space. It was crafted into political movements and imperatives as diverse, on the one end, as the Paineites whose radical artisan constituency redefined independence and pushed at the outer limits of republican citizenship, and, on the other, of proslavery planters who sought in it a reactionary counterweight to the insurgent democratic movements of the Western world.

But while republicanism had a long and complex history in the United States, it had one consistent feature: the distinction between independent men, in whom the public trust could confidently be placed, and dependents, in whom it could not. Those who called themselves republicans, whether Paineites or Populists or proslavery yeomen, were committed to that distinction.[44] No matter how the definition of independence was reworked or the boundaries stretched—and there were those redeeming moments—republicanism was defined by the

---

[42]Townsend, *The South Alone Should Govern the South*, 40, 9.

[43]Contrast this argument with that of Ford, that slavery had made South Carolina yeomen the political equals, and possibly superiors, of planters: Ford, *Origins of Southern Radicalism*, esp. 372–73.

[44]The recognition that republicanism was defined by its boundaries and exclusions and that relations of personal domination are properly the stuff of political history could prompt a different emphasis in the treatment of radical artisan republicanism than that offered by Eric Foner and Sean Wilentz or of anticapitalist yeoman Populists than that offered by Steven Hahn. See Eric Foner, *Tom Paine and Revolutionary America* (New York, 1976); Sean Wilentz, *Chants Democratic: New York City and the Rise of the American Working Class* (New York, 1984); Hahn, *Roots of Southern Populism*.

principle of exclusion. The exclusion of women, or slaves, or propertyless workers, or any other so-called dependent class marked not simply the limits of republicanism but one of its defining characteristics. In the antebellum South, this was dramatically evident, for in some regions more than 80 percent of the population was excluded from the privileges of citizenship. But everywhere in the United States, from the early days of the republic to the Civil War, the commitment to government by the virtuous and independent lent a special and contradictory character to political culture and ideology. In some times and places, it generated universal manhood suffrage; in others, an abhorrent and brutal program of geographical expansion; in yet others, the defense of slavery through Civil War. And always the disfranchisement of women.

Stephanie McCurry

I am a nineteenth century American historian with a strong interest in the history of women and gender. I was pulled into the study of history by a preoccupation with the question of power and how it works in particular societies and that remains the central focus of my work. It is an interest that comes from my experience growing up in Belfast, Northern Ireland in the 1960s and early 1970s during British military occupation. The violence of British imperial power was apparent, but so was the power of men over women within families in my community. I got hooked on the history of slavery and the American South in college at the University of Western Ontario, in a year-long survey course taught by Professor Craig Simpson. I went to graduate school at the University of Rochester and trained in two parallel, but not yet connected, areas: the U.S. South and feminist approaches to history. The fruits of that work appeared in my dissertation, first article (excerpted in this collection) and book, *Masters of Small Worlds: Yeoman Households, Gender Relations, and the Political Culture of the South Carolina Low Country*. I went on to write a book about the Confederacy and the destruction of slavery which, like all of my work, involves a rethinking of the terms of political history and the connections between the private and public spheres. I have taught at a number of universities in my career including the University of California, San Diego, Northwestern University, and the University of Pennsylvania. In September 2015 I joined the faculty of Columbia University.

QUESTIONS FOR CONSIDERATION

1. What argument does McCurry make to justify considering the private sphere of the household as essential to understanding the public role of politics in antebellum South Carolina?
2. In what ways did South Carolinian politics, religion, and gender roles unite to justify the slave system in the 1830s? Who was the primary audience for this justification of slavery? Why might this audience find this justification appealing?
3. How did Garrisonian feminists and abolitionists assume a similar position regarding the status of slaves and wives in order to make opposing arguments?
4. Why did yeoman farmers, many of whom did not own slaves themselves, subscribe to the slave-holding justifications of antebellum South Carolina?
5. Compare McCurry's article to Cornell's "Aristocracy Assailed: The Ideology of Backcountry Anti-Federalism." How do McCurry and Cornell approach political history in different ways? What are some similarities in their methods?

CHAPTER FIFTEEN

"We Are Engaged as a Band of Sisters": Class and Domesticity in the Washingtonian Temperance Movement, 1840–1850[1]

Ruth M. Alexander

Throughout the winter and spring of 1842, the women of the Ladies' Chelsea Temperance Benevolent Society visited the houses, alleys, and streets of their Manhattan neighborhood searching for families and individuals who suffered from the ravages of alcohol. Led by "Directress" Bowrason, a butcher's wife, the Chelsea devotees of the Washingtonian temperance movement offered cash, clothing, and the message of abstinence from alcohol to impoverished inebriates. Among those aided were three women "restored" to sobriety by the actions of the female Washingtonians. The first woman was destitute, drunk, "nearly naked," and "sick from exposure" when members of the society found her. She was persuaded to take the pledge of total abstinence, food and medical care were provided for her, and society members helped her find employment and board. Later she became a "worthy member" of the organization. The second, a young woman who was destitute and "without friends," took the pledge and was clothed, boarded, and assisted in obtaining work with a sympathetic family. The third, a mother so poor and drunken that local authorities had taken her children from her, was able to resume care of her family after receiving help from the Washingtonian women.[2]

News of these striking transformations may have caused admiration and amazement among those who read of the society's work in the pages of the *Olive Plant and Ladies' Temperance Advocate*, a monthly newspaper dedicated to women's "systematic and persevering exertions" in aid of the Washingtonian temperance movement. But lest the sympathetic readers of the *Olive Plant* be overawed

---

[1] Interested students are encouraged to read this essay in the original form. Ruth M. Alexander, "'We Are Engaged as a Band of Sisters': Class and Domesticity in the Washingtonian Temperance Movement, 1840–1850," *Journal of American History* 75 (3) (Dec. 1988), 763–85.

[2] *Olive Plant and Ladies' Temperance Advocate*, July 15, 1842, p. 5.

by the successes of the Chelsea women, the society's report ended with the modest claim, "We have not any cases of thrilling interest. . . . Our tale will be unvarnished, we have no disposition to shine."[3]

Feminine modesty, charity, the "rescue" of destitute or degraded females, and attentiveness to the reform of personal habits, all evident in the report from the Ladies' Chelsea Temperance Benevolent Society, were common features of the reform efforts spearheaded by middle-class women during the nineteenth century. In the antebellum era thousands of wives from the homes of merchants, manufacturers, professionals, and politicians left well-appointed parlors, nurseries, and kitchens to champion benevolent and reform causes. Numerous historians have asserted that this enthusiastic activism was inspired in part by middle-class women's adherence to the tenets of domesticity—an ideology that sharply differentiated the "public" world of men from the "private" world of women and yet ultimately prompted many matrons to take their message of moral probity into the temperance, moral reform, antislavery, and woman's rights movements.[4]

However, the Washingtonian cause, to which the Chelsea society claimed loyalty, drew its constituents largely from the working and lower middle classes. Its most visible leaders were skilled artisans newly converted to the cause of total abstinence, and Washingtonianism marked the first time that American women of relatively low rank joined and played a prominent role in reform. The thousands of women who established Martha Washington societies in the 1840s throughout the Northeast and Midwest were, like Mrs. Bowrason, primarily from the homes of laborers, artisans, shopkeepers, and clerks. (See Figure 15.1.) As one contemporary observer of the Marthas in New York and New Jersey wrote, their societies were "composed mostly of women whose earthly comforts are derived mainly from the labor of their own hands." Later in the decade the temperance benevolent societies disbanded, yet women of the working and lower middle classes remained active in the cause and organized new temperance mutual benefit societies. (See Figure 15.2.) Women of higher status and privilege

---

[3]Ibid., July 15, 1841, p. 12; ibid., July 15, 1842, p. 5.

[4]Carroll Smith-Rosenberg, "Beauty, the Beast, and the Militant Woman," *American Quarterly* 23 (Oct. 1971), 562–84; Keith Melder, *Beginnings of Sisterhood: The American Woman's Rights Movement, 1800–1850* (New York, 1977); Barbara Berg, *The Remembered Gate: Origins of American Feminism: The Woman and the City, 1800–1860* (New York, 1978); Ellen Carol DuBois, *Feminism and Suffrage: The Emergence of an Independent Women 's Movement in America, 1848–1869* (Ithaca, 1978); Mary Beth Norton, "The Paradox of Women's Sphere," in *Women of America,* ed. Carol Berkin and Mary Beth Norton (New York, 1979); Ruth Bordin, *Woman and Temperance: The Quest for Power and Liberty, 1873–1900* (Philadelphia, 1981); Jed Dannenbaum, "The Origins of Temperance Activism and Militancy among American Women," *Journal of Social History* 15 (Winter 1981), 235–52; Barbara Epstein, *The Politics of Domesticity: Women, Evangelism, and Temperance in Nineteenth-Century America* (Middletown, 1981); Mary P. Ryan, *Cradle of the Middle Class: The Family in Oneida County, New York, 1790–1865* (New York, 1981); Ian R. Tyrrell, "Women and Temperance in Antebellum America, 1830–1860," *Civil War History,* 28 (June 1982), 128–52; Nancy Hewitt, *Women's Activism and Social Change: Rochester, New York, 1822–1872* (Ithaca, 1984); Lori D. Ginzberg, "'Moral Suasion Is Moral Balderdash': Women, Politics, and Social Activism in the 1850s," *Journal of American History* 73 (Dec. 1986), 601–22.

Figure 15.1   Occupational Status of Officers of Martha Washington Temperance Benevolent Societies

	NEW YORK CITY 1842–1843 (15 SOCIETIES)	HARTFORD 1842–1850 (1 SOCIETY)	ROCHESTER 1844 (1 SOCIETY)	NEW HAVEN 1842–1846 (1 SOCIETY)
A. HUSBAND'S OR FATHER'S OCCUPATION				
Manufacturer		1		1
Merchant		2		
Professional	4	1	1	5
Artisan	8	7	2	2
Shopkeeper	2	7		4
Clerk	4	3	3	
Laborer	4	3		
B. FEMALE OFFICER'S OCCUPATION				
Boarding school director				1
Teacher	1			
Boardinghouse keeper			1	
Dressmaker		1		
Corsetmaker	1			
N	24	25	7	13

Sources: On New York City women, see the *Olive Plant and Ladies' Temperance Advocate*, April 1, 1842, pp. 151–52; ibid., Feb. 1, 1843, pp. 118–19; and John Doggett, *New York City Directory* (New York, 1843). On Hartford, see E. Geer, *Geer's Hartford City Directory* (9 vols., Hartford, 1842–1850). On Rochester, see James L. Elwood and Dellon M. Dewey, *A Directory and Gezeteer of the City of Rochester for 1844* (Rochester, 1844). On New Haven, see J. M. Patten, *Patten's New Haven Directory* (2 vols., New Haven, 1842–1846).

Figure 15.2   Occupational Status of Female Officers of Ten Washingtonian Mutual Benefit Societies New York City, 1847

	HUSBAND'S OR FATHER'S OCCUPATION	FEMALE OFFICER'S OCCUPATION
Manufacturer		
Merchant		
Professional	1	
Artisan	20	
Shopkeeper	2	
Clerk	1	
Laborer	6	
Boardinghouse keeper	1	
Shoe binder	1	

Sources: *Pearl*, March 27, 1847; John Doggett, *New York City Directory* (New York, 1846).
Note: I have been unable to locate membership lists for women in mutal benefit societies outside of New York City.

were not absent from the movement, especially in small cities and towns, but the leadership of most female Washingtonian societies was probably in the hands of women of humble background and social standing. What motivated such women to join the temperance cause? How are we to interpret their sentiments and their activism?[5]

The deleterious effects of alcohol within the family setting may have been the principal concern of the women who joined the Washingtonian movement. Certainly that was true in New York State, one of the most active and well-documented centers of Washingtonianism, and the region upon which this study is largely based. Many Martha Washingtonian societies were auxiliaries to men's societies, with family ties bringing men and women into the movement. Moreover, the *Olive Plant's* editor noted that female Washingtonians were often the wives and daughters of reformed inebriates, and that Washingtonian meetings were "deeply affecting, especially where women have been seen urging their husbands to come up and sign the pledge."[6]

The workingmen who pleased wives and daughters by signing the pledge of total abstinence sought by individual reform, or what Jed Dannenbaum calls "worldly redemption," to save themselves from the destructive uncertainties of the antebellum economy. Yet as numerous historians have argued, male Washingtonians' new devotion to sobriety signaled only a partial acquiescence to the values of efficiency and self-control dear to the emerging middle classes. Washingtonian men took as much inspiration from the artisan ethic of self-improvement as they did from new middle-class prescriptions. Indeed, many of the new pledge takers vociferously defended the honor, self-respect, and lively social traditions of laboring and artisan men.[7]

Although historians have been extremely attentive to the class and social identity of Washingtonian men, they have given only superficial analysis to Washingtonian women's enthusiasm for total abstinence and their apparent adherence to domesticity.... [H]istorians [have not] investigated differences between the domesticity of [Washingtonian] women of high and low

---

[5]Lorenzo Dow Johnson, *Martha Washingtonianism; or, A History of the Ladies' Temperance Benevolent Societies* (New York, 1843), 22; Hewitt, *Women's Activism and Social Change,* 59; Ryan, *Cradle of the Middle Class,* 133–34. E. Geer, *Geer's Hartford City Directory* (9 vols., Hartford, 1842–1850). See also Table 1.

[6]T. W. Johnson, *A Brief History of the Rise and Fall of the Temperance Reformation* (Glen's Falls, 1845), 29; *Journal of the American Temperance Union,* Jan. 1842, p. 6; *Olive Plant and Ladies' Temperance Advocate,* July 15, 1842, pp. 5–7; ibid., Aug. 15, 1842, pp. 22, 28; ibid., July 15, 1841, pp. 13–14. Of forty female Washingtonian societies in New York City, twenty-six were listed as the auxilliaries of men's groups. See *Crystal Fount and Rechabite Recorder,* Dec. 30, 1843.

[7]Jed Dannenbaum, *Drink and Disorder: Temperance Reform in Cincinnati from the Washingtonian Revival to the W.C.T.U.* (Urbana, 1984), 32–42, esp. 36; Dannenbaum, "Origins of Temperance Activism and Militancy among American Women," 235–52; Sean Wilentz, *Chants Democratic: New York City and the Rise of the American Working Class, 1788–1850* (New York, 1985); Ian R. Tyrrell, *Sobering Up: From Temperance to Prohibition in Antebellum America, 1800–1860* (Westport, 1979), 159–224; Bruce Laurie, "Nothing on Impulse," *Labor History* 15 (Summer 1974), 337–66; Emil Christopher Vigilante, "The Temperance Reform in New York State, 1829–1851" (PhD diss., New York University, 1964); John Allen Krout, *The Origins of Prohibition* (New York, 1925), 182–222.

socioeconomic status. They did not consider how the values, actions, or aspirations of women in the movement reflected their actual experience within working-class and lower middle-class communities. Nor have they reconciled the apparent contradiction between Washingtonian men's stubborn loyalty to artisan traditions and Washingtonian women's fascination with (supposedly) middle-class ideology.[8]

Failure to explain adequately Washingtonian domesticity may derive in part from the long-held assumption that domesticity had little positive meaning for women of the working classes. . . . Fresh efforts to understand the meanings of gender and domesticity in the Washingtonian movement can draw upon recent developments in social, labor, and women's history. During the past decade many historians have analyzed class formation in the nineteenth century.[9] They have given little direct attention to the gender ideologies of the working classes, but their work suggests that the ideology and practice of domesticity had varied meanings and sources and found adherents even among women of poor or marginal means.

Social and labor historians have discovered permeable and shifting class boundaries and dramatic rates of upward and downward mobility throughout the antebellum period and well into the postbellum years. The social and economic instability of the nineteenth century created conditions for the forging of ambitions and identities and the appropriation of behaviors based not only on immediate socioeconomic circumstances but on past experience and an anticipated or imagined future as well. Furthermore, within the shifting boundaries of both working-class and middle-class life, the location and nature of women's and men's social and economic duties were becoming increasingly disparate. Working-class women might earn money by doing piecework in their homes, by taking in boarders, or by accepting domestic positions or factory employment, but their wage-earning capabilities were far below those of the men in their families. And as male artisans and apprentices were forced out of small home-based workshops and into an industrial wage economy, they lost immediate oversight of domestic affairs. Working-class women's responsibilities in caring for the needs of the family, like those of more affluent women, gained in scope and importance.[10]

---

[8]Wilentz, *Chants Democratic*, 311; Tyrrell, *Sobering Up*, 179–83; Tyrrell, "Women and Temperance in Antebellum America," 140–41; Dannenbaum, "Origins of Temperance Activism and Militancy among American Women," 235–37; Ryan, *Cradle of the Middle Class*, 139–42.

[9]Stuart Blumin, *The Urban Threshold: Growth and Change in a Nineteenth-Century American Community* (Chicago, 1976); Susan E. Hirsch, *Roots of the American Working Class. The Industrialization of Crafts in Newark, 1800–1860* (Philadelphia, 1978); Bruce Laurie, *Working People of Philadelphia, 1800–1850* (Philadelphia, 1980); Wilentz, *Chants Democratic*; Ryan, *Cradle of the Middle Class*.

[10]Alice Kessler-Harris, *Out to Work: A History of Wage-Earning Women in the United States* (New York, 1982), 45–55; Carol Groneman, "'She Earns as a Child, She Pays as a Man': Women Workers in a Mid-Nineteenth Century New York City Community," in *Class, Sex, and the Woman Worker*, ed. Milton Cantor and Bruce Laurie (Westport, 1977); Hirsch, *Roots of the American Working Class*, 26–27, 38–41.

Building on suggestions that widespread social instability and cross-class patterns of sex role differentiation made domesticity attractive to members of both the working and middle classes, historians have begun to investigate the meanings of gender and the sources of gender ideologies within the working classes.... They have been especially sensitive to the ways in which working-class women's (and men's) responses to labor struggles were conditioned by attempts to reconcile traditional gender roles with changing socioeconomic circumstances."[11]

Mary H. Blewett's work on New England's nineteenth-century female shoe binders offers an especially intriguing analysis of gender consciousness within the changing artisan household of the antebellum era. Blewett argues that female shoe binders tended to identify themselves, neither as wageworkers nor as artisans, but rather as females dedicated to family interests who had to squeeze poorly paid shoe-binding jobs into their already busy lives. Women began binding shoes in the 1780s to increase the earnings of their families, but the mode of their integration into the production process left intact the traditional apprenticeship system and the dominance of men in artisan families. Sewing shoe uppers alone in their own kitchens, shoe binders had no craft status and were isolated from the discussions of work, politics, and religion that took place in the all-male workshops where the shoes were lasted and finished. During the antebellum period shoe binders rarely organized to demand higher wages because they found it difficult to reconcile "contradictions between perceptions of the proper gender role for women in the family and their consciousness as workers in production." Similarly, they were reluctant to join artisan and journeyman shoemakers in political efforts to uphold the integrity of their work and culture. "Gender-based ideology and work experience cut [these] women off from the . . . vital tradition of collective resistance." In 1860, when young female shoe binders employed in steam-powered factories sought to increase their wages by forging an alliance with female shoe binders still working at home, the home-workers remained loyal to traditional notions of gender and to the "preindustrial family

---

[11]Carol Groneman and Mary Beth Norton, eds., *"To Toil the Livelong Day": America's Women at Work, 1780-1980* (Ithaca, 1987). Mary H. Blewett, "The Sexual Divison of Labor and the Artisan Tradition in Early Industrial Capitalism: The Case of New England Shoemaking, 1780-1860," ibid., 35-46; and Carole Turbin, "Beyond Conventional Wisdom: Women's Wage Work, Household Economic Contribution, and Labor Activism in a Mid-Nineteenth-Century Working-Class Community" ibid., 47-68. See also Thomas Dublin, *Women at Work: The Transformation of Work and Community in Lowell, Massachusetts, 1826-1860* (New York: 1979); Ava Baron, "Women and the Making of the American Working Class: A Study of the Proletarianization of Printers," *Review of Radical Political Economics* 14 (Fall 1982), 23-42; Ruth Milkman, ed., *Women, Work, and Protest: A Century of US Women's Labor History* (Boston, 1985); Jacquelyn Dowd Hall, "Disorderly Women: Gender and Labor Militancy in the Appalachian South," *Journal of American History* 73 (Sept. 1986), 354-82; Jacqueline Jones, *Labor of Love, Labor of Sorrow: Black Women, Work, and the Family from Slavery to the Present* (New York, 1985); Dolores Janiewski, *Sisterhood Denied: Race, Gender, and Class in a New South Community* (Philadelphia, 1985); Kathy Peiss, *Cheap Amusements: Working Women and Leisure in Turn-of-the-Century New York* (Philadelphia, 1986); and Christine Stansell, *City of Women: Sex and Class in New York, 1789-1869* (New York, 1986).

wage system" and shunned association with shoe binders who proposed "to regard women as fellow workers outside of family relationships."[12]

The importance of Blewett's work lies in its location of the basis of a gender ideology, in this instance one of domesticity, in the discrepancy between men's and women's duties and prerogatives, whatever their level of wealth. She emphasizes the reciprocity between experience and ideology and the historical agency of laboring-class women, rather than the prescriptive role played by ideologues or reformers of the middle class. Blewett's assessment of the shoe binders' domesticity is negative, since it impeded class activism. Nevertheless, she succeeds in outlining a "class basis for the cult of domesticity among working women." Blewett's recognition that female domesticity existed independently of material comforts or social privilege and drew on long-standing traditions of artisan family organization establishes the starting point for an analysis of Washingtonian women.[13]

The women who joined the Washingtonian movement during its first phase, from approximately 1840 to 1843, dedicated themselves to four principal tasks in aid of the cause. Their temperance benevolent societies sought to provide material aid to those in want and to persuade both hardened and moderate drinkers to sign the pledge of total abstinence. They offered instruction to mothers to prevent them from leading their offspring to intemperate habits. Finally, the Martha Washingtonians took messages of inspiration and moral fortitude to recently reformed groups of young men. In each task, Washingtonian women revealed their deep absorption in the affairs of the home and the conviction that the use of alcohol was inimical to family happiness.[14]

The early Martha Washingtonians declared that their foremost duty was to provide reforming inebriates with material aid. Society members gathered as often as once a week to sew and repair clothing, and they distributed garments, furniture, bedding and cash in a constant round of visits to the homes of the newly abstinent. A few groups formed primitive employment agencies that helped reformed men and women locate jobs with employers who supported the Washingtonian movement and were themselves temperate.[15]

---

[12]Mary Blewett, "Work, Gender, and the Artisan Tradition in New England Shoemaking, 1780–1860," *Journal of Social History* 17 (Winter 1983), 221–48, esp. 239, 240; Blewett, "Sexual Division of Labor and the Artisan Tradition in Early Industrial Capitalism," 43–45.

[13]For a recent argument that differs from Blewett's, see Stansell, *City of Women*, 46–62, 213–14. Stansell argues that the values of domesticity were irrelevant to women of the laboring classes, who could ill afford to cultivate the delicate sensibilities or carefully guarded privacy of genteel women.

[14]Sources on the Martha Washingtonians include newspapers, contemporary histories, almanacs, and printed copies of association laws and constitutions. Sources of particular importance are the *Olive Plant and Ladies' Temperance Advocate* (published in New York, 1841–1843) and the *Pearl* (New York, 1846–47), two Washingtonian newspapers edited by women and devoted exclusively to female activists.

[15]*Journal of the American Temperance Union*, Aug. 1841, p. 119; *Olive Plant and Ladies' Temperance Advocate*, April 20, 1842, p. 159.

Underlying Washingtonian women's material assistance was the belief that alcoholic men and women were unfit to support or properly care for their families. Personal experience and observation had shown them that inebriates and their loved ones lived in conditions of "wretchedness and despair." The Martha Washington Society of New York City reported that its members decided to "form ourselves into an association" in aid of temperance because they had seen that "the use of all intoxicating drinks has caused, and is causing, incalculable evils to individuals and families, and has a tendency to prostrate all means adapted to the moral, social, and eternal happiness of the whole human family." Every issue of the *Olive Plant* was filled with society reports and personal testimonials that revealed Washingtonian women's intimate knowledge of alcoholism. In bringing aid to reforming inebriates Washingtonian women stressed the interdependence of the family group and the effects of intemperance on both employability and "domestic happiness." As the Lady Dorcas Temperance Society of Albany, New York, reported, their object was "to relieve the necessity of the reformed inebriate, and those that suffer with him or her, by all consistent and proper means that are in our power."[16]

Second, like Washingtonian men, the Marthas sought to bring the pledge of total abstinence to those who still used alcohol. The women's societies were particularly concerned with reclaiming inebriates of their own sex, thereby laying the foundation for the "moral resurrection" of homes "previously given to vice and cruelty." Many Martha Washingtonian societies claimed large numbers of formerly alcoholic women as members, including some "inveterate cases."[17] The Lady Howard Temperance Society of New York City established a home for "previously intemperate widows" and their families where mothers would no longer be "beset with every temptation to vice" and the children would be plucked from "the sure road to depravity." "In a convenient, well-ordered home [the mothers] will learn to support themselves, and both parents and offspring receive sound and regular instruction." . . .[18]

Efforts to rehabilitate alcoholic females rested on the conviction that it was women's duty to establish order and stability in the domestic setting. They also demonstrated profound faith in the plasticity of the female character. In telling of a woman who had successfully reformed after twenty years as a drunkard, one society asked, "to whom could she have appealed had there been no similar association?" Washingtonian women were willing to accept previously intemperate women into their ranks as full members, believing that even an utterly degraded

---

[16]Johnson, *Martha Washingtonianism*, 9–10. On Washingtonian women's knowledge of alcoholism, see, for example, the letter by "M.C.C.," in which a woman recounts the destruction wrought by her husband's alcoholism, *Olive Plant and Ladies' Temperance Advocate*, April 1, 1842, p. 148. Ibid., April 20, 1842, p. 159.

[17]"Guide to Societies," *Olive Plant and Ladies' Temperance Advocate*, July 15, 1842, p. 5. On formerly alcoholic women, see, for example, "First Annual Report, Lady Howard Temperance Society," ibid., March 1842, p. 8; "Reports," ibid., June 1, 1842, p. 184; "Guide to Societies," ibid., July 15, 1842, p. 5, esp. report of the Ladies' Chelsea Temperance Benevolent Society.

[18]Ibid., Jan. 15, 1842, p. 110; ibid., July 15, 1841, p. 13.

woman might be identified with, comforted, and redeemed. As the Lady Mount Vernon Temperance Benevolent Society of New York City reported:

> Instead of reproaching the fallen of our sex with harsh rebukes, we offer the friendship and confidence of our ladies. After signing the pledge, they are visited and their immediate wants supplied, as far as possible, and employment secured for them. Thus, real and efficient sympathy give them a motive for good action and rarely do they disappoint us.[19]

Both the distribution of charitable aid and the search for converts to the cause required that Martha Washingtonians visit homes throughout their communities. Such visits served to reinforce the experience and knowledge that Washingtonian women already had of the violence that alcoholic men did to their families, and the tragedy that alcoholic mothers wrought in their children's lives. The Martha Washingtonian Temperance Union of Utica, New York, reported visiting a home that neighbors had been too fearful to enter. The wife had broken her pledge of abstinence and while drunk got into a fight with her similarly inebriated husband. "It was long before she would show us her face and when she did, we almost shuddered as we gazed upon it. It was one continuous bruise, her eyes so swollen she could hardly open them." The visitors' dismay was overcome, and their courage rewarded, when the "penitent" woman renewed her pledge, her husband shortly following suit. . . .[20]

Washingtonian women acted out of sympathy for the entire family group and sought out the most disreputable members of their communities. They and their brothers in the movement sought to construct an alternative to the middle-class mainstream of the temperance movement where the drunkard "was likely to be ridiculed, or denounced, or perhaps turned out of doors." As the Lady Howard Temperance Society of Manhattan wrote, members had "witnessed the awful havoc that intemperance has made upon individuals and the well-being of the community" and were pledged to seek out "degraded inebriates . . . [even] though they may . . . die at their posts doing good."[21]

Concern for the well-being of families and children also prompted Washingtonian women to attempt to teach mothers to overcome the "deeply rooted . . . prejudices and propensities" that might endanger their children's future happiness. As charity visitors they urged mothers to set a healthful example to their children by pledging "not to use or provide for other's use, directly or indirectly, as an article of entertainment or beverage, any intoxicating liquors." Martha Washingtonians were also active in the formation of juvenile temperance societies that flourished in New York, Massachusetts, and Connecticut. . . .[22]

---

[19]Johnson, *Martha Washingtonianism*, 20, 69.

[20]*Olive Plant and Ladies' Temperance Advocate*, Aug. 15, 1842, pp. 29–30.

[21]D. C. Burdick, *Evolution of Washingtonianism*; or, *Society Mirror* (Owego, 1843), 4; *Olive Plant and Ladies' Temperance Advocate*, March 1842, p. 8.

[22]*Olive Plant and Ladies' Temperance Advocate*, July 15, 1842, p. 9. On the growth of juvenile temperance societies, see American Temperance Union, *Report of the Executive Committee* (New York, 1849); and Connecticut Washington Total Abstinence Society, *First Annual Report* (New Haven, 1845).

Figure 15.3
"The Husband, in a state of furious drunkeness, kills his wife with the bottle." –*New York Organ and Temperance Safeguard,* February 19, 1848. Courtesy New York State Library.

Washingtonian women's fourth field of activity—inspirational work—reflected the primacy of their concern for the family, while perhaps offering relief from the emotional and physical rigors of home visits. Washingtonian women insisted that it was primarily through women's exertions that drinking "fashions" could be altered. As one female activist asserted, women "must trample . . . the accursed social practice of wine drinking beneath their feet."[23] Unfurling banners that proclaimed Let the Rising Generation Be a Temperate One or Our Cause Is Righteous and Will Prevail, Martha Washingtonians took the message of abstinence to gatherings of Washingtonian men or, more often, to volunteer fire companies. Fire fighters were generally young men of socioeconomic backgrounds similar to those of the Washingtonians. In many cases they were newcomers to the city, independent of their families for the first time, and "at the most reckless excitable stage of life." Urban fire companies functioned as social fraternities, but they were notorious for the "riotous and disorderly" conduct of their members. Moreover, they enjoyed the "sport" of fire fighting so much that they were of dubious value in protecting property.[24]

Despite their poor reputation, youthful fire fighters won the interest, rather than the scorn, of Martha Washingtonians. Believing that the companies encouraged intemperance, Washingtonian women acted as surrogate mothers and intervened to save impressionable young men from becoming fixed in habits that

---

[23]*Olive Plant and Ladies' Temperance Advocate,* July 15, 1841, p. 12.

[24]Johnson, *Martha Washingtonianism,* 45, 74. A nineteenth-century history of fire companies is quoted in Joseph F. Kett, *Rites of Passage: Adolescence in America, 1790 to the Present* (New York, 1977), 91.

would surely produce misery for them and their families. As the Wallabout Martha Washingtonian Society of Brooklyn declared in presenting a silk and tasseled banner to Engine Company No. 12,

> To you and your honorable company we now surrender the keeping of this momento; take it as proof of the interest we feel in your moral welfare, and whenever the armies of Temperance are summoned to the bloodless combat, rally around it, and bear it proudly there.[25]

At a banner presentation in Middletown, New York, Martha Washingtonians warned their masculine audience, "Heaven forbid that you ever prove recreant to the confidence now so fully reposed in you." And in lower Manhattan, the Ladies' Cold Spring Benevolent Society sought to reinforce a young men's temperance society's dedication to the cause by declaiming:

> Your generous enlistment in this noble cause . . . is truly worthy of the high born spirit of your patriotism. . . . Who can be independent when thousands of weeping mothers and sisters have followed their nearest and dearest relatives, broken-hearted, to a drunkard's grave?[26]

Although morally righteous, Martha Washingtonians were obviously not unsympathetic to alcoholic men. The drunken husband, father, or son was believed to be both physically addicted to the substance of alcohol and unable to break away from social companions or settings that encouraged drink. He was thus as much the victim of a disease as his family was.[27] However, if Washingtonian women were convinced of the efficacy of the "cold water cure," they agreed that the reforming inebriate could not succeed without guidance. In their presentation of material aid and temperance banners to reforming inebriates, they combined an understanding of the alcoholic's lack of will and susceptibility to outside influence with a belief in their special capacity, as women, to provide moral resolve and direction.

The activism and rhetoric of the early Martha Washingtonians attests to their belief in the centrality of women's role in nurturing and protecting the family. The Washingtonian emphasis on women's maternal and moral responsibilities paralleled values and behaviors of the nineteenth century's new middle class. Yet that emphasis had been forcefully shaped, not by domestic privacy and comfort, but by familiarity with poverty, insecurity, and violence. It reflected

---

[25]*Olive Plant and Ladies' Temperance Advocate*, Jan. 15, 1842, p. 140.

[26]Ibid., Aug. 15, 1842, p. 29; ibid., Nov. 15, 1842, p. 80.

[27]On the etiology of alcoholism as viewed by the Washingtonians, see Burdick, Evolution of Washingtonianism, 4; *Olive Plant and Ladies' Temperance Advocate*, Jan. 15, 1842, p. 108; Sarah Ellis, "Intemperance As It Operates upon Individual Character," *Cold Water Magazine* 3 (July 1843), 12–15. Earlier temperance advocates were not unmindful of alcohol's impact on the family, but they were most concerned about its detrimental impact on industrial productivity and national growth. See Samuel Chipman, *Report of an Examination of Poor-Houses, Jails, etc., in the State of New York and in the Counties of Berkshire, Massachusetts; Litchfield, Connecticut; and Bennington, Vermont, etc.* (Albany, 1834); and Nathanial Scudder Prime, *The Pernicious Effects of Intemperance in the Use of Ardent Spirits and the Remedy of That Evil* (Brooklyn, 1812).

Washingtonian women's precarious dependence on men who might squander their meager but much-needed earnings at the corner tavern or turn on their families with a drunkard's wrath. Washingtonian domesticity was inspired too by the responsibility that the Marthas felt for children who might lose all protection if their mothers gave in to the temptations of drink.

Yet if Washingtonian women's domesticity was shaped by fear and urgency, it was also inspired by a fundamental desire to reaffirm what they perceived as the normative, traditional, and reciprocal obligations of men and women in artisan and laboring households. Washingtonian women were convinced that as wives and mothers they could not afford to remain silent while men, struggling to protect jobs, skills, and status in a changing economy, succumbed to the temporary pleasures of drink. Ultimately, Washingtonian domesticity rested on the conviction that if workingmen were to continue to be dutiful breadwinners, women must take responsibility for "keeping the morals of our brothers." The female editor of the *Olive Plant* summarized those sentiments when she declared,

> In a war like this, where the enemy has entrenched himself in the strongholds of domestic life, woman as the guardian of the sanctuary, must do battle for herself and for those dearer to her than her own heart's blood.[28]

As early as 1842, the Washingtonian movement showed signs of weakening as it was beset with internal disputes over its inexperienced leaders, lack of organization, alienation of elite temperance and religious leaders, and "low-class" social affairs. The resolve of many new abstainers wore thin and most societies suffered from high rates of "backsliding." Both the men's and women's societies were affected, and the *Olive Plant* did not hesitate to print news of female Washingtonians' distress at the declining appeal of their cause. In one such report, the Martha Washingtonians of Gloversville, New York, shared their disappointment over recent "violations" of the pledge among members. From Albany came the lament that the Marthas were no longer winning new converts and that there were many "with whom our efforts have as yet proved unavailing." And the Washingtonian lecturer Lorenzo Dow Johnson complained that the women's societies were "wanting in active and interested members of the poorer and working classes."[29]

Washingtonian men and women soon began to regroup, forming mutual benefit societies that adopted strict rules regarding the admission and day-to-day behavior of their members. Giving up their efforts to rescue the unreformed, they concentrated on providing support to those who had already demonstrated a basic, if still somewhat faltering, commitment to the pledge. Women were less frequently called upon to seek out and extend aid and sympathy to destitute drunkards, and most female Washingtonians gave up their charitable work and banner presentations. Instead, they turned their attention to a closer scrutiny of behavior within their own societies and within the ranks of the movement as a

---

[28]*Olive Plant and Ladies' Temperance Advocate*, July 15, 1841, p. 12; ibid., Aug. 2, 1841, p. 20.

[29]Tyrrell, *Sobering Up*, 195–206; Dannenbaum, *Drink and Disorder*, 38–42; *Olive Plant and Ladies' Temperance Advocate*, Feb. 1, 1843, p. 118; ibid., July 15, 1842, p. 8; ibid., Feb. 1, 1843, p. 118.

whole. Washingtonian men gave up the rambunctious and emotional "experi-ence meetings" and the all-male entertainments that had distinguished their early years, and Washingtonian women took charge of planning social activities for the movement.

Those organizational adjustments were part of an effort to rebuild and pre-serve the Washingtonian cause. Historians argue that they also signaled a deep-ening commitment among Washingtonian men to middle-class standards of behavior. The men's mutual benefit societies, organized under the direction of new national organizations such as the Sons of Temperance, gained most of their support from professionals or artisans who hoped to translate their traditional skills into profitable talents or commodities. The new societies failed to win wide-spread support from unskilled laborers, who were less likely to achieve status or security in an industrial economy. By the late 1840s the men's mutual benefit societies had lost the organizational autonomy and distinctive social identity that had characterized the Washingtonian movement in its early years and had merged with the middle-class mainstream of the temperance movement.[30]

What of Washingtonian women? Many of their temperance benevolent soci-eties disbanded in 1842 and 1843, new mutual benefit societies replacing them almost overnight. First notice of a female mutual benefit society appeared in November 1842 when the Lady Prospect Temperance Benevolent Society in Manhattan announced the "novel features" of its organization to the readers of the *Olive Plant*. In return for an initiation fee of fifty cents and weekly dues of twelve and a half cents members could be assured of two dollars per week in sick benefits and twenty dollars in death benefits. With eighty-two members, the society already had sixty dollars in its treasury. . . .[31]

Some of the female mutual benefit societies declared their loyalty to the old "Martha Washington principle" of going into "the abodes of poverty and misery and ministering to the wants of the wretched and downtrodden."[32] This senti-ment was especially common in societies affiliated with the Daughters of Rechab, a competitor to the larger Daughters of Temperance. Still, it was the rare society that submitted reports of charitable work to the *Pearl*, a New York newsweekly that reported on Washingtonian women's mutual benefit societies.

Instead, the new groups had three basic functions: to care for one another in illness and at the hour of death, to advance the cause of temperance by fostering female unity, and to organize excursions and entertainments for the enjoyment of all adherents to cold-water principles. These concerns appear quite different from those of the early Martha Washingtonians, but underlying both was a per-sistent dedication to the protection of home and family against the misfortunes that haunted the working and lower middle classes. Having witnessed the effects of backsliding in the movement and in their own homes and communities,

---

[30]Tyrrell, *Sobering Up*, 195–206; Wilentz, *Chants Democratic*, 311–14, 324; Laurie, *Working People of Philadelphia*, 122–24; Dannenbaum, *Drink and Disorder*, 41–42.

[31]*Olive Plant and Ladies' Temperance Advocate*, Nov. 15, 1842, p. 79.

[32]*Pearl*, Dec. 19, 1846, p. 228; ibid., Feb. 20, 1847, p. 299.

female members of the mutual benefit societies sought to help one another with-stand the unpredictability of adversity. Having seen reformed husbands once again "fall" into "bad company and environment," Washingtonian women had learned that the "right to a sober husband" had not yet been secured.[33] That real-ization led them to refine and further elaborate their domestic ideology, high-lighting their own moral virtue as the best protection against the sudden loss of support from husband or father.

The seriousness with which the women's mutual benefit societies regarded their duty to provide illness and death benefits to dues-paying members in good standing is revealed in their printed advertisements and reports. Weekly notices in the back pages of the *Pearl* disclosed the precise amount that each society had collected, and if the society was fortunate enough to have an account, the name of the bank in which savings were kept and the rate at which interest accrued. The handful of annual reports published by the *Pearl* specified dues collected, benefits and other expenses paid, and "balances on hand." They showed that societies could expect to spend at least one-half of their yearly savings on direct benefit disbursements. . . .[34]

The practical care offered by the mutual benefit societies easily shaded into efforts to improve female unity. A "poor widow . . . with three young daughters" became a member of the Rechabina Tent in New York City and soon discovered the "beautiful operation of the association."

> No sooner was it known that she was ill than she found friends and sisters at her bedside. She was provided with money, medical attendance, medicines—all that was needful; every night she had careful watchers, and, at last, when the scene of mortal life drew to its close, she breathed out her parting soul in the arms of three Daughters of Rechab—comforted in her last hour to know that those she loved, the orphans she was leaving, would neither be friendless nor destitute.[35]

Indeed, female unity was the centerpiece of the mutual benefit societies, even when it was not required by the illness or death of a member. Washingto-nian women had come to understand female unity as the foundation of domes-ticity and as a preventive to intemperance, poverty, and suffering. It was not a mere social contrivance, but rather the product of deliberately cultivated moral virtues. By "improving [their] social and moral condition, and elevating the female character," members would achieve "unity of action, and advance the cause of Virtue, Love, and Temperance."[36]

Female unity was also served by the close ties that mutual benefit societies established with neighborhood churches. There the society members found

---

[33]*Pearl*, June 6, 1846, p. 4; ibid., July 18, 1846, p. 52.

[34]The ratio of dues collected to benefits paid by four societies (all in their second year) were as follows: Harper Union, $1028/$503; Palm Tent, $481/$342; American Union, $337/$250; Washington Union, $1175/$1137. *Pearl*, Dec. 19, 1846, Feb. 20, Feb. 27, March 6, 1847.

[35]*Crystal Fount and Rechabite Recorder*, Oct. 3, 1846, p. 14.

[36]"Brooklyn Union No. 4, Daughters of Temperance," *Pearl*, Dec. 12, 1846, p. 224.

spiritual affirmation of their belief in the moral and social importance of the female sex. In thanks for a Bible received from the Mariners' Church, a young woman of the Perseverance Union declared:

> the beautiful Book . . . gives to woman her true position. We look to other lands where its influence has never been felt . . . and we see our sex degraded, ignorant, and menial . . . and we thank our God that our lot has been cast here. We are engaged as a band of sisters; enlisted in the heaven directed work of ameliorating the condition of society.[37]

If solidarity was achieved in part through mutual benefit and religiosity, it was also enhanced by strict standards governing the admission and subsequent conduct of Washingtonian women. The earliest Martha Washingtonian societies had no requirements for membership save a willingness to sign the pledge of total abstinence. But in the temperance mutual benefit societies (both male and female) members were also required to be of "good moral standing" and in good health. Men had to show proof of ability to earn a living; women had to show visible means of support. The standards were not taken lightly, for without them the societies would have been unable to collect regular dues and offer benefits. The strict standards also gave Washingtonian women ground rules for judging their own behavior and the character and behavior of others. Without such standards Washingtonian women might have felt less secure in their ability "to raise up the downtrodden, bind up the broken-hearted, and [secure] the eternal banishment of intemperance from our families, our homes, and our land. . . ."[38]

Given their requirements, the women's societies attracted few members who still drank or suffered from alcoholism. The Harper Union of the Daughters of Temperance in New York City was one of many societies dedicated to "preventing" female intemperance, "For it must be admitted (however painful the admission) that Intemperance is not confined to Man alone." But none of the women's mutual benefit societies ever reported the "rescue" of female inebriates as the early Martha Washingtonians had. Virginia Allen, editor of the *Pearl*, was deeply troubled by that characteristic of the new mutual benefit societies. Noting the arrest in a single week of two hundred New York City women on charges of drunkenness, she wrote:

> Where are our Martha Washingtonians? Where those who once waited not for such objects to meet their sight, but rather sought them out and encouraged them in the pure joys of the paths of Temperance? Alas, alas, we are becoming selfish and care no more for the wretched beings whom we once delighted to rescue from misery and starvation.[39]

---

[37]Ibid., April 10, 1847, p. 358.

[38]"First Annual Report, Vigilant Union No. 14, Daughters of Temperance?" ibid., Oct. 10, 1846, p. 149.

[39]"First Annual Report, Harper Union No. 11, Daughters of Temperance," *Pearl*. Oct. 10, 1846, p. 150; ibid., Oct. 3, 1846, p. 141.

Allen's plaintive cry suggests that the temperance mutual benefit societies were unable to promote female solidarity without imposing standards of social exclusivity and rejecting from their ranks the female inebriates whom they had originally hoped to restore "to the paths of virtue and respectability." By the mid-1840s female Washingtonians may have lost much of their former sympathy for female alcoholics, viewing them as women who lived in defiance of the parameters of acceptable womanhood. While they still treated male inebriates as victims reclaimable by womanly persuasion, they may have come to see female inebriates as lacking the moral will essential to "true women." To women intent on proving the power of a peculiarly feminine sensibility in the face of "the grovelling cares and perplexities of ordinary life," female frailty must have seemed a threat to their survival and their sense of worth.[40]

Finally, the female mutual benefit societies took charge of organizing temperance recreation for members of local societies, both male and female, and their families. The women were talented social directors, and the *Pearl* and the *Crystal Fount and Rechabite Recorder* were filled with announcements and reports of banquets, performances by temperance choirs, boating excursions, and temperance festivals in and around New York City. Over four hundred men and women assembled for dinner, dancing, and singing to celebrate the anniversary of Branch Tent No. 2 of the United Daughters of Rechab in October 1846. And though the hall was crowded, Allen was pleased to inform her readers that "perfect respect and decorum prevailed. . . ."[41]

[T]he women who continued to join New York City's mutual benefit societies well into the late 1840s gave no outward sign of caring for the pretensions of leaders at the top of the mutual benefit hierarchies. It is possible that the social affairs of Washingtonians in the late 1840s were faithful imitations of recreations observed among society's elites. More obviously an immediate concern of Washingtonian women was to retain oversight over men who, without the watchful eye and steadying hand of women, might "relapse" into intemperance and again be unable to provide for their families. Their carefully engineered social events, mixed gatherings of women and men (and sometimes children) that replaced the all-male affairs of the early Washingtonians, made oversight possible and relapse less likely.

Women's work in the Washingtonian temperance movement—in both benevolent and mutual benefit societies—cannot be fully understood without considering Washingtonian men's response to it. The available evidence may never allow us to reenter the homes of Martha Washingtonians to evaluate the reactions of men, members and nonmembers alike, to the moral and practical strategies of the "cold water army's" female partisans. We can, however, gain some idea of male perceptions of those strategies by surveying the scattered published comments of male Washingtonians on female participation in the movement. Such

---

[40]*Organ of the Washingtonians and Sons of Temperance*, Oct. 26, 1844, p. 131; *Pearl*, Feb. 20, 1847, p. 299.

[41]*Pearl*, Oct. 24, 1846, p. 165.

evidence reveals that, whatever their actual impact on drinking habits, Washingtonian women did impress their special concerns on Washingtonian men. The women may have been instrumental in encouraging men to weigh not just the economic obligation of husbands toward their wives but also the quality of the relationship between spouses.

During the first years of the movement, men's discussion of women's activism centered on two themes: the severe suffering caused women by intemperate mates and the sympathy and kindness that Washingtonian women offered the reforming inebriate. Washingtonian men were explicit in their discussions of the victimized wife, arguing that the "direst misfortunes" of intemperance fell "most heavily" on innocent women. Typical of this treatment was a Washingtonian newspaper's report about a drunken man who drove his sleigh off a bridge and was killed, leaving a poor widow with nine young children.[42] Such reports were undoubtedly intended to make readers feel guilty, to strengthen their commitment to the pledge or hasten their readiness to sign it. Drawing out the comparison between female innocence and male culpability, men in the movement also remarked Washingtonian women's compassion for the inebriate, however hateful his past actions, and the energy that they devoted to his reform. In his report on the work of the Martha Washingtonian society in Hudson, New York, the editor of the *Columbia Washingtonian* wrote,

> The drunkard is peculiarly sensitive—he has so long been the subject of scorn and contempt, and so unused to kindness that a soft word accompanied by a benevolent action toward him, at once breaks down his stubborn heart, and then, the voice of love may easily call him from the paths of vice.[43]

Praise for the Martha Washingtonians came also from an 1841 national convention of Washingtonians at Saratoga Springs, New York, where a resolution was passed commending the "unwearied labors" of women in the cause. And upon receiving a temperance banner from the Lady Dorcas Temperance Society in Albany, the president of the men's Washingtonian society thanked the ladies for their "approbation," which "will ever nerve our efforts and add new vigor to the blessed cause in which we are engaged."[44]

Those early comments revolved around a simple equation: The drinking habits of men caused their dependents intolerable suffering. Such behavior therefore should be stopped. The mechanics, carpenters, clerks, and laborers who joined the Washingtonian cause tried to sustain their new commitment to abstinence by stressing the importance of their traditional duties as heads of households. Encomiums to feminine devotion merely served to highlight the baseness and irresponsibility of masculine intemperance. The simplicity of the equation paralleled the straightforward character of women's charitable and inspirational work in the early temperance benevolent societies, work directed toward one end—the restoration of family happiness through the termination of alcoholic habits.

---

[42]*Columbia Washingtonian*, April 20, 1843, p. 2.

[43]Ibid., Aug. 18, 1842, p. 2.

[44]*Olive Plant and Ladies' Temperance Advocate*, Aug. 2, 1841, p. 21; ibid., Aug. 15, 1842, p. 27.

The Washingtonian women who joined mutual benefit societies in the mid-1840s had learned that the reform of drinking men depended on more than charity, sermonizing, and supplication; it required subtle and persistent surveillance as well. The men's mutual benefit societies took on some of that burden but Washingtonian women's recreational engineering and heightened moralism extended the scope and power of a specifically feminine surveillance. Comments by male Washingtonians during the late 1840s suggest that female oversight was carried into the home as well. The men's comments are the more fascinating because they emphasize, not the outward form of female surveillance, but the affection and moral strength inspiring it. They reveal as well men's attentiveness, absent at the start of the movement, to the intimate and emotional content of familial relationships, especially within the "conjugal union," and to the desirability of the home as a refuge for both husband and wife.

George Catlin praised the "earnest, consecrated power of female influence" at an 1844 meeting of New York City's Ashland Tent of the Sons of Temperance. In doing so, he described that "power" in terms of the several roles of women within the family. A sister's "affectionate admonition" might save her brother, a mother's "protection, guidance, and encouragement" might keep her child from harm, and a wife as "tender helpmate and . . . affectionate reprover" might be the salvation of her errant husband.[45]

Catlin's remarks acknowledged the range of feminine attachments to be found within the home and praised the moral power and emotional sensitivity that a young unmarried girl might bring to the domestic setting and the temperance cause. In an 1847 address Robert Beatty, a local officer in the Independent Order of Rechabites, suggested that the father too could be drawn into the intimacies of the domestic circle, that his emotional involvement in the family would increase not only his own happiness but that of his wife and children as well.

> Here was a Temperance Home. . . . Contentment beamed in every feature of the father's face; he seemed only anxious to make those about him happy; his wife, ceaseless in her cares to add joy to their home, shared with the laughing daughter and the romping son, his caresses.[46]

Sentimentality aside, Beatty must have hoped that his thoughts and feelings would be appreciated by his fellow members. Some men may have been unmoved, but the public pronouncements of Beatty and other male Washingtonians demonstrate facility with the language of domesticity, and the expectation that it was understandable to others in their ranks. As female Washingtonians endeavored to interpret the necessity and suffering that burdened their lives and to assess the relative importance of men's breadwinning and women's caretaking roles, they succeeded in reminding at least some men in the movement that the secure family was an intensely interdependent unit. In it the distinct economic obligations, moral virtues, and emotional sensibilities of its members were intertwined and mutually reinforcing.

---

[45]*Organ of the Washingtonians and Sons of Temperance*, Oct. 19, 1844, p. 122.

[46]*Crystal Fount and Rechabite Recorder*, Feb. 20, 1847, p. 169.

Figure 15.4
"A re-union—the mother and children restored to a happy temperance home." –*New York Organ and Temperance Safeguard*, April 15, 1848. Courtesy New York State Library.

The history of the Martha Washingtonians adds welcome subtlety to our understanding of the connections between domesticity, class, and reform in antebellum America. The language of domesticity played a critical role in bringing Washingtonian women to an awareness of their social and economic standing, and to an appreciation of the kinds of leverage that they might realistically use to redress their grievances. Washingtonian women were preoccupied with the meaning of gender, with an assessment of their special duties as women in the home and the community. Their sharp focus on gender permitted both a penetrating analysis of the particular effects of alcoholism on female dependency and the family circle and an acute awareness of the special vulnerability of the working and lower middle classes to the destructive power of drink.

Although an ideology of domesticity helped Washingtonian women articulate the realities of their socioeconomic position, it did not prompt them to express outright class consciousness. The absence of evidence that Washingtonian women asserted or struggled over class identity strongly suggests that class loyalty had less salience for women in the movement than for men. Society reports sent to the *Olive Plant* and the *Pearl* revealed obvious class pride in only a few instances. The women of the Ocean Union No. 5 of the Daughters of Temperance declared that it was because of their efforts as the wives, daughters, and sisters of sailors, that "an influence has . . . been exerted on that noble and useful class of men, who have so long with their families been neglected by the moral and religious community."[47]

---

[47]*Pearl*, April 10, 1847, p. 357.

As a rule, however, Washingtonian domesticity appears to have undercut or lowered sensitivity to the barriers or differences between classes. Despite the class consciousness that at first informed the organization of the movement, Washingtonians relied on the power of association to secure the reform of the individual and gave little thought to institutional barriers to social or economic advancement. The domesticity of Washingtonian women further accentuated the movement's ambiguous position on class solidarity. In placing family, morality, and the reciprocal relations of husband and wife above all other considerations, Washingtonian women supplanted the language and consciousness of class with a much stronger consciousness of domestic relations. For Washingtonian women the most promising guarantee of social and economic stability was the adoption of standards of behavior that reflected a sense of responsibility to the family and an emotional attachment to its members.

Some evidence suggests that Washingtonian women gradually acceded to middle-class values: Their eventual ostracism of female inebriates, strict rules of membership, and elaborate social affairs all point to the cultivation of behaviors and values separating and protecting them from the humiliations of impoverished lower-class life. Clearly, Washingtonian women shared in the belief in female moralism and familial devotion at the core of middle-class domesticity. The women's mutual benefit societies may have alienated many poor women who could not afford the dues or did not care to have their backgrounds and habits carefully investigated. So too, some Washingtonian men may have resented the feminine and "respectable" character that Washingtonian women brought to the movement's social events in the mid-1840s.

Yet to argue that Washingtonian women simply embraced middle-class standards or to conclude that nineteenth-century domesticity was essentially a middle-class construct is to ignore the actual operation of domesticity within the Washingtonian movement. Washingtonian women actively interpreted the meanings of gender and domesticity and elaborated a domestic ideology rooted in the exigencies of working-class and lower middle-class families and communities. They successfully combined a domestic ideology with Washingtonian faith in the fundamental worth of artisans and laborers and in the capacity of workingmen to join with one another and their families for the purposes of self-improvement. They were not prevented by lack of wealth or obscurity of rank from finding positive affirmation in domesticity, neither were they prevented from molding it to answer to their particular circumstances. That Washingtonian women appear to have found more certainty in gender than in class identity, to have compensated for economic insecurity and wifely dependence by elaborating and laying heavy emphasis on normative gender behaviors, does not point to a betrayal of class origins. Rather it suggests the immediacy of the family in their daily lives, and their less-than-constant exposure to social or working situations in which class relations were of decisive importance. The activism of Washingtonian women is evidence of the power of domestic ideology, the viability of a domestic model for women who had little material security, and of the fluidity of concepts of domesticity in antebellum life.

Ruth M. Alexander

I became interested in history as a child negotiating the streets of New York City during the tumultuous 1960s. Later, at the City College of New York, Eric Foner, Joan Kelly Gadol, and Barbara Engel encouraged my budding interest in the histories of race, gender, and human liberation. Throughout my career I have explored relationships of power that are associated with modernity, especially modern dynamics of gender and sexuality, race, and humans' relationship to nature. I have published *The 'Girl Problem': Female Sexual Delinquency in New York, 1900–1930* (1995), and I co-edit with Sharon Block and Mary Beth Norton, *Major Problems in American Women's History: Documents and Essays*, now in its fifth edition (2014). My work has appeared in the *Journal of American History, American Quarterly, Small Worlds: Childhood and Adolescence in America, 1850–1950* (1992) and *Sexual Borderlands* (2003). I am presently writing an article that examines the efforts of Jane Jacobs, Rachel Carson, and Betty Friedan to question American modernity's "distortion" of human and non-human nature in the 1960s. I am also writing a book on the environmental history of Longs Peak in Rocky Mountain National Park that examines the intersecting cultures of recreational climbers, park managers, and natural resource scientists and their combined impacts on the mountain landscape during the twentieth century. In addition to being a Professor in the History Department at Colorado State University, I am Faculty Council Chair of the Public Lands History Center at CSU. I provide administrative leadership in the Center and serve as a principal investigator on environmental, social, and oral history projects for public lands agencies. I am also a faculty member in CSU's School of Global and Environmental Sustainability.

QUESTIONS FOR CONSIDERATION

1. According to Alexander, what have historians traditionally argued regarding female reformers and middle class "tenets of domesticity?" How does she propose to change these arguments?
2. How did the working class status of the women of the Martha Washington Society shape their approach to reform? In what ways did context shape the reform impulse among these women?
3. Compare the reform efforts of the Martha Washington Society to other middle class reform organizations. What explains some of the similarities and differences between this working class organization and those dominated by the middle class?
4. Alexander claims that as early as 1842, the Washingtonian movement showed "signs of weakening." What were these signs and how did the Washingtonian

movement counter it? How did the Martha Washingtonians in particular seek to counter it? To what extent were these efforts successful?

5. In what ways did the rising standards for membership change the focus of the organizations that followed in the Washingtonian legacy? To what extent did these mutual benefit societies represent a change from the early years of the Washingtonian movement and to what extent did they represent a continuation of former reform efforts?

CHAPTER SIXTEEN

The Slave Trader, the White Slave, and the Politics of Racial Determination in the 1850s[1]

Walter Johnson

In January of 1857 Jane Morrison was sold in the slave market in New Orleans. The man who bought her was James White, a longtime New Orleans slave trader, who had recently sold his slave pen and bought land just up the river from New Orleans, in Jefferson Parish, Louisiana. Morrison, apparently, was to be one of his last speculations as a trader or one of his first investments as a planter. Sometime shortly after her sale, however, Morrison ran away. By the time White saw her again, in October 1857, they were in a courtroom in Jefferson Parish where Morrison had filed suit against him. Before it was settled, that suit would be considered by three different juries, be put before the Louisiana Supreme Court twice, and leave a lasting record of the complicated politics of race and slavery in the South of the 1850s. The reason for the stir would have been obvious to anyone who saw Morrison sitting in court that day: the fifteen-year-old girl whom White claimed as his slave had blond hair and blue eyes.

Morrison began her petition to the Third District Court by asking that William Dennison, the Jefferson Parish jailer, be appointed her legal representative and that she be sequestered in the parish prison to keep White from seizing and selling her. In her petition, Morrison asked that she be declared legally free and white and added a request that the court award her ten thousand dollars damages for the wrong that White had done her by holding her as a slave. She based her case on the claim that her real name was Alexina, not Jane, that she was from Arkansas, and that she had "been born free and of white parentage," or, as she put it in a later affidavit, "that she is of white blood and free and entitled to her

---

[1]Interested students are encouraged to read this essay in the original form. Walter Johnson, The Slave Trader, the White Slave, and the Politics of Racial Determination in the 1850s," *Journal of American History* 87 (1) (June 2000), 13–38.

Sale of Estates, Pictures and Slaves in the Rotunda, New Orleans

Figure 16.1

Slave sales—whether public auctions in the rotunda of one
of a city's grand hotels, like this one, or exchanges made
behind the high walls of the traders' pens—were public
events, part of the process by which ideas about race and
mastery were daily given material shape in the antebellum
South. Courtesy the Historic New Orleans Collection, acc. no. 1981.147.

freedom and that *on view this is manifest.*" Essentially, Alexina Morrison claimed
that she was white because she looked that way.[2]

In his response, White claimed that he had purchased Morrison (he still
called her Jane) from a man named J. A. Halliburton, a resident of Arkansas.
White exhibited an unnotarized bill of sale for Morrison (which would have been
legal proof of title in Arkansas, but was not in Louisiana) and offered an alternative explanation of how the young woman had made her way into the courtroom
that day. Morrison, he alleged, was a runaway slave. . . . White blamed Dennison
. . . and . . . "abolitionist" supporters of committing a crime: stealing and harbor-
ing his slave.[3]

. . . As codified in the statutes of the state of Louisiana and generally interpreted by the Louisiana Supreme Court, the legal issues posed by the case were
simple enough: If Alexina Morrison could prove she was white, she was entitled to
freedom and perhaps to damages; if James White could prove that her mother had
been a slave at the time of Morrison's birth or that Morrison herself had been a

---

[2]Testimony of William Dennison, June 19, 1858, *Morrison v. White*, Louisiana Supreme Court
case 442, 16 La. Ann. 100 (1861), Supreme Court of Louisiana Collection (Earl K. Long Library,
University of New Orleans, New Orleans, LA). Plaintiff's Petition, Oct. 19, 1857, ibid.; Answer, Nov.
22, 1857, ibid.; Petitioner's Affidavit, Oct. 19, 1857, ibid. Emphasis added.

[3]Answer, Nov. 22, 1857, ibid.

slave (and had not been emancipated), he was entitled to her service; if she was not proved to be either white or enslaved, her fate would be decided by the court on the basis of a legal presumption of "mulattoes'" freedom under Louisiana law. Captured in the neat hand of the legal clerk who prepared the record of the lower court hearings of the case, however, are circumstances that were apparently considerably more complicated than the ones envisioned by those who had made the laws.[4]

Testimony from the lower court hearings of *Morrison v. White* provides a pathway into the complex history of slavery, class, race, and sexuality in the changing South of the 1850s: particularly into slaveholders' fantasies about their light-skinned and female slaves; the role of performance in the racial identities of both slaves and slaveholders; the ways anxieties about class and capitalist transformation in the South were experienced and expressed as questions about racial identity; the babel of confusion surrounding the racial ideal on which the antebellum social structure was supposedly grounded; the relationship of the law of slavery as made by legislators and appellate judges to its everyday life in the district courtrooms of the antebellum South; and the disruptive effects of one woman's effort to make her way to freedom through the tangle of ideology that enslaved her body. In the South of the 1850s, Alexina Morrison's bid for freedom posed a troubling double question: Could slaves become white? And could white people become slaves?

WHITENESS AND SLAVERY

By the time *Morrison v. White* went to trial, Alexina Morrison would claim that her whiteness made her free, but when Morrison and White first met, in the slave market, it might simply have made her more valuable. It is well known that slaveholders favored light-skinned women such as Morrison to serve in their houses and that those light-skinned women sold at a price premium. What is less often realized is that in the slave market apparent differences in skin tone were daily formalized into racial categories—the traders were not only marketing race but also making it. In the slave market, the whiteness that Alexina Morrison would eventually try to turn against her slavery was daily measured, packaged, and sold at a very high price.[5]

. . . When people such as Morrison were sold, they were generally advertised by the slave traders with a racial category. Ninety percent of the slaves sold in the New Orleans market were described on the Acts of Sale that transferred their ownership with a word describing their lineage in terms of an imagined blood quantum—such as "Negro," "Griffe," "Mulatto," or "Quadroon." Those words described pasts that were not visible in the slave pens by referring to parents and grandparents who had been left behind with old owners. In using them, however, the traders depended upon something that was visible in the pens, skin color.

---

[4]See Judith Kelleher Schafer, *Slavery, the Civil Law, and the Supreme Court of Louisiana* (Baton Rouge, 1994), 90–95.

[5]Laurence Kotlikoff, "The Structure of Slave Prices in New Orleans, 1804–1862," *Economic Inquiry,* 17 (Oct. 1979), 515; Walter Johnson, *Soul by Soul: Life inside the Antebellum Slave Market* (Cambridge, MA, 1999), 150–56. See also Thomas C. Holt, "Marking Race: Race-Making and the Writing of History," *American Historical Review* 100 (Feb. 1995), 1–20.

When buyers described their slave market choices they often made the same move from the visible to the biological. . . .[6] The words the buyers used—*griffe, mulatto, quadroon*—preserved a constantly shifting tension between the "blackness" favored by those who bought slaves to till their fields, harvest their crops, and renew their labor forces and the "whiteness" desired by those who went to the slave market in search of people to serve their meals, mend their clothes, and embody their fantasies. . . .

As Monique Guillory has suggested in her work on the New Orleans quadroon balls, the gaze of the consumer projected a fantasy of white masculinity onto the bodies of light-skinned women. . . . [T]hat fantasy was particularly associated with the notorious "fancy trade" to New Orleans. . . . The word "fancy" has come down to us an adjective modifying the word "girl," a word that refers to appearances perhaps or manners or dress. But the word has another meaning; it designates a desire: He fancies. . . . The slave market usage embarked from this second meaning: "Fancy" was a transitive verb made noun, a slaveholder's desire made material in the shape of a woman like the one slave dealer Philip Thomas described seeing in Richmond: "13 years old, Bright Color, nearly a fancy for $1135." An age, a sex, a complexion, and a slaveholder's fantasy. . . . The slave dealer James Blakenly made the density of the traffic between phenotype and fantasy explicit when he described Mary Ellen Brooks: "A very pretty girl, a bright mulatto with long curly hair and fine features . . . Ellen Brooks was a fancy girl: witness means by that a young handsome girl of fourteen or fifteen with long curly hair." Solomon Northup, a free black who had himself been kidnapped and sold in the New Orleans market, remembered slave dealer Theophilus Freeman's account of the price that light-skinned Emily would bring in New Orleans: "There were heaps and piles of money to be made for such an extra fancy piece as Emily would be. She was a beauty—a picture—a doll one of your regular bloods—none of your thick-lipped, bullet-headed, cotton [pick]ers."[7]

. . . [A]ccording to the ideology of slaveholders' racial economy . . . light-skinned and slender, these women were the embodied opposites of those sought

---

[6]The figure of 90 percent is drawn from Robert W. Fogel and Stanley L. Engerman, eds., "The New Orleans Slave Sample," database available from the Inter-University Consortium for Political and Social Research, P.O. Box 1248, Ann Arbor, MI 48106. The word "griff" denoted the offspring of someone labeled "Negro" and someone labeled "Mulatto." Alexina Morrison was described as "yellow" on a bill of sale entered as evidence in her case. Bill of Sale, Morrison v. White; Testimony of Pascal Lebesque, *Landry v. Peterson and Stuart*, case 1025, 4 La. Ann. 96 (1849), Supreme Court of Louisiana Collection; Testimony of Dr. Richard Lee Fern, *Bloodgood v. Wilson*, case 3272, 10 La. Ann. 302 (1855), ibid.; Plaintiff's Petition, *Frierson v. Irvin*, case 1050, 4 La. Ann. 277 (1849), ibid.

[7]Monique Guillory, "Some Enchanted Evening on the Auction Block: The Cultural Legacy of the New Orleans Quadroon Balls" (PhD diss., New York University, 1999). . . . [S]ee Frederic Bancroft, *Slave Trading in the Old South* (Baltimore, 1931), 38, 50–51, 57, 102, 131, 251, 280, 328–30. Philip Thomas to William Finney, July 26, 1859, William A. J. Finney Papers, *The Records of Antebellum Southern Plantations on Microfilm*, ed. Kenneth Stampp; Testimony of James Blakenly, *White v. Slatter*, case 943, 5 La. Ann. 27 (1849), ibid.; Solomon Northup, *Twelve Years a Slave*, ed. Joseph Logsdon and Sue Eakin (Baton Rouge, 1968), 58.

as field hands; their whiteness unfitted them for labor. For slave buyers, near-white enslaved women symbolized the luxury of being able to pay for service . . . that had no material utility—they were "fancies," projections of the slaveholders' own imagined identities as white men and slave masters. . . .[8]

And so, at a very high price, whiteness was doubly sold in the slave market. In the first instance the enslaved women's whiteness was packaged by the traders and imagined into meaning by the buyers—into delicacy and modesty, interiority and intelligence, beauty, bearing, and vulnerability. These descriptions of enslaved light-skinned women, however, were projections of slaveholders' dreamy interpretations of the meaning of their own skin color. Indeed, in the second instance it was the buyers' own whiteness that was being bought. . . . [T]heir slaves were the showpieces of their pretensions; their own whiteness was made apparent in the bodies of the people they bought. . . .[9]

Slaves had to be made, sometimes violently, to enact the meaning slaveholders assigned to their bodies. . . . [M]ore than simply getting slaves to look the part, the buyers had to make sure they would play it. Stubbornness, recalcitrance, or simple inability on the part of their slaves could make a mockery of slaveholders' projected pretensions by revealing how much their own identities depended upon the behavior of their slaves. And so slaveholders were willing to pay a lot of money for the right kind of performance. The better the slaves' performance, the greater the value produced out of the synergetic whiteness of slave and slaveholder.[10]

Ironically, these slave market syntheses of whiteness and slavery, these costly flirtations with hybridity, were underwritten by slaveholders' ideology of absolute racial difference. The saving abstraction "black blood" held the power to distinguish nearly white women from really white ones, to distinguish what was essentially performance from what was the performance of essence—slaveholders generally believed that "black blood," if present, would be apparent in the countenance, conversation, or carriage of the one who bore its taint.[11] When a performance of enslaved whiteness was too good, however, the combination of "white" appearance and behavior could overwhelm the intended distinction; a slave could become "too white to keep," likely to slip aboard a ship or hop onto a train and escape to freedom. A virtuoso performance of whiteness could breach the categories designed to contain and commodify hybridity; a slave could step over the color line and onto the other side. Perhaps the slave trader who sold Morrison to White was thinking of that type of performance when he remembered that she was "too white." And perhaps that is why James White had apparently curled the young woman's hair and dyed it black after he brought her home from the slave market.[12]

---

[8]Testimony of Blakenly, *White v. Slatter.*

[9]Johnson, *Soul by Soul,* 78–116, 135–61.

[10]Johnson, *Soul by Soul,* 197–207.

[11]See Guillory, "Some Enchanted Evening on the Auction Block," 149–81; and Sollors, *Neither Black nor White Yet Both,* 142–61, 220–45.

[12]Olmsted, *Journey in the Seaboard Slave States,* 639–41. On worries about slaves who were "too white to keep," see Martha Hodes, *White Women, Black Men: Illicit Sex in the Nineteenth-Century South* (New Haven, 1997), 118–20. Testimony of W. J. Martin, June 19, 1858, *Morrison v. White*; Testimony of Dennison, June 19, 1858, ibid.

Figure 16.2
Slaves in the market were subjected to detailed physical
examinations as buyers assigned meaning to their bodies
based upon antebellum ideas about blackness and whiteness.
Courtesy the Historic New Orleans Collection, acc. no. 1981.3.

MORRISON VERSUS WHITE

According to most versions of the southern social order, Alexina Morrison—
whether as enslaved white or passing slave—was not supposed to exist at all. But
the color-coding, black slaves and white supremacy, that characterized most of
the political debate over slavery was unreliable as a description of the institution's
everyday life. First, there was racial mixture and sexual predation: throughout
the history of American slavery it was not always easy to tell who was "black."[13]
Second, there was manumission: just as racial mixture made it harder to tell who
was "black," manumission made it harder to tell who was a slave. The ultimate
expression of slaveholders' property right—the right to alienate their property
however they pleased—increasingly undermined the ability of slaveholders as a
class to keep race and slavery coextensive.[14] Finally, there were the slave trade and
interregional migration: The antebellum South was a rootless society. The broad
transition from an upper South tobacco economy to a lower South cotton economy and the domestic slave trade, through which as many as two-thirds of a
million people may have passed in the antebellum period, had removed hundreds
of thousands of people such as Alexina Morrison from the communities in which
their identities were rooted. Through acts as small as lying about their past in the
slave market or as audacious as running away and claiming to be white, many of

---

[13]Ira Berlin, *Slaves without Masters: The Free Negro in the Antebellum South* (New York, 1974),
365–70; Thomas D. Morris, *Southern Slavery and the Law, 1619–1860* (Chapel Hill, 1996), 35–36;
Ariela J. Gross, "Litigating Whiteness: Trials of Racial Determination in the Nineteenth Century
South," *Yale Law Journal* 108 (Oct. 1998), 109–88.

[14]Morris, *Southern Slavery and the Law*, 371–423.

Figure 16.3
By the late antebellum period, southern legislatures and judges—recognizing complexities suggested in this photograph of recently emancipated slaves from Louisiana—were increasingly concerned with the erosion of boundaries between black and white and slave and free. Courtesy the Library Company of Philadelphia.

the enslaved people forcibly transported by the trade worked their deracination against their slavery.[15]

By 1857, when Alexina Morrison ran away and sued the slave trader, southern lawmakers already had at least two centuries' experience with the ambiguities of a social order in which not all slaves were black and not all nonwhite people were slaves. Throughout the nineteenth century, southern states passed ever-more-detailed laws defining the acceptable limits of drinking, gambling, and lovemaking along the lines of race and slavery. Those laws attempted to control sites where black and white, slave and free, bargained and socialized freely with one another, places where the white supremacist ideology upon which the defense of slavery increasingly relied was daily undermined in practice. . . .[16]

The most explicit legislative consideration of race, however, came in the framing of presumptions assigning legal status as slave or free to an otherwise unknown person. Taken together, the presumption laws outlined two ways of thinking about race: South Carolina, Georgia, and Delaware assigned status on

[15]Bancroft, *Slave Trading in the Old South*; Michael Tadman, *Speculators and Slaves: Masters, Traders, and Slaves in the Old South* (Madison, 1989); Steven H. Deyle, "The Domestic Slave Trade in America" (PhD diss., Columbia University, 1995); and Johnson, *Soul by Soul.*

[16]Olmsted, *Journey in the Seaboard Slave States*, 639–41; Morris, *Southern Slavery and the Law*, 31–36; Richard C. Wade, *Slavery in Cities: The South, 1820–1860* (New York, 1964), 80–110; Barbara Jeanne Fields, *Slavery and Freedom on the Middle Ground: Maryland during the Nineteenth Century* (New Haven, 1985), 40–89; Victoria E. Bynum, *Unruly Women: The Politics of Social and Sexual Control in the Old South* (Chapel Hill, 1996), 88–110; Hodes, *White Women, Black Men*, 116–22; Morris, *Southern Slavery and the Law*, 17–36; Schafer, *Slavery, the Civil Law, and the Supreme Court of Louisiana*, 179.

the basis of observation and reputation; other slaveholding states, including Louisiana, attempted to establish presumptions of freedom based upon fractions of "black blood": halves, fourths, eighths, sixteenths, and so on down to one drop, which was the standard only in Arkansas during the antebellum period. The first standard emphasized appearance and performance; the second, more popular standard relied on a supposedly scientific estimation of an imagined blood quantum. The presumptions did not mean that the in-between people who came before the courts were free: Other evidence could overcome the legal presumption, most notably historical evidence that the person before the court had been held as a slave or born to an enslaved woman.[17]

Faced with a person of indeterminate identity, then, antebellum legislators and litigators had three conceptually distinct (though often practically interrelated) ways of locating them in the grid of acceptable social identities: personal history, race science based on discerning "black blood," and performance—the amalgam of appearance and reputation, of body, behavior, and scripted social role. And over the of the nineteenth century, in cases that resulted from the presumption laws, in cases that arose out of disputes over inheritance and other property claims, and in cases where enslaved people such as Morrison claimed they were white, judges throughout the slaveholding South (not just in Louisiana) were asked hundreds of times to stabilize the visible confusion of a hybrid reality into the stable degrees of difference demanded by a ruling class that wanted to see the world in black and white. Thus, when Alexina Morrison sued the slave trader for possession of her whiteness, she was entering a much broader ongoing contest over the tools used to determine the race of indeterminate bodies.[18]

There are only hints of how Alexina Morrison might have made sense of herself before she sued James White. In 1850, when the census takers passed through Matagorda County, Texas, the household of Moses Morrison included himself, three other white men, and, listed separately on the slave schedule, a woman aged thirty and labeled mulatto, five children aged between one and thirteen, also labeled mulatto, and an enslaved man, listed beneath this apparent slave family, aged thirty-eight and labeled black.[19] Of the children, one was a seven-year-old girl, most likely Alexina Morrison. That the children were listed as mulatto like their mother and that the only enslaved man in the household was

---

[17]For the broader legal context of *Morrison v. White*, see Morris, *Southern Slavery and the Law*, 17–36; Schafer, *Slavery, the Civil Law, and the Supreme Court of Louisiana*, 220–88; Hodes, *White Women, Black Men*, 96–122; Peter Bardaglio, *Reconstructing the Household: Families, Sex, and the Law in the Nineteenth-Century South* (Chapel Hill, 1995); Adrienne D. Davis, "Identity Notes Part One: Playing in the Light," *American University Law Review* 45 (Feb. 1996), 695–720; and Gross, "Litigating Whiteness," 109–88. For racial definition and law generally, see Virginia R. Dominguez, *White by Definition: Social Classification in Creole Louisiana* (New Brunswick, 1986); and Ian Haney-Lopez, *White by Law: The Legal Construction of Race* (New York, 1996).

[18]For other states, see Morris, *Southern Slavery and the Law*, 17–36; and Gross, "Litigating Whiteness," 109–88.

[19]Manuscript Population Schedules, Matagorda County, Texas, Seventh Census of the United States, 1850, household 93. Slave Schedules, ibid. Deposition of Benjamin F. Giles, March 1, 1858, *Morrison v. White*.

not suggests that their father was white—perhaps Moses Morrison or one of the men who boarded with him.

There is no way of knowing the internal life hidden behind the census taker's rendering of the Morrison household in Matagorda, of knowing who was treated as a slave in that household and who, perhaps, as a daughter. . . . Nor is there any way of knowing whether Alexina Morrison was treated as property or company as she subsequently passed through the households of various members of the Morrison family, whether she thought she was being sold or just moving on. . . . But two things are as clear as day: By the time she ended up in White's possession Alexina Morrison was a slave, and by the time she escaped she was white.

When Alexina Morrison escaped from James White, her jailer/protector remembered, the first thing she said was that she was white. And when she brought suit against White, she did so by building this assertion into a story: that she was born of white parents and taken away from her home in Arkansas by "gross fraud," that she had been held by force and falsely claimed as a slave. . . .

Morrison's claim of whiteness drew its power from three sources: her appearance, her behavior, and the idea that "black blood," if present at all, would necessarily be visible. Most simply, her case took the form of outright description. "From his opinion," one witness testified, "the girl is white. Says he judges she is white from her complexion." Or: "Has seen plaintiff and been intimately acquainted with her. From witness' judgment of plaintiff arising from his intimacy she has not the features of the African Race." Other witnesses placed a greater emphasis on behavior when they described what it meant to be white: "Had witness been introduced to the girl without knowing her, he would have taken her for a white girl . . . Has had opportunity of Judging her, and she conducted herself as a white girl. She is so in her conduct and actions. She has none of the features of an African." If there had been any of "the African race" in Alexina Morrison, they argued, it would have been outwardly and objectively visible in the way she looked and acted, but from the moment she had made her initial claim of whiteness, there had been no outward sign that she was anything but white all the way through. . . . Trying to make Alexina Morrison make sense to the court, Morrison's lawyers and witnesses drew on a set of images of feminine whiteness—modest carriage, unimposing gentility, emotional transparency. Indeed, it was Morrison's performance of her womanhood as much as of her whiteness that seems to have transfixed the white men who supported her cause: Alexina Morrison, they were arguing, was white because white womanhood was always as it seemed. By centering their case in the "flaxen haired, blue eyed," and presumably well-behaved young woman in the courtroom, Morrison and her lawyers had drawn on one of the sacred premises of the antebellum social order—the visible, unquestionable, objective character of race—as it was embodied in the most precious fetish of white supremacy, a white woman.[20]

_____

[20]Testimony of J. B. Clawson, June 19, 1858, *Morrison v. White*; Testimony of S. N. Cannon, June 19, 1858, ibid.; Testimony of Kemper, June 19, 1858, ibid.

The slave trader's case began with simple negation. Where Morrison's witnesses looked at the young woman and saw white, White's witnesses looked at her and saw black. Immediately after stating that he would not himself have bought Morrison because she was "too white," W. J. Martin, the dealer who brokered the sale of Morrison to White, testified that "from the appearance of the girl" he nevertheless judged "that she has African Blood." Martin's opinion was seconded by J. A. Breaux, who located Morrison's "African Blood" in "the shape of her cheek Bones and the conformation of the lower part of her mouth." The case by negation, however, was itself vulnerable to negation. In cross-examining Breaux, Morrison's lawyers posed alternative interpretations of the shape of the young woman's face: Had Breaux ever traveled among Indians or been to Mexico, the Antilles, or the West Indies? Had he noticed how straight Alexina Morrison's hair was? Had he looked at the color of her skin, at her hands or her feet? Would he describe Mr. Hall, a spectator in the courtroom, as having high cheekbones?[21] By providing alternative explanations for the supposedly nonwhite characteristics that seemed to show through Morrison's white skin, Morrison's lawyers hinted for the first time at the high stakes they were willing to bring to bear in the case. If Alexina Morrison could be judged black, was there any certainty that others might not be so judged: racial others like Indians, extranational others like Mexicans and West Indians, and indeed other white people like Mr. Hall, sitting right there in the courtroom? If Alexina Morrison was black, they hinted, there was no telling who else might be.

The indeterminacy of the visual evidence and the threat that all kinds of difference might be blackened by the slave trader's claim pushed White's lawyers into the awkward posture of trying to convince a jury of southern white men that they could not believe their eyes. . . . They did so by drawing on history, by which they hoped to prove that Alexina Morrison was a slave; race science, by which they hoped to undermine the idea that she was white; and, finally, a different set of images of race and gender performance—images that located the young woman's race in allusion to her sexuality rather than her demeanor.

The slave trader's history came from depositions taken in Texas and Arkansas where people remembered the young woman as a slave. Moses Morrison could not remember in whose house she was born, but he remembered buying Alexina, her siblings, and her mother in 1848; he remembered keeping her for four or five years and then taking her to his nephew's house in Little Rock, where she was to learn to sew and do housework. That was the last he had seen of her. She would have, he added, to highlight the importance of personal history and reputation in regulating hybridity, "passed for a white child anywhere if not known." From Arkansas, Morrison's nephew remembered Moses Morrison bringing Alexina out from Texas in 1850 and trying to give her to his (Moses') niece, Ellen. Ellen's father had said that "he did not want so white a Negro about him" and advised Moses Morrison to sell Alexina. Morrison, instead, gave her to

---

[21]Testimony of Martin, June 19, 1858, *Morrison v. White*; Testimony of J. A. Breaux, June 19, 1858, ibid.

his nephew, who remembered entrusting her to a slave trader, who took her to New Orleans at the beginning of 1857 and sold her to James White. From Morrison to his nephew to the trader to White: James White's lawyers tried to locate Alexina Morrison's apparent whiteness in a traceable history of slavery. Step by step, they outlined a story rooted in the moment in 1848 when she was sold with her mother as a slave to Moses Morrison; according to the standards of historical and legal record, that sale made Alexina Morrison a slave.[22]

And yet in a society as rootless as the antebellum South, the seemingly stable category of "slave" was a less certain legal tool than it might seem to a historian bent on figuring out whether or not Alexina Morrison "really" was what she said she was. The history provided by the slave trader, after all, occurred at a distance of time and space that made it untrustworthy; indeed, one of the judges who heard the case as it passed through the court system threw it out on the grounds that the depositions had been improperly taken and could not be relied upon as authentic.[23] The textual rendering of testimony given in Texas and Arkansas was apparently not history enough to convince him that the fate of the blond-haired and blue-eyed young woman who stood before him in the court should be decided by the depositions of distant witnesses testifying about a shadowy past as a slave.

While White's lawyers concentrated on tracing the young woman's history in their own effort to prove that she was a slave (for if they could prove that, it did not legally matter what color she was), the bulk of their cross-examination concentrated on undermining her lawyers' claim that she was white, a claim they clearly feared would influence the jury. In questioning Morrison's witnesses, the slave trader's lawyers asked repeatedly about hybridity, trying to work their way back to essential blackness from apparent whiteness. What were, they asked each of Morrison's witnesses, the distinctive features of the African race when removed to the fourth or fifth degree? Had not the witness seen people removed to the fourth degree with blue eyes before? Did the witness believe in the unity of the races? . . .[24]

Faced with the unquestionably blue-eyed and blond Alexina Morrison, the defendant's lawyers tried to resolve the mystery of hybridity back into the constancy of blackness by making the argument that "black blood" could disappear without a trace into apparent whiteness but still be present. Even if Morrison's witnesses were right and White's were wrong, even if the young woman standing in court was free of any visible trace of "the African," they were arguing, she could still be black. This line of questioning revealed how far White's lawyers were willing to go in contesting Morrison's claim to whiteness: To believe that Alexina Morrison was white, they implied, was to ignore one of the major

---

[22]Deposition of Morrison, July 26, 1858, *Morrison v. White*; Deposition of Giles, March 1, 1858, ibid.

[23]Defendant's Bill of Exceptions in the Fifth District Court hearing of the case, 1858, *Morrison v. White*.

[24]Cross-examination of G. H. Lyons, June 19, 1858, *Morrison v. White*; Cross-examination of Clawson, June 19, 1858, ibid.; Cross-examination of Cannon, June 19, 1858, ibid.

foundations of much white supremacist and proslavery thought, polygenesis—the idea that blacks and whites were created separately and so should ever remain. . . .[25]

The plaintiff's witnesses, however, refused to yield the point. G. H. Lyons told the court that he "knew the difference between the Caucasian and African races" and was "opposed to amalgamation," but he still thought that Morrison was white. . . . And S. N. Cannon assured the court that "colored blood will stick out" even in crosses of the fourth or fifth degree. It was in "the shape of the hairs being curled, the white of the eyes . . . in the shape of the nose and lips." But it was, they all agreed, nowhere in Alexina Morrison.[26]

In the end, the slave trader's effort to summon Morrison's evanescent "black blood" to the surface of her skin through a science lesson about crosses of the fourth and fifth degree was sidetracked at every turn by countersciences and slaveholding common sense. . . . No matter the seeming simplicity of the legal presumption that portions of "black blood" could be made manifest and measured, race science in practice was broadly contested.

White's lawyers apparently adjudged a distant history of slavery and a contested lesson about race science too uncertain to prove their case, and so it was with social practice and sexual performance that they concluded their effort. Where did you meet Alexina Morrison, they asked S. N. Cannon; was it at a ball? The witness responded that he had never seen her at a ball, and for the moment the matter ended there. But by the end of the third hearing of the case in the lower courts, the defense was asking the man: "Are you the father of the child of plaintiff?" And when the plaintiff's lawyers objected to that: "Is not the plaintiff in the family way for you now?" Shortly after, the witness was recalled and testified, under cross-examination, that he had been Morrison's jailer for five years, that she had spent nineteen months of those years out of jail, and that she had a child while in jail.[27]

This line of questioning aimed to establish Alexina Morrison's evanescent blackness by slotting her into one of the prefabricated categories that antebellum slaveholders used to mediate between the confusing hybridity they saw all around them and the imagined racial essences on which they grounded their society. By alluding to her public appearance at local balls and her extramarital sexuality, they drew on the racialized and sexualized image of the quadroon mistress to

[25]On polygenesis (and its opposite, monogenesis), the nineteenth-century debate about them, and the religious and scientific context of the arguments, see William Stanton, *The Leopards Spots: Scientific Attitudes toward Race in America, 1815–1859* (Chicago, 1960); Thomas Gossett, *Race: The History of an Idea in America* (Dallas, 1963); George M. Fredrickson, *The Black Image in the White Mind: The Debate over Afro-American Character and Destiny, 1817–1914* (New York, 1971); and Reginald Horsman, *Josiah Nott of Mobile: Southerner, Physician, and Racial Theorist* (Baton Rouge, 1987).

[26]Cross-examination of Lyons, June 19, 1858, *Morrison v. White*; Cross-examination of Cannon, June 19, 1858, ibid.

[27]Testimony of Cannon, June 19, 1858, June 30, 1862, *Morrison v. White*; Testimony of Dennison, May 18, 1859, ibid.

locate Alexina Morrison's origins.... Her sexuality, they implied, was proof of an essential blackness that no elegant dress could conceal. The final story they told about Alexina Morrison contested the imagery of transparent white womanhood used by Morrison's own witnesses. If race was evident in gendered versions of deportment, they were arguing, Alexina Morrison was playing a different part outside the courtroom than inside.[28]

There, the defense rested; the judge gave oral instructions (which the court reporter did not record), and the jury retired. When they returned, they reported to the court that there was "no possibility of any agreement upon a verdict." Faced with Alexina Morrison, the twelve white men who made a jury in Jefferson Parish could not decide whether to believe their eyes or the ways of seeing provided by legal practice, medical science, and white supremacist sexual ideology. Through the repeated and contradictory application of the fixed terms of the antebellum conversation about race to the body of the young woman in the courtroom, the witnesses in the Third District courtroom had called into question something that they all professed to believe was common sense: the idea that there were black people and white people. They left the case to be decided upon retrial.

WHITENESS VERSUS SLAVERY

The year 1857, when Alexina Morrison ran away and sued the slave trader, was a banner year in the history of American proslavery. For in 1857 the efforts of southern politicians to shore up the positive-good defense of slavery by erasing any evidence that black people could thrive (or even survive) outside slavery and to circumscribe the freedom of the potential free Negro enemy within seemed to take on new importance throughout the South. In 1857 Chief Justice Roger Taney's famous *obiter dictum* in *Dred Scott v. Sandford* abolished the rights of black Americans—not just slaves—to seek redress in the nation's courts. In 1857 there were continued calls for the reopening of the African slave trade ... [and] for the forcible enslavement of free people of color in states from Maryland to Louisiana. In the heat of the ongoing conflict over slavery, southern judges and legislators were, to all appearances, attempting to eliminate the ambiguities of the southern social order in favor of a fixed equivalence of race and status—of blackness with slavery and whiteness with slaveholding.[29]

The debates over the enslavement proposal, however, reveal that the solidifying South was shot through with a tension ... between the privileges of whiteness

[28]Petition for Change of Venue, July 1, 1858, *Morrison v. White*. On the image of the quadroon and octoroon mistresses, see Guillory, "Some Enchanted Evening on the Auction Block"; and Joseph Roach, *Cities of the Dead: Circum-Atlantic Performance* (New York, 1996), 211–24.

[29]See Don E. Ferenbacher, *The Dred Scott Case: Its Significance in American Law and Politics* (New York, 1978). For the African slave trade, see John Ashworth, *Slavery, Capitalism, and Politics in the Antebellum Republic, Vol. I: Commerce and Compromise* (Cambridge, England, 1995), 268–69. On the "enslavement crisis," see Berlin, *Slaves without Masters*, 369–80; Michael P. Johnson and James L. Roark, *Black Masters: A Free Family of Color in the Old South* (New York, 1984), 233–88; and Fields, *Slavery and Freedom on the Middle Ground*, 63–89.

and those of slaveholding. . . . On one side was a fundamentalist vision of the political economy of whiteness in which any free black was a potential threat to all whites; on the other was a straight-out adherence to the political economy of slavery in which any slaveholder, even a black slaveholder, was a potential ally in the fight against abolition. The poles of the discussion . . . starkly outline the existence of two—sometimes contending, sometimes overlapping—versions of the southern social order. In the late 1850s sectional tension was giving new urgency to a very old question: Was the southern social order based on race or on slavery?[30]

Like other southern states in the years leading up to 1857, Louisiana had taken legislative and judicial action to clarify the relationship of race and slavery. In the 1850s the legislature and courts of Louisiana tried to curb manumission, eliminate such states of "quasi-slavery" as *in futuro* emancipation, enforce a stricter segregation of social relations between black and white (especially drinking, gambling, and dancing), and regulate the public behavior of free people of color and slaves more vigilantly. . . . Morrison's case, then, went to the jury at a time when Louisiana was rebalancing the categories of southern social life by gradually abolishing the very liminal spaces from which she seems to have emerged. But Morrison did not claim to be liminal, she claimed to be white, and in Jefferson Parish in the 1850s that seems to have made all the difference in the world.[31]

The jury that heard *Morrison v. White* was chosen the way most antebellum juries were, from among the voters who lived in the court's ambit.[32] What is striking about the Jefferson Parish jurors who heard Alexina Morrison's case is how hard they are to track down. . . .[33] Taken together . . . the known jurors reflect the character of the community they represented: they were men in motion in a town dominated by steamboat and railroad, immigrants and transients in a newly populated parish, agents of change in a state that, even in the nineteenth century, celebrated aristocratic stasis. . . . And, with the exception of one juror who owned a sixty-year-old man and a fifty-three-year-old woman in 1860, the known jurors were nonslaveholders in a society based on slavery. They were the type of men for

---

[30]Berlin, *Slaves without Masters*, 369–70; Johnson and Roark, *Black Masters*, 169; Fields, *Slavery and Freedom on the Middle Ground*, 67–89.

[31]Morris, *Southern Slavery and the Law*, 29–36, 371–423; Berlin, *Slaves without Masters*, 318–40; Schafer, *Slavery, the Civil Law, and the Supreme Court of Louisiana*, 179.

[32]Ariela Gross, "Pandora's Box: Slavery, Character, and Southern Culture in the Courtroom, 1800–1860" (PhD diss., Stanford University, 1996), 217–21. Judgment on Prayer for Change of Venue, July 24, 1858, *Morrison v. White*.

[33]The jurors whom I have been able to trace, followed by the sources in which they appear, are: B. N. Fortier, Manuscript Population Schedules, Jefferson Parish, Louisiana, Eighth Census of the United States, 1860, p. 659. P. Mulligan, Manuscript Population Schedules, Jefferson Parish, Seventh Census, 1850, p. 225; Manuscript Population Schedules, Jefferson Parish, Eighth Census, 1860, p. 522. Louis Gabb, ibid., 493. J. Sutton, Manuscript Population Schedules, Jefferson Parish, Seventh Census, 1850, p. 88. W. W. Thompson, ibid., 192; Manuscript Population Schedules, Jefferson Parish, Eighth Census, 1860, p. 585. Those whom I have not been able to track are: C. Maderre, J. Kilborg, M. Evendt, F. Commo, E. I. Bufford, and P. Flouring.

whom "the wages of whiteness" held the promise of a daily psychological supplement to the portion they gained from their work, the type of men for whom slavery posed its own double question: Did they share in the society of slaveholders? Or were they in danger of being themselves enslaved?[34]

It is by now a threadbare truth that whiteness gave nonslaveholders a stake in slavery.[35] Nonslaveholding white men were potential slaveholders. More than that, they were shareholders in a society based on racial caste, entitled to public deference from people of color and involved in the daily discipline of slavery through slave catching and patrols. Finally, they were a constituency for the broad proslavery argument that identified the interests of all white people with those of slaveholders: In a slaveholding society, only black people were treated as slaves. . . .[36]

But the imagery of white slavery was dangerously unstable in an economy that was changing as fast as that of the urban South in the 1850s. It was in 1857, after all, that George Fitzhugh finalized his own famous solution to the anomalous presence of a white working class in a society based upon black slavery: Enslave them all. And, indeed, even as prosperous slaveholders were spending thousands of dollars at a time to buy near-white slaves to work in their households, they were employing increasing numbers of whites (and those, like the Irish, who were in the process of becoming white) as wage laborers, tenant farmers, and domestic servants. New Orleans in the 1850s, as the Louisiana physician and racial theorist Samuel Cartwright described it, daily offered more concrete examples of "white slavery" than did distant strikes or living conditions. "Here in New Orleans," Cartwright wrote in *DeBow's Review*, "the larger part of the drudgery-work requiring exposure to the sun, as rail-road making, street-paving, dray-driving, ditching, building, etc. is performed by white people . . . a class of persons who make Negroes of themselves in this hot climate." . . . According to

---

[34]The slaveholder on the jury was J. J. Guttierez, who appears on the Jefferson slave schedule for 1860, but not on the census. Thus, although I can tell that he was a slaveholder, I have no other information about his origins, household, occupation, or property. J. J. Guttierez also appears in the Jefferson Parish Police Jury minutes as the tax collector for the police jury on the left bank of the Mississippi River. Manuscript Population Schedules, Jefferson Parish, Eighth Census, 1860: Slave Schedule, p. 553; Jefferson Parish Police Jury, Minutes, Oct. 4, 1858, transcription, vol. 3 (1858–1864) (New Orleans Public Library, New Orleans, LA). On the class tensions expressed in southern jury trials, see Bertram Wyatt-Brown, "Community, Class, and Snopesian Crime: Local Justice in the Old South," in *Class, Conflict, and Consensus: Antebellum Southern Community Studies*, ed. Orville Vernon Burton and Robert C. McMath Jr. (Westport, 1982), 173–206. David R. Roediger, *The Wages of Whiteness: Race and the Making of the American Working Class* (London, 1991).

[35]Edmund Morgan, *American Slavery, American Freedom: The Ordeal of Colonial Virginia* (New York, 1976); Kathleen M. Brown, *Good Wives, Nasty Wenches, and Anxious Patriarchs: Gender, Race, and Power in Colonial Virginia* (Chapel Hill, 1996), 137–86, 247–82.

[36]Cheryl I. Harris, "Whiteness as Property," *Harvard Law Review*, 106 (June 1993), 1709–91; Walter Johnson, "Inconsistency, Contradiction, and Complete Confusion: The Everyday Life of the Law of Slavery," *Law and Social Inquiry*, 22 (Spring 1997), 425–30; Noel Ignatiev, *How the Irish Became White* (London, 1995), 69; Eugene D. Genovese, *The World the Slaveholders Made: Two Essays in Interpretation* (Middletown, 1969), 208–11; Roediger, *Wages of Whiteness*, 65–92.

Cartwright, the Irish were not becoming white, they were, like the white workingmen with whom they shared their days, turning black.[37]

In the image of a resentful white laborer put out to do the dirty work of capitalist transformation beneath the summer sun—draining swamps and building levees, digging canals and filling railbeds, work regarded as too dangerous for any (valuable) slave to do—we see a less familiar version of the southern political economy. In the urban South of the 1850s, class differences between slaveholder and nonslaveholder were sometimes experienced and expressed in terms of race. . . . Doubts about the commitment of the Irish workingmen of New Orleans to slavery . . . plagued local nativists and slaveholders throughout the 1850s. Indeed, in 1856 both local and national elections in the city had been marked by nativist violence against Irish and German immigrants who tried to vote. As they told the story of a vulnerable white servant sold as a slave, Morrison's lawyers were drawing rhetorical force from the daily experience of the white men who sat on the jury: In the slaveholders' economy, nonslaveholding white people were increasingly being treated like slaves.[38]

Or, even more pointedly, nonslaveholding white women were. One thing that differentiated nonslaveholding white men from slaves in the antebellum South, one dimension of their whiteness, was that they were legally able to protect their dependents from sexual violation, state attachment, and sale. Indeed, as Stephanie M. McCurry has shown, it was by asserting control over their own households that these men could claim, like their slaveholding neighbors, to be "masters"—an equal partnership in patriarchy that underwrote their supposedly equal participation in politics. And yet, as their wives and daughters daily went to work in the homes of their prosperous slaveholding neighbors, the domestic authority of nonslaveholding white men in urban areas such as New Orleans was being eroded in favor of the class privilege of their slaveholding neighbors.[39] It was on the embattled line between the slaveholders' economy and the inner circle of nonslaveholding white patriarchy that Alexina Morrison staked her claim to freedom when she ran away from James White. Morrison's first legal action, remember, was to ask that her jailer be appointed her legal guardian: She gave the jail in which she was being held the legal shape of a household and took for herself

---

[37]George Fitzhugh, *Cannibals All! Or, Slaves Without Masters*, ed. C. Vann Woodward (1857; Cambridge, MA, 1960); Genovese, *World the Slaveholders Made*, 208–11; and Ashworth, *Slavery, Capitalism, and Politics in the Antebellum Republic*, I, 228–46.

[38]Roediger, *Wages of Whiteness*, 84. Frederick Law Olmsted, *The Cotton Kingdom: A Traveler's Observations on Cotton and Slavery in the American Slave States*, ed. Arthur M. Schlesinger (1861; New York, 1962), 232; Ignatiev, *How the Irish Became White*, 19–23; Shugg, *Origins of Class Struggle in Louisiana*, 146–47; Mary Niall Mitchell, "Raising Freedom's Child: Race, Politics, and the Lives of Black Children in Nineteenth-Century Louisiana," draft PhD diss., New York University, 2000 (in Walter Johnson's possession), chap. 1.

[39]Stephanie M. McCurry, *Masters of Small Worlds: Yeoman Households, Gender Relations, and the Political Culture of the Antebellum South Carolina Lowcountry* (New York, 1995), viii, 5–35; Shugg, *Origins of Class Struggle in Louisiana*, 88–94; Burton and McMath, eds., *Class, Conflict, and Consensus*; Wade, *Slavery in Cities*, 274–75. See also Hasia Diner, *Erin's Daughters in America: Irish Women in the Nineteenth Century* (Baltimore, 1983).

the role of white dependent within that household. And in the months between her escape and her trial, she passed through the households of a number of nonslaveholding white men. First the house of her jailer, William Dennison, where she was placed by leave of the district attorney and from which she was seen walking with the jailer's wife, and later the house of J. B. Clawson, a clerk in whose home she was living at the time of the trial.[40]

But Morrison was not just living in Clawson's household, she was working there as a housekeeper.[41] In return for a place within the protective perimeter of this white household, Morrison was providing its members with access to an unfamiliar region of the world of whiteness and distinction. . . . [S]he was giving [nonslaveholders] an experience of whiteness usually reserved for those who owned slaves. The service she was rendering Clawson suggests that we should not . . . misconstrue the relationship between her protectors and Morrison as being merely benign or even wholly centered on her emancipation. Indeed, Alexina Morrison, in her effort to get free, had been forced to accept attention from white men—many of them nonslaveholders—that went well beyond their identification with her plight. "Saw her naked to the waist"—spoken by Morrison's supporters, those words circulate through the trial record like a *leitmotiv*. Indeed, in the weeks after the mistrial, Morrison's half-naked body seems to have been the center of a festival of whiteness in Jefferson Parish. P. C. Perret remembered seeing her "frequently" exhibited at the hotel in Carrollton after the first trial. . . . These witnesses, part of an apparently leering and possibly threatening group of white men, did things to Alexina Morrison that they would never have done to a white woman in public—not to a maid, not to a dancing girl, not to a prostitute.[42]

Publicly exhibited, stripped to the waist, and examined: Alexina Morrison was paying for her freedom with a performance straight out of the slave market. For the men at the hotel in Carrollton, Morrison's liminal body—now protected, now violated; now free, now enslaved; now white, now black; now Mexican, now Indian, now Caribbean—was a symbol of everything whiteness promised them: that they would never themselves be slaves, but that they were entitled to benefit from race as slaveholders did from slavery—through control and sexual access. Alexina Morrison had passed from the property regime of slavery into that of whiteness, from being subject to the prerogatives that defined mastery in the antebellum South to being subjected to those that defined white patriarchy.[43]

---

[40]Nicole Hahn Rafter, *Partial Justice: Women in State Prisons, 1800–1935* (Boston, 1985). Testimony of Dennison, June 19, 1858, *Morrison v. White*; Testimony of Clawson, June 19, 1858, ibid.; Testimony of Cannon, June 19, 1858, ibid.

[41]Testimony of Clawson, June 19, 1858, *Morrison v. White*.

[42]Testimony of Seaman Hopkins, May 18, 1859, *Morrison v. White*; Testimony of Perret, May 18, 1859, ibid.

[43]Johnson, *Soul by Soul*, 135–61. Harris, "Whiteness as Property."

VERDICT AND CONCLUSION

In the aftermath of the mistrial, James White claimed that "a few days before the last trial" when he had ridden out to Carrollton with one of his witnesses to look at Alexina Morrison, he was "surrounded by a lawless mob" that threatened him with "personal violence because he dared to assert his property in his own slave, who said mob declared to be a white person." Faced with the claim of a man who had once made his living selling slaves who might have been as white as themselves, some citizens of Jefferson Parish were apparently willing to risk their lives in defense of Alexina Morrison's claim. . . . [T]he judge in the Third District Court thought it one of the most extraordinary things he had ever heard. Noting that he had never before transferred a case, that Morrison had been "taken in the Society of white persons" and "was even seen dancing at a ball in Carrollton," that he had it on good authority that someone claiming her as his slave was risking his life, and that it would be several sessions of the court before an unprejudiced jury could be impaneled in Jefferson Parish, he sent the case to the Fifth District Court in New Orleans to be retried.[44]

There, in May 1859, both sides called new witnesses and elaborated arguments made in the first trial. . . . The judge in the Fifth District Court excluded both the unnotarized "private act of sale" presented by White's lawyers and the testimony of the slave trader's witnesses from Texas and Arkansas as "not legally authenticated." . . . Without the evidence of sale and the depositions from Texas and Arkansas, there was no proof whatsoever that Morrison was a slave, and so, apparently following the presumption of freedom in favor of mulattoes under Louisiana law, the New Orleans jury declared unanimously for her freedom.[45]

The lawyers for the slave trader appealed to the state supreme court, which declared that the evidence of the sale and the depositions from Texas and Arkansas had been improperly excluded, voided the verdict of the jury, and remanded the case to the Fifth District with the advice that the Supreme Court found "full proof" that Morrison had been born a slave and the order that "the presumption of freedom arising from her color . . . must yield to a proof of her servile origin." Going beyond questions of both fact and procedure in the lower court, however, the Supreme Court considered the case as a matter of public policy: "The Legislature has not seen fit to declare that any number of crosses between the Negro and the white shall emancipate the offspring of the slave, and it does not fall within the province of the judiciary to establish any such rule of property." . . . [T]he court reframed the case as part of the broader ongoing effort to achieve a more perfect equivalence of blackness and slavery and implied that history in Jefferson Parish was moving the wrong way: As the legislature in Louisiana, like those all over the South, was establishing firmer racial boundaries around slavery, in Jefferson Parish those boundaries seemed to be daily falling away.[46]

---

[44]Prayer for Change of Venue, July 1, 1858, *Morrison v. White*; Judgment on Prayer for Change of Venue, July 24, 1858, ibid.

[45]Reasons for Refusing New Trial, May 30, 1859, *Morrison v. White*; Decree of the Supreme Court, Feb. 4, 1861, ibid.

[46]Decree of the Supreme Court, Feb. 4, 1861, *Morrison v. White*.

The case was heard in the lower courts for the third time in New Orleans, where, on January 30, 1862, Alexina Morrison was herself "exhibited to the Jury in evidence." Following the instructions of the Supreme Court, the judge admitted the depositions from Arkansas. . . . After retiring for "some time," the jury sent word that its members were unable to agree upon a verdict and requested that they be allowed to decide by majority. Present in the courtroom, Morrison consented, and the jury returned to announce that it had voted 10 to 2 in her favor. White's lawyers again appealed to the Supreme Court, where the case was delayed during the Civil War occupation of New Orleans, redocketed five days after the assassination of Abraham Lincoln, and continued a few times until 1870, when it was placed on the delay docket where it sits today, apparently awaiting action on Morrison's request for damages.[47]

It is tougher to track Alexina Morrison. On the Jefferson Parish census of 1860 she is listed as a free white woman, living with her little girl in a house next door to that of William Dennison, the man whom she had first met as her jailer. Morrison's daughter, like the little girl who lived in Dennison's house, was called Mary.[48] Perhaps . . . her daughter was Morrison's best hope for a legacy of freedom. For, by the third hearing of the case (in 1862), Alexina Morrison was apparently back in jail, coughing blood, and fearful for her life. And there the trail ends: Neither Alexina nor Mary Morrison appears in the 1870 census of Jefferson or Orleans parishes.

Alexina Morrison was a woman who left her fellow slaves behind to make her bid for freedom alone, framed her case in the grammar of white supremacist patriarchy by presenting herself as a white woman in need, ceded the power over her situation to a legal system that supported slavery, delivered her body from the hands of the slaver to that of the jailer and from the property regime of slavery to that of whiteness. The Louisiana Supreme Court remained ever ready to ensure that the local chaos in Jefferson Parish did not interfere with the state's progress toward a more perfect equivalence of blackness and slavery. Morrison herself may have died of the illness she had contracted in prison. In the eyes of many, hers would be a story of hegemony: of agency without autonomy, opposition without effect, resistance without revolution; of a woman becoming ever more entangled in the logic of slavery as she tried to get free.[49] Judged by the history recorded in law books and legislative records and according to the Louisiana Supreme Court that had ultimate jurisdiction over her fate, Morrison was swimming against the current of history, finally unable, in spite of her extraordinary effort, to escape the inexorable consolidation of slaveholding power in the years before the Civil War.

But if we pay attention to the local as well as the legal importance of the case and the everyday as well as the systemic impact of individual acts of resistance, if we think about what it must have been like to wake up in Jefferson Parish on the

---

[47]Verdict, Jan. 30, 1862, *Morrison v. White*; Bond of Appeal, Feb. 11, 1862, ibid.; Supreme Court of Louisiana Docket Record, Supreme Court of Louisiana Collection. For post–Civil War action on cases involving slavery, see Schafer, *Slavery, the Civil Law, and the Supreme Court of Louisiana*, 289–304.

[48]Manuscript Population Schedules, Jefferson Parish, Eighth Census, 1860, dwellings 1470 and 1471.

[49]This is the argument made in Eugene D. Genovese, *Roll, Jordan, Roll: The World the Slaves Made* (New York, 1974), 25–49, 587–98. See also Mindie Lazarus-Black and Susan F. Hirsch, *Contested States: Law, Hegemony, and Resistance* (New York, 1994).

morning after the district court had decided Morrison's case and moved on to other business, historical time has a different scale and Alexina Morrison's story offers a different moral. The covering rhetoric of white supremacy may have remained unquestioned and the power of the Supreme Court to dampen subversive appropriations of that rhetoric by refusing the verdicts coming from the lower courts intact. But Alexina Morrison had raised troubling possibilities in a society based on racial slavery: that a slave might perform whiteness so effectively as to become white; that behavior thought to indicate natural difference might, instead, be revealed as the product of education, construction, and, even, commodification; that one could seem white without really being that way; that the whiteness by which the slaveholding social order was justified might one day be turned against it. The problems Morrison posed were particularly acute when addressed to the white workingmen who increasingly inhabited the antebellum South: How could they continue to claim to be their own masters if they or their wives and daughters worked for someone else? Did race really give them a stake in slavery? Would their whiteness really protect them from enslavement? No longer could a Jefferson Parish jury be trusted to try the case of the slave trader and the white slave; no longer could slaveholders be sure that the property claims of slavery would be supported by the logic of whiteness. Indeed, the notions of a supposedly commonsense differentiation between black and white that were broached in the Third District Court were so various and so contradictory that by the end of 1857 it would have been hard for anyone in Jefferson Parish to say for sure what people there meant when they talked about "race." Whether they realized it or not, as they tugged Alexina Morrison back and forth across a color line that they all thought they could plainly see, the white participants in *Morrison v. White* revealed that line as an effect of social convention and power, not nature.

Indeed, the local history of *Morrison v. White* seems to stand in direct contradiction to its legal history; the relation of race and law over time—the legal history of race—was running in one direction if you were sitting in the Third District Court in Jefferson Parish and another if you were sitting a few miles away in the Supreme Court in New Orleans. Beneath the gathering tide of proslavery in the 1850s, beneath the proslavery crackdown on interracial socializing and the curtailment of manumission laws, beneath *Dred Scott* and the self-enslavement laws, beneath the prognostications of Samuel Cartwright and the pronouncements of George Fitzhugh, beneath legal definitions of race and textbook versions of proper legal practice, ran an undercurrent of discontented whiteness. . . . *Morrison v. White*, a suit in which the slave sued the slave trader, illuminates the complexity of the relation between the economic system of slavery and the ideology of white supremacy by which it was increasingly justified. Though they remained wedded in the official rhetoric of the antebellum South—in the courtrooms and congresses—in the changing political economy of the 1850s, white supremacy and slavery were not coextensive paradigms of social order. Standing before the Third District Court, Alexina Morrison embodied the conflicting property claims of whiteness and slavery, claims that by running away and suing the slave trader she had brought into apparently irreconcilable conflict. In Jefferson Parish at least, the historic bargain at the heart of the southern social order—black slavery for white freedom—was less an accomplished fact than an open argument.

Walter Johnson

In 1999, I published a book about the interstate slave trade, entitled *Soul by Soul*. The aspiration of the book was to provide readers with an eye-level, everyday account of the intimate violence and hedged-in possibilities of resistance that characterized the history of the slave market in New Orleans, the nation's largest. This piece in this collection is an offshoot of that book. In the meantime, I have written methodological articles on how to think about the history of slavery and claims for reparations, about how historians' use the idea of "agency," and about whether or not slavery was capitalist (short answer: yes). In 2013 I published a book about slavery, capitalism, and imperialism in the nineteenth-century Mississippi Valley, *River of Dark Dreams*. Since then I have re-learned much of the American history I have forgotten since graduate school by quizzing my daughter as she worked her way through AP US History at the Cambridge Rindge and Latin School. In the fall of 2014 I began work on a book about St. Louis Missouri (my home state) from the time of Lewis and Clark up until the killing of Michael Brown and the subsequent uprising in Ferguson.

QUESTIONS FOR CONSIDERATION

1. Johnson claims that in antebellum New Orleans, "whiteness was packaged by traders and imagined into meaning by the buyers. . . ." What does he mean by "packaged" and "imagined" here? How did slaveholders maintain racial lines between white and black while still purchasing "whiteness" in slave markets?

2. Describe the ways in which Alexina Morrison's witnesses utilized common white American conceptions of race to convince themselves that she was white. How did James White use contemporary scientific theories of racial blackness to convince the jury that she was black?

3. In what ways did both sides of this debate use stereotypes of femininity to establish their case?

4. Why did James White's attempt to return Alexina Morrison to slavery raise such anxiety in some white Americans? What ambiguities in the categories of race and class did this anxiety expose?

5. Johnson claims that "the white participants in *Morrison v. White* revealed [the color] line as an effect of social convention and power, not nature." He also claims that Morrison's case revealed underlying tensions between racial and economic categories, namely, between whiteness and slavery. How did Alexina Morrison utilize these contextual factors to make her appeal? How did those contextual factors also constrain her pursuit of freedom?